OPENING DOORS

Understanding College Reading

OPENING DOORS

Understanding College Reading

Second Edition

JOE CORTINA
JANET ELDER

Richland College
Dallas County Community College District

The McGraw-Hill Companies, Inc.

New York St. Louis San Francisco Auckland Bogotá Caracas
Lisbon London Madrid Mexico City Milan Montreal
New Delhi San Juan Singapore Sydney Tokyo Toronto

OPENING DOORS

Understanding College Reading

5 6 7 8 9 0 DOC DOC 9 0 9

ISBN 0-07-024470-7

This book was set in Times Roman by Ruttle, Shaw, & Wetherill, Inc.
The editors were Sarah Moyers, Larry Goldberg, and Peggy Rehberger;
the design manager was Charles A. Carson;
the production supervisor was Richard A. Ausburn.
Cover photo by Petrisse Briel/The Image Bank.
The permissions editor was Cheryl Besenjak.
R. R. Donnelley & Sons Company was printer and binder.

Library of Congress Cataloging-in-Publication

Cortina, Joe.
Opening doors: understanding college reading. — 2nd ed. / Joe Cortina, Janet Elder.
p. cm.
Includes index.
ISBN 0-07-024470-7
1. College readers. 2. Reading (Higher education) I. Elder, Janet. II. Title.
PE1122.C697 1997
808'.0427—dc21 97–16752
CIP

http://www.mhcollege.com

ABOUT THE AUTHORS

Joe Cortina

Janet Elder

Joe Cortina and Janet Elder are professors in the Human and Academic Development Division of Richland College, a member of the Dallas County Community College District, where they both teach courses in basic and advanced reading improvement and study skills. Their combined teaching experience spans elementary, secondary, and undergraduate levels, as well as clinical remediation. Both are trained as reading specialists.

The authors have worked together as a writing team since 1985. Their first book, *Comprehending College Textbooks: Steps to Understanding and Remembering What You Read,* written with their former colleague, Katherine Gonnet, is now in its third edition. The first edition of *Opening Doors: Understanding College Reading* was published in 1995 and was also written with Katherine Gonnet. In addition, Dr. Elder and Dr. Gonnet co-authored the reading section of *How to Prepare for the TASP, Second Edition,* a study guide for entering college students who must take the Texas Academic Skills Program Test.

JOE CORTINA earned his B.A. degree in English from San Diego State University and his master's degree and doctoral degree in curriculum and instruction in reading from the University of North Texas. He has taught undergraduate teacher education courses in reading at the University of North Texas and Texas Woman's University. In 1981 he was selected to represent the Dallas County Community College District as a nominee for the Piper Award for Teaching Excellence. In addition, Dr. Cortina was chosen as his division's Piper Award nominee for excellence in teaching in 1987, 1988, and 1993. In 1992 he was selected as an honored alumnus by the Department of Elementary, Early Childhood, and Reading Education of the University of North Texas, and in 1994 he was a recipient of an Excellence Award given by the National Institute for Staff and Organizational Development. In addition to teaching reading courses at Richland College, he has served on interdisciplinary teaching teams for honors English courses and as a faculty leader of Richland's Writing Across the Curriculum Program. Dr. Cortina has served as a member of the editorial advisory board of *The Journal of Adolescent and Adult Literacy.* He is a frequent speaker at professional meetings.

JANET ELDER was graduated summa cum laude from the University of Texas in Austin with a B.A. in English and Latin. She is a member of Phi Beta Kappa. She was the recipient of a government fellowship for Southern Methodist University's Reading Research Program, which resulted in a master's degree. Her Ph.D in curriculum and instruction in reading is from Texas Woman's University, where the College of Education presented her the Outstanding Dissertation Award. She established the Richland College Honors Program and directed it for many years. She periodically serves as a member of the teaching teams in honors English and humanities courses. She has served on a task force that reevaluated Richland's college-wide writing program. She received the Extra Mile Award from special services students, has been her division's Piper Award nominee for excellence in teaching, and in 1993 received an Excellence Award from the National Institute for Staff and Organizational Development. She used a recent sabbatical to create multimedia instructional materials. Dr. Elder serves as a presenter at many professional conferences.

CONTENTS

TO THE INSTRUCTOR

Opening Doors is designed to help college students move from a pre-college reading level to a college reading level. It presents a systematic way of approaching college textbook material that can make students more efficient in their reading and studying. The heart of the text is Part Two, *Comprehension* (Chapters 4 through 8), but in addition *Opening Doors* presents study skills that are integral to success in college.

The scope of this book is broad, but the focus is always on comprehension. Moreover, the skills are integrated, and there is continual application of skills once they have been introduced. Although this text emphasizes essential main ideas and supporting details (Part Two, *Comprehension*), it includes skills that range from predicting and questioning actively as you read (Part One, *Orientation*) to selecting, organizing, and rehearsing textbook material to be learned for a test (Part Three, *Systems for Studying Textbooks*). In Part Three, students learn to use textbook features to full advantage, to underline and annotate textbook material, and to organize material several ways in writing so that it can be mastered for a test.

Although *Opening Doors* is designed for developmental readers, we have chosen to use only college textbook excerpts and other materials students would be likely to encounter in college. *Their selection is the result of field-testing with hundreds of our students over several semesters to identify selections that are interesting, informative, and appropriate. Field-testing also revealed that, with coaching and guidance from the instructor, students can comprehend these selections.* (We believe that this extensive field-testing provides a much more useful indicator of appropriateness than a readability formula.) Equally important is that students like dealing with "the real thing"—actual college textbook material—since that is what they will encounter in subsequent college courses. This type of practice enables them to transfer skills to other courses and avoid the frustration and disappointment of discovering that their reading improvement course did not prepare them for "real" college reading. Finally, these passages help students acquire and extend their background knowledge in a variety of subjects.

College textbook material contains many words students do not know but need to learn. However, underprepared students and English-as-a-second-language students tend to focus on *words* rather than ideas. Therefore, we present all vocabulary in context. It will also be important for you, the instructor, to help students view words as a means of accessing content rather than as ends unto themselves.

The practice exercises in *Opening Doors* are extensive. They prepare students to read and allow them to apply comprehension and study skills during and after reading. All vocabulary words are from the chapter reading selections and are presented in context. Comprehension questions are the same type that content-area teachers ask on tests (rather than "The main idea of the selection is . . . ," etc.). There are also critical reading exercises, with options for students to work collaboratively. Single paragraphs and short excerpts are used to introduce and illustrate skills; however, students *apply* these skills to *full-length selections.* Exercises call for both objective responses and essay answers. Despite our belief that having students "write out" their responses to questions about a selection is the most complete way to assess their comprehension, we realize that students need practice with traditional multiple-choice items as well.

FEATURES OF THE SECOND EDITION

We have retained the following features in the second edition of *Opening Doors:*

- A thorough reading comprehension core as the heart of the text (Part Two)
- Clear explanations and understandable examples of each essential reading comprehension skill
- Numerous textbook passages for application of reading and study skills
- Three full-length reading selections in each of the first eight chapters (typically, two of these are from college textbooks and one is a nontext selection). Chapters 9 and 10 each present an *actual textbook chapter* as the reading selection
- Exercises that integrate writing and reading and call for both objective and essay responses
- Cumulative review and application of skills
- Presentation of vocabulary and study skills as they relate to learning from college textbooks and other college-level materials
- Flexibility, allowing instructors to adapt assignments to the specific needs of their own students
- Skills typically included on state-mandated reading competency tests are addressed, as well as tips for scoring well on standardized reading tests
- Consistency in philosophy and approach with *Comprehending College Textbooks,* our other reading comprehension textbook
- An *Instructor's Manual* contains answer keys, teaching strategies, and pages that can be used to make transparency masters

Changes and New Features in the Second Edition

- Five new reading selections with accompanying activities and exercises
- The relocation of information about figurative language and connotations and denotations (Chapter 2)
- A section on critically evaluating written material (Chapter 8)
- A section on interpreting graphic material (Chapter 9)
- A test bank that appears in the *Instructor's Manual,* which consists of tests on the contents of each chapter that students can prepare for by completing and studying the chapter review cards
- Also in the *Instructor's Manual,* supplemental reading selections with accompanying questions

While many instructors will choose to use the 10 chapters in *Opening Doors* in the order in which they are presented, others may choose an alternative sequence (three possible sequences are included in the *Instructor's Manual*) that suits their specific course. For this reason, the previewing prompts and the instructions for completing chapter review cards are deliberately repeated in each chapter. Similarly, the previewing prompts and instructions for the practice exercises that accompany each reading selection are included with each selection so that instructors may assign the reading selections in any order.

We hope that you, along with your students, will learn new and interesting things in the selections in this book. Your enthusiasm for acquiring new information, your willingness to become engaged with the material, and your pleasure in learning will serve as a model for your students.

We wish you success in using *Opening Doors* to prepare your students to read textbooks effectively and to be successful in college. We hope the endeavor will be enjoyable and rewarding for both you and your students.

ACKNOWLEDGMENTS

We are grateful to Sarah Moyers, English Editor at McGraw-Hill, for her encouragement and assistance with this edition. Special thanks go to Laura Lynch, Susan Gamer, and Peg Markow for lending the boundless and generous talent and expertise that transformed our manuscript into the second edition of *Opening Doors.*

Our reviewers served us well with their constructive criticisms, suggestions, and supportive comments.

For the second edition, we are grateful to: Patricia A. Hale, Kilgore College; Kevin Hayes, Essex County College; Amy Kurata, Kapiolani Community College; Barbara Levy, Nassau Community College; Judith Y. McNeill, Portland Community College; Mitye Jo Richey, Community College of Allegheny County.

For the first edition, we are grateful to: Ellen Bell, Manatee Community College; Ada H. Belton, Keystone Jr. College; Roel Carmona, Del Mar College;

Gertrude Coleman, Middlesex County College; Diana Fink, Miramar College; Nancy Hanley, Anderson College; Susan L'Heureux, Sinclair Community College; Sandra Lloyd, Tomball College; Carol McPhillips, Villa Maria College; Maureen O'Brien, Springfield Tech Community College; Marianne Reynolds, Mercer County Community College; and Laurie Stevens, University of St. Thomas.

Our students at Richland College offered wonderful suggestions and encouraging comments during the field-testing of this edition. They continue to be among our best and most helpful critics.

We dedicate this new edition to our former colleague, Katherine Gonnet, who was our co-author on the first edition of *Opening Doors.* We miss collaborating with this valued friend, but know she will be pleased with the improvements.

Joe Cortina
Janet Elder

TO THE STUDENT

"Didn't I realize that reading would open up whole new worlds? *A book could open doors for me.* It could introduce me to people and show me places I never imagined existed."

Richard Rodriguez, *Hunger of Memory*

Dear Student,

Welcome to *Opening Doors.* We hope that this reading improvement textbook will, in fact, "open doors," doors for you to succeed in college. To accomplish this, *Opening Doors* contains some special features.

First, every reading selection in this book comes from a widely used college textbook or other materials that you are likely to encounter in your college reading. They were chosen to give you the practice, skill, and confidence you need to handle subsequent college courses successfully.

Second, this book focuses on helping you improve your ability to *comprehend—to understand*—what you read. This is the most critical ability you must have to be a successful reader. *Opening Doors* presents specific strategies to enable you to identify, comprehend, and remember important information in your college textbooks.

Third, *Opening Doors* is organized around the three areas that are essential to a student's success:

- *Part I: Orientation—Preparing and Organizing Yourself for Success in College*

This section includes chapters on making yourself a success in college (goal-setting, motivation, and time management), making sense of college reading, and approaching textbook assignments effectively.

- *Part II: Comprehension—Understanding Your College Textbooks by Reading for Ideas*

This section is the heart of this book. Comprehending what you read is vital to your success as a college student. The reading comprehension skills that are included in this section are:

identifying the topic and stated main idea,
formulating implied main idea sentences,
identifying supporting details,

understanding the organization of the details (the authors' writing patterns), and critical reading skills.

- *Part III: Study Systems—Developing a Textbook Study System that Works for You*

This section deals with selecting and organizing essential textbook information and rehearsing the information in order to learn it for a test. To provide you with an opportunity to practice these study skills, two full-length chapters from college textbooks are included in this section. We think you will enjoy applying the skills you learn in this section to actual textbook chapters.

All of the reading selections in Chapters 1 through 8 (three selections per chapter) are excerpts taken from college textbooks and other types of materials you are likely to encounter in college. These selections provide important practice, and they will increase your background knowledge in a variety of interesting subjects. Each reading selection is accompanied by preliminary and follow-up exercises. In order, the exercises are:

1. *Prepare Yourself to Read.* This exercise allows you to use techniques (such as previewing and making predictions) that will help you read the selection more actively and effectively.
2. *Apply Comprehension Skills.* This activity lets you *apply* to the reading selection the reading skills and techniques you are learning.
3. *Comprehension Quiz.* This exercise consists of a 10-item objective test on the content of the selection. You will answer questions that a college instructor might ask on a test about information, concepts, and facts in the selection.
4. *Extend Your Vocabulary by Using Context Clues.* In this exercise, you will determine the meaning of 10 important words that appear in the selection. In addition, the pronunciation is given for each word.
5. *Respond in Writing.* In these essay-type exercises, you will be asked to react in writing to the selection.

As noted above, Chapters 9 and 10 contain chapter-length selections. By the end of the semester, you will have learned important and effective study techniques and be able to apply them to these selections.

As you work through this book, you will discover that you are becoming a better reader. Not only will you have a clearer understanding of reading comprehension skills, you also will have had a great deal of practice with them. You will also discover that you are able to use these skills in your other college courses.

We welcome you to *Opening Doors.* We hope your journey through this textbook is an enjoyable and rewarding experience.

Joe Cortina
Janet Elder

OPENING DOORS

Understanding College Reading

ORIENTATION

Preparing and Organizing Yourself for Success in College

CHAPTERS IN PART ONE

CHAPTER 1

MAKING YOURSELF SUCCESSFUL IN COLLEGE

IN THIS CHAPTER YOU WILL LEARN
THE ANSWERS TO THESE QUESTIONS:

What do successful college students do?

How can I set goals for myself?

How can I motivate myself to do well in college?

How can I manage my time more effectively?

CHAPTER 1 CONTENTS

Well begun is half done.

DOING WHAT SUCCESSFUL STUDENTS DO

Some students are more successful than others. Why? One answer is that successful students know how to set goals for themselves, motivate themselves, and manage their time. In this chapter, you will learn how to do these things. If you start now and consistently apply the techniques and strategies in the chapter, you will become a more successful college student.

The Greek philosopher Aristotle observed, "We are what we repeatedly do. Excellence then is not an act, but a habit." This is valuable advice. If you make good study techniques a habit, each semester you can become a better, more effective student.

It is helpful to look more closely at exactly what successful students do. One research study involved college students who were highly effective despite the fact that they did not have high entrance scores. The researchers discovered that these students all shared five important characteristics:

1. *Effective students are highly motivated.* Successful students have an inner drive to do well. They are goal-oriented; they have specific careers in mind. They believe that they are responsible for their own success or failure; they attribute nothing to "good luck" or "bad luck."
2. *Effective students plan ahead.* Successful students are organized. They develop good study habits. They establish a study schedule and stick to it. They study at the same time each day, and in the same place.
3. *Effective students focus on understanding.* Successful students use verbal and written feedback to monitor their progress and make changes if necessary. They assess their own strengths and weaknesses on the basis of instructors' comments in class, evaluations of homework assignments, and grades on tests. If they start to do poorly or fall behind in a subject, they adjust their schedule to spend more time on it, and they immediately seek help from an instructor, a tutor, or a friend.
4. *Effective students are highly selective.* Successful students concentrate on main ideas and important supporting details when they read assignments. They do not try to memorize everything. To identify important information, they pay attention to signals in their textbooks and class notes. They use instructors' suggestions, course outlines, and textbook features to guide their efforts.

5. *Effective students are involved and attentive.* Successful students are focused on their academic work in class and outside of class. In class, they pay attention, take notes, and participate in discussions. They make a point of arriving early, and they help themselves concentrate by sitting near the front. Outside of class, they study in quiet places to avoid distractions. They put academic work ahead of social life, and they limit television watching. They study with others who are serious about school. They concentrate on the present rather than worrying about the past or daydreaming too much about the future.

Source: Adapted from John Q. Easton, Don Barshis, and Rick Ginsberg, "Chicago Colleges Identify Effective Teachers, Students," *Community and Junior College Journal,* December–January 1983–1984, pp. 27–31.

Perhaps the most interesting aspect of this description of successful college students is that nothing in it is especially complicated or difficult. With planning and determination, any student can make these behaviors part of his or her own life in college.

SETTING YOUR GOALS

Most successful students (in fact, most successful people) have this in common: they establish goals, and they put their goals *into writing.* They write down *what* they want to accomplish and *when* they want to accomplish it. Goals that are not written down are not much better than wishes. Writing your goals helps you make a commitment to them and gives you a yardstick for measuring your progress. Putting your goals in writing is a very simple tool that can help you turn wishes into reality.

You will probably find that your goals fall into several categories: educational, financial, spiritual, personal (including family matters), physical (health and fitness), and career-related. An example of an educational goal might be, "To complete all my courses this semester and earn at least a B in each."

Sometimes it becomes necessary to choose between two or more competing goals. For example, suppose that you wanted to attend college full time and work full time. You would have to give one goal or the other priority in order to allow for studying. Or you would have to modify both goals, deciding to attend college part time and work part time. Competing goals do not make it necessary to give up a goal, but they do make it necessary to be realistic, to set priorities, and to adjust your time and efforts.

One expert in time management, Alan Lakein, gives these recommendations for setting goals:

- *Be specific.* A vague goal like "I will do better" is not very helpful.

- *Be realistic.* An unrealistic goal like "I will work full time and attend college full time for the next 4 years" is not helpful.
- *Revise your goals at regular intervals.* It is important to revise goals regularly (probably every semester) because your situation may change.

Source: Alan Lakein, *How to Get Control of Your Time and Your Life,* Signet, New York, 1973, pp. 30–37, 64–65.

Putting Your Goals in Writing

Take a few minutes to write down your goals. Write at least three goals for each category. (These are personal and private, and they do not have to be shared with anyone.)

What are my long-term goals?

On the lines below, write three things you want to accomplish and achieve during your lifetime.

1. ______________________________
2. ______________________________
3. ______________________________

What are my intermediate goals?

On the lines below, write three things you want to accomplish during the next 3 to 5 years.

1. ______________________________
2. ______________________________
3. ______________________________

What are my short-term goals?

On the lines below, write three things you want to accomplish this semester.

1. ______________________________
2. ______________________________
3. ______________________________

Key terms

Long-term goal: Goal you want to accomplish during your lifetime.
Intermediate goal: Goal you want to accomplish in the next 3 to 5 years.
Short-term goal: Goal you want to accomplish in the next 3 to 6 months.

Lakein also recommends setting three types of goals: long-term, intermediate, and short-term. ***Long-term goals*** relate to your entire life; ***intermediate goals*** relate to the next 3 to 5 years; ***short-term goals*** relate to the next 3 to 6 months. (For a student, short-term goals would have to do with the current semester.) Your short-term goals should help you achieve your intermediate goals, which in turn should help you achieve your long-term, lifetime goals. For instance, improving your reading skills is a short-term goal that will contribute to the intermediate goal of earning a college degree, and ultimately to the long-term goal of an interesting, satisfying career.

The box on page 7 will give you the experience of formulating and writing down long-term, intermediate, and short-term goals. When you have recorded some goals in writing, identify one or two from each category that are especially important to you now. Whenever you must decide how to use your time, choose activities that help you reach those goals.

Keep a copy of your goals where you can see and read them often. You might keep them at the front of a notebook, for instance, or on your desk. Some of your goals will be achieved quickly and removed from your list; but you may find that some of them will remain on your list for a long time, perhaps a lifetime.

MOTIVATING YOURSELF

In college, you are responsible for motivating yourself. Developing an interest in and a commitment to your courses is not your instructors' responsibility; it is your responsibility.

Fortunately, motivating yourself is easier than you may think. For one thing, college is a stimulating place to be! As you progress through college, you will find that learning becomes increasingly pleasurable and satisfying. Also, there are specific, effective self-motivational techniques you can use. Here are a dozen motivational strategies that you can use to get yourself motivated and stay motivated throughout a semester.

1. *Write down your educational goals for the semester.* The act of writing down goals for the semester can be motivating in and of itself. Clear goals can also motivate you to use your time well. Specific goals (for class attendance and participation, homework, and grades) help you select activities that will move you toward your goals. In addition, achieving a worthwhile goal is a deeply satisfying experience that will motivate you to achieve more goals.
2. *Visualize success.* Visualize successful situations that you want to make happen in the near future, such as earning a high grade on an assignment or completing the semester successfully. Then visualize the future further ahead: imagine yourself graduating from college and being offered a good

job. Make your mental images as sharp and vivid as possible; imagine the pride you will feel in your accomplishment.

3. *Think in terms of earning what you want.* The truly valuable and worthwhile things in life are seldom easy; you have to pay a price for them.
4. *Think of classes as your easiest learning sessions.* If you spend 3 hours a week in class for a course, look on those hours as your *easiest* 3 hours of learning and studying for the course. Your instructor, who is an expert, is present to explain and to answer questions.
5. *View your courses as opportunities.* Especially if a course is difficult, consider it a challenge rather than a problem or an obstacle. Accept the fact that you are required to take a variety of courses to broaden your educational background. Later in life, you will most likely come to appreciate these courses more than you can now.
6. *Develop strategies for difficult courses.* To keep from feeling overwhelmed, a good strategy is to study one thing at a time. Another strategy is to consider the feeling of accomplishment that comes from mastering a difficult subject, and the pride you can take in succeeding at a challenging subject. Realize, too, that you can enjoy a subject even if you may never become an expert in it.
7. *Take tips from good students in your courses.* Ask them what they are doing to be successful. If they like a course that seems difficult or boring to you, ask them why they enjoy the subject.
8. *Choose the right friends.* Choose friends who will support and encourage your studying. Find a "study buddy" or form a small study group. Be sure to choose people who are also serious about school. It is also helpful to find a mentor (a wise and trustworthy counselor or instructor) who can give you advice, support, and encouragement.
9. *Plan activities to achieve your goals.* Break big projects into sequences of smaller, more manageable tasks. Then set priorities. (For instance, a 20-page reading assignment can be divided into four shorter readings of 5 pages each, and you may even want to read these during short study sessions on different days.)
10. *Give yourself rewards.* Reward yourself for successfully completing an activity such as a homework assignment or studying for a test. Watch a favorite television program, have a snack, work out, or take a walk.
11. *Make positive "self-talk" a habit.* Say encouraging things to yourself: "I think I can do this assignment, even though it might take a while." "If other students in my class can do this, I can too." Also, use a technique called *thought stopping* to shut off negative self-talk: when you find that you are giving yourself negative feedback, just say "Stop!" and substitute some *positive* self-talk. Don't let frustration overcome you and destroy your productivity. Recognizing that frustration is a normal part of learning (and of life) will help you develop tolerance for it.

12. *Think in terms of doing your best.* Reassure yourself. If you really do your best, you can feel satisfied with your effort. You will not have to wonder whether you might have done better if only you had tried harder.

Motivation leads to success; success increases motivation; increased motivation leads to more success; and so on! In other words, motivation and success go hand in hand to reinforce each other.

MANAGING YOUR TIME

Managing your time means making decisions about how you choose to spend time. When you look at the numbers in the box below, you will realize how much decision making is necessary in order to gain control of your time. Fortunately, there are several reliable strategies that you can use to control your time. In this section, you'll learn how to set up a weekly study schedule and make the most of your study sessions; you'll also look at two important planning tools: a monthly calendar and a daily list of things to do.

Making Decisions about How to Schedule Your Time

There are 168 hours in a week.

If you sleep 8 hours a night, you spend 56 hours a week sleeping.

If you spend 1 hour at each meal, you spend 21 hours a week eating.

If you have a full college schedule, you spend about 12 to 20 hours a week attending classes and labs.

This leaves you about 70 hours a week, or 10 hours a day, for everything else: studying, recreation, personal chores, and so on.

For 10 out of every 24 hours, you must make decisions about how you will spend your time.

Setting Up a Weekly Study Schedule

Key term

Study schedule: Weekly schedule with specific times set aside for studying.

If you promise yourself that you will study "whenever you find time," you may never "find time." To be a truly efficient student, you must set aside time for studying. In other words, it is essential to have a ***study schedule.*** A realistic, well-thought-out weekly schedule will assure you of ample study time.

College students often say that they have too much to do in too little time. In fact, they consider this their number one source of stress. Scheduling your time can work like a charm to lower this kind of stress, reducing tension, worries, and inefficiency. A schedule does not turn you into a robot; it frees you from constant decision making and lets you make the best use of your time.

It's important to balance study time and relaxation time. *Study first; then relax or have fun:* that's the rule for successful students. If you stick to this rule, you'll enjoy your free time more because you won't feel guilty about unfinished work. Free time becomes your reward for completing your studying.

To develop your weekly study schedule, use the planning form on page 13, and follow these steps:

- *Step 1.* Identify times that are already committed to other activities (classes, meals, work, travel time, sleep, organizations, etc.) and are therefore definitely unavailable for study. Write these activities in on your weekly planner.
- *Step 2.* Identify time when you probably would be unable to study (times for household and personal chores, family, rest, and leisure activities). Write them in on your weekly planner. These are more flexible parts of your schedule because you have more control over when to do them.
- *Step 3.* Identify the best times for you to study by checking off the times when you are most alert and energetic:

  Early morning (6–9 A.M.)_____

  Midmorning (9 A.M. to noon)_____

  Early afternoon (12–3 P.M.)_____

  Late afternoon (3–6 P.M.)_____

  Early evening (6–9 P.M.)_____

  Late evening (9 P.M. to midnight)_____

  Late night (after midnight)_____

  Studying when you are alert and rested allows you to accomplish more in less time. Try to schedule as much studying as possible during the hours you identified as your "best times."
- *Step 4.* Determine how much study time you need. Allow *at least* 1 hour of study time for each hour you spend in class. For a typical three-credit course, that would be a minimum of 3 hours of study per week; difficult courses may require more time. Then set aside the appropriate number of study hours for each course and write these times in on your weekly planner ("Study psychology," "Accounting homework," "Study history," etc.).

As you work on step 4, be sure to plan enough study time for each subject. College students are expected to be much more independent in their learning than high school students, and many new college students are surprised at how much time studying takes. Keep in mind that 1 hour of study for each hour of class is a *minimum.* If a course is difficult for you or if the assignments are time-consuming, you should schedule more study time. You will also need to schedule more study time if you are a slow reader or if you have not yet developed ef-

Sample Weekly Study Schedule

Here is a sample of a weekly study schedule that has been completed according to the directions on page 11. Notice that *specific study times have been identified for each course.* Use the blank form on page 13 to create your own weekly study schedule.

Time	*Sunday*	*Monday*	*Tuesday*	*Wednesday*	*Thursday*	*Friday*	*Saturday*
6:00 A.M.				← Get ready for school →			
7:00				Travel to school			
8:00		Accounting	**Read English**	Accounting	**Review English**	Accounting	
9:00		History	English	History	English	History	Tennis
10:00	Family time	Psychology		Psychology		Psychology	
11:00		Lunch	Biology	Lunch	Biology	Lunch	
12:00 noon		**Accounting homework**		**Accounting homework**		**Accounting homework**	Work
1:00 P.M.		**English**	Lunch	**English**	Lunch	**English**	
2:00		**assignments**	Biology lab	**assignments**	**Biology**	**assignments**	
3:00	Tennis	**Study biology**		**Study biology**	**study group**	Snack	
4:00		Dinner		Dinner		Work	
5:00		Work	**Read history**	Work	**Read history**		
6:00	**Read Biology**		**text**		**text**		Spend time
7:00	**assignments**		Dinner		Dinner		with friends
8:00	**English**		**Read**		**Read**		
9:00	**assignments**		**psychology text**		**psychology text**		
10:00	Sleep	Relax/watch news	Relax/watch news	Relax/watch news	Relax/watch news	Relax/watch news	
11:00		Sleep	Sleep	Sleep	Sleep	Sleep	Sleep
12:00 midnight							
1:00 A.M.							

Weekly Study Schedule

▪ ▪ ▪ ▪ ▪ ▪

Time	*Sunday*	*Monday*	*Tuesday*	*Wednesday*	*Thursday*	*Friday*	*Saturday*
6:00 A.M.							
7:00							
8:00							
9:00							
10:00							
11:00							
12:00 noon							
1:00 P.M.							
2:00							
3:00							
4:00							
5:00							
6:00							
7:00							
8:00							
9:00							
10:00							
11:00							
12:00 midnight							
1:00 A.M.							

fective study habits. Plan as much study time as you will need to meet the challenge of college courses.

The sample weekly planner on page 12 has been filled in to show you how a typical study schedule might look.

Once you have set up your study schedule, keep it where you can see it—*then follow it.* You will probably need about 3 weeks to become accustomed to a new schedule. Adjust it if you need to, but make a genuine effort to stick to it. Each time you deviate from your schedule, returning to it becomes harder. Sticking with it will get you past the hard part, which is simply getting started. Having a regular study routine makes it easier to become an effective student.

Making the Most of Your Study Time

Once you have set up a weekly study schedule, it is important to develop ways to make the most of your study time. There are a variety of steps you can follow to get the most out of your study sessions. Here are some key strategies:

1. *Find or create a suitable place to study.* Your study place can be at home or elsewhere. A library or any other quiet place on campus can serve well. Buy whatever materials and supplies you will need, and have them on hand in a drawer or book bag. Decide that when you are in your study place, you are there to study!
2. *Study in the same place at the same time every day.* Also, don't use your study place for any purpose except studying. This will help you "get into" studying immediately because it makes studying automatic, a habit. Knowing when, where, and what you are going to study will keep you from procrastinating.
3. *Try to make your study hours more productive.* Strive for, say, 1 or 2 productive study hours rather than 3 or 4 unproductive hours. To keep your study time productive, remember that just sitting at a desk is not studying, and just looking at a book is not reading. If you find yourself daydreaming, stop and refocus your thinking. After 1 or 2 hours of study, you may begin to tire and your ability to concentrate may decrease. If so, take a break or switch to another subject to maintain your efficiency. Be sure, however, to take your break at a logical stopping point—not in the middle of a task that is going well.
4. *Study as soon as possible after lecture classes.* One hour spent studying immediately or soon after a class will do as much to develop your understanding of the material as several hours of studying a few days later. Review and improve your lecture notes while they are still fresh in your mind. Start assignments while your understanding of the directions and the material is still accurate. If there are points you do not understand, take steps immediately to clear them up: look up an unknown word, make a note to ask the instructor about something that confused you, etc.

5. *Take advantage of short periods of free time for studying.* Scattered, brief periods of time (for instance, periods of 15 to 45 minutes before, between, and after classes) are often wasted. Use these brief times for study. Before a lecture class, for instance, it's wise to spend a few minutes reviewing your notes from the previous lecture or going over the reading assignment. When you look for short periods of free time to use, keep in mind that (in general) daytime study is more efficient than nighttime study: what you can accomplish in 1 hour during the day might take 2 hours at night. Also, don't overlook usable time on Saturdays and Sundays.
6. *Don't study your most difficult subject last.* You may have favorite subjects that you enjoy studying. It is tempting to focus on these subjects first and leave the harder subjects until last. But if you do this, you will often find that you have run out of time for a difficult subject or are too tired to work on it. Study your most difficult subjects when you still have the time and energy to do a good job on them.
7. *If you can't study at a scheduled time, take some time from another activity.* When unexpected events arise that take up time you had planned to use for studying, decide immediately where in your schedule you can make up the study session you missed, and make a temporary adjustment in your schedule. Don't overlook weekends, including Saturday and Sunday evening. Successful students often take advantage of weekends by using them as productive, unrushed study times.
8. *At the end of each week, review your class notes and textbook annotations.* Regular reviews of your week's class notes and textbook markings help you learn and remember the material. These reviews will save you time later, when you prepare for tests. Reviews also reduce stress because, long before a test, they give you a chance to discover anything you do not understand while there is enough time to correct the situation.

Planning Further Ahead: Creating a Monthly Assignment Calendar and Using a Daily "To Do" List

Two useful strategies for planning ahead are a monthly assignment calendar and a daily "to do" list. In this section you'll learn about each of these.

Students sometimes discover too late that they have three tests, a paper, and a project all due the same week. To alert themselves to especially busy weeks and give themselves an overview of the semester, effective students use a ***monthly assignment calendar.*** Planning ahead with a monthly calendar helps them meet each deadline and produce better work. As a result, they feel more in control, experience less stress, and enjoy the semester more.

Key term

Monthly assignment calendar: Calendar showing test dates and due dates in all courses for each month of a semester.

Monthly Assignment Calendar

Sunday	Monday	Tuesday	Wednesday	Thursday	Friday	Saturday

Sample Monthly Assignment Calendar

■ ■ ■ ■ ■ ■ ■

Month of September

Sunday	Monday	Tuesday	Wednesday	Thursday	Friday	Saturday
			1	2	3	4
5	6 History group report	7	8	9	10	11
12	13	14	15 Accounting Project due	16	17 English paper due	18
19	20	21	22	23	24	25
26	27					

Month of October

Sunday	Monday	Tuesday	Wednesday	Thursday	Friday	Saturday
					1 Psychology midterm	2
3	4 History test	5 Math test	6	7	8	9
10	11	12	13 English paper due	14	15	16
17	18	19	20	21	22	23
24 / 31	25					

Month of November

Sunday	Monday	Tuesday	Wednesday	Thursday	Friday	Saturday
	1	2	3 English oral report due	4	5	6
7	8	9	10	11	12 Psychology project due	13
14	15	16 Math test	17	18	19	20
21	22	23	24	25	26	27
28	29					

Month of December

Sunday	Monday	Tuesday	Wednesday	Thursday	Friday	Saturday
			1	2	3	4
5	6 History Test	7	8	9	10 English Paper due	11
12 Finals Begin	13 History Exam	14	15 Psy & English Exams	16 Math Exam	17 Acct Exam	18
19	20	21	22	23	24	25
26	27	28	29	30	31	

Setting up a monthly calendar is simple. As soon as you receive the syllabi for your courses, transfer all the test dates and due dates (for projects, papers, oral reports, etc.) to *one* calendar. If you see that several due dates coincide in one week, plan to finish some of the projects ahead of time. (To complete a project comfortably in advance of its deadline, break it into smaller parts.) Or, if several tests coincide, begin reviewing for them well ahead of time.

The boxes on pages 16–17 show monthly assignment calendars. The sample has been filled in to give you an idea of how a typical student's calendar might look. Make photocopies of the blank calendar for your own use.

Key term

"To do" list: Prioritized items to be accomplished in a single day.

Another good planning strategy is a daily ***"to do" list,*** a list of things to be done *today.* "To do" lists are recognized as a proven way to get more accomplished. Make the list up every morning or, if you prefer, make it up each evening for the next day. Be sure to make a list *every day.* An index card, which is both small and sturdy, works well for a "to do" list.

Sample "To Do" List

▪ ▪ ▪ ▪ ▪ ▪ ▪

A-1 Study for history test
A-2 Write draft of English paper
A-3 Schedule dental appointment
A-4 Pay bills

B-1 Return library books
B-2 Cleaners
B-3 Birthday present for Pat

C-1 Buy stamps
C-2 Call Lynn
C-3 Wash car

One important aspect of a "to do" list is that you identify which items you consider high priorities and which ones you consider less important. This helps you resist the temptation to do easy tasks first and postpone challenging tasks. If you use "to do" lists, you will be more productive and have more free time.

Here are the steps to follow when making a "to do" list:

- *Step 1.* Write down every significant thing you would like to accomplish today (or tomorrow, if you are making the list the night before). You can include activities related to long-term goals (such as "practice the piano" or "exercise for 45 minutes") as well as activities related to short-term goals.

- *Step 2.* Now decide how important each item on your list is by marking an item A if it is very important, B if it is moderately important, and C if it is of less importance. In other words, set priorities. Step 2 is crucial: if you do not set priorities, you may spend your time on easy but unimportant items while the important items are left undone.
- *Step 3.* Now you must set final priorities by ranking your A's, B's, and C's. Consider all the A's and label them A-1, A-2, A-3, etc. Do the same for the B's and C's. *This gives you the order in which you should do the items on the list.* (You may want to copy the list over at this point, putting the items in their final order.)

The box on page 18 shows a sample of a finished "to do" list which will give you an idea of how your own lists might look.

When you make your next "to do" list for the following day, look at the items on the current day's list that you did not complete. If they still need to be done, carry them over onto the new list. Priorities may change from day to day, of course.

A WORD ABOUT LEARNING STYLES

Key term

Learning style: Way in which an individual learns best.

In addition to managing your study time, you will need to think about your learning style. Your ***learning style*** is the way you, as an individual, learn best. Some of us are *visual learners* who prefer to see or read the material to be learned and will benefit from books, class notes, review cards, test review sheets, and the like. Others are *auditory learners,* preferring to hear the material, in the form of lectures and discussions. Auditory learners often benefit from reciting material or reading aloud to themselves, making audiotapes, and working in study groups. Still others are *tactile learners* who benefit from writing information down or manipulating materials physically. Tactile learners prefer laboratory work and other hands-on projects. Finally, of course, some of us combine more than one style. (The three basic styles are summarized in the box on page 20.)

You might also want to think about another aspect of learning: whether you prefer to work by yourself or with others. If you are a person who finds it advantageous to study with others, you will probably like being part of a study group. It's important to select other students who are motivated. Also, keep in mind that participating in a study group does not guarantee success. To prepare yourself to work with a group, you must still read and study on your own first.

Learning Styles

▪ ▪ ▪ ▪ ▪ ▪ ▪

Style	*Preferred sources of information*
Visual (prefers to read or see information)	Textbooks Class notes Chapter review cards Test review sheets
Auditory (prefers to hear information)	Class lectures and discussions Recitation Reading aloud to oneself Audiotapes Study groups
Tactile (prefers to write material down or to manipulate materials physically)	Note-taking during lectures and study sessions Laboratory work Hands-on projects (science, engineering, computer projects, and other technical subjects)

DEVELOPING CHAPTER REVIEW CARDS

Review cards, or *summary cards,* are an excellent study tool. They are a way to select, organize, and review the most important information in a textbook chapter. The process of creating review cards helps you organize information in a meaningful way and, at the same time, transfer it into long-term memory. The cards can also be used to prepare for tests (see Part Three). The review card activities in this book give you structured practice in creating these valuable study tools. Once you have learned how to make review cards, you can create them for textbook material in your other courses.

Now, complete the seven review cards for Chapter 1 by answering the questions or following the directions on each card. When you have completed them, you will have summarized: (1) what successful college students do, (2) important information about setting goals, (3) ways to motivate yourself, (4) ways to make the most of study time, (5) how to develop a monthly assignment calendar, (6) steps to take in making up a "to do" list, and (7) three learning styles.

Doing What Successful Students Do

What are five things successful college students do? (See pages 5–6.)

1. ______________________________

____

2. ______________________________

____

3. ______________________________

____

4. ______________________________

____

5. ______________________________

____

Chapter 1: Making Yourself Successful in College

Setting Goals

1. Why should goals be *written down?* (See page 6.)

____

____

____

2. What are Lakein's three recommendations for setting goals? (See pages 6–7.)

____

____

____

3. What are the three types of goals? (See page 8.)

____

____

____

Chapter 1: Making Yourself Successful in College

Motivating Yourself

What are twelve ways to motivate yourself? (See pages 8–10.)

1. ____
2. ____
3. ____
4. ____
5. ____
6. ____
7. ____
8. ____
9. ____
10. ____
11. ____
12. ____

Chapter 1: Making Yourself Successful in College

Making the Most of Your Study Time

What are eight ways to make the most of your study time? (See pages 14–15.)

1. ____________________
2. ____________________
3. ____________________
4. ____________________
5. ____________________
6. ____________________
7. ____________________
   ____
8. ____________________
   ____

Chapter 1: Making Yourself Successful in College

Developing a Monthly Assignment Calendar

How can you prepare a monthly assignment calendar? (See pages 15–19.)

1. What should you do as soon as you receive the syllabi for your courses?

   ____
   ____

2. What should you do if several project or test dates coincide?

   ____
   ____

Chapter 1: Making Yourself Successful in College

Making Up a "To Do" List

Describe briefly the three steps to follow in making a daily "to do" list. (See pages 18–19.)

Step 1: ____________________

____

____

Step 2: ____________________

____

____

Step 3: ____________________

____

____

Chapter 1: Making Yourself Successful in College

Learning Styles

Briefly describe these three learning styles. (See pages 19–20.)

Visual learners:

____

____

Auditory learners:

____

____

Tactile learners:

____

____

Chapter 1: Making Yourself Successful in College

Selection 1-1

Nonfiction

EDUCATION: THE BEST INVESTMENT

FROM *THE ROAD AHEAD*
BY BILL GATES

Prepare Yourself to Read

Directions: Do these exercises *before you read Selection 1-1.*

1. First, read and think about the title and the author. What do you already know about computers in education? What do you already know about Bill Gates?

   ____

   ____

2. Next, complete your preview by reading the following:

   Introduction (in *italics*)
   First paragraph (paragraph 1)
   First sentence of each paragraph
   All of the last paragraph (paragraph 15)

   On the basis of your preview, what does Bill Gates seem to suggest about the future of information technology in education?

   ____

   ____

Apply Comprehension Skills

Directions: Do these exercises *as you read Selection 1-1.* Apply two skills from this chapter:

Set your goal for reading. What do you hope to learn about how computers will be used in school in the future?

____

Plan your time. Estimate how long it will take you to read Selection 1-1.

____

EDUCATION: THE BEST INVESTMENT

In 1975 Bill Gates cofounded Microsoft Corporation, the world-famous software company, because he believed that there would eventually be a personal computer on every desktop and in every home. With regard to schools, he says, "I believe most countries will decide to make increased investments in education, and computer use in schools will catch up to its use in homes and businesses. Over time—longer in less developed countries—we are likely to see computers installed in every classroom in the world." Although "a classroom will still be a classroom," Gates believes that technology will transform education in a variety of ways. This selection from his book explains several of the changes he sees on "the road ahead." (In this selection Bill Gates often mentions CD-ROMS, compact disks with read-only memory that contain software programs.)

1 At first, new information technology will just provide incremental improvements over today's tools. Wall-mounted video white boards will replace a teacher's chalkboard handwriting with readable fonts and colorful graphics drawn from millions of educational illustrations, animations, photographs, and videos. Multimedia documents will assume some of the roles now played by textbooks, movies, tests, and other educational materials. And because multimedia documents will be linked to servers on the information highway, they will be kept thoroughly up-to-date.

2 CD-ROMs available today offer a taste of the interactive experience. The software responds to instructions by presenting information in text, audio, and video forms. CD-ROMs are already being used in schools and by kids doing their assignments at home, but they have limitations the highway won't. CD-ROMs can offer either a little information about a broad range of topics the way an encyclopedia does, or a lot of information about a single topic, such as dinosaurs, but the total amount of information available at one time is limited by the capacity of the disc. And, of course, you can use only the discs you have available. Nevertheless, they are a great advance over just-paper texts. Multimedia encyclopedias provide not only a research tool, but all sorts of material that can be incorporated into homework documents. These encyclopedias are available with teacher's guides that include suggestions for ways to use the encyclopedias in the classroom or as part of assignments. I have been excited to hear from teachers and students about the ways they have used our products—only a few of which we had anticipated.

CD-ROMs are one clear precursor to the 3
highway. The Internet's World Wide Web is another. The Web offers access to interesting, educational information, although most of it is still plain text. Creative teachers are already using on-line services to devise exciting new kinds of lessons.

Fourth-graders in California have done on- 4
line searches of newspapers to read about the challenges Asian immigrants face. Boston University has created software for high school students that shows detailed visual simulations of chemical phenomena, such as salt molecules dissolving in water.

Christopher Columbus Middle School in 5
Union City, New Jersey, was a school created out of crisis. In the late 1980s, the state test scores were so low and the absentee and the dropout rates were so high among the children of the school district that the state was considering taking it over. The school system, the teachers, and the parents (well over 90 percent of whom were of Hispanic extraction and didn't

Source: "Education: The Best Investment," from *The Road Ahead,* by Bill Gates with Nathan Myhrvold and Peter Rinearson, New York, Viking, 1995, pp. 193–196.

speak English as a first language) came up with an innovative five-year plan to rescue their schools.

6 Bell Atlantic (the local telephone company) agreed to help find a special networked, multimedia system of PCs linking the students' homes with the classrooms, teachers, and school administrators. The corporation initially provided 140 multimedia PCs, enough for the homes of the seventh-graders, the homes of all seventh-grade teachers, and at least four per classroom. The computers were networked and linked with high-speed lines and connected to the Internet, and the teachers were trained in using the PCs. The teachers set up weekend training courses for the parents, over half of whom attended, and encouraged the students to use e-mail and the Internet.

7 Two years later, parents are actively involved with their childrens' use of the home PCs and employ them themselves to keep in touch with teachers and administrators; the dropout rate and absenteeism are both almost zero, and the students are scoring nearly three times higher than the average for all New Jersey inner-city schools on standardized tests. And the program has been expanded to include the entire middle school.

8 Raymond W. Smith, chairman of the board and CEO of Bell Atlantic, comments, "I believe a combination of a school system ready for fundamental change in teaching methods, a parent body that was supportive and wanted to be involved, and the careful but intensive integration of technology into both the homes and classrooms . . . created a true learning community in which the home and school reinforce and support each other."

9 At Lester B. Pearson School, a Canadian high school serving an ethnically diverse neighborhood, computers are an integral part of every course in the daily curriculum. For the 1,200 students there are more than 300 personal computers, and more than 100 different software titles are in use. The school says its dropout rate, 4 percent, when compared with a national average of 30 percent, is Canada's lowest. Thirty-five hundred people a year visit to see how a high school can "incorporate technology in every aspect of school life."

When the information highway is in operation, the texts of millions of books will be available. A reader will be able to ask questions, print the text, read it on-screen, or even have it read in his choice of voices. He'll be able to ask questions. It will be his tutor. 10

Computers with social interfaces will figure out how to present information so that it is customized for the particular user. Many educational software programs will have distinct personalities, and the student and the computer will get to know each other. A student will ask, perhaps orally, "What caused the American Civil War?" His or her computer will reply, describing the conflicting contentions: that it was primarily a battle over economics or human rights. The length and approach of the answer will vary depending on the student and the circumstances. A student will be able to interrupt at any time to ask the computer for more or less detail or to request a different approach altogether. The computer will know what information the student has read or watched and will point out connections or correlations and offer appropriate links. If the computer knows the student likes historical fiction, war stories, folk music, or sports, it may try to use that knowledge to present the information. But this will be only an attention-getting device. The machine, like a good human teacher, won't give in to a child who has lopsided interests. Instead it will use the child's predilections to teach a broader curriculum. 11

Different learning rates will be accommodated, because computers will be able to pay individual attention to independent learners. Children with learning disabilities will be particularly well served. Regardless of his or her ability or disability, every student will be able to work at an individual pace. 12

Another benefit of computer-aided learning will be the way many students come to view 13 tests. Today, tests are pretty depressing for many kids. They are associated with falling short: "I got a bad grade," or "I ran out of time," or "I wasn't ready." After a while, many kids who haven't done well on tests may think to themselves, I'd better pretend tests aren't important to me, because I can never succeed at them. Tests can cause a student to develop a negative attitude toward all education.

14 The interactive network will allow students to quiz themselves anytime, in a risk-free environment. A self-administered quiz is a form of self-exploration, like the tests Paul Allen and I used to give each other. Testing will become a positive part of the learning process. A mistake won't call forth a reprimand; it will trigger the system to help the student overcome his misunderstanding. If someone really gets stuck, the system will offer to explain the circumstances to a teacher. There should be less apprehension about formal tests and fewer surprises, because ongoing self-quizzing will give each student a better sense of where he or she stands.

15 Many educational software and textbook companies are already delivering interactive computer products in mathematics, languages, economics, and biology that build basic skills this way. For example, Academic Systems of Palo Alto, California, is working on an interactive multimedia instructional system for colleges, to help teach basic math and English courses. The concept is called "mediated learning," and it blends traditional instruction with computer based learning. Each student begins by taking a placement test to determine which topics he or she understands and where instruction is required. The system then creates a personalized lesson plan for the student. Periodic tests monitor the student's progress, and the lesson plan can be modified as the student masters concepts. The program can also report problems to the instructor, who can then give the student individual help. So far, the company has found that students in pilot programs like the new learning materials, but the most successful classes are those in which an instructor is more available. The results underscore the point that new technology, by itself, is not sufficient to improve education.

Comprehension Quiz

True or false

Directions: In the blank provided, indicate whether each statement is true or false.

______ 1. The CD-ROMs that we have today give us a good idea of the types of things the information highway will make available to us when it is fully operational.

______ 2. In a "learning community" project in a New Jersey middle school that linked computers in students' homes with classrooms, the students' dropout and absenteeism rates went down, but they failed to increase their standardized test scores.

______ 3. Because computers will be able to pay individual attention to independent learners, students with different learning rates will be accommodated.

______ 4. Bill Gates believes that using an interactive network's self-administered quizzes will reduce students' fear and apprehension about formal tests.

Multiple-choice

Directions: For each item, select the best answer.

_____ 5. In the future, schools may use multimedia documents to replace
   a. tests.
   b. encyclopedias.
   c. textbooks.
   d. all of the above.

_____ 6. Multimedia documents can be kept thoroughly up-to-date because they will
   a. be continuously revised by students.
   b. not require an extensive amount of memory.
   c. be inexpensive.
   d. be linked to servers on the information highway.

_____ 7. When the information highway becomes fully operational, a student will be able to use it
   a. for self-testing.
   b. to ask questions.
   c. as a tutor.
   d. all of the above.

_____ 8. Bill Gates believes that interactive software will give students a better sense of what they are learning because of
   a. user-friendly directions.
   b. constant risk taking.
   c. ongoing self-quizzing.
   d. consistent reprimands.

_____ 9. Results of pilot programs which used mediated learning suggest that
   a. new technology, by itself, is not sufficient to improve education.
   b. students do not like new learning materials.
   c. students often learn best without an instructor.
   d. students who work at their own pace learn less than students who follow a prescribed schedule.

_____ 10. Bill Gates suggests all of the following are likely to happen *except:*
   a. Computers will improve many students' attitudes toward tests.
   b. Computers will dramatically change the way students learn in school.
   c. Computers will replace teachers.
   d. Computers will encourage students to collaborate more with each other as they learn.

Extend Your Vocabulary by Using Context Clues

Directions: ***Context clues*** are words in a sentence or paragraph that allow the reader to deduce (reason out) the meaning of an unfamiliar word. For each item in this exercise, a sentence from Selection 1-1 containing an important word (*italicized, like this*) is quoted first. Next, there is an additional sentence using the word in the same sense and providing another context clue. Use the context clues to deduce the meaning of each italicized word. *The definition you choose should make sense in both sentences.*

Pronunciation key: ă **pat** ā **pay** âr **care** ä **father** ĕ **pet** ē **be** ĭ **pit** ī **tie** îr **pier** ŏ **pot** ō **toe** ô **paw** oi **noise** ou **out** ŏŏ **took** ōō **boot** ŭ **cut** yōō **abuse** ûr **urge** th **thin** *th* **this** hw **which** zh **vision** ə **about**

_____ 1. "At first, new information technology will just provide *incremental* improvements over today's tools."

Acquiring and refining effective study skills doesn't happen overnight; it's an *incremental* process.

incremental (ĭn krə mĕnt´ l) means:

a. increasing rapidly by large amounts
b. occurring suddenly
c. increasing gradually by small amounts
d. new and difficult

_____ 2. "CD-ROMs are one clear *precursor* to the highway."

Flocks of birds flying south are a *precursor* of winter.

precursor (prē kûr´ sər) means:

a. one that precedes and indicates, suggests, or announces something to come
b. one thing that follows another
c. the final item in a lengthy series of items
d. an unusual solution to a problem

_____ 3. "Boston University has created interactive software for high school students that shows detailed visual *simulations* of chemical phenomena, such as salt molecules dissolving in water."

As part of pilot training, airlines use computer *simulations* of in-flight emergencies.

simulations (sĭm yə lā´ shənz) means:

a. representations, models
b. counterfeit copies
c. distorted images
d. games

_____ 4. "The school system, the teachers, and the parents (well over 90 percent of whom were of Hispanic *extraction* and didn't speak English as a first language) came up with an innovative five-year plan to rescue their schools."

Many large urban community colleges have a multitude of students of various ethnic *extractions.*

extraction (ĭk străk´ shən) means:

a. pulling something out by using great force
b. removal
c. obtaining something without resistance
d. family origin or ancestry

_____ 5. "At Lester B. Pearson School, a Canadian high school serving an ethnically diverse neighborhood, computers are an *integral* part of every course in the daily curriculum."

The kitchen is an *integral* part of the American home.

integral (ĭn´ tĭ grəl) means:

a. entire; total
b. essential or necessary for completeness
c. little used; secondary
d. technologically challenging

_____ 6. "A student will ask, perhaps orally, 'What caused the American Civil War?' His or he computer will reply, describing the conflicting *contentions:* that it was primarily a battle over economics or human rights."

The Miles brothers finally dissolved their business partnership; they were never able to resolve their *contentions* regarding the company's finances.

contentions (kən tĕn´ shənz) means:

a. loud, noisy disagreements
b. opposing views held by those in a dispute
c. beliefs held long and deeply
d. contests

______ 7. "The machine, like a good human teacher, won't give in to a child who has lopsided interests. Instead it will use the child's *predilections* to teach a broader curriculum."

When children are given choices between outdoor activities and indoor ones, their *predilections* are usually for outdoor ones.

predilections (prĕd´ l ĕk shənz) means:

a. intense dislikes
b. events that precede other events in time
c. preferences for one thing over another
d. natural talents or abilities

______ 8. "Different learning rates will be *accommodated,* because computers will be able to pay individual attention to independent learners."

If you are a vegetarian or have special dietary restrictions, you can be *accommodated* by airlines if you notify them ahead of time of your needs.

accommodated (ə kŏm´ ə dāt əd) means:

a. allowed for; specially provided for
b. settled; reconciled
c. improved
d. ignored; not paid attention to

______ 9. "A mistake won't call forth a *reprimand;* it will trigger the system to help the student overcome his misunderstanding."

The police officer received an official *reprimand* from the chief of police for her unprofessional handling of the protesters.

reprimand (rĕp´ rə mănd) means:

a. praise; complimentary words
b. certificate of appreciation
c. an explanation
d. harsh criticism or severe disapproval

______ 10. "So far, the company has found that students in *pilot* programs like the new learning materials, but the most successful classes are those in which an instructor is more available."

Because the "casual dress" *pilot* project received such a positive response from the employees, the company changed its dress code permanently.

pilot (pī´ lət) means:

a. pertaining to the operation of an aircraft
b. experimental; trial
c. follow-up
d. pertaining to a television program produced as a prototype for a possible series

Respond in Writing

Directions: As Oliver Wendell Holmes observed, "Writing is good for us because it brings our thoughts out into the open." These are essay-type exercises that will help you bring your thoughts into the open. Refer to Selection 1-1 as necessary to answer them.

Option for collaboration: It has been said that "None of us is as smart as all of us." Adults, in particular, learn well from each other. For this reason, your instructor may prefer that you work collaboratively—that is, with other students—on some of the "Respond in Writing" exercises. These exercises are identified in the margin. *If your instructor directs you to work collaboratively on any of these items,* form groups of three or four classmates to complete the exercise together. Discuss your answers with each other and have one member of the group record the answers. A member of the group may be asked to share the group's answers with the class.

1. Describe at least three surprising or interesting facts you learned about the impact of information technology on education.

Option

Exercise 2 may be completed collaboratively.

2. What information technology resources (such as computer labs and multimedia) are available at your college? Which of the new forms of information technology have you already used to further your learning at school or at home?

3. Which of the possibilities offered by information technology do you think would help you learn more effectively in college? Why?

Option

Exercise 4 may be completed collaboratively.

4. Predictably, Gates discusses only positive aspects of information technology in education. List some potential problems, limitations, or even disadvantages you think might be associated with using this technology in schools.

Option

Exercise 5 may be completed collaboratively.

5. What is the most important overall message the writer wants the reader to understand about information technology in education? Try to answer this question in one sentence.

Selection 1-2

Literature

SAVED

FROM *THE AUTOBIOGRAPHY OF MALCOLM X*
AS TOLD TO ALEX HALEY

Prepare Yourself to Read

Directions: Do these exercises *before you read Selection 1-2.*

1. First, read and think about the title. What do you already know about Malcolm X?

____

____

2. Next, complete your preview by reading the following:

   Introduction (in *italics*)
   First paragraph (paragraph 1)
   All of the last paragraph (paragraph 19)

   On the basis of your preview, what aspect of Malcolm X's life do you think will be discussed?

   ____

   ____

Apply Comprehension Skills

Directions: Do these exercises *as you read Selection 1-2.* Apply two skills from this chapter:

Set your goal for reading. What do you hope to learn about Malcolm X?

____

Plan your time. Estimate how long it will take you to read Selection 1-2.

____

SAVED

Born Malcolm Little in 1925, Malcolm X was a member of the American Black Muslims (1952–1963), an organization which advocated separatism and black pride. Before Malcolm X became a prominent Black Muslim and political leader, he served time in prison.

In this selection, Malcolm X describes a life-changing experience he had while he was in prison. His desire to write letters to Elijah Muhammad during this time motivated Malcolm X to make this profound change in his life. (Elijah Muhammad was an activist and leader of the Black Muslims in this country from 1934 to 1975; he favored political, social, and economic independence for black Americans.)

Malcolm X eventually separated from the Black Muslims and converted to orthodox Islam. He founded the Organization of Afro-American Unity in 1964. In 1965, Malcolm X was assassinated in Harlem as he was about to give a speech.

1 It was because of my letters that I happened to stumble upon starting to acquire some kind of a homemade education.

2 I became increasingly frustrated at not being able to express what I wanted to convey in letters that I wrote, especially those to Mr. Elijah Muhammad. In the street, I had been the most articulate hustler out there—I had commanded attention when I said something. But now, trying to write simple English, I not only wasn't articulate, I wasn't even functional. How would I sound writing in slang, the way I would *say* it, something such as, "Look, daddy, let me pull your coat about a cat, Elijah Muhammad—"

3 Many who today hear me somewhere in person, or on television, or those who read something I've said, will think I went to school far beyond the eighth grade. This impression is due entirely to my prison studies.

It had really begun back in the Charlestown Prison, when Bimbi first made me feel envy of his stock of knowledge. Bimbi had always taken charge of any conversation he was in, and I had tried to emulate him. But every book I picked up had few sentences which didn't contain anywhere from one to nearly all of the words that might as well have been in Chinese. When I just skipped those words, of course, I really ended up with little idea of what the book said. So I had come to the Norfolk Prison Colony still going through only book-reading motions. Pretty soon, I would have quit even these motions, unless I had received the motivation that I did. 4

I saw that the best thing I could do was get hold of a dictionary—to study, to learn some words. I was lucky enough to reason also that I should try to improve my penmanship. It was sad. I couldn't even write in a straight line. It was both ideas together that moved me to request a dictionary along with some tablets and pencils from the Norfolk Prison Colony school. 5

I spent two days just riffling uncertainly through the dictionary's pages. I'd never realized so many words existed! I didn't know which words I needed to learn. Finally, just to start some kind of action, I began copying. 6

In my slow, painstaking, ragged handwriting, I copied into my tablet everything printed on that first page, down to the punctuation marks. 7

I believe it took me a day. Then, aloud, I read back, to myself, everything I'd written on the tablet. Over and over, aloud, to myself, I read my own handwriting. 8

I woke up the next morning, thinking about those words—immensely proud to realize that not only had I written so much at one time, but I'd written words that I never knew were in the world. Moreover, with a little effort, I also could 9

Source: "Saved," from *The Autobiography of Malcolm X* with the assistance of Alex Haley, Ballantine, New York, 1992, pp. 171–174, 179.

remember what many of these words meant. I reviewed the words whose meanings I didn't remember. Funny thing, from the dictionary first page right now, that "aardvark" springs to my mind. The dictionary had a picture of it, a long-tailed, long-eared, burrowing African mammal, which lives off termites caught by sticking out its tongue as an anteater does for ants.

10 I was so fascinated that I went on—I copied the dictionary's next page. And the same experience came when I studied that. With every succeeding page, I also learned of people and places and events from history. Actually the dictionary is like a miniature encyclopedia. Finally the dictionary's A section had filled a whole tablet—and I went on into the B's. That was the way I started copying what eventually became the entire dictionary. It went a lot faster after so much practice helped me to pick up handwriting speed. Between what I wrote in my tablet, and writing letters, during the rest of my time in prison I would guess I wrote a million words.

11 I suppose it was inevitable that as my word-base broadened, I could for the first time pick up a book and read and now begin to understand what the book was saying. Anyone who has read a great deal can imagine the new world that opened. Let me tell you something: from then until I left that prison, in every free moment I had, if I was not reading in the library, I was reading on my bunk. You couldn't have gotten me out of books with a wedge. Between Mr. Muhammad's teachings, my correspondence, my visitors—usually Ella and Reginald—and my reading of books, months passed without my even thinking about being imprisoned. In fact, up to then, I never had been so truly free in my life.

12 The Norfolk Prison Colony's library was in the school building. A variety of classes was taught there by instructors who came from such places as Harvard and Boston universities. The weekly debates between inmate teams were also held in the school building. You would be astonished to know how worked up convict debaters and audiences would get over subjects like "Should Babies Be Fed Milk?"

13 Available on the prison library's shelves were books on just about every general subject. Much of the big private collection that Parkhurst had willed to the prison was still in crates and boxes in the back of the library—thousands of old books. Some of them looked ancient: covers faded, old-time parchment-looking binding. Parkhurst, I've mentioned, seemed to have been principally interested in history and religion. He had the money and the special interest to have a lot of books that you wouldn't have in general circulation. Any college library would have been lucky to get that collection.

14 As you can imagine, especially in a prison where there was heavy emphasis on rehabilitation, an inmate was smiled upon if he demonstrated an unusually intense interest in books. There was a sizable number of well-read inmates, especially the popular debaters. Some were said by many to be practically walking encyclopedias. They were almost celebrities. No university would ask any student to devour literature as I did when this new world opened to me, of being able to read and *understand.*

15 I read more in my room than in the library itself. An inmate who was known to read a lot could check out more than the permitted maximum number of books. I preferred reading in the total isolation of my own room.

16 When I had progressed to really serious reading, every night at about ten P.M. I would be outraged with the "lights out." It always seemed to catch me right in the middle of something engrossing.

17 Fortunately, right outside my door was a corridor light that cast a glow into my room. The glow was enough to read by, once my eyes adjusted to it. So when "lights out" came, I would sit on the floor where I could continue reading in that glow.

18 At one-hour intervals the night guards paced past every room. Each time I heard the approaching footsteps, I jumped into bed and

feigned sleep. And as soon as the guard passed, I got back out of bed onto the floor area of that light-glow, where I would read for another fifty-eight minutes—until the guard approached again. That went on until three or four every morning. Three or four hours of sleep a night was enough for me. Often in the years in the streets I had slept less than that. . . .

19 I have often reflected upon the new vistas that reading opened to me. I knew right there in prison that reading had changed forever the course of my life. As I see it today, the ability to read awoke inside me some long dormant craving to be mentally alive. I certainly wasn't seeking any degree, the way a college confers a status symbol upon its students. My homemade education gave me, with every additional book that I read, a little bit more sensitivity to the deafness, dumbness, and blindness that was afflicting the black race in America. Not long ago, an English writer telephoned me from London, asking questions. One was, "What's your alma mater?" I told him, "Books." You will never catch me with a free fifteen minutes in which I'm not studying something I feel might be able to help the black man.

Comprehension Quiz

True or false

Directions: In the blank provided, indicate whether each statement is true or false.

______ 1. There were a small number of well-read inmates at the prison in which Malcolm X served time.

______ 2. Despite Malcolm's initially limited ability to read and write, he was a person capable of learning.

______ 3. Norfolk Prison Colony liked prisoners to exhibit an interest in rehabilitating themselves while in prison.

______ 4. Malcolm's prison experience provided him with no opportunity to improve his reading or writing skills.

Multiple-choice

Directions: For each item, select the best answer.

______ 5. What did Malcolm X mean when he said, "In fact, up to then, I had never been so truly free in my life"?

a. He had been freed from prison.
b. He was able to explore a "new world" of books and ideas even though he was in prison.
c. He could devote as much time as he wanted to learning.
d. He felt carefree.

_____ 6. According to Malcolm X, he felt a need to begin to acquire more education because of

a. his inability to express himself well in conversation.
b. his desire to write letters and his envy of Bimbi.
c. the influence of Parkhurst.
d. the encouragement of a certain prison guard.

_____ 7. Prison inmates who were outstanding debators were

a. looked down on by other inmates.
b. regarded almost as celebrities by other inmates.
c. ignored by other inmates.
d. disliked.

_____ 8. The Norfolk Prison Colony was exemplary because of

a. its strong emphasis on rehabilitation.
b. its unusually large library.
c. the quality of instructors in the prison school.
d. all of the above.

_____ 9. Parkhurst was

a. the prison warden.
b. a teacher who taught at the prison.
c. the donor of the library books.
d. Malcolm's cellmate.

_____ 10. The dictionary was the book that opened the door of learning for Malcolm X; he used it

a. as a miniature encyclopedia which provided background knowledge about a variety of subjects.
b. to improve his penmanship by copying its pages.
c. to improve and expand his vocabulary.
d. all of the above.

Extend Your Vocabulary by Using Context Clues

Key term

Context clues: Words in sentences or paragraphs from which the meaning of an unfamiliar word can be deduced.

Directions: ***Context clues*** are words in a sentence or paragraph that allow the reader to deduce (reason out) the meaning of an unfamiliar word. For each item in this exercise, a sentence from Selection 1-2 containing an important word *(italicized, like this)* is quoted first. Next, there is an additional sentence using the word in the same sense and providing another context clue. Use the context clues to deduce the meaning of each italicized word. *The definition you choose should make sense in both sentences.*

Pronunciation key: ă **pat** ā **pay** âr **care** ä **father** ĕ **pet** ē **be** ĭ **pit** ī **tie** îr **pier** ŏ **pot** ō **toe** ô **paw** oi **noise** ou **out** ŏŏ **took** ōō **boot** ŭ **cut** yōō **abuse** ûr **urge** th **thin** *th* **this** hw **which** zh **vision** ə **about**

______ 1. "I had become increasingly frustrated at not being able to express what I wanted to *convey* in letters that I wrote, especially those to Mr. Elijah Muhammad."

I am sorry that I was unable to attend your uncle's funeral; please *convey* my sympathy to your aunt.

convey (kən vā´) means:

a. remember
b. achieve
c. write
d. communicate

______ 2. "In the street, I had been the most *articulate* hustler out there—I had commanded attention when I said something."

Because Prime Minister Winston Churchill was so *articulate,* his speeches are considered some of the finest ever given.

articulate (är tĭk´ yə lət) means:

a. using clear, expressive language
b. liking to talk
c. talking extensively
d. talking rapidly

______ 3. "Bimbi had always taken charge of any conversation he was in, and I had tried to *emulate* him."

Parents should be good role models, since children often *emulate* them.

emulate (ĕm´ yə lāt) means:

a. surpass by diligent effort
b. try to equal or excel, especially through imitation
c. reject
d. ridicule or make fun of

______ 4. "In my slow, *painstaking,* ragged handwriting, I copied into my tablet everything printed on that first page, down to the punctuation marks."

Rebuilding and restoring an antique automobile is a *painstaking* process.

painstaking (pānz´ tā kĭng) means:

a. rapid
b. confusing
c. painful
d. careful

_____ 5. "With every *succeeding* page, I also learned of people and places and events from history."

In the years *succeeding* his presidency, Jimmy Carter and his wife Rosalynn participated in numerous humanitarian projects.

succeeding (sək sēd´ ĭng) means:

a. coming next or after
b. coming before
c. inserted or inserted in
d. preceding.

_____ 6. "I suppose it was *inevitable* that as my word-base broadened, I could for the first time pick up a book and read and now begin to understand what the book was saying."

It is *inevitable* that summer follows spring.

inevitable (ĭn ĕv´ ĭ tə bəl) means:

a. likely to happen
b. uncertain
c. incapable of being prevented or avoided
d. unreasonable.

_____ 7. "Much of the big private collection that Parkhurst had *willed* to the prison was still in crates and boxes in the back of the library—thousands of old books."

Since my grandmother is no longer alive, I treasure the piano she *willed* to me.

willed (wĭld) means:

a. kept in storage
b. taken back
c. received as a gift
d. granted in a legal will; bequeathed

_____ 8. "As you can imagine, especially in a prison where there was heavy emphasis on *rehabilitation,* an inmate was smiled upon if he demonstrated an unusually intense interest in books."

It took six months of *rehabilitation* for the quarterback to recover fully from his back injury.

rehabilitation (rē hĭ bĭl ĭ tā´ shən) means:

a. regaining useful life through education or therapy
b. hard physical labor
c. rest and relaxation
d. cooperation

______ 9. "Fortunately, right outside my door was the *corridor* light that cast a glow in the room."

When the fire alarm sounded, students quickly left their classroom and walked down the *corridor* to the exit.

corridor (kôr′ ĭ dər) means:

a. door that leads to an exit
b. large room
c. passageway with rooms opening into it
d. an open area outside a building

______ 10. "Each time I heard the approaching footsteps, I jumped into bed and *feigned* sleep."

Have you ever *feigned* illness so that you wouldn't have to go to work?

feigned (fānd) means:

a. endured
b. experienced
c. pretended; gave a false appearance of
d. suffered or felt pain

Respond in Writing

Directions: As Oliver Wendell Holmes observed, "Writing is good for us because it brings our thoughts out into the open." These are essay-type exercises that will help you bring your thoughts into the open. Refer to Selection 1-2 as necessary to answer them.

Option for collaboration: For some of the "Respond in Writing" exercises, your instructor may prefer that you work collaboratively, that is, with other students. These exercises are identified in the margin. *If your instructor directs you to work collaboratively on any of these items,* form groups of three or four classmates to complete the exercise together. Discuss your answers with each other and have one member of the group record the answers. A member of the group may be asked to share the group's answers with the class.

1. State at least three surprising or interesting facts you learned about Malcolm X.

____

____

____

____

2. Why did Malcolm X want to become a better writer and reader?

3. Although Malcolm X may not have realized it, he used many of the same learning techniques that effective college students use. What were some of them?

Option

Exercise 4 may be completed collaboratively.

4. What are at least three ways in which Malcolm X's prison experience may have "saved" him?

Option

Exercise 5 may be completed collaboratively.

5. What is the most important overall message the writer wants the reader to understand about Malcolm X's experience in prison? Try to answer this question in one sentence.

Selection 1-3

Study skills

THE TIME MESSAGE

BY ELWOOD N. CHAPMAN

Prepare Yourself to Read

Directions: Do these exercises *before you read Selection 1-3.*

1. First, read and think about the title. What do you already know about time management?

 ____

 ____

2. Next, complete your preview by reading the following:

 Introduction (in *italics*)
 First paragraph (paragraph 1)
 Headings (in **bold print**)
 All of the last paragraph (paragraph 20)

 On the basis of your preview, what aspects of time management do you think will be discussed?

 ____

 ____

Apply Comprehension Skills

Directions: Do these exercises *as you read Selection 1-3.* Apply two skills from this chapter:

Set your goal for reading. What do you hope to learn about time management?

____

Plan your time. Estimate how long it will take you to read Selection 1-3.

____

THE TIME MESSAGE

In this chapter from a college orientation handbook, Chapman discusses what he calls the number-one problem of college students: time management. Read each of Chapman's ten messages to determine which ones you might need to apply for efficient management of your time.

1 You may have been exposed to this idea before, but this time try to hear. Pull out your earplugs! Turn up the volume! There is a message that is trying to reach you, and it is important that it get through loud and clear. It's beamed to all college freshmen. The message?

2 Time management!

3 Time is elusive and tricky. It is the easiest thing in the world to waste—the most difficult to control. When you look ahead, it may appear you have more than you need. Yet it has a way of slipping through your fingers like sand. You may suddenly find that there is no way to stretch the little time you have left to cover all your obligations. For example, as a beginning student looking ahead to a full semester or quarter you may feel that you have an oversupply of time on your hands. But toward the end of the term you may panic because time is running out. The answer?

4 Control.

5 Time is dangerous. If you don't control it, it will control you. If you don't make it work for you, it will work against you. You must become the master of time, not the servant. In other words, as a college student time management will be your number-one problem.

6 Study hard and play hard is an old adage, but it still makes sense. You have plenty of time for classes, study, work, and play if you use your time properly. It is not how much time you allocate for study that counts but how much you learn when you do study. Remember! You won't have a good time when you do go out on the town if you have a guilty feeling about your studies.

Too much wasted time is bad medicine. The 7
more time you waste, the easier it is to continue wasting time. Soon, doing nothing becomes a habit you can't break. It becomes a drug. You are hooked and out of control. When this happens, you lose your feeling of accomplishment and you fall by the wayside. A full schedule is a good schedule.

Some students refuse to hear the time mes- 8
sage. They refuse to accept the fact that college life demands some degree of time control. There is no escape. So what's the next step? If you seriously wish to get the time message, this chapter will give it to you. Remember—it will not only improve your grades but also free you to enjoy college life more.

Message 1. Time is valuable—control it from the beginning.

Time is today, not tomorrow or next week. 9
Get in the driver's seat *now.* Start your plan at the beginning of the term and readjust it with each new project. Thus you can spread your work time around a little.

Message 2. Get the notebook habit.

Go to the student bookstore today and buy a 10
pocket-size appointment notebook. There are many varieties of these special notebooks. Select the one you like best. Use it to schedule your study time each day. You can also use it to note important dates (such as announced exams or deadlines for papers), appointments, addresses, and telephone numbers (in case you need to check with professors or classmates about assignments). Keep it with you at all times.

Source: Elwood N. Chapman, "The Time Message," in Frank Christ, ed., *SR/SE Resource Book,* SRA, Chicago, Ill., 1969; abridged from chap. 1, pp. 3–8.

Message 3. Prepare a weekly study schedule.

11 The main purpose of the notebook is to help you prepare a weekly study schedule. Once prepared, follow the same pattern every week with minor adjustments. Sunday is an excellent day to make up your schedule for the following week. Write in your class schedule first. Add your work hours, if any. Then write in the hours each day you feel you must allocate for study. Keep it simple.

Message 4. Be realistic.

12 Often you know from experience how long it takes you to write a 500-word composition, to study for a quick quiz, to prepare a speech, or to review for a final. When you plan time for these things, be realistic. Don't underestimate. Overestimate, if possible, so that emergencies that arise don't hang you up. Otherwise your entire routine may get thrown off balance while you devote night and day to crash efforts.

Message 5. Make study time fit the course.

13 Some authorities say you should schedule three hours of study for every hour in class; others say two hours of preparation should be sufficient. How *much* study time you schedule for each classroom hour depends on four factors: (1) your ability, (2) the difficulty of the class, (3) the grades you hope to achieve, and (4) how well you use your study time. One thing, however, is certain: you should schedule a minimum of one hour of study for each classroom hour. In many cases, more will be required.

Message 6. Keep your schedule flexible.

14 It is vital that you re-plan your schedule on a weekly basis so that you can keep a degree of flexibility as you move through a semester. For example, as you approach mid-terms or final exams you will want to juggle your schedule to provide more time for review purposes. When a research project is assigned, you will want to provide an additional block of time to squeeze it in. A good schedule must have a little give so that special projects can be taken care of properly. Think out and prepare your schedule each week and do no become a slave to an inflexible pattern. Adjust it as you deem necessary. Experiment. A schedule is nothing more than a predetermined plan to make the best possible use of your time. Don't permit it to handcuff your ability to meet unexpected demands.

Message 7. Use the 20-20-20 formula.

For those students who must work about twenty hours each week and take a full college load, the 20-20-20 formula makes sense. This means you will be in classes (or labs) approximately 20 hours each week, you will work 20 hours, and you will study a minimum of 20 hours. 15

Message 8. Study first—fun later.

You will enjoy your fun time more *after* you have completed your study responsibilities. So, where possible, schedule your study hours in advance of fun activities. This is a sound principle to follow, so keep it in mind as you prepare your first schedule. 16

Message 9. Study some each class day.

Some concentrated study each day is better than many study hours one day and nothing the next. As you work out your individual schedule, attempt to include a minimum of two study hours each day. This will not only keep the study habit alive but also keep you up to date on your class assignments and projects. 17

Message 10. Free on Saturday—study on Sunday.

Many students think that it is psychologically good to back away from all study endeavors for one full day. Most students choose Saturday because of work, sporting events, or social activi- 18 ties. Sunday, on the other hand, seems to be an excellent study day for many students. It is a good day to catch up on back reading and other assignments. Give it some thought; it may be best for you too. Such a plan has the added advantage of warming you up for getting back into the weekday swing.

▪

19 Few beginning freshmen can control their time effectively without a written schedule, so why kid yourself into thinking you don't need one? You do. Later on, when you have had more experience and you have the time-control habit, you may be able to operate without it. Of course the schedule is only the first step. Once you have it prepared, you must stick with it and follow it faithfully. You must push away the many temptations that are always present or your schedule is useless. Your schedule will give you control only if you make it work.

20 Here's the message once more: You have plenty of time to take a full college load, study, work up to twenty hours a week, get sufficient sleep, take care of personal responsibilities, and have a good, healthy social life—if you control your time. It's your decision, and your life. So no excuses, please.

Comprehension Quiz

True or false

Directions: In the blank provided, indicate whether each item is true or false.

_____ 1. According to the author, few beginning college students can control their time effectively without a written schedule.

_____ 2. "Study hard and play hard" is an adage that the author believes no longer makes sense.

_____ 3. All college students realize the importance of controlling their time.

_____ 4. The more time you waste, the easier it is to continue wasting time.

_____ 5. According to the selection, many college students think it is psychologically beneficial to back away from all study tasks for two full days on the weekend.

_____ 6. Some concentrated study each day is better than many study hours one day and none the next.

Multiple-choice

Directions: For each item, select the best answer.

_____ 7. The author wrote this article to convince students that

a. they must become masters of their time.
b. time is the easiest thing in the world to waste.
c. time management is the number one problem of college students.
d. all of the above.

_____ 8. Your weekly study schedule for college classes should have all of the following characteristics *except* that

a. the same pattern must be followed exactly every week.
b. the same pattern should be followed every week with only minor adjustments.
c. some concentrated study for each class should be included each day.
d. a pocket-size calendar should be used to record your study schedule.

_____ 9. The author believes that a college student should schedule

a. a minimum of 1 hour study time for each classroom hour.
b. 2 hours of study each day.
c. a minimum of 3 hours of study each day.
d. 3 hours of study for every hour in class.

_____ 10. According to the selection, how much study time you schedule for each classroom hour depends on all of the following *except*

a. your ability.
b. the difficulty of class assignments and tests.
c. your work schedule.
d. how well you use your time.

Extend Your Vocabulary by Using Context Clues

Directions: ***Context clues*** are words in a sentence or paragraph that allow the reader to deduce (reason out) the meaning of an unfamiliar word. For each item in this exercise, a sequence from Selection 1-3 containing an important word *(italicized, like this)* is quoted first. Next, there is an additional sentence using the word in the same sense and providing another context clue. Use the context clues to deduce the meaning of each italicized word. *The definition you choose should make sense in both sentences.*

Pronunciation key: ă **pat** ā **pay** âr **care** ä **father** ĕ **pet** ē **be** ĭ **pit**
ī **tie** îr **pier** ŏ **pot** ō **toe** ô **paw** oi **noise** ou **out** o͝o **took** o͞o **boot**
ŭ **cut** yo͞o **abuse** ûr **urge** th **thin** *th* **this** hw **which** zh **vision** ə **about**

______ 1. "You may have been *exposed* to these ideas before, but this time try to hear."

College students are *exposed* to many new concepts and different points of view.

exposed (ĭk spōzd′) means:

a. convinced
b. made aware of
c. displayed
d. repeated frequently

______ 2. "Time is *elusive* and tricky."

Because certain mathematical concepts are *elusive,* it can take considerable thought to comprehend them.

elusive (ĭ lo͞o′ sĭv) means:

a. easy
b. unable to be captured
c. difficult to grasp
d. impossible to understand

______ 3. "Study hard and play hard is an old *adage,* but it still makes sense."

My grandmother's favorite *adage* is, "To have a friend, you must be one."

adage (ăd′ ĭj) means:

a. proverb or short saying
b. saying used only in a family
c. proverb made up by a famous person
d. saying whose origin in unknown

______ 4. "It is not how much time you *allocate* for study that counts but how much you learn when you do study."

Tom and Margaret *allocate* approximately one-third of their monthly income to pay for housing and utilities.

allocate (ăl′ ə kāt) means:

a. assign; allot
b. waste; throw away
c. misuse
d. earn

_____ 5. "Once prepared, follow the same pattern each week with *minor* adjustments."

My professor said that my paper was well written and needed only *minor* corrections.

minor (mī´ nĕr) means:

a. weekly
b. done on a regular basis
c. small in amount, size, or importance
d. done by a professional

_____ 6. "When you plan time for these things, be realistic. Don't *underestimate.*"

The soccer team tended to *underestimate* the ability of their opponents.

underestimate (ŭn dər ĕs´ tə māt) means:

a. judge a value or amount too low
b. guess wildly
c. predict accurately
d. value highly

_____ 7. "Think out and prepare your schedule each week and do not become a slave to an *inflexible* pattern."

Professor Little is so *inflexible* that he will not make any exceptions to his course requirements or his grading policies.

inflexible (ĭn flĕk´ sə bəl) means:

a. variable; changing
b. rigid; unalterable
c. unpleasant
d. difficult

_____ 8. "A schedule is nothing more than a *predetermined* plan to make the best possible use of your time."

Some insurance companies insist that each doctor publish a list of *predetermined* charges for medical services.

predetermined (prē dĭ tûr´ mĭnd) means:

a. decided by a group of people
b. incapable of being changed
c. determined or decided in advance
d. incapable of being known or determined

_____ 9. "This is a sound *principle* to follow, so keep it in mind as you prepare your first schedule."

"Isaac Newton is credited with formulating the *principle* of gravity."

principle (prĭn´ sə pəl) means:

a. basic truth, law, or assumption
b. person who directs a public school
c. false belief
d. reason

_____ 10. "Many students think that it is psychologically good to back away from all study *endeavors* for one full day."

Because he works so hard, my father is highly successful in nearly all of his business *endeavors.*

endeavors (ĕn dĕv´ ərz) means:

a. sessions
b. routines
c. carefully made plans
d. attempts or efforts

Respond in Writing

Directions: Refer to Selection 1-3 as necessary to answer these essay-type exercises.

Option for collaboration: For some of the "Respond in Writing" exercises, your instructor may prefer that you work collaboratively, that is, with other students. These exercises are identified in the margin. *If your instructor directs you to work collaboratively on any of these items,* form groups of three or four classmates to complete the exercise together. Discuss your answers with each other and have one member of the group record the answers. A member of the group may be asked to share the group's answers with the class.

1. Which of the "time messages" mentioned in the article do you use now? What *other* things do you do that help you manage your time effectively?

____

____

____

____

____

____

2. Which of the "time messages" mentioned in the article do you still need to "hear"? How would learning these help you? What other changes would enable you to manage your time better?

Option

Exercise 3 may be completed collaboratively.

3. What are some problems that prevent you from using your time as productively as you would like?

What solutions do you propose for the problems listed above?

Option

Exercise 4 may be completed collaboratively.

4. The author calls time management the number-one problem of college students. Is this true for you? Explain why you agree or disagree with the author's statement. If you disagree, describe what you consider *your* number one problem. Is that problem in any way *related* to time management?

Option

Exercise 5 may be completed collaboratively.

5. What is the most important overall message the writer wants the reader to understand about time? Try to answer this question in one sentence.

CHAPTER 2

APPROACHING COLLEGE READING

IN THIS CHAPTER YOU WILL LEARN
THE ANSWERS TO THESE QUESTIONS:

What do I need to know about the reading process?

How can I improve my reading?

Why should I make predictions as I read?

How can I monitor my comprehension while I read?

What do I need to know about adjusting my reading rate?

How can I develop a college-level vocabulary?

What are denotations and connotations?

What is figurative language?

CHAPTER 2 CONTENTS

▪ ▪ ▪ ▪ ▪ ▪ ▪

SKILLS

UNDERSTANDING THE READING PROCESS

IMPROVING YOUR READING

Predicting as You Read

Monitoring Your Comprehension

Adjusting Your Reading Rate

Factors influencing reading rate: Purpose and difficulty

When to slow down

When to speed up

DEVELOPING A COLLEGE-LEVEL VOCABULARY

Using Context Clues

Using Word-Structure Clues

Using a Dictionary Pronunciation Key

Understanding Denotations and Connotations of Words

Understanding Figurative Language

CREATING YOUR SUMMARY

DEVELOPING CHAPTER REVIEW CARDS

READINGS

Selection 2-1 ▪ "A Whale of a Survival Problem" by John Postlethwait and Janet Hopson *(Biology)*

Selection 2-2 ▪ "The Yellow Ribbon" by Pete Hamill *(Literature)*

Selection 2-3 ▪ "What Computers Can, Cannot, and Should Not Do" by Timothy Trainor and Diane Krasnewich *(Computer science)*

To read without reflecting is like eating without digesting.
Edmund Burke

UNDERSTANDING THE READING PROCESS

Understanding the reading process can make you a better reader and help you study more effectively. You should be aware of several important points about reading.

1. *Reading is a form of thinking.* It is your brain that does the reading, not your eyes. Your eyes merely transmit images to the brain for it to interpret. (To understand this, consider a blind person reading Braille: in this case, it is the fingertips that transmit images to the brain.) Therefore, improving your reading means improving your *thinking.* Remember that meaning resides in the reader's mind, not in symbols printed on a page. It is the readers who construct meaning by associating their knowledge and experience with what is on the printed page.
2. *Reading requires no unique mental or physical abilities.* The processes you typically use when you read are the same processes of vision, reasoning, and memory that you use in other areas of your daily life.
3. *The reading process includes three stages.* The three stages of reading are *preparing yourself to read, processing information,* and *reacting to what you read.* These stages overlap, but all three are needed for the reading process to be complete. In Chapter 3, this process will be explained as it applies to college reading.
4. *Effective reading is interactive.* Effective reading requires that you interact with the material you are reading. One way to interact with an author's ideas is to mentally ask yourself questions as you read and then seek answers to these questions. Another way to interact with material you are reading is by relating your own experience and knowledge to the author's ideas. Reading interactively also means being aware of how the material is organized. Finally, interactive reading means that you monitor your comprehension of what you read, and that you take steps to correct the situation when you are *not* comprehending.
5. *Comprehension problems often result from a reader's lack of background knowledge.* Many comprehension problems are not strictly reading comprehension problems but instead are more general comprehension problems that occur when the reader lacks sufficient background knowledge. To put it another way, comprehension problems occur when a reader

does not possess enough information about a subject to understand what an author is saying about it. This means that if you are having difficulty understanding new or unfamiliar material, you may need to increase your background knowledge. (For example, you could read a simplified explanation in an encyclopedia first.) Finding out more about an unfamiliar topic can clear up this kind of problem.

6. *Your reading rate and your comprehension are related.* The more you know about a topic and the better you understand the material, the faster you can read it. Conversely, if you know very little about a topic, you should reduce your reading rate.
7. *Your reading strategies should fit your purpose for reading.* You read for many different purposes, and your reason for reading any particular material affects the way you approach it. (For example, your approach to reading a newspaper or a letter from a friend will be different from your approach to reading and studying a college textbook.) You should choose reading strategies that fit your purpose.

IMPROVING YOUR READING

Predicting as You Read

Key term

Predicting: Anticipating what is coming next as you read.

Predicting means making educated guesses about what is coming next as you read. Predicting is often a natural part of reading, but you may not always do when you are reading a college textbook. As you read an assignment, you should make a conscious effort to anticipate the author's writing pattern. (Chapter 7 examines authors' writing patterns.)

Of course, when you preview a chapter or reading selection you are predicting in a general way what it will be about and how the material is organized. However, when you read and study carefully, you should continue to make predictions *as* you read. For example, if an author presents one side of an issue, you might predict that he or she is going to discuss the other side as well. If a paragraph begins with the question, "Why do people have nightmares?" you would expect the author to explain the reason or reasons.

Predicting helps you concentrate and comprehend; it focuses your attention, because you will then want to read to determine if your prediction was correct. Predicting helps you stay involved with the material you are reading.

Instead of passively waiting to see what comes up next when you are reading, try to anticipate what the author will say or present. You will discover that making predictions helps you become a more active, effective reader.

Monitoring Your Comprehension

Key term

Monitoring your comprehension: Evaluating your understanding as you read and correcting the problem whenever you realize that you are not comprehending.

Monitoring your comprehension means evaluating your understanding as you read and correcting the problem whenever you realize that you are *not* comprehending. You should monitor your comprehension whenever you read and study college textbooks.

To monitor your comprehension, follow these three steps. First, ask yourself, "*Am I understanding what I am reading?*" If you do not understand what you are reading, take a second step and ask yourself, "*Why* don't I understand?" If you can determine why you are not comprehending, you should take a final step: do whatever is needed to correct the situation.

Several specific strategies for correcting comprehension problems are listed in the box on page 60. Make monitoring your comprehension a habit. After all, unless you comprehend what you are reading, you are not really reading.

Adjusting Your Reading Rate

Have you ever been asked, "What's your reading rate?" The fact is that each reader has, or should have, *several* reading rates. Reading everything at the same rate without comprehending is a sign of poor reading, even if the rate is a fast one.

Having flexible reading rates is an important skill. You will find it helpful to begin developing flexibility in your reading rates right away. To become a flexible reader, you may find it useful to think of developing a "collection" of reading speeds. The information below provides a brief introduction to adjusting your reading rate. A range of reading rates and when to use each are presented in the box on page 61.

Factors influencing reading rate: Purpose and difficulty

In order to be flexible, efficient readers adjust their reading rate according to two factors: their *purpose* for reading, and *how difficult* the material is for them.

Obviously, you read for many different purposes. For instance, your purpose in reading a textbook may be to understand and learn the material thoroughly for a test. Or there may be some specific bit of information you are searching for, such as the definition of a term in a textbook, a name in an index, or the starting time of a movie in a newspaper listing. Sometimes, of course, you read a magazine or a book just for pleasure.

What determines how difficult certain material will be for you to read? Actually, there are several factors, such as vocabulary level, writing style, and "idea density." However, the most important factor is *how much you already know about the subject.* If you are reading about computers, for instance, and you already know a great deal about them, then you will easily understand the terms and concepts you encounter. The information will make more sense to you than it would to someone who knows nothing about computers.

Strategies for Correcting Certain Comprehension Problems

Problems	Solutions
I am not understanding because the subject is completely new to me. College reading frequently introduces you to subjects you have not learned about before. Textbooks contain a great deal of new information, sometimes even within a single paragraph.	▪ Keep reading to see if the material becomes clearer. ▪ Ask for a brief explanation from someone who is knowledgeable about the topic. ▪ Read supplemental material or simpler material on the same topic (perhaps an encyclopedia, another textbook, or a book from the library).
I am not understanding because there are words I do not know. College material often contains new words and specialized or technical vocabulary that you must learn.	▪ Try to use the rest of the sentence or paragraph (the context) to figure out the meaning of an unfamiliar word. ▪ Look up unfamiliar words in a dictionary or in the glossary at the back of the textbook. ▪ Ask someone the meaning of unfamiliar words.
I am not understanding because I am not concentrating as I read. Distractors are interfering with my concentration. Your mind may sometimes wander while you are reading long or difficult passages.	▪ Identify what is bothering you. Is it a *physical distraction* (such as a noisy room or being tired) or is it a *psychological distraction* (such as being worried or daydreaming)? ▪ Take some action that will help you eliminate the distraction. For example, close the door or move to a quiet room. ▪ Turn off the television. Turn off the music. Don't answer the telephone. ▪ If you are worrying about a personal problem or worrying about finding time for important errands (for example, jot the items down on a "to do" list). Then, after studying, tackle your "to do" list. The point is to take some action toward solving problems that are distracting you. ▪ Make a deliberate decision to concentrate on what you are reading. Concentration does not happen automatically.

When you are assigned to read a textbook chapter, you should look through it first. Ask yourself why you are reading it and how much you already know about it. If the material is new to you, then you will need to read more slowly. If you are very familiar with the material, you can probably read it at a faster rate. The point is to read flexibly, adjusting your rate as needed. Often, you must continue to adjust your rate *as* you are reading.

Flexible Reading: Information-Gathering Techniques and Reading Rates

	Approximate rate (wpm)	*Uses*
Information-gathering techniques:		
Scanning	1,500 words per minute (wpm) or more	To find a particular piece of information (such as a name, date, or phone number)
Skimming	800–1,000 wpm	To get an overview of the highlights of the material
Reading rates:		
Rapid reading	300–500 wpm	For fairly easy material; when you want only important facts or ideas; for leisure reading
Average reading	200–300 wpm	For textbooks, complex magazines and journals, and literature
Study reading	50–200 wpm	For new vocabulary, complex concepts, technical material, and retaining details (such as legal documents, material to be memorized, and material of great interest or importance)

When to slow down

Here are some situations in which you should slow down your reading:

- You know very little about the topic, or it is entirely new to you.
- A passage consists of complicated or technical material that you need to learn.
- A passage has details you need to remember.
- A passage contains new or difficult vocabulary.
- There are directions that you must follow.
- The material is accompanied by charts or graphs to which you must shift your attention as you read.
- The material requires you to visualize something in your mind (a section on the digestive system in a biology text would be an example).
- The writing is beautiful, artistic, descriptive, or poetic and invites you to linger and enjoy each word. (You may want to read such material aloud to yourself.)
- The material contains ideas you want to consider carefully (such as two sides of an argument) or "words to live by" (such as philosophical, religious, or inspirational writing).

When to speed up

Here are some situations in which you can speed up your reading:

- The whole passage is easy; there are no complicated sentences, no complex ideas, and no difficult terms.
- There is an easy passage within a longer, more difficult section.
- A passage gives an example of something you already understand, or explains it in different words.
- You are already knowledgeable about the topic.
- You want only main ideas and are not concerned about details.
- The material is not related to your purpose for reading (for example, a section of a magazine article that does not pertain to the topic you are researching).

Here are four useful tips for increasing your reading rate on easy material:

1. Practice regularly with easy, interesting material, such as a newspaper, a magazine (like *Reader's Digest*), or a short, easy novel.
2. Read for 15 minutes each day, pushing yourself to read at a rate that is slightly too fast for you—in other words, a rate that is slightly uncomfortable. Once it becomes comfortable, push yourself a little more.

3. Monitor your concentration. If you are momentarily distracted, return immediately to your reading.
4. Keep track of the number of pages you read each day.

As you continue to practice, you will find that you are able to read more pages in the same amount of time. You will also find that you can usually understand the important points in a passage even though you are reading it at a faster rate. There is another bonus: As you read each day, you will be adding to your background knowledge. This will enable you to read related material more effectively in the future.

DEVELOPING A COLLEGE-LEVEL VOCABULARY

Developing a powerful vocabulary is a process that takes time; but every time you read, you have an opportunity to expand your vocabulary. The more you read, the better your vocabulary can become—if you develop a real interest in words and their meanings. Remember that writers take special care to select words that convey precisely what they want to say.

Developing a large vocabulary will make your college work easier, and your speech and your writing will become more interesting and more precise. If all that is not enough, your increased vocabulary may ultimately lead to an increased salary. Research tells us that the size of a person's vocabulary correlates with his or her income. Thinking of each word you learn as "money in the bank" may be an incentive for you to pay attention to new words and add them to your vocabulary!

There are three techniques that you can use to develop and expand your vocabulary as you read:

1. *Use context clues.* Figure out the meaning of an unfamiliar word from clues provided by the surrounding words and sentences.
2. *Use word-structure clues.* Determine a word's meaning on the basis of its prefix, root, or suffix.
3. *Use a dictionary.* Use a dictionary to determine a word's pronunciation and meaning as it is used in the passage you are reading.

The vocabulary exercises that follow each of the reading selections in *Opening Doors* will give you many opportunities to use context clues and practice pronouncing words correctly.

Using Context Clues

Writers want you to understand what they have written. When they use words that they think might be unfamiliar to their readers, they often help the reader by offering various clues in the rest of the sentence so that the reader can deduce (reason out) the meaning of the word. Such clues are called ***context clues.*** (The word *context* refers to the sentence and the paragraph in which the unknown word appears.) Since context clues can help you figure out the meaning of an unfamiliar word, think of them as gifts the writer is giving you to make your job easier.

Key term

Context clues: Other words in a sentence or paragraph which help the reader deduce the meaning of an unfamiliar word.

How can you take advantage of these "gifts"? You can often determine a word's meaning by reading a sentence carefully and by paying attention to the words and other sentences surrounding the unfamiliar word. Some of the most common types of context clues are summarized in the box on page 65.

Using Word-Structure Clues

Key term

Word-structure clue: Root, prefix, or suffix that helps you determine a word's meaning.

Although context clues will be your greatest aid in determining the meaning of unknown words, ***word-structure clues*** or *word-part clues* can also help you determine meanings. A list of important and useful word parts appears in Appendix 1.

To use word-structure clues, examine an unfamiliar word to see if it has any of the following word parts:

- *Root.* Base word that has a meaning of its own.
- *Prefix.* Word part attached to the beginning of a root that adds its meaning to the root.
- *Suffix.* Word part attached to the end of a root word.

Prefixes and suffixes are also called *affixes,* since they are "fixed" (attached or joined) to a root or base word. A word may consist of:

Root only (such as *graph*)
Prefix and root (*tele* • *graph*)
Root and suffix (*graph* • *ic*)
Prefix, root, and suffix (*tele* • *graph* • *ic)*

Learning about prefixes and suffixes not only increases your vocabulary but can help you improve your spelling as well. For instance, if you know the meaning of the prefix *mis* ("bad" or "wrong"), then you will understand why the word *misspell* has two *s*'s: one is in the prefix and one in the root word.

Key term

Root: Base word that has a meaning of its own.

Roots are powerful vocabulary-building tools, since whole "families" of words in English often come from the same root. For example, if you know that the root *aud* means "to hear," then you will understand the connection between *audience* (people who come to *hear* something or someone), *auditorium* (a place where people come to *hear* something), *audit* (enrolling in a course just to *hear* about a subject, rather than taking it for credit), *auditory* (pertaining to *hearing,* as in *auditory nerve*), and *audiologist* (a person trained to evaluate *hearing*).

Using Context Clues to Determine the Meaning of Unfamiliar Words

▪ ▪ ▪ ▪ ▪ ▪ ▪

Type of clue	*What to ask yourself*	*What to look for*	*Example*
1. Definition clue	Are there *definition clues* accompanied by a definition?	Definition clues: *is defined as, is called, is, that is, refers to, meaning, characterized by*	***Interiority*** *is defined as* the tendency toward looking within during middle age.
2. Synonym clue	Is there a *synonym* for an unfamiliar word? Is there a synonym set off by commas, parentheses, a colon, dashes or brackets? (See page 313.)	Synonym clues: *in other words, or, that is to say, also known as, by this we mean*	The garden was ***redolent,*** or *fragrant,* with the scent of orange blossoms.
3. Contrast clue	Is the meaning of an unfamiliar word explained by a contrasting word or phrase with the *opposite* meaning?	Words indicating opposite meanings: *instead of, but, in contrast, on the other hand, however, unlike*	*Instead of* helping my back injury, the new exercises were ***deleterious.***
4. Experience *clue*	Can your own *experience and background knowledge* help you deduce the meaning of an unfamiliar word?	A sentence that contains *a familiar experience* can help you logically figure out the meaning of a new word.	The campers *were warned that hiking up that steep mountain trail would* ***enervate*** even the strongest members of their group.
5. Example clue	Are there *examples* that illustrate the meaning of an unfamiliar word?	Words that introduce examples: *for example, such as, to illustrate, like*	He enjoys *swimming, scuba diving, water skiing,* and other ***aquatic*** sports.
6. Clue from another sentence	Is there *another sentence* in the paragraph that explains the meaning of an unfamiliar word?	*Additional information in another sentence* may help explain an unfamiliar word.	When studying for his final exams, the student was told to ***eschew*** television. *"Just give TV up!"* was his roommate's advice.

Knowing the meaning of a word's root makes it easier to remember the meaning of that word.

Key term

Prefix: Word part attached to the beginning of a root that adds its meaning to the root.

Prefixes change the meaning of a root by adding their meaning to the root. For example, adding the prefix *tele* ("distant" or "far") to the root word *scope* ("to see") creates the word *telescope,* a device that lets you *see* things which are *far* away. Try adding the prefixes *pre* ("before") and *re* ("back") to the root *cede* ("to go" or "to move"). *Precede* means "go before" something or someone else; *recede* means "move back."

By thinking of roots and prefixes as parts of a puzzle, you can often figure out the meaning of an unfamiliar word. Remember, however, that just because a word begins with the same letters as a prefix, it does not necessarily contain that prefix. The words *malt, mall, male,* and *mallard* (a type of duck), for example, have no connection with the prefix *mal* ("wrong" or "bad").

Key term

Suffix: Word part attached to the end of a root word.

Suffixes sometimes add their meaning to a root. Other suffixes change a word's part of speech or inflection. For example, consider these forms of the word *predict:* predict*ion,* predict*ability,* predict*or* (nouns); predict*able* (adjective); predict*ably* (adverb). Examples of suffixes that serve as inflectional endings include adding *s* to make a word plural or *ed* to make a verb past tense.

Suffixes are not as helpful as roots or prefixes in determining the meaning of unfamiliar words because many suffixes have similar or even the same meanings. Also, some root words change their spelling before a suffix is added. For instance, when certain suffixes are added to *happy* the *y* becomes an *i: happier, happiness, happily.*

The most common and helpful roots, prefixes, and suffixes in English come from Latin and ancient Greek. These Latin and Greek word parts not only help you figure out the meaning of a word, they also serve as built-in memory aids that make it easy to recall the meaning.

Spanish, French, Italian, Portuguese, and Romanian are called *romance languages* because they draw so heavily on Latin. (Latin was the "Roman" language because it was spoken in ancient Rome.) Although English is not one of the romance languages (it is a Germanic language), English still has many words derived from Latin and ancient Greek. In particular, a considerable number of terms in science, medicine, and technology are derived from Latin and Greek, so learning word parts from these two older languages can be useful to you if you are considering a career in those fields.

Key term

Etymology: Origin and history of a word.

A word's ***etymology*** (origin and history) will indicate whether it contains Latin or Greek word parts. For this reason, dictionaries often give the etymology of a word in brackets [ ] before or after the definition. These etymologies are frequently helpful; look for familiar word parts in them.

You may want to familiarize yourself with the common roots, prefixes, and suffixes in Appendix 1. Then watch for them in new words you encounter. Use these word-structure clues whenever possible to help you confirm your "educated guess" about a word's meaning. When you look up a word in the dictionary, take an extra minute to check the etymology for word-structure clues that you might recognize. This technique will help you learn and remember the meaning of many roots and affixes.

Using a Dictionary Pronunciation Key

Most college students already know how to locate a word in the dictionary efficiently and accurately, and how to determine which definition is appropriate for their needs. But like many students, you may still not be proficient at or feel confident using a ***dictionary pronunciation key.*** Being able to use a pronunciation key is important, because when you need to remember words, one of the most helpful things you can do is learn their correct pronunciation and say them aloud. Checking and then practicing a word's pronunciation takes only a moment or two.

A complete pronunciation key appears at the beginning of a dictionary. Typically, it looks like the example shown in the box on page 68.

In most dictionaries an abridged pronunciation key, showing only vowel sounds and the more unusual consonant sounds, appears at or near the bottom of each page. It looks something like this:

Pronunciation key: ă **pat** ā **pay** âr **care** ä **fa**ther ĕ **pet** ē **be** ĭ **pit** ī **tie** îr **pier** ŏ **pot** ō **toe** ô **paw** oi **noi**se ou **out** ŏŏ **took** ōō **boot** ŭ **cut** yōō ab**u**se ûr **ur**ge th **thin** *th* **this** hw **wh**ich zh vision ə **a**bout

Your instructor can give you guidance in using a dictionary pronunciation key. In *Opening Doors,* you will have numerous opportunities to practice this skill, since the pronunciation is given for each term in the vocabulary quizzes following the reading selections. To help you interpret the symbols, the sample pronunciation key is repeated in each vocabulary section.

Understanding Denotations and Connotations of Words

Key terms

Denotation: Literal, explicit meaning of a word—its dictionary definition.

Connotation: Additional, nonliteral meaning associated with a word.

The literal, explicit meaning of a word—its dictionary definition—is called its ***denotation.*** But many words also have connotations. A ***connotation*** is an additional, nonliteral meaning associated with a word. For example, the two words *weird* and *distinctive* have similar denotations (something out of the ordinary). It is their connotations that would cause us to choose one of these words instead of the other when describing someone or something. You might describe the traits of someone you admire as *distinctive,* but those of someone you dislike as *weird.* Because *distinctive* has a positive connotation and *weird* has a negative one, most people, for example, would rather be thought of as having *distinctive* clothes than *weird* clothes. *Distinctive* is associated with positive qualities; *weird* is associated with negative ones.

Dictionary Pronunciation Key

▪ ▪ ▪ ▪ ▪ ▪ ▪

Spellings	*Symbols*	*Spellings*	*Symbols*
pat	ă	pop	p
pay	ā	roar	r
care	âr	sauce	s
father	ä	ship, dish	sh
bib	b	tight, stopped	t
church	ch	thin	th
deed, milled	d	this	*th*
pet	ĕ	cut	ŭ
bee	ē	urge, term, firm,	ûr
fife, phase, rough	f	word, heard	
gag	g	valve	v
hat	h	with	w
which	hw	yes	y
pit	ĭ	abuse, use	yo͞o
pie, by	ī	zebra, xylem	z
pier	îr	vision, pleasure,	zh
judge	j	garage	
kick, cat, pique	k	*a*bout, it*e*m, ed*i*ble,	
lid, needle	l (nēd´l)	gall*o*p, circ*u*s	ə
mum	m	butter	ər
no, sudden	n (sŭd´n)		ə
thing	ng	FOREIGN	
pot	ŏ	*French* feu,	œ
toe, hose	ō	*German* schön	
caught, paw	ô	*French* tu,	ü
noise	oi	*German* über	
took	o͝o	*German* ich,	KH
boot	o͞o	*Scottish* loch	
out	ou	*French* bon	N

STRESS

Primary stress ´ bi ol´ o gy (bī ŏl´ ə jē)

Secondary stress ´ bi´ o log´ ical (bī´ ə lŏj´ i kəl)

Source: American Heritage Dictionary, 2d College Paperback ed., Houghton Mifflin, Boston, Mass., 1983, p. xiii. Copyright © 1983 by Houghton Mifflin Company. Reprinted by permission. Abbreviated keys are adapted from the same source.

As suggested above, there are many words whose connotations evoke either a positive or a negative response. For instance, consider your responses to the following pairs of adjectives, nouns, and verbs. They have similar denotations, but different connotations. For example, the word

distinctive	has a more positive connotation than	*weird*
slender		*skinny*
assertive		*pushy*
preowned		*used*
computer whiz		*computer nerd*
correctional facility		*prison*
political activist		*demagogue*
study		*cram*
exaggerate		*lie*
borrow		*plagiarize*

Careful readers ask themselves, "Does this word have a connotation as well as a denotation?" That is, "Is there a positive or negative association in addition to the word's literal meaning?"

Here is an excerpt from an essay on gambling by George Will. Notice the effect of the author's use of the word *lust*. The author chose this word because of its negative connotation:

> Gambling is debased speculation, a lust for sudden wealth that is not connected with the process of making society more productive of goods and services.
>
> *Source:* George F. Will, "Lotteries Cheat, Corrupt the People," Washington Post Writers' Group, 1994. © 1994, Washington Post Writers' Group. Reprinted with permission.

According to the dictionary, one denotation (definition) of *lust* is "overwhelming craving"; another definition is "excessive or unrestrained sexual desire." In this passage, the author uses *lust* because of its negative connotations: pursuit of something evil or bad for us, lack of self-control, impurity. The author could have said simply "a *need* for sudden wealth" or "a *desire* for sudden wealth," but he has used a stronger word to convey that gamblers have an excessive desire for sudden wealth: they crave it.

Understanding Figurative Language

Key term

Figurative language: Imagery; words that create unusual comparisons, vivid pictures, and special effects; also called ***figures of speech.***

Figurative language is language that uses imagery: unusual comparisons, vivid words that create certain effects, words that paint a picture in the reader's or listener's mind. Figurative expressions are also called ***figures of speech.*** You use *figurative language* every day, although you may not know it by that name. Whenever you say something such as "That chemistry test was a monster" or "My mother is a saint," you are using figurative language.

Because figures of speech do not literally mean what the words say, the reader or listener must interpret their meaning. If you say, "My landlord is a prince," you do not actually or literally mean that he is royalty. You expect your listener to interpret your words to mean that you appreciate your landlord, perhaps because he is cooperative and pleasant. If you say, "My landlord is a rat,"you do not literally mean that he is a rodent. You expect your listener to interpret your words to mean that you dislike your landlord, perhaps because he has proved to be untrustworthy or unfair.

Four especially common figures of speech are *metaphor, simile, hyperbole,* and *personification.* Let's look at each of these.

Key term

Metaphor: Figure of speech implying a comparison between two essentially dissimilar things, usually by saying that one of them *is* the other.

Metaphors and similes both make unusual comparisons. A ***metaphor*** is an implied comparison between two things that, on the surface, seem very different from each other, yet are alike in some significant way. In other words, a metaphor usually states that one thing *is* something else. The author assumes that readers will not take his or her words literally, but will understand that this is a figure of speech. (That is, the sentence is to be taken figuratively, not literally.) For example, in the sentence "Katherine's *garden is a rainbow,*" the writer is making a comparison between a garden and a rainbow to help the reader envision the colorful flowers in the garden. To interpret this metaphor correctly, the reader must compare a garden and a rainbow and determine what they have in common: a multitude of colors. (The author does not mean that the garden was literally a rainbow.) Another example of a metaphor would be "Joe's *desk was a mountain of paper.*" It creates a vivid image of how high ("a mountain") the paper was stacked on the desk. As noted, metaphor usually states that one thing *is* something else (in these cases, that a garden *is* a rainbow or that a stack of papers *was* a mountain).

Key term

Simile: Figure of speech stating a comparison between two essentially dissimilar things by saying that one of them is *like* the other.

A ***simile*** is also a comparison between two essentially dissimilar things, but instead of saying that one thing *is* something else, the author says that one thing is *like* something else. A simile is usually introduced by the words *like* or *as.* "Janet felt *like a lottery winner* when she received the scholarship" and "The marine stood at attention *as rigid as an oak"* are examples of similes. In the first sentence, receiving a scholarship is compared to winning a lottery. The author wants us to understand that receiving the scholarship made Janet feel as excited as if she has won a great deal of money in the lottery. In the second sentence, a marine, because of his stiff posture, is compared to an oak tree. To repeat: a simile says that one thing is *like* another. To understand it, you must determine which things are being compared and the important way in which the author considers them to be similar.

Key term

Hyperbole: Figure of speech using obvious exaggeration for emphasis.

Another type of figurative language is ***hyperbole,*** in which obvious exaggeration is used for emphasis. "My parents will *explode* if I get one more speeding ticket" is an example of hyperbole. The parents would not literally "explode," but the exaggeration conveys how angry they would be.

Key term

Personification: Figure of speech giving human traits to nonhuman or nonliving things.

In ***personification,*** nonliving or nonhuman things are given human characteristics or qualities. "My *car groaned, coughed,* and *wheezed,* then *crawled* to a stop" gives human qualities to an automobile, to suggest that the car made strange noises and then quit running. Cars, of course, cannot groan, cough, wheeze, and crawl in the same sense that a person would.

Figurative Language

▪ ▪ ▪ ▪ ▪ ▪ ▪

Figures of speech	*Examples*
Metaphor: Implied comparison between two dissimilar things	Television is a junkyard of violence and stupidity.
Simile: Stated comparison between two dissimilar things, usually introduced by the word *like* or *as*	Ted finally found his car keys, but after his search, his apartment looked as if it had been hit by a tornado.
Hyperbole: Obvious exaggeration for emphasis	I'm so excited about graduation I won't be able to sleep for a month.
Personification: Attribution of human characteristics or qualities to nonhuman or nonliving things	The drab, dilapidated building looked tired and unhappy until it received a face-lift.

Careful readers ask themselves, "Is the author using figurative language?" "What things are being compared, and how are they alike?" "What image is being conveyed?"

The box above summarizes metaphor, simile, hyperbole, and personification.

Understanding figurative language can help you grasp an author's message exactly, and it also makes material more interesting and enjoyable to read.

Here are some examples of figurative language by famous or well-known authors. The figure of speech is italicized. On the lines beside each one, write the meaning of the figure of speech.

What is the meaning of the figurative language?

Metaphor

"A *good laugh is sunshine in the house.*" ______________________________

William Makepeace Thackeray ______________________________

"*Time is money.*" ______________________________

Edward Bulwer-Lytton ______________________________

"*Money is a good servant but a bad master.*" ______________________________

____

Sir Francis Bacon ______________________________

"*Grief is itself* a *medicine.*" ______________________________

William Cowper ______________________________

"Debt is a bottomless sea."

Thomas Carlyle

"All the world's a stage,
And all the men and women merely players:
They have the exits and their entrances;
And one man in his time plays many parts."

William Shakespeare
As You Like It, 1599–1600

"Hope is a good breakfast, but it is a bad supper."

Francis Bacon

"This is what is left of our army! Only rags to mop up China's blood."

Amy Tan
The Kitchen God's Wife

"Because the Internet originated as a computer-science project rather than a communications utility, it has always been a magnet for hackers—programmers who turn their talents toward mischief or malice by breaking into the computer systems of others."

Bill Gates
The Road Ahead

Simile

Much of the Internet culture will seem as quaint to future users of the information highway as stories of wagon trains and pioneers on the Oregon Trail do to us today.

Bill Gates
The Road Ahead

"The water from the spring," she said, "is heavy as gold, sweet as honey, but clear as glass. If you look into the pool you can see your face, just like in a mirror."

Amy Tan
The Kitchen God's Wife

Hyperbole

"Here once the embattled farmers stood, And fired the shot heard round the world."

Ralph Waldo Emerson,
"Concord Hymn"

"Everybody had made a 'ton of money' in the last few years and expected to make a ton more."

Richard Ford,
Independence Day

"He had a big mustache yellowed by eight million Pall Malls."

Richard Ford,
Independence Day

Personification

"Those were the kinds of thoughts that crawled into my head."

Amy Tan
Joy Luck Club

"Chance makes our parents, but choice makes our friends."

Delille

"Misery loves company."

English proverb

"Misfortunes always come in by a door that has been left open for them."

Czech proverb

"When money speaks, the truth is silent."

Russian proverb

DEVELOPING CHAPTER REVIEW CARDS

Review cards, or *summary cards,* are an excellent study tool. They are a way to select, organize, and review the most important information in a textbook chapter. The process of creating review cards helps you organize information in a meaningful way and, at the same time, transfer it into long-term memory. The cards can also be used to prepare for tests (see Part Three). The review card activities in this book give you structured practice in creating these valuable study tools. Once you have learned how to make review cards, you can create them for textbook material in your other courses.

Now, complete the seven review cards for Chapter 2 by answering the questions or following the directions on each card. When you have completed them, you will have summarized important information about: (1) the process of reading, (2) predicting as you read, (3) monitoring your comprehension as you read, (4) adjusting your reading rate, (5) using context clues to determine the meaning of unfamiliar words, (6) word-structure clues, and (7) figurative language.

Understanding the Reading Process

List seven important points about the reading process. (See pages 57–58.)

1. ______________________________
2. ______________________________
3. ______________________________
4. ______________________________
5. ______________________________
6. ______________________________
7. ______________________________

Chapter 2: Approaching College Reading

Predicting As You Read

1. What is predicting? (See page 58.)

____

____

____

2. Why is predicting helpful? (See page 58.)

____

____

____

Chapter 2: Approaching College Reading

Monitoring Your Comprehension

1. What does *monitoring your comprehension* mean? (See page 59.)

____

____

2. Describe the three steps in monitoring your comprehension as you read. (See page 59.)

First: ____

____

Second: ____

____

Third: ____

____

Chapter 2: Approaching College Reading

Adjusting Your Reading Rate

Efficient readers adjust their rate according to two factors. (See page 59.)

Factor 1: ______________________________

Factor 2: ______________________________

List several situations in which it is appropriate to *slow down* your reading rate. (See page 62.)

____

____

____

List several situations in which it is appropriate to *speed up* your reading rate. (See page 62.)

____

____

____

Chapter 2: Approaching College Reading

Using Context Clues to Find Meanings of Words

What are *context clues?* (See pages 63–64.)

____

____

What are six types of context clues? (See the box on page 65.)

1. ______________________________
2. ______________________________
3. ______________________________
4. ______________________________
5. ______________________________
6. ______________________________

Chapter 2: Approaching College Reading

Using Word-Structure Clues

Define the following. (See pages 64–66.)

Word-structure clues: ______________________________

____

Root: ______________________________

____

Prefix: ______________________________

____

Suffix: ______________________________

____

Etymology: ______________________________

____

Figurative Language

Define the following. (See pages 69–70.)

Figurative language: ______________________________

____

Metaphor: ______________________________

____

Simile: ______________________________

____

Hyperbole: ______________________________

____

Personification: ______________________________

____

Chapter 2: Approaching College Reading

READINGS

Selection 2-1

Biology

A WHALE OF A SURVIVAL PROBLEM

FROM *THE NATURE OF LIFE*
BY JOHN POSTLETHWAIT AND JANET HOPSON

Prepare Yourself to Read

Directions: Do these exercises *before you read Selection 2-1.*

1. First, read and think about the title. What do you already know about whales?

 ____

 ____

2. Next, complete your preview by reading the following:

 Introduction (in *italics*)
 First paragraph (paragraph 1)
 First sentence of each paragraph
 Words in *italics*
 Diagram
 All of the last paragraph (paragraph 4)

 On the basis of your preview, what problems threaten a whale's survival?

 ____

 ____

Apply Comprehension Skills

Directions: Do these exercises *as you read Selection 2-1.*

Adjust your reading rate. On the basis of your preview and your prior knowledge of how whales survive, do you think you should read Selection 2-1 slowly or rapidly? ______________________________

Develop a college-level vocabulary. Did you notice any unfamiliar words while you were previewing Selection 2-1? If so, list them here.

____

Predict as you read. As you read Selection 2-1, make predictions about what the author will discuss next. Write your predictions in the blanks provided.

A WHALE OF A SURVIVAL PROBLEM

Have you ever wondered how an animal's size and its survival are related? This textbook selection sheds light on that question and also explains, in part, why people find whales fascinating.

Practice exercises

Directions: At each of the points indicated below, answer the question, "What do you predict will be discussed next?"

1 An intrepid visitor to the perpetually frozen Antarctic could stand at the coastline, raise binoculars, and witness a dramatic sight just a few hundred meters offshore: a spout as tall and straight as a telephone pole fountaining upward from the blowhole of a blue whale (*Balaenoptera musculus),* then condensing into a massive cloud of water vapor in the frigid air. The gigantic animal beneath the water jet would be expelling stale air from its 1-ton lungs after a dive in search of food. Then, resting at the surface only long enough to take four deep breaths of fresh air, the streamlined animal would raise its broad tail, thrust mightily, and plunge into the ocean again. The observer on shore might see such a sequence only twice per hour, since the the blue whale can hold its breath for 30 minutes as it glides along like a submarine, swallowing trillions of tiny shrimp-like animals called krill.

2 It is difficult to comprehend the immense proportions of the blue whale, the largest animal ever to inhabit our planet. At 25 to 30 m (80 to 100 ft) in length, this marine mammal is longer than three railroad boxcars and bigger than any dinosaur that ever lumbered on land. It weighs more than 25 elephants or 1600 fans at a basketball game. Its heart is the size of a beetle—a Volkswagen beetle. And that organ pumps 7200 kg (8 tons) of blood through nearly 2 million kilometers (1.25 million miles) of blood vessels, the largest of which could accommodate an adult person crawling on hands and knees. The animal has a tongue the size of a grown elephant. It has 45,500 kg (50 tons) of muscles to move its 54,500 kg (60 tons) of skin,

Source: John Postlethwait and Janet Hopson, "A Whale of a Survival Problem," in *The Nature of Life,* McGraw-Hill, New York, 1992, chap. 20, pp. 430–431. Reproduced with permission of McGraw-Hill.

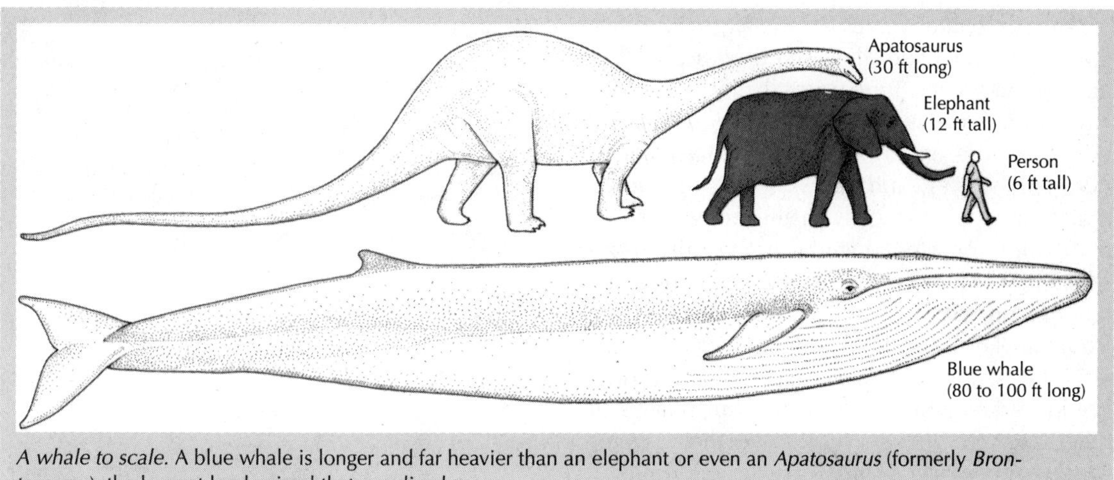

A whale to scale. A blue whale is longer and far heavier than an elephant or even an *Apatosaurus* (formerly *Brontosaurus*), the longest land animal that ever lived.

bones, and organs. And this living mountain can still swim at speeds up to 48 km (30 mi) per hour!

3 Leviathan proportions aside, it is difficult to grasp the enormous problems that so large an organism must overcome simply to stay alive. For starters, a blue whale is a warm-blooded animal with a relatively high metabolic rate; to stay warm and active in an icy ocean environment, it must consume and burn 1 million kilocalories a day. This it does by straining 3600 kg (8000 lb) of krill from the ocean water each day on special food-gathering sieve plates. In addition, each of the trillions of cells in the whale's organs must exchange oxygen and carbon dioxide, take in nutrients, and rid itself of organic wastes, just as a single-celled protozoan living freely in seawater must do. Yet a given whale cell—a liver cell, let's say—can lie deep in the body, separated from the environment by nearly 2 m (6 ft) of blubber, muscle, bone, and other tissues. For this reason, the whale needs elaborate transport systems to deliver oxygen and nutrients and to carry away carbon dioxide and other wastes. Finally, the galaxy of living cells inside a whale must be coordinated and controlled by a brain, a nervous system, and chemical regulators (hormones) so that the organism can function as a single unit.

Practice exercise

What do you predict will be discussed in paragraph 3?

____

Practice exercise

What do you predict will be discussed in paragraph 4?

____

4 Although blue whales are the largest animals that have ever lived, they share with all other animals the same fundamental physical problems of day-to-day survival: how to extract energy from the environment; how to exchange nutrients, wastes, and gases; how to distribute materials to all the cells in the body; how to maintain a constant internal environment despite fluctuations in the external environment; how to support the body; and how to protect it from attackers or from damaging environmental conditions. Blue whales have evolved with unique adaptations of form and function that meet such challenges and leave the animals suited to their way of life.

Comprehension Quiz

True or false

Directions: In the blank provided, indicate whether each statement is true or false.

_____ 1. The blue whale expels water through its blowhole.

_____ 2. The blue whale can hold its breath for more than 1 hour as it glides under water.

_____ 3. The blue whale feeds daily on trillions of tiny shrimplike animals called krill.

_____ 4. Although large, the blue whale is not the largest animal ever to inhabit our earth.

_____ 5. A human adult could crawl on hands and knees through the largest blood vessels of a blue whale.

Multiple-choice

Directions: For each item, select the best answer.

_____ 6. In paragraph 1, "a spout as tall and straight as a telephone pole fountaining upward from the blowhole of a blue whale," refers to

a. ice.
b. saltwater.
c. fresh air.
d. stale air that has condensed into water vapor.

______ 7. The "living mountain" mentioned in paragraph 2 refers to

a. the dinosaur.
b. 8,000 pounds of krill.
c. the blue whale.
d. a grown elephant.

______ 8. After diving for food, the blue whale surfaces and

a. expels stale air through its blowhole, then dives again.
b. expels stale air, rests long enough to take four breaths of fresh air, then dives again.
c. expels stale air, rests on the surface for 30 minutes, then dives again.
d. none of the above.

______ 9. Which of the following problems of day-to-day survival does the blue whale share with all other animals?

a. how to extract energy (food) from the environment.
b. how to distribute materials to all the cells in the body.
c. how to balance the internal environment with the changes in the external environment.
d. all of the above.

______ 10. Because the blue whale is a warm-blooded animal and has a relatively high metabolic rate, it must

a. rid itself of organic wastes.
b. expel stale air through its blowhole.
c. consume and burn 1 million kilocalories a day in order to stay warm and active in the icy ocean.
d. take four deep breaths of fresh air before diving again for food.

Extend Your Vocabulary by Using Context Clues

Directions: ***Context clues*** are words in a sentence or paragraph that allow the reader to deduce (reason out) the meaning of an unfamiliar word. For each item in this exercise, a sentence from Selection 2-1 containing an important word *(italicized, like this)* is quoted first. Next, there is an additional sentence using the word in the same sense and providing another context clue. Use the context clues to deduce the meaning of each italicized word. *The definition you choose should make sense in both sentences.*

Pronunciation key: ă **pat** ā **pay** âr **care** ä **father** ĕ **pet** ē **be** ĭ **pit** ī **tie** îr **pier** ŏ **pot** ō **toe** ô **paw** oi **noise** ou **out** o͝o **took** o͞o **boot** ŭ **cut** yo͞o **abuse** ûr **urge** th **thin** *th* **this** hw **which** zh **vision** ə **about**

_____ 1. "An *intrepid* visitor to the perpetually frozen Antarctic could stand at the coastline, raise binoculars, and witness a dramatic sight just a few hundred meters off shore."

Columbus was an *intrepid* explorer who set sail for the unknown New World.

intrepid (ĭn trĕp´ ĭd) means:

a. extremely cold
b. fun-loving
c. fearless; bold
d. weary; fatigued

_____ 2. "An intrepid visitor to the *perpetually* frozen Antarctic could stand at the coastline, raise binoculars, and witness a dramatic sight just a few hundred meters off shore."

The Earth moves *perpetually* around the sun.

perpetually (pər pĕch´ o͞o əl lē) means:

a. forever
b. partially
c. slowly
d. once a month

_____ 3. "An intrepid visitor to the perpetually frozen Antarctic could stand at the coastline, raise binoculars, and witness a dramatic sight just a few hundred meters off shore: a spout as tall and as straight as a telephone pole fountaining upward from the blow hole of a blue whale, then *condensing* into a massive cloud of water vapor in the frigid air."

When you turn on your car heater in the winter, water vapor may start *condensing* and running down the inside of the windows.

condensing (kən dĕns´ ĭng) means:

a. turning into steam
b. changing from a gas into a liquid
c. becoming colder
d. changing from a liquid into a solid

______ 4. "An intrepid visitor to the perpetually frozen Antarctic could stand at the coastline, raise binoculars, and witness a dramatic sight just a few hundred meters off shore: a spout as tall and as straight as a telephone pole fountaining upward from the blow hole of a blue whale, then condensing into a massive cloud of water vapor in the *frigid* air."

Snowflakes began to fall from the gray, *frigid* sky.

frigid (frĭj´ ĭd) means:

a. smoky
b. dry
c. cloudy
d. extremely cold

______ 5. "The gigantic animal beneath the water jet would be *expelling* stale air from its 1-ton lungs after a dive in search of food."

Our college is *expelling* five students for cheating on an exam.

expelling (ĭk spĕl´ ĭng) means:

a. maintaining
b. breathing out
c. forcing out or ejecting
d. preventing

______ 6. "*Leviathan* proportions aside, it is difficult to grasp the enormous problems that so large an organism must overcome simply to stay alive."

The deep-sea fishermen swore they had seen a *leviathan*—a shark so huge that it was larger than their boat.

leviathan (lə vī´ ə thən) means:

a. something unusually large of its kind
b. measuring device
c. large shark
d. huge ship

______ 7. "For starters, a blue whale is a warm-blooded animal with a *relatively* high metabolic rate; to stay warm in an icy ocean environment, it must consume and burn 1 million kilocalories a day."

Our boss is usually very talkative, but he was *relatively* quiet at the staff meeting today.

relatively (rĕl´ ə tĭv lē) means:

a. pertaining to social relationships
b. pertaining to reality
c. pertaining to a member of the family
d. in comparison with something else

______ 8. "For starters, a blue whale is a warm-blooded animal with a relatively high *metabolic* rate; to stay warm in an icy ocean environment, it must consume and burn 1 million kilocalories a day."

Exercise and stress increase a person's *metabolic* rate.

metabolic (mĕt ə bŏl′ ĭk) means:

a. pertaining to the speed at which an organism moves
b. pertaining to bodily physical and chemical processes that maintain life
c. pertaining to breathing and respiration
d. pertaining to survival

______ 9. "For this reason, the whale needs *elaborate* transport systems to deliver oxygen and nutrients and to carry away carbon dioxide and wastes."

The plans for the queen's coronation were so *elaborate* that it took a staff of 500 people to carry out the arrangements.

elaborate (ĭ lăb′ ər ĭt) means:

a. time-consuming
b. very complex
c. difficult to understand
d. simple

______ 10. "Finally, the *galaxy* of living cells inside a whale must be coordinated and controlled by a brain, a nervous system, and chemical regulators (hormones) so that the organism can function as a single unit."

From the dazzling *galaxy* of toys in the toy department, my young nephew finally selected a remote-controlled car.

galaxy (găl′ ək sē) means:

a. stars in the universe
b. numerous collection of things
c. system
d. display

Respond in Writing

Directions: Refer to Selection 2-1 as necessary to answer these essay-type questions.

Option for collaboration: For some of the "Respond in Writing" exercises, your instructor may prefer that you work collaboratively, that is, with other students. These exercises are identified in the margin. *If your instructor directs you to work collaboratively on any of these items,* form groups of three or four classmates to complete the exercise together. Discuss your answers with each other and have one member of the group record the answers. A member of the group may be asked to share the group's answers with the class.

1. Describe the three comparisons the author uses to illustrate the enormous size of the blue whale's body.

   First comparison:

   ____

   ____

   ____

   Second comparison:

   ____

   ____

   ____

   Third comparison:

   ____

   ____

   ____

Option

Exercise 2 may be completed collaboratively.

2. Because of its size, what are three special problems that blue whales must overcome to survive?

   One problem:

   ____

   ____

   ____

   Another problem:

   ____

   ____

   ____

   A third problem:

   ____

   ____

   ____

Option

Exercise 3 may be completed collaboratively.

3. What is the most important overall message the writer wants the reader to understand about the survival of whales? Try to answer this question in one sentence.

____

____

____

____

____

Selection 2-2

Literature

THE YELLOW RIBBON

BY PETE HAMILL

Prepare Yourself to Read

Directions: Do these exercises *before you read Selection 2-2.*

1. First, read *only* the title, the introduction (in *italics*), and the first paragraph. What comes to your mind when you think of a yellow ribbon?

   ____

   Who are the characters in the story?

   ____

   What is taking place?

   ____

2. As you read the rest of the selection, try to answer these questions:

   Who is Vingo?

   Why is he on the bus?

Apply Comprehension Skills

Directions: Do the practice exercises *as you read Selection 2-2.*

Adjust your reading rate. On the basis of your preview and your prior knowledge about computers, do you think you should read Selection 2-2 slowly or rapidly? ______________________________

Develop a college-level vocabulary. Did you notice any unfamiliar words while you were previewing Selection 2-2? If so, list them here.

____

Predict as you read. As you read Selection 2-2, make predictions about what the author will discuss next. Write your predictions in the blanks provided.

THE YELLOW RIBBON

Today, ribbons of different colors are often worn to show support for various causes. For Vingo, the main character in this story, yellow "ribbons" take on a very special significance.

Practice exercises

Directions: At each of the points indicated below, answer the question, "What do you predict will happen next?"

1 They were going to Fort Lauderdale, the girl remembered later. There were six of them, three boys and three girls, and they picked up the bus at the old terminal on 34th Street, carrying sandwiches and wine in paper bags, dreaming of golden beaches and the tides of the sea as the gray cold spring of New York vanished behind them. Vingo was on board from the beginning.

2 As the bus passed through Jersey and into Philly, they began to notice that Vingo never moved. He sat in front of the young people, his dusty face masking his age, dressed in a plain brown ill-fitting suit. His fingers were stained from cigarettes and he chewed the inside of his lip a lot, frozen into some personal cocoon of silence.

3 Somewhere outside of Washington, deep into the night, the bus pulled into a Howard Johnson's, and everybody got off except Vingo. He sat rooted in his seat, and the young people began to wonder about him, trying to imagine his life: Perhaps he was a sea captain, maybe he had run away from his wife, he could be an old soldier going home. When they went back to the bus, the girl sat beside him and introduced herself.

Practice exercise

What do you predict will happen next?

____

____

4 "We're going to Florida," the girl said brightly. "You going that far?"

5 "I don't know," Vingo said.

6 "I've never been there," she said. "I hear it's beautiful."

7 "It is," he said quietly, as if remembering something he had tried to forget.

8 "You live there?"

Source: Pete Hamill, "The Yellow Ribbon," *New York Post,* 1972.

9 "I did some time there in the Navy. Jacksonville."

10 "Want some wine?" she said. He smiled and took the bottle of Chianti and took a swig. He thanked her and retreated again into his silence. After a while, she went back to the others, as Vingo nodded in sleep.

11 In the morning they awoke outside another Howard Johnson's, and this time Vingo went in. The girl insisted that he join them. He seemed very shy and ordered black coffee and smoked nervously, as the young people chattered about sleeping on the beaches. When they went back on the bus, the girl sat with Vingo again, and after a while, slowly and painfully and with great hesitation, he began to tell his story. He had been in jail in New York for the last four years, and now he was going home.

12 "Four years!" the girl said. "What did you do?"

13 "It doesn't matter," he said with quiet bluntness. "I did it and I went to jail. If you can't do the time, don't do the crime. That's what they say and they're right."

14 "Are you married?"

15 "I don't know."

16 "You don't know?" she said.

17 "Well, when I was in the can I wrote to my wife," he said. "I told her, I said, Martha, I understand if you can't stay married to me. I told her that. I said I was gonna be away a long time, and that if she couldn't stand it, if the kids kept askin' questions, if it hurt her too much, well, she could just forget me. Get a new guy—she's a wonderful woman, really something—and forget about me. I told her she didn't have to write me or nothing. And she didn't. Not for three-and-a-half years."

18 "And are you going home now, not knowing?"

19 "Yeah," he said shyly. "Well, last week, when I was sure the parole was coming through I wrote her. I told her that if she had a new guy, I understood. But if she didn't, if she would take me back she should let me know. We used to live in this town, Brunswick, just before Jacksonville, and there's a great big oak tree just as

Practice exercise

What do you predict will happen next?

____

____

you come into town, a very famous tree, huge. I told her if she would take me back, she should put a yellow handkerchief on the tree, and I would get off and come home. If she didn't want me, forget it, no handkerchief, and I'd keep going on through."

20 "Wow," the girl said. "Wow."

21 She told the others, and soon all of them were in it, caught up in the approach of Brunswick, looking at the pictures Vingo showed them of his wife and three children, the woman handsome in a plain way, the children still unformed in a cracked, much-handled snapshot. Now they were 20 miles from Brunswick and the young people took over window seats on the right side, waiting for the approach of the great oak tree. Vingo stopped looking, tightening his face into the ex-con's mask, as if fortifying himself against still another disappointment. Then it was 10 miles, and then five and the bus acquired a dark hushed mood, full of silence, of absence, of lost years, of the woman's plain face, of the sudden letter on the breakfast table, of the wonder of children, of the iron bars of solitude.

22 Then suddenly all of the young people were up out of their seats, screaming and shouting and crying, doing small dances, shaking clenched fists in triumph and exaltation. All except Vingo.

23 Vingo sat there stunned, looking at the oak tree. It was covered with yellow handkerchiefs, 20 of them, 30 of them, maybe hundreds, a tree that stood like a banner of welcome blowing and billowing in the wind, turned into a gorgeous yellow blur by the passing bus. As the young people shouted, the old con slowly rose from his seat, holding himself tightly, and made his way to the front of the bus to go home.

Practice exercise

What do you predict will happen next?

____

Comprehension Quiz

True or false

Directions: In the blank provided, indicate whether each statement is true or false.

_______ 1. Six young people boarded a bus for a summer vacation in Florida.

_______ 2. Vingo told his story to a young woman on the train.

_______ 3. The author states that Vingo's wife was foolish.

_______ 4. Vingo was traveling to his home in Jacksonville, Florida.

Multiple-choice

Directions: For each item, select the best answer.

_______ 5. Vingo's prison experience had left him

a. unfeeling and uncaring.
b. feeling that he had paid his debt to society by serving his jail sentence.
c. feeling suicidal.
d. feeling that he had been imprisoned unjustly.

_______ 6. According to the author, when Vingo saw the yellow handkerchiefs, he felt

a. relieved.
b. sad.
c. stunned.
d. disappointed.

_______ 7. To Vingo, the yellow handkerchiefs tied to the oak tree meant

a. an approaching holiday.
b. welcome home for returning soldiers.
c. nothing.
d. forgiveness and a new start.

_______ 8. At the end of the story, we can conclude that Vingo's wife was

a. forgiving.
b. bitter.
c. unforgiving.
d. revengeful.

_______ 9. The group of young people were traveling to Florida from

a. New Jersey.
b. Philadelphia.
c. New York.
d. Washington.

______ 10. Perhaps the lesson the young people learned from Vingo's story is that

a. despite the hardships of life, there is an opportunity for happiness if one is willing to try again.
b. Vingo's wife was justified in not allowing him to return.
c. for an ex-con, there not much chance for happiness.
d. there are some things that no marriage can survive.

Extend Your Vocabulary by Using Context Clues

Directions: ***Context clues*** are words in a sentence or paragraph that allow the reader to deduce (reason out) the meaning of an unfamiliar word. For each item in this exercise, a sentence from Selection 2-2 containing an important word *(italicized, like this)* is quoted first. Next, there is an additional sentence using the word in the same sense and providing another context clue. Use the context clues to deduce the meaning of each italicized word. *The definition you choose should make sense in both sentences.*

Pronunciation key: ă **pat** ā **pay** âr **care** ä **father** ĕ **pet** ē **be** ĭ **pit** ī **tie** îr **pier** ŏ **pot** ō **toe** ô **paw** oi **noise** ou **out** o͝o **took** o͞o **boot** ŭ **cut** yo͞o **abuse** ûr **urge** th **thin** *th* **this** hw **which** zh **vision** ə **about**

______ 1. "There were six of them, three boys and three girls, and they picked up the bus at the old *terminal* on 34th Street."

Before the days of airplanes, the train *terminal* was found in small and large towns and was a very busy place.

terminal (tûr′ mə nal) means:

a. fatal illness
b. dock or pier
c. bus stop
d. station, especially one that is the final stop at either end of a railway or bus line

______ 2. "They were dreaming of golden beaches and the tides of the sea as the gray cold spring of New York *vanished* behind them."

No one knew what happened to Mrs. Martin's ring; it simply *vanished* from her jewelry box during the dinner party.

vanished (văn′ ĭsht) means:

a. disappeared
b. intensified
c. grew smaller
d. exploded

_____ 3. "His fingers were stained from cigarettes and he chewed the inside of his lip a lot, frozen into some personal *cocoon* of silence."

The sleeping bag provided as a cozy *cocoon* for the sleeping child.

cocoon (kə ko͞on´) means:

a. wool blanket
b. pupal case spun by the larvae of moths and other insects
c. protective covering
d. coat

_____ 4. "He sat *rooted* in his seat, and the young people began to wonder about him, trying to imagine his life."

Connie wanted to run from the large barking dog, but she was so terrified that her feet seemed *rooted* in the ground.

rooted (ro͞ot´ əd) means:

a. buried
b. bored or uninterested
c. frightened
d. firmly established or anchored

_____ 5. "He smiled and took the bottle of Chianti and took a *swig*."

The hot, thirsty tennis player finished his soft drink in a single *swig*.

swig (swĭg) means:

a. glance
b. insult or offense
c. large swallow or gulp
d. taste

_____ 6. "Well, when I was in the *can*, I wrote to my wife."

Mike said that John was sentenced to 30 days in the *can* for reckless driving.

can (kăn) means:

a. rehabilitation center
b. jail or prison
c. food container
d. small town

_____ 7. "Vingo stopped looking, tightening his face into an ex-con's mask, as if *fortifying* himself against still another disappointment."

During half-time, the coach was *fortifying* the team's sagging morale.

fortifying (fôr´ tə fī ĭng) means:

a. improving
b. strengthening
c. fooling by means of a clever trick
d. making happy or cheerful

______ 8. "Then it was 10 miles, and then five and the bus acquired a dark hushed mood, full of silence, of absence, of lost years, of the woman's plain face, of the sudden letter on the breakfast table, of the wonder of children, of the iron bars of *solitude*."

Because he liked *solitude*, the artist often took long walks on the deserted beach in the early morning hours.

solitude (sŏl´ ĭ to͞od) means:

a. isolation or being alone
b. quietude or silence
c. loneliness
d. beauty

______ 9. "Then suddenly all of the young people were up out of their seats, screaming and shouting and crying, doing small dances, shaking clenched fists in triumph and *exaltation*."

Nothing could top the *exaltation* I felt when I received my college diploma at the graduation ceremony.

exaltation (ĭgs əl tā´ shən) means:

a. calm, reflective mood
b. disappointment
c. delight or elation
d. memory or recollection

______ 10. "The tree was covered with yellow handkerchiefs, 20 of them, 30 of them, maybe hundreds, a tree that stood like a banner of welcome blowing and *billowing* in the wind."

The sails of the boat were *billowing* like open parachutes.

billowing (bĭl´ ō ing) means:

a. folding and unfolding
b. disintegrating
c. swelling or surging
d. flapping

Respond in Writing

Directions: Refer to Selection 2-2 as necessary to answer these essay-type items.

Option for collaboration: For some of the "Respond in Writing" exercises, your instructor may prefer that you work collaboratively, that is, with other students. These exercises are identified in the margin. *If your instructor directs you to work collaboratively on any of these items,* form groups of three or four classmates to complete the exercise together. Discuss your answers with each other and have one member of the group record the answers. A member of the group may be asked to share the group's answers with the class.

1. Yellow ribbons are still used to welcome someone home. Can you think of some examples?

2. Ribbons of different colors are often worn to show support for various causes. Give one or more examples. Describe the color of the ribbon and the cause.

Option

Exercise 3 may be completed collaboratively.

3. How did you feel when you read about the "gorgeous yellow blur" that awaited Vingo?

Option

Exercise 4 may be completed collaboratively.

4. On the basis of what you learned about Vingo in this selection, do you feel he deserved to be forgiven? Explain your answer.

Option

Exercise 5 may be completed collaboratively.

5. This story seems to illustrate several truths about life. What are some of the truths that the story reveals?

Option

Exercise 6 may be completed collaboratively.

6. What is the most important overall message the writer wants the reader to understand? Try to answer this question in one sentence.

Selection 2-3

Computer science

WHAT COMPUTERS CAN, CANNOT, AND SHOULD NOT DO

FROM *COMPUTERS,* BY TIMOTHY TRAINOR AND DIANE KRASNEWICH

Prepare Yourself to Read

Directions: Do these exercises *before you read Selection 2-3.*

1. First, read and think about the title. What do you already know about computers?

   ____

   ____

2. Next, complete your preview by reading the following:

   Introduction (in *italics*)
   First paragraph (paragraph 1)
   First sentence of each paragraph
   Listed items
   All of the last paragraph (paragraph 6)

   On the basis of your preview, what can computers do? What can they *not* do?

   ____

   ____

Apply Comprehension Skills

Directions: Do these exercises *as you read Selection 2-3.*

Adjust your reading rate. On the basis of your preview and your prior knowledge about computers, do you think you should read Selection 2-3 slowly or rapidly? ________________________

Develop a college-level vocabulary. Did you notice any unfamiliar words while you were previewing Selection 2-3? If so, list them here.

____

Predict as you read. As you read Selection 2-3, make predictions about what the author will discuss next. Write your predictions in the blanks provided.

WHAT COMPUTERS CAN, CANNOT, AND SHOULD NOT DO

Are you intimidated by computers? Do you worry that computers will take over everything? See what these textbook authors, computer scientists, have to say on the subject.

1 Computers exist to benefit and assist people, not to replace them. Computers cannot, for example, make emotional judgments, disobey instructions entered by humans, read people's minds, or replace interpersonal relationships. On the contrary, people must be extremely explicit in instructing a computer to perform even the simplest commands. What computers can do, however, is extremely helpful. They can

- Store data in vast amounts
- Process data quickly and accurately
- Simulate possible outcomes based on a given set of conditions
- Recommend or take action based on output

2 Computers cannot be effective unless the people using them are able to identify what results they need and how to achieve those results. Ultimately, computers are dependent upon people.

3 Accordingly, people should not relinquish their decision-making responsibilities to computers. Humans need to be on hand to interpret conditions reported by computers, particularly if medical treatment, national defense, air traffic control, or even loan processing is involved. Nonprogrammable, human factors must complement computer read-outs for a complete and fair analysis.

4 At times computers may appear to make decisions. In monitoring a refinery, for example, a computer might trigger a fire-extinguishing system. Another computer, used for monitoring vital signs, might regulate the flow of oxygen to a patient. In both cases, however, although the

Practice exercises

Directions: At each of the points indicated below, answer the question, "What do you predict will be discussed next?"

Practice exercise

What do you predict will be discussed next?

____

Source: Timothy Trainor and Diane Krasnewich, "What Computers Can, Cannot, and Should Not Do," in *Computers,* 4th ed., McGraw-Hill, New York, 1994, pp. 12–14.

computer initiates action, it does not make a decision. Rather, the decisions of these process control systems were made by the human beings who programmed the machines to respond to a particular set of conditions. Therefore people must take complete responsibility for a computer's actions. They must anticipate all potential problems and direct computers to avoid them.

5 While computers may be able to enhance a person's capabilities, they can never adequately replace interpersonal relationships. Even the most sophisticated computing machinery cannot supplant parent-to-child and teacher-to-student relationships. Similarly, the rapport between physician and patient is essential for successful treatment.

6 People, then, are an integral part of any computer system that accepts input, processes it, and delivers output. People control computer systems through program design, by monitoring operations, and by making final decisions based upon computer output. They should not give up decision-making responsibilities because the human qualities of analysis, reasoning, and compassion are required to interpret computer-delivered results.

Practice exercise

What do you predict will be discussed next?

____

Comprehension Quiz

True or false

Directions: In the blank provided, indicate whether each statement is true or false.

_____ 1. People must tell computers what to do.

_____ 2. Computers can store large quantities of information.

_____ 3. The authors believe that people should relinquish decision making to computers.

_____ 4. A computer cannot be effective unless the people using it are able to identify the results they need.

_____ 5. Computers may eventually replace people.

Multiple-choice

Directions: For each item, select the best answer.

_____ 6. Computers can do all of the following *except*

a. recommend or take action on the basis of output.
b. make emotional judgments.
c. store vast amounts of data.
d. process data accurately and quickly.

_____ 7. *Programming* a computer means that a person is

a. using a computer.
b. giving a computer instructions.
c. repairing a computer.
d. analyzing a computer's output.

_____ 8. Computers can

a. read people's minds.
b. disobey instructions entered by people.
c. simulate possible outcomes on the basis of a given set of conditions.
d. take the place of interpersonal relationships.

_____ 9. One way people can control computer systems is to

a. process data quickly and accurately.
b. make final decisions themselves on the basis of computer output.
c. reduce the processing time of projects.
d. use nonprogrammable factors.

_____ 10. Ultimately, complete responsibility for a computer's actions rests with

a. people.
b. programs.
c. outcomes.
d. data contained in the computer's system.

Extend Your Vocabulary Using Context Clues

Directions: ***Context clues*** are words in a sentence or paragraph that allow the reader to deduce (reason out) the meaning of an unfamiliar word. For each item in this exercise, a sentence from Selection 2-3 containing an important word *(italicized, like this)* is quoted first. Next, there is an additional sentence using the word in the same sense and providing another context clue. Use the context clues to deduce the meaning of each italicized word. *The definition you choose should make sense in both sentences.*

Pronunciation key: ă **pat** ā **pay** âr **care** ä **father** ĕ **pet** ē **be** ĭ **pit** ī **tie** îr **pier** ŏ **pot** ō **toe** ô **paw** oi **noise** ou **out** ŏŏ **took** ōō **boot** ŭ **cut** yōō ab**u**se ûr **urge** th **thin** *th* **this** hw **which** zh vision ə **about**

_____ 1. "On the contrary, people must be extremely *explicit* in instructing a computer to perform even the simplest commands."

Because Maria gave us *explicit* directions, we were able to find her house without any trouble.

explicit (ĭk splĭs′ ĭt) means:

a. patient
b. reasonable
c. precise
d. cheerful

_____ 2. "Computers store data in *vast* amounts."

Sam Walton's *vast* fortune from his hundreds of Wal-Mart stores made him one of the wealthiest men in the nation.

vast (văst) means:

a. huge
b. unknown
c. varying
d. small

_____ 3. "Ultimately, computers are *dependent* upon people."

Small children are *dependent* upon their parents for food, clothing, and protection.

dependent (dĭ pĕn′ dənt) means:

a. not connected with
b. relying upon
c. not related to
d. comfortable with

_____ 4. "Accordingly, people should not *relinquish* their decision-making responsibilities to computers."

The judge ordered the man to *relinquish* possession of his boss's car.

relinquish (rĭ lĭng′ kwĭsh) means:

a. fight for
b. practice
c. take
d. give up

______ 5. "Nonprogrammable, human factors must *complement* computer readouts for a complete and fair analysis."

Mark selected a blue-and-red striped tie to *complement* his white shirt, navy sports coat, and white slacks.

complement (kŏm´ plə mənt) means:

a. make something complete
b. make something attractive
c. improve
d. change

______ 6. "Another computer, used for monitoring *vital* signs, might regulate the flow of oxygen to a patient."

Air and water are *vital* for human survival.

vital (vīt´ l) means:

a. helpful
b. difficult
c. pleasant to have
d. essential for life

______ 7. "In both cases, however, although the computer *initiates* action, it does not make a decision."

Today our store *initiates* its new advertising campaign to attract more teenage and young adult customers.

initiates (ĭ nĭsh´ ē āts) means:

a. tries
b. begins
c. cancels
d. prevents

______ 8. "They must anticipate all *potential* problems and direct computers to avoid them."

Senator Barnes is an outstanding legislator and a *potential* candidate for president.

potential (pə tĕn´ shəl) means:

a. possible
b. dangerous
c. unusual
d. unimportant

_____ 9. "While computers may be able to *enhance* a person's capabilities, they can never adequately replace interpersonal relationships."

Most people select clothing that will *enhance* their appearance.

enhance (ĕn hănz´) means:

a. ruin
b. limit
c. improve
d. change

_____ 10. "Similarly, the *rapport* between physician and patient is essential for successful treatment."

Michael has such *rapport* with children that he had decided to become an elementary school teacher.

rapport (ră pôr´) means:

a. limited contact
b. harmonious relationship
c. poor communication
d. brief experience

Respond in Writing

Directions: Refer to Selection 2-3 as necessary to answer these essay-type questions.

Option for collaboration: For some of the "Respond in Writing" exercises, your instructor may prefer that you work collaboratively, that is, with other students. These exercises are identified in the margin. *If your instructor directs you to work collaboratively on any of these items,* form groups of three or four classmates to complete the exercise together. Discuss your answers with each other and have one member of the group record the answers. A member of the group may be asked to share the group's answers with the class.

1. According to this selection, what are some things computers can do and cannot do?

Things computers can do	*Things computers cannot do*
_____	_____
_____	_____
_____	_____
_____	_____
_____	_____

Option

Exercise 2 may be completed collaboratively.

2. What kinds of decisions should *never* be turned over to a computer?

____

____

____

____

____

____

Option

Exercise 3 may be completed collaboratively.

3. What is the most important overall message the writer wants the reader to understand about a computer's capabilities? Try to answer this question in one sentence.

____

____

____

____

____

____

____

CHAPTER 3

APPROACHING COLLEGE ASSIGNMENTS: READING TEXTBOOKS AND FOLLOWING DIRECTIONS

IN THIS CHAPTER YOU WILL LEARN
THE ANSWERS TO THESE QUESTIONS:

What is an effective way to read and study a college textbook?

How can I prepare to read an assignment?

How can I guide my reading by asking questions?

How can I review material by rehearsing?

What are the keys to following directions on college assignments and tests?

CHAPTER 3 CONTENTS

SKILLS

If you need a helping hand, look at the end of your sleeve.

COLLEGE TEXTBOOKS: A PROCESS FOR READING AND STUDYING EFFECTIVELY

Students often ask, "When should I start studying for final exams?" The answer is, "At the beginning of the semester." From the first day of classes, you should read and study your textbook assignments as if you were preparing for the final exam. If you read and study your assignments effectively the first time, you won't have to start over again and reread them when it is time for a unit test or major exam.

Reading your textbooks requires more than casually looking at the pages. Reading and studying take time and effort. Moreover, you must make reading and studying textbook material an *active* process, not a passive one.

How can you understand and remember what you read in your textbooks? This chapter presents an effective approach for reading a college textbook assignment that will ultimately save you time. This approach is based on *doing it right the first time,* so that when you prepare for a test, you will not have to spend additional hours rereading textbook chapters. This approach helps you learn more *the first time* you read your textbook assignments.

The basic steps of this study-reading process are:

- Prepare to read.
- Ask and answer questions as you read.
- Review by rehearsing the answers to your questions.

The box on the following two pages shows all three steps of this study-reading process in detail. Each of these steps is explained in detail below.

Key term

Preparing to read: Previewing a chapter, assessing your prior knowledge, and planning your time.

Step 1: Prepare to Read

Before you begin to read a textbook assignment, you should spend a few minutes preparing to read. ***Preparing to read*** involves previewing the chapter, assessing your prior knowledge, and planning your reading and study time.

Preview the chapter

Key term

Previewing: Examining reading material to determine its topic and organization.

Previewing can give you a general idea of what an entire assignment will be about and allows you to see how the material is organized. This not only helps you comprehend what you read but also helps improve your concentration, motivation, and interest in what you are about to read. (That is why each of the reading selections in *Opening Doors* is preceded by an activity called "Prepare Yourself to Read.")

A Three-Step Process for Studying College Textbooks

▪ ▪ ▪ ▪ ▪ ▪ ▪

Step 1: Prepare to Read

Preview the selection to see what it contains and how it is organized:

- Read the title.
- Read the introduction.
- Read headings and subheadings in each section.
- Read words in italics or bold print.
- Look over illustrations, charts, and diagrams.
- Read any questions that are included in the chapter or the study guide.
- Read the summary.

Ask yourself:

- "What topics does the author seem to be emphasizing?"
- "How are the topics organized?"

Assess your prior knowledge. Ask yourself:

- "What do I already know about the topic?"
- "How familiar am I with this topic?"

Plan your reading and study time. Ask yourself:

- "How can I best allot my time for this assignment?"
- "Do I need to divide the assignment into smaller units?"

Step 2: Ask and Answer Questions as You Read

Guide your reading by asking and answering questions:

- Turn chapter headings into questions.
- Create questions based on what the paragraphs or sections appear to be about.
- If the author has included questions, use them.
- Use questions in a study guide, if there is one accompanying the course or textbook.
- Use questions given by the instructor.

Read actively:

- Look for answers to your questions.

Record the answers to your questions:

- Write the answers on notebook paper or in the margins of the textbook.
- Create review cards for the material.
- Emphasize the answers by highlighting or underlining them.

Step 3: Review by Rehearsing the Answers to Your Questions

Review the material and *transfer it into long-term memory* by rehearsing (practicing):

- Recite (say aloud) the answers to your questions.
- Try to write the important points from memory.

To preview a chapter assignment:

- *First, read the chapter title.* This should tell you the overall topic of the chapter.
- *Next, read the chapter introduction.* A chapter introduction (if there is one) usually presents some of the important points to be made in the chapter, or it may give some background information that you will need.
- *Read the heading of each section.* Turn through the chapter to read the headings and subheadings. These will tell you what topics the author has included and can provide an outline of how information in the chapter is organized.

- *Read words in italic or bold print.* Notice any words that appear in *italics* or **bold print;** these are often important terms you will be expected to understand and remember.
- *Look at illustrations.* Be sure to look at any *pictures, charts, diagrams,* and *graphs* you find in the chapter. These give you visual representations of the material.
- *Read any questions that are included in the chapter or the study guide.* They will alert you to important information you should watch for as you read.
- *Finally, read the chapter summary.* If there is a chapter summary, it will contain many of the important ideas of the chapter in brief form. A chapter summary (like a chapter introduction) is especially useful. Take advantage of it.

As you preview, you should make some predictions—"educated guesses"—about what is in the chapter you are about to read. Ask yourself, "What topics does the author seem to be emphasizing?" and "How are the topics organized?"

Assess your prior knowledge

As you learned in Chapter 2, when you lack background knowledge in a subject—and this is often the case when you are reading college textbooks—you may have difficulty comprehending the material. Assessing your ***prior knowledge*** (in other words, what you already know about the topic) will enable you to decide whether you need help with the assignment and whether you need to allow additional time. To assess your prior knowledge, simply ask yourself, "What do I already know about this topic?" Previewing the chapter can help you determine this. By introducing you to the chapter topics, previewing allows you to predict whether or not you will be dealing with familiar material.

Key term

Prior knowledge: What you already know about a topic; background knowledge.

If the material is new to you, you may need to take extra steps to deal with an assignment successfully. While you are previewing, while you are reading, or after you finish reading, you may discover that you do not understand the material adequately, and you may decide that you need to increase your background knowledge. If so, it is your responsibility to take some or all of these steps to fill in missing background information:

- Reading other, perhaps easier, textbooks on the same subject (these might be other college textbooks or more general study aids, such as an outline of American history or a text with a title such as *Accounting Made Easy*)
- Consulting an encyclopedia, a good dictionary, or some other reference book
- Talking with someone who is knowledgeable about the subject

These steps require effort, and obviously there are no shortcuts. But going the extra mile to get necessary background information is part of being a responsible, mature learner and student. As a bonus, you may discover that it is exciting and satisfying to understand new or difficult material through your own efforts. You may also find that when you take responsibility for your own learning, you will feel good about yourself as a student. (Remember that a *student* is someone who *studies.*)

Plan your reading and study time

By previewing an assignment, you will be able to decide whether you can read the entire assignment in just one study session or whether you need to divide it into smaller parts.

If you decide that you need more than one study session, you should divide the assignment into several shorter segments and read them at times when you know you can concentrate best. For example, a 15-page chapter may be too much for you to read and study effectively all at once. You could divide the assignment into three 5-page segments and read them on three separate days, perhaps including a weekend. Or you could divide this long assignment into three 1-hour study sessions on the same afternoon, perhaps at 1, 5, and 8 P.M. In any case, *plan* your study-reading session and follow your plan. (Then, reward yourself after you complete your studying!)

Step 2: Ask and Answer Questions to Guide Your Reading

The second step in reading and studying a college textbook assignment is *guiding your reading by asking and answering questions.* To read and study effectively, you need to read and understand *each paragraph or section.* This means that you must determine what is important to learn and remember in each section. To put it another way, you need to read for a specific purpose. Reading for a specific purpose will increase your interest and concentration, and it will enable you to monitor (evaluate) your comprehension while you are reading. One of the best ways to learn the material in a reading assignment is to ask and answer questions about the material as you read.

Ask questions as you read

Creating one or more questions for each section of a reading assignment will guide you to the pertinent, important information and help you remember that information. When you read to seek answers to questions, you will be reading with a specific purpose; in other words, you will be reading *selectively* and *purposefully.*

Turning chapter headings and subheadings into questions is the easiest way to accomplish this step. For example, if a section in a history textbook has a heading "The Spanish-American War Begins," you might want to ask, "*Why* did the war begin?" You may also want to ask, "*When* did it begin?" (In Chapters 9 and 10 you will be working with actual college textbook chapters which have headings that can be turned into useful questions.)

When a section or paragraph has no heading, it is a good idea to create a question based on what that section or paragraph appears to be about. If you see a term or phrase in **bold print** or *italics,* you might create a question about that term or phrase. You can also create questions about names of people, places, events, and so on. Of course, you will be able to refine your questions later, when you read the material more carefully.

In addition to creating your own questions as you read each section of a textbook, you may find that the author has included questions for you. These may appear at the end of a chapter, at the beginning of a chapter, throughout a chapter (perhaps in the margins), or in an accompanying study guide. If a textbook chapter contains such questions, read them *before* you read the chapter. Then keep them in mind as you read. When you have finished reading the chapter, you should be able to answer these questions. In fact, you will very probably be asked some of these same questions on a test. Chapter questions also enable you to monitor your comprehension: *Are you getting from the chapter the important information the author (and your instructor) expect you to know?*

Finally, your instructor may give you questions to guide you as you read a chapter. Of course, you should be able to answer these questions by the time you finish reading and studying the chapter.

Answer questions as you read

As you read each paragraph or section, look for answers to your questions. Then, *after* you have read that paragraph or section, record the answers by writing them down. A word of warning: Do *not* try to record answers while you are reading a section. Trying to read and write at the same time will disrupt your comprehension and greatly slow you down. The time to write your answers is immediately after you *finish* reading a section, not while you are reading it for the first time.

There are several effective ways to record your answers. One of the most effective is to write the questions and answers on notebook paper or in the margins of your textbook. Another effective way of recording answers is to make review cards for the material. In addition, you may want to mark information that answers your questions by going over it with a highlighter pen.

What if you cannot locate or formulate an answer to one of your questions? In that case, there are several things you can do:

- Read ahead to see if the answer becomes apparent.
- If the question involves an important term you need to know, look the term up in the glossary or in a dictionary.
- Go back and reread the paragraph.
- Make a note to ask a classmate or your instructor about the point in question.

- If you still cannot answer all of your questions after you have read an assignment, note which questions remain unanswered. Put a question mark in the margin, or make a list of the unanswered questions. One way or another, be sure to find the answers.

As you can see, actively seeking answers to questions encourages you to concentrate and focus on *understanding* as you read. Reading for a purpose—to answer specific questions—can help you remember more and ultimately score higher on tests. Often, you will discover that questions on tests are identical to the ones you asked yourself as you studied. When this happens, you will be glad that you took the time to use this technique while you were studying.

Step 3: Review by Rehearsing Your Answers

Experienced college students know that if they want to remember what they read in their textbooks, they need to take certain steps to make this happen. They also know that it is essential to take these steps *immediately* after they finish reading a section or a chapter, while the material is still in short-term memory: that is, while the material is still fresh in their minds. Good readers understand that forgetting occurs very rapidly and that they need to rehearse material immediately in order to remember it: that is, transfer it into permanent, or long-term, memory. The shocking fact is that unless you take some special action beyond simply reading a textbook assignment, you will forget half of what you read by the time you finish the chapter!

One highly effective way to rehearse important points in a chapter is to *recite* your questions and answers about the material. Simply rereading your answers is not good enough; you should say them aloud. Remember, "If you can't say it, you don't know it."

Another highly effective way to rehearse important points in a chapter is to *write them from memory.* When you take the time to give yourself a "practice test" in this way, you are transferring the material into long-term memory. When you check your answers, make corrections and add any information needed to make your answers complete.

Taking the time to review and rehearse immediately after you finish reading a chapter will not only help you remember what you learned. It will also give you a feeling of accomplishment, which in turn will encourage you to continue learning. One success will build on another.

To recapitulate, here is the three-step process: (1) *Prepare to read* by previewing, assessing your prior knowledge, and planning your study time. (2) *Ask and answer questions to guide your reading.* (3) *Review by rehearsing your answers.* This process will enable you to learn more as you complete your textbook reading assignments, and it will also be a foundation for effective test preparation. Remember that preparing for a test *begins* with reading textbook assignments effectively. (Specific techniques for preparing for tests are discussed in Chapters 9 and 10. They include annotating textbooks by writing marginal study notes, outlining, "mapping," writing summaries, creating review cards, and developing test review sheets.)

FOLLOWING DIRECTIONS IN TEXTBOOKS AND ON TESTS

An important part of college reading is following written directions. In particular, it is important for you to understand directions in order to do your assignments correctly, carry out procedures in classes and labs (such as computer labs and science labs), and earn high grades on tests.

You have probably learned from experience that problems can arise from misunderstanding or failing to follow directions. Perhaps you have answered an entire set of test questions instead of some specific number stated in the directions ("Answer *any five* of the following seven essay questions . . ."). Or you may have had points deducted from your grade on a research paper because you did not follow the correct format ("Double-space your paper and number the pages . . ."). When you do not follow directions, you can waste time and lower your grade.

Guidelines for Following Directions

There are a few simple things to remember about following written directions:

- *Read the entire set of directions carefully before doing any of the steps.* This is a time when you must slow down and pay attention to every word.
- *Make sure you understand all the words in the directions.* Although directions may use words you see very often, you may still not know precisely what each of the words means. For example, on an essay test you might be asked to *compare* two poems or *contrast* two pieces of music. Do you know the difference between *compare* and *contrast?* Unless you do, you cannot answer the question correctly. Other typical words in test questions include *enumerate, justify, explain,* and *illustrate.* Each has a specific meaning. General direction words include *above, below, consecutive, preceding, succeeding, former, and latter.* In addition, directions in college textbooks and assignments often include many specialized terms that you must understand. For example, in a set of directions for a biology lab experiment, you might be instructed to "stain a tissue sample on a slide." The words *stain, tissue,* and *slide* have very specific meanings in biology.
- *Circle signals that announce steps in directions and underline key words.* Not every step in a set of directions will have a signal word, of course, but steps in sets of directions frequently are introduced by letters or numbers (*a, b, c,* or 1, 2, 3, etc.) or words such as *first, second, third, next, then, finally,* and *last* to indicate the sequence or order of the steps.

You should mark directions *before* you begin following them, since you must understand what you are to do *before* you try to do it. This means finding and numbering steps if they are not already numbered. A single sentence sometimes contains more than one step. (For example, "Type your name, enter your I.D. number, and press the Enter key.") When you are busy working on a test or an assignment, it is easy to become distracted and do the steps in the wrong order or leave a step out. Another reason it is important to number steps in a set of directions is that even though the steps may not include signal words, you are still responsible for finding each step. Especially on tests, then, you should number each step and mark key words in directions.

Example: Directions from a Textbook

Look at the box below, which shows a set of directions from a textbook entitled *Getting Started with the Internet.* The directions explain how to "log on" in order to establish a connection with a network. It is necessary to log on so that you can use e-mail, visit Internet websites, and access certain software programs.

Notice that the steps in the directions are numbered. If you were actually following these directions, you would want to read the entire set first, then mark key words. Notice also that before you can carry out these directions, you must

Exercise 1: Logging On

▪ ▪ ▪ ▪ ▪ ▪ ▪

The method for logging on may vary by site. The following steps are very general. Check with your instructor for specific steps at your site.

1. Turn on system.
2. Choose Host Name: ____________
3. Username: Enter your assigned username.
4. Password: (Enter the last four digits of Soc. Sec. #)
5. The first time you may have to change the password to something of your choice. It should be at least 6 characters (alpha, numeric, or a combination of both). Enter your selection and then verify it by entering the same value again. Remember it or you will not be able to log in again!
6. A $, >, or % prompt will appear. You are now on the network. (We will be using the $ as the prompt in our examples.)
7. When you are finished with all your exercises for the day, you exit the system with

   $logout or *$lo*

Source: Joan Lumpkin and Susan Durnbaugh, *Getting Started with the Internet,* Wiley, New York, 1995, pp. 12–13.

understand certain terms (such as *system, host name, alpha,* and *numeric*) and know certain information (such as your assigned *username* and the last four digits of your social security number). Notice also that step 5 is written as a single paragraph. This makes it easy to overlook the fact that there are *two* important parts in this step: after typing your password the first time, you must verify it by typing it again.

Example: Directions for a Test

The box at the bottom of this page shows a set of directions from a unit test for a psychology course. Read these directions carefully.

Notice that this unit has two distinct parts: Part I—Content Questions, and Part II—Discussion Questions. Part I of the test consists of multiple-choice questions, whereas Part II requires the student to write essay answers.

Notice that each multiple-choice question in Part I is worth 2 points (for a total of 50 points), and that the student must use a machine-scorable answer sheet and a number two pencil. Also, notice that Part I is to be completed *before* beginning Part II.

In Part II, notice that each question is worth a possible 25 points (for a total of 50 points). Next, notice a key point in the directions: *only two* of the four discussion questions are to be answered. Notice that notebook paper is required for these two essay answers, but either pen or pencil may be used. Finally, notice that the answer to each discussion question must be at least 3 paragraphs long, but not longer than 5 paragraphs.

Marking the test directions as shown in the box on the next page would help you follow them accurately.

Unit Test: Psychological Disorders

▪ ▪ ▪ ▪ ▪ ▪ ▪

Directions:

Part I—Content Questions. (2 points each.) Answer the 25 multiple-choice questions using the machine-scorable answer sheet provided. (You must use a number two pencil on this answer sheet.) Complete this part of the test before you begin Part II.

Part II—Discussion Questions. (25 points each.) Answer two of the four discussion questions, using notebook paper. (You may use pen or pencil for this portion of the test.) The answer to each discussion question should be 3–5 paragraphs in length.

Sample of Marked Directions
Unit Test: Psychological Disorders

▪ ▪ ▪ ▪ ▪ ▪ ▪

Directions:

50 points

1.

Part I—Content Questions. (2 points each.) Answer the 25 multiple-choice questions using the machine-scorable answer sheet provided. (You must use a number two pencil on this answer sheet.) Complete this part of the test before you begin Part II.

50 points

2.

Part II—Discussion Questions. (25 points each.). Answer two of the four discussion questions, using notebook paper. (You may use pen or pencil for this portion of the test.) The answer to each discussion question should be 3–5 paragraphs in length.

DEVELOPING CHAPTER REVIEW CARDS

Review cards, or *summary cards,* are an excellent study tool. They are a way to select, organize, and review the most important information in a textbook chapter. The process of creating review cards helps you organize information in a meaningful way and, at the same time, transfer it into long-term memory. The cards can also be used to prepare for tests (see Part Three). The review card activities in this book give you structured practice in creating these valuable study tools. Once you have learned how to make review cards, you can create them for textbook material in your other courses.

Now, complete the seven review cards for Chapter 3 by answering the questions or following the directions on each card. When you have completed them, you will have summarized important information about: (1) preparing to read, (2) previewing a textbook chapter, (3) assessing your prior knowledge, (4) guiding your reading, (5) answering questions as you read, (6) reviewing and rehearsing, and (7) following directions in textbooks and on tests.

The Three-Step Process for Reading and Studying: Step 1

What is the first step of the three-step study-reading process? What does this step consist of? (See pages 109–113.)

Step 1: ______________________________

Step 1 involves these three parts:

____

____

____

Chapter 3: Approaching College Assignments

Previewing a Textbook Chapter

One part of step 1 in the study-reading process is previewing a chapter. List seven things to do in previewing. (See pages 110–112.)

1. ____________________
2. ____________________
3. ____________________
4. ____________________
5. ____________________
6. ____________________
7. ____________________

Chapter 3: Approaching College Assignments

Assessing Your Prior Knowledge

Assessing your prior knowledge is part of step 1 in the study-reading process. Define *prior knowledge.* (See page 112.)

____

____

List three things you can do if you need to increase your prior knowledge about a topic. (See page 112.)

1. ____________________
2. ____________________
3. ____________________

Chapter 3: Approaching College Assignments

The Three-Step Process for Reading and Studying: Step 2

What is the second step of the three-step study-reading process? (See page 113.)

Step 2: ______________________________

List at least four chapter features or other sources which you can base your own questions to ask as you read. (See pages 113–114.)

____

____

____

____

____

____

Chapter 3: Approaching College Assignments

Answering Questions as You Read

When should you record the answers to your questions about a passage? (See page 114.)

____

List three ways to record your answers. (See page 114.)

____

____

____

Describe some things you can do if any of your questions remain unanswered when you have finished a passage. (See pages 114–115.)

____

____

____

Chapter 3: Approaching College Assignments

The Three-Step Process for Reading and Studying: Step 3

What is the third step of the three-step study-reading process? (See page 115.)

Step 3: ______________________________

When should you rehearse the answers to your questions about material in a reading assignment?

____

List two effective ways to rehearse:

____

____

Chapter 3: Approaching College Assignments

Following Directions

List three things to remember about following written directions. (See pages 116–117.)

1. ______________________________

   ____

2. ______________________________

   ____

3. ______________________________

   ____

Chapter 3: Approaching College Assignments

READINGS

Selection 3-1

Human development

COLLEGE

FROM *HUMAN DEVELOPMENT*
BY DIANE E. PAPALIA AND SALLY WENDKOS OLDS

Prepare Yourself to Read

Directions: Do these exercises *before you read Selection 3-1.*

1. First, read and think about the title. What does this selection seem to be about?

____

____

2. Next, complete your preview by reading the following:

   Introduction (in *italics*)
   First paragraph (paragraph 1)
   Headings for each section
   Words in *italics*
   All of the last paragraph (paragraph 19)

   On the basis of your preview, what aspects of college do you think will be discussed?

   ____

Apply Comprehension Skills

Directions: Do these exercises *as you read Selection 3-1.*

Ask and answer questions as you read. Complete the practice exercises by creating questions based on what each paragraph seems to be about.

Read actively to find answers to your questions. Record the answers to your questions. Write the answer in the margin or highlight the answer in the text.

Review by rehearsing the answers to your questions. Recite your answers or write them down from memory.

COLLEGE

Today, more people than ever attend college. Even though there is no longer one "typical" college experience, most students feel that attending college will have a significant effect on their lives. As you read, think about what you hope to gain from attending college and the ways in which your experience as a college student is the same as or different from those of students described in this selection.

1 College can mean anything from a 2-year community college stressing vocational training or a small 4-year liberal arts school to a large university with graduate divisions. Most colleges today are coeducational, but a few are still all-male or all-female. With such diversity, it is hard to generalize about the college experience.

WHO GOES TO COLLEGE?

2 Today's college classrooms include many different kinds of students. Juanita, for example, entered college directly from high school, having already decided on a premedical program. Vince worked for 2 years after high school and is now taking courses in music and journalism, unsure which to follow as a career. Otis wants a master's degree in business administration as the first step on his route to a six-figure salary. Marilyn came to college looking for a husband. Consuela interrupted her education to marry and raise three children; now that they are in college, she herself came back to earn a degree. Todhio, retired from business after a lifetime supporting a family, now has time to expand his intellectual horizons.

3 Nearly 14.2 million students are enrolled in American colleges and universities. Fifty-five percent are women, and an increasing percentage are ages 35 and older (National Center for Education Statistics, NCES, 1989a, 1991).

Practice exercises

Directions: For each paragraph,

- Create a question based on what the paragraph seems to be about. Ask *who, what, when, where, why,* or *how.*
- Write your question in the spaces provided.
- Write the answer to your question in the margin or highlight it in the text.

Doing this will help you understand and remember the material.

Practice exercise

Question about paragraph 1:

____

____

Practice exercise

Question about paragraph 2:

____

____

Practice exercise

Question about paragraph 3:

____

____

Source: Human Development, 6th ed., by Diane E. Papalia and Sally Wendkos Olds, McGraw-Hill, New York, 1995, pp. 426–428.

INTELLECTUAL GROWTH IN COLLEGE

4 College can be a time of intellectual discovery and personal growth. For traditional students—those in transition from adolescence to adulthood—college offers a chance to question assumptions held over from childhood and thus to mold a new adult identity. Sometimes this questioning may lead to an identity crisis and to serious problems: abuse of alcohol or drugs, eating disorders, risk taking, and even suicide. Fortunately, however, it more often fosters healthy development.

5 Students change in response to other students who challenge long-held views and values; to the student culture itself, which is different from the culture of society at large; to the curriculum, which offers new insights and new ways of thinking; and to faculty members, who often take a personal interest in students and provide new role models (Madison, 1969).

6 A 4-year longitudinal study of 165 undergraduates in three disciplines found that students majoring in the *natural sciences* (biology, chemistry, microbiology, physics), *humanities* (communications, English, history, journalism, linguistics, philosophy), or *social sciences* (psychology, anthropology, economics, political science, sociology) showed improvements in reasoning from their first year of their college to their fourth (Lehman & Nisbett, 1990).

7 Students in all three fields improved the quality of their everyday reasoning. This shows that reasoning skills can be taught and suggests that such teaching can help people change the way they think about uncertainty in everyday life. The different major courses of study taught different kinds of reasoning abilities. For example, undergraduate training in the social sciences produced gains in statistical and methodological reasoning, or the ability to generalize patterns. Students majoring in the other two categories had better conditional reasoning, or the ability to use formal deductive logic, like that used in computer programming and mathematics. And all the students except the social

Practice exercise

Question about paragraph 4:

____

____

Practice exercise

Question about paragraph 5:

____

____

Practice exercise

Question about paragraph 6:

____

____

Practice exercise

Question about paragraph 7:

____

____

science majors improved their verbal reasoning, the ability to recognize arguments, evaluate evidence, and detect analogies in reading passages. (These findings suggest that a narrow education in a single major field is not enough to realize one's intellectual potential.)

8 One avenue of self-discovery in college is the exploration of new, more realistic career choices. For example, Lucas was first attracted to a career in astronomy; but after exploring other fields, he decided that he really wanted to work with people.

Practice exercise

Question about paragraph 8:

____

____

9 The academic and social challenges of college can lead to intellectual and moral growth. In a study that has inspired much of the research on postformal thought, William Perry (1970) interviewed 67 Harvard and Radcliffe students throughout their undergraduate years and found that their thinking progressed from rigidity to flexibility and ultimately to freely chosen commitments:

- As students encounter a wide variety of ideas, they accept the coexistence of several different points of view, and they also accept their own uncertainty. They consider this stage temporary, however, and expect to learn the "one right answer eventually."
- Next they see the relativism of all knowledge and values: they recognize that different societies, different cultures, and different individuals work out their own value systems. They now realize that their opinions on many issues are as valid as anyone else's.
- Finally they affirm their identity through the values and commitments they choose for themselves.

Practice exercise

Question about paragraph 9:

____

____

GENDER DIFFERENCES IN ACHIEVEMENT IN COLLEGE

10 Looking around you at your classmates, you can probably see many signs of the rapid change in women's roles—in college enrollment, in the courses women choose, and in their personal, educational, and occupational

Practice exercise

Question about paragraph 10:

____

____

goals. In the 1970s, high school girls were less likely than boys to go to college and less likely to finish. Today girls are *more* likely than boys to go to college and about as likely to pursue advanced degrees (National Center for Education Statistics, NCES, 1989a, 1991).

11 And women are earning more degrees today than in the past. More than half of the bachelors and masters degrees awarded in 1990–1991, and about 40 percent of doctoral and professional degrees, were awarded to women (NCES, 1991). And in recent years the percentage of women among students of dentistry, medicine, veterinary medicine, and law took large leaps (Congressional Caucus for Women's Issues, 1987).

Practice exercise

Question about paragraph 11:

____

____

12 Yet as recently as the late 1970s, some of the same girls who had outshone boys throughout high school slipped behind in college. Even the ablest female students had lower self-esteem and more limited aspirations than males. Women were avoiding academic risks and steering away from mathematics (Sells, 1980). Many overprepared for class and took careful notes, but panicked over assignments and examinations and felt less confident than their male classmates about their preparation for graduate study (Leland et al., 1979). Even highly gifted women tended to go to less selective colleges than men and were less likely to go on to prestigious graduate schools and high-status occupations (Kerr, 1985).

Practice exercise

Question about paragraph 12:

____

____

13 These patterns may well have resulted from gender socialization, since during adolescence girls tend to become more focused on relationships and boys tend to become more focused on careers (Kerr, 1985). Society gives girls messages that emphasize the roles of wife and mother and stress the difficulty or even the impossibility of combining personal achievement with love and family. Young men are given no reason to believe that their roles as future husbands might interfere with developing their career potential.

Practice exercise

Question about paragraph 13:

____

____

14 These gender-based messages to young people may help to explain why differences still persist today between adult men and women. The great majority of engineering, architecture, and science students are male, while most of the students of teaching, foreign languages, and home economics are female (Newhouse News Service, 1987).

Practice exercise

Question about paragraph 14:

LEAVING COLLEGE

15 The *college dropout* is variously defined as a student who leaves a college and takes some time off before resuming studies at the same school, or ends college studies altogether. About half of entering college students never earn a degree at all (National Institute of Education, NIE, 1984).

Practice exercise

Question about paragraph 15:

16 There is no "typical" college dropout. Students leave school for many reasons—marriage, the desire to be close to a loved one, a change in occupational status, or dissatisfaction with their school. Ability may be a factor; able students are more likely than they were in the early 1970s to remain in college (U.S. Department of Education, 1987). But although most dropouts have lower average aptitude scores than those who stay in school, they are usually doing satisfactory work.

Practice exercise

Question about paragraph 16:

17 Leaving college temporarily can be a positive step. Many students gain more by working for a while, enrolling at a more compatible institution, or just allowing themselves time to mature. After 2 years of academic work and 1 year of art school, for example, Sally's [one of the author's] daughter Dorri took 2 years out to pursue a long-held dream of a career in rock music. She worked as a waitress and took music lessons while she was out of school—but then decided against following this route. Having learned more about herself, her goals, and the music business, she decided to go back to the school of design in which she had been enrolled, which had allowed her to "stop out" for up to 2 years without having to reapply. Dorri majored in illustration, received her Bachelor of

Practice exercise

Question about paragraph 17:

Fine Arts degree, and is now working as a graphic artist.

18 Many colleges make it easy for students to take leaves of absence, to study part time and to earn credit for independent study, life experiences, and work done at other institutions. "Stopping out," then, is generally not a major problem; but students who drop out and never earn degrees at all may limit their opportunities.

Practice exercise

Question about paragraph 18:

____

____

19 Formal education need not—and often does not—end in the early twenties. It can continue throughout adulthood. The trend toward lifelong learning can be seen in growing college enrollments over the past decade by people over 30, and especially by those over 35 (National Center for Education Statistics, NCES, 1989b).

Practice exercise

Question about paragraph 19:

____

____

Comprehension Quiz

True or false

Directions: In the blank provided, indicate whether each statement is true or false.

______ 1. Students today attend college for a wide variety of reasons and under a variety of circumstances.

______ 2. Almost 14.2 million students graduate from American colleges and universities each year.

______ 3. The majority of college students today are men, and an increasing percentage are ages 35 and older.

______ 4. A four-year study found that college students majoring in the natural sciences, humanities, or social sciences showed improvement in reasoning from their first year to their fourth year of college.

______ 5. The researcher William Perry found that students come to college expecting to learn the "one right answer," but they later learn to form their own opinions and values and to make intellectual and moral commitments.

______ 6. "Stopping out" of college can be a positive step if, for example, a student reenrolls at a more compatible institution.

Multiple-choice

Directions: For each item, select the best answer.

_____ 7. College students often experience intellectual and personal growth as they respond to

a. faculty members, who often provide new role models.
b. the curriculum, which offers new insights and new ways of thinking.
c. other students, who challenge long-held views and values.
d. all of the above.

_____ 8. Today, girls are

a. less likely than they were in the past to study dentistry, medicine, and law.
b. more likely than men to go to college.
c. more likely to attend college at younger ages than boys.
d. less likely than boys to attend community colleges.

_____ 9. Female college students may sometimes have lower self-esteem and lower aspirations than males because of

a. insufficient preparation for college courses.
b. gender socialization.
c. parental pressures.
d. all of the above.

_____ 10. Growing college enrollment during the past decade by people age 30 and over suggests

a. that colleges offer more challenging courses today.
b. that more and more students avoid college during their twenties.
c. a need for new college majors in technical careers.
d. a trend toward lifelong learning.

Extend Your Vocabulary by Using Context Clues

Directions: ***Context clues*** are words in a sentence or paragraph that allow the reader to deduce (reason out) the meaning of an unfamiliar word. For each item in this exercise, a sentence from Selection 3-1 containing an important word *(italicized, like this)* is quoted first. Next, there is an additional sentence using the word in the same sense and providing another context clue. Use the context clues to deduce the meaning of each italicized word. *The definition you choose should make sense in both sentences.*

Pronunciation key: ă pat ā pay âr care ä father ĕ pet ē be ĭ pit ī tie îr pier ŏ pot ō toe ô paw oi noise ou out o͝o took o͞o boot ŭ cut yo͞o abuse ûr urge th thin *th* this hw which zh vision ə about

_______ 1. "College can mean anything from a 2-year community college stressing vocational training or a small 4-year *liberal arts* school to a large university with graduate divisions."

Academic disciplines such as languages, literature, history, philosophy, mathematics, and science are the core of a *liberal arts* curriculum.

liberal arts (lĭb′ ər əl ärtz) means:

a. free from political bias
b. of general cultural concern
c. not strict or rigorous
d. noncredit

_______ 2. "Sometimes this questioning may lead to an identity crisis and to serious problems. . . . Fortunately, however, it more often *fosters* healthy development."

Special training, along with encouragement from adults, *fosters* children's artistic and musical talent.

fosters (fŏs′ tərz) means:

a. receives parental care from someone other than the natural parents
b. lessens; decreases
c. promotes the growth or development of
d. cherishes; values highly

_______ 3. "And all the students except the social science majors improved their verbal reasoning, the ability to recognize arguments, evaluate evidence, and *detect* analogies in reading passages."

If you *detect* evidence that someone has tampered with any new bottle of medicine, you should immediately return it to the store where you purchased it.

detect (dĭ tĕkt′) means:

a. create; cause to exist
b. overlook; fail to notice
c. deliberately choose to ignore
d. discover the presence of

_______ 4. "And all the students except the social science majors improved their verbal reasoning, the ability to recognize arguments, evaluate evidence, and detect *analogies* in reading passages."

To make concepts about the computer easier to understand, *analogies* are often made between it and the human brain.

analogies (ə nal´ ə jēz) means:

a. meanings that are implied rather than stated
b. comparisons between things that are similar in some respects but otherwise are dissimilar
c. forms of deductive reasoning consisting of a major premise, a minor premise, and a conclusion
d. conclusions reached by deriving general principles from particular facts

_______ 5. "In a study that has inspired much of the research on postformal thought, William Perry (1970) interviewed 67 Harvard and Radcliffe students throughout their undergraduate years and found that their thinking progressed from *rigidity* to flexibility and ultimately to freely chosen commitments."

Our supervisor was eventually fired because of his *rigidity;* he followed every rule even when there were circumstances that called for an exception.

rigidity (rĭ jĭd´ ĭ tē) means:

a. inability or unwillingness to adapt to change
b. condition of not being able to be bent
c. extreme coldness
d. hostility; anger

_______ 6. "As students encounter a wide variety of ideas, they accept the *coexistence* of several different points of view, and they also accept their own uncertainty."

The *coexistence* of war and peace in the same place and at the same moment is an impossibility.

coexistence (kō ĭg zĭst´ əns) means:

a. getting along peacefully
b. conflicting, irreconcilable aims
c. a cease-fire between hostile forces
d. state of existing together at the same time despite differences

_____ 7. "Next they see the *relativism* of all knowledge and values: they recognize that different societies, different cultures, and different individuals work out their own value systems."

The ancient but once widely accepted belief that the sun revolved around the earth suggests that *relativism* exists.

relativism (rĕl´ ə tĭ vĭz əm) means:

a. a theory that concepts of truth and moral values are absolute throughout time
b. a theory that one's family and relatives determine the moral values appropriate for a person
c. a theory that concepts of truth and moral values are not absolute but are relative to the persons or groups holding them
d. a theory that knowledge and values of any sort can never be determined by the individual

_____ 8. "Even the ablest female students had lower self-esteem and more limited *aspirations* than males."

Ever since Bill Clinton was a young man, he had *aspirations* to become the president of the United States.

aspirations (as pə rā´ shənz) means:

a. high ambitions; goals involving high achievement
b. unfulfilled desires
c. unusual accomplishments
d. vague, unspecified goals

_____ 9. "But although most dropouts have lower average *aptitude* scores than those who stay in school, they are usually doing satisfactory work."

Sir Isaac Newton, the greatest and most influential scientist who ever lived, showed considerable mechanical *aptitude* as a child, but he was a poor student whose brilliance in science and math was not evident until young adulthood.

aptitude (ap´ tĭ to͞od) means:

a. an inherent ability, as for learning; a talent
b. physical strength and coordination
c. resolute determination
d. the ability to remember everything

______ 10. "Many college students gain more by working for a while, enrolling at a more *compatible* institution, or just allowing themselves time to mature."

The judge granted the Smiths a divorce on the basis that they were no longer *compatible.*

compatible (kəm pat´ ə bəl) means:

a. prestigious; having high social standing
b. wealthy; prosperous
c. capable of existing in harmonious or agreeable combination
d. not well-suited; inappropriate

Respond in Writing

Directions: Refer to Selection 3-1 as necessary to answer these essay-type questions.

Option for collaboration: For some of the "Respond in Writing" exercises, your instructor may prefer that you work collaboratively, that is, with other students. These exercises are identified in the margin. *If your instructor directs you to work collaboratively on any of these items,* form groups of three or four classmates to complete the exercise together. Discuss your answers with each other and have one member of the group record the answers. A member of the group may be asked to share the group's answers with the class.

Option

Item 1 may be completed collaboratively.

1. Today colleges or universities may be 2- or 4-year institutions, large or small, public or private; and they may offer technical, vocational, or liberal arts degrees. What do you see as the benefits of the existence of such a variety of institutions?

____

____

____

____

____

____

____

2. The writers note a trend toward "lifelong learning," indicated by an increase in students over age 30 and especially over age 35. Give at least three reasons why lifelong learning is becoming so important.

Option

Item 3 may be completed collaboratively.

3. What is the most important overall message the writers want the reader to understand about the experience of going to college? Try to answer this question in one sentence.

Selection 3-2

Art appreciation

ART IN THE SERVICE OF RELIGION

FROM *LIVING WITH ART* BY RITA GILBERT

Prepare Yourself to Read

Directions: Do these exercises *before you read Selection 3-2.*

1. First, read and think about the title. What does this selection seem to be about?

 ____

 ____

2. Next, complete your preview by reading the following:

 Introduction (in *italics*)
 First paragraph (paragraph 1)
 First sentence of each paragraph
 Words in *italics*
 Picture and caption
 All of the last paragraph (paragraph 12)

 On the basis of your preview, how do you think art is used to serve religion?

 ____

Apply Comprehension Skills

Directions: Do these exercises *as you read Selection 3-2.*

Ask and answer questions as you read. Complete the practice exercises by creating questions based on what each paragraph seems to be about.

Read actively to find answers to your questions. Record the answers to your questions. Write the answer in the margin or highlight the answer in the text.

Review by rehearsing the answers to your questions. Recite your answers or write them down from memory.

ART IN THE SERVICE OF RELIGION

Think about various churches, synagogues, mosques, temples, shrines, and other religious structures you have attended or visited. Have you ever considered how the architecture of a place of worship is related to the activities that occur there? In this selection from an art appreciation textbook, the author explains the relationship between three different religions and the architecture of their places of worship.

1 Since earliest times art has served religion in two important ways. First, artists have erected the sacred temples where believers join to profess their faith and follow the observances faith requires. Second, art attempts to make specific and visible something that is, by its very nature, spiritual, providing images of the religious figures and events that make up the fabric of faith. In this section we shall explore how the theme of religious art has been adapted for different purposes, for different faiths, in different parts of the world.

2 A very large portion of the magnificent architecture we have was built in the service of religion. Naturally the architectural style of any religious structure reflects the culture in which it was built, but it is also dependent on the particular needs of a given religion. Three examples will show this.

3 On a high hill, the Acropolis, overlooking the city of Athens stands the shell of what many consider the most splendid building ever conceived: the Parthenon. The Parthenon was erected in the 5th century B.C. as a temple to the goddess Athena, patroness of the city, and at one time its core held a colossal statue of the goddess. However, the religion associated with the Parthenon was not confined to worship of a diety. In ancient Greece, veneration of the gods was closely allied to the political and social

Practice exercises

Directions: For each paragraph,

- Create a question based on what the paragraph seems to be about. Ask *who, what, when, where, why,* or *how.*
- Write your question in the spaces provided.
- Write the answer to your question in the margin or highlight it in the text.

Doing this will help you understand and remember the material.

Practice exercise

Question about paragraph 1:

____

____

Practice exercise

Question about paragraph 2:

____

____

Practice exercise

Question about paragraph 3:

____

____

Source: Rita Gilbert, "Art in the Service of Religion," in *Living with Art,* 3d ed., McGraw-Hill, New York, 1992, pp. 63–65. Reproduced with permission of McGraw-Hill. *Photo:* Archeological Survey of India, Janpath, New Delhi.

ideals of a city-state that celebrated its own greatness.

4 Rising proudly on its hill, visible from almost every corner of the city, and for miles around, the Parthenon functioned as a symbol of the citizens' aspirations. Its structure as a religious shrine seems unusual for us in that it turns outward, toward the city, rather than in upon itself. Worshipers were not meant to gather inside the building; actually, only priests could enter the inner chamber, or *cella,* where the statue of Athena stood. Religious ceremonies on festal occasions focused on processions, which began down in the city, wound their way up the steep path on the west side of the Acropolis, and circled the Parthenon and other sacred buildings at the top.

Practice exercise

Question about paragraph 4:

____

____

5 Most of the Parthenon's architectural embellishment was intended for the appreciation of the worshipers outside. All four walls of the exterior were decorated with sculptures high up under the roof, and originally portions of the marble facade were painted a vivid blue and red. In a later chapter we shall consider details of the Parthenon's structure; here we concentrate on the theme of religion and on the Parthenon's purpose, which is both religious *and* political exaltation.

Practice exercise

Question about paragraph 5:

____

____

6 At about the same time the Parthenon was being constructed in Athens, but half a continent away, one of the world's great religions was developing and beginning to form its own architecture. Buddhism derives its principles from the teachings of Gautama Siddhartha, later known as the Buddha, who was born in India about 563 B.C. Although of noble birth, the Buddha renounced his princely status and life of ease. When he was about twenty-nine, he began a long period of wandering and meditation, seeking enlightenment. He began with the supposition that humans are predisposed to live out lives of suffering, to die, then to be reborn and repeat the pattern. Ultimately, he worked out a doctrine of moral behavior that he believed could break the painful cycle of life and death, and he attracted many followers.

Practice exercise

Question about paragraph 6:

____

____

7 Buddhism is predominantly a personal religion, and its observances depend less on communal worship than on individual contemplation. It places great emphasis on symbolism, much of it referring to episodes in the Buddha's life. Both of these aspects—the personal and the symbolic—are evident in one of Buddhism's finest early shrines, the Great Stupa at Sanchi, in India. Like the Parthenon, the Great Stupa turns more outward than inward, but its moundlike form is more sculptural, intended as a representation of the cosmos. At the very top is a three-part "umbrella," symbolizing the three major aspects of Buddhism—the Buddha, the Buddha's law, and the Monastic Order.

8 Buddhist shrines—the word *stupa* means "shrine"—often housed relics of the Buddha, and worship rituals called for circumambulation ("walking around") of the stupa. Thus, on the outside of the Great Stupa of Sanchi we see a railed pathway, where pilgrims could take the ritual clockwise walk following the Path of Life around the World Mountain. Elsewhere the stupa is embellished richly with carvings and sculpture evoking scenes from the Buddha's life. Every part of the stupa is geared to the pursuit of personal enlightenment and transcendence.

9 If the Buddhist temple is dedicated to private worship, then its extreme opposite can be found in the total encompassment of a community religious experience: the medieval Christian cathedral. And the supreme example of that ideal is the Cathedral of Notre Dame de Chartres, in France. Chartres Cathedral was built, rebuilt, and modified over a period of several hundred years, but the basic structure, which is in the Gothic style, was established in the 13th century. A cathedral—as opposed to a church—is the bishop's domain and therefore is always in a town or a city. This one fact is crucial to understanding the nature of Chartres and the role it played in the people's lives.

10 The cathedral towers magnificently over the surrounding city, much as the Parthenon does over Athens, but here the resemblance ends.

Practice exercise

Question about paragraph 7:

____

____

Practice exercise

Question about paragraph 8:

____

____

Practice exercise

Question about paragraph 9:

____

____

The Great Stupa. Sunga and early Andhra periods. Third century B.C. to first century A.D. Sanchi, India.

Whereas the Parthenon is above and apart from the city, accessible only by a steep path, Chartres Cathedral is very much a living presence *within* the city. In the Middle Ages houses and shops clustered right up to its walls, and one side of the cathedral formed an edge of the busy marketplace. The cathedral functioned as a hub of all activities, both sacred and secular, within the town.

11 Medieval France had one dominant religion, and that was the Christianity of Rome. One could assume that almost every resident of the town of Chartres professed exactly the same faith, and so the church was an integral part of everyday life. Its bells tolled the hours of waking, starting work, praying, and retiring for the evening rest. Its feast days were the official holidays. Chartres Cathedral and its counterparts served the populace not only as a setting for religious worship but as meeting hall, museum, concert stage, and social gathering place.

Practice exercise

Question about paragraph 10:

____

____

Practice exercise

Question about paragraph 11:

____

____

Within its walls business deals were arranged, goods were sold, friends met, young couples courted. Where else but inside the cathedral could the townsfolk hear splendid music? Where else would they see magnificent art?

12 Three religious structures: the Parthenon, the Great Stupa, and Chartres Cathedral. Each was built in the service of religion but for each we can find another slightly different purpose. For the Parthenon the purpose is also *political;* for the Great Stupa there is the purely *private* observance of religion; and for Chartres the *social* role is as important as the religious.

Practice exercise

Question about paragraph 12:

____

____

Comprehension Quiz

True or false

Directions: In the blank provided, indicate whether each statement is true or false.

______ 1. Throughout history, art has served religion in three important ways.

______ 2. The Parthenon was built as a temple of the Greek goddess Diana.

______ 3. Greek citizens gathered inside the Parthenon to worship their gods.

______ 4. Many consider the Parthenon the most splendid building ever.

______ 5. The Buddhist religion and its architecture were developing in India at approximately the same time as the Parthenon was being constructed in Greece.

______ 6. "Circumambulation" is a Buddhist religious ritual that involves walking clockwise around the stupa, a Buddhist shrine.

Multiple-choice

Directions: For each item, select the best answer.

______ 7. Which of the following does *not* describe early Buddhism?

a. It is a personal religion.
b. It requires individual contemplation and a search for enlightenment.
c. It requires communal worship.
d. It involves a ritual of walking.

_____ 8. One of the finest Buddhist shrines, the Great Stupa of Sanchi in India, is characterized by all of the following *except* that it

a. contains a railed pathway.
b. resembles the cosmos with its moundlike form.
c. does not contain any carving or sculptures.
d. houses relics of the Buddha.

_____ 9. In medieval France, the cathedral served as a

a. place of worship.
b. concert stage and meeting hall.
c. museum housing fine religious paintings and sculpture.
d. all of the above.

_____ 10. Chartres Cathedral in France was built, rebuilt, and modified over a period of

a. 25 years.
b. 50 years.
c. 100 years.
d. several hundred years.

Extend Your Vocabulary by Using Context Clues

Directions: ***Context clues*** are words in a sentence or paragraph that allow the reader to deduce (reason out) the meaning of an unfamiliar word. For each item in this exercise, a sentence from Selection 3-2 containing an important word *(italicized, like this)* is quoted first. Next, there is an additional sentence using the word in the same sense and providing another context clue. Use the context clues to deduce the meaning of each italicized word. *The definition you choose should make sense in both sentences.*

Pronunciation key: ă **pat** ā **pay** âr **care** ä **father** ĕ **pet** ē **be** ĭ **pit** ī **tie** îr **pier** ŏ **pot** ō **toe** ô **paw** oi **noise** ou **out** o͝o **took** o͞o **boot** ŭ **cut** yo͞o **abuse** ûr **urge** th **thin** *th* **this** hw **which** zh **vision** ə **about**

_____ 1. "First, artists have erected the sacred temples where believers join to *profess* their faith and follow the observances faith requires."

Although the scientists were willing to *profess* loyalty to the country, they were deported as spies.

profess (prə fĕs´) means:

a. discuss
b. lie about
c. deny
d. declare

_____ 2. "In ancient Greece, *veneration* of the gods was closely allied to the political and social ideals of a city-state that celebrated its own greatness."

In Asian cultures older people, such as grandparents, are treated with great respect and *veneration.*

veneration (vĕn ə rā´ shən) means:

a. reverence
b. courtesy
c. fondness
d. patience

_____ 3. "All four walls of the exterior were decorated with sculptures high up under the roof, and originally, portions of the marble *facade* were painted a vivid blue and red."

The architect updated the *facade* of the old hotel by adding a beautiful new brick veneer and elegant bronze doors.

facade (fə säd´) means:

a. front of a building
b. decorative trim
c. columns; pillars
d. steps or stairs

_____ 4. "Although of noble birth, the Buddha *renounced* his princely status and life of ease."

When my brother became a Catholic priest, he *renounced* all of his worldly possessions.

renounced (rĭ nounst´) means:

a. ignored
b. gave up, especially by formal announcement
c. described in someone else's words
d. collected; gathered together

_____ 5. "He began with the *supposition* that humans are predisposed to live out lives of suffering, to die, then to be reborn and repeat the pattern."

Under the American judicial system, we begin with the *supposition* that a person is considered innocent until proven guilty.

supposition (sŭp ə zĭsh´ ən) means:

a. scientific conclusion
b. religious belief
c. assumption
d. hope

_____ 6. "Like the Parthenon, the Great Stupa turns more outward than inward, but its moundlike form is more sculptural, intended as a representation of the *cosmos*."

Every culture has its own explanation of the creation of the *cosmos*.

cosmos (kŏz´ məs) means:

a. city
b. mountains
c. the universe regarded as an orderly, harmonious whole
d. life after death

_____ 7. "Buddhist shrines—the word 'stupa' means 'shrine'—often housed *relics* of the Buddha, and worship rituals called for circumambulation ('walking around') of the stupa."

The museum presented a splendid exhibit of Russian icons and other religious *relics*.

relics (rĕl´ ĭks) means:

a. objects of religious veneration
b. pieces of art
c. personal belongings
d. paintings

_____ 8. "Elsewhere the stupa is *embellished* richly with carvings and sculpture evoking scenes from the Buddha's life."

The Sistine Chapel in Rome is *embellished* with magnificent frescoes by Michelangelo.

embellished (ĕm bĕl´ ĭsht) means:

a. made colorful and bright
b. painted
c. made in a shape of a bell
d. adorned; made beautiful

_____ 9. "Every part of the stupa is geared to the pursuit of personal enlightenment and *transcendence*."

The monk spent his days in solitude, meditation, and prayer as a way of seeking *transcendence*.

transcendence (trăn sĕn´ dĕns) means:

a. suffering
b. existence above or independent of the material universe
c. a change from one physical place to another
d. recognition; honor

_____ 10. *Medieval* France had one dominant religion, and that was the Christianity of Rome."

Our favorite childhood stories were about *medieval* kings, queens, and castles.

medieval (mē dē ē´ vəl) means:

a. pertaining to the Middle Ages, a 1,000-year period of European history between antiquity and the Renaissance
b. pertaining to the period of American history between the Civil War and the present
c. pertaining to a period in European history between the fourteenth and sixteenth centuries, a time of revived intellectual and artistic achievement
d. pertaining to a period in European history characterized by absence of artistic achievement

Respond in Writing

Directions: Refer to Selection 3-2 as necessary to answer these essay-type questions.

Option for collaboration: For some of the "Respond in Writing" exercises, your instructor may prefer that you work collaboratively, that is, with other students. These exercises are identified in the margin. *If your instructor directs you to work collaboratively on any of these items,* form groups of three or four classmates to complete the exercise together. Discuss your answers with each other and have one member of the group record the answers. A member of the group may be asked to share the group's answers with the class.

Option

Exercise 1 may be completed collaboratively.

1. The Great Stupa of Sanchi was designed strictly for the private observance of religion by individuals. However, the Parthenon and Chartres Cathedral served other purposes besides such private observance. In addition to religious worship, what *other purposes* did each of them serve?

   Parthenon:

   ____

   ____

   ____

Chartres Cathedral:

Option

Exercise 2 may be completed collaboratively.

2. What is the most important overall message the writer wants the reader to understand about religious structures like the Parthenon, the Great Stupa of Sanchi, and Chartres Cathedral? Try to answer this question in one sentence.

Selection 3-3

Human development

PARENTHOOD

FROM *HUMAN DEVELOPMENT*
BY DIANE E. PAPALIA AND SALLY WENDKOS OLDS

Prepare Yourself to Read

Directions: Do these exercises *before you read Selection 3-3.*

1. First, read and think about the title. What does this selection seem to be about?

 ____

 ____

2. Next, complete your preview by reading the following:

 Introduction (in *italics*)

 First paragraph (paragraph 1)

 Headings for each section

 Examine the bar graph and explanation beside it

 All of the last paragraph (paragraph 17)

 On the basis of your preview, what aspects of parenthood do you think will be discussed?

 ____

Apply Comprehension Skills

Directions: Do these exercises *as you read Selection 3-1.*

Ask and answer questions as you read. Complete the practice exercises by creating questions based on what each paragraph seems to be about.

Read actively to find answers to your questions. Record the answers to your questions. Write the answer in the margin or highlight the answer in the text.

Review by rehearsing the answers to your questions. Recite your answers or write them down from memory.

PARENTHOOD

"Just wait until you *have children of your own!" At one time or another in our lives, we have all heard these words. Becoming a parent and being a parent affect every area of a person's life. In this selection, the authors present some of the new, interesting, and sometimes surprising research findings about parenthood.*

1 The birth of a baby marks a major transition in the parents' lives. Moving from an intimate relationship between two people to one involving a totally dependent third person changes individuals and changes marriages. Parenthood is a developmental experience, whether the children are biological offspring, are adopted, or are the children of only one spouse.

WHY PEOPLE HAVE CHILDREN

2 At one time, the blessing offered newlyweds in the Asian country of Nepal was, "May you have enough sons to cover the hillsides!" (B. P. Arjyal, personal communication, Feb. 12, 1993). Having children has traditionally been regarded as not only the primary reason for marriage, but its ultimate fulfillment. In preindustrial societies, large families were a necessity: children helped with the family's work and eventually cared for their aging parents. And because the death rate in childhood was high, fewer children reached maturity. Because economic and social reasons for having children were so powerful, parenthood—especially motherhood—had a unique aura.

3 Today, Nepali couples are wished, "May you have a very bright son." Although sons are still preferred over daughters there, even boys are not wished for in such numbers as in the past, in the face of the lessening or even reversal of previous reasons for having children. Because of technological progress, fewer workers are

Practice exercises

Directions: For each paragraph,

- Create a question based on what the paragraph seems to be about. Ask *who, what, when, where, why,* or *how.*
- Write your question in the spaces provided.
- Write the answer to your question in the margin or highlight it in the text.

Doing this will help you understand and remember the material.

Practice exercise

Question about paragraph 1:

____

____

Practice exercise

Question about paragraph 2:

____

____

Practice exercise

Question about paragraph 3:

____

____

Source: Human Development, 6th ed., by Diane E. Papalia and Sally Wendkos Olds, McGraw-Hill, New York, 1995, pp. 455–456 and 459–461.

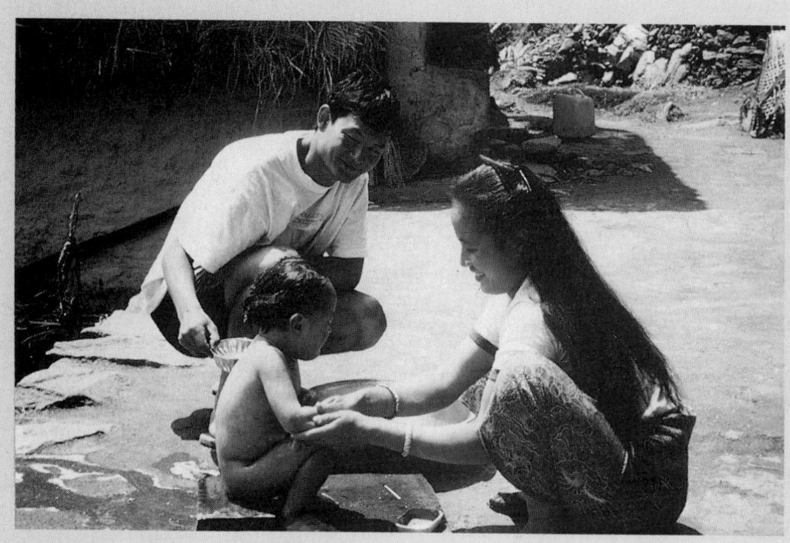

These Nepalese parents enjoy the fun and stimulation of having a child—although by now Kusum's parents have realized that parenthood also has other aspects, especially when their 2 1/2-year-old is unenthusiastic about being bathed. The physical, psychological, and financial stresses of rearing children contribute to the parents' own development. One of the best things about parenthood is that it is never predictable: parents must constantly meet the challenges of their children's changing needs. (*Sally Wendkos Olds*)

needed; because of modern medical care, most children survive; and because of government programs, some care of the aged is being provided. Overpopulation is a major problem in many parts of the world, and children are an expense rather than an economic asset. Furthermore, children can have negative, as well as positive, effects on a marriage.

4 Still, the desire for children is almost universal. Why? Psychoanalytic theorists like Freud maintain that women have a deep instinctual wish to bear and nurture infants. Ego psychologists like Erikson see generativity—a concern with establishing and guiding the next generation—as a basic developmental need. Functionalist sociologists attribute reproduction to people's need for immortality, achieved by replacing themselves with their children. Other theorists consider parenthood a part of nature, universal in the animal world. There is also continuing cultural pressure to have children, on the assumption that all normal people want them. For the subjects in one study of 199 married couples—nonparents to parents of four—the chief motivations for parenthood were the wish for a close relationship with another

Practice exercise

Question about paragraph 4:

____

____

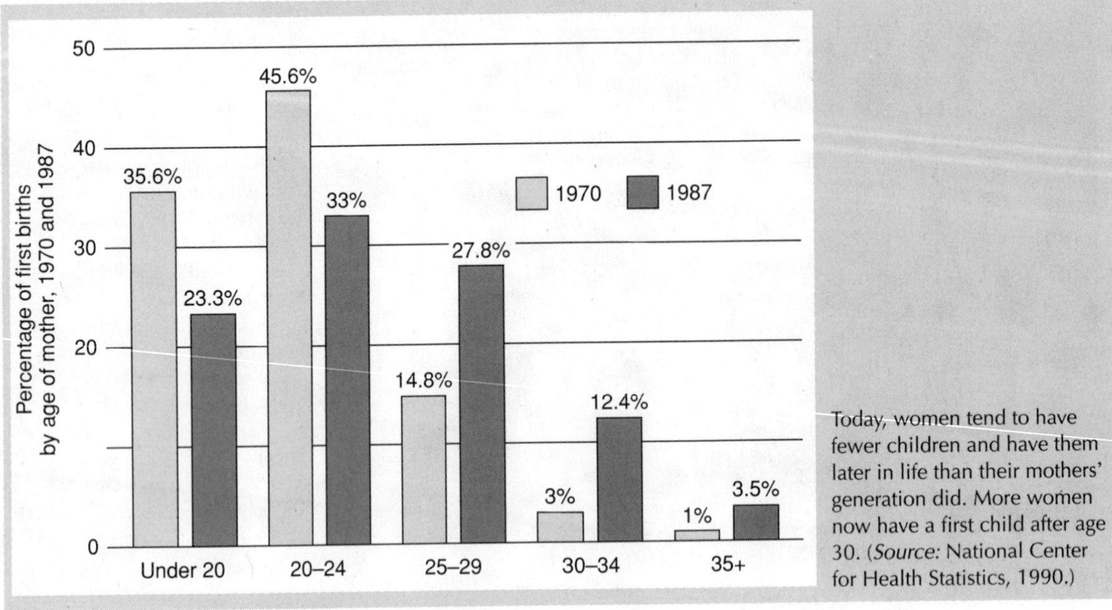

Today, women tend to have fewer children and have them later in life than their mothers' generation did. More women now have a first child after age 30. (*Source:* National Center for Health Statistics, 1990.)

human being and the desire to educate and train a child (F. L. Campbell, Townes, & Beach, 1982).

WHEN PEOPLE HAVE CHILDREN

5 The authors of this book exemplify changing trends in parenthood over the past 30 years. Sally [Wendkos Olds] was 23 years old in 1957, when she had her first child; not until after her third child was born, 5 years later, did she actively pursue her writing career. Diane [Papalia], who is younger, established her academic career first and was 39 when she and Jonathan adopted Anna in 1986.

6 By and large today's couples have fewer children and have them later in life than the previous generation did; now many people spend the early years of their marriage finishing an education and starting a career. More contemporary women—16 percent in 1987 versus 4 percent in 1970—have a first child after age 30 (National Center for Health Statistics, 1990).

Practice exercise

Question about paragraph 5:

____

____

Practice exercise

Question about paragraph 6:

____

____

7 This pattern is not an accident: today's women see a later "ideal age" for first birth. The most recently married women, the best educated, and the most strongly feminist choose the latest ideal ages (Pebley, 1981). And more educated women actually do have their children later; educational level is the most important predictor of the age when a woman will first give birth (Rindfuss, Morgan, & Swicegood, 1988; Rindfuss & St. John, 1983).

Practice exercise

Question about paragraph 7:

____

____

8 The trend toward later motherhood seems to be a blessing for babies. Although mothers over 35 have a higher risk of birth-related complications, the risk to the baby's health is only slightly higher than for infants of younger women (Berkowitz, Skovoron, Lapinski, & Berkowitz, 1990). On the positive side, babies of older mothers seem to benefit from their mothers' greater ease with parenthood. When 105 new mothers aged 16 to 38 were interviewed and observed with their infants, the older mothers reported more satisfaction with parenting and spent more time at it. They were more affectionate and sensitive to their babies and more effective in encouraging desired behavior (Ragozin, Basham, Crinic, Greenberg, & Robinson, 1982).

Practice exercise

Question about paragraph 8:

____

____

THE TRANSITION TO PARENTHOOD

9 Both women and men often feel ambivalent about becoming parents. Along with excitement, they usually feel some anxiety about the responsibility of caring for a child and about the permanence that a pregnancy seems to impose on a marriage. Pregnancy also affects a couple's sexual relationship, sometimes making it more intimate, but sometimes creating barriers.

Practice exercise

Question about paragraph 9:

____

____

10 What happens in a marriage from the time of the first pregnancy until the child's third birthday? That varies considerably. One research team followed 128 middle- and working-class

couples during this time; at the beginning of the study the husbands' ages averaged 29 years and wives' 27 years. Although some marriages improved, many suffered overall, especially for the wives. Many spouses loved each other less, became more ambivalent about their relationship, argued more, and communicated less. This was true no matter what the sex of the child was and whether or not the couple had the second child by the time the first was 3 years old. But when the researchers looked, not at the *overall* quality of the marriage, but at such *individual* measures as love, conflict, ambivalence, and effort put into the relationship, at least half of the sample showed either no change on a particular measure or a small positive change (Belsky & Rovine, 1990).

Practice exercise

Question about paragraph 10:

____

____

11 What distinguishes marriages that deteriorate after parenthood from those that improve? This study found no single determining factor. Rather, a number of different factors related to both parents and child seemed influential. In deteriorating marriages, the partners were more likely to be younger and less well educated, to earn less money, and to have been married for fewer years. One or both partners tended to have low self-esteem, and husbands were likely to be less sensitive (Belsky & Rovine, 1990). The mothers who had the hardest time were those with babies who had irregular temperaments and were therefore harder to take care of. . . .

Practice exercise

Question about paragraph 11:

____

____

12 Two surprising findings emerged from Belsky and Rovine's study. First, couples who were most romantic "pre-baby" had more problems "post-baby," perhaps because they had unrealistic expectations. Second, women who had planned their pregnancies were unhappier, possibly because they had expected life with a baby to be better than it turned out to be. Another finding of unmet expectations emerged from a study of married, middle-class white women. These mothers too expected things to be better 1 year after their first babies were born—in terms of their relationships with their husbands, their own physical well-being, and their maternal competence and satisfaction—

Practice exercise

Question about paragraph 12:

____

____

than they turned out to be, and had trouble adjusting (Kalmuss, Davidson, & Cushman, 1992).

13 One often violated expectation involves the division of chores. When a couple has shared them fairly equally before the baby is born, and the, post-baby, the burden shifts to the wife, marital happiness tends to decline, especially for nontraditional wives (Belsky, Land, & Huston, 1986).

Practice exercise

Question about paragraph 13:

___

___

PARENTHOOD AS A DEVELOPMENTAL EXPERIENCE

14 As hard as it may be to take on the role of parent, keeping it up is even more demanding. Parenting has rich rewards, but anyone with children will testify that those rewards are earned. Caring for small children can be unsettling, irritating, frustrating, and overwhelming, as well as fulfilling and amusing.

Practice exercise

Question about paragraph 14:

___

___

15 About one-third of mothers find mothering both enjoyable and meaningful, a third find it neither, and another third have mixed feelings (L. Thompson & Walker, 1989). Among couples who do not have children, husbands consider having children more important and are more apt to want them than their wives do (Seccombe, 1991). However, once the children come, although fathers treasure and are emotionally committed to them, they enjoy looking after them less than mothers do. Although fathers generally believe they should be involved in their children's lives, most are not nearly as involved as mothers are (Backett, 1987; Boulton, 1983; LaRossa, 1988). Still, men's families are very important to them.

Practice exercise

Question about paragraph 15:

___

___

16 In resolving conflicts about their personal roles (parent versus spouse versus worker), most successful parents define their situation positively. They believe that in any conflict, parental responsibilities clearly come first. They concentrate on one set of responsibilities at a time. And they compromise some standards when necessary, letting the furniture go undusted or becoming less active in community affairs to spend more time with their children

Practice exercise

Question about paragraph 16:

___

___

(B.C. Miller & Myers-Walls, 1983; Myers-Walls, 1984; Paloma, 1972). As children develop, parents do too.

17 Unfortunately, some people cannot meet the physical, psychological, and financial demands and challenges of parenthood. They may abuse, neglect, maltreat, or abandon their children; or they may become physically or emotionally ill themselves. Most parents, however, do cope, sometimes with the help of their family, friends, and neighbors; books and articles about child rearing; and professional advice.

Practice exercise

Question about paragraph 17:

____

____

Comprehension Quiz

True or false

Directions: In the blank provided, indicate whether each statement is true or false.

_____ 1. Psychoanalytic theorists like Freud believe that women have a deep instinctual wish to bear and nurture children.

_____ 2. One study found that a chief motivation for parenthood is the wish for a close relationship with another human being.

_____ 3. In general, today's couples have fewer children and have them earlier in life than the previous generation did.

_____ 4. Women with less education tend to have their children later in life.

_____ 5. Both men and women often feel excited about becoming parents, yet anxious about the responsibility of caring for a child.

_____ 6. Eventually, all mothers find mothering both enjoyable and meaningful.

Multiple-choice

Directions: For each item, select the best answer.

_____ 7. Although the desire to have children is almost universal,

a. people seem to want fewer children today.
b. people seem to want bigger and bigger families.
c. fewer children reach maturity in preindustrial societies.
d. people in industrialized societies need more children

_____ 8. There is ongoing cultural pressure to have children because

a. motherhood seems to have a unique aura.
b. today children are economic assets.
c. it is generally assumed that all normal people want them.
d. all of the above.

_____ 9. One study that interviewed and observed new mothers aged 16 to 35 found that the older mothers

a. spent more time parenting.
b. were more affectionate to their babies.
c. reported more satisfaction with parenting.
d. all of the above.

_____ 10. Once a couple become parents, their marital happiness can decline if

a. the pregnancy was unplanned.
b. the couple have a second child by the time their first child is 3 years old.
c. the burden of most of the previously shared chores shifts to the wife.
d. the couple have been married for more than 15 years.

Extend Your Vocabulary by Using Context Clues

Directions: ***Context clues*** are words in a sentence or paragraph that allow the reader to deduce (reason out) the meaning of an unfamiliar word. For each item in this exercise, a sentence from Selection 3-3 containing an important word *(italicized, like this)* is quoted first. Next, there is an additional sentence using the word in the same sense and providing another context clue. Use the context clues to deduce the meaning of each italicized word. *The definition you choose should make sense in both sentences.*

Pronunciation key: ă **pat** ā **pay** âr **care** ä **father** ĕ **pet** ē **be** ĭ **pit**
ī **tie** îr **pier** ŏ **pot** ō **toe** ô **paw** oi **noise** ou **out** o͝o **took** o͞o **boot**
ŭ **cut** yo͞o **abuse** ûr **urge** th **thin** *th* **this** hw **which** zh **vision** ə **about**

_____ 1. "The birth of a baby marks a major *transition* in the parents' lives."

Although it represents a milestone in a person's life, the *transition* from college student to full-time employee is often difficult.

transition (trăn zĭsh′ ən) means:

a. unexpected or unanticipated change
b. passage from one state to another
c. slow, gradual change
d. unwanted event or occurrence

______ 2. "Parenthood is a *developmental* experience, whether the children are biological offspring, are adopted, or are the children of only one spouse."

Many new or underprepared college students find that *developmental* reading, writing, and math courses provide the necessary background for subsequent college courses.

developmental (dĭ vĕl əp mənt´ əl) means:

a. progressing from a simpler stage to a stage that is more advanced, mature, or complex
b. noncredit
c. frustrating
d. decreasing in complexity or sophistication

______ 3. "In *preindustrial* societies, large families were a necessity: children helped with the family's work and eventually cared for their aging parents."

In *preindustrial* times, many items that are now mass-produced by machines were produced singly, by hand.

preindustrial (prē ĭn dŭs´ trē əl) means:

a. relating to a society whose industries do not yet produce manufactured goods on a large scale
b. relating to a society in which all individuals are engaged in industry
c. relating to a society in which all industry exists for profit
d. relating to a society whose economic well-being rests only on the production of manufactured goods

______ 4. "Because economic and social reasons for having children were so powerful, parenthood—especially motherhood—had a unique *aura*."

Even though final election returns were not yet in, an *aura* of defeat pervaded the candidate's headquarters.

aura (ôr´ ə) means:

a. distinctive but intangible quality of gloom
b. distinctive but intangible quality of joy that seems to disappear and reappear
c. distinctive but intangible quality associated with famous persons
d. distinctive but intangible quality that seems to surround a person or thing

_____ 5. "Still, the desire for children is almost *universal*."

Love is a *universal* emotion.

universal (yo͞o nə vûr′ səl) means:

a. knowledgeable about many subjects
b. existing all over the world
c. pertaining to the universe
d. cosmic

_____ 6. "Psychoanalytic theorists like Freud maintain that women have a deep *instinctual* wish to bear and nurture infants."

Because most birds have an *instinctual* fear of snakes, many gardeners place rubber snakes in their gardens to scare them away.

instinctual (ĭn stĭngk′ cho͞o əl) means:

a. learned from repeated experience
b. discovered by chance
c. modified by subsequent experience or learning
d. derived from a natural tendency or impulse

_____ 7. "Both men and women often feel *ambivalent* about becoming parents."

Many citizens and physicists have *ambivalent* feelings about nuclear energy, since it can be used for both constructive and destructive purposes.

ambivalent (ăm bĭv′ ə lənt) means:

a. able to use both the right and the left hand equally skillfully
b. positive
c. clear and distinct; unequivocal
d. having opposing attitudes or feelings at the same time

_____ 8. "Along with the excitement, they usually feel some anxiety about the responsibility of caring for a child and about the permanence that a pregnancy seems to *impose* on a marriage."

Because dictators have total control, they can *impose* their will and their decisions on all who live in their country.

impose (ĭm pōz′) means:

a. to become inconvenient
b. to make available
c. to force something on someone
d. to remove

_____ 9. "Another finding of *unmet* expectations emerged from a study of married, middle-class white women."

The bank robber refused to free his hostages unless the police agreed to his *unmet* demands.

unmet (ŭn mĕt´) means:

a. not formally introduced
b. not familiar
c. not known by the general public
d. not satisfied; unfulfilled

_____ 10. "They may abuse, neglect, *maltreat,* or abandon their children; or they may become physically or emotionally ill themselves."

The SPCA (Society for the Prevention of Cruelty to Animals) is an organization that works to prevent and stop those who *maltreat* pets or animals.

maltreat (măl trēt´) means:

a. abuse; treat in a rough or cruel way
b. ignore; pay no attention to
c. send away to a distant place
d. refuse to interact with

Respond in Writing

Directions: Refer to Selection 3-3 as necessary to answer these essay-type questions.

Option for collaboration: For some of the "Respond in Writing" exercises, your instructor may prefer that you work collaboratively, that is, with other students. These exercises are identified in the margin. *If your instructor directs you to work collaboratively on any of these items,* form groups of three or four classmates to complete the exercise together. Discuss your answers with each other and have one member of the group record the answers. A member of the group may be asked to share the group's answers with the class.

1. According to the authors, what factors seem to be associated with making parenthood a successful and satisfying experience?

____

____

____

____

____

Option

Item 2 may be completed collaboratively.

2. If couples wait until they are older, more mature, and better educated before becoming parents, what effects do you think this might have *on their children?* List at least three effects.

Option

Item 3 may be completed collaboratively.

3. If couples are older, more mature, and better educated when they became parents, what effects do you think this might have *on society?* List at least three effects.

Option

Item 4 may be completed collaboratively.

4. What is the most important overall message the writers want the reader to understand about parenthood? Try to answer this question in one sentence.

COMPREHENSION

Understanding College Textbooks by Reading for Ideas

CHAPTERS IN PART TWO

CHAPTER 4

DETERMINING THE TOPIC AND THE STATED MAIN IDEA

IN THIS CHAPTER YOU WILL LEARN
THE ANSWERS TO THESE QUESTIONS:

Why is it important to determine the topic of a paragraph?

How can I determine the topic of a paragraph?

Why is the stated main idea of a paragraph important?

How can I locate the stated main idea sentence of a paragraph?

CHAPTER 4 CONTENTS

A person who does not read has no advantage over someone who cannot read.

THE TOPIC OF A PARAGRAPH

What is the Topic of a Paragraph, and Why Is It Important?

Key term

Topic: Word or phrase that tells what an author is writing about.

Every paragraph has a topic because every paragraph is written *about* something. That "something" is the topic. A ***topic*** is a word or phrase that tells what the author is writing about in a paragraph. (There are other names for the topic of a paragraph. In a writing course or an English course, you may hear the topic referred to as the *subject* or *subject matter.* These are simply different terms for the topic.)

The topic may be mentioned several times within the paragraph, and each sentence in a paragraph should relate in some way to the topic. The topic may be expressed as a single word (for instance, *procrastination*) or as a phrase consisting of two or more words (for instance, *childhood diseases* or *the number of women in Congress*).

Determining the topic is the essential first step in understanding a passage that you are reading and studying. This step focuses your attention and helps you understand complex paragraphs precisely.

Determining and Expressing the Topic

When you read a paragraph, you can determine its topic by asking yourself, "Who or what is this paragraph about?" and then answering this question. Paragraphs in textbooks contain various clues that will help you answer the question.

The topic of a textbook paragraph is often obvious because it is a *word, name,* or *phrase* that:

- Appears as a *heading* or *title*
- Appears in special type such as **bold print,** *italics,* or color
- Is *repeated* throughout the paragraph
- Appears at the beginning of the paragraph and is then referred to throughout the paragraph by *pronouns* (or other words)

A paragraph does not usually contain all these clues, but every paragraph will probably have at least one of them. Let's look at each clue in more detail.

The topic may appear as a heading or title

Textbook authors typically use the topic of an important section as the heading or title for that section. The following paragraph from a textbook on business communications illustrates this clue (as well as some others). Read the paragraph, using its heading (and other clues) to determine its topic.

LEARNING ABOUT A CULTURE THROUGH ITS LANGUAGE

The best way to prepare yourself to do business with people from another culture is to study their culture in advance. If you plan to live in another country or do business there repeatedly, learn the language. The same holds true if you must work closely with a subculture that has its own language, such as Vietnamese-Americans or Hispanic-Americans. Even if you end up doing business with foreigners in your own language, you may show respect by making the effort to learn their language. In addition, you will learn something about the culture and its customs in the process. If you do not have the time or opportunity to actually learn a new language, at least learn a few words.

Source: Courtland Bovée and John Thill, *Business Communication Today,* 3d ed., McGraw-Hill, New York, 1992, p. 570. Reproduced with permission of McGraw-Hill.

Notice that in this excerpt, the heading *Learning about a Culture through Its Language* tells you what the topic is. This phrase describes everything that is discussed in the paragraph: it expresses the topic that all the sentences in the paragraph have in common. (Notice also that the words *culture* and *learn* are repeated throughout the paragraph.)

Annotate

Go back to the excerpt. Underline or highlight the heading, which indicates the topic.

It is important to understand that although the heading of a paragraph is often a clue to the topic, it may not express the topic completely or accurately. To determine the topic, do not rely *only* on headings; you must also read the paragraph and ask yourself, "Who or what is this paragraph about?"

The topic may appear in special print

A second clue to the topic of a paragraph is the use of special print (such as **boldface,** *italic,* or color) to emphasize a word, phrase, or name. The paragraph below is from a textbook on criminal justice. Read this paragraph, watching for special print that indicates its topic.

Written criminal codes in all jurisdictions make distinctions between felonies and misdemeanors, and sometimes lesser offenses called "violations" or "infractions." A **felony** is a serious crime with correspondingly harsh penalties including such civil disabilities as loss of voting privileges after conviction as well as criminal punishment of more than 1 year in prison. A **misdemeanor** is a minor offense, less serious than a felony, subject to penalties such as a fine or a jail term of less than 1 year.

Source: Patrick R. Anderson and Donald J. Newman, *Introduction to Criminal Justice,* 5th ed., McGraw-Hill, New York, 1993, p. 7.

Annotate

Go back to the excerpt. Underline or highlight the words in bold print, which indicate the topic.

Notice the words in bold print: **felony** and **misdemeanor.** These words, together, indicate the topic; the paragraph discusses *felonies and misdemeanors.* Keep in mind that the topic can also appear in italics, and that in many college textbooks such key words are printed in color. Special print, then, can often help you recognize the topic.

The topic may be repeated throughout the paragraph

A third clue to the topic is repetition of a word, phrase, or name throughout a paragraph. Read the paragraph below from a psychology textbook, using this clue to determine its topic.

> Claustrophobia. Acrophobia. Xenophobia. Although these sound like characters in a Greek tragedy, they are actually members of a class of psychological disorders known as phobias. Phobias are intense, irrational fears of specific objects or situations. For example, claustrophobia is a fear of enclosed places, acrophobia a fear of high places, and xenophobia a fear of strangers. Although the objective danger posed by an anxiety-producing stimulus is typically small or nonexistent, to the individual suffering from the phobia it represents great danger, and a full-blown panic attack may follow exposure to the stimulus.

Source: Robert S. Feldman, *Understanding Psychology,* 3d ed., McGraw-Hill, New York, 1993, p. 562.

Annotate

Go back to the excerpt. Underline or highlight the repeated word, which indicates the topic.

Notice that the word *phobia* or *phobias* appears three times in this paragraph, indicating its topic. In addition, three types of phobias are given as examples.

The topic may appear once and then be referred to by pronouns or other words

A fourth clue to the topic of a paragraph is a word, phrase, or name that appears at the beginning of the paragraph and is then referred to throughout the paragraph by a pronoun (such as *he, she, it, they, his, her, its,* etc.). Here is a paragraph from a physics textbook. Determine its topic by using this clue.

> Before the age of 30, Isaac Newton had invented the mathematical methods of calculus, demonstrated that white light contained all the colors of the rainbow, and discovered the law of gravitation. His was a lonely and solitary life. His father died before he was born, and after his mother remarried, he was raised by an aged grandmother. In 1661, he was admitted to Cambridge University, where he worked for the next eight years, except for one year at home to escape the plague. During those years, he made his major discoveries, although none were published at that time. His genius was nonetheless recognized, and in 1669 he was appointed Lucasion Professor of Mathematics at Cambridge University, a position he retained until 1695. His major scientific work was completed prior to 1692, when he suffered a nervous

Source: Frederick Bueche, *Principles of Physics,* 5th ed., McGraw-Hill, New York, 1988, p. 70.

breakdown. After his recovery, he determined to lead a more public life, and soon became the Master of the Mint in London. He was elected president of the Royal Society in 1703, and held that position until his death.

Notice that Newton's name appears only in the first sentence, but it is obvious from the pronouns *he* and *his* that the rest of the paragraph continues to discuss him. Therefore, *Isaac Newton* is the topic of this paragraph.

You should also be aware that sometimes a word, phrase, or name indicating the topic may appear at the beginning and then be replaced throughout the paragraph by one or more other words rather than by pronouns. For instance, a paragraph might began "Pneumonia is . . ." and then might say something such as "This disease is characterized by . . ." and "The condition worsens when . . ." and "The disorder is typically treated by . . ." In this case, the words *disease, condition,* and *disorder* refer to pneumonia and indicate that *pneumonia* is the topic of the paragraph.

Annotate

Go back to the excerpt. Underline or highlight the topic and the pronouns that stand for it.

Precision is important when you express a topic. If the words you use are too general or too specific, they will not describe the topic accurately. A topic described in terms that are *too general,* or too broad, will go beyond what is discussed in the paragraph. A topic described in terms that are *too specific,* or too narrow, will fail to cover everything discussed in the paragraph. Suppose, for instance, that the topic of a paragraph is *causes of gang violence.* The word *gang* or *violence* or the phrase *gang violence,* would be too general to express this topic precisely; and the phrase *lack of parental supervision as a cause of gang violence* would be too specific, even though "lack of parental supervision" is mentioned in the paragraph as one of the causes. Also, keep in mind that it is possible to express a topic in more than one way. For example, the topic of a paragraph could be correctly expressed as *Winston Churchill's childhood, the childhood of Winston Churchill, Churchill's life as a child, Churchill's boyhood,* or *Churchill's youth,* since these all mean the same thing.

Determining a topic precisely is the starting point in comprehending as you read. It is also a key to locating the main idea sentence in a paragraph, as you will see in the next section of this chapter.

THE STATED MAIN IDEA OF A PARAGRAPH

What Is a Stated Main Idea, and Why Is It Important?

Every paragraph has a main idea. A ***stated main idea*** is a sentence within a paragraph that expresses the most important point the author wants the reader to understand about the topic of the paragraph. (There are various terms for a stated main idea. In a writing course or an English course, the main idea sentence of a paragraph may be called a *topic sentence.*)

Key term

Stated main idea: Sentence in a paragraph that expresses the most important point about the topic.

As you have learned in the first part of this chapter, the topic of a paragraph can be expressed as a single word, a phrase, or a name. A main idea sentence expresses the *most important point* about the topic. Because the word *main* means "*most* important," there can be only *one* main idea. The main idea sentence in a paragraph whose topic is *procrastination* might be, "Procrastination is the major cause of stress for college students." (This sentence tells you the important point the author wants readers to understand about procrastination.)

A main idea is called a *stated* main idea when the author presents it (in other words, states it) as one of the sentences in the paragraph. A *stated main idea sentence* may appear at the beginning or end of a paragraph, or in the middle. Of course, only one sentence can be the *most* important sentence in a paragraph.

In this chapter, you will practice with paragraphs that contain stated main ideas. Sometimes, however, an author does not state the main idea of a paragraph directly. In that case, the main idea is called an *implied* main idea, and the reader must create a sentence that states the author's main point. (Implied main ideas are discussed in Chapter 5.)

There are three major reasons why it is important to determine main ideas when you are studying:

- To increase your comprehension
- To enable you to mark textbooks effectively and take notes as you study
- To help you remember important material for tests

For these reasons, effective readers focus on main ideas as they read.

Locating the Stated Main Idea Sentence

Two steps to follow

Since a stated main idea is one of the sentences in the paragraph, your task is simply to determine *which* sentence is the main idea. Often, the stated main idea will be obvious. To identify the stated main idea sentence, find the sentence that contains both the topic and the most important point about it.

To locate the stated main idea, follow these two steps:

- *Step 1.* After you have read the paragraph, determine the topic by asking yourself, "Who or what is the passage about?" and then answering this question. (Use the clues you learned in the first part of this chapter for determining the topic.)
- *Step 2.* Locate the main idea sentence by asking yourself, "What is the most important point the author wants me to understand about this topic?" Then search for the sentence that answers this question. That sentence is the stated main idea.

Here is a simple formula for identifying a stated main idea sentence:

TOPIC	+	AUTHOR'S MOST IMPORTANT POINT ABOUT THE TOPIC	=	MAIN IDEA SENTENCE

Where a stated main idea sentence may appear

The stated main idea sentence may appear at the beginning of the paragraph. The first sentence of a paragraph is often the main idea. The following excerpt from a textbook on career planning is an example in which the stated main idea appears at the *beginning* of the paragraph. The topic of this paragraph is *beginning a new job.* Read the paragraph and ask yourself, "What is the most important point the authors want me to understand about beginning a new job?" The sentence that answers this question, the first sentence, is the main idea.

Beginning a new job is always exciting and sometimes intimidating. There is an invigorating feeling of a fresh start and a clean slate. You face new challenges and draw on a renewed sense of energy as you approach them. But you may also feel apprehensive about this new adventure. Will it actually turn out as well as you hope? You are entering a strange environment, and you must learn to work with new associates. If you were fired from your last job, you may feel particularly sensitive. "What if it happens again?" you ask yourself.

Source: William Morin and James Cabrera, *Parting Company: How to Survive the Loss of a Job and Find Another,* Harcourt, Brace, San Diego, Calif., 1982, p. 238.

The first sentence in the excerpt is a general one which mentions two different types of feelings people often have as they start a new job. Since the most important thing the authors want you to understand is that people may have *both* types of feelings, this sentence is the main idea of the paragraph: *Beginning a new job is always exciting and sometimes intimidating.* The rest of the paragraph supports this sentence as the main idea: the first half of the paragraph explains why starting a new job is exciting, and the last half of the paragraph explains why it can be intimidating. In this paragraph, then, the first sentence states the main idea, and the rest of the sentences are details that tell us more about it.

Annotate

Go back to the excerpt. Underline or highlight the stated main idea sentence.

The stated main idea sentence may appear at the end of the paragraph. Frequently, the *last sentence* of a paragraph is the stated main idea. That is, the stated main idea appears at the *end* of the paragraph. Read the excerpt below, from a sociology textbook. The topic of this paragraph is *ethnocentrism.* As you read the paragraph, ask yourself, "What is the most important point the authors want me to understand about the term *ethnocentrism?*" The sentence that answers this question, the last sentence, is the stated main idea.

When members of a dominant culture become suspicious of subcultures and seek to isolate or assimilate them, it is often because the members of the dominant culture are making value judgments about the beliefs and practices of the subordinate groups. Most Anglo-Americans, for instance, see the extensive family obligations of Hispanics as a burdensome arrangement that inhibits individual freedom. Hispanics, in contrast, view the isolated nuclear family of Anglo-Americans as a lonely institution that cuts people off from the love and assistance of their kin. This tendency to view one's own cultural patterns as good and right and those of others as strange or even immoral is called **ethnocentrism.**

Source: Craig Calhoun, Donald Light, and Susanne Keller, *Sociology,* 6th ed., New York, McGraw-Hill, 1994, p. 65.

Annotate

Go back to the excerpt. Underline or highlight the stated main idea sentence.

In this paragraph, the first sentence is an introductory one that explains how and why members of a dominant culture may react to members of subcultures. It is followed by two examples. However, the last sentence of the paragraph is the main idea because it states the authors' most important point: that *ethnocentrism* is the term used to describe this tendency to view one's own cultural patterns as superior and other cultures as inferior or wrong. Notice that this stated main idea sentence contains the topic.

The stated main idea sentence may appear within the paragraph. Sometimes the stated main idea sentence is neither the first nor the last sentence of a paragraph, but rather one of the other sentences in the paragraph. That is, the stated main idea appears *within* the paragraph. Here is a paragraph from a government textbook in which the second sentence is the main idea sentence. The topic is *television commercials and presidential campaigns.* As you read this paragraph, ask yourself, "What is the most important point the author wants me to understand about television commercials and presidential campaigns?"

The television campaign includes political advertising. Televised commercials are by far the most expensive part of presidential campaigns. Since 1976, political commercials on television have accounted for about half of the candidates' expenditures in the general election campaign. In 1992 Bush and Clinton each spent more than $30 million on advertising in the general election, and Perot spent even more. Perot relied heavily on "infomercials"—30-minute and hour-long commercials that emphasized substance over slogans.

Source: Thomas E. Patterson, *The American Democracy,* 3d ed., McGraw-Hill, New York, 1996, p. 398. Reproduced with permission of McGraw-Hill.

Annotate

Go back to the excerpt. Underline or highlight the stated main idea sentence.

The second sentence presents the author's most important point: *Televised commercials are by far the most expensive part of presidential campaigns.* Each of the other sentences presents facts demonstrating how expensive televised campaign commercials have become.

How to Tell If You Have Identified the Stated Main Idea Sentence

How can you tell if you have *correctly* identified the stated main idea sentence of a paragraph? You have found the stated main idea sentence if:

- The sentence contains the topic.
- The sentence states the *one* most important point about the topic.
- The sentence is general enough to cover all the information in the paragraph.
- The other sentences explain or tell more about the main idea sentence.
- The sentence makes complete sense by itself (in other words, you can understand it without having to read the rest of the paragraph).

How to avoid two common errors in locating a stated main idea

You have learned that a stated main idea sentence is often the first or last sentence of a paragraph, and so you may be tempted to take a shortcut by looking only at the first and last sentences. This is a common error which should be avoided. You must read the entire paragraph to determine the main idea accurately. Unless you read the whole paragraph, you may miss a stated main idea sentence that appears somewhere in the middle.

A second common error can occur when a paragraph is difficult. In this case, you may be tempted to decide that a sentence is the main idea because it contains familiar or interesting information or because it seems to "sound important." These are *not* good reasons for identifying a sentence as the stated main idea. To avoid this second error, remember that the stated main idea sentence must always answer the question, "What is *the one most important point* the author wants me to understand about the topic?"

A Word about the Stated Overall Main Idea in a Longer Passage

Determining stated main ideas is a skill that can also be applied to passages longer than a single paragraph, such as sections of a textbook chapter, short reading selections, and essays. You will sometimes discover a sentence in a longer passage (usually an introductory or concluding sentence) that expresses the most important point or the overall message of the *entire passage.* Each of the reading selections at the end of each chapter in this book includes an exercise which gives you practice in determining a main idea that expresses the overall message of the entire selection.

STANDARDIZED READING TESTS: TOPICS AND STATED MAIN IDEAS

College students may be required to take standardized reading tests as part of an overall assessment program, in a reading course, or as part of a state-mandated "basic skills" test. A standardized reading test typically consists of a series of passages followed by multiple-choice questions, to be completed within a specified time limit. Included in Part Two of *Opening Doors* are tips that should help you score as high as possible on standardized reading tests. The tips below have to do with determining topics and stated main ideas.

To begin with, you should be aware that students sometimes miss questions on reading tests because they do not realize what they are being asked. If the wording of an item is even slightly unfamiliar, they may not recognize that they are being asked to apply a reading comprehension skill they already know. Therefore, you should learn to recognize certain *types* of questions no matter how they are worded, just as you recognize your friends no matter what they are wearing.

You are being asked to select the *topic of a passage* when the test question begins:

The best title for this selection is . . .

This passage discusses . . .

This passage focuses mainly on . . .

The topic of this passage is . . .

This passage is mainly about . . .

This passage mainly concerns . . .

The problem the author is discussing in this passage is . . .

The author is explaining the nature of . . .

To find the right answer, simply ask yourself, "Who or what is this passage about?" Then see which of the choices offered most closely matches your answer. Remember to use the four clues for determining topics: titles or headings, emphasized words, repetition, and pronouns (or other words).

If you are being asked to select the *main idea,* the question may be worded:

The author's main point is that . . .

The principal idea of this passage is that . . .

Which of the following best expresses the main idea of this paragraph (or a specifically identified paragraph)?

Which of the following best expresses the main idea of the entire passage?

To find the right answer, ask yourself, "What is the most important point the author wants me to understand about the topic?" Next, search the passage for a single sentence that answers this question. Then read each of the choices offered to see which one is the same as the sentence you selected or says much the same thing.

DEVELOPING CHAPTER REVIEW CARDS

Review cards, or *summary cards,* are an excellent study tool. They are a way to select, organize, and review the most important information in a textbook chapter. The process of creating review cards helps you organize information in a meaningful way and, at the same time, transfer it into long-term memory. The cards can also be used to prepare for tests (see Part Three). The review card activities in this book give you structured practice in creating these valuable study tools. Once you have learned how to make review cards, you can create them for textbook material in your other courses.

Now, complete the seven review cards for Chapter 4 by answering the questions or following the directions on each card. When you have completed them, you will have summarized: (1) what the topic of a paragraph is and (2) how to determine it; (3) what a stated main idea sentence is and (4) how to locate it; (5) where the stated main idea sentence of a paragraph may appear; (6) how to tell if you have identified a stated main idea sentence correctly; and (7) how to avoid two errors in identifying stated main idea sentences.

The Topic of a Paragraph

1. What is the topic of a paragraph? (See page 169.)

____

____

2. Why is determining the topic important? (See page 169.)

____

____

3. To determine the topic, what question should you ask yourself? (See page 169.)

____

____

Chapter 4: Determining the Topic and the Stated Main Idea

Determining the Topic of a Paragraph

What four clues will help you determine the topic? (See pages 169–172.)

1. ______________________________

2. ______________________________

3. ______________________________

4. ______________________________

Chapter 4: Determining the Topic and the Stated Main Idea

The Stated Main Idea of a Paragraph

1. What is a stated main idea sentence? (See page 172.)

____

2. What are three reasons why it is important to determine a stated main idea? (See page 173.)

Reason: ______________________________

Reason: ______________________________

Reason: ______________________________

Chapter 4: Determining the Topic and the Stated Main Idea

Locating a Stated Main Idea Sentence

What are two steps to follow in locating a stated main idea sentence? (See page 173.)

Step 1: ____

____

Step 2: ____

____

What is a formula for identifying a stated main idea sentence? (See page 174.)

Formula:

Chapter 4: Determining the Topic and the Stated Main Idea

Where a Stated Main Idea Sentence May Appear

Where in a paragraph may the stated main idea sentence appear? List three places. (See pages 174–175.)

1. ____

   ____

2. ____

   ____

3. ____

   ____

Chapter 4: Determining the Topic and the Stated Main Idea

Checking Your Identification of a Stated Main Idea Sentence

List five ways you can tell if you have identified the stated main idea sentence correctly. (See page 176.)

You have selected the stated main idea sentence if:

1. ____

2. ____

3. ____

4. ____

5. ____

Chapter 4: Determining the Topic and the Stated Main Idea

Avoiding Errors in Determining a Stated Main Idea Sentence

What are two common errors in determining stated main idea sentence? Describe how each can be avoided. (See page 176.)

Error: ____

How to avoid it: ____

Error: ____

How to avoid it: ____

Chapter 4: Determining the Topic and the Stated Main Idea

Selection 4-1

Government

THE CAMPAIGN FOR ELECTION

FROM *THE AMERICAN DEMOCRACY* BY THOMAS E. PATTERSON

Prepare Yourself to Read

Directions: Do these exercises *before you read Selection 4-1.*

1. First, read and think about the title. What do you already know about the presidential campaign of 1992?

____

____

2. Next, complete your preview by reading the following:

   Introduction (in *italics*)
   First paragraph (paragraph 1)
   Subheading
   First sentence of each paragraph
   Map
   Last paragraph (paragraph 7)

   On the basis of your preview, what aspects of the 1992 presidential campaign does the selection seem to be about?

____

____

Apply Comprehension Skills

Directions: Do the Annotation Practice Exercises *as you read Selection 4-1.* Apply two skills from this chapter:

Determine the topic. When you read a paragraph, ask yourself, "What or who is this about?"

Identify the stated main idea. As you read, ask yourself, "What is the most important point the author wants me to understand about the topic?" Then search for the sentence that answers this question.

Complete the Annotation Practice Exercises. In these exercises, you will work only with paragraphs that have stated main ideas.

THE CAMPAIGN FOR ELECTION

Do you think of yourself as a Democrat? A Republican? An independent? Most Americans say they belong to one of the two major political parties and vote in presidential elections. However, many people also acknowledge that they do not have an understanding of election strategies. What makes a presidential campaign successful? In the selection below, from a government text, the author describes factors that shape presidential campaign strategies.

1 The winner in the November general election is almost certain to be either the Republican or the Democratic nominee. A minor-party or independent candidate, such as George Wallace in 1968, John Anderson in 1980, or Ross Perot in 1992, can draw votes away from the major-party nominees but stands almost no chance of defeating them.

2 A major-party nominee has the critical advantage of support from the party faithful. Although party loyalty has declined in recent decades, two-thirds of the nation's voters still identify themselves as Democrats or Republicans, and most of them support their party's presidential candidate. Even Democrat George McGovern, who had the lowest level of party support among recent nominees, was backed in 1972 by nearly 60 percent of his party's voters.

3 Republican nominees have usually found it easier to keep their party's loyalists in line. The GOP [Grand Old Party, that is, the Republican Party] has been the more homogeneous party, and campaign appeals to traditional social values, patriotism, restrained government spending, lower taxes, and a strong defense have usually maintained the Republican vote. In 1992, however, a weak economy hurt the Republican effort. George Bush received the votes of 73 percent of Republicans, while Perot got 17 percent and Bill Clinton 10 percent. . . .

Annotation practice exercises

Directions: For each exercise below,

- Write the topic of the paragraph on the lines beside the paragraph.
- Underline or highlight the stated main idea sentence of the paragraph.

This will help you remember the topic and the main idea.

Annotation exercise

- Topic of paragraph 2:

____

____

- Underline or highlight the stated main idea of paragraph 2.

Source: Thomas E. Patterson, "The Campaign for Election," from *The American Democracy,* 3d ed., McGraw-Hill, New York, 1996, pp. 394–396. Reproduced with permission of McGraw-Hill. *Photo:* Andy Clark/Reuters/Bettmann.

George Bush, Ross Perot, and Bill Clinton *(left to right)* take questions from citizens during the second debate of the 1992 presidential campaign, at the University of Richmond.

Election strategy

4 Presidential candidates act strategically. In deciding whether to pursue a course of action, they try to estimate its likely impact on the voters. For incumbents and challengers alike, some of these issues will be questions of past performance. During the 1992 campaign, a sign on the wall of Clinton's headquarters in Little Rock read, "The Economy, Stupid." The slogan was the idea of James Carville, Clinton's chief strategist, and was meant as a reminder to the candidate and the staff to keep the campaign focused on the nation's sluggish economy, which ultimately was the issue that defeated Bush. As in 1980, when incumbent Jimmy Carter lost to Ronald Reagan during tough economic times, the voters were motivated largely by a desire for change.

Annotation exercise

- Topic of paragraph 4:

____

____

- Underline or highlight the stated main idea of paragraph 4.

5 Candidates try to project a strong leadership image. Whether voters accept this image, however, depends more on external factors than on a candidate's personal characteristics. In 1991,

after the Persian Gulf War, Bush's approval rating reached 91 percent, the highest level recorded since polling began in the 1930s. A year later, with the Gulf War a receding memory and the nation's economy in trouble, Bush's approval rating dropped below 40 percent. Bush tried to stir images of his strong leadership of the war, but voters remained preoccupied with the economy.

6 The candidates' strategies are shaped by many considerations, including the constitutional provision that each state shall have electoral votes equal in number to its representation in Congress. Each state thus gets two electoral votes for its Senate representation and a varying number of electoral votes depending on its House representation. All together, there are 538 electoral votes (including three for the District of Columbia, even though it has no voting representatives in Congress). To win the presidency, a candidate must receive at least 270 votes, an electoral majority.

7 The importance of the electoral votes is magnified by the existence of the *unit rule;* all the states except Maine and Nebraska grant all their electoral votes as a unit to the candidate who wins the state's popular vote. For this reason, candidates are particularly concerned with winning the most populous states, such as California (with 54 electoral votes), New York (33), Texas (32), Florida (25), Pennsylvania (23), Illinois (22), and Ohio (21). Victory in the eleven largest states alone would provide an electoral majority, and presidential candidates therefore spend most of their time campaigning in those states. Because of the unit rule, a relatively small popular-vote margin can produce a lopsided electoral-vote margin. Clinton received only 43 percent of the popular vote in 1992, compared with Bush's 38 percent and Perot's 19 percent; but Clinton won in states that gave him an overwhelming 370 electoral votes, compared with 168 for Bush and none for Perot (see map).

Annotation exercise

- Topic of paragraph 6:

  ____

  ____

- Underline or highlight the stated main idea of paragraph 6.

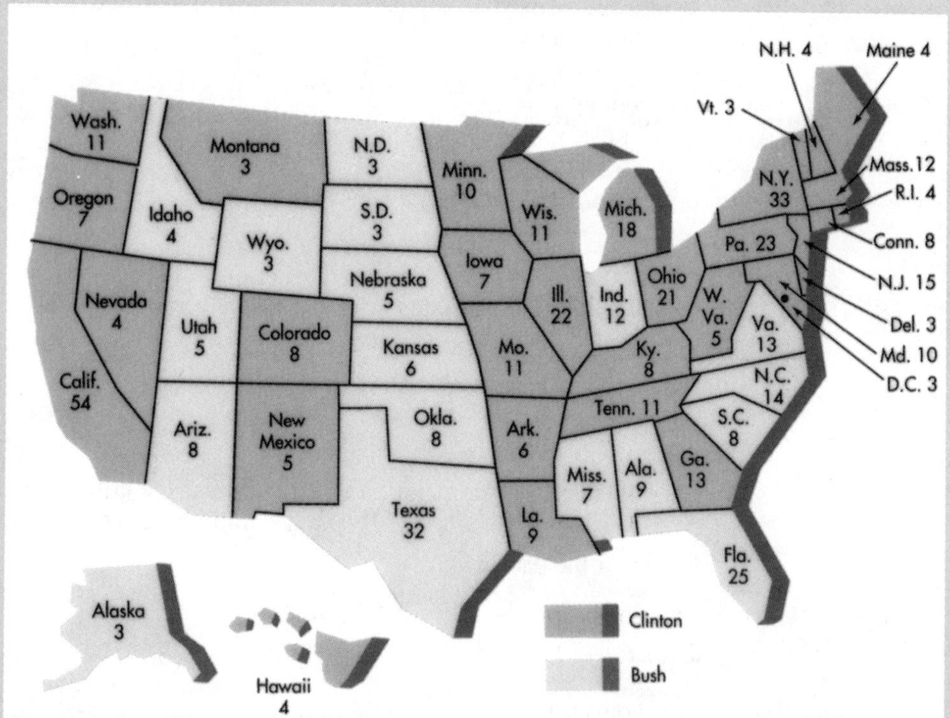

Electoral votes in the fifty states and states carried by the presidential candidates in the 1992 election. The larger the population of a state, the more electoral votes it has—and the more important it is to presidential candidates. Each state's electoral votes are shown here, along with the states carried by candidates Bill Clinton and George Bush in the 1992 election. To win the presidency, a candidate must receive 270 of the national total of 538 electoral votes. Clinton won 32 states and the District of Columbia for 370 electoral votes, while Bush took 18 states and 168 electoral votes. Ross Perot did not finish first in any state and thus received no electoral votes.

Comprehension Quiz

True or false

Directions: In the blank provided, indicate whether each statement is true or false.

______ 1. Republican nominees have traditionally found it easier than Democratic nominees to keep party loyalists in line.

______ 2. The author believes that a minor-party or independent candidate has a good chance of defeating the major-party nominees.

______ 3. In 1992, the issue that ultimately defeated George Bush and elected Bill Clinton was the Persian Gulf War.

_____ 4. To win the presidency, a candidate must receive 270 of the national total of 538 electoral votes.

_____ 5. Each state has one electoral vote for each of its two senators plus a varying number of electoral votes based on its representation in the House.

Multiple-choice

Directions: For each item, select the best answer.

_____ 6. The three most populous states, with the most electoral votes, are:

a. Florida, New York, Texas
b. California, New York, Texas
c. California, New York, Florida
d. Texas, California, Florida

_____ 7. The author states that "a major party nominee has the critical advantage of support from the party faithful." By *party faithful* he means:

a. leaders of the parties
b. people who make at least one financial contribution to the party of their choice
c. people who vote for the same party year after year
d. voters with religious faith

_____ 8. According to this selection, of all voters, how many identify themselves as either Democrats or Republicans?

a. half
b. two-thirds
c. three-fourths
d. all

_____ 9. In the presidential election of 1992, which of the following hurt the Republican effort?

a. the Persian Gulf War
b. low unemployment
c. Bush's foreign policy
d. a weak economy and a conflict within the Republican party

_____ 10. According to the map, which of the most populous states cast its electoral votes for Bush in the 1992 election?

a. California
b. Florida
c. New York
d. Texas

Extend Your Vocabulary by Using Context Clues

Directions: **Context clues** are words in a sentence or paragraph that allow the reader to deduce (reason out) the meaning of an unfamiliar word. For each item in this exercise, a sentence from Selection 4-1 containing an important word *(italicized, like this)* is quoted first. Next, there is an additional sentence using the word in the same sense and providing another context clue. Use the context clues to deduce the meaning of each italicized word. *The definition you choose should make sense in both sentences.*

Pronunciation key: ă **pat** ā **pay** âr **care** ä **father** ĕ **pet** ē **be** ĭ **pit** ī **tie** îr **pier** ŏ **pot** ō **toe** ô **paw** oi **noise** ou **out** o͝o **took** o͞o **boot** ŭ **cut** yo͞o ab**use** ûr **ur**ge th **thin** *th* **this** hw **wh**ich zh vi**si**on ə **a**bout

_____ 1. "Republican nominees have usually found it easier to keep their party's *loyalists* in line."

When their team fell behind by three touchdowns, most of the fans left, but the *loyalists* stayed until the end.

loyalists (loi′ ə lĭsts) means:

a. people who are members of royalty
b. British subjects
c. people who are faithful to a group or an ideal
d. traitors

_____ 2. "The GOP has been the more *homogeneous* party, and campaign appeals to traditional social values, patriotism, restrained government spending, lower taxes, and a strong defense have usually maintained the Republican vote."

The southern part of the city is *homogeneous;* the people who live there are mostly blue-collar factory workers.

homogeneous (hō mə jē′ nē əs) means:

a. uniform; the same throughout
b. consisting of a variety of things
c. consisting only of men
d. pertaining to a celebration

_____ 3. "In 1991, after the Persian Gulf War, Bush's approval rating reached 91 percent, the highest level recorded since *polling* began in the 1930s."

Nearly all political *polling* is conducted by volunteers who staff telephone banks.

polling (pōl ĭng) means:

a. favors granted to members of a political party
b. official outcome or result
c. voting
d. sample of public opinion to acquire information

_____ 4. "The candidates' strategies are shaped by many considerations, including the constitutional provision that each state shall have *electoral* votes equal in number to its representation in Congress."

A political science or government course often provides students with their first true understanding of the United States' *electoral* process.

electoral (ĭ lĕk´ tĕr əl) means:

a. pertaining to an election
b. pertaining to the presidency
c. pertaining to Congress
d. pertaining to politics

_____ 5. "Because of the unit rule, a relatively small popular-vote *margin* can produce a lopsided electoral-vote *margin*."

Because the astronomer's instruments were not set properly, the *margin* of error in all of the measurements was large.

margin (mär´ jĭn) means:

a. border or edge
b. a lower standard of quality
c. small amount
d. measure, quantity, or degree of difference

_____ 6. "Presidential candidates act *strategically*."

By recycling and planning *strategically*, the company saved half a million dollars last year.

strategically (strə tē´ jĭk lē) means:

a. by use of specific, goal-directed methods and procedures
b. by involvement of a large group of people
c. spontaneously
d. fatefully or luckily

_____ 7. "For *incumbents* and challengers alike, some of these issues will be questions of past performance."

Because State Senator Blum and Mayor Nguyen are the *incumbents,* they are better known than their opponents.

incumbents (ĭn kûm´ bənts) means:

a. famous people
b. newcomers
c. people currently holding political office
d. candidates for political office

_____ 8. "The slogan was meant as a reminder to keep the campaign focused on the nation's *sluggish* economy, which ultimately was the issue that defeated Bush."

Business was so *sluggish* during the holiday season that many stores held clearance sales before Christmas.

sluggish (slŭg´ ĭsh) means:

a. feeling ill
b. slow or inactive
c. busy or brisk
d. unchanged

_____ 9. "The candidates' strategies are shaped by many considerations, including the constitutional *provision* that each state shall have electoral votes equal in number to its representation in Congress."

My grandfather included a *provision* in his will establishing a scholarship fund at our local university.

provision (prə vĭzh´ ən) means:

a. stipulation or condition of an agreement
b. stock of necessary supplies, such as food
c. something that is prevented
d. something that is deliberately omitted

_____ 10. "Candidates are particularly concerned with winning the most *populous* states."

California is the most *populous* state in the nation.

populous (pŏp´ yə ləs) means:

a. well-liked
b. trend-setting
c. heavily populated
d. having a high proportion of students

Respond in Writing

Directions: Refer to Selection 4-1 as necessary to answer these essay-type items.

Option for collaboration: For some of the "Respond in Writing" exercises, your instructor may prefer that you work collaboratively, that is, with other students. These exercises are identified in the margin. *If your instructor directs you to work collaboratively on any of these items,* form groups of three or four classmates to complete the exercise together. Discuss your answers with each other and have one member of the group record the answers. A member of the group may be asked to share the group's answers with the class.

Option

Exercise 1 may be completed collaboratively.

1. According to the author, there are several reasons why George Bush lost the 1992 presidential election and several reasons why Bill Clinton won. List at least three reasons for each.

   Reasons George Bush lost:

   ____

   ____

   ____

   ____

   Reasons Bill Clinton won:

   ____

   ____

   ____

   ____

Option

Exercise 2 may be completed collaboratively.

2. What are three factors that influence presidential candidates' strategies?

   Factor 1:

   ____

   ____

   Factor 2:

   ____

   ____

   Factor 3:

   ____

   ____

Option

Exercise 3 may be completed collaboratively.

3. What is the most important overall message the author wants the reader to understand about the 1992 presidential campaign? Try to answer this question in one sentence.

____

____

____

____

____

____

____

Selection 4-2

History

MUHAMMAD

FROM *THE 100: A RANKING OF THE MOST INFLUENTIAL PERSONS IN HISTORY* BY MICHAEL K. HART

Prepare Yourself to Read

Directions: Do these exercises *before you read Selection 4-2.*

1. First, read and think about the title. What do you already know about Muhammad?

   ____

   ____

2. Next, complete your preview by reading the following:

   Introduction (in *italics*)
   First paragraph (paragraph 1)
   First sentence of each paragraph
   Words in *italics*
   Last paragraph (paragraph 9

   On the basis of your preview, what information about Muhammad does this selection seem to present?

   ____

   ____

Apply Comprehension Skills

Directions: Do the Annotation Practice Exercises *as you read Selection 4-2.* Apply two skills from this chapter:

Determine the topic. When you read a paragraph, ask yourself, "What or who is this about?"

Identify the stated main idea. As you read, ask yourself, "What is the most important point the author wants me to understand about the topic?" Then search for the sentence that answers this question.

Complete the Annotation Exercises. In these exercises, you will work only with paragraphs that have stated main ideas.

MUHAMMAD

Of the billions of human beings who have populated the earth, which ones do you think have most influenced the world and the course of history? The historian Michael Hart attempts to answer this fascinating question in his book. He emphasizes that he was seeking to identify the "most influential" persons in history, not necessarily the "greatest." On his list of the top 100, the first ten are: (1) Muhammad, (2) Isaac Newton, (3) Jesus Christ, (4) Buddha, (5) Confucius, (6) St. Paul, (7) Ts'ai Lun, (8) Johann Gutenberg, (9) Christopher Columbus, (10) Albert Einstein. Perhaps you were surprised to see Muhammad listed first. In the selection below, Hart describes why he considers Muhammad to be the "most influential person in history."

1 My choice of Muhammad to lead the list of the world's most influential persons may surprise some readers and may be questioned by others, but he was the only man in history who was supremely successful on both the religious and secular levels.

2 Of humble origins, Muhammad founded and promulgated one of the world's great religions, and became an immensely effective political leader. Today, thirteen centuries after his death, his influence is still powerful and pervasive.

3 The majority of the persons in this book had the advantage of being born and raised in centers of civilization, highly cultured and politically pivotal nations. Muhammad, however, was born in the year 570, in the city of Mecca, in southern Arabia, at that time a backward area of the world, far from the centers of trade, art, and learning. Orphaned at age six, he was reared in modest surroundings. Islamic tradition tells us that he was illiterate. His economic position improved when, at the age of twenty-five, he married a wealthy widow. Neverthe-

Annotation practice exercises

Directions: For each exercise below,

- Write the topic of the paragraph on the lines beside the paragraph.
- Underline or highlight the stated main idea sentence of the paragraph.

This will help you remember the topic and the main idea.

Source: Michael Hart, *The 100: A Ranking of the Most Influential Persons in History,* Carol Publishing Group, 1978, from pp. 33–39.

less, as he approached forty, there was little outward indication that he was a remarkable person.

4 Most Arabs at that time were pagans, who believed in many gods. There were, however, in Mecca, a small number of Jews and Christians; it was from them no doubt that Muhammad first learned of a single, omnipotent God who ruled the entire universe. When he was forty years old, Muhammad became convinced that this one true God (Allah) was speaking to him, and had chosen him to spread the true faith.

Annotation exercise

- Topic of paragraph 4:

___

___

- Underline or highlight the stated main idea of paragraph 4.

5 For three years, Muhammad preached only to close friends and associates. Then, about 613, he began preaching in public. As he slowly gained converts, the Meccan authorities came to consider him a dangerous nuisance. In 622, fearing for his safety, Muhammad fled to Medina (a city some 200 miles north of Mecca), where he had been offered a position of considerable political power.

6 The flight, called the *Hegira,* was the turning point of the Prophet's life. In Mecca, he had had a few followers. In Medina, he had many more, and he soon acquired an influence that made him a virtual dictator. During the next few years, while Muhammad's following grew rapidly, a series of battles were fought between Medina and Mecca. This war ended in 630 with Muhammad's triumphant return to Mecca as conqueror. The remaining two and one-half years of his life witnessed the rapid conversion of the Arab tribes to the new religion. When Muhammad died, in 632, he was the effective ruler of all of southern Arabia.

Annotation exercise

- Topic of paragraph 6:

___

___

- Underline or highlight the stated main idea of paragraph 6.

7 How, then, is one to assess the overall impact of Muhammad on human history? Like all religions, Islam exerts an enormous influence upon the lives of its followers. It is for this reason that the founders of the world's great religions all figure prominently in this book. Since there are roughly twice as many Christians as Moslems in the world, it may initially seem strange that Muhammad has been ranked higher than Jesus. There are two principal reasons for that decision. First, Muhammad played

a far more important role in the development of Islam than Jesus did in the development of Christianity. Although Jesus was responsible for the main ethical and moral precepts of Christianity (insofar as these differed from Judaism), St. Paul was the main developer of Christian theology, its principal proselytizer, and the author of a large portion of the New Testment.

8 Muhammad, however, was responsible for both the theology of Islam and its main ethical and moral principles. In addition, he played the key role in proselytizing the new faith, and in establishing the religious practices of Islam. Moreover, he is the author of the Moslem holy scriptures, the *Koran,* a collection of certain of Muhammad's insights that he believed had been directly revealed to him by Allah. Most of these utterances were copied more or less faithfully during Muhammad's lifetime and were collected together in authoritative form not long after his death. The Koran, therefore, closely represents Muhammad's ideas and teachings and to a considerable extent his exact words. No such detailed compilation of the teachings of Christ has survived. Since the Koran is at least as important to Moslems as the Bible is to Christians, the influence of Muhammad through the medium of the Koran has been enormous. It is probable that the relative influence of Muhammad on Islam has been larger than the combined influence of Jesus Christ and St. Paul on Christianity. On the purely religious level, then, it seems likely that Muhammad has been as influential in human history as Jesus.

9 Furthermore, Muhammad (unlike Jesus) was a secular as well as a religious leader. In fact, as the driving force behind the Arab conquests, he may well rank as the most influential political leader of all time.

Annotation exercise

- Topic of paragraph 9:

  ____

  ____

- Underline or highlight the stated main idea of paragraph 9.

Comprehension Quiz

True or false

Directions: In the blank provided, indicate whether each statement is true or false.

_____ 1. The author believes that everyone will agree with his choice of Muhammad as the most influential person in history.

_____ 2. The author chose Muhammad simply because of Muhammad's success as a religious leader.

_____ 3. Muhammad was born and raised in what was then called Arabia, a highly cultured and pivotal nation.

_____ 4. According to the author, Muhammad learned about a single, all-powerful God from the small number of Christians and Jews living in Mecca.

Multiple-choice

Directions: For each item, select the best answer.

_____ 5. Muhammad began preaching that Allah was the one true God when Muhammad was

a. still in his teens.
b. 26 years old.
c. 30 years old.
d. 40 years old.

_____ 6. The *Hegira* was Muhammad's flight

a. from Arabia.
b. from Medina to Mecca.
c. from Mecca to Medina.
d. to southern Arabia.

_____ 7. Since there are roughly twice as many Christians as Moslems, why does the author rank Muhammad higher than Jesus, the founder of Christianity?

a. The author feels that Muhammad played a larger role in the development of Islam than Jesus did in the development of Christianity.
b. The author is a Moslem.
c. More books have been written about Muhammad than about Jesus.
d. Muhammad, who died at age 62, lived longer than Jesus did.

_____ 8. The Koran is

a. the Bible translated into Arabic.
b. another name for the Hegira.
c. the Moslem holy scriptures.
d. Muhammad's family name.

_____ 9. Of the statements below about Muhammad's life, which one is *not* true?

a. He was orphaned at age 6.
b. He preached to close friends for 3 years and then began preaching in public.
c. He never married.
d. He was a driving force behind Arab conquests.

_____ 10. The author maintains that Muhammad should top the list of the world's most influential persons because

a. Muhammad was responsible for the theology of Islam and its main principles.
b. In Mecca, he became a virtual dictator.
c. Muhammad was a great military leader.
d. Muhammad was an influential religious and secular leader.

Extend Your Vocabulary by Using Context Clues

Directions: ***Context clues*** are words in a sentence or paragraph that allow the reader to deduce (reason out) the meaning of an unfamiliar word. For each item in this exercise, a sentence from Selection 4-2 containing an important word *(italicized, like this)* is quoted first. Next, there is an additional sentence using the word in the same sense and providing another context clue. Use the context clues to deduce the meaning of each italicized word. *The definition you choose should make sense in both sentences.*

Pronunciation key: ă **pat** ā **pay** âr **care** ä **father** ĕ **pet** ē **be** ĭ **pit** ī **tie** îr **pier** ŏ **pot** ō **toe** ô **paw** oi **noise** ou **out** o͝o **took** o͞o **boot** ŭ **cut** yo͞o **abuse** ûr **urge** th **thin** *th* **this** hw **which** zh **vision** ə **about**

_____ 1. "Of humble origins, Muhammad founded and *promulgated* one of the world's great religions, and became an immensely effective political leader."

In the State of the Union address, the President *promulgated* the new administration's policy on gun control.

promulgated (prŏm´ əl gāt əd) means:

a. reversed or changed
b. made known or put into effect by public declaration
c. refused to reveal
d. denounced as untrue

_______ 2. "Today, thirteen centuries after his death, his influence is still powerful and *pervasive.*"

The drug problem in the United States is difficult to deal with because it is so *pervasive.*

pervasive (pər vā´ sĭv) means:

a. important
b. widespread
c. decreasing or diminishing
d. popular

_______ 3. "The majority of the persons in this book had the advantage of being born and raised in centers of civilization, highly cultured or politically *pivotal* nations."

Supreme Court Justice O'Connor's opinion was the *pivotal* one that reversed the lower court's decision.

pivotal (pĭv´ ə təl) means:

a. causing rotation
b. pertaining to religion
c. determining a direction or effect; crucial
d. going in two different directions

_______ 4. "Orphaned at age six, he was reared in *modest* surroundings."

Even after Norrises won the lottery, they continued to live in a *modest* apartment and drive inexpensive cars.

modest (mŏd´ ĭst) means:

a. plain rather than showy
b. shy or reserved
c. luxurious
d. rural; pertaining to the country

_______ 5. "*Islamic* tradition tells us that [Muhammad] was illiterate."

Mosques are *Islamic* houses of worship.

Islamic (ĭs läm´ ĭc) means:

a. pertaining to the Christian religion based on the teachings of Jesus
b. pertaining to the Buddhist religion based on the teachings of Buddha
c. pertaining to the Moslem religion based on the teachings of Muhammad
d. pertaining to the Confucian religion based on the teaching of Confucius

______ 6. "Furthermore, Muhammad (unlike Jesus) was a *secular* as well as a religious leader."

While some people view abortion as a religious issue, others view it as a purely *secular* issue.

secular (sek´ yə lər) means:

a. private
b. pertaining to worship
c. spiritual
d. not related to religion

______ 7. "There were, however, in Mecca, a small number of Jews and Christians; it was from them no doubt that Muhammad first learned of a single, *omnipotent* God who ruled the entire universe."

Hitler was a madman who thought he was *omnipotent.*

omnipotent (ŏm nĭp´ ə tənt) means:

a. having unlimited power or authority
b. having limited power or authority
c. having authority given by the citizens of a country
d. having no power or authority

______ 8. "As he slowly gained *converts,* the Meccan authorities came to consider him a dangerous nuisance."

The new political party in India rapidly gained *converts.*

converts (kŏn´ vûrts) means:

a. people who revert to previously held beliefs
b. people who adopt a new religion or belief
c. people who cling to long-held beliefs
d. people who have no religious beliefs

______ 9. "Although Jesus was responsible for the main ethical precepts of Christianity, St. Paul was the main developer of Christian *theology,* its principal proselytizer, and the author of a large portion of the New Testament."

Although he decided not to become a minister and left the seminary, he continued to read Christian *theology* throughout his life.

theology (thē ŏl´ ə jē) means:

a. system or school of opinions about God and religious questions
b. study of beliefs throughout the world
c. study of ancient religious rituals
d. study of the lives of saints

______ 10. "In addition, Muhammad played the key role in *proselytizing* the new faith, and in establishing the religious practices of Islam."

The evangelists were *proselytizing* loudly on busy downtown street corners, stopping anyone who was willing to listen to them tell them about their religious beliefs.

proselytizing (prŏs´ ə lə tī z ĭng) means:

a. speaking loudly or shouting
b. deceiving with trickery
c. declaring false or untrue
d. attempting to convert from one belief or faith to another

Repond in Writing

Directions: Refer to Selection 4-2 as necessary to answer these essay-type items.

Options for collaboration: For some of the "Respond in Writing" exercises, your instructor may prefer that you work collaboratively, that is, with other students. These exercises are identified in the margin. *If your instructor directs you to work collaboratively on any of these items,* form groups of three or four classmates to complete the exercise together. Discuss your answers with each other and have one member of the group record the answers. A member of the group may be asked to share the group's answers with the class.

Option

Exercise 1 may be completed collaboratively.

1. List three reasons the author chose Muhammad as the most influential person in history.

Reason 1:

______

______

______

Reason 2:

______

______

______

Reason 3:

______

______

______

Option

Exercise 2 may be completed collaboratively.

2. Michael Hart, the author of *The 100: A Ranking of the Most Influential Persons in History,* selected 99 other important people for his book. List 10 names *you* would include in a list of the world's most influential people, and state your reasons for including them.

Person 1: ______________________________

Reason: ______________________________

Person 2: ______________________________

Reason: ______________________________

Person 3: ______________________________

Reason: ______________________________

Person 4: ______________________________

Reason: ______________________________

Person 5: ______________________________

Reason: ______________________________

Person 6: ______________________________

Reason: ______________________________

Person 7: ______________________________

Reason: ______________________________

Person 8: ______________________________

Reason: ______________________________

Person 9: ______________________________

Reason: ______________________________

Person 10: ______________________________

Reason: ______________________________

Option

Exercise 3 may be completed collaboratively.

3. What is the most important overall message the writer wants the reader to understand about Muhammad? Try to answer this question in one sentence.

____

____

____

____

Selection 4-3

Biology

THE SCIENTIFIC METHOD: ORGANIZED COMMON SENSE

FROM *BIOLOGY! BRINGING SCIENCE TO LIFE*
BY JOHN POSTLETHWAIT, JANET HOPSON, AND RUTH VERES

Prepare Yourself to Read

Directions: Do these exercises *before you read Selection 4-3.*

1. First, read and think about the title. What do you already know about the scientific method?

   ____

   ____

2. Next, complete your preview by reading the following:

   Introduction (in *italics*)
   First paragraph (paragraph 1)
   First sentence of each paragraph
   Words in *italics* and ***boldface***
   Last paragraph (paragraph 5)

3. On the basis of your preview, how many steps are there in the scientific method?

   ____

Apply Comprehension Skills

Directions: Do the Annotation Practice Exercises *as you read Selection 4-3.* Apply two skills from this chapter:

Determine the topic. When you read a paragraph, ask yourself, "What or who is this about?"

Identify the stated main idea. As you read, ask yourself, "What is the most important point the author wants me to understand about the topic?" Then search for the sentence that answers this question.

Complete the Annotation Practice Exercises. In these exercises, you will work only with paragraphs that have stated main ideas.

THE SCIENTIFIC METHOD: ORGANIZED COMMON SENSE

Perhaps you have never taken biology or chemistry, and the "scientific method" sounds like something that only scientists would use. You will be pleased to learn, however, that although you may not know the scientific method by its proper name, you already apply this technique of "organized common sense" in many ordinary situations.

1 A biologist is rarely happy just to describe a curious event, such as the disappearance of a tadpole's tail as the young frog becomes an adult. Scientists instead want to learn what causes the event. To investigate the natural world in the most organized way, scientists use the ***scientific method.*** They:

1. Ask a *question* or identify a problem to be solved based on observations of the natural world.
2. Propose a *hypothesis,* a possible answer to the question or a potential solution to the problem.
3. Make a *prediction* of what they will observe in a specific situation if the hypothesis is correct.
4. *Test* the prediction by performing an experiment.

2 If the hypothesis predicts the results correctly, the scientist makes other predictions based on the same hypothesis and tests them. Scientific research requires logic, analytical skills, and perseverance. Only after researchers create and test several likely hypotheses and find one that consistently predicts what they see in nature will they tentatively accept a hypothesis as correct.

3 While the steps of the scientific method may sound very regimented, they are really little more than an organized commonsense approach—one you use regularly in your own

Annotation practice exercises

Directions: For each exercise below,

- Write the topic of the paragraph on the lines beside the paragraph.
- Underline or highlight the stated main idea sentence of the paragraph.

This will help you remember the topic and the main idea.

Annotation exercise

- Topic of paragraph 1:

____

____

- Underline or highlight the stated main idea of paragraph 1.

Source: John Postlethwait, Janet Hopson, and Ruth Veres, "The Scientific Method: Organized Common Sense," from *Biology! Bringing Science to Life,* McGraw-Hill, New York, 1991, pp. 16–17. Reproduced with permission of McGraw-Hill.

life. Let's say that one evening, you observe that your desk lamp stops working. You would pose a question (step 1): "What made my desk lamp go out?" And you would probably create a hypothesis (step 2): "Maybe the light bulb burned out." Next you would make a prediction (step 3): "If the bulb burned out, then when I replace it with a working bulb, the lamp should light." Finally, you would perform an experiment (step 4): You would remove a bulb from a floor lamp that works, screw it into your desk lamp, and watch the result. When you performed the test, you would include what scientists call a *control,* a check that all factors of the experiment are the same except for the one in question. Here, the control is the borrowed bulb that works in the floor lamp. If the borrowed bulb fails to work in the desk lamp, you could conclude, based on your control, that a burned-out bulb is not the problem. You would next discard the faulty-bulb hypothesis and ask new questions: "Is the lamp itself broken? Is something wrong with the wiring to the wall socket?" You could then make new hypotheses, new predictions, and perform new tests until you discovered why your lamp went out.

Annotation exercise

- Topic of paragraph 3:

____

____

- Underline or highlight the stated main idea of paragraph 3.

4 While an orderly approach to exploring nature, the scientific method is by no means rigid, rote, or unimaginative in practice. Once a scientist has observed a curious phenomenon, it takes creativity to dream up a clear, testable hypothesis. It also takes logic, talent, experience, imagination, and intuition to follow through with cleverly designed experiments and alternative hypotheses. Finally, it takes an ability to communicate clearly through writing and speaking to share results with others.

Annotation exercise

- Topic of paragraph 4:

____

____

- Underline or highlight the stated main idea of paragraph 4.

5 No tool is more powerful for understanding the natural world than the scientific method, although it does not apply, however, to matters of religion, politics, culture, ethics, or art. These valuable ways of approaching the world and its problems proceed along different lines of inquiry and experience. Nevertheless, many of the world's current problems have underlying biological bases, and thus they mainly demand biological solutions.

Comprehension Quiz

True or false

Directions: In the blank provided, indicate whether each statement is true or false.

_____ 1. Biologists are content merely to describe curious events in the natural world.

_____ 2. Scientists accept a hypothesis as correct if the hypothesis consistently predicts what scientists see in nature.

_____ 3. The scientific method differs completely from the organized commonsense approach that a person may use regularly in his or her own life.

_____ 4. The scientific method is a valuable way of understanding matters such as religion, politics, culture, and ethics.

_____ 5. A control is a check that all factors in an experiment are the same except for the one in question.

Multiple-choice

Directions: For each item, select the best answer.

_____ 6. The scientific method is based on all of the following steps except:

a. identifying a problem.
b. proposing a hypothesis.
c. making a prediction.
d. publishing the results.

_____ 7. Once a hypothesis predicts results correctly, the scientist

a. is free to identify new problems in the natural world.
b. makes other predictions related to other problems.
c. makes other predictions based on the same hypothesis.
d. publishes the results.

_____ 8. Which of the words below correctly describes the scientific method?

a. unimaginative
b. logical
c. rigid
d. rote

_____ 9. A scientist should possess which of the following attributes?

a. creativity and talent
b. experience and imagination
c. intuition
d. all of the above

_____ 10. The scientific method is also important because

a. not much is known about the natural world.
b. many of the world's current problems have underlying biological causes.
c. it can be applied to art.
d. it teaches scientists to be logical and to communicate clearly.

Extend Your Vocabulary by Using Context Clues

Directions: ***Context clues*** are words in a sentence or paragraph that allow the reader to deduce (reason out) the meaning of an unfamiliar word. For each item in this exercise, a sentence from Selection 4-3 containing an important word *(italicized, like this)* is quoted first. Next, there is an additional sentence using the word in the same sense and providing another context clue. Use the context clues to deduce the meaning of each italicized word. *The definition you choose should make sense in both sentences.*

Pronunciation key: ă **pat** ā **pay** âr **care** ä **father** ĕ **pet** ē **be** ĭ **pit**
ī **tie** îr **pier** ŏ **pot** ō **toe** ô **paw** oi **noise** ou **out** o͝o **took** o͞o **boot**
ŭ **cut** yo͞o **abuse** ûr **urge** th **thin** *th* **this** hw **which** zh **vision** ə **about**

_____ 1. "A biologist is rarely happy just to describe a *curious* event, such as the disappearance of a tadpole's tail as the young frog becomes an adult."

The young man had a *curious* appearance: he wore an enormous top hat, striped pants, gloves, and bowling shoes.

curious (kyo͝or′ e əs) means:

a. unimportant
b. interesting
c. shocking
d. unusual

_____ 2. "They *propose* a hypothesis, a possible answer to the question or a potential solution to the problem."

The two senators want to *propose* a new law that would help protect children from drug dealers.

propose (prə pōz′) means:

a. review
b. suggest
c. oppose
d. offer marriage to someone

_____ 3. "They propose a *hypothesis,* a possible answer to the question or a potential solution to the problem."

The scientists did not have a way to test their *hypothesis* about why dinosaurs disappeared millions of years ago.

hypothesis (hī pŏth´ ĭ sĭs) means:

a. possible answer to a question; potential solution to a problem
b. conclusion about a scientific theory
c. story told throughout the ages
d. event that cannot be explained

_____ 4. "They make a *prediction* of what they will observe in a specific situation if the hypothesis is correct."

We thought the meteorologist's *prediction* of rain was right, so we canceled our plans for a picnic.

prediction (prĭ dĭk´ shən) means:

a. falsehood; lie
b. description of something before it happens
c. description of something that has already happened
d. explanation of why something has happened

_____ 5. "While these steps may sound very *regimented,* they are really little more than an organized commonsense approach—one you use regularly in your own life."

The elementary school principal likes everything *regimented,* so he makes the children walk down the halls in straight lines.

regimented (rĕj´ ə mĕn təd) means:

a. put into strict order
b. simple to do
c. unclear
d. ordinary

_____ 6. "If the borrowed bulb fails to work in the desk lamp, you could *conclude,* based on your control, that a burned-out bulb is not the problem."

Because the man could prove that he was in another city when the robbery occurred, the jury was able to *conclude* that he had not robbed the bank.

conclude (kən klo͞od´) means:

a. be unsure
b. hope
c. be unaware
d. determine

______ 7. "You would next *discard* the faulty-bulb hypothesis and ask new questions: 'Is the lamp itself broken? Is something wrong with the wiring to the wall socket?'"

Rather than *discard* clothes she no longer wears, Lynn donates them to charity.

discard (dĭs kärd´) means:

a. reconsider
b. save
c. throw out
d. be amused by

______ 8. "While an orderly approach to exploring nature, the scientific method is by no means rigid, *rote,* or unimaginative in practice."

Many children dislike the *rote* process of memorizing multiplication tables.

rote (rōt) means:

a. done with great speed
b. creative
c. entertaining
d. done by repetition

______ 9. "It also takes logic, talent, experience, imagination, and *intuition* to follow through with cleverly designed experiments and alternative hypotheses."

Since the detective did not have many clues, she solved the case by using *intuition.*

intuition (ĭn to͞o ĭsh´ ən) means:

a. knowing by instinct rather than by reasoning
b. careful reasoning
c. wild guess
d. strong emotion

______ 10. "These valuable ways of approaching the world and its problems proceed along different lines of *inquiry* and experience."

There will be a formal *inquiry* into the cause of those airplane crashes last winter.

inquiry (ĭn kwīr´ ē) means:

a. explanation
b. investigation
c. request
d. report

Respond in Writing

Directions: Refer to Selection 4-3 as necessary to answer these essay-type items.

Option for collaboration: For some of the "Respond in Writing" exercises, your instructor may prefer that you work collaboratively, that is, with other students. These exercises are identified in the margin. *If your instructor directs you to work collaboratively on any of these items,* form groups of three or four classmates to complete the exercise together. Discuss your answers with each other and have one member of the group record the answers. A member of the group may be asked to share the group's answers with the class.

Option

Exercise 1 may be completed collaboratively.

1. One measure of how well a person understands something is his or her ability to explain the concept to someone else. Suppose that, as an out-of-class project in a biology course, you have been asked to explain the scientific method to a seventh-grade science class. You are preparing notes for your presentation so that you can explain the four steps of the scientific method *in very simple language.* You will probably need to use several short sentences to describe each step. Use the space below to write your simplified explanation of the scientific method.

SIMPLIFIED EXPLANATION OF THE SCIENTIFIC METHOD

Step 1: Question ______________________________

____

____

____

Step 2: Hypothesis ______________________________

____

____

____

Step 3: Prediction ______________________________

____

____

____

Step 4: Test ______________________________

____

____

____

Option

Exercise 2 may be completed collaboratively.

2. Apply the four steps of the scientific method to this problem: You insert a cassette into your tape player and press the "play" button, but nothing happens. Solve this problem scientifically by posing a question (step 1), creating a hypothesis (step 2), making a prediction (step 3), and testing the hypothesis by performing an experiment (step 4) *Write down what you hope to learn by performing each step.*

APPLYING THE SCIENTIFIC METHOD

Step 1: Pose a question.

____

____

____

____

____

Step 2: Create a hypothesis.

____

____

____

____

____

Step 3: Make a prediction.

____

____

____

____

____

Step 4: Test the hypothesis.

____

____

____

____

____

Option

Exercise 3 may be completed collaboratively.

3. What is the most important overall message these writers want the reader to understand about the scientific method? Try to answer this question in one sentence.

____

____

____

____

____

____

____

____

CHAPTER 5

FORMULATING IMPLIED MAIN IDEAS

IN THIS CHAPTER YOU WILL LEARN THE ANSWERS TO THESE QUESTIONS:

What is an implied main idea of a paragraph?

Why is the implied main idea important?

How can I formulate implied main idea sentences?

How can I know when a formulated main idea sentence is correct?

CHAPTER 5 CONTENTS

If you want to climb mountains, do not practice on molehills.

IMPLIED MAIN IDEAS IN PARAGRAPHS

What Is an Implied Main Idea?

Key term

Implied main idea: Main point that is not stated directly as one sentence and therefore must be inferred and formulated by the reader.

Every paragraph has a main idea, of course, but not every paragraph includes a *stated* main idea sentence. When an author suggests the most important point without stating it directly, the main idea is *implied.* That is, a paragraph has an ***implied main idea*** when the author gives you the information needed to understand the main point but does not state that point directly as a single sentence. When an author implies the main idea, *you,* the reader, must use information in the paragraph to infer (reason out) the main idea and formulate (create) a sentence that expresses it.

Sometimes you must infer that information from two or more sentences in the paragraph has to be *combined* to formulate one complete main idea sentence. At other times, you will have to formulate a *general* sentence that expresses the most important (but unstated) point the author is trying to illustrate or prove. When you grasp the main idea in these ways, you are *inferring* it.

In other words, if a paragraph presents facts, descriptions, explanations, or examples that only *suggest* the main point the author wants you to understand, it is up to you to formulate the main idea.

Why Is the Implied Main Idea Important?

Your comprehension will be limited unless you understand both stated main ideas and implied main ideas. In addition to increasing your comprehension, you will remember material better if you take these steps to formulate main ideas whenever they are implied. College instructors assume that students will read carefully enough to understand paragraphs with implied main ideas. Often, they base test items on implied main ideas as well as on more obvious stated main ideas.

To be an effective reader, then, you must be able to identify stated main ideas and be able to formulate main idea sentences for any paragraphs in which the main idea is implied.

FORMULATING AN IMPLIED MAIN IDEA

Three Steps to Follow

Of course, you will not know until you read a paragraph whether its main idea is stated or implied. When you cannot locate a stated main idea sentence, formulate the implied main idea by following these steps:

1. First, after you have read the paragraph, *determine the topic* by asking yourself, "Who or what is this passage about?"
2. Next, *determine the main idea* by asking yourself, "What is the most important idea the author wants me to *infer* about this topic?"
3. Then, use information in the paragraph to *formulate a main idea sentence* that answers the question in step 2. The sentence you formulate will be the main idea.

How to Use Information in a Paragraph to Formulate the Main Idea

Even when authors do not directly state a main idea as one sentence, they still provide you with information you need to infer and formulate the main idea. Authors may provide such information in three ways, and those three ways are the basis for "formulas" for creating main idea sentences.

Formula 1: Add an essential word or phrase to a sentence already in the paragraph

Sometimes, an author may express *most* of the main idea in one sentence of the paragraph, yet that sentence lacks some essential piece of information—a piece of information that you must insert to make the sentence a *complete* main idea sentence. To put it another way, a paragraph may contain a sentence that *almost* states the author's main idea, but you must add certain information to that sentence to make it express the main idea completely. For instance, a sentence may need to have the topic inserted to make it express the main idea fully.

When a sentence in the paragraph almost states the main idea but lacks essential information, use ***formula 1*** to create a main idea sentence:

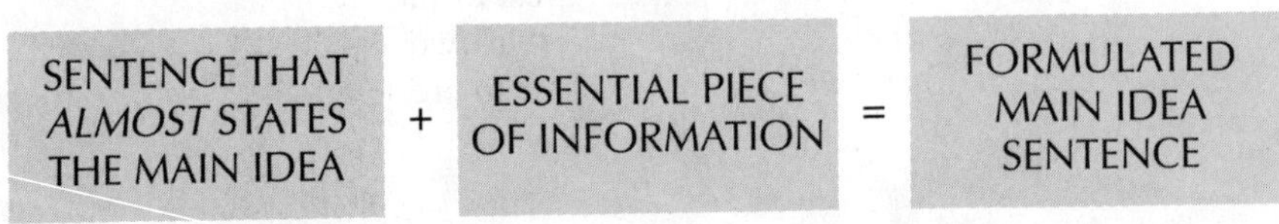

Here is an example of formulating an implied main idea using formula 1. The following paragraph is from a sociology textbook. The topic of this passage is *ethnocentrism.* The last sentence almost states the authors' most important point—the definition of ethnocentrism—but it lacks the word *ethnocentrism.* A complete main idea sentence can be formulated by adding the topic, *ethnocentrism,* to the last sentence of the paragraph. This formulated main idea sentence will express the most important point the authors want you to understand about ethnocentrism, its definition.

Each person is born into a particular society that has its own particular culture. At an early age, children begin to learn many aspects of this culture, such as language, standards of behavior, and beliefs. They also begin to learn many of the group's values concerning judgments of good and bad, proper and improper, and right and wrong. This learning continues into and throughout adulthood as people internalize, accept, and identify with their group's way of living. This feeling is called ***ethnocentrism.*** It is the basic inclination to judge other cultures in terms of the values and norms of one's own culture.

Formulated main idea sentence

____

____

____

____

____

____

____

____

Source: Daniel Hebding and Leonard Glick, *Introduction to Sociology,* McGraw-Hill, New York, 1992, p. 62.

Annotate

Go back to the excerpt. Write a formulated main idea sentence by adding essential information to the sentence which almost states the main idea.

The last sentence becomes a complete main idea sentence when the essential word *ethnocentrism* is added. *Ethnocentrism is the basic inclination to judge other cultures in terms of the values and norms of one's own culture.*

Formula 2: Combine two sentences from the paragraph into a single sentence

Sometimes a paragraph contains two sentences that each give *part* of the complete main idea. Both sentences contain important information, yet neither sentence by itself expresses the complete main idea. Therefore, since the author has not stated the main idea in a single sentence, *you* must combine these two sentences to formulate one sentence that expresses the complete main idea. The two sentences may follow one another, or they may be separated. (For example, the first sentence of the paragraph may present part of the main idea, and the last sentence may give the rest of the main idea.)

When you realize that two sentences in a paragraph each state part of the main idea, use ***formula 2*** to create a main idea that is a single sentence:

SENTENCE THAT EXPRESSES *PART* OF THE MAIN IDEA	+	SENTENCE THAT EXPRESSES *REST* OF THE MAIN IDEA	=	FORMULATED MAIN IDEA SENTENCE

Here is an example of formula 2. The paragraph below is from a textbook on sociology. Its topic is *tastes.* A main idea sentence for this paragraph can be formulated by combining its last two sentences into a single sentence. This formulated main idea sentence will express the most important point the authors want you to understand about tastes.

Tastes—we all have them. You prefer certain styles of art, certain kinds of food and clothing, certain types of music, certain ways of decorating your room. The list could go on and on. *De gustibus non est disputandum,* the old saying goes—there is no accounting for taste. Tastes just seem to spring from somewhere inside us, rather mysteriously. We can't really say why we prefer rock to Mozart, burgers to pâté, jeans to neatly pressed slacks. Tastes are simply part of us, our individual selves. But tastes are also part of culture, which is a broader social phenomenon.

Formulated main idea sentence

____

____

____

____

____

____

____

____

Source: Craig Calhoun, Donald Light, and Susanne Keller, *Sociology,* 6th ed., McGraw-Hill, New York, 1994, p. 68.

Annotate

Go back to the excerpt. Write a formulated main idea sentence by combining the two sentences in the paragraph that state part of the main idea.

The two most important sentences are the last two: "Tastes are simply part of us, our individual selves" and "But tastes are also part of culture, which is a broader social phenomenon." Neither sentence by itself expresses the complete main idea. The first sentence addresses taste on a personal level; the other sentence addresses it as part of culture. You must combine the sentences to formulate a complete main idea sentence: *Tastes are simply part of us, our individual selves, but tastes are also part of culture, which is a broader social phenomenon.* (Of course, it would be equally correct to express this same main idea in other ways, such as, *Although tastes are simply part of us, our individual selves, tastes are also part of culture, which is a broader social phenomenon.*)

Formula 3: Summarize ideas from several sentences into one general sentence

Sometimes, a paragraph consists only of details. When this is the case, you must formulate a main idea sentence by inferring the *general* point the author is illustrating or proving with the details, and then express this idea as a single sentence. This is not a matter of combining the details into one long sentence, but rather of writing a sentence that *sums up* the details the author presents. In other words, you have to create a general sentence that *summarizes* the details. When you write this formulated main idea sentence, you will usually have to use some (or even several) of your own words.

When several sentences in a paragraph contain important information, ***formula 3*** can be used to infer and express the main idea as a single sentence:

READER'S GENERAL INFERENCE *BASED ON* THE DETAILS	=	FORMULATED MAIN IDEA SENTENCE

Here is an example of formulating an implied main idea using formula 3. The following excerpt is from a special section in an algebra textbook that introduces interesting information to be used in solving verbal problems. The topic of this paragraph is *pesticides.* The paragraph has an implied main idea that can be formulated from information given throughout the paragraph. As you read the paragraph, try to reason out (infer) the most important general point the authors are making about pesticides.

Pesticides kill plants and animals other than the pests they are intended for. Pesticides pollute water systems. Some pests develop immunity to frequently used pesticides. Some pesticides such as DDT and its relatives can remain in the environment for many years beyond the time necessary to do their intended job. Some pesticides have been linked to cancer and other health problems in humans.

Formulated main idea sentence

____

____

____

____

____

____

Source: James Streeter, Donald Hutchison, and Louis Hoelzle, *Beginning Algebra,* 3d ed., McGraw-Hill, New York, 1993, p. 370.

Annotate

Go back to the excerpt. Formulate a general main idea sentence that summarizes the important information from several sentences into a single sentence.

In this paragraph, you must write a general statement about the important information in *several* sentences to formulate a main idea sentence. You need to examine the information, think about it, and ask yourself, "What is the most important general point the authors want me to understand about pesticides?" To answer that question, you will need to use some of your own words.

Although the phrase *dangerous effects* does not appear in it, this paragraph is obviously describing dangerous effects of pesticides. It is up to the reader to infer (reason out or deduce) the main idea and use a general phrase such as *dangerous effects.* An example of a correctly formulated main idea sentence for the paragraph would be: *Pesticides have dangerous effects on the environment, plants, animals, and human beings.* This formulated main idea sentence expresses the general point the authors want you to understand about pesticides.

The example given above for the formulated main idea sentence is *not* the only possible "correct" formulation. Another possible formulated main idea sentence would be: *Pesticides have several dangerous effects.* Still another possibility is: *Certain effects of pesticides are dangerous.* There are other possibilities as well. What is important is not the exact wording but that the sentence express the authors' main point.

Requirements for Correctly Formulated Main Idea Sentences

When you formulate an implied main idea sentence (in other words, when you use one of the formulas above), there is a way to check to be sure that your formulated main idea sentence is correct. A *correctly* formulated implied main idea sentence is one that meets these four requirements.

1. A formulated main idea must be a complete sentence that includes the *topic* of the paragraph.
2. A formulated main idea sentence must express the author's most important *general* point about the topic. (In other words, if the formulated main idea sentence were placed at the beginning of the paragraph, the other sentences would explain, prove, or tell more about it).
3. A formulated main idea sentence must not contain any of the supporting details.
4. A formulated main idea sentence must make complete sense by itself (without anyone's having to read the rest of the paragraph). For example, the following sentence would not be meaningful by itself, since the reader would not know who "him" refers to: *Most historians consistently rank him among the five greatest presidents of the United States.* Therefore, this sentence could not be a correct main idea. On the other hand, this next sentence could be a main idea sentence, since it makes sense by itself: *Most historians consistently rank Abraham Lincoln among the five greatest presidents of the United States.*

If your formulated main idea sentence meets these four requirements, it will be correct. Remember that an implied main idea sentence can be worded in various ways, all of which would be correct as long as they meet the four requirements.

A Word about the Implied Overall Main Idea in a Longer Passage

Of course, the ability to formulate implied main ideas is a skill that can be applied not only to paragraphs but also to longer passages, such as a section of a textbook chapter, a short reading selection, or an essay. In fact, you will often want to formulate the main idea of an entire passage in order to express its most important point or its overall message. Throughout this book, the reading selections at the end of each chapter include exercises that will give you practice in formulating main idea sentences expressing the main point of the entire selection.

STANDARDIZED READING TESTS: IMPLIED MAIN IDEAS

College students may be required to take standardized reading tests as part of an overall assessment program, in a reading course, or as part of a state-mandated "basic skills" test. A standardized reading test typically consists of a series of passages followed by multiple-choice questions, to be completed within a specified time limit. Here are some tips about formulating implied main ideas that should help you score as high as possible on standardized tests.

Remember that test items about main ideas may be worded in several different ways. Possible wordings include these:

> The author's main point is that . . .
>
> The principal idea of this passage is that . . .
>
> Which of the following best expresses the main idea of the entire passage?
>
> Which of the following best expresses the main idea of this paragraph (or a specifically identified paragraph)?

To answer test items like these, first determine the subject matter of the passage: the topic. Then ask yourself, "What is the most important idea the author wants me to understand about the topic?" If you cannot find a single sentence in the passage that answers this question, write your own formulation of the main idea on scratch paper or in the margin next to the passage. Next, examine the choices offered as answers, comparing each choice with your own formulation. Look for a choice that is similar *in meaning* to your own answer, but remember that the wording may be different. If none of the choices is at least partially similar to your formulation, you may need to reread the passage and make another attempt at formulating the main idea.

DEVELOPING CHAPTER REVIEW CARDS

Review cards, or *summary cards,* are an excellent study tool. They are a way to select, organize, and review the most important information in a textbook chapter. The process of creating review cards helps you organize information in a meaningful way and, at the same time, transfer it into long-term memory. The cards can also be used to prepare for tests (see Part Three). The review card activities in this book give you structured practice in creating these valuable study tools. Once you have learned how to make review cards, you can create them for textbook material in your other courses.

Now, complete the five review cards for Chapter 5 by answering the questions or following the directions on each card. When you have completed them, you will have summarized important information about implied main ideas: (1) what they are, (2) why they are important, (3) what steps and methods to follow in formulating them, (4) how to check to see if your formulations are correct, and (5) how to formulate them in longer passages.

Implied Main Ideas

1. What is an implied main idea? (See page 217.)

____

____

____

____

____

2. Why is the implied main idea important? (See page 217.)

____

____

____

____

____

Chapter 5: Formulating Implied Main Ideas

Steps to Follow in Formulating an Implied Main Idea Sentence

What are three general steps to follow in formulating an implied main idea sentence? (See page 218.)

Step 1: ____

____

____

Step 2: ____

____

____

Step 3: ____

____

____

Chapter 5: Formulating Implied Main Ideas

Formulas for Creating Implied Main Idea Sentences

What are three formulas for creating implied main idea sentences? (See pages 218–221.)

Formula 1:

Formula 2:

Formula 3:

Chapter 5: Formulating Implied Main Ideas

Requirements for Correctly Formulated Main Idea Sentences

What are four requirements for a correctly formulated main idea sentence? (See page 222.)

Requirement 1: ____________________

____

Requirement 2: ____________________

____

Requirement 3: ____________________

____

Requirement 4: ____________________

____

Chapter 5: Formulating Implied Main Ideas

Implied Main Ideas in Longer Passages

1. The skill of formulating implied main ideas can be applied to longer reading assignments, such as (see page 222): ____________________

   ____

   ____

2. A purpose of formulating the main idea of an entire passage is to do the following (see page 222):

   ____

   ____

Chapter 5: Formulating Implied Main Ideas

Selection 5-1

Sociology

THE CHANGING ROLES OF MEN AND WOMEN

BY MERRILL McLOUGHLIN WITH TRACY L. SHRYER, ERICA E. GOODE, AND KATHLEEN McALIFFE

Prepare Yourself to Read

Directions: Do these exercises *before you read Selection 5-1.*

1. First, read and think about the title. What do you already know about the roles of men and women?

   ___

   ___

2. Next, complete your preview by reading the following:

   Introduction (in *italics*)
   First paragraph (paragraph 1)
   Headings
   First sentence of each paragraph
   Words in **bold print** and *italics*
   Last paragraph (paragraph 7)

   On the basis of your preview, how do the roles of men and women seem to be changing?

   ___

   ___

Apply Comprehension Skills

Directions: Do the Annotation Practice Exercises *as you read Selection 5-1.* Apply the skills from this chapter:

Formulate implied main ideas. Follow these general steps: first determine the topic; then ask what the author's most important point about the topic is; then create a sentence that expresses the author's most important point. Use the appropriate formula to "formulate" an implied main idea sentence based on information in the paragraph.

Check your formulated main idea sentences. Be sure each of your main idea sentences meets the requirements on page 222.

In these exercises, you will work only with paragraphs that have implied main ideas.

THE CHANGING ROLES OF MEN AND WOMEN

Undoubtedly you have heard people refer to the "gender gap." What are the truly significant differences between men and women? Read the conclusions of sociologists and compare them with your opinions.

In politics and management, the "gender gap" is real

1 There is one difference between the sexes on which virtually every expert and study agree: Men are more aggressive than women. It shows up in 2-year-olds. It continues through school days and persists into adulthood. It is even constant across cultures. And there is little doubt that it is rooted in biology—in the male sex hormone testosterone.

2 If there's a feminine trait that's the counterpart of male aggressiveness, it's what social scientists awkwardly refer to as "nurturance." Feminists have argued that the nurturing nature of women is not biological in origin, but rather has been drummed into women by a society that wanted to keep them in the home. But the signs that it is at least partly inborn are too numerous to ignore. Just as tiny infant girls respond more readily to human faces, female toddlers learn much faster than males how to pick up nonverbal cues from others. And grown women are far more adept than men at interpreting facial expressions: A recent study by University of Pennsylvania brain researcher Ruben Gur showed that they easily read emotions such as anger, sadness, and fear. The only such emotion men could pick up was disgust.

3 What difference do such differences make in the real world? Among other things, women appear to be somewhat less competitive—or at least competitive in different ways—than men.

Annotation practice exercises

Directions: For each exercise below,

- Write the topic of the paragraph on the lines provided.
- Formulate the implied main idea of the paragraph and write it on the lines provided.

This will help you remember the topic and the main idea.

Annotation exercise

- Topic of paragraph 1:

____

____

- Formulate the implied main idea of paragraph 1:

____

____

____

____

____

Source: Merrill McLoughlin with Tracy Shryer, Erica Goode, and Kathleen McAliffe, "Men versus Women," in Daniel Hebding and Leonard Glick, *Introduction to Sociology,* McGraw-Hill, New York, 1992, from pp. 111–112. Abridged from an excerpt from *U.S. News and World Report,* August 8, 1988, pp. 50–56, from *Men versus Women.*

At the Harvard Law School, for instance, female students enter with credentials just as outstanding as those of their male peers. But they don't qualify for the prestigious *Law Review* in proportionate numbers, a fact some school officials attribute to women's discomfort in the incredibly competitive atmosphere.

4 Students of management styles have found fewer differences than they expected between men and women who reach leadership positions, perhaps because many successful women deliberately imitate masculine ways. But an analysis by Purdue social psychologist Alice Eagly of 166 studies of leadership style did find one consistent difference: Men tend to be more "autocratic"—making decisions on their own—while women tend to consult colleagues and subordinates more often.

5 Studies of behavior in small groups turn up even more differences. Men will typically dominate the discussion, says University of Toronto psychologist Kenneth Dion, spending more time talking and less time listening.

Annotation exercise

- Topic of paragraph 4:

____

____

- Formulate the implied main idea of paragraph 4:

____

____

____

____

____

Political fallout

6 The aggression-nurturance gulf even shows up in politics. The "gender gap" in polling is real and enduring: Men are far more prone to support a strong defense and tough law-and-order measures such as capital punishment, for instance, while women are more likely to approve of higher spending to solve domestic social problems such as poverty and inequality. Interestingly, there is virtually no gender gap on "women's issues," such as abortion and day care; in fact, men support them slightly *more* than women. . . .

7 Applied to the female of the species, the word "different" has, for centuries, been read to mean "inferior." At last, that is beginning to change. And in the end, of course, it's not a question of better or worse. The obvious point—long lost in a miasma of ideology—is that each sex brings strengths and weaknesses that may check and balance the other; each is half of the human whole.

Annotation exercise

- Topic of paragraph 7:

____

____

- Formulate the implied main idea of paragraph 7:

____

____

____

____

____

Comprehension Quiz

True or false

Directions: In the blank provided, indicate whether each statement is true or false.

_______ 1. The one difference between the sexes that experts seem to agree on is that men are more aggressive than women.

_______ 2. Feminists argue that "nurturance" (the nurturing nature of women) has been drummed into women by a society that wants to keep them at home.

_______ 3. According to recent studies, women are far more adept than men at interpreting facial expressions.

_______ 4. Women appear to be less competitive than men, or at least competitive in a different way from men.

_______ 5. Researchers who study management styles have found more differences than they expected between men and women who reached leadership positions.

Multiple-choice

Directions: For each item, select the best answer.

_______ 6. After analyzing 166 studies of leadership style, Alice Eagly found that

a. men tended to make more decisions on their own.
b. women tended to consult colleagues and subordinates less often.
c. men and women were similar.
d. there were no differences between men and women.

_______ 7. Polls on political issues report that

a. men are less prone to support strong defense and tough law-and-order measures.
b. women are less likely to approve of higher spending to solve domestic social problems.
c. there is a definite "gender gap" on "women's issues."
d. none of the above.

_______ 8. Applied to the female of the species, the word *different* has, for centuries, been interpreted to mean

a. physically different.
b. inferior.
c. more nurturing.
d. all of the above.

______ 9. Studies of men and women in small groups have found that

a. men typically dominate the discussion and spend less time listening.
b. women typically dominate the discussion and spend less time listening.
c. there are no differences between men and women.
d. there is no consistent pattern.

______ 10. The authors of this selection conclude that

a. differences between the sexes will continue to create difficulties for the societies of the world.
b. each sex brings strengths and weaknesses that may check and balance the other, since each is half of the human whole.
c. no further research is needed.
d. there is essentially no difference between the sexes.

Extend Your Vocabulary by Using Context Clues

Directions: ***Context clues*** are words in a sentence or paragraph that allow the reader to deduce (reason out) the meaning of an unfamiliar word. For each item in this exercise, a sentence from Selection 5-1 containing an important word *(italicized, like this)* is quoted first. Next, there is an additional sentence using the word in the same sense and providing another context clue. Use the context clues to deduce the meaning of each italicized word. *The definition you choose should make sense in both sentences.*

Pronunciation key: ă **pat** ā **pay** âr **care** ä **father** ĕ **pet** ē **be** ĭ **pit**
ī **tie** îr **pier** ŏ **pot** ō **toe** ô **paw** oi **noise** ou **out** o͝o **took** o͞o **boot**
ŭ **cut** yo͞o **abuse** ûr **urge** th **thin** *th* **this** hw **which** zh **vision** ə **about**

______ 1. "In politics and management, the '*gender* gap' is real."

By using certain medical tests, it is possible to determine the *gender* of a baby before it is born.

gender (jĕn´ dər) means:

a. pertaining to business
b. pertaining to classification by sex
c. pertaining to males
d. pertaining to females

_____ 2. "Feminists have argued that the *nurturing* nature of women is not biological in origin, but rather has been drummed into women by a society that wanted to keep them at home."

A *nurturing* teacher can often help timid children overcome their shyness.

nurturing (nûr´ chər ing) means:

a. constantly busy
b. quiet
c. new; inexperienced
d. supportive; fostering growth

_____ 3. "Just as tiny infant girls respond more *readily* to human faces, female toddlers learn much faster than males how to pick up nonverbal cues from others."

When confronted with the stolen articles, the shoplifter *readily* admitted her guilt.

readily (rĕd´ l ē) means:

a. promptly
b. happily
c. reluctantly
d. coldly

_____ 4. "At the Harvard Law School, for instance, female students enter with *credentials* just as outstanding as those of their male peers."

He tried to get a job as a realtor, but he lacked experience and the necessary *credentials.*

credentials (krĭ dĕn´ shəlz) means:

a. qualifications
b. applications
c. certificates
d. goals and objectives

_____ 5. "But women don't qualify for the *prestigious* Law Review in proportionate numbers."

The late Supreme Court Justice Thurgood Marshall received many *prestigious* awards for his lifetime of outstanding service.

prestigious (prĕ stĭj´ əs) means:

a. little known
b. highly esteemed; valued
c. competitive
d. existing for many years

_____ 6. "Men tend to be more '*autocratic*'—making decisions on their own—while women tend to consult colleagues and subordinates more often."

The citizens hated many of the policies of their country's *autocratic* dictator.

autocratic (ô tō kră´ tĭc) means:

a. irrational
b. unfair
c. friendly
d. making decisions without consulting others

_____ 7. "Men tend to be more 'autocratic'—making decisions on their own—while women tend to consult colleagues and *subordinates* more often."

The district manager gave her *subordinates* a bonus because they achieved a new sales record last month.

subordinates (sə bôr´ də nĭts) means:

a. people of lower rank or under the authority of another
b. people of equal rank; peers
c. supervisors
d. people whose rank is not known or cannot be determined

_____ 8. "The aggression-nurturance *gulf* even shows up in politics."

After their terrible argument, there was a great *gulf* between the father and his son.

gulf (gŭlf) means:

a. wide gap; separating distance
b. large body of water that is partially enclosed by land
c. ill-will or hostility
d. confusion

_____ 9. "Men are far more *prone* to support a strong defense and tough law-and-order measures such as capital punishment."

Lee is an impulsive person who is *prone* to act without thinking first.

prone (prōn) means:

a. lying face down
b. opposed to
c. unwilling
d. having a tendency; likely

_____ 10. "Women are more likely to approve higher spending to solve *domestic* social problems such as poverty and inequality."

Rather than focusing on international affairs, the president concentrated on *domestic* issues such as welfare, the national economy, and education.

domestic (də mĕs´ tĭk) means:

a. pertaining to business
b. pertaining to women
c. pertaining to a country's national or internal affairs
d. pertaining to pets and farm animals

Respond in Writing

Directions: Refer to Selection 5-1 as necessary to answer these essay-type items.

Option for collaboration: For some of the "Respond in Writing" exercises, your instructor may prefer that you work collaboratively, that is, with other students. These exercises are identified in the margin. *If your instructor directs you to work collaboratively on any of these items,* form groups of three or four classmates to complete the exercise together. Discuss your answers with each other and have one member of the group record the answers. A member of the group may be asked to share the group's answers with the class.

Option

Exercise 1 may be completed collaboratively.

1. Complete the chart below, which compares and contrasts the six characteristics the authors present for women and those they present for men.

Men	*Women*
1. _______________	Nurturing
2. Competitive	_______________
3. _______________ _______________ _______________	Likely to consult subordinates and colleagues in decision-making
4. Likely to dominate small-group discussions	_______________ _______________
5. _______________ _______________	In favor of higher government spending on domestic problems
6. Tending to support women's issues	_______________ _______________

Option

Exercise 2 may be completed collaboratively.

2. What is the most important overall message these writers want the reader to understand about the roles of men and women? Try to answer this question in one sentence.

____

____

____

____

____

____

Selection 5-2

Magazine article

LAUGH YOUR STRESS AWAY

BY STEPHEN LALLY

Prepare Yourself to Read

Directions: Do these exercises *before you read Selection 5-2.*

1. First, read and think about the title. What do you already know about stress?

   ____

   ____

2. Next, complete your preview by reading the following:

   Introduction (in *italics*)
   First paragraph (paragraph 1)
   Headings
   First sentence of each paragraph

   On the basis of your preview, what advice is the author going to give about handling stress?

   ____

   ____

Apply Comprehension Skills

Directions: Do the Annotation Practice Exercises *as you read Selection 5-2.* Apply the skills from this chapter:

Formulate implied main ideas. Follow these general steps: first determine the topic; then ask what the author's most important point about the topic is; then create a sentence that expresses the author's most important point. Use the appropriate formula to "formulate" an implied main idea sentence based on information in the paragraph.

Check your formulated main idea sentences. Be sure each of your main idea sentences meets the requirements on page 222.

In these exercises, you will work only with paragraphs that have implied main ideas.

LAUGH YOUR STRESS AWAY

Feeling a little stressed? Tense? Edgy? If fast relief is what you're after, laughter really is the best medicine.

1 Humor is one of the best on-the-spot stress busters around. It's virtually impossible to belly laugh and feel bad at the same time. If you're caught in a situation you can't escape or change (a traffic jam, for example), then humor may be the healthiest form of temporary stress release possible.

2 Even when you *can* change the situation, humor helps. Research by Alice M. Isen, Ph.D., a psychologist at Cornell University, in Ithaca, New York, shows that people who had just watched a short comedy film were better able to find creative solutions to puzzling problems than people who had either just watched a film about math or had just exercised. In other studies, Dr. Isen found that shortly after watching or experiencing comedy, people were able to think more clearly and were better able to "see" the consequences of a given decision.

3 The physiological effects of a good laugh work against stress. After a slight rise in heart rate and blood pressure during the laugh itself, there's an immediate recoil: Muscles relax and blood pressure sinks below prelaugh levels, and the brain may release endorphins, the same stress reducers that are triggered by exercise. A hearty ha-ha-ha also provides a muscle massage for facial muscles, the diaphragm and the abdomen. Studies show it even temporarily boosts levels of immunoglobulin A, a virus-fighter found in saliva.

4 While our cave-dwelling ancestors were stressed by actual life-threatening situations like bumping into a woolly mammoth, times have changed. "Nowadays, stress is usually not caused by the situation itself, but by how we perceive that situation," says Allen Elkin, Ph.D., program director of Manhattan's Stress Man-

Annotation practice exercises

Directions: For each exercise below,

- Write the topic of the paragraph on the lines provided.
- Formulate the implied main idea of the paragraph and write it on the lines provided.

This will help you remember the topic and the main idea.

Source: Stephen Lally, "Laugh Your Stress Away," *Prevention,* June 1991, from pp. 50–53. Reprinted by permission of *Prevention* magazine.

agement and Counseling Centers. Getting a new perspective is what comedy is all about. Several philosophers and writers have pointed out that comedy and tragedy are different ways of looking at the same stressful event.

5 Comedy works by stepping back from a situation and playing up its absurdities. The same kind of disinterested observation makes the tale of your disastrous vacation seem funny—after you get safely home. For stress busting, the trick is to find ways to laugh at the situation *while it's happening.* Even if you don't consider yourself much of a comedian, here are a few simple techniques you can use:

The Bart Simpson maneuver

6 How would your favorite cartoon character or comedian react to the situation? "Imagining what would happen can give you a chuckle, making the situation less annoying. You can even pretend *you're* the star of a TV comedy, and this frustrating episode is tonight's plot," says Steve Allen Jr., M.D., an assistant professor of family medicine at SUNY Health Science Center, Syracuse (yes, he's the son of well-known comedian Steve Allen).

Ballooning

7 In your mind, consciously exaggerate the situation: Blow it completely out of proportion and into absurdity—into a comedy routine. In that long, long checkout line, don't say "This waiting is killing me; I hate this." Say: "I'll *never* get to the front of this line. The woman ahead of me is covered in cobwebs. The guy in front of her grew a beard standing in line. The cashier must be part snail. The continental drift moves faster." This maneuver helps take the edge off the situation, redirects your tension, and helps you see things as not so impossible after all. Your running commentary, however, is probably best kept to yourself. If people stare at you because you seem to be laughing for no

Annotation exercise

- Topic of paragraph 6:

____

- Formulate the implied main idea of paragraph 6:

____

Annotation exercise

- Topic of paragraph 7:

____

- Formulate the implied main idea of paragraph 7:

____

reason, pretend you're reading the scandal sheets. You don't have to be a master of one-liners to be funny. There are gentler forms of humor that can defuse anxiety in a group without making anyone feel like the butt of a joke.

Pick a safe subject

8 Making fun of your own foibles can save face in an embarrassing situation—you'll have people laughing *with* you, rather than *at* you. Inanimate sources of frustration, like computers and copying machines, are also safe objects of humor.

Lay it on the line

9 Sometimes just telling the truth or pointing out the obvious can get a laugh. People are accustomed to exaggeration and truth bending (too many TV commercials, perhaps), so plain speaking can come as a refreshing shock. For example, after delivering a series of lengthy explanations during a question-and-answer period, some people have been known to put everyone in stitches by simply replying to the next question with "Gee, I don't know." This kind of humor is a way of fighting stress by accepting our shortcomings," says Joel Goodman, Ed.D., director of the HUMOR Project in Saratoga Springs, New York.

Annotation exercise

- Topic of paragraph 9:

____

____

- Formulate the implied main idea of paragraph 9:

____

____

____

____

____

Clip a cartoon

10 Keep a file of jokes and cartoons that make *you* laugh. Paste a few up where you're likely to need them—at work, on the refrigerator, wherever.

Comprehension Quiz

True or false

Directions: In the blank provided, indicate whether each statement is true or false.

_____ 1. The author believes that humor may be the healthiest way to relieve stress.

_____ 2. During a good laugh, there is a slight rise in heart rate and blood pressure.

_____ 3. After a good laugh, blood pressure rises steadily.

_____ 4. Our cave-dwelling ancestors were stressed by life-threatening situations.

_____ 5. The trick to stress busting is find ways to laugh at the situation after it has happened.

_____ 6. Getting a new perspective is what comedy is all about.

Multiple-choice

Directions: For each item, select the best answer.

_____ 7. Alice Isen, Ph.D., concluded that after watching or experiencing comedy, people

a. felt better temporarily but then became depressed again.
b. were able to think more clearly and see the consequences of a given decision.
c. reported no difference.
d. gradually became more relaxed and cheerful.

_____ 8. The physiological effects of a good laugh include

a. relaxation of the muscles.
b. lowering of blood pressure.
c. release of endorphins.
d. all of the above.

_____ 9. The Bart Simpson maneuver for reducing stress is to imagine

a. yourself removed from the stressful situation.
b. yourself as Bart Simpson.
c. how your favorite cartoon character or comedian would react.
d. none of the above.

_____ 10. Ballooning, a technique to reduce stress, consists of
   a. seeing yourself attached to a balloon which is floating away from the stressful situation.
   b. consciously exaggerating the situation by blowing it out of proportion into absurdity.
   c. releasing your tension by inhaling and exhaling deeply.
   d. visualizing your stress as a balloon that explodes and disappears.

Extend Your Vocabulary by Using Context Clues

Directions: ***Context clues*** are words in a sentence or paragraph that allow the reader to deduce (reason out) the meaning of an unfamiliar word. For each item in this exercise, a sentence from Selection 5-2 containing an important word *(italicized, like this)* is quoted first. Next, there is an additional sentence using the word in the same sense and providing another context clue. Use the context clues to deduce the meaning of each italicized word. *The definition you choose should make sense in both sentences.*

Pronunciation key: ă **pat** ā **pay** âr **care** ä **father** ĕ **pet** ē **be** ĭ **pit** ī **tie** îr **pier** ŏ **pot** ō **toe** ô **paw** oi **noise** ou **out** o͝o **took** o͞o **boot** ŭ **cut** yo͞o **abuse** ûr **urge** th **thin** *th* **this** hw **which** zh **vision** ə **about**

_____ 1. "The *physiological* effects of a good laugh work against stress."

Exercise has both *physiological* and psychological benefits.

physiological (fĭz ē ə lŏj′ ə kəl) means:
   a. pertaining to the emotions
   b. pertaining to the body
   c. pertaining to nutrition
   d. pertaining to the lifespan of an organism

_____ 2. "After a slight rise in heart rate and blood pressure during the laugh itself, there's an immediate *recoil.*"

After he fired the powerful shotgun, the *recoil* knocked him backwards.

recoil (rē′ koil) means:
   a. clicking sound
   b. winding something in loops
   c. increase
   d. drop or movement backwards

_____ 3. "Muscles relax and blood pressure sinks below prelaugh levels, and the brain may release *endorphins,* the same stress reducers that are triggered by exercise."

Exercising, eating chocolate, and being in love release *endorphins* in the body.

endorphins (ĕn dôr´ fĭnz) means:

a. hormones in the brain that cause hunger
b. chemicals in the brain that cause drowsiness and confusion
c. hormones in the body that cause feelings of sadness and depression
d. chemicals in the brain that reduce pain and produce a sense of well-being

_____ 4. "Muscles relax and blood pressure sinks below prelaugh levels, and the brain may release endorphins, the same stress reducers that are *triggered* by exercise."

The rioting in the city was *triggered* by the judge's unfair ruling.

triggered (trĭg´ ərd) means:

a. activated; initiated
b. pulled a trigger
c. prevented
d. decreased; diminished

_____ 5. "While our cave-dwelling ancestors were stressed by actual life-threatening situations like bumping into a woolly *mammoth,* times have changed."

Scientists do not know for sure why the *mammoth* disappeared.

mammoth (măm´ əth) means:

a. type of large moth
b. animal that looks similar to a human being
c. extinct type of elephant once found throughout the northern hemisphere
d. rare bird

_____ 6. "The same kind of *disinterested* observation makes the tale of your disastrous vacation seem funny—after you get safely home."

To be effective, referees and umpires must be *disinterested* in who wins the games they officiate at.

disinterested (dĭs ĭn´ trĭ stĭd) means:

a. deeply interested
b. overly concerned
c. knowledgeable
d. impartial or free from bias

_____ 7. "The *continental* drift moves faster."

During World War II, *continental* warfare enveloped nearly all of Europe.

continental (kŏn tə nĕn´ tl) means:

a. pertaining to a continent or principal land mass of the earth
b. pertaining to water or the ocean
c. related to travel
d. pertaining to technology

_____ 8. "This *maneuver* helps take the edge off the situation, redirects your tension, and helps you see things as not so impossible after all."

I tried to talk the police officer out of giving me a speeding ticket by being friendly and polite, but the *maneuver* failed.

maneuver (mə nü´ vər) means:

a. joke
b. strategy
c. excuse
d. mistaken idea

_____ 9. "Making fun of your own *foibles* can save face in an embarrassing situation—you'll have people laughing with you, rather than at you."

He was a practical joker and a nonstop talker, but he was so talented that we overlooked these *foibles*.

foibles (foi´ bəlz) means:

a. admirable qualities in one's character
b. unforgivable mistakes
c. minor weaknesses of character
d. humiliating experiences

_____ 10. "*Inanimate* sources of frustration, like computers and copying machines, are also safe objects of humor."

The actor's performance was so stiff that he seemed almost *inanimate*.

inanimate (ĭn ăn´ ə mĭt) means:

a. unfamiliar
b. lively; spirited
c. like a cartoon character
d. lacking lifelike qualities

Respond in Writing

Directions: Refer to Selection 5-2 as necessary to answer these essay-type items.

Options for collaboration: For some of the "Respond in Writing" exercises, your instructor may prefer that you work collaboratively, that is, with other students. These exercises are identified in the margin. *If your instructor directs you to work collaboratively on any of these items,* form groups of three or four classmates to complete the exercise together. Discuss your answers with each other and have one member of the group record the answers. A member of the group may be asked to share the group's answers with the class.

Consider the following situation:

Stephen Lally says, "Stress is not usually caused by the situation itself, but by how we perceive the situation." Suppose that you are to give a presentation in one of your classes. A few minutes before class, someone spills coffee on you in the cafeteria. You have a large coffee stain on your shirt, but there is no time to change before class.

Option

Exercises 1 and 2 may be completed collaboratively.

1. Explain at least two ways you could perceive this situation.

____

____

____

____

____

____

2. Now explain how you could apply one or more of Lally's five stress-busting techniques to help you deal with the situation.

____

____

____

____

____

____

Option

Exercise 3 may be completed collaboratively.

3. Develop an original technique for stress-busting. (It must be safe and legal!)

____

____

____

____

____

____

Option

Exercise 4 may be completed collaboratively.

4. What is the most important overall message the writer wants the reader to understand about stress? Try to answer this question in one sentence.

____

____

____

____

____

____

Selection 5-3

Government

WHY VOTE? POLITICIANS ARE ALL THE SAME

BY JANET FLAMMANG, DENNIS GORDON, TIMOTHY LUKES, AND KENNETH SMORSTEN

Prepare Yourself to Read

Directions: Do these exercises *before you read Selection 5-3.*

1. First, read and think about the title. When was the last time you voted? If you have never voted, why not?

   ____

   ____

2. Next, complete your preview by reading the following:

   Introduction (in *italics*)
   First paragraph (paragraph 1)
   First sentence of each paragraph
   Last paragraph (paragraph 5)

   On the basis of your preview, what do you think this selection is about?

   ____

   ____

Apply Comprehension Skills

Directions: Do the Annotation Practice Exercises *as you read Selection 5-3.* Apply the skills from this chapter:

Formulate implied main ideas. Follow these general steps: first determine the topic; then ask what the author's most important point about the topic is; then create a sentence that expresses the author's most important point. Use the appropriate formula to "formulate" an implied main idea sentence based on information in the paragraph.

Check your formulated main idea sentence. Be sure each of your main idea sentences meets the requirements on page 222.

In these exercises, you will work only with paragraphs that have implied main ideas.

WHY VOTE? POLITICIANS ARE ALL THE SAME

Why do people vote even when they know that their vote will not influence the outcome of the election? Read this selection from a government text to find the reasons the authors give.

1 Given the fact that each person is only one of approximately 90 million voters in this country, does it make sense to believe that one person's participation, one vote, will have any impact on a major election? Simply to raise the question "What if everyone felt the same way?" does not remove the lingering impression that a single person is dwarfed by the enormous number of people who do trek to the polls, especially in a national election.

2 Supporters of the ruling elite theory insist that even though voters are given a choice among candidates, their choice is restricted to a narrow range of similar-minded individuals sanctioned by the ruling elite. Elections do not express what most people want or need, nor do they provide guidance for politicians (even if they want it) on what policies to enact. In this view, elections are primarily just rituals that perform a symbolic function for society.

3 Still, since most people continue to show their faces at the polls at one time or another, what arguments can be made in favor of voting? One argument is that voting does have significance, if not in individual impact, then in group pressure. Because citizens collectively have the power to give or withhold votes, they directly control the tenure of elected officials. Even if the choice is between Tweedledee and Tweedledum, Tweedledee knows that a day of reckoning is fixed by law and that minimally he or she must strive to avoid displeasing the constituents or lose the job.

4 But perhaps political efficacy and impact in voting are not the only considerations anyway.

Annotation practice exercises

Directions: For each exercise below,

- Write the topic of the paragraph on the lines provided.
- Formulate the implied main idea of the paragraph and write it on the lines provided.

This will help you remember the topic and the main idea.

Annotation exercise

- Topic of paragraph 1:

____

____

- Formulate the implied main idea of paragraph 1:

____

____

____

____

____

Source: Janet Flammang, Dennis Gordon, Timothy Lukes, and Kenneth Smorsten, "Why Vote? Politicians Are All the Same," from *American Politics in a Changing World,* 3d ed., Harcourt Brace, 1990, p. 304.

People do not vote only to influence policy. Millions go to the effort to register and vote for a variety of other reasons as well. Some people may participate just to avoid feeling guilty about not voting. They may have been taught that is their patriotic duty to vote and that they have no right to complain about the outcome if they stay at home. Still others may vote to derive satisfaction from feeling that they are somehow participants, not just spectators, in an exciting electoral contest.

5 Even if their one vote may not be crucial to the outcome, it nevertheless affirms their role in and support for the political process. Indeed, perhaps it is this final need that fuels the desire for full democratic participation among people in many nations of the world.

Annotation exercise

- Topic of paragraph 4:

____

____

- Formulate the implied main idea of paragraph 4:

____

____

____

____

____

Annotation exercise

- Topic of paragraph 5:

____

____

- Formulate the implied main idea of paragraph 5:

____

____

____

____

____

Comprehension Quiz

True or false

Directions: In the space provided, indicate whether each statement is true or false.

______ 1. The writers of this passage believe that a person should still vote even though that person is only one of approximately 9 million voters.

______ 2. Voters may vote a politician out of office if he or she displeases the constituents.

______ 3. Voting does have significance, if not in individual impact, then in group pressure.

_____ 4. Voters go to the polls for a single reason.

_____ 5. Most people believe that elections are primarily just rituals that perform a symbolic function for society.

_____ 6. Voters cannot directly control the tenure of elected officials.

Multiple-choice

Directions: For each item, select the best answer.

_____ 7. Supporters of the ruling elite theory believe that

a. people vote as a way to influence policy.
b. elections express what people want and need.
c. there is a narrow range of similar-minded candidates for voters to choose from.
d. voters find electoral contests exciting.

_____ 8. People continue to vote for all of the following reasons *except* that they

a. feel their one vote is crucial to the outcome of the election.
b. want to avoid feeling guilty about not voting.
c. feel it is patriotic to do so.
d. feel as if they are participants in the electoral process and not just spectators.

_____ 9. The example of the twins Tweedledum and Tweedledee (characters in the book *Alice in Wonderland*) is used by these writers to illustrate that

a. the world of politics is a "wonderland."
b. voters do not control how long a candidate will be in office.
c. people need to vote.
d. voters sometimes have to choose between remarkably similar candidates.

_____ 10. The authors believe that in the final analysis, eligible voters

a. vote because they have overcome doubts that their one vote is useless.
b. do not vote, because they have not overcome their doubts.
c. vote because voting affirms their role in and supports the political process.
d. vote because they have strong ties to the political party of their choice.

Extend Your Vocabulary by Using Context Clues

Directions: ***Context clues*** are words in a sentence or paragraph that allow the reader to deduce (reason out) the meaning of an unfamiliar word. For each item in this exercise, a sentence from Selection 5-3 containing an important word *(italicized, like this)* is quoted first. Next, there is an additional sentence using the word in the same sense and providing another context clue. Use the context clues to deduce the meaning of each italicized word. *The definition you choose should make sense in both sentences.*

Pronunciation key: ă **pat** ā **pay** âr **care** ä **father** ĕ **pet** ē **be** ĭ **pit** ī **tie** îr **pier** ŏ **pot** ō **toe** ô **paw** oi **noise** ou **out** o͝o **took** o͞o **boot** ŭ **cut** yo͞o **abuse** ûr **urge** th **thin** *th* **this** hw **which** zh **vision** ə **about**

______ 1. "Supporters of the ruling elite theory insist that even though voters are given a choice among candidates, their choice is restricted to a narrow range of similar-minded individuals sanctioned by the ruling *elite*."

The *elite* usually live in large homes, are well educated, hold positions of power in their jobs, shop at expensive specialty stores, eat in fine restaurants, and drive luxury cars.

elite (ĭ lēt´) means:

a. men in a social group
b. older members of a social group
c. superior members of a social group
d. new members of a social group

______ 2. "Elections do not express what most people want or need, nor do they provide guidance for politicians (even if they want it) on what policies to *enact*."

Congress must go through a lengthy process to *enact* a piece of proposed legislation.

enact (ĕn ăkt´) means:

a. make a bill into a law
b. act out on a stage
c. pretend
d. write

______ 3. "Because citizens *collectively* have the power to give or withhold votes, they directly control the tenure of elected officials."

The club members believed, *collectively*, that their president should resign; and because they all felt that way, he turned in his resignation.

collectively (kə lĕk´ tĭv lē) means:

a. in a manner pertaining to a collection of objects
b. for a reason
c. in a manner pertaining to a country
d. by a number of individuals acting as one group

______ 4. "Because citizens collectively have the power to give or withhold votes, they directly control the *tenure* of elected officials."

Supreme Court justices have a lifetime *tenure* and serve until they retire, resign, or die.

tenure (tĕn´ yər) means:

a. power held by a person in office
b. length of time a person holds office
c. salary paid to a person who holds office
d. success of a person who holds office

______ 5. "Even if the choice is between Tweedledee and Tweedledum, Tweedledee knows that the day of reckoning is fixed by law and that *minimally* he or she must strive to avoid displeasing the constituents or lose the job."

With just a high school diploma, he was only *minimally* prepared to start a career.

minimally (mĭn´ ə məl ē) means:

a. to the greatest degree or amount possible
b. to the same amount or degree
c. to an unknown amount or degree
d. to the least amount or degree

______ 6. "Even if the choice is between Tweedledee and Tweedledum, Tweedledee knows that the day of reckoning is fixed by law and that minimally he or she must strive to avoid displeasing the *constituents* or lose the job."

Because the *constituents* were unhappy with the mayor's performance, they did not reelect him.

constituents (kən stĭch´ o͞o ənts) means:

a. people who are represented by an elected official
b. people who favor an elected official
c. people who vote in every election
d. people who plan to seek public office

______ 7. "But perhaps political *efficacy* and impact in voting are not the only consideration anyway."

Tim was thankful for the *efficacy* of the new medicine; it stopped his terrible headaches.

efficacy (ĕf´ ĭ kə sē) means:

a. prescription
b. weakness
c. ability to produce a desired effect
d. formula

______ 8. "Still others may vote to *derive* satisfaction from feeling that they are somehow participants, not just spectators, in an exciting electoral contest."

With a positive attitude, you can *derive* enjoyment even from ordinary, day-to-day tasks.

derive (dĭ rīv′) means:

a. wish for
b. avoid
c. delay
d. obtain

______ 9. "Still others may vote to derive satisfaction from feeling that they are somehow participants, not just spectators, in an exciting *electoral* contest."

Many people criticize the *electoral* process, but it is still one of the fairest systems for choosing government officials.

electoral (ĭ lĕk′ tər əl) means:

a. pertaining to an election
b. pertaining to Congress
c. pertaining to political campaigns
d. pertaining to luck

______ 10. "Even if their one vote may not be crucial to the outcome, it nevertheless *affirms* their role in and support for the political process."

The homeless man says that people's kindness to him since his accident *affirms* his faith in human goodness.

affirms (ə fûrmz′) means:

a. reduces
b. declares or maintains to be true
c. proves wrong
d. reveals or shows

Respond in Writing

Directions: Refer to Selection 5-3 as necessary to answer these essay-type items.

Options for collaboration: For some of the "Respond in Writing" exercises, your instructor may prefer that you work collaboratively, that is, with other students. These exercises are identified in the margin. *If your instructor directs you to work collaboratively on any of these items,* form groups of three or four classmates to complete the exercise together. Discuss your answers with each other and have one member of the group record the answers. A member of the group may be asked to share the group's answers with the class.

1. According to the selection, what are three reasons that people should vote?

2. List the three reasons the authors present for why people do not vote.

Option

Exercise 3 may be completed collaboratively.

3. Suppose that only a very small number of citizens in the United States voted in presidential elections. Discuss what you think might happen to our country by the year 2010 if no more than one or two out of every 100 qualified voters bothered to vote.

Option

Exercise 4 may be completed collaboratively.

4. What is the most important overall message these writers want the reader to understand about voting? Try to answer this question in one sentence.

CHAPTER 6

IDENTIFYING SUPPORTING DETAILS

IN THIS CHAPTER YOU WILL LEARN THE ANSWERS TO THESE QUESTIONS:

What are supporting details in a paragraph?

Why is it useful to understand supporting details?

How can I identify supporting details in paragraphs?

How can I list supporting details clearly?

CHAPTER 6 CONTENTS

▪ ▪ ▪ ▪ ▪ ▪ ▪

SKILLS

Little by little does the trick.

Key term

Supporting details: In a paragraph, additional information necessary for understanding the main idea.

SUPPORTING DETAILS IN PARAGRAPHS

What Are Supporting Details?

A paragraph consists of more than a topic and a main idea. The other sentences in the paragraph are supporting details. The topic and the main idea are essential to understanding the paragraph, but the ***supporting details*** provide additional information that enables you to understand the main idea *completely.*

Supporting details may consist of names, dates, places, descriptions, statistics, or other information explaining or illustrating the main idea. Specific types of supporting details that authors use to organize ideas into paragraphs include steps in a process, lists of characteristics, reasons, results, items in a series, similarities, and differences. (See Chapter 7.)

Be careful not to confuse the main idea with the supporting details. They are related to the main idea, but they are not the same thing. The main idea expresses an important *general* point that is based on the supporting details or is explained by them.

Why Are Supporting Details Important?

As noted above, the supporting details in a paragraph have an important connection with the main idea. Often, supporting details lead you to the stated main idea, since all of them explain more about the main idea. Similarly, supporting details contain important information that will help you formulate a main idea when it is implied.

In addition, it is useful to identify and understand supporting details because they can help you grasp the *organization* of a paragraph. If you understand *how* the supporting details explain, illustrate, or support the main idea of the paragraph, that makes it easier to remember the material, to take notes, and to mark your textbooks effectively.

Listing the supporting details after you read can help you study more efficiently. There are many instances when you will want to list supporting details in order to learn and remember them. For example, you would want to include important details on chapter review cards. Instructors often ask test questions based on supporting details—names, dates, places, and other important information.

Along with determining the topic and the main idea, then, identifying supporting details will help you become a more successful reader and student.

IDENTIFYING AND LISTING SUPPORTING DETAILS

To identify the supporting details of a paragraph, ask yourself, "*What else* does the author want me to know so that I can understand the main idea completely?" One way to approach this is by turning the main idea sentence into a question, using the words *who, what, where, when, why,* and *how.*

For example, suppose that the main idea of a paragraph is: *In a corporation, the chief financial officer is responsible for many basic functions.* You could change this sentence into the question, "*What* are the basic functions of a chief financial officer?" That question would lead you to the details that describe the basic functions, and therefore explain the main idea.

Often, you will find that supporting details are introduced by signal words such as *for example, first, second, next, also, in addition,* and *moreover.* Also, watch for numbers (1, 2, 3) and letters (*a, b, c*) that signal lists of details.

Here is an excerpt from a music appreciation textbook. Its topic is *the role of American colleges and universities in our musical culture.* The first sentence is the main idea: *American colleges and universities have played an unusually vital role in our musical culture.* Turn this main idea into the question, "*What* role have American colleges and universities played in our musical culture?" Then read the paragraph to identify the details that answer this question.

> American colleges and universities have played an unusually vital role in our musical culture. They have trained and employed many of our leading composers, performers, and scholars. Music courses have expanded the horizons and interests of countless students. And since the middle of the century, many universities have sponsored performing groups specializing in twentieth-century music. In addition, they have housed most of the electronic music studios.

Source: Roger Kamien, *Music: An Appreciation,* 5th ed., McGraw-Hill, New York, 1992, p. 444.

There are four details that answer the question, "*What* role have American colleges and universities played in our musical culture?"

- They trained and employed many leading composers, performers, and scholars.
- They expanded the horizons and interests of students through music courses.
- Since mid-century, they have sponsored performing groups specializing in twentieth-century music.
- They have housed most of the electronic music studios.

Key term

Paraphrasing: Restating an author's material in your own words.

Annotate

Go back to the excerpt. Locate the four supporting details and number them. Use the two signal words to help you locate the last two details.

Notice that in this list, the supporting details are not written out exactly as they appear in the paragraph. When you are listing supporting details, you will often want to use some of your own words in order to keep them brief. Rewriting someone else's material in your own words is called ***paraphrasing.***

Notice also, in this excerpt, the words *And* and *In addition* in the last two sentences. These words signal to the reader that two separate details are being given. But notice that not every detail is introduced by a signal word.

Since you are often responsible for understanding the supporting details in a textbook paragraph, you will also, after you have read the paragraph, find it helpful to go back and insert a *number* next to each detail. Numbering the supporting details is helpful for at least three reasons. First, it helps you locate all the details. Second, it helps you remember how many details there were in the paragraph. Third, it prevents you from overmarking the paragraph by underlining or highlighting too much.

In the next excerpt, the topic is *Richard Feynman* (pronounced FINEman), an American physicist and writer. Feynman was a Nobel Prize laureate, worked on the atomic bomb, reinvented quantum mechanics (the mathematics describing atomic processes), and exposed the fatal error by NASA that had caused the explosion of the space shuttle *Challenger.* The first sentence of the paragraph is the stated main idea: *Mr. Feynman was one of the great characters of modern physics.* Change this main idea sentence into the question, "*Why* was Feynman considered a 'character'?" Then read the paragraph to identify the details that answer this question.

Mr. Feynman was one of the great characters of modern physics. He was a jokester who figured out how to crack safes in Los Alamos offices while working on atomic bomb research in World War II. He was a computational wizard, once besting early computers in a contest to track a rocket launch. He could demolish other physicists whose presentation contained an error or humiliate them by producing in minutes a complicated calculation that took them weeks or months.

Source: Tom Siegfried, "Exploring the Mind of a Genius," *The Dallas Morning News,* October 25, 1992, sec. J.

The question "*Why* was Feynman considered a 'character'?" is answered by these three details:

- He was a jokester.
- He was a computational wizard.
- He could demolish and humiliate other physicists with his brilliance.

Annotate

Go back to the excerpt. Locate the three supporting details and number them.

Notice how briefly these supporting details can be written and how clearly they stand out when they are listed on separate lines. Listing the supporting details this way makes it easy to see the information that explains why Feynman was considered a "character." Notice also that some of the information from the last sentence of the paragraph has been paraphrased. As mentioned above, when you are listing supporting details it is not necessary to use the exact words of the paragraph, and it is not necessary to use complete sentences. Finally, did you notice that there are no signal words in this paragraph to indicate the supporting details?

The excerpt below has a number of important details. It is from a book on English composition. The topic of this paragraph is *careless writing and readers who get lost,* and the stated main idea is: *If the reader is lost, it's usually because the writer hasn't been careful enough.* Turn the main idea into the question, "*What* are some ways careless writers cause readers to get lost?" Now read the paragraph to find the supporting details that answer this question.

> It won't do to say that the reader is too dumb or too lazy to keep pace with the train of thought. If the reader is lost, it's usually because the writer hasn't been careful enough. The carelessness can take any number of forms. Perhaps a sentence is so excessively cluttered that the reader, hacking through the verbiage, simply doesn't know what it means. Perhaps a sentence has been so shoddily constructed that the reader could read it in several ways. Perhaps the writer has switched pronouns in mid-sentence, or has switched tenses, so the reader loses track of who is talking or when the action took place. Perhaps Sentence B is not a logical sequel to Sentence A—the writer, in whose head the connection is clear, has not bothered to provide the missing link. Perhaps the writer has used an important word incorrectly by not taking the trouble to look it up. The writer may think "sanguine" and "sanguinary" means the same thing, but the difference is a bloody big one. The reader can only infer (speaking of big differences) what the writer is trying to imply.

Source: William K. Zinsser, *On Writing Well,* 5th ed., Harper and Row, New York, 1994, pp. 9, 12.

There are five details that answer the question, "*What* are some ways careless writers cause readers to get lost?"

- careless writers clutter sentences with too many words
- they write sentences that can be read in several ways
- they switch pronouns or tenses
- they don't supply links between sentences
- they use words incorrectly

Annotate

Go back to the excerpt. Locate the five supporting details using the word *perhaps* to identify them. Then number each of them.

Notice that some of the details listed above have been shortened or reworded to make them easier to understand and remember. Notice also that none of the common signal words (such as *also, and,* and *another*) were used in this paragraph. Instead, repeated use of the words *perhaps* signals each supporting detail in the paragraph. (Inserting small numbers next to the details would make them easy to locate, even though the details are spread throughout the paragraph.)

The final sample paragraph is from a health textbook. As the heading indicates, its topic is *water.* Its implied main idea is: *Water serves many important functions in the body.* Turn this main idea into a question, "*What* important functions does water serve in the body?" Then read the paragraph to find the details that answer this question.

WATER

Like fiber, water has no nutritional value, yet is a very important food component. It is used to transport nutrients to the cells and to remove cellular waste products. In addition, it acts as a medium for digestion, regulates body temperature, and helps cushion the vital organs. An inadequate water intake will restrict the function of all body systems. Finally, water and some of the chemicals it carries are responsible for bodily structure since, on average, 60 percent of the body is water.

Source: Marvin Levy, Mark Dignan, and Janet Shirreffs, *Targeting Wellness: The Core,* McGraw-Hill, New York, 1992, p. 52. Reproduced with permission of McGraw-Hill.

Eight details answer the question, "*What* important functions does water serve in the body?" Notice that they have been paraphrased and shortened.

- Water is an important food component.
- It transports nutrients to cells.
- It removes cellular waste.
- It acts as a medium for digestion.
- It regulates body temperature.
- It helps cushion vital organs.
- Inadequate intake of water restricts functions of all body systems.
- It is partly responsible for body structure because the body is 60 percent water.

Annotate

Go back to the excerpt. Identify the eight supporting details, using the two signal words to help you. Then number each detail.

As you can see, a single sentence can contain more than one supporting detail. In this paragraph, although there are five sentences, there are eight supporting details. The second sentence contains two details, and the third sentence contains three. There are two signals in the paragraph, *In addition* and *Finally.*

There are other ways besides listing to organize supporting details you want to learn. These techniques are presented in Chapter 10.

STANDARDIZED READING TESTS: SUPPORTING DETAILS

College students may be required to take standardized reading tests as part of an overall assessment program, in a reading course, or as part of a state-mandated "basic skills" test. A standardized reading test typically consists of a series of passages followed by multiple-choice questions, to be completed within a specified time limit.

Standardized reading tests always include questions about supporting details. The purpose of such questions is to see if you can locate and comprehend specific information stated in a passage.

Questions about supporting details often begin with phrases such as the following:

According to the passage . . .

According to the information in the passage . . .

The author states . . .

The author states that . . .

Questions may also refer to specific information in a passage, as in the following examples:

One function of water in the body is . . .

The museum mentioned in the passage is located in . . .

World War I began in the year . . .

The height of the tower was . . .

To answer an item about supporting details, read the question carefully to determine exactly what information you need (for instance, a place, a person's name, or a date). Then *skim* the passage, looking for that information. When you come to the part of the passage that has what you are looking for, slow down and read it more closely.

Don't be fooled by a question that is worded somewhat differently from the passage. For instance, a passage might state that a child was rescued by a "police officer," but the correct answer choice might be "an officer of the law." Or a passage might specifically mention "the Vanderbilts and the Rockefellers," but the correct answer choice might be "two wealthy Eastern families." In cases like this, you need to look for information that *means the same thing,* even if the words are different.

DEVELOPING CHAPTER REVIEW CARDS

Review cards, or *summary cards,* are an excellent study tool. They are a way to select, organize, and review the most important information in a textbook chapter. The process of creating review cards helps you organize information in a meaningful way and, at the same time, transfer it into long-term memory. The cards can also be used to prepare for tests (see *Part Three*). The review card activities in this book give you structured practice in creating these valuable study tools. Once you have learned how to make review cards, you can create them for textbook material in your other courses.

Now, complete the five review cards for Chapter 6 by answering the questions or following the directions on each card. When you have completed them, you will have summarized: (1) what supporting details are, (2) why they are important, (3) how to find them in a paragraph, (4) how to list them, and (5) how to mark them.

What Supporting Details Are

Define *supporting details.* (See page 261.)

____

____

Supporting details may consist of (see page 261):

____

____

____

____

____

Chapter 6: Identifying Supporting Details

Why Supporting Details Are Important

Describe three reasons why supporting details are important. (See page 261.)

1. ____

2. ____

3. ____

Chapter 6: Identifying Supporting Details

How to Find Supporting Details

To identify supporting details in a paragraph, what question should you ask yourself? (See page 262.)

____

List some signal words that can introduce supporting details. (See page 262.)

____

Besides signal words, what are two other ways authors indicate supporting details? (See page 262.)

____

Is every supporting detail introduced by a signal of some sort? (See page 263.)

____

Chapter 6: Identifying Supporting Details

How to Write Down Supporting Details

To write down supporting details in a way that will make them stand out clearly, what is a good format to use? (See page 263.)

____

Define *paraphrasing.* (See page 263.)

____

____

Why is paraphrasing useful when you are writing down supporting details? (See page 263.)

____

____

Chapter 6: Identifying Supporting Details

How to Mark Supporting Details

How can you make supporting details easy to locate after you have read a paragraph? (See page 263.)

____

____

____

Give three reasons why this is a helpful technique. (See page 263.)

Reason 1: ______________________________

____

Reason 2: ______________________________

____

Reason 3: ______________________________

____

Chapter 6: Identifying Supporting Details

Selection 6-1

Business

COMMUNICATION CLOSE-UP AT BEN AND JERRY'S HOMEMADE

FROM *BUSINESS COMMUNICATION TODAY*
BY COURTLAND BOVÉE AND JOHN THILL

Prepare Yourself to Read

Directions: Do these exercises *before you read Selection 6-1.*

1. First, read and think about the title. What do you already know about Ben and Jerry's as a company? What do you know about its ice cream?

   ____

   ____

2. Next, complete your preview by reading the following:

   Introduction (in *italics*)
   First paragraph (paragraph 1)
   First sentence of each paragraph
   Last paragraph (paragraph 10)

   On the basis of your preview, what does the selection seem to be about?

   ____

   ____

Apply Comprehension Skills

Directions: Do the Annotation Practice Exercises *as you read Selection 6-1.*

Determine the topic. When you read a paragraph, ask yourself, "What or who is this about?"

Locate or formulate the main idea. As you read, ask yourself, "What is the most important point these authors want me to understand about the topic?"

Identify and list supporting details. As you read, ask yourself, "What else do these authors want me to know so that I can understand the main idea completely?" List the supporting details.

COMMUNICATION CLOSE-UP AT BEN AND JERRY'S HOMEMADE

Anyone who has ever tasted Ben and Jerry's ice cream knows that this is no ordinary ice cream. Neither is Ben and Jerry's Homemade an ordinary company. There really is a Ben, and there really is a Jerry. Here's their story.

1 Down at the factory in Waterbury, Vermont, they're known as "the boys." They are Ben Cohen and Jerry Greenfield, arguably America's most famous purveyors of ice cream and certainly two of America's most colorful entrepreneurs. They've been friends since seventh grade and business partners since 1978 when they opened their first scoop shop, using techniques gleaned from a $5 correspondence course on how to make ice cream. Their firm, Ben & Jerry's Homemade, sold more than $76 million worth of super premium ice cream in 1990 and employs around 300 people, give or take a few, depending on the season.

2 Ben and Jerry have stong personalities and strong opinions. They believe that work should be fun, or else it isn't worth doing. They also believe in helping the unfortunate, protecting the environment, and treating people fairly. They want their company to be a happy, humanitarian place where everybody feels good about coming to work and producing a top-notch product.

3 One person who helps the company accomplish this goal is Maureen Martin, the coordinator of employee communication. Her job is to see that everyone knows what's going on at the company's two production plants, five company-owned retail outlets, and 82 franchised scoop shops. The theory at Ben & Jerry's is that sharing information builds trust and helps people do their jobs better. To that end, Martin publishes a monthly newsletter and organizes staff meetings, which are held every six to eight

Annotation practice exercises

Directions: For each paragraph indicated, write in the spaces provided:

- Main idea sentence
- Supporting details

Doing this will help you remember main ideas and details.

Practice exercise

Main idea sentence of paragraph 1:

____

____

Supporting details:

____

____

____

____

____

____

Source: Courtland Bovée and John Thill, "Communication Close-Up at Ben & Jerry's Homemade," in *Business Communication Today,* 3d ed., McGraw-Hill, New York, 1992, pp. 26–28. Reproduced with permission of McGraw-Hill. *Photo:* Courtesy of Ben and Jerry's, photo by Glen Moody.

Ben Cohen and Jerry Greenfield

weeks at each of the two factories. Additionally, she handles internal publicity for a variety of special events and activities.

4 The staff meetings are an important channel of communication because they give all the employees a chance to interact directly with top management—and vice versa. The feedback gives Ben and Jerry insight into what the employees are thinking. According to Martin, the meetings combine the qualities of a "pep rally" and a financial briefing. Most are designed to convey information about Ben & Jerry's performance and operating plans, but some are held to deal with a specific agenda or to obtain employee input. "We sometimes break up into small discussion groups so that employees can express their opinions," Martin explains. "One meeting was held to discuss the topic of improving employee communications. We talked about what was working and what wasn't and possible solutions." Martin tries to keep the style of the meetings light and upbeat, and she uses a variety of media—sound effects, videotapes, and overhead transparencies.

5 To publicize special events, Martin relies on a combination of written and oral communication. She might send out a memo, post notices on bulletin boards, run an article in the newsletter, and pass the word informally as she

Practice exercise

Main idea sentence of paragraph 4:

____

____

Supporting details:

____

____

____

____

____

____

talks with people about various matters. The repetition in various formats gives the message maximum exposure and builds anticipation.

6 The special events are, in themselves, a form of communication in that they express management's concept of a desirable working environment. Many of the events are dreamed up by the Joy Gang, an official, but informal, group headed by Jerry Greenfield himself, whose title is now Minister of Joy. (Greenfield has partially distanced himself from day-to-day management.) The committee's function is to spread cheer and build camaraderie. One of the group's recent events was Elvis Day, held in honor of Presley's birthday. "A bunch of people dressed up like Elvis, and we played Elvis tunes all day long," Martin explains. "We even served Elvis's favorite food at lunch." At various times, the Joy Gang has also hired a masseuse to take the kinks out of weary production workers, rented a synchroenergizer to induce mental tranquillity, and purchased roller skates so that employees would not wear themselves out running around.

7 In many respects, actions speak louder than words at Ben & Jerry's. Plenty of companies publicize their commitment to community service, but very few match Ben & Jerry's financial contribution to charity. The firm donates 7.5 percent of its annual pretax profits to a foundation that funds environmentalists, the disadvantaged, and children.

8 Actions also telegraph Ben & Jerry's commitment to an egalitarian work environment: the open office arrangement, the bright colors, the pictures of cows and fields hanging on warehouse walls, the employee committees (so many that Maureen Martin is publishing a directory), the casual clothes, the first-name relationships, the compressed pay scale that keeps executive salaries in balance with lower-level compensation, the free health club memberships for everyone, the upcoming on-site daycare facility. And the free ice cream. Three pints a day per person. Now that's communication at its best!

Practice exercise

Main idea sentence of paragraph 6:

____

____

Supporting details:

____

____

____

____

____

____

9 Whether you work for a free-spirited company like Ben & Jerry's or a more conventional organization, you will discover that when all is said and done, what's done is more important that what's said. Action is the ultimate form of communication. It speaks with an unmistakable voice. The diaper changing tables in both the men's and women's rooms at Ben & Jerry's say more about the company's commitment to family values than any pronouncement in a policy manual possibly could. At the same time, when Ben Cohen tears his remaining hair and laments that the company is growing too fast, the employees give each other knowing looks and hustle to meet production targets. They've noticed that for a man who hates growth, Ben sure sells a lot of ice cream.

10 Perhaps a certain amount of inconsistency between words and actions is unavoidable. Life is full of ambiguities, and most of us have mixed feelings about things from time to time. We don't always say what we really mean; in fact, we don't always *know* what we really mean. Under the circumstances, no wonder we sometimes have trouble figuring out all the surface and underlying messages that we send and receive. Unraveling the mysteries of communication requires perception, concentration, and an appreciation of the communication process.

Comprehension Quiz

True and false

Directions: In the blank provided, indicate whether each statement is true or false.

______ 1. Ben and Jerry feel that communication is less important than other aspects of their business.

______ 2. Ben and Jerry personally handle all of the communication responsibilities for their company.

______ 3. The authors of this selection believe that unraveling the mystery of communication requires perception, concentration, and luck.

_____ 4. The authors state that we do not always say what we really mean, and that we do not always know what we really mean.

_____ 5. The authors' position is that action is the ultimate form of communication.

Multiple-choice

Directions: For each item, select the best answer.

_____ 6. Ben Cohen and Jerry Greenfield
a. were experienced in the ice cream business before they started their own company.
b. became friends after college and then became business partners later.
c. started their business in Maine.
d. none of the above.

_____ 7. Ways of facilitating communication at Ben and Jerry's Homemade include
a. monthly newsletters and employee committees.
b. staff meetings every 6 to 8 weeks.
c. special events dreamed up by the "Joy Gang."
d. all of the above.

_____ 8. The authors describe Ben and Jerry's Homemade as a business that is
a. pleasant but conventional.
b. in need of revitalization.
c. free-spirited.
d. an example of poor business communication.

_____ 9. Special activities at Ben and Jerry's Homemade have included
a. having an "Elvis Day."
b. buying roller skates for employees.
c. hiring a masseuse for the employees.
d. all of the above.

_____ 10. Employees at Ben and Jerry's have expressed a need for
a. a free health club.
b. more casual dress at work.
c. brighter, and more pleasant working conditions.
d. none of the above.

Extend Your Vocabulary by Using Context Clues

Directions: ***Context clues*** are words in a sentence or paragraph that allow the reader to deduce (reason out) the meaning of an unfamiliar word. For each item in this exercise, a sentence from Selection 6-1 containing an important word *(italicized, like this)* is quoted first. Next, there is an additional sentence using the word in the same sense and providing another context clue. Use the context clues to deduce the meaning of each italicized word. *The definition you choose should make sense in both sentences.*

Pronunciation key: ă **pat** ā **pay** âr **care** ä **father** ĕ **pet** ē **be** ĭ **pit** ī **tie** îr **pier** ŏ **pot** ō **toe** ô **paw** oi **noise** ou **out** o͝o **took** o͞o **boot** ŭ **cut** yo͞o **abuse** ûr **urge** th **thin** *th* **this** hw **which** zh **vision** ə **about**

______ 1. "They are Ben Cohen and Jerry Greenfield, *arguably* America's most famous purveyors of ice cream."

AIDS is *arguably* the most dangerous health crisis facing the world today.

arguably (ar´ gyo͞o əb lē) means:

a. by quarreling or bickering
b. by defeating someone in a dispute
c. illogically
d. able to be supported with reasons in an argument

______ 2. "They are Ben Cohen and Jerry Greenfield, arguably America's most famous *purveyors* of ice cream."

British firms take great pride in serving as *purveyors* of fine goods to the royal family.

purveyors (pər vā´ ərz) means:

a. people who supply or furnish something
b. people who purify something
c. people who invent something
d. people who ship or send something

______ 3. "They opened their first scoop shop using techniques *gleaned* from a $5 correspondence course on how to make ice cream."

By searching through state and local records and old newspaper clippings, Martha *gleaned* information about her great-grandparents.

gleaned (glēnd) means:

a. sneaked or stole
b. learned in depth
c. collected bit by bit
d. misinterpreted

______ 4. "They want their company to be a happy, *humanitarian* place where everybody feels good about coming to work and producing a top-notch product."

The Red Cross is perhaps the most famous *humanitarian* organization in the world.

humanitarian (hyōō măn ĭ târ´ ē ən) means:

a. devoted to human welfare
b. devoted to improving working conditions
c. pertaining to life in poor countries
d. devoted to helping people during disasters

______ 5. "The repetition in various formats gives the message maximum *exposure* and builds anticipation."

Political candidates often appear on local and national talk shows in order to gain as much free public *exposure* as possible.

exposure (ĭk spō´ zher) means:

a. being subjected to light
b. being subjected to humiliation
c. being liked
d. being made known

______ 6. "The committee's function is to spread cheer and build *camaraderie*."

The *camaraderie* among the members of the swimming team lasted long after they had all finished college.

camaraderie (kä mə rä´ də rē) means:

a. happiness
b. skill or talent
c. goodwill among friends
d. competitiveness

______ 7. "At various times, the Joy Gang has also hired a *masseuse* to take the kinks out of weary production workers."

A *masseuse* accompanied the United States women's track team to the Olympics.

masseuse (mă soez´) means:

a. woman who monitors employees' health
b. woman trained in relaxation techniques
c. woman who trains athletes
d. woman who gives massages professionally

______ 8. "Actions also telegraph Ben and Jerry's commitment to an *egalitarian* work environment: the open office arrangement, the employee committees, the casual clothes, the first-name relationships, the compressed pay-scale that keeps executive salaries in balance with lower-level compensation, and the free health club memberships for everyone."

Community colleges are *egalitarian* institutions that are open to any qualified member of the community.

egalitarian (ĭ găl ĭ târ′ ē ən) means:

a. favoring or advocating equality for all
b. pertaining to things that are not alike
c. favoring certain groups
d. pertaining to education

______ 9. "The diaper changing tables in both the men's and the women's rooms at Ben and Jerry's say more about the company's commitment to family values than any *pronouncement* in a policy manual could."

The Surgeon General's *pronouncement* about the effects of secondhand smoke is proving to be correct.

pronouncement (prə nouns′ mənt) means:

a. formal declaration or statement
b. words articulated clearly
c. guide to pronunciation
d. posted statement of an official or an employer

______ 10. "Life is full of *ambiguities,* and most of us have mixed feelings about things from time to time."

We were puzzled and amused by one of the *ambiguities* in her previous employer's reference: "You will be lucky to get her to work for you."

ambiguities (ăm bĭ gyōō′ ĭ tēz) means:

a. statements that can cause pain
b. statements that can be interpreted in more than one way
c. statements that can cause frustration
d. statements that are easy to comprehend

Respond in Writing

Directions: Refer to Selection 6-1 as necessary to answer these essay-type items.

Option for collaboration: For some of the "Respond in Writing" exercises, your instructor may prefer that you work collaboratively, that is, with other students. These exercises are identified in the margin. *If your instructor directs you to work collaboratively on any of these items,* form groups of three or four classmates to complete the exercise together. Discuss your answers with each other and have one member of the group record the answers. A member of the group may be asked to share the group's answers with the class.

Option

Item 1 may be completed collaboratively.

1. The authors use Ben and Jerry's Homemade as an illustration of a company with effective communication strategies. Develop a list of the communication techniques and strategies described in the selection. You may write them in your own words.

____

____

____

____

____

____

Option

Item 2 may be completed collaboratively.

2. What is the most important overall message these writers want the reader to understand about effective communication? Try to answer this question in one sentence.

____

____

____

____

____

____

____

____

Selection 6-2

Essay

HOW TO FIND TIME TO READ

BY LOUIS SHORES

Prepare Yourself to Read

Directions: Do these exercises *before you read Selection 6-2.*

1. First, read and think about the title. Do you have enough time to read? Why or why not?

   ____

   ____

2. Next, complete your preview by reading the following:

   Introduction (in *italics*)

   First paragraph (paragraph 1)

   First sentence of each paragraph

   Last paragraph (paragraph 10)

   On the basis of your preview, do you think the author believes that everyone can find time to read?

   ____

   ____

Apply Comprehension Skills

Directions: Do the Annotation Practice Exercises *as you read Selection 6-2.*

Determine the topic. When you read a paragraph, ask yourself, "What or who is this about?"

Locate or formulate the main idea. As you read, ask yourself, "What is the most important point this author wants me to understand about the topic?"

Identify and list supporting details. As you read, ask yourself, "What else does the author want me to know so that I can understand the main idea completely?" List the supporting details.

HOW TO FIND TIME TO READ

This article about finding time for leisure reading was written for a general audience. However, finding time for this kind of reading is an even greater problem for busy college students. If you spend considerable time on your required academic reading, you may feel that you have no time to read magazines, newspapers, or books for pleasure. The author of this selection gives a simple solution to the problem of "how to find time to read."

1 If you are an average reader you can read an average book at the rate of 300 words per minute. You cannot maintain that average, however, unless you read regularly every day. Nor can you attain that speed with hard books in science, mathematics, agriculture, business, or any subject that is new or unfamiliar to you. The chances are you will never attempt that speed with poetry or want to race through some passages in fiction over which you wish to linger. But for most novels, biographies, and books about travel, hobbies, or personal interests, if you are an average reader you should have no trouble at all absorbing meaning and pleasure out of 300 printed words every 60 seconds.

2 Statistics are not always practicable, but consider these: If the average reader can read 300 words a minute of average reading, then in 15 minutes he can read 4,500 words. Multiplied by 7, the days of the week, the product is 31,500. Another multiplication by 4, the weeks of the month, makes 126,000. And final multiplication by 12, the months of the year, results in a grand total of 1,512,00 words. That is the total number of words of average reading an average reader can do in just 15 minutes a day for one year.

3 Books vary in length from 60,000 to 100,000 words. The average is about 75,000 words. In one year of average reading by an average

Annotation practice exercises

Directions: For each paragraph indicated, write in the spaces provided:

- Main idea sentence
- Supporting details

Doing this will help you remember main ideas and details.

Practice exercise

Main idea sentence of paragraph 1:

____

____

Supporting details:

____

____

____

____

____

____

Source: From Louis Shores, "How to Find Time to Read," in Frank Christ, ed., *SR/SE Resource Book,* Chicago, Ill., SRA, 1969, pp. 105–107, abridged.

reader for 15 minutes a day, 20 books will be read. That's a lot of books. It is 4 times the number of books read by public-library borrowers in America. And yet it is easily possible.

4 One of the greatest of all modern physicians was Sir William Osler. He taught at the Johns Hopkins Medical School. He finished his teaching days at Oxford University. Many of the outstanding physicians today were his students. Nearly all of the practicing doctors of today were brought up on his medical textbooks. Among his many remarkable contributions to medicine are his unpublished notes on how people die.

5 His greatness is attributed by his biographers and critics not alone to his profound medical knowledge and insight but to his broad general education, for he was a very cultured man. He was interested in what men have done and thought throughout the ages. And he knew that the only way to find out what the best experiences of the race had been was to read what people had written. But Osler's problem was the same as everyone else's, only more so. He was a busy physician, a teacher of physicians, and a medical-research specialist. There was no time in a 24-hour day that did not rightly belong to one of these three occupations, except the few hours for sleep, meals, and bodily functions.

6 Osler arrived at his solution early. He would read the last 15 minutes before he went to sleep. If bedtime was set for 11:00 P.M., he read from 11:00 to 11:15. If research kept him up to 2:00 A.M., he read from 2:00 to 2:15. Over a very long lifetime, Osler never broke the rule once he had established it. We have evidence that after a while he simply could not fall asleep until he had done his 15 minutes of reading.

7 In his lifetime, Osler read a significant library of books. Just do a mental calculation for half a century of 15-minute reading periods daily and see how many books you get. Consider what a range of interests and variety of subjects are possible in one lifetime. Osler read widely out-

Practice exercise

Main idea sentence of paragraph 5:

____

____

Supporting details:

____

____

____

____

____

____

side of his medical specialty. Indeed, he developed from the 15-minute reading habit an avocational specialty to balance his vocational specialization. Among scholars in English literature, Osler is known as an authority on Sir Thomas Browne, a seventeenth-century English prose master, and Osler's library on Sir Thomas is considered one of the best anywhere. A great many more things could be said about Osler's contribution to medical research, to the reform of medical teaching, to the introduction of modern clinical methods. But the important point for us here is that he answered supremely well for himself the question all of us who live a busy life must answer: How can I find time to read?

8 No universal formula can be prescribed. Each of us must find our own 15-minute period each day. It is better if it is regular. Then all additional spare minutes are so many bonuses. And, believe me, the opportunity for reading-bonuses are many and unexpected. Last night an univited guest turned up to make five for bridge. I had the kind of paperback book at hand to make being the fifth at bridge a joy.

9 The only requirement is the will to read. With it you can find the 15 minutes no matter how busy the day. And you must have the book at hand. Not even seconds of your 15 minutes must be wasted starting to read. Set that book out in advance. Put it into your pocket when you dress. Put another book beside your bed. Place one in your bathroom. Keep one near your dining table.

10 You can't escape reading 15 minutes a day, and that means you will read half a book a week, 2 books a month, 20 a year, and 1,000 or more in a reading lifetime. It's an easy way to become well read.

Practice exercise

Main idea sentence of paragraph 7:

____

____

Supporting details:

____

____

____

____

____

____

Comprehension Quiz

True or false

Directions: In the blank provided, indicate whether each statement is true or false.

_____ 1. The author states that the average reader reads 400 words per minute.

_____ 2. According to the author, it is possible to read books in science and math at the same rate of speed as novels and biographies.

_____ 3. The author stresses that readers should never read for more than 15 minutes a day.

_____ 4. By reading for 15 minutes a day, the average reader can read 20 books a year.

_____ 5. William Osler maintained a schedule of wide reading by reading 15 minutes each day at bedtime.

_____ 6. William Osler had time to read only medical books.

Multiple-choice

Directions: For each item, select the best answer.

_____ 7. Which of the following statements about William Osler is *false?*

a. He was an outstanding teacher at Johns Hopkins Medical School and Oxford University.
b. He wrote widely used medical textbooks.
c. He was noted for his profound medical knowledge and his broad general knowledge.
d. He rarely broke his habit of daily reading once he had established it.

_____ 8. A lifetime habit of reading enabled William Osler to

a. read widely outside his medical specialty.
b. become an authority on a famous English writer, Sir Thomas Browne.
c. become cultured and highly regarded as a man of broad general knowledge.
d. all of the above.

_____ 9. It is the writer's opinion that an average reader

a. can become well-read by reading for 15 minutes a day.
b. should build a collection of books he or she has read.
c. should read at least four different types of books.
d. should become an expert in a particular area.

_____ 10. In the United States, users of public libraries typically read

a. 5 books a year.
b. 10 books a year.
c. 20 books a year.
d. 40 books a year.

Extend Your Vocabulary by Using Context Clues

Directions: ***Context clues*** are words in a sentence or paragraph that allow the reader to deduce (reason out) the meaning of an unfamiliar word. For each item in this exercise, a sentence from Selection 6-2 containing an important word *(italicized, like this)* is quoted first. Next, there is an additional sentence using the word in the same sense and providing another context clue. Use the context clues to deduce the meaning of each italicized word. *The definition you choose should make sense in both sentences.*

Pronunciation key: ă **pat** ā **pay** âr **care** ä **father** ĕ **pet** ē **be** ĭ **pit** ī **tie** îr **pier** ŏ **pot** ō **toe** ô **paw** oi **noise** ou **out** o͝o **took** o͞o **boot** ŭ **cut** yo͞o ab**u**se ûr **urge** th **thin** *th* **this** hw **which** zh vi**s**ion ə **a**bout

_____ 1. "The chances are you will never attempt a fast speed with poetry or race through some passages in fiction over which you wish to *linger.*"

After the final football game of a winning season, some students always *linger* at the victory party long after midnight.

linger (lĭng′ gər) means:

a. finish quickly
b. read slowly
c. stay as though reluctant to leave
d. be with friends

_____ 2. "Statistics are not always *practicable,* but consider these: If the average reader can read 300 words a minute of average reading, then in 15 minutes he can read 4,500 words."

The engineer's first plan for stabilizing the bridge was too difficult and expensive to be *practicable.*

practicable (prăk′ tĭ kə bəl) means:

a. feasible or suitable
b. requiring practice
c. reliable; dependable
d. accomplished without practice

_____ 3. "Nearly all of the *practicing* doctors of today were brought up on his medical textbooks."

Judge Carver continued to be a *practicing* judge until the day he died at age 76.

practicing (prăk´ tĭs ĭng) means:

a. gaining experience
b. not held in high regard
c. working a limited number of hours per week
d. actively engaged in a profession

_____ 4. "His greatness is attributed by his biographers and critics not alone to his *profound* medical knowledge and insight but to his broad general education, for he was a very cultured man."

The Greek philosopher Plato had a *profound* respect for the power of reason.

profound (prə found´) means:

a. limited; partial
b. lifelong
c. absolute; complete
d. incorrect

_____ 5. "His greatness is attributed by his biographers and critics not alone to his profound medical knowledge and insight but to his broad general education, for he was a very *cultured* man."

Knowledge of music, art, and literature is considered a characteristic of a *cultured* person.

cultured (kûl´ chərd) means:

a. pretentious; snobbish
b. having a college degree
c. elderly
d. having refined intellectual and artistic taste

_____ 6. "Indeed, he developed from this 15-minute reading habit an *avocational* specialty to balance his vocational specialization."

Marty is a pilot, so it is not surprising that his *avocational* interests include making and flying radio-controlled model airplanes.

avocational (ăv ə kā´ shən l) means:

a. pretaining to food or cuisine
b. pertaining to a hobby
c. pertaining to a profession or career
d. pertaining to the voice

______ 7. "Indeed, he developed from this 15-minute reading habit an avocational specialty to balance his *vocational* specialization."

Vocational courses at our college include data processing, bookkeeping, automotive technology, and robotics.

vocational (vō kā´ shən l) means:

a. pertaining to an occupation
b. pertaining to a college or university
c. pertaining to a vacation or leisure time
d. pertaining to salary or income

______ 8. "Among scholars in English literature, Osler is known as an authority on Sir Thomas Browne, a seventeenth-century English *prose* master."

Most students feel that *prose* is easier to understand than poetry.

prose (prōz) means:

a. ordinary speech and writing instead of verse
b. sonnets and love songs
c. plays written by Shakespeare
d. literature by British writers

______ 9. "A great many more things could be said about Osler's contribution to medical research, to the *reform* of medical teaching, to the introduction of modern clinical methods."

Congress wants a *reform* of the federal tax code, which is too complex and confusing for the average person to understand.

reform (rĭ fôrm´) means:

a. creation; development
b. abuse or malpractice
c. improvement by correction of errors or removal of defects
d. a return to the beginning

______ 10. "But the important point for us is that he answered *supremely* well for himself the question all of us who live a busy life must answer: How can I find time to read?"

The Simpsons were *supremely* happy after they retired and moved to Hawaii.

supremely (sə prēm´ lē) means:

a. finally
b. temporarily
c. slightly
d. to the best or greatest extent

Respond in Writing

Directions: Refer to Selection 6-2 as necessary to answer these essay-type items.

Options for collaboration: For some of the "Respond in Writing" exercises, your instructor may prefer that you work collaboratively, that is, with other students. These exercises are identified in the margin. *If your instructor directs you to work collaboratively on any of these items,* form groups of three or four classmates to complete the exercise together. Discuss your answers with each other and have one member of the group record the answers. A member of the group may be asked to share the group's answers with the class.

1. How much leisure reading (reading other than your assigned reading) do you do each day?

   ____

   ____

   ____

2. If you do not already spend at least 15 minutes a day on leisure reading, when during your day could you perhaps fit in 15 minutes?

   ____

   ____

   ____

3. Most Americans are not regular users of public libraries. According to the author, those who do borrow library books read only five books a year. How often do you check out books from a public library or a college library? How often do you go to bookstores?

   ____

   ____

   ____

4. In what areas would you like to do more reading? List the types of books, magazines, and newspapers that you already enjoy reading or think you might enjoy reading.

   ____

   ____

   ____

Option

Item 5 may be completed collaboratively.

5. What is the most important overall message the writer wants the reader to understand about finding time to read? Try to answer this question in one sentence.

____

____

____

____

____

____

____

____

Selection 6-3

Economics

FROM A BEGINNER'S GUIDE TO THE WORLD ECONOMY

BY RANDY CHARLES EPPING

Prepare Yourself to Read

Directions: Do these exercises *before you read Selection 6-3.*

1. First, read and think about the title. Do you have any knowledge of the "world economy"? What approach do you think a "beginner's guide" might take?

   ____

   ____

2. Next, complete your preview by reading the following:

   Introduction (in *italics*)
   First paragraph (paragraph 1)
   Section headings
   Last paragraph (paragraph 17)

   On the basis of your preview, what three aspects of the Third World will be discussed?

   ____

   ____

Apply Comprehension Skills

Directions: Do the Annotation Practice Exercises *as you read Selection 6-3.*

Determine the topic. When you read a paragraph, ask yourself, "What or who is this about?"

Locate or formulate the main idea. As you read, ask yourself, "What is the most important point this author wants me to understand about the topic?"

Identify and list supporting details. As you read, ask yourself, "What else does the author want me to know so that I can understand the main idea completely?" List the supporting details.

A BEGINNER'S GUIDE TO THE WORLD ECONOMY

Most adults feel intimidated by the subject of economics because they know so little about it. This selection shows that the concepts of economics can be explained in a way that makes them more comprehensible. After reading it, you should have a basic understanding of the economic concept of the "Third World," the roots of Third World poverty, and what can be done to improve the situation.

What Is the Third World?

1 The term *Third World* was based on the idea that the "first" and "second" worlds were made up of the free-market and centrally planned countries with advanced industrial economies. This developed world was seen to include most of the countries of Eastern and Western Europe as well as Australia, New Zealand, Japan, the United States, and Canada.

2 The developing and relatively poor countries that are said to make up the Third World can be divided into three groups: those developing rapidly, those developing moderately, and the poorest few whose economies are not developing at all.

3 At the top of the list of Third World nations are the rapidly developing countries called Newly Industrialized Countries (NIC). Most lists of NICs include Brazil, Argentina, Hong Kong, Israel, Singapore, South Africa, South Korea, Taiwan, and Thailand. These "lucky few" are seen to be on their way to joining the ranks of the advanced economies of the world.

4 The bulk of the Third World consists of a large group of moderately developing economies that includes most of the countries in Africa, Asia, and Latin America. The most populous countries in this group are India, China, Indonesia, and Malaysia, which together comprise more than half of the world's population.

Annotation practice exercises

Directions: For each paragraph indicated, write in the spaces provided:

- Main idea sentence
- Supporting details

Doing this will help you remember main ideas and details.

Practice exercise

Main idea sentence of paragraph 1:

____

____

Supporting details:

____

____

____

____

____

____

Source: From Randy Charles Epping, *A Beginner's Guide to the World Economy,* Vintage/Random House, New York, 1992, pp. 83–86, 93–94.

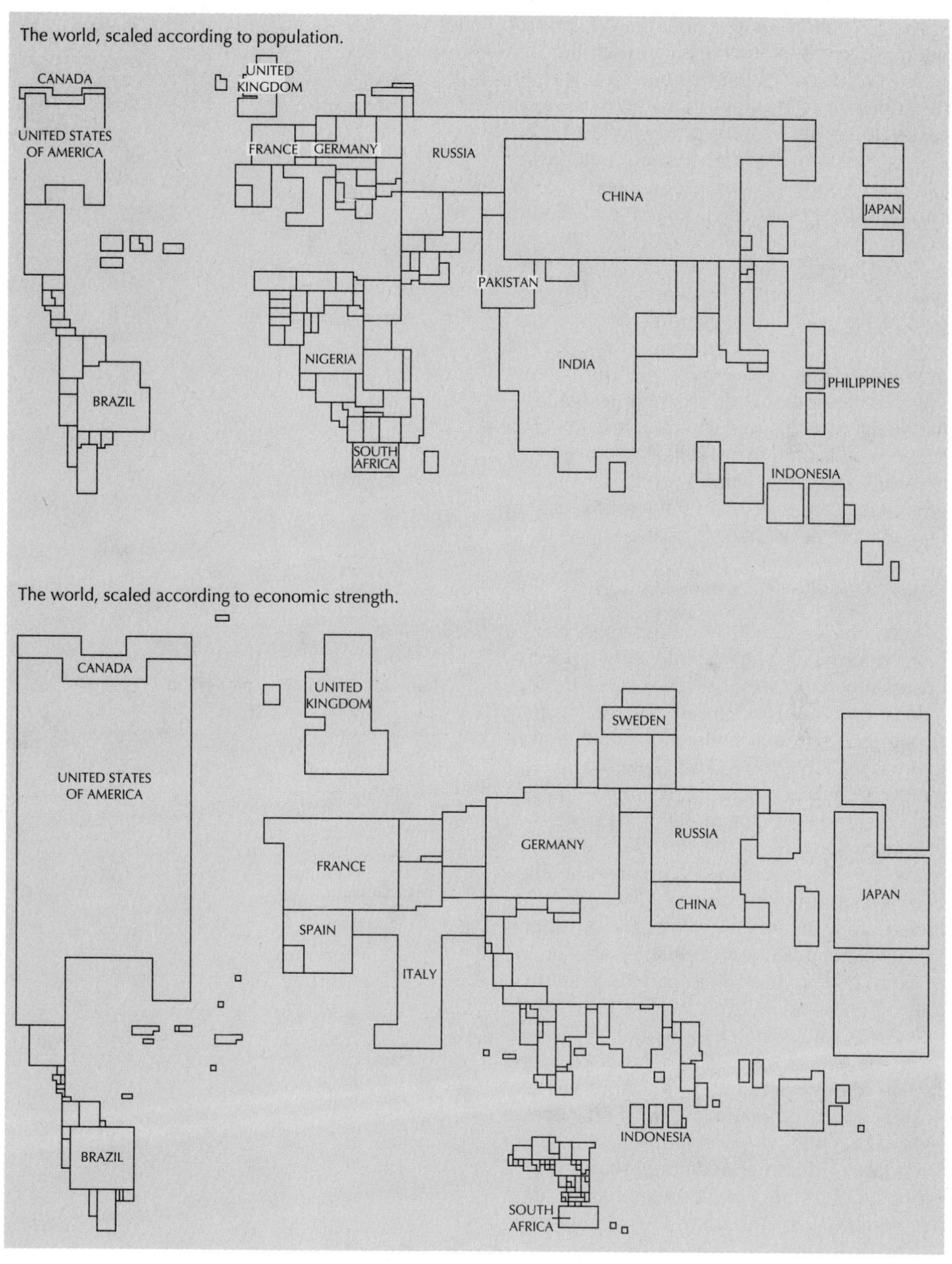
The world, scaled according to population.
CANADA
UNITED KINGDOM
UNITED STATES OF AMERICA
FRANCE
GERMANY
RUSSIA
CHINA
JAPAN
PAKISTAN
NIGERIA
INDIA
PHILIPPINES
BRAZIL
SOUTH AFRICA
INDONESIA
The world, scaled according to economic strength.
CANADA
UNITED KINGDOM
SWEDEN
UNITED STATES OF AMERICA
RUSSIA
GERMANY
FRANCE
JAPAN
CHINA
SPAIN
ITALY
BRAZIL
INDONESIA
SOUTH AFRICA

5 At the bottom of this list are the world's poorest countries, found mainly in sub-Saharan Africa, which have so few resources and so little money that it is virtually impossible for them to develop at all. In Somalia and Sudan, for example, there are essentially no natural resources on which to base economic growth. This group is sometimes called the "Fourth World."

6 Although the Third World comprises three quarters of the world's population and 90 percent of the world's population growth, it provides only 20 percent of the world's economic production. And even though the Third World holds much of the world's natural resources—including vast petroleum reserves in Latin America, Asia, and the Middle East—many raw materials from the Third World are shipped abroad for consumption in the world's wealthier and more developed countries.

What Are the Roots of Third World Poverty?

7 Economic and political misjudgment can be blamed for much of the Third World's poverty, but an important factor has also been the population explosion. This caused many developing countries to see their populations double in as little as twenty years. The growth was due mainly to lack of birth control, improved medical care, and declining mortality rates.

8 Extreme poverty in the Third World has led many parents to create ever larger families, hoping that their children could work and increase family income. But the economic opportunities were often not available, and unemployed children and their parents ended up moving into already overcrowded Third World cities in a fruitless search for work.

9 By the end of the 1980s, most Third World nations found themselves in a vicious circle of poverty and overpopulation, with no hope in sight. The flood of poor families into major Third World cities put additional strains on the economic infrastructure. Growing urban areas like Bombay, São Paulo, and Shanghai became

Practice exercise

Main idea sentence of paragraph 7:

____

____

Supporting details:

____

____

____

____

____

____

centers of glaring poverty and unemployment with extensive slums and squatter settlements ringing overgrown and polluted city centers.

10 Saddled with enormous debt payments, hyperinflation, surging populations, and mounting unemployment, many Third World countries in the late 1980s struggled just to keep their economies afloat. In many cases, with no money available for investment, even the infrastructure, such as roads and water systems, literally began to fall apart. The solution for many overburdened Third World governments was to simply increase debt in order to keep money flowing. But rampant inflation often ends up eroding most of these efforts, creating an ever-widening gap between the Third World's poorest and richest nations.

11 While many economies in Latin America, Africa, and Asia stagnated, the economies of the elite developing countries of the Pacific Rim rose to levels that rivaled Japan's in the 1960s. The success of many Third World countries in growing their way out of poverty can be traced largely to effective economic policy. By efficiently producing and exporting manufactured goods, countries such as Taiwan and Korea earned enormous amounts of money that they have been able to reinvest in their growing economies.

Practice exercise

Main idea sentence of paragraph 11:

____

____

Supporting details:

____

____

____

____

____

____

What Can Be Done to Promote Third World Development?

12 Economic growth cannot possibly solve all the problems facing the billions of poor and undernourished people in the Third World, but because of rapid population growth, their problems would almost certainly get worse without it.

13 In order to provide the basic food, clothing, and shelter for their citizens, the underdeveloped Third World countries need to stimulate their stagnating economies caught in a vicious circle of low growth and declining export earnings. One of the first steps in encouraging development would be to reduce the Third

World's debt and supply additional funds to revive their moribund economies. One such plan was formulated in the 1980s by U.S. Treasury Secretary Nicholas Brady, who called for the commercial banks to forgive part of the debt owed to them and to increase new lending. The basic goal of the Brady plan was to encourage economic growth in the Third World.

14 The Brady Plan also called upon the world's major development banks and funds, such as the World Bank and the International Monetary Fund, to provide substantial "project loans" to rebuild the infrastructure in the Third World. In addition, continued bank lending in the form of "adjustment loans" would help with the payment of interest and principal on previous loans. Basically, the Brady Plan called for a net transfer of funds back to the developing countries.

15 Another way to promote Third World development is to increase development funds provided by regional development banks with the backing of the developed countries. The Inter-American Development Bank, for example, was set up to provide low-interest loans to developing countries in the Western Hemisphere. In this way, funds from wealthy countries can be channeled to less-developed nations in the form of "development loans."

16 Wealthy creditor governments also have the option of writing off their debt, accepting that it will never be repaid. France, for example, decided in the 1980s that most of its development loans to African countries need not be repaid, in an effort to encourage further economic growth in the region.

17 In order to provide further assistance to Third World debtors, the world's wealthy countries can also work through specialized organizations such as the Lomé Convention, which channels development aid from the European Community to poor Third World countries; and the Paris Club, which helps governments of debtor nations "reschedule" or delay repayment of their loans until their economies are in better shape.

Comprehension Quiz

True or false

Directions: In the blank provided, indicate whether each statement is true or false.

______ 1. The *first* and *second worlds* are defined as the free-market countries and the centrally planned countries with advanced industrial economies.

______ 2. The first and second worlds were considered to include most of the countries of eastern and western Europe, Australia, New Zealand, Japan, the United States, and Canada.

______ 3. The author believes that the economic problems of Third World countries cannot be solved.

______ 4. The Third World can be divided into three groups: countries with rapidly developing economies, countries with moderately developing economies, and countries whose economies are not developing at all.

______ 5. The bulk of the Third World consists of a large group of moderately developing countries.

______ 6. According to the author, economic growth cannot solve all the problems faced by billions of undernourished people in the Third World.

Multiple-choice

Directions: For each item, select the best answer.

______ 7. Newly Industrialized Countries (NIC) that seem to be on their way to joining the rank of advanced economies include

a. Somalia and Sudan.
b. India, China, Indonesia, and Malaysia.
c. South Africa, South Korea, Taiwan, and Thailand.
d. all of the above.

______ 8. Third World poverty is caused by

a. economic and political misjudgment.
b. enormous debt payments.
c. overpopulation.
d. all of the above.

_____ 9. The author's position is that Third World development will require that

a. Third World countries pay off their debts completely.
b. commercial banks press hard for debt payment from Third World countries.
c. wealthy countries discontinue making development loans to Third World countries.
d. none of the above.

_____ 10. The author believes that wealthy creditor nations can aid Third World development by

a. agreeing to follow the Brady Plan.
b. channeling funds in the form of development loans.
c. writing off the debt owed by Third World countries.
d. all of the above.

Extend Your Vocabulary by Using Context Clues

Directions: ***Context clues*** are words in a sentence or paragraph that allow the reader to deduce (reason out) the meaning of an unfamiliar word. For each item in this exercise, a sentence from Selection 6-3 containing an important word *(italicized, like this)* is quoted first. Next, there is an additional sentence using the word in the same sense and providing another context clue. Use the context clues to deduce the meaning of each italicized word. *The definition you choose should make sense in both sentences.*

Pronunciation key: ă **pat** ā **pay** âr **care** ä **father** ĕ **pet** ē **be** ĭ **pit** ī **tie** îr **pier** ŏ **pot** ō **toe** ô **paw** oi **noise** ou **out** o͝o **took** o͞o **boot** ŭ **cut** yo͞o **abuse** ûr **urge** th **thin** *th* **this** hw **which** zh **vision** ə **about**

_____ 1. "The term Third World was based on the idea that the 'first' and 'second' worlds were made up of the *free-market* and centrally planned countries with advanced industrial economies."

Currently, several countries are struggling to shift from a planned economy which the government controlled to a competitive *free market.*

free market (frē mär′ kĭt) means:

a. market in which everything is free
b. economic system in which resources are allocated by private decisions rather than by the government
c. completely unregulated economy
d. economic system in which the government is free to do whatever it pleases

______ 2. "At the top of the list of Third World nations are the rapidly developing countries called Newly *Industrialized* Countries (NIC)."

Advanced technology is characteristic of highly *industrialized* countries such as Japan and Germany.

industrialized (ĭn dŭs´ trē ə līzd) means:

a. having highly developed industries that produce goods and services
b. struggling
c. controlled by industries
d. busy or hardworking

______ 3. "And even though the Third World holds much of the world's natural resources, many raw materials from the Third World are shipped abroad for *consumption* in the world's wealthier and more developed countries."

The level of energy *consumption* in the United States has risen dramatically during the twentieth century.

consumption (kən sŭmp´ shən) means:

a. use of consumer goods or serivces
b. spending
c. ingestion of food
d. debilitating illness

______ 4. "The flood of poor families into major Third World cities put additional strains on the economic *infrastructure*."

The President pledged to improve two parts of the nation's *infrastructure:* public transportation and health care.

infrastructure (ĭn´ frə strŭk chər) means:

a. government buildings
b. hospitals
c. construction in rural areas
d. basic services and facilities needed by a society

______ 5. "Saddled with enormous debt payments, *hyperinflation,* surging populations, and mounting unemployment, many Third World countries in the late 1980s struggled just to keep their economies afloat."

When Germany experienced *hyperinflation* in the 1920s, it took a wheelbarrow full of money to buy a single loaf of bread.

hyperinflation (hī pər ĭn flā´ shən) means:

a. decrease in inflation
b. rapid input of air
c. excessive rate of increase in consumer prices
d. rapid accumulation of debt

______ 6. "Saddled with enormous debt payments, hyperinflation, *surging* populations, and mounting unemployment, many Third World countries in the late 1980s struggled just to keep their economies afloat."

When the storm hit, the *surging* sea water flooded the beaches and low-lying areas of the city.

surging (sûrj´ ĭng) means:

a. decreasing
b. angry
c. increasing suddenly
d. poor

______ 7. "But *rampant* inflation often ends up eroding most of these efforts, creating an ever-widening gap between the Third World's poorest and richest nations."

In poverty-stricken areas of many large cities, crime is *rampant.*

rampant (răm´ pənt) means:

a. tolerated or accepted
b. decreasing
c. controlled
d. growing or spreading unchecked

______ 8. "While many economies in Latin America, Africa, and Asia *stagnated,* the economies of the elite developing countries of the Pacific Rim rose to levels that rivaled Japan's in the 1960s."

The aging actor's career had *stagnated* for several years, but then he suddenly achieved fame in a blockbuster movie.

stagnated (stăg´ nā təd) means:

a. rotted
b. improved
c. smelled bad
d. failed to change or develop

______ 9. "One of the first steps in encouraging development would be to reduce the Third World's debt and supply additional funds to revive their *moribund* economies."

The doctor summoned the family to the bedside of the *moribund* woman when she had only moments to live.

moribund (môr´ ə bŭnd) means:

a. abundant
b. dead
c. almost at the point of death
d. ill

_____ 10. "Wealthy *creditor* governments also have the option of writing off their debt, accepting that it will never be repaid."

Because the Newtons charged too many purchases on their credit cards and were unable to pay their debts, they were hounded by one *creditor* after another.

creditor (krĕd´ ĭ tər) means:

a. one to whom money is owed
b. one who deserves financial credit
c. one who is trustworthy
d. one who owes money

Respond in Writing

Directions: Refer to Selection 6-3 as necessary to answer these essay-type items.

Option for collaboration: For some of the "Respond in Writing" exercises, your instructor may prefer that you work collaboratively, that is, with other students. These exercises are identified in the margin. *If your instructor directs you to work collaboratively on any of these items,* form groups of three or four classmates to complete the exercise together. Discuss your answers with each other and have one member of the group record the answers. A member of the group may be asked to share the group's answers with the class.

1. The author presents three essential questions that he expects you to be able to answer after you have read this selection. In the spaces below and on the following page, write a complete answer to each question.

   What is the Third World?

   (Note: Before reading this selection, you may not have known exactly what the *Third World* is. Now that you have read the selection, define this term in your own words.)

   ____

   ____

   ____

   ____

   ____

What are the roots of Third World poverty?

What can be done to promote Third World development?

Option

Item 2 may be completed collaboratively.

2. Could the United States ever become a Third World country? (In other words, are there circumstances that could cause a "first" or "second" world country to become a Third World country?) Explain your answer.

Option

Item 3 may be completed collaboratively.

3. Third World countries fall into three categories (Newly Industrialized Countries, moderately developed countries, and the world's poorest countries—"fourth world" countries). What would a Third World country have to do to become a "first" or "second" world country? Is there anything a "fourth world" country could do to improve its situation?

Option

Item 4 may be completed collaboratively.

4. What is the most important overall message the writer wants the reader to understand about the Third World and its economy? Try to answer this question in one sentence.

CHAPTER 7

RECOGNIZING AUTHORS' WRITING PATTERNS

IN THIS CHAPTER YOU WILL LEARN THE ANSWERS TO THESE QUESTIONS:

What is meant by an author's writing pattern?

Why is it helpful to be aware of writing patterns?

How can I recognize list, sequence, definition, comparison-contrast, and cause-effect patterns when I read?

What are mixed patterns?

How can I recognize these patterns?

CHAPTER 7 CONTENTS

If you don't know where you're going, you may end up somewhere else.

PATTERNS OF WRITING

Key term

Writing patterns: Ways authors organize and present their ideas.

In this chapter you will learn another skill to help you improve your reading comprehension: recognizing authors' patterns of writing. ***Writing patterns*** are authors' ways of organizing information and presenting it logically in paragraphs and longer passages. You may also hear writing patterns referred to as *patterns of organization, patterns of development, rhetorical patterns,* and *thinking patterns.* These are all names for the same thing.

What Patterns Do Writers Use?

All of us use certain patterns to organize our thoughts. When people write, they use these same patterns to organize information in ways that seem logical to them. If you can identify the pattern a writer is using and "think along" with the author as you read, then you will find it easier to comprehend what he or she is saying. The specific pattern an author uses depends on the relationship among the ideas he or she wants to emphasize. In this chapter you will be introduced to five common writing patterns used by textbook authors. These patterns are:

- List
- Sequence
- Definition
- Comparison-contrast
- Cause-effect

You will also be introduced to what are called *mixed patterns:* passages that contain more than one pattern.

It is important for you to understand that, as mentioned above, the patterns that authors use are the same thinking patterns that you use every day. The box on page 308 gives examples of how college students use these patterns every day in typical comments they make. Although you use these patterns yourself when you speak or write, you still may not be aware of them when you read. This chapter will show you how to recognize the patterns when you read.

Examples of Thinking Patterns in Everyday Comments

"I'm taking four courses this semester: history, psychology, reading, and math." ***(list)***

"I have a history paper due on Tuesday, a math quiz on Thursday, a vocabulary quiz in reading on Friday morning, and a psychology test Friday afternoon!" ***(sequence)***

"To me, success means always giving your best effort, even if the results aren't perfect." ***(definition)***

"Psychology focuses on the behavior of the individual, but sociology focuses on human behavior in groups." ***(comparison-contrast)***

"When I stick to my study schedule, I learn more, do better on tests, and feel less stress." ***(cause-effect)***

Why Is Recognizing Writing Patterns Important?

Recognizing authors' writing patterns as you read provides several advantages:

- *Comprehension.* You will comprehend more because you will be able to follow the writer's ideas more accurately and more efficiently.
- *Prediction.* As soon as you identify a pattern, you can make predictions about what is likely to come next in a paragraph. As you learned in Chapter 2, effective readers are active readers who make logical predictions as they read.
- *Memorization.* You can memorize information more efficiently when you understand the way it is organized. If you can grasp an author's pattern of organization, you will not only learn the information more quickly but also retain it more easily.
- *Improvement in your own writing.* Using these patterns yourself will enable you to write better, more organized paragraphs. For example, you can write better answers on essay tests when you use appropriate patterns to organize the information.

RECOGNIZING AUTHORS' WRITING PATTERNS

The five common writing patterns are described below, with textbook excerpts that illustrate each pattern. As you may already know, every pattern has certain words and phrases that are associated with it and serve as signals of it. Moreover, the main idea sentence often contains clues about which pattern is being used. As you read, ask yourself, "What pattern did the author use to organize the main idea and supporting details?"

List Pattern

Key term

List pattern: Series of items in no particular order, since order is unimportant.

As its name indicates, the ***list pattern*** (sometimes called *listing pattern*) presents a series, or list, of items. The order of the items is not important. If the items in the paragraph were rearranged, it would not matter.

Clues in a paragraph that typically indicate a listing pattern are *and, also, another, moreover, in addition,* and words such as *first, second, third, fourth, finally.* Sometimes authors use numbers (1, 2, 3) or letters *(a, b, c)*, even though the order is not important. Watch for words or numbers that announce categories *(two types, five ways, several kinds*). Sometimes bullets (•) or asterisks (*) are used to set off individual items in a list. Their purpose is to ensure that the reader will notice each separate item as well as the total number of items. It is important to remember that your task is to identify *all* the items in the list.

Here is a paragraph from an economics textbook. The topic is *the financing of corporate activity.* The first sentence states the main idea: *Generally speaking, corporations finance their activity in three different ways.* The authors have listed details that help you understand more about this main idea. Notice that these details are in no special order. As you read this paragraph, ask yourself, "What are the *three different ways* that corporations finance their activity?"

> Generally speaking, corporations finance their activity in three different ways. First, a very large portion of a corporation's activity is financed internally out of undistributed corporate profits. Second, like individuals or unincorporated businesses, corporations may borrow from financial institutions. For example, a small corporation which wants to build a new plant or warehouse may obtain the funds from a commercial bank, a savings and loan institution, or an insurance company. Also, unique to corporations, common stocks and bonds can be issued.
>
> *Source:* Campbell McConnell and Stanley Brue, *Economics: Principles, Problems, and Policies,* McGraw-Hill, New York, 1990, p. 110.

Annotate

Go back to the excerpt. Underline or highlight the words that signal a list. Then number each supporting detail.

In this paragraph, the authors use the phrase *three different ways* and the clue words *first, second, also* to signal that the reader should expect a list of three supporting details: three ways of financing corporate activities. The order in which the items are listed is not important. What is important is that there are three different ways, and what those ways are.

The next excerpt is from a health and fitness textbook. It illustrates the listing pattern in a very obvious way: the items in the list are numbered. The topic of the paragraph is *signs of alcoholism,* and its implied main idea (to be formulated by the reader) is, *The diagnosis of alcoholism is often imprecise and difficult for nonprofessionals to make, but there are certain changes in behavior that can warn of possible alcoholism.* On the basis of the topic and the main idea, what do you predict will be listed?

SIGNS OF ALCOHOLISM

The diagnosis of alcoholism is not something that can be precise, and it is often difficult for nonprofessionals to make. The disease carries such a stigma that the alcoholic, friends, and family often postpone seeking treatment. Meanwhile, it is not unusual for the alcoholic to deny the problem and rationalize continued drinking. Certain changes in behavior that warn of possible alcoholism include:

1. Surreptitious, secretive drinking
2. Morning drinking (unless that behavior is not unusual in the person's peer group)
3. Repeated, conscious attempts at abstinence
4. Blatant, indiscriminate use of alcohol
5. Changing beverages in an attempt to control drinking
6. Having five or more drinks daily
7. Having two or more blackouts while drinking

Source: Martin Levy, Mark Dignan, and Janet Shirreffs, *Targeting Wellness: The Core,* McGraw-Hill, New York, 1992, p. 251. Reproduced with permission of McGraw-Hill.

Annotate

Go back to the excerpt. Underline or highlight the clues that signal a list.

At the end of this paragraph, the list of warnings of possible alcoholism is actually set off from the text, indicated by a colon (:) and announced by the phrase *Certain changes in behavior that warn of possible alcoholism include.* The topic *signs of alcoholism* in the heading and the words *certain changes* in the main idea sentence help readers predict that a list will be given. The authors list seven supporting details (behavioral changes) and number these details even though they are not in any particular order. The numbers are included to make sure that the reader notices each separate item. (Numbering items in a list is referred to as *enumeration.*)

Sequence Pattern

Key term

Sequence pattern: List of items in a specific, important order.

The ***sequence pattern*** presents a list of items in a *certain specific order* because the order is important. The sequence pattern is a type of list, but it differs from a simple list because the order of the items is significant. A very common type of sequence is based on occurrence of events in time, and therefore a sequence pattern is often called *time order* or *chronological order.* Sets of directions are examples of sequences that students encounter daily.

Words that signal a sequence pattern include *first, second, third, then, next, finally.* Words that refer to time, such as dates and phrases like *during the eighteenth century* or *in the last decade,* may also signal sequences. Watch also for enumerations (1, 2, 3, etc.), letters (*a, b, c,* etc.), and signal words such as *steps, stages, phases, progression,* and *series.*

Below is an excerpt in which authors use a sequence pattern to show the order in which certain events occur. The topic of this paragraph is *the alcohol continuum.* Read the paragraph and notice the list of details and the *order* in which they are given.

THE ALCOHOL CONTINUUM

Alcoholism is a progressive disease that develops as a series of stages through which any drinker may pass. At one end of the spectrum is occasional and moderate social drinking with family or friends on special occasions. At the other end is long-term, frequent, uncontrollable drinking with severe physical, psychological, and social complications. The full continuum can be summarized as follows:

1. **Occasional drinker** drinks in small quantities only on special occasions.
2. **Light drinker** drinks regularly in small and nonintoxicating quantities.
3. **Social drinker** drinks regularly in moderate and nonintoxicating quantities.
4. **Problem drinker** drinks to intoxication with no pattern to episodes, gets drunk without intending to or realizing it.
5. **Binge drinker** drinks heavily in recurrent episodes, often brought on by disturbances in work, home, or social life.
6. **Excessive drinker** experiences frequent episodes of uncontrollable drinking affecting work, family, and social relationships.
7. **Chronic alcoholic** is in serious trouble from long-term, frequent, and uncontrollable drinking; experiences physical complications including organic dysfunction, tolerance, and dependence; and develops severe work, home, and social problems.

Source: Martin Levy, Mark Dignan, and Janet Shirreffs, *Targeting Wellness: The Core,* McGraw-Hill, New York, 1992, pp. 250–256.

Annotate

Go back to the excerpt. Underline or highlight the clues that signal a sequence.

The details in this paragraph are numbered, announced by a colon, and clearly listed after the phrase *can be summarized as follows.* But there are other clues indicating that a sequence pattern is being used: the words *progressive disease, continuum, series of stages,* and *spectrum.* In this paragraph, the order of the information is obviously important.

Now read this excerpt from a music textbook, in which the author also uses the sequence pattern. Notice the dates that are associated with important events in the Beatles' career.

THE BEATLES

The Beatles—the singer-guitarists Paul McCartney, John Lennon, and George Harrison, and the drummer Ringo Starr—have been the most influential performing group in the history of rock. Their music, hairstyle, dress, and lifestyle were imitated all over the world, resulting in a phenomenon known as Beatlemania. All four Beatles were born during the early 1940s in Liverpool, England, and dropped out of school in their teens to devote themselves to rock. Lennon and McCartney, the main songwriters of the group, began working together in 1956 and were joined by Harrison about two years later. In 1962 Ringo Starr became their new drummer. The group gained experience by performing in Hamburg, Germany, and in Liverpool, a port to which sailors brought the latest American rock, rhythm-and-blues, and country-and-western records. In 1961, the Beatles made their first record, and by 1963 they were England's top rock group. In 1964, they triumphed in the United States, breaking attendance records everywhere and dominating the record market. Audiences often became hysterical, and the police had to protect the Beatles from their fans. Beatle dolls, wigs, sweatshirts, and jackets flooded the market. Along with a steady flow of successful records, the Beatles made several hit movies: *A Hard Day's Night, Help!* and *Yellow Submarine.*

Source: Roger Kamien, *Music: An Appreciation,* 5th ed., McGraw-Hill, New York, 1992, p. 608.

Annotate

Go back to the excerpt. Underline or highlight the clues that signal a sequence.

The details supporting the main idea—that the Beatles were the most influential group in the history of rock—are given in chronological order: the order in which they occurred. The author uses dates throughout the paragraph to tell when each important event occurred. In addition, the phrases *were born during the early 1940s* and *dropped out of school in their teens* indicate the sequence of events in the Beatles' history.

Definition Pattern

Key Term

Definition pattern: Pattern presenting the meaning of an important term discussed throughout a passage.

The ***definition pattern*** presents the meaning of an important term that is discussed throughout the passage. The details in the rest of the paragraph discuss or illustrate the term.

Definitions are easy to identify because the terms being defined often appear in **bold print** or *italics.* Moreover, they are typically introduced by signal words: *is, is defined as, means, is known as, refers to, the term, is called,* and so forth.

Sometimes a synonym (a word or phrase with the same meaning as the term) will be signaled by the word *or, in other words,* or *that is.* For example, in the sentence, "Many women perceive a *glass ceiling,* or barrier of subtle discrimination, that keeps them from the top position in business," the word *or* introduces words *(barrier of subtle discrimination)* that mean the same thing as *glass ceiling.*

Also, definitions can be signaled by certain punctuation marks. All the examples below define *anorexia nervosa.* Use the punctuation clues to help you find the definition.

- *Commas* (,)

  Anorexia nervosa, an eating disorder that can lead to starvation, occurs most often in teenage girls.

  Teenage girls are the most common victims of *anorexia nervosa,* an eating disorder that can lead to starvation.
- *Parentheses* ( )

  Anorexia nervosa (an eating disorder that can lead to starvation) occurs most often in teenage girls.
- *Brackets* [ ]

  Anorexia nervosa [an eating disorder than can lead to starvation] occurs most often in teenage girls.
- *Dashes* (—)

  Anorexia nervosa—an eating disorder that can lead to starvation—occurs most often in teenage girls.
- *Colon* (:)

  An illness affecting primarily teenage girls is *anorexia nervosa:* an eating disorder that can lead to starvation.

Here is a paragraph from a business textbook in which the authors define two forms of *sexual harassment* in the workplace. Notice that the entire paragraphs defines *sexual harassment.*

> Another sensitive issue concerning primarily women in the workplace is **sexual harassment.** As defined by the Equal Employment Opportunity Commission, sexual harassment takes two forms: the obvious request for sexual favors with an implicit reward or punishment related to work, and the more subtle creation of sexist environment in which employees are made to feel uncomfortable by off-color jokes, lewd remarks, and posturing.

Source: David Rachman, Michael Mescon, Courtland Bovée, and John Thill, *Business Today,* McGraw-Hill, New York, 1993, p. 110. Reproduced with permission of McGraw-Hill.

Annotate

Go back to the excerpt. Underline or highlight the clues that signal a definition.

In this paragraph, the phrases *as defined by* and *takes two forms* signal to the reader that there are two distinct definitions of sexual harassment in the workplace. Notice that a colon (:) announces the two definitions. Notice also that although the term *sexual harassment* appears in the first sentence, it is actually defined in the following sentence.

Below is an excerpt from a psychology textbook in which the author presents a definition as the main idea and then goes on to explain it more fully by giving an example. The term the author is defining is the *foot-in-the-door principle.*

FOOT-IN-THE-DOOR PRINCIPLE

People who sell door-to-door have long recognized that once they get a foot in the door, a sale is almost a sure thing. To state the **foot-in-the-door principle** more formally, a person who agrees to a small request is later more likely to comply with a larger demand. Evidence suggests, for instance, that if someone asked you to put a large, ugly sign in your front yard to promote safe driving, you would refuse. If, however, you had first agreed to put a small sign in your window, you would later be much more likely to allow the big sign to be placed in your yard.

Source: Dennis Coon, *Essentials of Psychology,* 5th ed., West, St. Paul., Minn., 1991, p. 627.

Annotate

Go back to the excerpt. Underline or highlight the clues that signal a definition.

In this paragraph the author first gives the definition of the foot-in-the-door principle in the main idea: *the tendency for a person who has first complied with a small request to be more likely later to fulfill a larger request.* To announce to the reader that the foot-in-the-door effect is being defined precisely, the author uses the phrase *To state the* ***foot-in-the-door*** *principle more formally.* Did you notice that the definition is set off by a comma, and that the important term appears in the heading and in bold print within the paragraph?

Comparison-Contrast Pattern

Key term

Comparison-contrast pattern: Pattern used to present similarities (comparisons), differences (contrasts), or both.

Often writers want to emphasize comparisons and contrasts. A *comparison* shows how two or more things are similar or alike. A *contrast* points out the differences between them. The ***comparison-contrast pattern*** presents similarities (comparisons), differences (contrasts), or both.

To signal comparisons, authors use the words *similarly, likewise, both, same,* and *also.* To signal contrasts, authors use clues such as *on the other hand, in contrast, however, while, whereas, although, nevertheless, different, unlike,* and *some . . . others.* Contrasts are also signaled by words in a paragraph that have opposite meanings, such as *advantages* and *disadvantages* or *assets* and *liabilities.*

In the following excerpt from an art textbook, the author presents important information about the advantages and disadvantages of the very slow rate at which oil paint dries. Read the paragraph to determine what she says about the positive and negative aspects of this characteristic.

The outstanding characteristic of oil paint is that it dries very slowly. This creates both advantages and disadvantages for the artist. On the plus side, it means that colors can be blended very subtly, layers of paint can be applied on top of other layers with little danger of separating or cracking, and the artist can rework sections of the painting almost indefinitely. This same assest becomes a liability when the artist is pressed for time—perhaps when an exhibition has been scheduled. Oil paint dries so *very* slowly that it may be weeks or months before the painting has truly "set." Another great advantage of oil is that it can be worked in an almost infinite range of consistencies, from very thick to very thin. The German Expressionist painter Oskar Kokoschka often used thick oil paints straight from the tube, occasionally squeezing them directly on the canvas without a brush. He could then mold and shape the thick paint with a palette knife (a spatula-shaped tool) to create actual three-dimensional depth on the canvas.

Source: Rita Gilbert, *Living with Art,* 3d ed., McGraw-Hill, New York, 1992, p. 200.

Annotate

Go back to the excerpt. Underline or highlight the clues that signal a comparison-contrast pattern.

In this paragraph, *advantages, disadvantages, on the plus side, asset,* and *liability* are clues or signals that the author is presenting both the positive and negative aspects of the slow rate at which oil paint dries.

Here is another paragraph from the same art textbook, which also uses the comparison-contrast pattern. (It appears in Selection 3-2 of *Opening Doors.*) Notice that the author presents similarities and differences between a Buddhist shrine and a medieval Christian cathedral.

Buddhist shrines—the word *stupa* means "shrine"—often housed relics of the Buddha, and worship rituals called for circumambulation ("walking around") of the stupa. Thus, on the outside of the Great Stupa of Sanchi we see a railed pathway, where pilgrims could take the ritual clockwise walk following the Path of Life around the World Mountain. Elsewhere the stupa is embellished richly with carvings and sculpture evoking scenes from the Buddha's life. Every part of the stupa is geared to the pursuit of personal enlightenment and transcendence. If the Buddhist temple is dedicated to private worship, then its extreme opposite can be found in the total encompassment of a community religious exerience: the medieval Christian cathedral. And the supreme example of that ideal is the Cathedral of Notre Dame de Chartres, in France. Chartres Cathedral was built, rebuilt, and modified over a period of several hundred years, but the basic structure, which is in the Gothic style, was established in the 13th century. A cathedral—as opposed to a church—is the bishop's domain and therefore is always in a town or a city. This one fact is crucial to understanding the nature of Chartres and the role it played in the people's lives.

Source: Rita Gilbert, *Living with Art,* 3d ed., McGraw-Hill, New York, 1992, pp. 64–65.

Annotate

Go back to the excerpt. Underline or highlight the clues that signal a comparison-contrast pattern.

In the middle of this passage, the author signals the major difference she is presenting between the Great Stupa and Chartres Cathedral by the words *extreme opposite.* She wants the reader to understand that these two structures were built to serve different religious purposes. More specifically, she wants the reader to understand that Buddhist stupas were designed for *personal enlightenment and private worship,* whereas Christian cathedrals were designed for a *community religious experience.* In this passage, the words *personal* and *private* are used in contrast to *community.* (Incidentally, there is an additional contrast in this excerpt. Near the end of the excerpt, a distinction is made between a cathedral and a church. The phrase *as opposed to* points up the difference.)

Cause-Effect Pattern

Key term

Cause-effect pattern: Pattern presenting reasons for (causes of) events or conditions and results (effects) of events or conditions.

The ***cause-effect pattern*** presents *reasons for* (causes of) events or conditions and *results* (effects) of events or conditions. Authors often use these words to indicate a cause: *because, the reasons, causes, reasons why, is due to, is caused by.* These words are often used to indicate an effect: *therefore, consequently, thus, as a consequence, led to, the results, as a result, the effect was, resulted in.*

The following excerpt from a health textbook uses the cause-effect pattern. Its topic is *lung cancer and the way an individual smokes.* The verb *affects* and the phrase *depending on* signal the cause-effect pattern.

> The *way* an individual smokes affects the chances of developing lung cancer. The risk increases depending on how many cigarettes are smoked each day, how deeply the smoker inhales, and how much tar and nicotine are contained in the cigarettes. . . . People who started smoking early in their lives are also at greater risk than those who have only smoked for a few years.

Source: Martin Levy, Mark Dignan, and Janet Shirreffs, *Targeting Wellness: The Core,* McGraw-Hill, New York, 1992, p. 261. Reproduced with permission of McGraw-Hill.

Annotate

Go back to the excerpt. Underline or highlight the clues that signal a cause-effect pattern.

In this paragraph, the authors present four *causes* that contribute to one effect, the smoker's increased risk of lung cancer: (1) how many cigarettes are smoked daily, (2) how deeply the smoker inhales, (3) the amount of tar and nicotine in the cigarettes, and (4) the age at which a person starts smoking. (Notice that three causes are mentioned in a single sentence.)

Here is an excerpt from a physics textbook which uses the cause-effect pattern. It explains *why* many people enjoy physics.

MANY PEOPLE ENJOY PHYSICS. WHY?

> There are several reasons physicists and many of those who study physics find it enjoyable. First, it is a joy to find out how the world behaves. Knowledge of the laws of nature allows us to look on the world with a fuller appreciation of its beauty and wonder. Second, we all enjoy discovering something new. Scientists take great satisfaction in exposing a facet of nature that was previously not seen or perhaps not understood. Imagine how Columbus must have felt when he sighted America. Scientists share a similar excitement when their work results in the discovery of a new aspect of nature. Fortunately, it seems that the more we discover about nature, the more there is to discover. The excitement of discovery drives science forward. Third, most of us enjoy the successful completion of a demanding task. That is why people of all ages work puzzles. Each question or problem in science is a new puzzle to be solved. We enjoy the satisfaction of success. Fourth, science benefits humanity. A substantial fraction of those who embark on scientific work do so because they wish to contribute to the progress of civilization. Call it idealistic, perhaps, but ask yourself what medical tools we would have today without the work of countless scientists in physics, chemistry, biology, and the re-

lated sciences. Our present civilization is heavily indebted not only to those in science but also to those in the general populace who know enough about science to support its progress.

Source: Frederick J. Bueche, *Principles of Physics,* 5th ed., McGraw-Hill, New York, 1988, p. 3. Reproduced with permission of McGraw-Hill.

Annotate

Go back to the excerpt. Underline or highlight the clues that signal a cause-effect pattern.

In the main idea sentence (the first sentence), this author uses the clue words *several reasons.* Then he uses *first, second, third,* and *fourth* to announce the four reasons which explain his main idea: *There are several reasons physicists and many of those who study physics find it enjoyable.* Even the word *Why?* in the title tells readers to expect a list of reasons (causes).

In the following excerpt from a business textbook, the authors present several effects (results) of employee assistance programs. This paragraph does not contain signal words such as *results* or *effects.* Instead, the authors assume that the reader will understand the relationship between these programs and their results. The phrase *Such programs have been reported to . . .* implies that employee assistance programs have certain effects. Read the paragraph and notice the four effects the authors present.

A number of companies have also instituted **employee assistance programs** (EAPs) for employees with personal problems, especially drug or alcohol dependence. Such programs have been reported (on the average) to reduce absenteeism by 66 percent, health-care costs by 86 percent, sickness benefits by 33 percent, and work-related accidents by 65 percent. Participation in EAPs is voluntary and confidential. Employees are given in-house counseling or are referred to outside therapists or treatment programs.

Source: David Rachman, Michael Mescon, Courtland Bovée, and John Thill, *Business Today,* McGraw-Hill, New York, 1993, pp. 283–284. Reproduced with permission of McGraw-Hill.

Annotate

Go back to the excerpt. Underline or highlight the clues that signal a cause-effect pattern.

In a single sentence, these authors present four beneficial effects of employee assistance programs: reductions in (1) absenteeism, (2) costs of health care, (3) costs of sickness benefits, and (4) work-related accidents. (Notice that all four effects are given in a single sentence.)

Note: How to avoid seeing everything as a "list"

When you are first learning about authors' writing patterns, you may mistakenly view every paragraph as having a "list pattern," since the same clue words can signal more than one pattern. For example, you may have noticed that some of the cause-effect clue words in the excerpt on physics (page 316) are the same clue words that could signal a simple list. The passage about physics, however, uses the clue words *first, second, third,* and *fourth* to present a *list of reasons.* Since a cause-effect relationship is what the author wants to emphasize, this excerpt should be considered to have a cause-effect pattern.

Whenever you encounter what appears to be a list, ask yourself, "a list of *what?*" Your answer should help you realize if the author is using one of the other patterns instead. For instance, if your answer is "a list of *events in a particular order,*" then the paragraph has a sequence pattern. If your answer is "a list of *similarities* or *differences,*" the paragraph has a comparison-contrast pattern. If your answer is "a list of *causes, reasons,* or *results,*" then the paragraph has a cause-effect pattern. View a paragraph as having a list pattern only when you are certain that no other pattern can be used to describe the way the ideas are organized.

Mixed Patterns

Key term

Mixed pattern: Combination of two or more writing patterns.

Each of the textbook excerpts presented so far in this chapter has been used to illustrate only one writing pattern, but you should be aware that authors frequently use two or more of the patterns at the same time. Such a combination is called a ***mixed pattern.***

Below is an example of a *mixed pattern in a single paragraph.* This excerpt, from a health and fitness textbook, uses both the definition pattern and the cause-effect pattern. The paragraph presents a definition of passive smoking, and it *also* presents effects of passive smoking.

PASSIVE SMOKING AND THE RIGHTS OF NONSMOKERS

Reports from the U.S. surgeon general's office suggest that tobacco smoke in enclosed indoor areas is an important air pollution problem. This has led to the controversy about **passive smoking**—the breathing in of air polluted by the second-hand tobacco smoke of others. Carbon monoxide levels of sidestream smoke (smoke from the burning end of a cigarette) reach a dangerously high level. True, the smoke can be greatly diluted in freely circulating air, but the 1 to 5 percent carbon monoxide levels attained in smoke-filled rooms can be sufficient to harm the health of people with chronic bronchitis, other lung disease, or cardiovascular disease. Nicotine also builds up in the blood of nonsmokers exposed to cigarette smoke hour after hour. It has been estimated that passive smoking can give nonsmokers the equivalent in carbon monoxide and nicotine of one to ten cigarettes per day.

Source: Martin Levy, Mark Dignan, and Janet Shirreffs, *Targeting Wellness: The Core,* McGraw-Hill, New York, 1992, pp. 262–263. Reproduced with permission of McGraw-Hill.

Annotate

Go back to the excerpt. Underline or highlight the clues that signal the two patterns in the mixed pattern.

In this paragraph, the bold print and the dashes **(passive smoking—)** are clues that the authors are defining a term. Although the authors do not use clue words that signal cause-effect, they are presenting a cause-effect relationship: passive smoking is the cause of a number of health problems. Therefore, this paragraph can be described as a mixed pattern because it includes both a definition *and* a cause-effect relationship.

Here is an excerpt from a textbook on American government that is an example of a *mixed pattern in a longer passage.* It consists of four paragraphs in which the author uses three patterns. In the first paragraph, the author presents a *definition* of regionalism (the tendency of people in a particular geographic area to defend their interests against those of people in other geographic areas). In the second paragraph, the author uses the *comparison-contrast* pattern to emphasize differences between two regions of the United States, the "Sunbelt" and the "Frostbelt." In the third paragraph, the author uses the *cause-effect* pattern to explain the conflict over federal aid that resulted from a shift of economic influence to the Sunbelt. In the fourth paragraph, the author again uses a *cause-effect* pattern to explain a shift of political influence (an increased number of seats in Congress) from the northeast and midwest (Frostbelt) to the southern and western states (Sunbelt). (Although the passage includes several references to time—*past two decades, in the first half of the 1980s,* etc.—the author is not emphasizing a sequence relationship.)

THE RESURGENCE OF REGIONALISM

An important characteristic of intergovernmental politics today is **regionalism,** the tendency of people in a particular geographic area to defend their interests against those of people in other geographic areas. Historic regionalism pitted North against South, as we saw, for example, in examining the conflicts at the Constitutional Convention. One central regional issue today is the competition between Sunbelt and Frostbelt for federal moneys.

The so-called **Sunbelt** region (the states of the South and Southwest) has experienced significant increases in population and economic development over the past two decades. During the same time, the Northeastern and Midwestern states of the so-called **Frostbelt** saw both their population and their economic growth lag behind that of the nation at large. In the first half of the 1980s, the North Central region actually *lost* more jobs than it gained. Southwestern oil states such as Texas and Oklahoma were also hit hard in the middle 1980s by the collapse of the oil boom. Nevertheless, the Sunbelt has grown in economic influence relative to the rest of the nation.

This shift of economic influence from the Frostbelt to the Sunbelt has prompted a sharp conflict between these regions in seeking greater amounts of federal aid. Frostbelt leaders have charged that their region pays more income taxes into the federal treasury than comes back in the form of grants-in-aid, and they subsequently have pressured Congress to rewrite funding formulas so that they will be more favorable to the Frostbelt. Faced with this challenge, Sunbelt leaders have also begun to lobby Washington for their version of how federal aid ought to be distributed.

The rise of the South and the West is seen not only in economic influence but in political influence as well. The reapportionment of congressional seats after the 1990 census saw a dramatic shift of congressional seats from the Northeast and Midwest to fast-growing Southern and Western states such as Florida and California.

Source: John Harrigan, *Politics and the American Future,* McGraw-Hill, New York, 1992, pp. 72–73. Reproduced with permission of McGraw-Hill.

Annotate

Go back to the excerpt. Underline or highlight the clues that signal the three patterns in the mixed pattern.

Here is another excerpt—from a business textbook—that illustrates the use of a mixed pattern in longer passage. In this excerpt, which discusses *crisis management,* the authors have used four patterns: *definition, cause-effect, comparison-contrast,* and *sequence.* As you read this excerpt, look for clue words that indicate which pattern is being used in each paragraph.

CRISIS MANAGEMENT

The most important goal of any business is to survive. But any number of problems may arise, some threatening the very existence of the company. An ugly fight for control of a company, a product failure (such as Microsoft's first two versions of the Windows program), breakdowns in an organization's routine operations (as a result of fire, for example)—any surprising event may develop into a serious and crippling crisis. **Crisis management,** the handling of such unusual and serious problems, goes a long way toward determining the company's future. For example, Johnson & Johnson is widely thought to have done a good job of coping with the two Tylenol poisoning scares, moving quickly to remove capsules from the shelves and to publicize the problem. As a result, the effects of the first scare had been almost completely overcome by the time the second hit.

In contrast, H.J. Heinz so badly handled a crisis that the future of its Canadian subsidiary of StarKist Foods was in doubt. StarKist was accused of shipping 1 millions cans of "rancid and decomposing" tuna, which were first rejected by Canadian inspectors but later passed by a high government official. Under the prodding of Canadian news media, the prime minister finally had the tainted tuna seized. All along, Heinz and StarKist maintained a story silence over "Tunagate," and their mishandling of the crisis cost plenty: The company that once controlled half of the Canadian tuna market watched its revenues fall 90 percent. After being closed for almost three years, the StarKist plant reopened in August 1988. Due to the economic downturn in 1989, StarKist closed the plant for good.

Companies that experience a crisis for which they are ill prepared seem to make a series of mistakes. First, warnings about possible problems are ignored at one or several management levels. Then the crisis hits. Under pressure, the company does the worst thing it could do: It denies the severity of the problem or it denies its own role in the problem. Finally, when the company is forced to face reality, it takes hasty, poorly-conceived action.

A better way does exist. Management experts caution that the first 24 hours of a crisis are critical. The first move is to explain the problem—both to the public and to the company's employees. Simultaneously, the offending product is removed from store shelves, and the offending action is stopped, or the source of the problem (whatever it is) is brought under control to the extent possible.

Source: David Rachman, Michael Mescon, Courtland Bovée, and John Thill, *Business Today,* McGraw-Hill, New York, 1993, pp. 169–170. Reproduced with permission of McGraw-Hill.

Annotate

Go back to the excerpt. Underline or highlight the clues that signal the four patterns in the mixed pattern.

STANDARDIZED READING TESTS: WRITING PATTERNS

College students may be required to take standardized reading tests as part of an overall assessment program, in a reading course, or as part of a state-mandated "basic skills" test. A standardized reading test typically consists of a series of passages followed by multiple-choice questions, to be completed within a specified time limit.

Questions about organization of material in a passage may be worded in several different ways. Sometimes you are asked to identify the *type* of pattern; sometimes you are asked about specific *information* that has been listed, presented in a sequence, defined, compared or contrasted, or discussed in terms of causes and effects.

Here are some examples of typical wording of questions and possible answer choices about authors' patterns of organization.

> Which of the following organization patterns does the author use to present information in this passage?
>
> In this passage the author presents . . . (*a comparison, a sequence of events,* etc.)
>
> How is the information in the selection organized?
>
> In this passage, what is compared with . . . ?
>
> According to this passage, what are effects of . . . ?
>
> This passage explains *(two, three, four)* similarities between . . .
>
> Which of the following is an effect of . . . ?
>
> Paragraph 3 contrasts childhood aggression with . . .
>
> The second step in the process of carbon filtration is . . .

To answer questions about organization, watch for clue words that signal each of the patterns. When you find clue words in a passage, *circle them* so that you can clearly see relationships among the ideas presented. You will also find it helpful to *number* items in lists and sequences, causes and effects, and similarities and differences so that you do not overlook any of them. Remember, too, that words in a stated main idea sentence may suggest a pattern (such words include *ways, factors, causes, reasons, series, stages, differences, similarities,* etc.)

DEVELOPING CHAPTER REVIEW CARDS

Review cards, or *summary cards,* are an excellent study tool. They are a way to select, organize, and review the most important information in a textbook chapter. The process of creating review cards helps you organize information in a meaningful way and, at the same time, transfer it into long-term memory. The cards can also be used to prepare for tests (see Part Three). The review card activities in this book give you structured practice in creating these valuable study tools. Once you have learned how to make review cards, you can create them for textbook material in your other courses.

Now, complete the three review cards for Chapter 7, following the directions on each card. When you have completed them, you will have summarized: (1) names and definitions of five writing patterns, (2) advantages of recognizing authors' patterns as you read, and (3) clues that serve to signal writing patterns.

Authors' Writing Patterns

Name and describe five writing patterns commonly used by authors. (See pages 309–316.)

Pattern: ______________________________

Description: ______________________________

Pattern: ______________________________

Description: ______________________________

Pattern: ______________________________

Description: ______________________________

Pattern: ______________________________

Description: ______________________________

Pattern: ______________________________

Description: ______________________________

Chapter 7: Recognizing Authors' Writing Patterns

Advantages of Identifying Writing Patterns

What are four advantages of identifying writing patterns as you read? (See page 308.)

1. ______

2. ______

3. ______

4. ______

Chapter 7: Recognizing Authors' Writing Patterns

Clues to Writing Patterns: Signal Words

What signal words identify each of the five writing patterns described in this chapter? (See pages 309–316.)

1. List: ______
2. Sequence: ______
3. Definition: ______
4. Comparison-contrast: ______
5. Cause-effect: ______

Chapter 7: Recognizing Authors' Writing Patterns

Selection 7-1

Computer Science

A GLOBAL WAREHOUSE OF INFORMATION

FROM NET.SEARCH: QUICKLY FIND ANYTHING YOU NEED ON THE INTERNET

Prepare Yourself to Read

Directions: Do these exercises *before you read Selection 7-1.*

1. First, read and think about the title. What do you already know about the Internet?

____

____

2. Next, complete your preview by reading the following:

Introduction (in *italics*)
Headings and subheadings
Words in **bold print**
Tables and figures
First paragraph (paragraph 1)
First sentence of each paragraph
Last paragraph (paragraph 20)

On the basis of your preview, what aspects of the Internet does this selection seem to be about?

____

____

Apply Comprehension Skills

Directions: Do the Annotation Practice Exercises *as you read Selection* 7-1.

Determine topics and main ideas. When you read a paragraph, ask yourself what it is about (topic) and what the author wants you to understand (main idea) about the topic.

Identify supporting details. As you read, ask yourself what else the author wants you to know so that you can understand the main idea.

Recognize the authors' writing patterns. As you read, ask yourself, "What pattern did the author use to organize the main idea and supporting details?" Watch for clue words that signal the pattern.

A GLOBAL WAREHOUSE OF INFORMATION

The following is an excerpt from an introductory chapter on the Internet. The "Internet," as the word itself suggests, is a linking between computer networks. It is, in reality, a "network of networks"—thousands upon thousands of them! For obvious reasons, every college student today should know how to access information on what the authors describe as "the world's biggest public library and electronic gathering place." This "global warehouse of information" is considered an essential resource in both the academic world and the business world. Once you become an "Internaut," you'll literally have the world at your fingertips.

1 Have you ever tried to put together one of those 5,000-piece jigsaw puzzles where the picture is something impossibly difficult like a photograph of jelly beans? You think you may go crazy trying to find the next piece. The Internet may seem like a giant puzzle. But, instead of thousands, there are literally millions of different pieces—text-based documents, images, software programs, video and audio files. Where do you begin to find the one piece that you need today, right now?

2 This chapter provides a foundation that you will be able to use as you learn about the specific Internet tools and systems that are available for Net searching. In this chapter you will learn the following:

- What types of information and resources are available on the Internet
- How searching the Internet for information can save time and money
- About the different information systems and search tools on the Internet and how to choose the best one to begin a search
- That the Internet is alive with more than 30

Annotation practice exercises

Directions: For each exercise, use the spaces provided to write:

- Main idea sentence of the paragraph
- Author's pattern for organizing supporting details (writing pattern)

Also, in the paragraph, number the supporting details and underline or highlight clue words that signal the writing pattern. This will help you remember main ideas, details, and writing patterns.

Source: William Eager, Larry Donahue, David Forsyth, Kenneth Mitton, and Martin Waterhouse, "A Global Warehouse of Information," in *NET.SEARCH, QUICKLY FIND ANYTHING YOU NEED ON THE INTERNET,* Indianapolis, Ind., 1995, pp. 9–16.

million people who can help you find information

INFORMATION CAN BE VALUABLE

3 The information that you locate from a search has real value. Information helps us make informed decisions—whether it's about which college to attend or how to save money when traveling abroad. You can also use information to save money and make money. You might want to do a search to find the most competitive price on a product or learn about new investment or employment opportunities.

4 Businesspeople can find information that can be of value in all aspects of running a company—from product development to marketing. The use of the Internet to gain a competitive edge in the marketplace can have tremendous economic value. Individuals and small companies can use the information resources of the Internet to level the playing field for locating and seizing international business opportunities. Using the Internet searching tools, it becomes possible to learn about new trading partners or requests for proposals. An Internet connection in Hong Kong becomes a gateway for doing business with China as you can access a database of more than 1,000 companies locating company contracts, financial data, product information, addresses, and phone numbers (Web address: **http://www.hk.super.net/~rlowe/bizhk/bhhome.html**).

5 Educators and students can use the Internet to find information useful for course curriculum, study programs, and class reports. As a reference source, the Internet provides "just-in-time" information. Log on to the Internet 10 minutes before you have to make a presentation or finish a report and get the information you need.

6 When you tap into the resources of the Internet, you can search for and retrieve information that will help with decision making, improve productivity, and even enhance your economic situation. There is another, almost hidden, value

in using the Internet to locate information. That's in the savings associated with the time and expense that it traditionally takes to find information. No longer do you have to drive to the library or make a long-distance phone call to find information. Now you can search a global warehouse of information by connecting to the Internet from your home or office. In the current "information age," the ability to quickly locate, retrieve, and use information has tremendous value for everyone. And, with its global connections and millions of users, the Internet is the world's biggest electronic library and public gathering place.

Practice exercise

Main idea sentence of paragraph 6:

____

____

____

____

____

Writing pattern:

____

WHAT TYPE OF INFORMATION CAN I FIND ON THE INTERNET?

7 Here you are reading the words on this page. Your brain translates the printed characters and words—which you learned back in grade school—into meaningful information. Words clearly are one form of information, but information also comes in several other forms. A symphony by Beethoven, a speech by Winston Churchill, a photograph by Ansel Adams, a movie by Steven Spielberg—all these different forms of media contain information. And every one of these forms of media can be converted into a digital format and saved as a computer file. Software programs, spreadsheets, and databases are also digital in form, and contain useful applications and information. For the remainder of this book all of these different things will be referred to as "information."

8 The term **multimedia** has come to define the capability of computer technology—especially CD-ROMs—to offer users a multisensory experience as you quickly move from a picture to sounds to movies. The Internet itself is perhaps the biggest multimedia system ever created. Table 1 identifies some of the media types that you'll find on the Internet computers, searched for by users like you, then distributed to your personal computer.

Practice exercise

Main idea sentence of paragraph 8:

____

____

____

____

____

Writing pattern:

____

Table 1
Media Types on the Internet

Types of Media	*Examples of Content*
Text	Articles, books, reports, periodicals
Images	Photographs, weather maps, digital art
Sound	Voice and music recordings
Movies	Short (10 second–2 minute) videos
Programs and files	Software, spreadsheets, databases

9 The digital format means that all of this information is accessible via the Internet. The subjects or categories of information that you will find on the Internet are vast. In fact, it would be difficult to think of a subject that you couldn't find on the Internet. What makes the Internet such a comprehensive warehouse of digital information is that you can use the various Internet systems to access computers and information maintained by governments, educational institutions, commercial companies, and nonprofit organizations all around the world. Here are a few examples of information and software programs you can access:

- Library catalogs and electronic books from libraries around the world, including the extensive collection at the U.S. Library of Congress.
- Commercial databases on thousands of subjects.
- Business catalogs that describe products and services.
- Information directories such as AT&T's Internet site, which offers a searchable index of companies that have 800-numbers.
- Publications and books. Thousands of quarterly, monthly, weekly, and daily periodicals, electronic versions of newsstand magazines, and the complete text of books.

- Vast repositories of government information. From searchable databases of space flight information offered by NASA to a directory of all of the towns and cities in Canada.
- Software programs and utilities for all computer platforms including financial, word-processing, graphics, educational, and Internet programs.

GLOBAL INFORMATION FROM A GLOBAL NETWORK

10 The overwhelming U.S. participation in the initial development of the Internet has one important ramification for Net searchers: English has become the de facto standard for text-based documents and interfaces to the various Internet systems. When you visit Internet computers in Japan, Germany, or Argentina the odds are that either you will get English language information on your computer screen or you will have an option that will take you to an English-based version of the information.

11 Although a significant portion of the users and computers that are connected to the Internet are in the United States, the Internet is truly a global communication system. More than 80 countries around the world have connected networks to the Internet. For example, Canada has the second largest Internet infrastructure in the world—with well over 1 million users. Other countries that have a significant presence on the Internet include France, Germany, the United Kingdom, Australia, and Japan—each operating more than 1,000 networks that connect to the Internet.

12 The global nature of the Internet means that it is just as easy to connect with and search through information on a computer in China or Australia as it is to access one that may be located in the United States. As foreign governments, educational institutions, and companies continue to connect to the Internet and allow Net searchers to access their information, it becomes increasingly easy to find information

Practice exercise

Main idea sentence of paragraph 10:

____

____

____

____

____

Writing pattern:

____

that previously would have been difficult or even impossible to locate.

13 For example, if you're planning a trip to India, you could visit a site that has a city-by-city menu that leads to descriptions of each town, directions of how to get there, local sightseeing opportunities, and lodging accommodations (Gopher address: **soochak.ncst.ernet.in**). You can even search and find obscure works of literature that you'd never find anyplace else. A site in Ireland, for example, collects and puts on-line Irish literature dating from 600 to 1600 A.D.

Note

14 There are several ways to measure the continual growth of the Internet. One is by the number of people who have access to the Internet. It's estimated that there are 40 million Internet users, and the number of users continues to increase at the rate of approximately 2 million each month. A second measure is in the number of host computers that are connected to the Internet. A **host computer** is a computer that is connected to the Internet on a continual basis, and you may connect to hosts all over the world during a Net search. The number of hosts has grown from 235 in May 1982 to more than 4 million in May 1995. And because each host can store lots of files, the quantity and variety of information that's available continues to grow at an amazing rate.

FROM ACADEMIC TO BUSINESS APPLICATIONS

15 Although you don't need a history lesson on how to search the Internet, a quick snapshot of the evolution of the Internet will give you some insight into the quantity and types of information that are available.

16 With more than 25 years of academic involvement, a significant portion of the hosts, information, and users of the Internet revolve around education. Approximately 900,000 educational and research organizations operate

Figure 1
An Internet search for "colleges" provides a list of more than 1,000 different U.S. educational institutions that maintain Internet sites. Here is the main page for Harvard University's World Wide Web site.

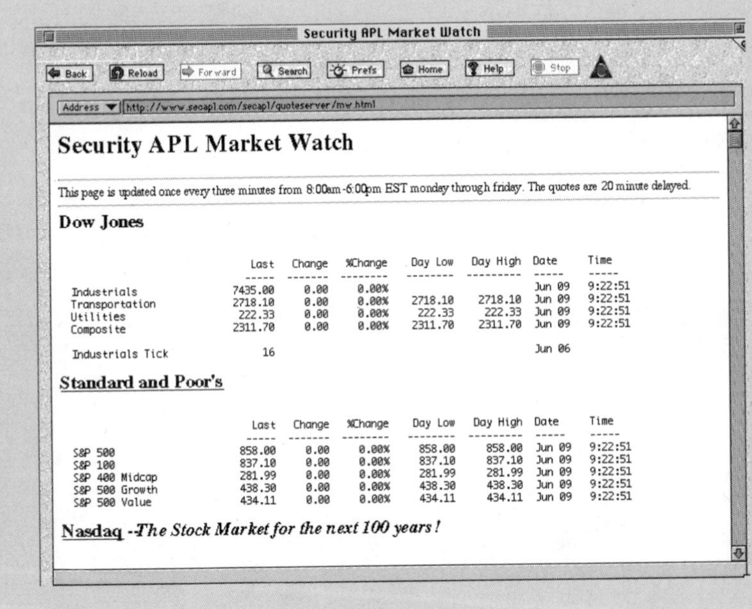

Security APL Market Watch

This page is updated once every three minutes from 8:00am-6:00pm EST monday through friday. The quotes are 20 minute delayed.

Dow Jones

	Last	Change	%Change	Day Low	Day High	Date	Time
Industrials	7435.00	0.00	0.00%			Jun 09	9:22:51
Transportation	2718.10	0.00	0.00%	2718.10	2718.10	Jun 09	9:22:51
Utilities	222.33	0.00	0.00%	222.33	222.33	Jun 09	9:22:51
Composite	2311.70	0.00	0.00%	2311.70	2311.70	Jun 09	9:22:51
Industrials Tick	16					Jun 06	

Standard and Poor's

	Last	Change	%Change	Day Low	Day High	Date	Time
S&P 500	858.00	0.00	0.00%	858.00	858.00	Jun 09	9:22:51
S&P 100	837.10	0.00	0.00%	837.10	837.10	Jun 09	9:22:51
S&P 400 Midcap	281.99	0.00	0.00%	281.99	281.99	Jun 09	9:22:51
S&P 500 Growth	438.30	0.00	0.00%	438.30	438.30	Jun 09	9:22:51
S&P 500 Value	434.11	0.00	0.00%	434.11	434.11	Jun 09	9:22:51

Nasdaq -*The Stock Market for the next 100 years!*

Figure 2
Information on the Internet is extremely current. This Internet site updates stock and security market information every three minutes.

Internet hosts—about 25 percent of the total hosts on the Internet. As a result, there are scholarly reports, studies, journals, images, and software programs encompassing every educational and scientific subject you can think of. Figure 1 shows the Harvard University Internet Web site and Figure 2 displays a sample of the financial information that is available on the Internet.

17 The commercial sector is rapidly getting a large presence on the Internet. The commercial sector now operates more than 800,000 hosts. According to telecommunications giant MCI, 38 percent of all publicly traded companies with sales that exceed $400 million have some type of presence on the Internet.

18 Fortunately, the trend for commercial Internet sites is for companies to offer product information, news, articles, interactive brochures, free software utilities, and even games as opposed to blatant advertising. A good example of this is Time Warner's Internet site, which is shown in Figure 3 (Web address: **http://www.pathfinder.com/**). Among other things, you'll find the "Virtual Garden," which maintains a collection of horticultural information and articles about gardening from *Sunset* and *Southern Living* magazines.

Note

19 When a college or company registers its Internet computer it has to pick a unique domain name or address that identifies its site. In the United States, educational sites get an address that ends with .edu. Commercial sites get addresses that end with .com, and government hosts end with .gov. This naming system makes it easy for you to quickly identify what type of site you are visiting—if you don't already know.

INTERNET ACCESS FROM AMERICA ONLINE AND "FRIENDS"

20 The tremendous publicity and rapid growth of the Internet have not gone unnoticed by commercial companies that provide online ser-

Figure 3
Commercial Internet sites offer a variety of useful information and software programs. The Pathfinder site is a gateway to articles and news from several Time Warner publications.

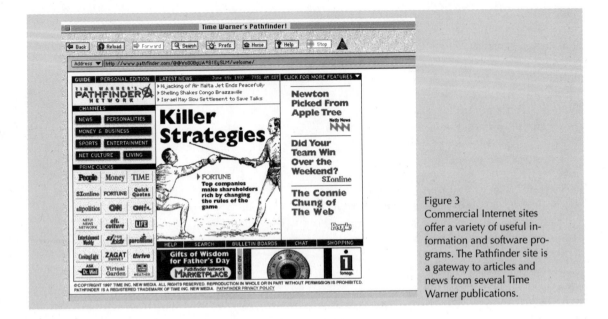

vices and access to databases. American Online (AOL), CompuServe, Prodigy, and Delphi all offer their users—more than 5 million people—access to the Internet. If you use the Internet, you can send electronic mail and have conversations with all of these people. These commercial online services also have software programs (known as browsers) that enable you to access the Internet World Wide Web system.

Comprehension Quiz

True or false

Directions: In the blank provided, indicate whether each statement is true or false.

_____ 1. According to the authors, using the Internet to locate information is faster and cheaper than finding information in traditional ways.

_____ 2. Today, forms of media such as photographs, speeches, movies, and even symphonies can be converted to a digital format and saved as a computer file.

_____ 3. Programs, files, and text are the only types of media that can be found on the Internet.

______ 4. Thousands of periodicals, magazines, and even complete books can be accessed using the Internet.

______ 5. English has become the standard language for the Internet because the United States was a leader in the initial development of the Internet.

Multiple-choice

Directions: For each item, select the best answer.

______ 6. A *host computer* is

a. a personal computer used to access the Internet from home.
b. a computer connected to the Internet on a continual basis that can store a huge number of files.
c. a computer in the United States that is linked to computers in other countries.
d. an Internet computer that converts text-based documents to digital format.

______ 7. The Internet can be characterized as

a. a reference source that can provide "just-in-time" information.
b. an electronic library.
c. a public library.
d. all of the above.

______ 8. Approximately 25 percent of the total hosts on the Internet are

a. educational and research organizations.
b. government agencies.
c. publicly traded companies.
d. Canadian, French, German, and British users.

______ 9. Today, there is a trend to use commercial Internet sites to

a. display multimedia advertising.
b. link global networks.
c. provide access to research information and government databases.
d. offer product information, news, articles, and free software utilities.

______ 10. American colleges must have which of the following at the end of their unique Internet domain names or addresses?

a. .com
b. .edu
c. .gov
d. .aol

Extend Your Vocabulary by Using Context Clues

Directions: **Context clues** are words in a sentence or paragraph that allow the reader to deduce (reason out) the meaning of an unfamiliar word. For each item in this exercise, a sentence from Selection 7-1 containing an important word (*italicized, like this*) is quoted first. Next, there is an additional sentence using the word in the same sense and providing another context clue. Use the context clues to deduce the meaning of each italicized word. *The definition you choose should make sense in both sentences.*

Pronunciation key: ă **pat** ā **pay** âr **care** ä **father** ĕ **pet** ē **be** ĭ **pit** ī **tie** îr **pier** ŏ **pot** ō **toe** ô **paw** oi **noise** ou **out** o͝o **took** o͞o **boot** ŭ **cut** yo͞o ab**use** ûr **urge** th **thin** *th* **this** hw **which** zh vision ə **about**

______ 1. "Information helps us make *informed* decisions—whether it's about which college to attend or how to save money when traveling abroad."

By becoming an *informed* consumer, you can buy wisely and avoid scams.

informed (ĭn fôrmd´) means:

a. knowing more than anyone else
b. knowledgeable; educated
c. knowing all that is known
d. thrifty; economical

______ 2. "Using Internet searching tools, it becomes possible to learn about new trading partners or requests for *proposals*."

The corporation's board of directors approved the *proposal* to open branch offices in six more cities.

proposal (prə pō´ zəl) means:

a. plan offered for consideration
b. offer of marriage
c. making one's intention known
d. merger

______ 3. "And every one of these forms of media can be *converted* into a digital format and saved as a computer file."

Water can be *converted* into ice by freezing it.

converted (kən vûrt´ əd) means:

a. adapted and used for a different purpose
b. persuaded to adopt a particular religion or belief
c. exchanged for something of equal value
d. changed into another form or state; transformed

______ 4. "The term *multimedia* has come to define the capability of computer technology—especially CD-ROMs—to offer users a multisensory experience as you move quickly from a picture to sounds to movies."

Movement, sound, and color make *multimedia* an especially appropriate format for educational and entertainment software.

multimedia (mŭl tē mē´ dē ə) means:

a. combined use of several media (such as movies, slides, and music)
b. use of several mass media (such as television, radio, and print)
c. type of political campaign
d. type of advertising campaign

______ 5. "What makes the Internet such a *comprehensive* warehouse of digital information is that you can use the various Internet systems to access computers and information maintained by governments, educational institutions, commercial companies, and nonprofit organizations all around the world."

Following President John F. Kennedy's assassination in 1963, the Warren Commission was created to carry out a *comprehensive* investigation of the incident.

comprehensive (kŏm prĭ hĕn´ sĭv) means:

a. showing extensive understanding
b. large in scope or content
c. covering the entire content of a college course
d. of immeasurable size

______ 6. "Library catalogs and electronic books from libraries around the world, including the *extensive* collection at the U.S. Library of Congress."

Albert Barnes acquired an *extensive* knowledge of impressionist art and assembled one of the world's greatest private collections of impressionist masterpieces.

extensive (ĭk stĕn´ sĭv) means:

a. acquired by one person
b. occurring over a brief period of time
c. pertaining to the eighteenth century
d. being large in extent, range, or amount

______ 7. "The overwhelming U.S. participation in the initial development of the Internet has one important *ramification* for Net searchers."

The law requiring child safety restraints in cars was the most significant *ramification* of that court case.

ramification (răm ə fĭ kā´ shən) means:

a. anticipated change that never occurs
b. negative or harmful effect
c. development or consequence that grows out of something else
d. undetected or unnoticed consequence

______ 8. "You can even search and find *obscure* works of literature that you'd never find anywhere else."

Obscure stars in distant galaxies have been detected with high-powered telescopes.

obscure (ŏb skyŏŏr´) means:

a. famous; widely known
b. far from centers of human population
c. boring; uninteresting
d. not readily seen or noticed; out of sight

______ 9. "The *commercial* sector is rapidly getting a large presence on the Internet."

Many of the books about the O.J. Simpson trial were written for *commercial* reasons.

commercial (kə mûr´ shəl) means:

a. of or relating to computers
b. having profit as a chief aim
c. supported by advertising
d. educational

______ 10. "The commercial *sector* is rapidly getting a large presence on the Internet."

The northern *sector* is the fastest-growing part of the city.

sector (sĕk´ tər) means:

a. part or division
b. division of an offensive military position
c. smallest unit possible
d. portion of a circle bounded by two radii and the included arc

Respond in Writing

Directions: Refer to Selection 7-1 as necessary to answer these essay-type items.

Option for collaboration: For some of the "Respond in Writing" exercises, your instructor may prefer that you work collaboratively, that is, with other students. These exercises are identified in the margin. *If your instructor directs you to work collaboratively on any of these items,* form groups of three or four classmates to complete the exercise together. Discuss your answers with each other and have one member of the group record the answers. A member of the group may be asked to share the group's answers with the class.

1. The authors describe several useful features of the Internet. List at least three ways you, as a colleage student, might use (or have already used) the Internet.

Option

Item 2 may be completed collaboratively.

2. One of the advantages of the Internet is its multimedia capabilities (such as images, sound, and movies). Describe several ways you think this feature could be used to enhance students' learning.

Option

Item 3 may be completed collaboratively.

3. The Internet is a network of networks that literally connects computers all over the world. How might college students benefit from the "global" nature of the Internet.

Option

Item 4 may be completed collaboratively.

4. What is the most important overall message the writer wants the reader to understand about the Internet and what it has to offer? Try to answer this question in one sentence.

____

____

____

____

____

____

____

Selection 7-2

Health

THE DECISION TO MARRY

FROM *TARGETING WELLNESS: THE CORE*
BY MARVIN LEVY, MARK DIGNAN, AND JANET SHIRREFFS

Prepare Yourself to Read

Directions: Do these exercises *before you read Selection 7-2.*

1. First, read and think about the title. In your opinion, why do people decide to marry?

   ____

   ____

2. Next, complete your preview by reading the following:

   Introduction (in *italics*)
   First paragraph (paragraph 1)
   Headings in *italics*
   First sentence of each paragraph
   Words in *italics*
   Last paragraph (paragraph 9)

   On the basis of your preview, what does this selection seem to be about?

   ____

   ____

Apply Comprehension Skills

Directions: Do the Annotation Practice Exercises *as you read Selection 7-2.*

Determine the topics and main ideas. When you read a paragraph, ask yourself what it is about (topic) and what the author wants you to understand (main idea) about the topic.

Identify supporting details. As you read, ask yourself what else the author wants you to know so that you can understand the main idea?

Recognize the author's writing pattern. As you read, ask yourself, "What pattern did the author use to organize the main idea and supporting details?" Watch for clue words that signal the pattern.

THE DECISION TO MARRY

Today, half of all marriages fail. Part of this can be attributed to getting married for the wrong reasons or marrying someone who is incompatible. What are poor reasons for getting married? What characterizes a successful, high-quality marriage? What determines a couple's compatibility? This textbook selection answers these questions.

1 Marriage is an institution that is changing. Traditionally, marriage has been an economic arrangement in which husbands have worked outside the home to provide financial security for their families, while wives have cared for the children and run the home. Today, however, this arrangement is changing. The roles of husband and wife are not as clearly defined as in the past, especially when both partners work and earn money for the family. Many people today expect and get more from marriage than economic benefits. They look to their spouses for sharing, emotional support, and intimacy. Happily married people often identify the spouse as their best friend.

2 *Why do people marry?* The pressures for a couple to marry can be enormous. This pressure often comes from parents and other relatives as well as from the media. Sometimes the members of a family, ethnic group, or religious group may pressure individuals to marry so that a new generation can be raised in the teaching and values of the group.

3 Aside from these pressures, people marry for a variety of reasons. Some still marry for economic reasons. For others, marriage is viewed as the only acceptable framework in which to enjoy sex freely. Some people marry to escape from an unhappy home life, on the rebound from another relationship, or to avoid loneliness.

4 Researchers have identified several patterns in "high-quality," or well-balanced marriages. Some

Annotation practice exercises

Directions: For each exercise, use the spaces provided to write:

- Main idea sentence of the paragraph
- Authors' pattern for organizing supporting details (writing pattern)

Also, in the paragraph, number supporting details and underline or highlight clue words that signal the writing pattern. This will help you remember main ideas, details, and writing patterns.

Practice exercise

Main idea sentence of paragraph 2:

____

____

____

____

____

Writing pattern:

____

Source: Marvin Levy, Mark Dignan, and Janet Shirreffs, "The Decision to Marry," in *Targeting Wellness: The Core,* McGraw-Hill, New York, 1992, pp. 122–123. Reproduced with permission of McGraw-Hill. *Photo:* Tony Freeman/PhotoEdit.

of these married people tend to focus their energies on joint activities. Their strongest wish is to spend time together, yet they also strike a balance between privacy and togetherness. Other couples focus their energies on being parents and on raising their children. Some dual-career couples, although they spend much of their energy on their individual careers, develop intimacy by sharing what is going on in their work. It thus seems that the desire to spend time together, raise children, and share other aspects of life and career are all healthy reasons for marrying.

5 *Love and romance* A basic element in most marriages is the love one person feels for another. There are many different types of love between persons, including parental love, fraternal love, and romantic love. Each requires caring and respect. Romantic love includes the qualities of deep intimacy and passion and begins with a feeling of intense attraction between two people.

6 Although most marriages are based on romantic love, few couples sustain that romance as the years go by. Romantic love often develops into a less intense and all-consuming type of love known as companionate love. A companionate love relationship is steadier than romantic love and is based on trust, sharing, affection, and togetherness. Maintaining the love in a marriage requires considerable effort and commitment. Married partners who succeed in communicating, giving physical warmth, and sharing interest and responsibilities are more likely to remain in love.

7 *Assessing compatibility* When people are looking for a mate, they tend to be attracted to potential partners whose ethnic, religious, economic, and educational background is similar to their own. Certain physical attributes are also significant factors. They are least likely to match up with a similar person in the area of compatibility of personality. Personality factors are not always easy to observe. Sometimes people do not reveal their true selves during courtship. Moreover, people with opposite personality

Practice exercise

Main idea sentence of paragraph 4:

____

Writing pattern:

____

Practice exercise

Main idea sentence of paragraph 6:

____

Writing pattern:

____

Since antiquity, the marriage ceremony has provided a formal setting in which a couple can publicly affirm their love for and commitment to each other.

types often attract each other, perhaps because one personality rounds out the other.

8 Unfortunately, great differences in personality can often lead to conflict later on. One study found that a source of marital dissatisfaction among husbands was a feeling that their wives were too possessive, neglectful, and openly admiring of other men. Dissatisfied wives complained that their husbands were possessive, moody, and openly attracted to other women. The study also found that sex is a source of great difficulties for unhappy married men and women. It found that women see sex as following from emotional intimacy, while men see it as a road to intimacy. As a result, men complain that their wives withhold sex from them and

women complain that their husbands are too sexually aggressive.

9 How can people be sure they are marrying people with whom they are truly compatible? One way is by taking plenty of time to get to know the other person. Researchers have found that couples seem to go through three stages in this process. First, each person tries to measure his or her good and bad qualities against those of the other person. People tend to be drawn to others who seem to have about the same assets and liabilities they themselves possess. Second, people look for compatible beliefs, attitudes, and interests to support the initial attraction. It is not until the third stage that people reveal to each other how they handle responsibility, react to disappointment, and cope with a wide variety of situations. The key to compatibility is for the couple to be sure that they have arrived at this last stage before they think seriously about marriage. Such people are less likely to be unpleasantly suprised than are those who marry quickly.

Comprehension Quiz

True or false

Directions: In the blank provided, indicate whether each statement is true or false.

______ 1. Marriage is an unchanging institution.

______ 2. According to the authors, people can experience enormous pressure to marry.

______ 3. Pressure to marry can come from many sources.

______ 4. Sometimes people do not reveal their true selves during courtship.

______ 5. As years go by in a marriage, most couples are able to sustain the intense attraction of romantic love.

______ 6. People with opposite personality types will not attract each other.

Multiple-choice

Directions: For each item, select the best answer.

_____ 7. Which of the following is *not* a characteristic of companionate love?
   a. steadiness
   b. all-consuming intensity of feeling
   c. mutual trustworthiness
   d. shared areas of responsibility

_____ 8. Which of the following is *not* a characteristic of "high quality" marriages?
   a. Energy is focused on the economic benefits of marriage.
   b. Energy is focused on joint activities.
   c. Energy is focused on being parents and raising children.
   d. A balance is struck between privacy and togetherness.

_____ 9. Which of these is a source of marital dissatisfaction?
   a. husbands' feeling that wives are too possessive, neglectful, and openly admiring of other men
   b. wives' feeling that husbands are possessive, moody, and openly attracted to other women
   c. conflicts over sex
   d. all of the above

_____ 10. Researchers have found that people seem to go through three stages in the process of selecting a mate. Which of the following is *not* a stage?
   a. A person measures his or her good and bad qualities against those of the other person.
   b. People evaluate the physical attractiveness of a possible partner.
   c. People look for compatible beliefs, attitudes, and interests in the other person.
   d. People reveal how they handle responsibility and disappointment.

Extend Your Vocabulary by Using Context Clues

Directions: ***Context clues*** are words in a sentence or paragraph that allow the reader to deduce (reason out) the meaning of an unfamiliar word. For each item in this exercise, a sentence from Selection 7-2 containing an important word *(italicized, like this)* is quoted first. Next, there is an additional sentence using the word in the same sense and providing another context clue. Use the context clues to deduce the meaning of each italicized word. *The definition you choose should make sense in both sentences.*

Pronunciation key: ă **pat** ā **pay** âr **care** ä **father** ĕ **pet** ē **be** ĭ **pit** ī **tie** îr **pier** ŏ **pot** ō **toe** ô **paw** oi **noise** ou **out** o͝o **took** o͞o **boot** ŭ **cut** yo͞o **abuse** ûr **urge** th **thin** *th* **this** hw **which** zh **vision** ə **about**

_____ 1. "Marriage is an *institution* that is changing."

The family is an *institution* that has been studied extensively.

institution (ĭn stĭ to͞o´ shən) means:

a. building
b. written agreement
c. political decision
d. established custom or practice

_____ 2. "Some people marry to escape from an unhappy home life, on the *rebound* from another relationship, or to avoid loneliness."

The senator was quickly on the *rebound* after losing the election, and soon began making plans to enter a new career.

rebound (rē´ bound) means:

a. recovery from disappointment
b. capture of something
c. sideways movement
d. ground

_____ 3. "There are many different types of love between persons, including parental love, *fraternal* love, and romantic love."

He joined a *fraternal* organization to make new friends and enjoy social activities.

fraternal (frə tûr´ nəl) means:

a. pertaining to friendship
b. pertaining to business
c. pertaining to hobbies
d. none of the above

_____ 4. "Although most marriages are based on romantic love, few couples *sustain* that romance as the years go by."

Although he was in an irreversible coma, his family asked the doctors to do everything possible to *sustain* his life.

sustain (sə stān´) means:

a. prevent
b. alter
c. end
d. maintain

_____ 5. "Romantic love often develops into a less intense and all-*consuming* type of love known as companionate love."

Sailing has become such a time-*consuming* hobby for Bob that he never has time for anything else on weekends.

consuming (kən sōōm´ ĭng) means:

a. engrossing; absorbing
b. confusing
c. wasting
d. saving

_____ 6. "Sometimes people do not reveal their true selves during *courtship.*"

Lynn and Pat's *courtship* lasted for 6 years before they decided to marry.

courtship (kôrt´ shĭp) means:

a. court case
b. voyage at sea
c. legal separation
d. seeking someone's affection with the hope of marrying him or her

_____ 7. "One study found that a source of *marital* dissatisfaction among husbands was a feeling that their wives were too possessive, neglectful, and openly admiring of other men."

Please indicate your *marital* status: single, married, divorced or widowed.

marital (măr´ ĭ tl) means:

a. pertaining to fighting
b. pertaining to marriage
c. pertaining to divorce
d. pertaining to a wedding

_____ 8. "People tend to be drawn to others who seem to have about the same assets and *liabilities* they themselves possess."

Not knowing how to use computers and lack of rapport with others are *liabilities* for anyone who plans to enter the business world.

liabilities (lī ə bĭl´ ĭ tēz) means:

a. handicap; something that holds one back
b. advantages, benefits
c. business skills
d. lies, deceptions

_____ 9. "Second, people look for compatible beliefs, attitudes, and interests to support the *initial* attraction."

The doctor changed her *initial* diagnosis after she received the patient's test results.

initial (ĭ nĭsh′ əl) means:

a. professional
b. inappropriate
c. first
d. puzzling

_____ 10. "The key to *compatibility* is for the couple to be sure that they have arrived at this last stage before they think seriously about marriage."

In families with step-children, psychological counseling can improve *compatibility.*

compatibility (kəm păt ə bĭl ə tē) means:

a. a successful marriage
b. financial security
c. existing in harmonious or agreeable combination
d. achievement of career goals

Respond in Writing

Directions: Refer to Selection 7-2 as necessary to answer these essay-type items.

Option for collaboration: For some of the "Respond in Writing" exercises, your instructor may prefer that you work collaboratively, that is, with other students. These exercises are identified in the margin. *If your instructor directs you to work collaboratively on any of these items,* form groups of three or four classmates to complete the exercise together. Discuss your answers with each other and have one member of the group record the answers. A member of the group may be asked to share the group's answers with the class.

1. What three reasons do the authors say are *inappropriate* reasons for marrying?

First inappropriate reason:

_____

_____

Second inappropriate reason:

_____

_____

Third inappropriate reason:

2. What three reasons do the authors say are *healthy* reasons for marrying?

First healthy reason:

Second healthy reason:

Third healthy reason:

Option

Item 3 may be completed collaboratively.

3. Suppose that two people are attracted to each other, and they share similar ethnic, religious, economic, and educational backgrounds. However, because their personalities are quite different, they are not sure they are compatible. According to the selection, what three steps can they take to determine whether their personalities are truly compatible?

Option

Item 4 may be completed collaboratively.

4. What is the most important overall message these writers want their readers to understand about the decision to marry? Try to answer this question in one sentence.

____

____

____

____

____

REACTIONS TO IMPENDING DEATH

FROM *ESSENTIALS OF PSYCHOLOGY* BY DENNIS COON

Selection 7-3

Psychology

Prepare Yourself to Read

Directions: Do these exercises *before you read Selection 7-3.*

1. First, read and think about the title. What do you already know about dying people's reactions to impending death?

   ____

   ____

2. Next, complete your preview by reading the following:

   Introduction (in *italics*)
   First paragraph (paragraph 1)
   Headings
   First sentence of each paragraph
   Words in **bold print** and *italics*
   Last paragraph (paragraph 16)

   On the basis of your preview, what does this selection seem to be about?

   ____

   ____

Apply Comprehension Skills

Directions: Do the Annotation Practice Exercises *as you read Selection 7-3.*

Determine topics and main ideas. When you read a paragraph, ask yourself what it is about (topic) and what the author wants you to understand (main idea) about the topic.

Identify supporting details. As you read, ask yourself what else the author wants you to know so that you can understand the main idea?

Recognize the author's writing pattern. As you read, ask yourself, "What pattern did the author use to organize the main idea and supporting details?" Watch for clue words that signal the pattern.

REACTIONS TO IMPENDING DEATH

The topic of death makes many people in our society uncomfortable. The author of this selection presents a well-known theory about terminally ill persons' reactions to their forthcoming death. (Note that even for a healthy person, a significant loss of any kind—loss of a long-held job, loss of a home to fire or flood, even the loss of a beloved pet—produces these same reactions.) In addition, the author includes helpful information on hospices and bereavement.

1 A direct account of emotional responses to death comes from the work of Elisabeth Kübler-Ross (1975). Kübler-Ross is a **thanatologist** (one who studies death) who spent hundreds of hours at the bedsides of the terminally ill. She found that dying persons tend to display several emotional reactions as they prepare for death. Five basic reactions are described here:

1. **Denial and isolation.** A typical first reaction to impending death is an attempt to deny its reality and to isolate oneself from information confirming that death is really going to occur. Initially the person may be sure that "It's all a mistake," that lab reports or X-rays have been mixed up, or that a physician is in error. This may proceed to attempts to ignore or avoid any reminder of the situation.
2. **Anger.** Many dying individuals feel anger and ask, "Why me?" As they face the ultimate threat of having everything they value stripped away, their anger can spill over into rage or envy toward those who will continue living. Even good friends may temporarily evoke anger because their health is envied.
3. **Bargaining.** In another common reaction the terminally ill bargain with themselves or with God. The dying person thinks, "Just

Annotation practice exercises

Directions: For each exercise, use the spaces provided to write:

- Main idea sentence of the paragraph
- Author's pattern for organizing supporting details (writing pattern)

Also, in the paragraph, number supporting details and underline or highlight clue words that signal the writing pattern. This will help you remember main ideas, details, and writing patterns.

Practice exercise

Main idea sentence of paragraph 1:

____

____

____

____

____

Writing pattern:

____

Source: Dennis Coon, "Reactions to Impending Death," in *Essentials of Psychology,* West, St. Paul, Minn., 1991, pp. 136–138. *Photo:* Alan Tannenbaum/Sygma.

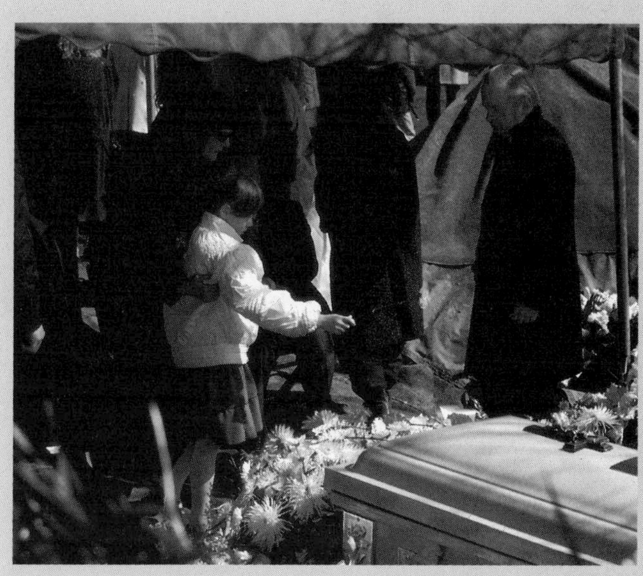

As cultural rituals, funerals encourage a release of emotion and provide a sense of closure for survivors, who must come to terms with the death of a loved one.

let me live a little longer and I'll do anything to earn it." Individuals may bargain for time by trying to be "good" ("I'll never smoke again"), by righting past wrongs, or by praying that if they are granted more time they will dedicate themselves to their religion.

4. **Depression.** As death draws near and the person begins to recognize that it cannot be prevented, feelings of futility, exhaustion, and deep depression may set in. The person recognizes that he or she will be separated from friends, loved ones, and the familiar routines of life, and this causes a profound sadness.

5. **Acceptance.** If death is not sudden, many people manage to come to terms with dying and accept it calmly. The person who accepts death is neither happy nor sad, but at peace with the inevitable. Acceptance usually signals that the struggle with death has been resolved. The need to talk about death ends, and silent companionship from others is frequently all that is desired.

2 Not all terminally ill persons display all these reactions, nor do they always occur in this order. Individual styles of dying vary greatly, according to emotional maturity, religious beliefs, age, education, the attitudes of relatives, and so forth. Generally, there does tend to be a movement from initial shock, denial, and anger toward eventual acceptance of the situation. However, some people who seem to have accepted death may die angry and raging against the inevitable. Conversely, the angry fighter may let go of the struggle and die peacefully. In general, one's approach to dying will mirror his or her style of living.

3 It is best not to think of Kübler-Ross' list as a fixed series of stages to go through in order. It is an even bigger mistake to assume that someone who does not show all the listed emotional reactions is somehow deviant or immature. Rather, the list describes typical and appropriate reactions to impending death. It is also interesting to note that many of the same reactions accompany any major loss, be it divorce, loss of a home due to fire, death of a pet, or loss of a job.

Question: How can I make use of this information?

4 First, it can help both the dying individual and survivors to recognize and cope with periods of depression, anger, denial, and bargaining. Second, it helps to realize that close friends or relatives of the dying person may feel many of the same emotions before or after the person's death because they, too, are facing a loss.

5 Perhaps the most important thing to recognize is that the dying person may have a need to share feelings with others and to discuss death openly. Too often, the dying person feels isolated and separated from others by the wall of silence erected by doctors, nurses, and family members. Adults tend to "freeze up" with a dying person, saying things such as, "I don't know how to deal with this."

6 Understanding what the dying person is going through may make it easier for you to offer support at this important time. A simple willingness to be with the person and to honestly share his or her feelings can help bring dignity, acceptance, and meaning to death. In many communities these goals have been aided by the hospice movement.

Hospice

7 A **hospice** is basically a hospital for the terminally ill. The goal of the hospice movement is to improve the quality of life in the person's final days. Hospices typically offer support, guidance, and companionship from volunteers, other patients, staff, clergy, and counselors. Pleasant surroundings, an atmosphere of informality, and a sense of continued living help patients cope with their illnesses. Unlimited around-the-clock visits are permitted by relatives, friends, children, and even pets. Patients receive constant attention, play games, make day trips, have pre-dinner cocktails if they choose, and enjoy entertainment. In short, life goes on for them.

8 At present most larger cities in the United States have hospices. They have been so successful that they are likely to be added to many more communities. At the same time, treatment for the terminally ill has dramatically improved in hospitals—largely as a result of pioneering efforts in the hospice movement.

Bereavement

9 After a friend or relative has died, a period of grief typically follows. Grief is a natural and normal reaction to death as survivors adjust to loss.

Practice exercise

Main idea sentence of paragraph 7:

____

____

____

____

____

Writing pattern:

____

10 Grief tends to follow a predictable pattern. Grief usually begins with a period of **shock** or numbness. For a brief time the bereaved remain in a dazed state in which they may show little emotion. Most find it extremely difficult to accept the reality of their loss. This phase usually ends by the time of the funeral, which unleashes tears and bottled-up feelings of despair.

11 Initial shock is followed by sharp **pangs of grief.** These are episodes of painful yearning for the dead person and, sometimes, anguished outbursts of anger. During this period the wish to have the dead person back is intense. Often, mourners continue to think of the dead person as alive. They may hear his or her voice and see the deceased vividly in dreams. During this period, agitated distress alternates with silent despair, and suffering is acute.

12 The first powerful reactions of grief gradually give way to weeks or months of **apathy, dejection,** and **depression.** The person faces a new emotional landscape with a large gap that cannot be filled. Life seems to lose much of its meaning, and a sense of futility dominates the person's outlook. The mourner is usually able to resume work or other activities after 2 or 3 weeks. However, insomnia, loss of energy and appetite, and similar signs of depression may continue.

13 Little by little, the bereaved person accepts what cannot be changed and makes a new beginning. Pangs of grief may still occur, but they are less severe and less frequent. Memories of the dead person, though still painful, now include positive images and nostalgic pleasure. At this point, the person can be said to be moving toward **resolution.**

14 As was true of approaching death, individual reactions to grief vary considerably. In general, however, a month or two typically passes before the more intense stages of grief have run their course. As you can see, grief allows survivors to discharge their anguish and to prepare to go on living.

Practice exercise

Main idea sentence of paragraph 10:

____

____

____

____

____

Writing pattern:

____

Question: Is it true that suppressing grief leads to more problems later?

15 It has long been assumed that suppressing grief may later lead to more severe and lasting depression. However, there is little evidence to support this idea. A lack of intense grief does not usually predict later problems. Bereaved persons should work through their grief at their own pace and in their own way—without worrying about whether they are grieving too much or too little. Some additional suggestions for coping with grief follow.

Practice exercise

Main idea sentence of paragraph 15:

____

____

____

____

____

Writing pattern:

____

Coping with Grief

- Face the loss directly and do not isolate yourself.
- Discuss your feelings with relatives and friends.
- Do not block out your feelings with drugs or alcohol.
- Allow grief to progress naturally; neither hurry nor surpress it.

16 The subject of death brings us full circle in the cycle of life.

Comprehension Quiz

True or false

Directions: In the blank provided, indicate whether each statement is true or false.

______ 1. Elisabeth Kübler-Ross found that every terminally ill patient displays the five basic reactions to dying.

______ 2. Kübler-Ross's list of reactions represents a fixed series of stages.

______ 3. Many of the reactions outlined by Kübler-Ross also accompany major losses such as divorce, loss of a job, and loss of a home in a fire.

______ 4. The primary goal of the hospice movement is to provide advanced medical treatment for the dying person.

______ 5. The hospice movement has had no effect on the quality of care that terminally ill patients receive in hospitals.

______ 6. Patients in a hospice may have a predinner cocktail if they choose to.

Multiple-choice

Directions: For each item, select the best answer.

______ 7. A thanatologist is one who studies

a. hospital care.
b. diseases.
c. death.
d. psychology.

______ 8. The author states that individual styles of dying are influenced by all of the following factors *except* the

a. attitude of relatives.
b. gender of the dying person.
c. age of the dying person.
d. emotional maturity of the dying person.

______ 9. Which of the following does *not* illustrate the value of Kübler-Ross's findings?

a. We can assume that someone who does not exhibit all the emotional reactions described by Kübler-Ross is immature.
b. The dying person who is familiar with Kübler-Ross's theory may be able to recognize, cope with, and discuss the various stages.
c. As survivors, we can better understand and support the terminally ill person.
d. Doctors and nurses may have a better understanding of the feelings of the terminally ill person.

______ 10. Hospice care is characterized by

a. restricted visits.
b. a hospital-like environment.
c. day trips, entertainment, and visits by the family (even pets), if the patient is able.
d. care, guidance, and support by doctors and staff only.

Extend Your Vocabulary by Using Context Clues

Directions: ***Context clues*** are words in a sentence or paragraph that allow the reader to deduce (reason out) the meaning of an unfamiliar word. For each item in this exercise, a sentence from Selection 7-3 containing an important word *(italicized, like this)* is quoted first. Next, there is an additional sentence using the word in the same sense and providing another context clue. Use the context clues to deduce the meaning of each italicized word. *The definition you choose should make sense in both sentences.*

Pronunciation key: ă **pat** ā **pay** âr **care** ä **father** ĕ **pet** ē **be** ĭ **pit** ī **tie** îr **pier** ŏ **pot** ō **toe** ô **paw** oi **noise** ou **out** o͝o **took** o͞o **boot** ŭ **cut** yo͞o **abuse** ûr **urge** th **thin** *th* **this** hw **which** zh **vision** ə **about**

______ 1. "As death draws near and the person begins to recognize that it cannot be prevented, feelings of *futility,* exhaustion, and deep depression may set in."

When they saw how vast the forest fire was, the firefighters realized the *futility* of their efforts to put it out and simply tried to prevent it from spreading further.

futility (fyo͞o tĭl′ ĭ tē) means:

a. reasonableness; sensibleness
b. uselessness; lack of useful results
c. cheerfulness
d. helpfulness

______ 2. "Acceptance usually signals the struggle with death has been *resolved.*"

My parents always *resolved* their problems by discussing them.

resolved (rĭ zŏlved′) means:

a. found a solution to; settled
b. ignored; paid no attention to
c. made known publicly
d. kept secret

_____ 3. "It is an even bigger mistake to assume that someone who does not show all the listed emotional reactions is somehow *deviant* or immature."

Children who are abused often exhibit *deviant* behavior later in their lives.

deviant (dē´ vē ənt) means:

a. kind, gentle
b. illegal; against the law
c. difficult to diagnose
d. differing from accepted standards

_____ 4. "Rather, the list describes typical and appropriate reactions to *impending* death."

We knew from the dark clouds that the *impending* storm could hit at any minute.

impending (ĭm pĕn´ dĭng) means:

a. about to take place
b. severe, harsh
c. delayed; later than expected
d. soothing

_____ 5. "For a brief time the *bereaved* remain in a dazed state in which they may show little emotion."

The *bereaved* widow of the police officer received dozens of letters expressing sympathy over the loss of her courageous husband.

bereaved (bĭ rēvd´) means:

a. peaceful; serene
b. young; childlike
c. suffering the loss of a loved one
d. suffering from a serious illness

_____ 6. "This phase usually ends by the time of the funeral, which *unleashes* tears and bottled-up feelings of despair."

When a hurricane *unleashes* its fury, it can cause millions of dollars of damage.

unleashes (ŭn lēsh´ əz) means:

a. releases
b. controls
c. calms; soothes
d. prevents

______ 7. "Initial shock is followed by sharp *pangs* of grief."

We had not eaten since morning, and our hunger *pangs* increased when we smelled the delicious aroma coming from the campfire that night.

pangs (păngz) means:

a. cravings; strong desires
b. strong, sudden sensations
c. sad, despondent feelings
d. strong dislikes

______ 8. "During this period, agitated distress alternates with silent despair, and suffering is *acute.*"

Everyone in the search party felt *acute* relief when the missing child was found.

acute (ə kyo͞ot´) means:

a. intense
b. mild
c. moderate
d. not noticeable

______ 9. "The first powerful reactions of grief gradually give way to weeks or months of apathy, *dejection,* and depression."

We could tell from their *dejection* that they had lost the final game of the baseball playoffs.

dejection (dĭ jĕkt´ shən) means:

a. agitation; nervousness
b. energy; liveliness
c. discouragement or low spirits
d. happiness; elation

______ 10. "Life seems to lose much of its meaning, and a sense of futility *dominates* the person's outlook."

The story of the president's resignation *dominates* our thoughts this week.

dominates (dŏm´ ə nāts) means:

a. controls or occupies
b. treats harshly
c. treats as unimportant
d. is excluded from

Respond in Writing

Directions: Refer to Selection 7-3 as necessary to answer these essay-type items.

Options for collaboration: For some of the "Respond in Writing" exercises, your instructor may prefer that you work collaboratively, that is, with other students. These exercises are identified in the margin. *If your instructor directs you to work collaboratively on any of these items,* form groups of three or four classmates to complete the exercise together. Discuss your answers with each other and have one member of the group record the answers. A member of the group may be asked to share the group's answers with the class.

1. The thanatologist Elisabeth Kübler-Ross found five basic reactions to death (or any major loss). Give examples of how each of these reactions might manifest itself in a person's behavior. You may add examples of your own to any the author gives. (For instance, one possible behavior accompanying the first emotional reaction is avoiding calling to get results of medical tests.)

Emotional reaction	*Possible behaviors accompanying the reaction*
Denial and isolation	______________________ ______________________
Anger	______________________ ______________________
Bargaining	______________________ ______________________
Depression	______________________ ______________________
Acceptance	______________________ ______________________

2. What are two important ways a person could benefit from knowledge of the five reactions Kübler-Ross describes?

____

____

____

3. How does a hospice differ from a hospital? In your answer, use words that signal contrasts (see page 314 for these words).

Option

Item 4 may be completed collaboratively.

4. With the exception of the "bargaining stage," there is a predictable pattern of grief, just as there is a predictable pattern of reactions to impending death. Review this comparison (presented at the end of the selection) and complete the table on the opposite page. (To get you started, the answers to be inserted opposite *Denial and isolation* are "shock or numbness" and "difficulty accepting the reality of the loss." Write them in the space provided.)

Reactions to death or loss	*Reactions to grief*
Denial and isolation	
Anger	
Bargaining	(No equivalent reaction)
Depression	
Acceptance	

Option

Item 5 may be completed collaboratively.

5. What is the most important overall message the writer wants the reader to understand about reactions to impending death? Try to answer this question in one sentence.

CHAPTER 8

READING CRITICALLY

IN THIS CHAPTER YOU WILL LEARN
THE ANSWERS TO THESE QUESTIONS:

What is critical reading?

How can I determine an author's purpose and intended audience?

How can I determine an author's point of view and tone?

How can I distinguish between facts and opinions?

How can I draw logical inferences and conclusions?

How can I evaluate written material?

CHAPTER 8 CONTENTS

It is not enough to have a good mind. The main thing is to use it well.
René Descartes

WHAT IS CRITICAL READING?

Key term

Critical reading: Going beyond basic comprehension to gain additional insights.

Going beyond basic comprehension to gain additional insights as you read is called ***critical reading.*** Whenever you read, you should identify basic information: topic, main idea, and supporting details. However, to gain a greater understanding, you will often need to go beyond these basic elements.

Reading critically requires you to ask certain questions *after* you read a passage and to *think* critically about what you have read. This also means taking time to reread and reconsider an author's message so that you can make careful evaluations and judgments about what you are reading. Critical reading requires you to understand implied (suggested) and figurative (nonliteral) meanings in addition to literal (stated) meanings.

CRITICAL READING SKILLS

The important, interrelated critical reading skills presented in this chapter are:

- Determining an author's purpose and intended audience
- Determining an author's point of view and tone
- Distinguishing between facts and opinions
- Making logical inferences and drawing conclusions
- Evaluating written material

Because these skills are *interrelated,* they are presented together in this chapter. As you will learn in this chapter, an author's *purpose* causes him or her to present certain facts and opinions, and to use a certain *tone* to convey a *point of view* and an *intended meaning* to an *intended audience.*

Determining an Author's Purpose and Intended Audience

Key term

Purpose: An author's reason for writing.

Authors write for specific purposes. An author's ***purpose*** is simply his or her reason for writing. The author's purpose may be to inform, to instruct, to entertain, or to persuade the reader to believe something or take a certain action. Most textbook authors write for the purpose of informing (giving information) and instructing (explaining how to do something).

Sometimes an author will state his or her purpose. For example, the author of a biology textbook might write, "The purpose of this section is to define and explain the two types of cell division." At other times, the author may feel that the purpose is so obvious and assumes that the reader can infer it.

Understanding an author's purpose means that you are aware of his or her motives for writing. This can help you understand what information the writer has chosen to present (for example, one side of an issue or both sides) and how the information is likely to be presented (objectively or with a bias). Understanding the author's purpose helps you evaluate the author's message accurately. Thus you can prevent yourself from being unknowingly influenced by the author's bias.

To determine an author's purpose, think about the words he or she has chosen to use, because words may be chosen deliberately to influence your thinking and elicit a certain response. For example, authors who have a bias may use phrases such as these to try to achieve their purpose:

Any reasonable person will agree that . . .

Only a fool could believe that . . .

The only intelligent choice, then, is . . .

Another way to determine an author's purpose is to examine whether or not both sides of an issue have been presented. Has important information been treated inadequately or left out altogether?

Remember that although an author may appear to be presenting unbiased information about both sides of an issue, the real purpose may be to pursuade you to believe or support one side. This is one reason why critical readers ask themselves, "Why did the author write this?"

Authors also have specific audiences in mind when they write. An author's ***intended audience*** is the *reader:* that is, the audience consists of people the author has in mind as readers, the people he or she is writing for. For instance, a psychologist writing a textbook may assume that his or her audience will be students taking a psychology course. The psychologist will have these students in mind while writing, and that will shape decisions about the material to be included and about the level of difficulty. "Who did the author intend to read this?" is a question critical readers always ask themselves.

Key term

Intended audience: People an author has in mind as readers; the people he or she is writing for.

Sometimes, of course, an author will state who the intended audience is. However, when *you* must determine an author's intended audience, look at the topic being discussed (technical or of general interest), the level of language used (simple, sophisticated, or specialized), and the purpose for writing (to instruct, inform, persuade, entertain, etc.).

Below is a paragraph from an article in *Prevention* magazine entitled "Laugh Your Stress Away" (Selection 5-2). After you read this paragraph, ask yourself, "Why did the author write this?" and "Who did the author intend to read this?"

Humor is one of the best on-the-spot stress busters around. It's vitually impossible to belly laugh and feel bad at the same time. If you're caught in a situation you can't escape or change (a traffic jam, for example), then humor may be the healthiest form of temporary stress release possible.

What is the author's purpose?

____

____

Who is the author's intended audience?

____

____

Source: Steven Lally, "Laugh Your Stress Away," *Prevention,* June 1991, p. 284. Reprinted by permission of *Prevention* magazine.

Annotate

Go back to the excerpt. Determine the author's purpose and intended audience, and write your responses in the spaces provided.

In this paragraph, the author's purpose is to *inform* the reader that humor can be an effective way to temporarily reduce stress. You can see that the author uses simple language and short sentences. Notice that the author uses informal language: *stress busters, belly laugh.* He also chooses a simple example: being stuck in a traffic jam. Because his topic requires no special prior knowledge and because his approach is uncomplicated, you can assume that the author's intended audience is the *general public.* Practically anyone could understand and benefit from the information he presents. Of course, the source of the passage, *Prevention* magazine, helps confirm that the general public is the intended audience.

After you read the next passage, from a business communication textbook, determine the authors' purpose and the audience they had in mind.

Think about the people you know. Which of them would you call successful communicators? What do these people have in common? Chances are, the individuals on your list share five qualities:

- *Perception.* They are able to predict how their message will be received. They anticipate your reaction and shape the message accordingly. They read your response correctly and constantly adjust to correct any misunderstanding.
- *Precision.* They create a "meeting of the minds." When they finish expressing themselves, you share the same mental picture.
- *Credibility.* They are believable. You have faith in the substance of their message. You trust their information and their intentions.
- *Control.* They shape your response. Depending on their purpose, they can

What is the authors' purpose?

____

____

____

Who is the authors' intended audience?

____

____

____

make you laugh or cry, calm down, change your mind, or take action.
▪ *Congeniality.* They maintain friendly, pleasant relations with the audience. Regardless of whether you agree with them, good communicators command your respect and goodwill. You are willing to work with them again, despite your differences.

What sets good communicators apart is their ability to overcome the main barriers to communication. They do this by creating their messages carefully, minimizing noise in the transmission process, and facilitating feedback.

Source: Courtland Bovée and John Thill, *Business Communication Today,* 3d ed., McGraw-Hill, New York, 1992, p. 44. Reproduced by permission of McGraw-Hill.

Annotate

Go back to the excerpt. Determine the authors' purpose and intended audience, and write your responses in the spaces provided.

In this excerpt, the authors' purpose is to *inform.* The authors list specific elements that characterize good communicators and describe how these people interact with others. The authors' intended audience is *students in a business course or other adults who want to know about characteristics of effective communication* (such as those who work in business situations or talk to large or small groups).

Here is a passage from a health textbook whose purpose and audience are easy to determine. In this passage, the authors use simple, factual language to describe to the reader the proper procedure to follow when someone is choking.

CHOKING

If a person who seems to be choking on food or a foreign object can speak, do not interfere with that individual's attempt to cough up the object. If the person is unable to speak, it is appropriate to provide emergency care by using the Heimlich maneuver. Stand behind the victim and place both arms around his or her waist. Grasp one fist with the other hand and place the thumb side of the fist against the victim's abdomen, slightly above the navel and below the rib cage. Press your fist into the victim's abdomen with a quick inward and upward thrust. Repeat this procedure until the object is dislodged. The Heimlich maneuver should not be used with infants under one year of age.

What is the authors' purpose?

____

____

____

Who is the authors' intended audience?

____

____

____

Source: Marvin Levy, Mark Dignan, and Janet Shirreffs, *Targeting Wellness: The Core,* McGraw-Hill, New York, 1992, pp. 284–285. Reproduced with permission of McGraw-Hill.

Annotate

Go back to the excerpt. Determine the authors' purpose and intended audience, and write your responses in the spaces provided.

The purpose of the passage is to *instruct* (to describe how to perform the Heimlich maneuver). The intended audience is students in a health course or a first aid course, or anyone else who might be interested in learning the Heimlich maneuver.

Here is a paragraph from a selection entitled "The Time Message" (Selection 1-3). After you have read it, ask yourself, "Why did the author write this?" and "Who did the author intend to read this?"

> Time is dangerous. If you don't control it, it will control you. If you don't make it work for you, it will work against you. You must become a master of time, not the servant. In other words, as a college student, time management will be your number-one problem.

What is the authors' purpose?

____

____

Who is the authors' intended audience?

____

____

Source: E. N. Chapman, "The Time Message," in Frank Christ, ed., *SR/SE Resource Book,* SRA, Chicago, Ill., 1969, p. 3.

Annotate

Go back to the excerpt. Determine the author's purpose and audience, and write them in the spaces provided.

Although the author of this paragraph informs the reader about the importance of controlling time, he hopes to *persuade* the reader to address this potentially "dangerous" problem. The author's intended audience is clearly stated in the last sentence of the paragraph: the *college student,* especially one who has not yet mastered time management skills.

Here is a paragraph written for a completely different purpose. It is from the best-seller *Having Our Say: The Delany Sisters' First 100 Years.* (See Selection 8-1.) In this excerpt, 103-year-old Bessie Delany describes her near-fatal bout with typhoid fever when she was 15 years old.

> When I got out of the hospital, I looked like death. They had cut off my hair, real short, and I weighed next to nothing. I could not get enough to eat. Mama was so worried that she fixed a small basket of fruit each morning for me to carry with me all day, so I could eat whenever I wanted. For a long time I was on crutches, and I was not expected to recover fully. They used to say that typhoid fever left its mark on people. Well, nothing has shown up yet, so I guess I'm in the clear!

What is the authors' purpose?

____

____

____

Who is the authors' intended audience?

____

____

____

Sarah and Elizabeth Delany with Amy Hill Hearth, *Having Our Say,* Dell, New York, 1993, p. 83.

Annotate

Go back to the excerpt. Determine the author's purpose and intended audience, and write your responses in the spaces provided.

As the last sentence suggests, the purpose of this paragraph is to entertain the reader: 88 years later Bessie Delany "guesses" she's "in the clear" and no longer needs to worry that any aftereffects of her bout with typhoid will show up. The intended audience is any member of the general public who would enjoy reading about the lives of two remarkable centenarian sisters.

Remember, part of critical reading is asking yourself, "Why did the author write this?" and "Who did the author intend to read this?"

Determining an Author's Point of View and Tone

Key term

Point of view: An author's position (attitude, belief, or opinion) on a topic.

Point of view refers to an author's position (attitude or belief) about a topic. In other words, an author's point of view is his or her opinion about that topic. Even though authors are generally experts in their fields, they do not always agree on every topic and issue.

Because authors may have different points of view and may disagree with other experts, it is important that you recognize what each author's point of view is. For example, one author's point of view might be, "Gun control is necessary if we are to have a safe society." The point of view of an author with the opposite bias would be, "Gun control would only make society less safe." An unbiased (neutral or objective) point of view would be, "Gun control has both advantages and disadvantages."

To determine the author's point of view, critical readers ask themselves, "What is the author's position on this issue?" and then look for words that reveal the author's point of view such as:

Supporting this new policy is *essential* because . . .

The proposed legislation *will benefit* all the citizens of Dallas county because . . .

It is *not in the best interest* of the country to . . .

Voters *should oppose* the creation of a state lottery because . . .

Key term

Tone: Manner of writing (choice of words and style) that reveal an author's attitude toward a topic.

An author's ***tone*** is a manner of writing that reveals or reflects the author's attitude toward a topic, just as tone of voice reveals a speaker's attitude. When someone is speaking, you can generally tell by the tone if he or she is serious, sarcastic, sympathetic, enthusiastic, etc. To convey a tone, a speaker relies on pitch, volume, and inflection, along with choice of words. (For example, if someone says, "I made a C on my biology test," you would need to know the speaker's tone to know whether he or she was excited, relieved, or disappointed.) In much the same way, writers depend on their choice of words and writing style to convey their tone.

Authors use tone just as speakers do. Authors, however, must rely on style of writing and choice of words to reveal their tone. They select words and writing styles that fit their purposes for writing (to inform, instruct, persuade, or entertain) and their point of view. In other words, they use tone (informal, serious, sincere, humorous, etc.) to help convey their purpose and point of view (for example, in favor of or opposed to something). Thus, you can determine an author's tone by examining his or her choice of words and style of writing. To determine an author's tone, ask yourself, "What do the author's choice of words and style of writing reveal about his or her attitude?'

As just noted, choice of words—or *word choice*—is one way the authors reveal their tone. For example, one writer might use the word *lie* to convey a critical, disapproving, or bitter tone; another might use *exaggerate* to convey a tolerant or even an amused tone. Compare the following two sentences; they contain the same message (taxpayers' money will be used to help the unemployed), but the word choice makes their tone very different:

> Once again, the American taxpayers have to foot the bill for those who are too lazy or unwilling to work.
>
> Once again, American taxpayers are showing their generosity by helping those unable to find employment.

Note the disapproving tone conveyed by the word choice in the first sentence *(foot the bill* and *too lazy or unwilling to work).* A more positive, compassionate tone is conveyed by the choice of words in the second sentence *(showing their generosity by helping* and *unable to find employment).*

Now consider how an author's *writing style* also conveys a tone. Each of these sentences contains the same message, but the writing style makes their tone quite different:

> Since there will be a significant increase in employment opportunities in the field of "virtual reality," computer science majors would be wise to investigate this fast-growing area.
>
> VR is becoming a really hot career field, so check it out!

These sentences present essentially the same information, but the first sentence has a more formal, factual tone. It is the type of sentence you might find in a career brochure or a computer science textbook. In the second sentence, however, the use of "VR," the phrase *really hot career field,* and the expression of *check it out* convey an informal and enthusiastic tone. This kind of sentence might appear in a computer magazine or on a poster advertising a computer job fair.

Although an author's tone is often obvious, there may be times when the tone is less clear and requires careful thought on your part. If you misunderstand an author's tone, you will misinterpret the message. For example, if you read a short story and you miss the author's ironic tone, you will mistakenly think his or her meaning is the opposite of what it actually is. In situations like this—when you overlook irony—you may think authors are being serious when they are actually joking; that they are calm when, in fact, they are angry; or that they are in favor of something when, in reality, they oppose it. Understanding the author's tone will enable you to grasp the ***intended meaning,*** even when the author's words appear on the surface to be saying something different. Critical readers ask themselves, "What is the author's *intended* meaning?"

Key term

Intended meaning: What an author wants you to understand even when his or her words seem to be saying something different.

When authors are being ironic, they create a deliberate contrast between their apparent meaning and their intended meaning; they say one thing but mean the opposite. That is, the words are intended to express something different from their literal meaning. You use irony every day in conversation. For example, you might say, "Well, that test was a breeze!" but your ironic tone makes it clear how difficult the test actually was. Another form of *irony* occurs when there is incongruity between what might be expected and what actually occurs. For example, it would be ironic if you won a new car in a contest the day after you bought a new one. (Students sometimes confuse irony with sarcasm. *Sarcasm* is a cutting, often ironic remark that is intended to convey contempt or ridicule. Sarcasm is always meant to hurt; irony is not.)

Some words that can be used to describe an author's tone are:

ambivalent	evasive	joking	sentimental
amused	factual	joyful	serious
angry	forgiving	malicious	shocked
approving	grim	mocking	skeptical
arrogant	hostile	negative	solemn
bitter	humorous	nostalgic	straightforward
cautious	impassioned	optimistic	supportive
compassionate	indifferent	pessimistic	sympathetic
conciliatory	indignant	positive	tolerant
critical	insulting	remorseful	urgent
cynical	intolerant	respectful	
disapproving	ironic	sarcastic	
disbelieving	irreverent	self-pitying	

You already know the meaning of many of these words, and you should familiarize yourself with the meaning of those you do not know. To be sure you understand an author's message correctly, you should ask the question critical readers ask, "Based on the author's tone, what is his or her intended meaning?"

Here is an excerpt from an essay by George Will, a well-known author and political columnist. His topic is legal gambling (state lotteries and betting on the sport of jai alai). As you read, notice that his disapproving tone helps convey his negative point of view toward legal forms of gambling.

Last year, Americans legally wagered $15 billion, up 8 percent over 1976. Lotteries took in 24 percent more. Stiffening resistance to taxes is encouraging states to seek revenues from gambling, and thus to encourage gambling. There are three rationalizations for this:

- State-run gambling controls illegal gambling.

What is the author's point of view?

______

______

______

What is the author's tone?

______

______

- Gambling is a painless way to raise revenues.
- Gambling is a "victimless" recreation, and thus is a matter of moral indifference.

Actually, there is evidence that legal gambling increases the respectability of gambling, and increases public interest in gambling. This creates new gamblers, some of whom move on to illegal gambling, which generally offers better odds. And as a revenue-raising device, gambling is severely regressive.

Gamblers are drawn disproportionately from minority and poor populations that can ill afford to gamble, that are especially susceptible to the lure of gambling, and that especially need a government that will not collaborate with gambling entrepreneurs, as in jai alai, and that will not become a gambling entrepreneur through a state lottery.

A depressing number of gamblers have no margin for economic losses and little understanding of the probability of losses. Between 1975 and 1977 there was a 140 percent increase in spending to advertise lotteries—lotteries in which more than 99.9 percent of all players are losers. Such advertising is apt to be especially effective, and cruel, among people whose tribulations make them susceptible to dreams of sudden relief.

Grocery money is risked for such relief. Some grocers in Hartford's poorer neighborhoods report that receipts decline during jai alai season. Aside from the injury gamblers do to their dependents, there is a more subtle but more comprehensive injury done by gambling. It is the injury done to society's sense of elemental equities. Gambling blurs the distinction between well-earned and "ill-gotten" gains.

State-sanctioned gambling institutionalizes windfalls, whets the public appetite for them, and encourages the delusion that they are more frequent than they really are. Thus do states simultaneously cheat and corrupt their citizens.

Source: George F. Will, "Lotteries Cheat, Corrupt the People," © 1994 Washington Post Writers' Group. Reprinted with permission.

This passage clearly shows George Will's point of view: he opposes legal gambling because he believes it harms the public in a variety of ways. His disapproving tone is created by his deliberate choice of words such as these:

rationalization (instead of *reasons*)

collaborating with (which suggests helping someone do something wrong)

the *lure* of gambling

a *depressing* number of gamblers

cruel

dreams of sudden relief (which will not really happen)

injury

ill-gotten gains

encourages the *delusion*

cheat and corrupt their citizens

Annotate

Go back to the excerpt. Determine this author's point of view and tone. Write them in the spaces provided.

In addition, Will's style of writing conveys his disapproving tone and point of view. He presents facts in a well-reasoned argument against gambling. Moreover, he appears extremely knowledgeable about his subject.

In the passage below, the authors' tone is completely different, since it is from a study skills textbook. Its purpose is to define *concentration* and explain an important point about concentration. As you read this paragraph, ask yourself, "What is the author's position on this issue?" and "What do the author's choice of words and style of writing reveal about his or her attitude?"

Psychologically defined, concentration is the process of centering one's attention over a period of time. In practical application, however, concentration is not as simple to cope with as the definition may imply. For this reason, it is important to keep the following points in mind.

What is the authors' point of view?

____

____

What is the authors' tone?

____

____

Source: William Farquar, John Krumboltz, and Gilbert Wrenn, "Controlling Your Concentration," in Frank Christ, ed., *SR/SE Resource Book,* SRA, Chicago, Ill., 1969, p. 119.

Annotate

Go back to the excerpt. Determine this author's point of view and tone. Write them in the spaces provided.

In this paragraph, the authors' tone is factual and straightforward rather than emotional and persuasive. The authors' point of view is that concentration is a more complicated process than it might seem.

It is obvious from these two examples that an author's tone is related to his or her purpose and point of view. Being aware of the author's tone will help you determine that purpose and point of view. (For example, the purpose may be to persuade you. The author's point of view is what he or she hopes to persuade you to believe.)

The chart below shows the *interrelationship* among author's purpose, tone, point of view, intended meaning, and intended audience.

How the Critical Reading Skills Are Interrelated

The author's ***purpose*** *causes him or her to use a certain* ***tone*** *to convey a* ***point of view*** *and an* ***intended meaning*** *to an* ***intended audience.***

The author's **purpose**

To inform. To instruct.
To persuade. To entertain.

causes him or her to use a certain **tone**

Serious. Formal. Sincere. Enthusiastic.
Disapproving. Sympathetic. Informal.
Humorous. Ironic, etc.

that conveys a **point of view** *and an* **intended meaning**

Supportive (for). Unsupportive (against). Objective (neutral).
Intended meaning: Argument. Overall main idea (thesis).

to an **intended audience**

General public. Specific group. A particular person.

The following chart tells you more about *how the author conveys* these elements.

The author's . . .

- ***purpose*** is supported by ***choice of writing pattern*** and ***choice of facts and opinions***
  - ***tone*** is reflected in ***word choice*** and ***writing style***
    - ***point of view*** and ***intended meaning*** are presented as an ***argument*** or an ***overall main idea***
      - ***intended audience*** may be the ***general public*** or a ***specific group***

Remember, part of reading critically is to ask yourself, "What is the author's position on this issue?" and "What do the author's choice of words and style of writing reveal about his or her attitude?"

Distinguishing between Facts and Opinions

Key term

Fact: Something that can be proved to exist or have happened or is generally assumed to exist or have happened.

Many students mistakenly believe that anything that appears in print, especially in a textbook, must be a fact. Although college textbooks may consist largely of facts, they often include many useful and valuable opinions as well.

What is the difference between a fact and an opinion? A ***fact*** is something that can be proved to exist or have happened, or is generally *assumed* to exist or have happened (for example, *In 1620 the Pilgrims landed in what is now Plymouth, Massachusetts,* or *Thousands of years ago, early people migrated from Asia to the North American continent by walking from Siberia to Alaska across the frozen Bering Strait.*) The process of proving that something is a fact (that it is true) is called *verification.* Verification requires experimentation and research or direct experience and observation.

Key term

Opinion: Belief or judgment that cannot be proved or disproved.

An ***opinion,*** on the other hand, is a belief or judgment. Opinions can be neither proved nor disproved. Therefore, when a statement cannot be found to be either factual or false, it represents an opinion. It is important to realize that although opinions cannot be proved, they can be supported by valid reasons and plausible evidence. Well-supported opinions are useful, since they are based on facts or on the ideas of knowledgeable people. Opinions in textbooks typically represent this type of valuable opinion, since they are the well-reasoned beliefs of the author or other experts. Scientific theories are also examples of "expert opinions." (If a theory could be proved, then it would no longer be a theory. It would be a fact.) Of course, poorly supported or unsupported opinions are not useful.

Students sometimes confuse incorrect information with opinions because they assume if something is not a fact, it must automatically be an opinion. However, information can be a fact (it is correct information), an opinion (it represents someone's belief), or a *false statement of fact* (it is not a fact or an opinion; it is simply incorrect information). The statements *January follows February* and *Water freezes at 212°F* are examples of false statements of fact. Since they can be proved incorrect, they are not facts or opinions.

Critical readers ask themselves, "Can the information the author presents be proved, or does it represent a judgment?" When an author includes opinions, it is important for you to evaluate these opinions, because not all opinions are valid or useful. An opinion is of little value if it is poorly supported, that is, if the author does not give good reasons for it. A well-supported opinion, on the other hand, can be as important and useful as a fact. To repeat: Even though opinions cannot be proved, they are valuable when supported by facts and other well-reasoned opinions; poorly supported opinions are of little value, even if the author writes persuasively. For example, consider the following two sets of support for this statement: *Ann Garcia would make an excellent governor.* (This statement is an opinion, of course, because of the use of the word *excellent.*) Note the difference between the two ways this opinion might be supported:

Opinion: Ann Garcia would make an excellent governor.

Well-reasoned support:
Law degree from Harvard (fact)
Chief legal counsel of a Fortune 500 company (fact)
Served 12 years as a senator (fact)
Appears to be extremely ethical (opinion)
Seems strongly committed to family values (opinion)
Would be an effective problem-solver (opinion)

Poor support
Her father served as an ambassador (fact)
Her brother is a millionaire (fact)
Married to the same man for twenty years (fact)
Has smart, beautiful children (opinion)
Is attractive (opinion)
Comes across well in TV ads (opinion)

Because opinions represent judgments, beliefs, or interpretations, authors often use certain words or phrases to indicate that they are presenting an opinion. The following words and phrases are typical of those that signal an opinion:

perhaps
apparently
presumably
one possibility is
one interpretation is
in our opinion
many experts believe
many people think that
it seems likely
this suggests
in our view
in the opinion of

In addition, words that indicate value judgments can signal opinions. These include words such as:

most
greatest
worst
best
excellent
interesting
beautiful
wealthy
successful
fascinating
effective

These words signal opinions because people may disagree about what is considered "successful," "fascinating," etc. For example, in the sentence *Adults must have a college degree in order to be successful,* the word *successful* could mean successful financially, personally, socially, or in all of these ways. Because there are different interpretations of what *successful* means, it would be impossible to prove a statement like this (although it could be supported with certain facts about college graduates). Consequently, the statement expresses an opinion. (Even though this may be a widely held opinion, it is still an opinion.) As you read, then, watch for judgmental words that can be interpreted in different ways by different people.

The following box summarizes important information on facts and opinions.

Facts and Opinions

Fact	False Statement	Opinion
Can be *proved* (correct information)	Can be *disproved* (incorrect information)	Cannot be proved *or* disproved (someone's belief or judgment)
Valuable	Of no value	▪ Valuable if *well supported* ▪ Of no value if *unsupported* or *poorly supported*

To distinguish between facts and opinions when reading critically, ask yourself these questions in this order:

1. Can the information in the statement be proved?
   (If so, it is correct information, a *fact.*)
2. Can the information in the statement be disproved?
   (If so, it is incorrect information, a *false statement of fact.*)
3. Is the information in the statement something that cannot be proved *or* disproved?
   (If so, it is an opinion.) If it is an opinion, ask yourself:
   - Is the opinion *well-supported* (based on valid reasons and plausible evidence)?

     (If so, it is a valuable opinion.)
   - Is the opinion *unsupported* or *poorly supported?*

     (If so, it is of little or no value.)

Following are two excerpts form *The Autobiography of Malcolm X.* (See Selection 1-2, "Saved.") The first contains facts that can be verified about the prison where Malcolm X served his sentence. In the second excerpt, Malcolm X gives his opinions about how learning to read changed him.

Facts

The Norfolk Prison Colony's library was in the school building. A variety of classes was taught there by instructors who came from such places as Harvard and Boston universities.

Notice that this passage contains information that can be verified by objective proof: the location of the prison library and the names of the universities the instructors came from.

In the second passage, Malcolm X states his opinions about reading and its effect on him:

Opinions

> I have often reflected upon the new vistas that reading opened to me. I knew right there in prison that reading had changed forever the course of my life. As I see it today, the ability to read awoke inside me some long dormant craving to be mentally alive.
>
> *Source:* Alex Haley, *The Autobiography of Malcolm X,* Ballantine, New York, 1992, pp. 173, 179.

Malcolm X's opinions are that reading opened new vistas to him, that it changed the course of his life forever, and that it awoke in him a craving to be mentally alive.

The next excerpt, from an American government textbook, discusses how historians and political scientists have ranked presidents of the United States. It includes a table that summarizes the results of three surveys. As this excerpt shows, experts often agree in their opinions. When such agreement exists, the opinions are especially valuable.

> Several surveys have asked American historians and political scientists to rank the presidents from best to worst. Although some presidential reputations rise or fall with the passage of time, there has been remarkable consistency in whom the scholars rank as the best and worst presidents. . . . The consistency of these results suggests that scholars use some unspoken criteria when assessing the presidents. At least four criteria stand out: the effectiveness of presidential policy, the president's vision of the office, the president's handling of crises, and the president's personality.

SCHOLARS RANK THE PRESIDENTS

> In three surveys conducted in the 1980s, scholars were asked to rank the presidents. The results below show only those presidents who clearly and consistently ranked near the top or bottom. The surveys included all presidents except Reagan (who was still in office and thus could not be assessed dispassionately), Bush (who had not yet served), and William Harrison and Garfield (whose terms were too short to be realistically assessed).

Greatest presidents (in top five on all three surveys)	*Failures* (in bottom five in all three surveys)
Abraham Lincoln	James Buchanan
George Washington	U.S. Grant
Franklin Delano Roosevelt	Warren G. Harding
Thomas Jefferson	Richard M. Nixon
Theodore Roosevelt	

Near-greats (in top ten on all three surveys)	*Near-failures* (in bottom ten on all three surveys)
Woodrow Wilson	Calvin Coolidge
Andrew Jackson	Millard Fillmore
Harry S. Truman	Andrew Johnson
	John Tyler
	Franklin Pierce

Sources: John J. Harrigan, *Politics and the American Future,* 3d ed., McGraw-Hill, New York, 1992, pp. 282–283. Table: 1982 poll of forty-nine scholars in *Chicago Tribune Magazine,* January 10, 1982, pp. 8–13, 15, 18 (Copyrighted, 1982 Chicago Tribune Company, all rights reserved, used with permission); and poll of forty-one scholars by David L. Porter in 1981, reprinted in Robert K. Murray and Tim H. Blessing, "The Presidential Performance Study: A Progress Report," *Journal of American History* 70, no. 3 (December 1983): 535–555.

Here are two final excerpts, one factual and one containing the author's opinion. Both are from an essay by John Ciardi entitled "Another School Year—What For?" As you read these excerpts, ask yourself, "Can the information the author presents be proved, or does it represent a judgment?"

It was January of 1940 and I was fresh out of graduate school starting my first semester at the University of Kansas City. Part of the reading for the freshman English course was *Hamlet.*

Fact or opinion?

____

If you have no time for Shakespeare, for a basic look at philosophy, for the continuity of the fine arts, for that lesson of man's development we call history—then you have no business in college.

Fact or opinion?

____

Source: John Ciardi, "Another School Year—What For?" Rutgers University Press. Reprinted by permission of the Ciardi family.

Did you recognize that the first excerpt consists of facts and the second excerpt gives an opinion?

Here are two additional points about facts and opinions: First, you should remember that although some paragraphs contain only facts or only opinions, they may consist of both facts and opinions and may even present both in the same sentence. Second, you should realize that it may be difficult, at times, to distinguish opinions from facts. An author may present opinions in such a way that they *seem* like facts. For example, a writer might introduce an opinion by stating, "The fact is . . ." ("The fact is, Hawaii's weather makes it the perfect place for a winter vacation.") Stating that something is a fact, however, does not make it a fact (Hawaii isn't the perfect place for your winter vacation if you want to do Alpine skiing). Ideally, of course, an author would always express an opinion in a way that makes it clear that it *is* an opinion. ("In this writer's opinion, Hawaii's weather makes it the perfect place for a winter vacation.") But authors do not always do this, and it is your job to think critically as you read, being alert for opinions. Then, when you identify an opinion, you can continue reading to determine whether or not it is well supported.

Making Logical Inferences and Drawing Conclusions

Key term

Inference: A logical conclusion based on what an author has stated.

A critical reader understands not only what an author states directly, but also what the author *suggests.* In other words, it is the responsibility of critical readers to make inferences, or draw conclusions. An ***inference*** is a logical conclusion that the reader makes. It goes beyond what the author states but must be based on what the author has said. To repeat: inferences go beyond what an author has stated directly, but they must be based on what the author says. Your inferences are conclusions *you* have made on the basis of the passage. Remember that you cannot use information *stated* by the author as an inference. This is logical: if the author has already stated it, there would be no reason for you to infer it.

When you read, you should ask yourself, "What logical conclusions can be based on what the author has stated?" To make an inference, the reader must deduce the author's meaning. That is, readers must use the "evidence" and facts the author presents in order to arrive at the inference the author wants them to make. Readers must make a connection between what an author says and what the author wants them to conclude or do. For example, a writer might describe the benefits of regular exercise but not state directly that you should exercise. This writer expects you to make the inference (draw the conclusion) that you should exercise regularly because exercise will benefit you.

Making inferences is not new to you. In fact, you make inferences continually in your daily life. You make deductions on the basis of descriptions, facts, opinions, experiences, and observations. Assume, for example, that a woman in your class arrives late. She seems frustrated and upset, and her hands are covered with grease and grime. It would be logical to infer that she has had a flat tire or some other trouble with her car and has had to fix the problem herself. Your inference would be based on your observations. Similarly, you make inferences every day about things you read. For instance, suppose that your roommate leaves you a note saying, "Hope you didn't need your brown jacket today. It looks great with my new jeans." You would infer that your roommate has borrowed—and is probably wearing—your brown jacket. This is your roommate's *intended meaning* ("I borrowed your jacket, and I'm wearing it"), even though this information doesn't appear in the message.

Chapter 5 of *Opening Doors,* "Formulating Implied Main Ideas," involves making inferences. When authors *suggest* a main idea but do not state it directly, they are *implying* it. When readers comprehend an implied main idea, they are *inferring* it. The writer implies the main idea; the reader infers it.

Sometimes, formulating an implied main idea is the only inference you need to make about a passage. Thinking critically, however, may involve making additional inferences and drawing conclusions about what you have read. You can make inferences on the basis of a single paragraph as well as longer passages.

Sometimes, of course, there are *no* inferences to be made about the material in textbook passages. In this case, you need only to understand the topic, main idea, and supporting details.

You can learn to make logical inferences by studying examples of correct inferences. Here is an excerpt from a business communications textbook about a well-known ice cream company, Ben and Jerry's Homemade (Selection 6-1). After reading this excerpt, you can draw some inferences about how the employees feel about Ben and Jerry and the company.

Down at the factory in Waterbury, Vermont, they're known as "the boys." They are Ben Cohen and Jerry Greenfield, arguably America's most famous purveyors of ice cream and certainly two of America's most colorful entrepreneurs. They've been friends since seventh grade and business partners since 1978 when they opened their first scoop shop, using techniques gleaned from a $5 correspondence course on how to make ice cream. Their firm, Ben & Jerry's Homemade, sold more than $76 million worth of super premium ice cream in 1990 and employs around 300 people, give or take a few, depending on the season.

Ben and Jerry have strong personalities and strong opinions. They believe that work should be fun, or else it isn't worth doing. They also believe in helping the unfortunate, protecting the environment, and treating people fairly. They want their company to be a happy, humanitarian place where everybody feels good about coming to work and producing a top-notch product.

What inferences do the authors want you to make about the employees of Ben and Jerry's?

____

____

____

____

____

____

> . . . Actions also telegraph Ben & Jerry's commitment to an egalitarian work environment: the open office arrangement, the bright colors, the pictures of cows and fields hanging on warehouse walls, the employee committees, the casual clothes, the first-name relationships, the compressed pay scale that keeps executive salaries in balance with lower-level compensation, the free health club memberships for everyone, the upcoming on-site day-care facility. And the free ice cream. Three pints a day per person. Now that's communication at its best.

Source: Courtland Bovée and John Thill, *Business Communication Today,* 3d ed., McGraw-Hill, New York, 1992, pp. 26, 28. Reproduced with permission of McGraw-Hill.

Because the owners of Ben and Jerry's Homemade provide their employees with a fair, supportive, informal, and comfortable work environment, it is logical to conclude that:

Employees who work there are happy.
They appreciate the company's philosophy.
They are likely to remain employees of Ben and Jerry's.

The following details from the passage are the ones on which these inferences are based:

Employees call Ben and Jerry "the boys."
Ben and Jerry believe that work should be fun.
Ben and Jerry are interested in protecting the environment.
They believe in treating people fairly.
They want their company to be a happy, humanitarian place.
They have an open office arrangement.
They use bright colors.
There are pictures on warehouse walls.
Employees wear casual clothes.
First names are used.
There is a compressed pay scale.
There is a free health club.
There will soon be an on-site day-care facility.
Employees receive free ice cream daily.

Annotate

Go back to the excerpt. In the spaces provided, write some of the logical inferences based on it.

You could draw other logical conclusions from these details as well. For example, you could conclude that companies can be humane and humanitarian yet still be extremely profitable. You could conclude that the public appreciates a high-quality product and is willing to pay for it. You might conclude that you would like to work for Ben and Jerry's.

Here is another textbook excerpt whose conclusion must be inferred by reading critically. The passage is from a health textbook, and its topic is *passive smoking.*

PASSIVE SMOKING AND THE RIGHTS OF NONSMOKERS

Reports from the U.S. surgeon general's office suggest that tobacco smoke in enclosed indoor areas is an important air pollution problem. This has led to the controversy about **passive smoking**—the breathing in of air polluted by the second-hand tobacco smoke of others. Carbon monoxide levels of sidestream smoke (smoke from the burning end of a cigarette) reach a dangerously high level. True, the smoke can be greatly diluted in freely circulating air, but the 1 to 5 percent carbon monoxide levels attained in smoke-filled rooms can be sufficient to harm the health of people with chronic bronchitis, other lung disease, or cardiovascular disease.

What inferences do the authors want you to make?

____

____

____

____

____

____

Source: Martin Levy, Mark Dignan, and Janet Shirreffs, *Targeting Wellness: The Core,* McGraw-Hill, New York, 1992, pp. 262–263. Reproduced with the permission of McGraw-Hill.

Annotate

Go back to the excerpt. In the spaces provided, write logical inferences based on it.

These authors want the reader to conclude that nonsmokers, especially those with certain health conditions, should avoid enclosed indoor areas in which there is cigarette smoke. Smokers should also conclude that they ought to refrain from smoking around others in an enclosed area. These are conclusions (inferences) the authors want the reader to make, even though they do not state them. These inferences are based on the statements that "carbon monoxide levels of sidestream smoke reach dangerously high levels" and that these levels "can be sufficient to harm the health of people with chronic bronchitis, other lung disease, or other cardiovascular disease."

When you read, remember to ask yourself, "What logical conclusions can be based on what the author has stated?"

The box on the next page illustrates the application of critical reading skills to an actual piece of writing, a review of an imaginary movie. It is designed to show that critical reading skills are a part of everyday life.

Example of Critical Reading Applied to a Critic's Review of a Movie

Here is a critic's review of *Cyberpunk,* a new science-fiction movie:

> Do you enjoy violence? Do you like vulgar language? Do you appreciate painfully loud sound effects? What about watching unknown actors embarrass themselves? Or sitting for three hours and ten minutes without a break? If so, and you've got $7.50 to burn, then "Cyberpunk" is the movie for you!

Questions	*Answers*
What is the author's purpose?	To present his evaluation of a new movie
Who is the author's intended audience?	The movie-going public
What is the author's point of view?	The movie is terrible.
What is the author's tone?	Sarcastic
What is the author's intended meaning?	The movie is not worth seeing.
Does the author include facts, opinions, or both?	Both
What logical inference (conclusion) does the author expect you to make?	Don't waste your time or money on this movie.

Evaluating Written Material

Key term

Argument: Point of view or position the author wants to persuade the reader to believe.

Key term

Credibility: Believability of an author's argument.

You will often need to critically evaluate material you have read. You should begin by accurately determining the author's argument. An author's ***argument*** is the point of view (position on an issue) the author believes and wants to persuade the reader to believe. (You may also hear the argument referred to as the *thesis,* and it is often the same as the overall main idea.) A written argument is not the same as an oral disagreement. The purpose of a written argument is to persuade the reader to believe something by "arguing" (presenting) a case for it. For example, an author might argue that "All college students should be required to take at least one computer course."

The term ***credibility*** refers to how believable an author's argument is. To be believable, the author's argument must be based on logic or evidence. In other words, critical readers consider an argument to be *credible* if it is based on sources of information that are objective and reliable, if it is well supported with relevant facts and examples, and if it is based on logical reasoning.

Here are the steps you must take to critically evaluate the credibility of the author's argument.

1. *Determine the author's argument.* Ask yourself, "What is the important overall point the author wants to convince the reader to believe?"
2. *Identify the assumptions on which the author bases his or her argument.* Assumptions are things the author takes for granted or accepts as true without proof. Ask yourself, "What assumptions has the author made?"
3. *Identify the types of support the author presents.* Does the author give facts, examples, case studies, research results, or expert opinions? Does he or she cite personal experience or observations, make comparisons, give reasons or evidence? Ask yourself, "What types of support does the author give?"
4. *Determine whether the support is relevant.* Support is relevant when it pertains directly to the argument. Ask yourself, "Is the support relevant?"
5. *Determine whether the argument is valid.* The term *valid* means that an argument is well supported because it has been correctly inferred or deduced from the information on which it is based. Ask yourself, "Is the argument valid?"
6. *Determine whether the author's argument is objective and complete.* The term *objective* means that an argument is based on facts and evidence instead of on the author's feelings or unsupported opinions. The term *complete* means that an author has not left out information because it might weaken or even disprove his or her argument. Ask yourself, "Is the argument objective and complete?"
7. *Evaluate the credibility of the author's argument.* Consider the author's assumptions, types of support, relevance, validity, objectivity and completeness to determine the believability of the author's argument. Ask yourself, "Is the argument credible?"

Consider the argument "All college students should be required to take at least one computer science course." To evaluate its credibility, you would examine the assumptions the author has made. For example, he or she obviously assumes that it is valuable to know about computers, that computers will continue to be important in people's personal and professional lives, etc. The types of support the author gives might include facts and research findings about the growing use of computers, several examples of ways college students benefit, and his or her personal experience. As a reader, you would have to decide whether or not the support is relevant (directly supports the argument), whether the argument is valid (correctly reasoned), whether it is objective (presents both sides of the issue), and whether it is complete (information that might support the other side of the issue was not omitted). Consideration of these elements would enable you to evaluate whether or not the author's argument has credibility.

Now read and evaluate an excerpt from a college textbook on health. This excerpt (from "The Decision to Marry," Selection 7-2) discusses the compatibility of couples who have opposite personality types. After you have read this passage, apply the steps above to evaluate it critically.

Unfortunately, great differences in personality can often lead to conflict later on. One study found that a source of marital dissatisfaction among husbands was a feeling that their wives were too possessive, neglectful, and openly admiring of other men. Dissatisfied wives complained that their husbands were possessive, moody, and openly attracted to other women. The study also found that sex is a source of great difficulties for unhappy married men and women. It found that women see sex as following from emotional intimacy, while men see it as a road to intimacy. As a result, men complain that their wives withhold sex from them and women complain that their husbands are too sexually aggressive.

What makes the authors' argument credible?

____

____

____

____

____

____

Source: Marvin Levy, Mark Dignan, and Janet Shirreffs, "The Decision to Marry," in *Targeting Wellness: The Core,* McGraw-Hill, New York, 1992, p. 123.

To determine the authors' argument, ask yourself, "What is the important overall point the authors want to persuade the reader to believe?" The answer to this question—their argument—is stated in the first sentence: "Unfortunately, great differences in personality can often lead to conflict later on."

To identify what the authors take for granted and base their argument on, ask yourself, "What assumptions have the authors made?" It is clear that the authors assume that personality traits can be accurately assessed and remain consistent throughout people's lives. They assume that what is true for dating couples is also true for married couples. The authors assume that if people are aware of the effects of great personality differences on relationships, they can make better decisions in selecting a spouse, and if they are married to spouses with "opposite personalities," that they can understand it can cause marital conflict. These assumptions seem reasonable.

To identify the kind of support the authors present, ask yourself, "What types of support do the authors give?" The authors refer to a research study that compares husbands' and wives' sources of dissatisfaction with each other.

To determine whether or not the support pertains directly to the point the authors are making, ask yourself, "Is the support relevant?" The research study the authors cite deals only with married couples, although not all couples who live together are married. Although the authors do not state that the couples in the study had great personality differences, the first finding of the study *does* support the argument that such differences can lead to conflict later on (since possessiveness, moodiness, and aggressiveness can be viewed as personality traits). On the other hand, the second finding of the study (on sex as a source of difficulties for unhappy married couples) does *not* directly support the authors' argument (since it is differences in attitudes toward sex rather than personality differences that appear to cause the problems). Moreover, the differing attitudes of husbands and wives appear to be related to gender rather than to personality. Therefore, this second finding of the study is not as relevant to the authors' argument.

The authors' argument would not be *valid* if it were based only on the second finding. Presenting research findings makes the argument more *objective* than if it were based only on the authors' observations and opinions. Although the authors present only one side of the issue, their argument nevertheless seems reasonably *complete.* However, unless readers are already quite familiar with this topic, it is not possible for them to knowledgeably evaluate the completeness of the authors' argument.

Annotate

Go back to the excerpt. List the elements that make the authors' argument credible.

A critical evaluation of this excerpt could be summed up as follows: The authors' argument (that great differences in personalities can ultimately lead to conflict between a married couple) has *credibility.* The authors' argument is believable because it is based on logical assumptions and is supported with a relevant finding from a research study.

The following chart shows the aspects of written material that must be considered when you wish to evaluate the credibility of an author's argument.

Evaluating Written Material

To evaluate the *credibility* of an *author's argument:*

- Identify the *assumptions* on which the argument is based.
- Evaluate the *types of support* presented.
- Decide whether the support is *relevant.*

Then, *decide:*

- If the argument is *valid.*
- If the argument is *objective.*
- If the argument is *complete.*

The credibility of an author's argument depends on the underlying assumptions, the types of support presented and their relevance, and whether the argument is valid, objective, and complete. An author's argument (overall main idea) has credibility (believability) only if it is based on logical assumptions, is defended with relevant support, and is valid, objective, and complete.

STANDARDIZED READING TESTS: CRITICAL READING

College students may be required to take standardized reading tests as part of an overall assessment program, in a reading course, or as part of a state-mandated "basic skills" test. A standardized reading test typically consists of a series of passages followed by multiple-choice questions, to be completed within a specified time limit.

There are several types of questions involving critical reading. Questions about the author's *purpose* may be worded:

The author's purpose for writing this passage is to . . .
The reason the author wrote this passage is . . .
It is likely that the author wrote this in order to . . .
The reason the author wrote this selection is primarily to . . .
The purpose of the author in writing this selection is to . . .
The author wrote this passage in order to . . .

Questions about the author's *intended audience* may be worded:

The author intended this passage to be read by . . .
The author's intended audience is . . .
The author expects this passage to be read by . . .

Questions about the author's *point of view* may be worded:

The passage suggests that the author's point of view is . . .
The passage suggests that the author's attitude toward . . . is . . .
It is clear that the author believes . . .
The passage suggests that the author's opinion about . . . is . . .
The author's opinion about . . . is . . .

Questions about *tone* may be worded:

The tone of this passage is . . . *(factual, ironic, etc.)*
The tone of this passage can be described as . . .
Which of the following words best describes the tone of the passage?

Questions about *fact* and *opinion* may be phrased:

Which of the following statements represents an opinion of the author's?

Which of the following statements expresses an opinion rather than a fact?

Which of the following does the first *(second, third, etc.)* sentence represent *(fact or opinion)?*

In dealing with questions about fact and opinion, watch for words (such as *perhaps, apparently, it seems, experts believe*) that signal opinions. Watch also for judgmental words (such as *best* or *beautiful*), which also indicate opinions.

Questions about *inferences* or *conclusions* may be worded:

Which of the following conclusions could be made about . . . ?

On the basis of information in this passage, the reader could conclude . . .

It can be inferred from the passage that . . .

The passage implies that . . .

In dealing with questions on inferences or conclusions, remember that an inference must be logical and must be based on information in the passage.

Questions about author's *intended meaning* may be worded:

The author wants the reader to understand . . .

The author's use of sarcasm suggests . . .

The author's true meaning is . . .

The author's use of irony indicates . . .

Questions about the author's *argument* may be worded:

The author's argument about . . . is . . .

In this selection, the author argues that . . .

The author's position on this issue is . . .

The author's point of view is . . .

The passage suggests that the author believes . . .

Questions about the author's *credibility* may be worded:

The author has credibility because . . .

The author establishes his credibility by . . . *(by presenting data, giving examples, etc.)*

The author's argument is believable because . . .

The author is believable because . . .

Questions about the author's *assumptions* may be worded:

The author bases his (or her) argument on which of the following assumptions?
Which of the following assumptions underlies the author's argument?
The author's argument is based on which of the following assumptions?

Questions about *types of support* the author presents may be worded:

The author presents which of the following types of support?
The author includes all of the following types of support except . . .

DEVELOPING CHAPTER REVIEW CARDS

Review cards, or *summary cards,* are an excellent study tool. They are a way to select, organize, and review the most important information in a textbook chapter. The process of creating review cards helps you organize information in a meaningful way and, at the same time, transfer it into long-term memory. The cards can also be used to prepare for tests (see Part Three). The review card activities in this book give you structured practice in creating these valuable study tools. Once you have learned how to make review cards, you can create them for textbook material in your other courses.

Now, complete the seven review cards for Chapter 8 by answering the questions or following the directions on each card. When you have completed them, you will have summarized important information about: (1) what critical reading is, (2) authors' purpose and intended audience, (3) authors' point of view and tone, (4) facts and opinions, (5) making inferences and drawing conclusions, and (6) evaluating written material.

Critical Reading

Define *critical reading.* (See page 369.)

____

____

List the skills of critical reading. (See page 369.)

1. ______________________________
2. ______________________________
3. ______________________________
4. ______________________________
5. ______________________________

Chapter 8: Reading Critically

Author's Purpose and Intended Audience

Define the author's *purpose* and list four common purposes for writing. (See page 369.)

What are two ways to determine an author's purpose? (See page 370.)

Define *intended audience.* (See page 370.)

To determine an author's intended audience, what three things can you look for? (See page 370.)

Chapter 8: Reading Critically

Author's Point of View and Tone

Define *point of view.* (See page 374.)

Give some examples of words that signal an author's point of view. (See page 374.)

Define *tone.* (See page 374.)

What two things can you examine to determine an author's tone? (See page 375.)

What is irony? (See page 376.)

Chapter 8: Reading Critically

Facts and Opinions

1. What is a *fact?* (See page 380.)

   ____

2. What is an *opinion?* (See page 380.)

   ____

3. What are some clues (signal words) which suggest that you are reading an opinion? (See page 382.)

   ____

   ____

4. What makes an opinion a valuable opinion? (See page 381.)

   ____

Chapter 8: Reading Critically

Making Logical Inferences and Drawing Conclusions

1. What is an *inference?* (See page 386.)

   ____

   ____

2. In reading critically, what question should you ask yourself in order to make an inference or draw a conclusion? (See page 386.)

   ____

   ____

Chapter 8: Reading Critically

Evaluating Written Material

List the seven steps you must take to critically evaluate the credibility of an author's argument. (See page 391.)

1. ______________________________
2. ______________________________
3. ______________________________
4. ______________________________
5. ______________________________
6. ______________________________
7. ______________________________

Selection 8-1

Literature

FROM *HAVING OUR SAY: THE DELANY SISTERS' FIRST 100 YEARS*

BY SARAH L. DELANY AND A. ELIZABETH DELANY WITH AMY HILL HEARTH

Prepare Yourself to Read

Directions: Do these exercises *before you read Selection 8-1.*

1. First, read *only* the title, the introduction, and the first three paragraphs.

   What comes to your mind when you read the title *Having Our Say: The Delany Sisters' First 100 Years?*

   ___

   ___

   ___

2. As you read the rest of the selection, keep in mind which sister is speaking.

Apply Comprehension Skills

Directions: Do the Annotation Practice Exercises *as you read Selection 8-1.* Read critically:

Think about the author's purpose, intended audience, point of view, tone, and intended meaning.

Distinguish between facts and opinions.

Make logical inferences and draw conclusions as you read.

FROM *HAVING OUR SAY*

What would it be like to live for more than 100 years? To be nearly half as old as the United States itself? Sarah Delany was born in 1889; her sister Elizabeth was born in 1891. Neither sister ever married, and the two lived together nearly all of their lives. Sarah Delany said that she and her sis-

Annotation practice exercises

Directions: For each of the exercises below, read critically to answer the questions. This will help you gain additional insights as you read.

Source: Sarah L. Delany and A. Elizabeth Delany with Amy Hill Hearth, *Having Our Say: The Delany Sisters' First 100 Years,* New York, Dell, 1993, pp. 3, 5, 287–290, 296–298.

ter probably know each other "better than any two human beings on this Earth." Their book, Having Our Say, *was published in 1993 and quickly went onto the* New York Times *best-seller list. In their book, they are described this way: "Sarah Delany and Dr. Elizabeth Delany were born in Raleigh, North Carolina, on the campus of St. Augustine's College. Their father, born into slavery, and freed by the Emancipation, was an administrator at the college and America's first elected black Episcopal bishop. Sarah received her bachelor's and master's degrees from Teachers College at Columbia University and was New York City's first appointed black home economics teacher on the high school level. Elizabeth received her degree in dentistry from Columbia University and was the second black woman licensed to practice dentistry in New York City. The sisters retired to Mt. Vernon, New York, thirty-nine years ago, where they still live today." [Note: Bessie Delany died in 1996 at the age of 104.]*

1 Both more than one hundred years old, Sarah ("Sadie") Delany and her sister, Annie Elizabeth ("Bessie") Delany, are among the oldest living witnesses to American history. They are also the oldest surviving members of one of the nation's preeminent black families, which rose to prominence just one generation after the Civil War.

2 Few families have ever achieved so much so quickly. Henry Beard Delany, the sisters' father, was born into slavery but eventually became the first elected "Negro" bishop of the Episcopal Church, U.S.A. All ten of his children were college-educated professionals at a time when few Americans—black or white—ever went beyond high school.

3 The Delany creed centered on self-improvement through education, civic-mindedness, and ethical living, along with a strong belief in God. The family motto was, "Your job is to help somebody." According to Bessie and Sadie Delany, this code applied to anyone who needed help, regardless of color. Their accomplishments could not shield them from discrimination and the pain of racism, but they held them-

Bessie at age 100.

Sadie at age 102.

selves to high standards of fair-minded idealism.

SADIE

4 One thing I've noticed since I got this old is that I have started to dream in color. I'll remember that someone was wearing a red dress or a pink sweater, something like that. I also dream

Bessie and Sadie Delaney at home in Mount Vernon.

more than I used to, and when I wake up I feel tired. I'll say to Bessie, "I sure am tired this morning. I was teaching all night in my dreams!"

5 Bessie was always the big dreamer. She was always talking about what she dreamed the night before. She has this same dream over and over again, about a party she went to on Cotton Street in Raleigh, way back when. Nothing special happens; she just keeps dreaming she's there. In our dreams, we are always young.

6 Truth is, we both forget we're old. This happens all the time. I'll reach for something real quick, just like a young person. And realize my reflexes are not what they once were. It surprises me, but I can't complain. I still do what I want, pretty much.

7 These days, I am usually the first one awake in the morning. I wake up at six-thirty. And the first thing I do when I open my eyes is smile, and then I say, "Thank you, Lord, for another day!"

8 If I don't hear Bessie get up, I'll go into her room and wake her. Sometimes I have to knock on her headboard. And she opens her eyes and says, "Oh, Lord, another day?" I don't think Bessie would get up at all sometimes, if it weren't for me. She stays up late in her room and listens to these talk-radio shows, and she doesn't get enough sleep.

9 In the mornings, Monday through Friday, we do our yoga exercises. I started doing yoga exercises with Mama about forty years ago. Mama was starting to shrink up and get bent down, and I started exercising with her to straighten her up again. Only I didn't know at that time that what we were actually doing was "yoga." We just thought we were exercising.

10 I kept doing my yoga exercises, even after Mama died. Well, when Bessie turned eighty she decided that I looked better than her. So she decided she would start doing yoga, too. So we've been doing our exercises together ever since. We follow a yoga exercise program on the TV. Sometimes, Bessie cheats. I'll be doing an exercise and look over at her, and she's just lying there! She's a naughty old gal.

11 Exercise is very important. A lot of older people don't exercise at all. Another thing that is terribly important is diet. I keep up with the latest news about nutrition. About thirty years ago, Bessie and I started eating much more healthy foods. We don't eat that fatty Southern food very often. When we do, we feel like we can't move!

12 We eat as many as seven different vegetables a day. Plus lots of fresh fruits. And we take vitamin supplements: Vitamin A, B complex, C, D, E, and minerals, too, like zinc. And Bessie takes tyrosine when she's a little blue.

13 Every morning, after we do our yoga, we each take a clove of garlic, chop it up, and

Practice exercise

In paragraph 7, what is the author's (Sadie's) point of view?

____

____

Practice exercise

What inference can you make about Bessie's outlook on life from paragraph 8?

____

____

____

Practice exercise

Write one fact and one opinion that the author (Sadie) gives in paragraph 10.

____

____

____

swallow it whole. If you swallow it all at once, there is no odor. We also take a teaspoon of cod liver oil. Bessie thinks it's disgusting, but one day I said, "Now, dear little sister, if you want to keep up with me, you're going to have to start taking it, every day, and stop complainin'." And she's been good ever since.

14 As soon as we moved to our house in 1957, we began boiling the tap water we use for our drinking water. Folks keep telling us that it's not necessary, that the City of Mount Vernon purifies the water. But it's a habit and at our age, child, we're not about to change our routine.

15 These days, I do most of the cooking, and Bessie does the serving. We eat our big meal of the day at noon. In the evening, we usually have a milk shake for dinner, and then we go upstairs and watch "MacNeil Lehrer" on the TV.

16 After that, we say our prayers. We say prayers in the morning and before we go to bed. It takes a long time to pray for everyone, because it's a very big family—we have fifteen nieces and nephews still living, plus all their children and grandchildren. We pray for each one, living and dead. The ones that Bessie doesn't approve of get extra prayers. Bessie can be very critical and she holds things against people forever. I always have to say to her, "Everybody has to be themselves, Bessie. Live and let live."

BESSIE

17 I wonder what Mr. Miliam would think of his granddaughters living this long. Why, I suppose he'd get a kick out of it. I know he'd have lived longer if Grandma hadn't died and it broke his heart. Sometimes, you need a reason to keep living.

18 Tell you the truth, I wouldn't be here without sister Sadie. We are companions. But I'll tell you something else. Sadie has taken on this business of getting old like it's a big *project.* She has it all figured out, about diet and exercise. Sometimes, I just don't want to do it, but she is my big sister and I really don't want to disappoint her. Funny thing about Sadie is she

Practice exercise

What is the author's (Sadie's) tone in paragraph 14?

____

____

____

rarely gets—what's the word?—depressed. She is an easygoing type of gal.

19 Now, honey, I get the blues sometimes. It's a shock to me, to be this old. Sometimes, when I realize I am 101 years old, it hits me right between the eyes. I say, "Oh Lord, how did this happen?" Turning one hundred was the worst birthday of my life. I wouldn't wish it on my worst enemy. Turning 101 was not so bad. Once you've past that century mark, it's just not as shocking.

20 There's a few things I have had to give up. I gave up driving a while back. I guess I was in my late eighties. That was terrible. Another thing I gave up on was cutting back my trees so we have a view of the New York City skyline to the south. Until I was ninety-eight years old, I would climb up on the ladder and saw those tree branches off so we had a view. I could do it perfectly well; why pay somebody to do it? Then Sadie talked some sense into me, and I gave up doing it.

21 Some days I feel as old as Moses and other days I feel like a young girl. I tell you what: I have only a little bit of arthritis in my pinky finger, and my eyes aren't bad so I know I could still be practicing dentistry. Yes, I am sure I could still do it.

22 But it's hard being old, because you can't always do everything you want, exactly as *you* want it done. When you get old as we are, you have to struggle to hang onto your freedom, your independence. We have a lot of family and friends keeping an eye on us, but we try not to be dependent on any one person. We try to pay people, even relatives, for whatever they buy for us, and for gasoline for their car, things like that, so that we do not feel beholden to them.

23 Longevity runs in the family. I'm sure that's part of why we are still here. As a matter of fact, until recently there were still five of us, of the original ten children. Then, Hurbert went to Glory on December 28, 1990, and Hap, a few weeks later, in February 1991. Laura, our dear

baby sister, passed on in August 1993. That leaves just me and Sadie.

24 Now, when Hurbert died, that really hurt. He was just shy of ninety years old. It never made a bit of difference to me that Hubert became an assistant United States attorney, a judge, and all that. He was still my little brother.

25 Same way with Hap. You know what? Even when he was ninety-five years old, Sadie and I still spoiled him. When he didn't like what they were cooking for dinner at his house, he would get up and leave the table and come over here and we'd fix him what he liked to eat.

26 Good ol' Hap knew he was going to Glory and he was content. He said, "I've had a good life. I've done everything I wanted to do, I think I've done right by people." We Delanys can usually say that when our time comes.

Comprehension Quiz

True or false

Directions: In the blank provided, indicate whether each statement is true or false.

______ 1. The Delany sisters have similar outlooks on living and growing older.

______ 2. Bessie can be pessimistic at times.

______ 3. The Delany sisters attribute their longevity to hard work and luck.

______ 4. Sadie is more optimistic and easygoing than Bessie.

______ 5. The Delany sisters pray twice each day.

Multiple-choice

Directions: For each item, select the best answer.

______ 6. Bessie Delany believes that one reason for her longevity is

a. determination.
b. genetics.
c. independence.
d. assistance from family members.

_____ 7. Bessie Delany started doing yoga exercises when she was

a. a young girl.
b. a teenager.
c. in her forties.
d. quite old.

_____ 8. In addition to exercise and eating healthy foods, the Delany sisters also

a. take vitamin supplements.
b. eat a clove of garlic every day.
c. take a teaspoon of cod liver oil each day.
d. all of the above.

_____ 9. The reason the Delany sisters still boil the tap water they use for drinking is that

a. it has simply become a habit.
b. their city does not have a water purification system.
c. they believe it is more healthful.
d. all of the above.

_____ 10. For Bessie Delany, one difficult part of old age is

a. fighting boredom.
b. worry about financial security.
c. struggling to maintain independence.
d. staying in contact with other family members.

Extend Your Vocabulary by Using Context Clues

Directions: ***Context clues*** are words in a sentence or paragraph that allow the reader to deduce (reason out) the meaning of an unfamiliar word. For each item in this exercise, a sentence from Selection 8-1 containing an important word *(italicized, like this)* is quoted first. Next, there is an additional sentence using the word in the same sense and providing another context clue. Use the context clues to deduce the meaning of each italicized word. *The definition you choose should make sense in both sentences.*

Pronunciation key: ă **pat** ā **pay** âr **care** ä **father** ĕ **pet** ē **be** ĭ **pit** ī **tie** îr **pier** ŏ **pot** ō **toe** ô **paw** oi **noise** ou **out** o͝o **took** o͞o **boot** ŭ **cut** yo͞o **abuse** ûr **urge** th **thin** *th* **this** hw **which** zh **vision** ə **about**

_____ 1. "They are also the oldest surviving members of one of the nation's *pre-eminent* black families, which rose to prominence just one generation after the Civil War."

Pearl Buck, William Faulkner, John Steinbeck, Ernest Hemingway, and Saul Bellow are *preeminent* twentieth-century American writers who have each won both the Pulitzer Prize and the Nobel Prize in Literature.

preeminent (pre ə̆m´ ə nənt) means:

a. possessing unusual academic skills
b. college-educated
c. unknown by the general public
d. outstanding; superior

_____ 2. "They are also the oldest surviving members of one of the nation's pre-eminent black families, which rose to *prominence* just one generation after the Civil War."

A former California governor, Earl Warren gained national *prominence* as Chief Justice of the Supreme Court and as the leader of a government commission that investigated the assassination of President John F. Kennedy.

prominence (prŏm´ ə nəns) means:

a. limited power or influence
b. vast wealth
c. being superior and widely known
d. great popularity

_____ 3. "The Delany *creed* centered on self-improvement through education, civic-mindedness, and ethical living, along with a strong belief in God."

Two important aspects of the architect Frank Lloyd Wright's innovative *creed* were uniting buildings with their surroundings and integrating technology into his structures.

creed (krēd) means:

a. slogan or motto
b. quotation whose source is unknown
c. selfishness and greed
d. system of beliefs, principles, or opinions

_____ 4. "The Delany creed centered on self-improvement through education, civic-mindedness, and *ethical* living, along with a strong belief in God."

Because of their honesty and integrity, George Washington and Abraham Lincoln are considered two of the most *ethical* men ever to serve as president of the United States.

ethical (ĕth′ ĭ kəl) means:

a. exceedingly popular
b. in accordance with other people's beliefs
c. plain; not fancy
d. in accordance with the accepted principles of right and wrong; moral

______ 5. "Their accomplishments could not shield them from discrimination and the pain of racism, but they held themselves to high standards of fair-minded *idealism.*"

The ruthlessness of the corporate world quickly destroyed the young employee's *idealism.*

idealism (ī dē′ ə lĭz əm) means:

a. pursuit of honorable or worthy principles or goals
b. enthusiasm; excitement
c. racial prejudice or biogotry
d. unhelpful, misguided beliefs

______ 6. "We have a lot of family and friends keeping an eye on us, but we try not to be *dependent* on any one person."

If you have *dependent* children for whom you provide the primary financial support, you must indicate this when you file your income tax.

dependent (dĭ pĕn′ dənt) means:

a. unreasonable
b. grateful; appreciative
c. relying on or requiring the aid of another for support
d. dependable; reliable

______ 7. "We try to pay people, even relatives, for whatever they buy for us, and for gasoline for their car, things like that, so that we do not feel *beholden* to them."

Because my wonderful parents helped pay for my college education, I will always be *beholden* to them.

beholden (bĭ hōl′ dən) means:

a. holding tightly to someone or something
b. owing something, such as gratitude, to another; indebted
c. feeling guilty; guilt-ridden
d. hostile

_______ 8. "*Longevity* runs in the family."

A healthy lifestyle and a positive outlook are two keys to *longevity.*

longevity (lŏn jĕv´ ĭ tē) means:

a. long life; great duration of life
b. being unusually tall
c. illness characterized by weakened muscles
d. addiction to harmful substances

_______ 9. "As a matter of fact, until recently, there were still five of us, of the *original* ten children."

Were you able to locate the *original* contract or only the later versions of it?

original (ə rĭj´ ə nəl) means:

a. creative or unusual in nature
b. new
c. preceding all others in time; first
d. fresh

_______ 10. "Good ol' Hap knew he was going to Glory and he was *content.*"

After serving twelve years as her company's chief executive, she was *content* to turn the role over to her capable vice president.

content (kən tĕnt´) means:

a. full; complete
b. dissatisfied
c. angry; resistant
d. willing; ready to accept

Respond in Writing

Directions: Refer to Selection 8-1 as necessary to answer these essay-type items.

Option for collaboration: For some of the "Respond in Writing" exercises, your instructor may prefer that you work collaboratively, that is, with other students. These exercises are identified in the margin. *If your instructor directs you to work collaboratively on any of these items,* form groups of three or four classmates to complete the exercise together. Discuss your answers with each other and have one member of the group record the answers. A member of the group may be asked to share the group's answers with the class.

1. What was the most surprising or interesting thing you learned about either or both of the Delany sisters?

Option

Item 2 may be completed collaboratively.

2. In what ways are Sadie and Bessie Delany alike? In what ways are they different?

3. Bessie states that "longevity runs in the family." In addition to heredity, however, to what do the Delanys credit their long lives?

4. Being educated made a significant difference in the Delanys' lives. How do you think *you* will look back on the time you spent in college? What difference do you think it might make in your life?

Option

Item 5 may be completed collaboratively.

5. Assuming that you were able to maintain good health, what do you think would be some of the *best* things about being 100 years old?

Option

Item 6 may be completed collaboratively.

6. What is the most important overall message the Delany sisters want the readers to understand about them and their lives? Try to answer this question in one sentence.

Selection 8-2

Health

FROM *LEGALIZING DRUGS*

BY RICHARD SCHLAAD AND PETER SHANNON

Prepare Yourself to Read

Directions: Do these exercises *before you read Selection 8-2.*

1. First, read and think about the title. What is your opinion about legalizing drugs?

   ____

2. Complete your preview by reading:

   Introduction (in *italics*)
   Headings
   First sentence of each paragraph

Apply Comprehension Skills

Directions: Do the Annotation Practice Exercises *as you read Selection 8-2.*

Think about the author's purpose, intended audience, point of view, tone, and intended meaning.
Distinguish between facts and opinions.
Make logical inferences and draw conclusions as you read.

LEGALIZING DRUGS

As the headings indicate, this article examines both sides of the controversial issue of making certain illegal drugs legal. As you read, think about which side contains stronger support and is presented more convincingly.

Annotation practice exercises

Directions: For each of the exercises below, read critically to answer the question. This will help you gain additional insights as you read.

Source: Richard Schlaad and Peter Shannon, "Legalizing Drugs," in Marvin Levy, Mark Dignan, and Janet Shirreffs, *Targeting Wellness: The Core,* McGraw-Hill, New York, 1992, p. 235. Reproduced with permission of McGraw-Hill.

Pro-Legalization: Weighing the Costs of Drug Use

1 For over 100 years this society has made the use of certain drugs illegal and has penalized illegal drug use. But during that time the use of marijuana, heroin and other opiates, and cocaine has become an epidemic. Most recently, Americans have spent billions of dollars on arresting and imprisoning sellers and importers of crack cocaine, with almost no effect on the supply or street price of the drug.

2 The societal costs of illegal drugs are immense. They include the costs of law enforcement, criminal proceedings against those arrested, and jails and prisons. They also include the spread of deadly diseases such as AIDS and hepatitis through the use of shared needles; the cost to society of raising "crack babies," children poisoned by drugs even before birth; and the cost of raising a generation of young people who see illegal drug selling and violence as their only escape from poverty and desperation. Finally, the societal costs include the emotional cost of the violence that no one can now escape.

3 Legalizing drug use in this country would eliminate many of these costs. Billions of dollars would be saved. This money could be spent on treatment of addicts, job training, and education programs to help many disadvantaged young people assume valuable roles in society. The government could make drug use legal for adults but impose severe penalties on anyone who sells drugs to young people. Drug sales could be heavily taxed, thus deterring drug purchases and giving society the benefit of tax revenues that could be used for drug treatment and education.

Practice exercise

What is the authors' purpose in paragraphs 1–3?

____

____

____

____

____

Anti-Legalization: Providing a Positive Role Model

4 Certain drugs are illegal because they are dangerous and deadly and provide no societal value. To make their possession or use legal would send a message to young people that using drugs is acceptable and that drugs are not treacherous or life-destroying.

5 Making drugs illegal has not increased the number of drug users or sellers, just as making alcohol legal after Prohibition did not reduce the number of people who drank. Recent law enforcement efforts have indeed made a difference. Over the past few years, as law enforcement efforts have sent more and more people to jail, the number of young people who use illegal drugs has steadily declined. Furthermore, education about the ill effects of drug use has begun to deter people from buying and using illegal drugs.

6 Recently, the incidence of drug-related deaths and violence has begun to level off even in the areas of the most hard-core drug use. This is proof that strict law enforcement is working. This country has begun to turn the corner on this drug epidemic.

Practice exercise

What is the authors' purpose in paragraphs 4–6?

____

____

____

____

____

Practice exercise

Who is the authors' intended audience?

____

____

____

____

Comprehension Quiz

True or false

Directions: In the blank provided, indicate whether each statement is true or false.

______ 1. According to the authors, one argument for not legalizing certain drugs is that it will send a message to young people that using drugs is acceptable.

______ 2. In the United States, the use of illegal drugs has become epidemic.

______ 3. The authors state that legalizing drugs would save Americans billions of dollars.

______ 4. The legalization of drugs has been a topic of serious public debate since the 1960s.

_____ 5. The authors propose that if drugs were made legal, drug sales to adults would be heavily taxed, and there would be severe penalties for anyone who sells drugs to young people.

_____ 6. Although the authors of this selection present both sides of the debate about legalizing drugs, they clearly support the legalization of drugs.

Multiple-choice

Directions: For each item, select the best answer.

_____ 7. The authors use the word *epidemic*
   a. because they want readers to be alarmed at how widespread the problem is.
   b. to suggest that drug use is a disease.
   c. to imply that drug use can be stopped.
   d. none of the above

_____ 8. Which of the following is *not* cited in the selection as an example of a societal cost of illegal drugs?
   a. cost of law enforcement, criminal proceedings, jails, and prisons
   b. cost for treatment of AIDS and hepatitis, diseases that are spread through the use of shared drug needles
   c. cost of educating lawyers and law enforcement officers
   d. cost of raising a generation of young people who see illegal drug selling and violence as their only escape from poverty

_____ 9. Law enforcement agencies oppose legalizing drugs because their efforts have
   a. already reduced the number of young people using drugs.
   b. resulted in jailing more and more people for drug-related crimes.
   c. resulted in a lower incidence of drug-related deaths and violence.
   d. all of the above

_____ 10. One of the arguments for legalizing drugs is that the billions of dollars that would be saved could instead be spent on
   a. the treatment of addicts.
   b. job training.
   c. education programs to help disadvantaged young people.
   d. all of the above

Extend Your Vocabulary by Using Context Clues

Directions: **Context clues** are words in a sentence or paragraph that allow the reader to deduce (reason out) the meaning of an unfamiliar word. For each item in this exercise, a sentence from Selection 8-2 containing an important word *(italicized, like this)* is quoted first. Next, there is an additional sentence using the word in the same sense and providing another context clue. Use the context clues to deduce the meaning of each italicized word. *The definition you choose should make sense in both sentences.*

Pronunciation key: ă **pat** ā **pay** âr **care** ä **father** ĕ **pet** ē **be** ĭ **pit** ī **tie** îr **pier** ŏ **pot** ō **toe** ô **paw** oi **noise** ou **out** o͝o **took** o͞o **boot** ŭ **cut** yo͞o ab**use** ûr **urge** th **thin** *th* **this** hw **which** zh vision ə **about**

______ 1. "One of the most serious problems in the United States in the late twentieth century is the *widespread* use of illegal drugs."

After the explosion at the nuclear power plant, there was *widespread* contamination from radioactive material.

widespread (wīd′ sprĕd′) means:

a. spread thickly
b. in great quantity
c. affecting many people
d. occurring widely

______ 2. "*Legalizing* drug use in this country would eliminate many of these costs."

The Supreme Court decision in Roe v. Wade, *legalizing* abortion in the United States, has been highly controversial.

legalizing (lē′ gə līz ĭng) means:

a. removing
b. arguing in court
c. authorizing by law
d. banning

______ 3. "Pro-Legalization: *Weighing* the Costs of Drug Use"

The judge explained to the jurors what is involved in *weighing* evidence and arriving at a verdict.

weighing (wā ĭng) means:

a. considering; evaluating
b. determining the weight of
c. disproving
d. ignoring

_____ 4. "But during that time the use of marijuana, heroin and other *opiates,* and cocaine has become an epidemic."

Because *opiates* such as tranquilizers, alcohol, and barbiturates depress the functioning of the central nervous system, they can produce drowsiness or even coma.

opiates (ō´ pē ĭts) means:

a. illegal drugs
b. narcotics that induce relaxation or sleep
c. drugs that stimulate the nervous system
d. black-market drugs

_____ 5. "But during that time the use of marijuana, heroin and other opiates, and cocaine has become an *epidemic.*"

Today there is an *epidemic* of violence in many large and small American cities.

epidemic (ĕp ĭ dĕm´ ĭk) means:

a. illness
b. problem affecting older people
c. rapid spread or development
d. decrease

_____ 6. "The *societal* costs of illegal drugs are immense."

Many *societal* problems cannot be solved by government alone.

societal (sə sī´ ĭ təl) means:

a. pertaining to the upper class
b. pertaining to colleges
c. pertaining to a society of people who share a common culture
d. pertaining to manners

_____ 7. "The societal costs of illegal drugs are *immense.*"

The blue whale is the most *immense* mammal on earth.

immense (ĭ mĕns´) means:

a. huge
b. dangerous
c. increasing
d. misunderstood

_____ 8. "The government could make drug use legal for adults but *impose* severe penalties on anyone who sells drugs to young people."

Please do not *impose* your opinions on everyone else; let us make up our own minds.

impose (ĭm pōz´) means:

a. inflict or force on
b. take unfair advantage of
c. remove
d. require by law

_____ 9. "To make their possession or use legal would send a message to young people that using drugs is acceptable and that drugs are not *treacherous* or life-destroying."

Driving in the *treacherous* ice storm was frightening.

treacherous (trĕch´ ər əs) means:

a. expensive
b. long-lasting
c. dangerous
d. illegal

_____ 10. "Furthermore, education about the ill effects of drug use has begun to *deter* people from buying and using illegal drugs."

If you are determined to achieve your goals, you will let nothing *deter* you from attaining them.

deter (dĭ tûr´) means:

a. prevent or discourage by means of fear or doubt
b. detain
c. speed up
d. encourage by supportive measures

Respond in Writing

Directions: Refer to Selection 8-2 as necessary to answer these essay-type items.

Option for collaboration: For some of the "Respond in Writing" exercises, your instructor may prefer that you work collaboratively, that is, with other students. These exercises are identified in the margin. *If your instructor directs you to work collaboratively on any of these items,* form groups of three or four classmates to complete the exercise together. Discuss your answers with each other and have one member of the group record the answers. A member of the group may be asked to share the group's answers with the class.

Option

Item 1 may be completed collaboratively.

1. Now that you have read this selection, what is your position on legalizing drugs? Explain why you favor or oppose their legalization.

Option

Item 2 may be completed collaboratively.

2. What are the weaknesses in your position on legalizing drugs? In other words, what reasons could someone present to argue against your position?

Option

Item 3 may be completed collaboratively.

3. What is the most important overall message the writers want the reader to understand about legalizing drugs? Try to answer this question in one sentence.

Selection 8-3

Literature

THE ACHIEVEMENT OF DESIRE

FROM *HUNGER OF MEMORY*
BY RICHARD RODRIGUEZ

Prepare Yourself to Read

Directions: Do these exercises *before you read Selection 8-3.*

1. First, read and think about the title. What does Selection 8-3 seem to be about?

   ____

2. Complete your preview by reading:

   Introduction (in *italics*)
   First paragraph (paragraph 1)
   First sentence of each paragraph
   Words in *italics*
   Last paragraph (paragraph 10)

Apply Comprehension Skills

Directions: Do the Annotation Practice Exercises *as you read Selection 8-3.* Read critically:

Think about the author's purpose, intended audience, point of view, tone, and intended meaning.
Distinguish between facts and opinions.
Make logical inferences and draw conclusions as you read.

THE ACHIEVEMENT OF DESIRE

What are your earliest memories connected with reading? How has your concept of reading changed since you first learned to read? In this selection, Richard Rodriguez recounts the evolution of his concept of reading from elementary school to college. Writing now from the perspective of a mature reader, Rodriguez candidly and poignantly describes his early, naive notions about reading.

1 OPEN THE DOORS OF YOUR MIND WITH BOOKS, read the red and white poster over the nun's desk in early September. It soon was apparent to me that reading was the classroom's central activity. Each course had its own book. And the information gathered from a book was unquestioned. READ TO LEARN, the sign on the wall advised in December. I privately wondered: What was the connection between reading and learning? Did one learn something only by reading it? Was an idea only an idea if it could be written down? In June, CONSIDER BOOKS YOUR BEST FRIENDS. Friends? Reading was, at best, only a chore. I needed to look up whole paragraphs of words in a dictionary. Lines of type were dizzying, the eye having to move slowly across the page, then down, and across. . . . The sentences of the first books I read were coolly impersonal. Toned hard. What most bothered me, however, was the isolation reading required. To console myself for the loneliness I'd feel when I read, I tried reading in a very soft voice. Until: "Who is doing all that talking to his neighbor?" Shortly after, remedial reading classes were arranged for me with a very old nun.

2 At the end of each school day, for nearly six months, I would meet with her in the tiny room that served as the school's library but was actually only a storeroom for used textbooks and a vast collection of *National Geographics.* Everything about our session pleased me: the small-

Annotation practice exercises

Directions: For each of the exercises below, read critically to answer the questions. This will help you gain additional insights as you read.

Practice exercise

What was the author's point of view about reading when he was first learning to read (paragraph 1)?

____

____

____

____

____

Source: Richard Rodriguez, "The Achievement of Desire," from *Hunger of Memory,* Bantam, New York, 1982, pp. 59–64.

ness of the room; the noise of the janitor's broom hitting the edge of the long hallway outside the door; the green of the sun, lighting the wall; and the old woman's face blurred white with a beard. Most of the time we took turns. I began with my elementary text. Sentences of astonishing simplicity seemed to me lifeless and drab: "The boys ran from the rain. . . . She wanted to sing. . . . The kite rose in the blue." Then the old nun would read from her favorite books, usually biographies of early American presidents. Playfully she ran through complex sentences, calling the words alive with her voice, making it seem that the author somehow was speaking directly to me. I smiled just to listen to her. I sat there and sensed for the very first time some possibility of fellowship between a reader and a writer, a communication, never *intimate* like that I heard spoken words at home convey, but one nonetheless *personal.*

3 One day the nun concluded a session by asking me why I was so reluctant to read by myself. I tried to explain; said something about the way written words made me feel all alone—almost, I wanted to add but didn't, as when I spoke to myself in a room just emptied of furniture. She studied my face as I spoke; she seemed to be watching more than listening. In an uneventful voice she replied that I had nothing to fear. Didn't I realize that reading would open up whole new worlds? A book could open doors for me. It could introduce me to people and show me places I never imagined existed. She gestured toward the bookshelves. (Bare-breasted African women danced, and the shiny hubcaps of automobiles on the back covers of the *Geographic* gleamed in my mind.) I listened with respect. But her words were not very influential. I was thinking then of another consequence of literacy, one I was too shy to admit but nonetheless trusted. Books were going to make me "educated." *That* confidence enabled me, several months later, to overcome my fear of the silence.

4 In fourth grade I embarked upon a grandiose reading program. "Give me the names of im-

portant books," I would say to startled teachers. They soon found out that I had in mind "adult books." I ignored their suggestions of anything I suspected was written for children. (Not until I was in college, as a result, did I read *Huckleberry Finn* or *Alice's Adventures in Wonderland.*) Instead, I read *The Scarlet Letter* and Franklin's *Autobiography.* And whatever I read I read for extra credit. Each time I finished a book, I reported the achievement to a teacher and basked in the praise my effort earned. Despite my best efforts, however, there seemed to be more and more books I needed to read. At the library I would literally tremble as I came upon whole shelves of books I hadn't read. So I read and I read and I read: *Great Expectations;* all the short stories of Kipling; *The Babe Ruth Story;* the entire first volume of the *Encyclopedia Britannica* (A–ANSTEY); the *Iliad; Moby Dick; Gone with the Wind; The Good Earth; Ramona; Forever Amber; The Lives of the Saints; Crime and Punishment: The Pearl. . . .* Librarians who initially frowned when I checked out the maximum ten books at a time started saving books they thought I might like. Teachers would say to the rest of the class, "I only wish the rest of you took reading as seriously as Richard obviously does."

5 But at home I would hear my mother wondering, "What do you see in your books?" (Was reading a hobby like her knitting? Was so much reading even healthy for a boy? Was it the sign of "brains"? Or was it just a convenient excuse for not helping around the house on Saturday mornings?) Always, "What do you see . . . ?"

6 What *did* I see in my books? I had the idea that they were crucial for my academic success, though I couldn't have said exactly how or why. In the sixth grade I simply concluded that what gave a book its value was some major idea or theme it contained. If that core essence could be mined and memorized, I would become learned like my teachers. I decided to record in a notebook the themes of the books that I read. After reading *Robinson Crusoe,* I wrote that its theme was "the value of learning

Practice exercise

What was the author's point of view about reading when he was in fourth grade (paragraph 4)?

____

____

____

Practice exercise

What was the author's point of view about reading when he was in sixth grade (paragraph 6)?

____

____

____

____

to live by oneself." When I completed *Wuthering Heights,* I noted the danger of "letting emotions get out of control." Rereading these brief moralistic appraisals usually left me disheartened. I couldn't believe that they were really the source of reading's value. But for many more years, they constituted the only means I had of describing to myself the educational value of books.

7 In spite of my earnestness, I found reading a pleasurable activity. I came to enjoy the lonely good company of books. Early on weekday mornings, I'd read in my bed. I'd feel a mysterious comfort then, reading in the dawn quiet—the blue-gray silence interrupted by the occasional churning of the refrigerator motor a few rooms away or the more distant sounds of a city bus beginning its run. On weekends, I'd go to the public library to read, surrounded by old men and women. Or, if the weather was fine, I would take my books to the park and read in the shade of a tree. A warm summer evening was my favorite reading time. Neighbors would leave for vacation and I would water their lawns. I would sit through the twilight on the front porches or in backyards, reading to the cool, whirling sounds of the sprinklers.

8 I also had favorite writers. But often those writers I enjoyed most I was least able to value. When I read William Saroyan's *The Human Comedy,* I was immediately pleased by the narrator's warmth and the charm of his story. But as quickly I became suspicious. A book so enjoyable to read couldn't be very "important." Another summer I determined to read all the novels of Dickens. Reading his fat novels, I loved the feeling I got—after the first hundred pages—of being at home in a fictional world where I knew the names of the characters and cared about what was going to happen to them. And it bothered me that I was forced away at the conclusion, when the fiction closed tight, like a fortune-teller's fist—the futures of all the major characters neatly resolved. I never knew how to take such feelings seriously, however. Nor did I suspect that these experiences could be part of a novel's meaning. Still, there were

pleasures to sustain me after I'd finish my books. Carrying a volume back to the library, I would be pleased by its weight. I'd run my fingers along the edge of the pages and marvel at the breadth of my achievement. Around my room, growing stacks of paperback books reinforced my assurance.

9 I entered high school having read hundreds of books. My habit of reading made me a confident speaker and writer of English. Reading also enabled me to sense something of the shape, the major concerns, of Western thought. (I was able to say something about Dante and Descartes and Engels and James Baldwin in my high school term papers.) In these various ways, books brought me academic success as I hoped that they would. But I was not a good reader. Merely bookish, I lacked a point of view when I read. Rather, I read in order to acquire a point of view. I vacuumed books for epigrams, scraps of information, ideas, themes—anything to fill the hollow within me and make me feel educated. When one of my teachers suggested to his drowsy tenth-grade English class that a person could not have a "complicated idea" until he had read at least two thousand books, I heard the remark without detecting either its irony or its very complicated truth. I merely determined to compile a list of all the books I had ever read. Harsh with myself, I included only once a title I might have read several times. (How, after all, could one read a book more than once?) And I included only those books over a hundred pages in length. (Could anything shorter be a book?)

10 There was yet another high school list I compiled. One day I came across a newspaper article about the retirement of an English professor at a nearby state college. The article was accompanied by a list of the "hundred most important books of Western Civilization." "More than anything else in my life," the professor told the reporter with finality, "these books have made me all that I am." That was the kind of remark I couldn't ignore. I clipped out the list and kept it for the several months it took me to read

Practice exercise

What inference does the author expect readers to make about his concept of "reading" when he was in high school (paragraphs 9–10)?

____

____

____

all of the titles. Most books, of course, I barely understood. While reading Plato's *Republic,* for instance, I needed to keep looking at the book jacket comments to remind myself what the text was about. Nevertheless, with the special patience and superstition of a scholarship boy, I looked at every word of the text. And by the time I reached the last word, relieved, I convinced myself that I had read *The Republic.* In a ceremony of great pride, I solemnly crossed Plato off my list.

Comprehension Quiz

True or false

Directions: In the blank provided, indicate whether each statement is true or false.

______ 1. Richard Rodriguez's early education began in a public elementary school.

______ 2. All of Rodriguez's earliest experiences with reading were pleasant.

______ 3. Richard Rodriguez was always recognized as an outstanding reader during his early elementary school years.

______ 4. As a child, Rodriguez felt that reading was a lonely activity.

______ 5. Richard Rodriguez began to be interested in reading books when he realized that by reading, whole new worlds would open up for him, he would become an educated person, and he could participate in a pleasurable activity.

Multiple-choice

Directions: For each item, select the best answer.

______ 6. Even as an adult, Rodriguez remembered all of the following posters in his elementary classroom *except*

a. OPEN THE DOORS OF YOUR MIND WITH BOOKS.
b. READING IS A FUNDAMENTAL ACTIVITY.
c. CONSIDER BOOKS YOUR BEST FRIEND.
d. READ TO LEARN.

______ 7. Richard Rodriguez entered high school having read
   a. fewer than 10 books.
   b. 50 books.
   c. 100 books.
   d. hundreds of books.

______ 8. Through his wide reading, Rodriguez began to
   a. share his love of reading with his siblings.
   b. be encouraged by his parents.
   c. become a confident speaker and writer of English.
   d. all of the above

______ 9. As an adult, Rodriguez could see that he had not been a mature reader in high school because he had
   a. thought that gaining wisdom from books was just a matter of reading as many books as possible.
   b. not been a critical reader; he did not have his own point of view.
   c. felt that books of less than 100 pages did not "count."
   d. all of the above

______ 10. At the time Richard Rodriguez crossed Plato's *Republic* off the list, he
   a. decided to read all of Plato's other works.
   b. felt that he understood it perfectly.
   c. felt that he had "read" it, even though he understood very little of it.
   d. all of the above

Extend Your Vocabulary by Using Context Clues

Directions: ***Context clues*** are words in a sentence or paragraph that allow the reader to deduce (reason out) the meaning of an unfamiliar word. For each item in this exercise, a sentence from Selection 8-3 containing an important word *(italicized, like this)* is quoted first. Next, there is an additional sentence using the word in the same sense and providing another context clue. Use the context clues to deduce the meaning of each italicized word. *The definition you choose should make sense in both sentences.*

Pronunciation key: ă **pat** ā **pay** âr **care** ä **father** ĕ **pet** ē **be** ĭ **pit** ī **tie** îr **pier** ŏ **pot** ō **toe** ô **paw** oi **noise** ou **out** o͝o **took** o͞o **boot** ŭ **cut** yo͞o **abuse** ûr **urge** th **thin** *th* **this** hw **which** zh **vision** ə **about**

_____ 1. "One day the nun *concluded* a session by asking me why I was so reluctant to read by myself."

The minister *concluded* the church service with a final prayer.

concluded (kən klo͞od´ əd) means:

a. finished; brought to an end
b. deduced by logic
c. interrupted
d. initiated

_____ 2. In an *uneventful* voice she replied that I had nothing to fear."

We were worried about driving through the mountains at night, but fortunately our trip was *uneventful.*

uneventful (ŭn ĭ vĕnt´ fəl) means:

a. exciting
b. evoking strong emotion
c. dangerous
d. occurring without disruption

_____ 3. "In fourth grade I *embarked* upon a grandiose reading program."

Columbus *embarked* upon his voyage to the New World with three small ships.

embarked (ĕm bärkt´) means:

a. completed or finished
b. won an award
c. started or began
d. became stuck in

_____ 4. "In fourth grade I embarked upon a *grandiose* reading program. 'Give me the names of important books,' I would say to startled teachers."

Even though he had no experience in business, he bragged about his *grandiose* plans for starting a multimillion-dollar computer software company right after graduation.

grandiose (grăn´ dē ōs) means:

a. sophisticated; suave
b. extensive
c. future
d. pompous; acting in a grand manner to achieve an effect

_____ 5. "What did I see in books? I had the idea that they were *crucial* for my academic success, though I couldn't have said exactly how or why."

It is *crucial* to your survival to take along the proper equipment and supplies if you go backpacking in the desert.

crucial (kro͞o´ shəl) means:

a. unrelated to
b. unnecessary
c. impeding progress or success
d. essential or critical

_____ 6. "After reading *Robinson Crusoe,* I wrote that its theme was 'the value of learning to live by oneself.' When I completed *Wuthering Heights,* I noted the danger of 'letting emotions get out of control.' Rereading these brief *moralistic* appraisals usually left me disheartened."

My boss was a *moralistic* man who believed in hard work, punctuality, and thriftiness.

moralistic (môr ə lĭs´ tĭk) means:

a. pertaining to friendship
b. pertaining to education
c. juvenile; childish
d. pertaining to moral principles

_____ 7. "Rereading these brief moralistic appraisals usually left me *disheartened.*"

Tony was *disheartened* when he did not get the job.

disheartened (dĭs här´ tənd) means:

a. having one's courage or spirit shaken or destroyed; discouraged
b. pleased
c. satisfied with one's own efforts; complacent
d. angry

_____ 8. "In spite of my *earnestness,* I found reading a pleasurable activity."

Because of the six-year-old's solemnness and *earnestness,* he seemed more like an adult than a child.

earnestness (ûr´ nĭst nəs) means:

a. frustration
b. seriousness
c. stubbornness
d. shyness

______ 9. "Around my room, growing stacks of paperback books reinforced my *assurance*."

One reason the company offered Maria the job was that the interviewer had been impressed with her *assurance*.

assurance (ə shŏŏr′ əns) means:

a. self-confidence; freedom from doubt
b. refusal
c. decision
d. promise or vow made under pressure

______ 10. "I vacuumed books for *epigrams,* scraps of information, ideas, themes—anything to fill the hollow within me and make me feel educated."

In my parents' high school yearbook, there were *epigrams* printed beside the seniors' pictures.

epigrams (ĕp′ ĭ grămz) means:

a. riddles; puzzles
b. pieces of advice
c. short, witty remarks or poems
d. epitaphs

Respond in Writing

Directions: Refer to Selection 8-3 as necessary to answer these essay-type items.

Option for collaboration: For some of the "Respond in Writing" exercises, your instructor may prefer that you work collaboratively, that is, with other students. These exercises are identified in the margin. *If your instructor directs you to work collaboratively on any of these items,* form groups of three or four classmates to complete the exercise together. Discuss your answers with each other and have one member of the group record the answers. A member of the group may be asked to share the group's answers with the class.

1. Richard Rodriguez states that despite the fact that he did not understand many of the books he read in high school, reading them helped him in three ways. What were the three ways?

   First way:

   ____

   ____

Second way:

Third way:

Option

Item 2 may be completed collaboratively.

2. In what ways do you think reading many books might help you?

Option

Item 3 may be completed collaboratively.

3. What is the most important overall message the writer wants the reader to understand about reading? Try to answer this question in one sentence.

PART THREE

SYSTEMS FOR STUDYING TEXTBOOKS

Developing a System That Works for You

CHAPTERS IN PART THREE

CHAPTER 9

SELECTING AND ORGANIZING TEXTBOOK INFORMATION

IN THIS CHAPTER YOU WILL LEARN THE ANSWERS TO THESE QUESTIONS:

How can I select important textbook information?

Why should I organize textbook information as I read?

How can I use textbook features to make my studying more efficient?

What are effective ways to mark textbooks?

What are effective ways to take notes from textbooks?

How can I interpret graphic material correctly?

CHAPTER 9 CONTENTS

One of the toughest things to learn is the ability to make yourself do the thing you have to do, when it ought to be done, whether you like it or not.

Thomas Huxley

STUDYING BETTER RATHER THAN HARDER

Chapter 1 of this book emphasized that it can take considerable time to learn the information in your textbooks. Although experienced college students know this, new students sometimes do not. Beginning students often have unrealistic expectations about the amount of time it will take to read and study textbooks and prepare for tests. In fact, they may be shocked to discover just how much time studying requires; and they may also conclude, mistakenly, that *they* are the only ones who have to spend so much time.

You already know, then, that one of the things it takes to be successful is allowing sufficient study time. However, you also need to recognize that simply spending large amounts of time studying will not by itself guarantee success: what you *do* during your study times is equally important.

Staring at a book is not the same as reading, and sitting at a desk is not the same as studying. Some students who claim they are studying often are only daydreaming. (Studying a little and daydreaming a lot do not add up to studying.) Other students do really invest many hours in studying yet are disappointed in the results. Still other students are successful at studying but feel discouraged because it seems to take them too much time. You yourself have undoubtedly had the experience of finishing an assignment, realizing that you did it the "hard way," and feeling frustrated because you know you worked harder and longer than you needed to. You are probably wondering, "Isn't there a better, more efficient way?"

The answer is yes: there *is* a better, more efficient way to study. This chapter and the next one describe specific techniques to help you read your textbooks more efficiently and learn to study *better,* rather than harder or longer. Often, what makes the difference between a successful student and a less successful one is *applying these study skills in a systematic way.*

You may already be familiar with some of these study techniques, or you may be learning them for the first time. In either case, by mastering and using these skills you can become a more effective student. These skills will serve you well in all your courses, adding new techniques to your study repertoire. They will also help you in a variety of other learning situations. There will always be situations in college and in the workplace in which you must organize, learn, and remember information.

Remember, however, that these study skills are not "magic." They simply allow you to study better rather than harder. The truth is that being a successful student demands time, effort, and dedication. You can become a better and better student each semester, but only if you are willing to invest enough time and effort, and if you bring enough dedication to the task.

THREE KEYS TO STUDYING COLLEGE TEXTBOOKS

The strategies in this chapter and Chapter 10 are based on three essentials of studying: three *keys* to studying better. The three keys are *selecting* essential information to study, *organizing* that information in a meaningful way, and *rehearsing* it in order to remember it. As you will see, selectivity, organization, and rehearsal are interrelated and interdependent.

Key 1: Selectivity

Key term

Selectivity: Identifying main ideas and important supporting details. First of three essential study strategies.

Selectivity is the first essential key to understanding and remembering what you read. Too many students think that they can (and must) learn and remember everything in their textbooks, but this is a mistaken idea that leads only to frustration. Generally, *it is necessary to identify and remember only main ideas and important supporting details.* Therefore, you must be selective as you read and study.

Chapters 4 through 8 (Part Two, the "comprehension core,") explained how to read selectively by focusing on main ideas and details. The techniques in the present chapter will further increase your ability to be selective: you will learn about textbook features, textbook marking, and textbook notes.

Key 2: Organization

Key term

Organization: Arranging main ideas and supporting details in a meaningful way. Second of three essential study strategies.

Organization is the second key to learning and remembering what you read. The reason is simple: *organized material is easier to learn, memorize, and recall* than unorganized material.

Part Two explained how to see relationships between main ideas and supporting details by identifying authors' patterns of writing. Those skills make learning and remembering easier. In this chapter, you will learn additional skills of organization. Using textbook features, along with your own textbook marking and notetaking, will help you to organize material more effectively.

Key 3: Rehearsal

Key term

Rehearsal: Saying or writing material to transfer it into long-term memory. Third of three essential study strategies.

Rehearsal, a concept introduced in Chapter 3, is the third key to learning and remembering textbook material. Rehearsal involves saying aloud or writing down material you want to memorize. It is *not* merely rereading, nor is it a casual overview. Rehearsal is a way of reviewing material that puts the material into your memory. Particularly with complex material, it is necessary to *rehearse information to transfer it to long-term (permanent) memory.*

It is important to understand that comprehending and remembering are two separate tasks. The fact that you comprehend textbook material does not necessarily mean that you will remember it. To *remember* material as well as understand it, you must take additional steps; that is, you must rehearse. Just as actors begin to memorize their lines long before a performance, students need to rehearse textbook material frequently, long before a test. (Rehearsal is discussed in detail in Chapter 10.)

Summary of the Three-Step Process for Studying College Textbooks

▪ ▪ ▪ ▪ ▪ ▪ ▪

Step 1: Prepare to read

Overview to see what the selection contains and how it is organized.
Assess your prior knowledge.
Plan your reading and study time.

Step 2: Ask and answer questions to guide your reading.

Use questions to guide your reading.
Read actively, looking for answers.
Record the answers to your questions.

Step 3: Review by rehearsing your answers.

Review the material by *rehearsing,* to transfer it to long-term memory.

Selectivity, organization, and rehearsal are the foundation for the study techniques in this chapter and in Chapter 10. At this point, however, it will be useful to look back at the three-step process for reading and studying textbooks presented in Chapter 3, since we will now be adding specific study skills to that general approach. The three-step process is shown again in the box above.

USING TEXTBOOK FEATURES

Key term

Textbook feature: Device used to emphasize important material and show how it is organized.

Using textbook features will help you locate, select, and organize material you want to learn. Taking advantage of textbook features is one way to study better rather than harder.

A ***textbook feature*** is a device an author uses to emphasize important material or to show how material is organized. It is a way authors help readers get the most out of a textbook. Another term for *textbook feature* is *learning aid.*

There are many kinds of textbook features, and in this section you will look at some of the most important. Though no single college textbook is likely to include all of these features, many of your textbooks will have several of them.

Keep in mind that different authors may call the same feature by different names. For example, what one author may call a *chapter summary* another may call a *chapter review, chapter highlights, key points, points to remember, a look back,* or *summing up.*

Be sure to take advantage of textbook features as you study; they are there to help you locate, select, and organize the material you must learn.

Prefaces

Key term

Preface: Introductory section in which authors tell readers about the book.

At the beginning of a textbook, you will usually find one or more kinds of introductory material. A ***preface*** (such as the example below from a communications textbook) is a section in which the author tells readers about the book. It is an important message from the author. Whether a preface is addressed to students, to instructors, or to both, it is likely to provide helpful information. It typically describes the author's approach to the subject, explains how the book is organized, and mentions special features the book contains. The author may also explain how the current edition of a book improves on the previous edition.

Regardless of what a preface is called (*Preface, To the Student, A Word to Students*), you should read it before you read anything else, because it gives important information and advice. For instance, in the example from a composition text on the opposite page, the authors explain the value of the list of words and definitions following each reading.

In *Opening Doors,* the section "To the Student" is a preface; it appears on pages xvii–xix. Did you read it? If not, you should do so now.

Preface

Human Communication is designed for introductory communication courses. Since it was first published twenty years ago, it has been used by over 125,000 students—a figure that makes us feel both humbled and encouraged. As in earlier editions, our commitment is to present students with a comprehensive theoretical base, an understanding of how modern communication has evolved and continues to change and grow, and a grasp of its immediate and long-term applications to their own lives.

Once again we focus on the traditional concerns of speech communication and link together contexts as various as two-person communication and mass communication. Our approach is to fuse current and classic communication theory, fundamental concepts, and important skills. Despite its complexities, we believe we can present our subject to introductory students without over-simplification, in language that is clear, vivid, and precise.

We have tried, as in previous editions, to create a text that is sensitive to diversity, one that reflects our long-term interest in gender and cultural issues. Thus, throughout our book we integrate examples and references that represent a wide variety of backgrounds, ages, and ethnic and cultural groups.

Source: Stewart L. Tubbs and Sylvia Moss, *Human Communication,* 7th ed., McGraw-Hill, New York, 1994, from p. xiii. Reproduced with permission of McGraw-Hill.

TO THE STUDENT

We have chosen these readings primarily to provide you with helpful models of style and structure. At the same time, we have tried hard to select pieces that you will enjoy and find enlightening. The idea is to encourage in you a fondness for language and a sharp eye for technique, both of which will serve to make you a more skillful writer.

The selections include poetry and stories as well as essays, and the writing assignments sometimes ask you to do what might be called "creative writing." You may want to know why you should ponder a poem or describe a fantasy when the writing you will need to do in the working world consists of ordering parts from the Acme Showcase Company, reporting on water damage from burst pipes, or describing right-of-way specifications for a city street. Although these quite different kinds of writing appear to have little in common, the creative exercises will stretch your imagination and bolster your confidence. Any practice that helps you to realize fully your power over words will prove worthwhile. The ease of expression you develop during creative writing (when no rules apply) will carry over into anything you choose to write. Of course, every writer has times when the words stubbornly have minds of their own, kicking each other in the shins and refusing to stand nicely in line; but the more you think about and practice writing, the briefer these little rebellions will be.

Many students feel confident that they can understand an essay, but turn into quivering masses of uncertainty when given a poem to read. Don't let yourself be intimidated by the unusual word patterns of poets. If the meaning is unclear on first reading, go over it again—aloud this time. Give yourself the pleasure of puzzling out the meaning. Assume an open, relaxed approach to the literary selections, and you will find that you can learn from them as much about rhetoric as you can from a comfortably paragraphed page of prose.

Your task will be made easier by the list of words and definitions following each reading. These definitions supply only the meaning of the word in the context of that selection. The words defined are those that may be new to you (like *interlocutor* or *vacuity*), those that carry a different meaning in the selection from the usual one (*exact* used as a verb, for example), and those that have changed meaning over time (*fancy* meaning "imagination," for instance).

Your most taxing work in using this text involves thinking. You will need to think critically in analyzing the selections, and you will have to think hard in planning and practicing your writing. But you should find, as you progress, that the line between work and pleasure grows steadily less distinct.

Source: Susan Day and Elizabeth McMahan, *The Writer's Resource: Readings for Composition,* 4th ed., McGraw-Hill, New York, 1994, p. xxv. Reproduced with permission of McGraw-Hill.

CONTENTS

Source: Richard E. Sullivan, Dennis Sherman, and John B. Harrison, *A Short History of Western Civilization,* 8th ed., McGraw-Hill, New York, 1994, p. iv. Reproduced with permission of McGraw-Hill.

Tables of Contents

Another feature at the beginning of a textbook is a ***table of contents.*** This may simply be a list of chapter titles, or (like the example on the opposite page) it may be more detailed, including major chapter headings. Some tables of contents show chapter subheadings as well. The table of contents is your first chance to get an overview of the organization of the textbook as a whole: the "big picture." Notice—in the example on the opposite page, that this history textbook is divided into major parts. Each part is in turn divided into chapters ("1/, 2/," etc.). The order of the chapters seems to be based both on chronology (time) and geography.

In addition to the main table of contents at the beginning of a textbook, there may also be a separate listing of some special sections or features. The example below, from a sociology text, lists "boxes" (a feature that will be discussed on page 454–455).

LIST OF BOXES

BOX

Source: Richard T. Schaefer and Robert P. Lamm, *Sociology: A Brief Introduction,* McGraw-Hill, New York, 1994, p. xiii. Reproduced with permission of McGraw-Hill.

Part Openings

Key term

Part Opening: Textbook feature that introduces a section (part) consisting of several chapters.

As you have just seen, chapters in a textbook may be grouped into larger sections or parts. *Opening Doors,* for example, has three major parts. ***Part openings*** are often useful features. A part opening may list the chapters contained in that part (as in *Opening Doors*), or it may present an opening statement or briefly describe each of its chapters (like the example from a sociology text on the opposite page). This gives you a quick overview of the material that will be covered by all chapters in the part and also suggests how those chapters are connected or interrelated.

Sometimes, important text material is given in the part opening, as in the example below from a theater textbook. (Note the definition of *Renaissance,* the dates, and the general historical background.) Information mentioned in a part opening may actually appear in several different chapters; by consolidating this information at the beginning of the part, the authors clarify it and make it easier to remember.

PART TWO

THEATERS OF THE RENAISSANCE

The Renaissance was an age of humanism, discovery, and exceptional art. *Renaissance* is a French word meaning "rebirth," and during this historical period—from roughly 1400 to 1650—European culture is said to have been reborn. Its rebirth included a rediscovery of earlier cultures, but equally important was a new view of human possibilities. In the Middle Ages, human beings had been seen as small, insignificant figures on the lower rungs of a sort of universal ladder, with the deity and other divinities at the top. In the Renaissance, people began to regard the individual as important and as having enormous potential.

A significant aspect of the Renaissance was, of course, the rediscovery of the civilizations of Greece and Rome. For the first time in several centuries, the heritage of these civilizations—their art, literature, and philosophy—became available, largely through the rediscovery of ancient manuscripts. The achievements and ideas of Greece and Rome struck a sympathetic chord in men and women of fourteenth-century Italy and France, who hoped to create a new classical civilization that would equal the old.

Other things were happening in addition to this rediscovery of the past. The major distinction between the Middle Ages and the Renaissance was a secularization of society—that is, a move away from religion. The dominance of the Roman Catholic church was eroded as Renaissance society became more concerned with "this world" than with the "next world," the afterlife in heaven.

Source: Edwin Wilson and Alvin Goldfarb, *Living Theater: A History,* 2d ed., McGraw-Hill, New York, 1994, from pp. 136–137. Reproduced with permission of McGraw-Hill.

PART

A sociologist can make a reasonably accurate prediction about where a child will end up in life on the basis of a few simple facts: the child's parents' incomes and education; whether the child is black, Hispanic, Asian American, or Anglo-American; and whether the child is male or female. To be sure, some youngsters will escape the sociologist's crystal ball. But most will not. The "crystal ball" in this case is an understanding of social stratification.

Chapter 8 explores the origins and consequences of social stratification. This chapter describes social class differences in the United States, with special emphasis on the poor, and shows how these differences affect not just how well people live but how long they live.

Chapter 9 examines inequalities based on race and ethnicity. This chapter begins by looking at intergroup relations in cross-cultural perspective; then traces the history of racial and ethnic inequality in the United States; analyzes where black, Hispanic, Native, and Asian Americans stand today; and suggests why efforts to reduce racial and ethnic inequality have proven so disappointing.

Chapter 10 focuses on gender and age. Clearly the roles women play in our society have changed dramatically in the past quarter century. But are American women better off than their mothers were? If not, why not? The position the elderly occupy in our society has also changed, in many ways for the better. What explains these two different patterns?

SOCIAL INEQUALITY

Source: Michael S. Bassis, Richard J. Gelles, and Ann Levine, *Sociology: An Introduction,* 4th ed., McGraw-Hill, New York, 1991, p. 213. Reproduced with permission of McGraw-Hill.

Chapter Outlines

Key term

Chapter outline: Textbook feature at the beginning of a chapter, listing the topics or headings in their order of appearance.

A ***chapter outline*** is a list of chapter topics or headings in their order of appearance in the chapter. It provides a preliminary overview of the chapter. This feature helps you see the content and organization of the entire chapter. It lets you know in advance not only what topics the chapter will cover, but how they fit together. Trying to read or study a chapter without first seeing its outline is like trying to solve a jigsaw puzzle without looking at the picture on the box. It can be done, certainly, but it takes longer and is much more difficult!

Chapter outlines may be called by various names such as *Chapter Contents, Chapter Topics, Preview, Overview,* or *In This Chapter;* or may have no title at all. They can also take various forms. They may or may not actually be set up in outline style; and they may be general or detailed.

Chapter outlines in *Opening Doors,* for instance, appear on separate pages, including headings and subheadings, and also list reading selections. The example on the opposite page (from a criminology text) is also in outline style; notice that next to it, in the second column, the chapter itself begins. The example shown below (from a text on social behavior) looks very different: it must be read "across," and subheadings are indicated by *italics* rather than indentations.

5

Some Interesting Differences in the Elements of Subjective Culture

❖

The Sapir-Whorf Hypothesis ◆ Gender Inequalities across the World ◆ *Foragers* ◆ *Horticultural Societies* ◆ *Pastoral Societies* ◆ *Agrarian Societies* ◆ *Industrial Societies* ◆ *Socialist Societies* ◆ *The Third World* ◆ *Information Societies* ◆ What Is Functional Is Good ◆ Cultural Differences in Attributions ◆ Cultures and Dealing with Time ◆ Culture and Marriage ◆ Culture and Social Distance ◆ Culture and Stereotypes ◆ *Sex Stereotypes* ◆ Summary

Source: Harry C. Triandis, *Culture and Social Behavior,* McGraw-Hill, New York, 1994, p. 120. Reproduced with permission of McGraw-Hill.

CHAPTER 18

Corrections: Prisons and Alternatives to Prisons

We like to think of ourselves as a civilized and humane society even with respect to criminals. Indeed, we call our prisons "correctional" institutions, presumably placing corrected behavior as the central goal. Surveys show that individual deterrence, reaffirmation of norms, and rehabilitation rank higher in American public opinion than do retribution, incapacitation, and revenge (Jacoby and Dunn, 1987). Yet the United States currently has the largest prison population in its history.

Criminologists generally believe that they approach the issues of punishment and imprisonment in a rational and humane way. For instance, they usually refer to punishment in terms of "just deserts," deterrence, selective incapacitation, rehabilitation, restitution, and community service. In fact, most studies of criminal punishment rarely employ the word **penology** (the study of punishment); rather they use the term "corrections." Again, the implication is that the punishment system is structured to change or reform the criminal's behavior.

Social scientists of both liberal and conservative orientations are skeptical of any reformative claims made by the penal system. If anything, there is at present a retributive mood among many policymakers and some scientists (Casper, 1988). Today the rehabilitation ideology is hardly mentioned in a positive light.

Source: Lydia Voigt, William E. Thornton, Jr., Leo Bartile, and Jerrold M. Seaman, *Criminology and Justice,* McGraw-Hill, New York, 1994, p. 518. Reproduced with permission of McGraw-Hill.

Chapter Objectives and Introductions

Key term

Chapter objectives: Textbook feature at the beginning of a chapter, telling you what you should know or be able to do after studying the chapter.

Authors often use a list of ***chapter objectives*** at the beginning of a chapter to tell you what you should know or be able to do after studying the chapter. Objectives appear in various forms and may also be called *Preview Questions, What You'll Learn, Goals,* etc. In the example below left (from a communication text), the authors state directly, "After finishing this chapter, you should be able to . . ." and they state the objectives like test items. Note the directions *define, explain, compare and contrast,* and *describe.* In the example below right (from a sociology text), the objectives are called "Looking Ahead" and are phrased as questions. In *Opening Doors,* chapter objectives are also written as questions.

Key term

Chapter introduction: Textbook feature at the beginning of a chapter, describing the overall purpose and major topics.

A ***chapter introduction*** is an opening passage which describes the overall purpose, major topics and their sequence, or how this chapter is linked to preceding chapters. Or it may "set the scene" by giving, for instance, a case study or an anecdote. A chapter introduction may (like the example at the top of the opposite page actually be called *Introduction,* or (like the other example opposite) it may be indicated by special type or a large ornamental letter at the beginning of the first word. Read chapter introductions carefully; they are a helpful guide to what lies ahead.

After finishing this chapter, you should be able to:

Define *listening*
Explain the nature of serial communication
State how much time you spend listening
Compare and contrast helpful and harmful listening habits
Distinguish between the processes of hearing and listening
Explain the "listening level–energy involvement" scale
Define *feedback*
Describe how feedback affects communication
Use different types of evaluative and nonevaluative feedback
Focus your attention while listening
Set appropriate listening goals
Listen to understand ideas
Listen to retain information
Listen to evaluate and analyze content
Listen empathically

Source: Teri Kwal Gamble and Michael Gamble, *Communication Works,* 4th ed., McGraw-Hill, New York, 1993, p. 141. Reproduced with permission of McGraw-Hill.

LOOKING AHEAD

- How are girls socialized to be "feminine" and boys to be "masculine"?
- How are gender roles apparent in everyday conversations between men and women?
- Why is it that, despite outnumbering men, women are viewed as a subordinate minority by sociologists?
- How pervasive is sex-typing of jobs? Are there many jobs viewed either as "men's work" or as "women's work"?
- When married women work outside the home, do their husbands assume equal responsibility for housework and child care?
- Why is it said that women from racial and ethnic minorities face a kind of "double jeopardy"?
- How does the world view of feminists involved in defending abortion rights differ from that of antiabortion activists?

Source: Richard T. Schaefer and Robert P. Lamm, *Sociology,* 4th ed., McGraw-Hill, New York, 1992, p. 324. Reproduced with permission of McGraw-Hill.

Introduction

In this chapter, you will be reading longer passages because college reading isn't limited to single paragraphs. Fortunately, one of the hallmarks of a mature reader is the ability to deal with increasingly longer, more complex textbook passages. For example, a reader moves from comprehending a sentence to comprehending a paragraph. The reader then connects the information in a paragraph with the information in the next paragraph, and the next (all the while following the writer's main ideas). Soon the reader has followed the writer's thoughts throughout the chapter and subsequently throughout all the chapters of the book.

In one sense, reading longer passages is easier. You can see the *overall subject matter* and the *overall main idea* instead of just smaller parts. Seeing the overall organization of a longer section of a textbook chapter (or even the entire chapter) promotes comprehension and recall.

In this chapter you will learn how to determine the overall subject matter and the overall main idea for a longer passage. You will also learn how to write a summary of a longer textbook selection. But first, you will find out how to read and study a textbook assignment in an organized, intelligent manner.

Source: Joe Cortina, Janet Elder, and Katherine Gonnet, *Comprehending College Textbooks,* 2d ed., McGraw-Hill, New York, 1992, p. 320. Reproduced with permission of McGraw-Hill.

Conflict is an inevitable part of the life of any group, and sooner or later it touches all group members. A conflict can be started by anyone and can occur at any point in a group's existence. Opposed or contradictory forces within us can create inner conflicts, or we can find ourselves experiencing tension as external forces build and create interpersonal conflicts. Thus, a conflict can originate within a single group member or between two or more group members.

A group experiences *conflict* whenever a member's thoughts or acts limit, prevent, or interfere with his or her own thoughts or acts or with those of any other member. If you think about your recent group experiences, you will probably discover that you have been involved in conflicts. Some involved only you; some involved you and another. Probably, some were mild and subtle; others were intense and hostile. In any case, probably all of them were interesting.

Our goal in this chapter is to explore what conflict is, how it arises, how it affects us as group members, and how we can handle it productively. In doing so, we will develop skills to help us deal more effectively with group problem solving and decision making.

Source: Teri Kwal Gamble and Michael Gamble, *Communication Works,* 4th ed., McGraw-Hill, New York, 1994, p. 283. Reproduced with permission of McGraw-Hill.

Lists and Sequences

When ***lists and sequences*** of important material are set off from a paragraph in some special way, they become helpful textbook features. A list or sequence is presented in this way in order to draw your attention to it. Items in a list sequence may be set in a row or rows (like the example below left from a sociology text), numbered (like the example at the top of the opposite page, from a music text), or lettered. The example below right is set in **boldface** and shows a symbol for each planet. The items in the sequence at the bottom of the opposite page (from a journalism text) have small marks called *bullets* (which are also used in *Opening Doors*). Notice also that the important stages here (*Phase 1, Phase 2,* etc.) are in a special typeface.

Note, too, that the authors of the astronomy text suggest a *mnemonic device* (memory aid). Mnemonic devices are often a good method to use with lists and sequences.

Cultural Universals

Like the hominids, human beings have made dramatic cultural advances. Despite their differences, all societies have attempted to meet basic human needs by developing cultural universals. ***Cultural universals,*** such as language, are general practices found in every culture.

Anthropologist George Murdock (1945:124) compiled a list of cultural universals. The examples identified by Murdock include the following practices:

Athletic sports	Housing
Bodily adornment	Language
Calendar	Laws
Cooking	Marriage
Courtship	Medicine
Dancing	Music
Decorative art	Myths
Family	Numerals
Folklore	Personal names
Food habits	Property rights
Food taboos	Religion
Funeral ceremonies	Sexual restrictions
Games	Surgery
Gestures	Toolmaking
Gift giving	Trade
Hairstyles	Visiting

Source: Richard T. Schaefer and Robert P. Lamm, *Sociology: A Brief Introduction,* McGraw-Hill, New York, 1994, p. 34. Reproduced with permission of McGraw-Hill.

A Survey of the Planets

The solar system is defined as the sun, its nine orbiting planets, their own satellites, and a host of small interplanetary bodies, such as asteroids and comets. Starting in the center of the solar system, the major bodies and their symbols are:

☉ **Sun**
☿ **Mercury**
♀ **Venus**
⊕ **Earth**
♂ **Mars**
♃ **Jupiter**
♄ **Saturn**
♅ **Uranus**
♆ **Neptune**
♇ **Pluto**

The symbols, mostly derived from ancient astrology, are sometimes used as convenient abbreviations today. A traditional memory aid for this outward sequence is "*M*en *V*ery *E*arly *M*ade *J*ars *S*tand *U*pright *N*icely, *P*eriod." Surely today's students can do better![1] To avoid confusion about the positions of Saturn, Uranus, and Neptune, remember that the *SUN* is a member of the system, too.

Source: William K. Hartman, *Astronomy: The Cosmic Journey,* Wadsworth, Belmont, Calif., 1988, p. 106. Reprinted by permission.

CHARACTERISTICS OF MUSIC SINCE 1950

Accurately describing the relatively recent past is a difficult task. Yet any overview of music since 1950 must include these major developments:

1. Increased use of the *twelve-tone system*
2. *Serialism*—use of the techniques of the twelve-tone system to organize rhythm, dynamics, and tone color
3. *Chance music,* in which a composer chooses pitches, tone colors, and rhythms by random methods, or allows a performer to choose much of the musical material
4. *Minimalist music,* characterized by a steady pulse, clear tonality, and insistent repetition of short melodic patterns
5. Works containing deliberate *quotations* from earlier music.
6. A *return to tonality* by some composers
7. *Electronic music*
8. *"Liberation of sound"*—greater exploitation of noiselike sounds
9. *Mixed media*
10. New concepts of *rhythm* and *form*

Source: Roger Kamien, *Music: An Appreciation,* 2d Brief ed., McGraw-Hill, New York, 1994, p. 305. Reproduced with permission of McGraw-Hill.

PHASES OF A DEVELOPING STORY

Whenever a major news event occurs, all the daily media strive to keep their audiences as up to date as possible. A story can be developed for hours or for months, and it is usually covered in four phases:

- *Phase 1.* The story first breaks. Journalists rush to the scene to report the news as it is happening, or they work the phones to put together an initial breaking story. They work on the story full time, and their primary function is to tell their audiences *what* happened, *when, where* and to *whom.* The story is front-page news. Reporters will usually write *mainbars,* primary stories that report the *breaking news;* and *sidebars,* supplemental stories that explain the news or report the human element.
- *Phase 2.* Journalists try to explain the *why* and *how* of the story, but they also continue to report late-breaking developments, such as cleanup operations or a final casualty count. This means that the story is likely to remain front-page news. *Second-day stories,* which report the latest news as well as summarize the earlier news, and sidebars are written to put the news into perspective for an audience.
- *Phase 3.* The story is no longer front-page news, unless something unusual happens to warrant front-page treatment, but reporters are still covering it full time or routinely. They look for something fresh, but they also analyze and continue to humanize the story. Follow-ups and features may be written for days afterward.
- *Phase 4.* Few reporters are working on the story full time any longer, but there may be a few pursuing specific angles. Reporters still make routine checks. Weeks or months later, there may be a major development as officials release their findings or investigative reporters come up with something. The story could become front-page news again.

Source: Bruce D. Itule and Douglas Anderson, *News Writing and Reporting for Today's Media,* 3d ed., McGraw-Hill, New York, 1994, p. 121. Reproduced with permission of McGraw-Hill.

Boxes

A ***box,*** or ***sidebar,*** is supplementary material that is separated from the regular text. It may appear at the bottom or top of a page of text (like the example opposite) or on one or more pages by itself. "Box" material may or may not be in an actual box; it may be set off in columns, in a different typeface, or by color.

Boxes can contain a variety of information: case studies, research studies, biographical sketches, interviews, excerpts from other works, controversial issues, practical applications—the possibilities are almost endless. Boxes may be numbered, and authors often create box titles to fit the subject matter: for example *Points to Ponder, Issues and Debate, Close-Up, Speaking Out, Current Research,* and *What Do You Think?*

Pay close attention to boxes: they clarify important points, provide vivid examples, and broaden and deepen your understanding of the material.

● CULTURE AND COMMUNICATION

A REFUSAL TO COMPETE

A new teacher—let's call her Mary—arrived at a Navaho Indian reservation. Each day in her classroom, something like this would occur. Mary would ask five of her young Navaho students to go to the chalkboard and complete a simple mathematics problem from their homework. All five students would go to the chalkboard, but not one of them would work the problem as requested. Instead, they would all stand silent and motionless.

Mary, of course, wondered what was going on. She repeatedly asked herself if she might possibly be calling on students who could not do the assigned problems. "No, it couldn't be that," she reasoned. Finally, Mary asked her students what the problem was. Their answer displayed an understanding not many people attain in a lifetime.

Evidently, the students realized that not everyone in the class would be able to complete the problems correctly. But they respected each other's uniqueness, and they understood, even at their young age, the dangers of a "win-lose" approach. In their opinion, no one would "win" if anyone was embarrassed or humiliated at the chalkboard, and so they refused to compete publicly with each other. Yes, the Navaho students wanted to learn—but not at the expense of their peers.

Where do you stand? In your opinion would typical American schoolchildren behave similarly? Why or why not? Should they behave like the Navahos?

Source: Teri Kwal Gamble and Michael Gamble, *Communication Works,* 4th ed., McGraw-Hill, New York, 1994, p. 290. Reproduced with permission of McGraw-Hill.

BOX 9-1

MARITAL POWER

Sociologists Robert Blood, Jr., and Donald Wolfe (1960) developed the concept of ***marital power*** to describe the manner in which decision making is distributed within families. They defined power by examining who makes the final decision in each of eight important areas that, the researchers argue, traditionally have been reserved entirely for the husband or for the wife. These areas include what job the husband should take, what house or apartment to live in, where to go on vacation, and which doctor to use if there is an illness in the family. Using this technique, Blood and Wolfe (1960:22–23) surveyed families in the Detroit area and concluded that the "aggregate balance of power falls slightly in the husband's direction." They added that, in general, it seemed appropriate to "label these as relatively egalitarian couples."

Recent research suggests that money plays a central role in determining marital power. Money has different meanings for members of each sex: for men it typically represents identity and power; for women, security and autonomy. Apparently, money establishes the balance of power not only for married couples but also for unmarried heterosexual couples who are living together. Married women with paying work outside the home enjoy greater marital power than full-time homemakers do (Blumstein and Schwartz, 1983; Godwin and Scanzoni, 1989; Kaufman, 1985).

Labor not only enhances women's self-esteem but also increases their marital power, because some men have greater respect for women who work at paying jobs. Sociologist Isik Aytac (1987) studied a national sample of households in the United States and found that husbands of women holding management positions share more of the domestic chores than other husbands. In addition, as a wife's proportional contribution to the family income increases, her husband's share of meal preparation increases. Aytac's research supports the contention that the traditional division of labor at home can change as women's position in the labor force improves and women gain greater marital power.

Comparative studies have revealed the complexity of marital power issues in other cultures. For example, anthropologist David Gilmore (1990) examined decision making in two rural towns in southern Spain. These communities—one with 8000 residents and the other with 4000—have an agricultural economy based on olives, wheat, and sunflowers. Gilmore studied a variety of decision-making situations, including prenuptial decisions over household location, administration of domestic finances, and major household purchases. He found that working-class women in these communities—often united with their mothers—are able to prevail in many decisions despite opposition from their husbands.

Interestingly, wives' control over finances in these towns appears to lessen with affluence. Among the wealthier peasants, husbands retain more rights over the family purse strings, especially in terms of bank accounts and investments. In some cases, they make investments without their wives' knowledge. By contrast, in the working class—where surplus cash is uncommon and household finances are often based on borrowing and buying on credit because of the uncertainties of household employment—it is the wife who "rules" the household economy, and the husband accepts her rule.

Some marital relationships may be neither male-dominated nor female-dominated. The third type of authority pattern, the ***egalitarian family,*** is one in which spouses are regarded as equals. This does not mean, however, that each decision is shared in such families. Mothers may hold authority in some spheres, fathers in others. In the view of many sociologists, the egalitarian family has begun to replace the patriarchal family as the social norm. A study of Detroit families by Robert Blood, Jr., and Donald Wolfe (1960) supports this contention (see Box 9-1).

Source: Richard T. Schaefer and Robert P. Lamm, *Sociology: A Brief Introduction,* McGraw-Hill, New York, 1994, p. 237. Reproduced with permission of McGraw-Hill.

Tables

Key term

Table: Material arranged in rows and columns.

A ***table*** consists of material arranged in rows and columns. Tables contain words, numbers, or both. They may also include symbols, calculations, diagrams, and other types of information.

A table is an important textbook feature because it summarizes a great deal of information in a clear, concise, and organized way, as you can see from the examples here. To understand a table, it is necessary to read its title and the headings of the rows and columns. (Later in this chapter is a section on interpreting graphic material.)

TABLE 14.1

Summary of Findings Concerning Child Abuse

	Infancy	Toddler and preschool period	Middle childhood	Adolescence
		Interpersonal		
Social	Insecure attachment: Mother — Child Rejecting; hostile — Avoidant (Type A) Neglecting — Ambivalent (Type C) Rejecting & neglecting — Avoidant & ambivalent (Type D)	Avoids familiar people;* aggressive response to positive overtures;* ambivalent approach;* aggressive or distressed response to distress*	Fewer social and communicative skills; fewer friends; difficulty decentering; less empathy	Less competent; dysfunctional family
Play		Less mature, less group and parallel play; aggressive;* withdrawn;† interacts with teachers†		
		Intrapersonal		
Adjustment			Increased internalizing and externalizing of problems; less initiative	Increased internalizing and externalizing of problems
Self		Visual recognition delayed and affectless; fewer words for own and others' inner states		

* Physically Abused
† Neglected

Source: Charles Wenar, *Developmental Psychopathology,* 3d ed., McGraw-Hill, New York, 1994, p. 386. Reproduced with permission of McGraw-Hill.

TABLE 19-2 FUNDAMENTAL BOSONS

Field	Particle	Mass	Spin	Couples to:
Electromagnetic	Photon	0	1	Charge
Strong nuclear	Gluon	0	1	Color
Weak nuclear	$W^{\pm}$	80,130	1	All fermions
	Z^0	91,180	1	
Gravity	Graviton?	0	2	Energy
Higgs?	Higgs?	?	0	Rest mass

Source: Robert H. March, *Physics for Poets,* 3d ed., McGraw-Hill, New York, 1992, p. 247. Reproduced with permission of McGraw-Hill.

TABLE 1–4
FOUR PERSPECTIVES ON HUMAN DEVELOPMENT

Perspective	Important Theories	Basic Belief	Technique Used
Psychoanalytic	Freud's psychosexual theory	Freud: Behavior is controlled by powerful unconscious urges.	Clinical observation
	Erikson's psychosocial theory	Erikson: Personality develops throughout life in a series of stages.	
Mechanistic	Behaviorism, or traditional learning theory (Pavlov, Skinner, Watson)	Behaviorism: People are responders; concern is with how the environment controls behavior.	Rigorous and scientific (experimental) procedures
	Social-learning theory (Bandura)	Social-learning theory: Children learn in a social context, by observing and imitating models; person is an active contributor to learning.	
Organismic	Piaget's cognitive-stage theory	There are qualitative changes in the way children think that develop in a series of four stages between infancy and adolescence. Person is an active initiator of development.	Flexible interviews; meticulous observation
Humanistic	Maslow's self-actualization theory	People have the ability to take charge of their lives and foster their own development.	Discussion of feelings

Source: Diane E. Papalia and Sally Wendkos Olds, *Human Development,* 5th ed., McGraw-Hill, New York, 1992, p. 22. Reproduced with permission of McGraw-Hill.

Graphic Aids

Key term

Graphic aid: Visual explanation of concepts and relationships.

Graphic aids, or ***illustrations,*** consolidate information and present it more clearly than would be possible with words alone. Graphic aids include figures, cartoons, and photographs.

Figures include maps, charts, diagrams, graphs, and "how-to" processes. They also include anatomical drawings (like the example below left) and drawings of laboratory apparatus (like the example below right).

Textbook figures are often numbered for reference (for example, "Figure 6a", "Figure 10-2"). They typically have *legends:* titles, descriptions, and explanations that appear above, below, or alongside the illustration. To understand a figure, you must read the legend and any labels within the figure. To understand a graph, be sure to read the *axes* (the labels that appear on the sides and bottom of the graph).

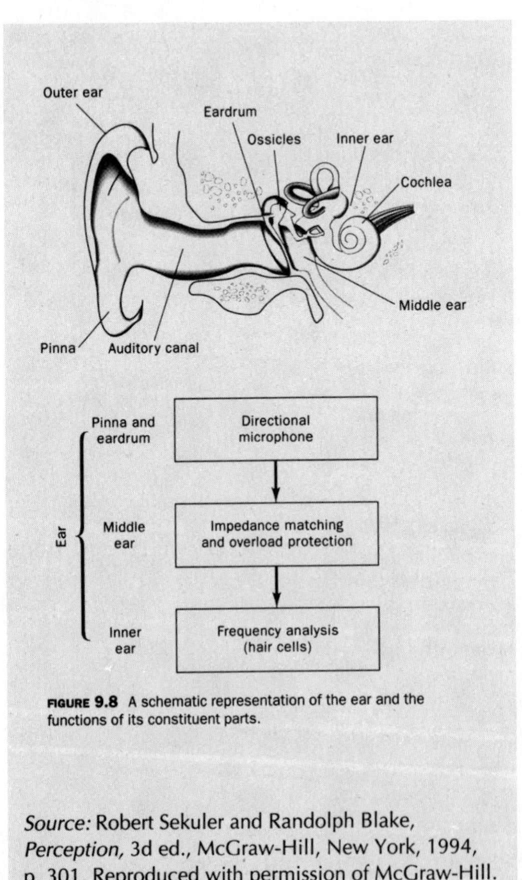

FIGURE 9.8 A schematic representation of the ear and the functions of its constituent parts.

Source: Robert Sekuler and Randolph Blake, *Perception,* 3d ed., McGraw-Hill, New York, 1994, p. 301. Reproduced with permission of McGraw-Hill.

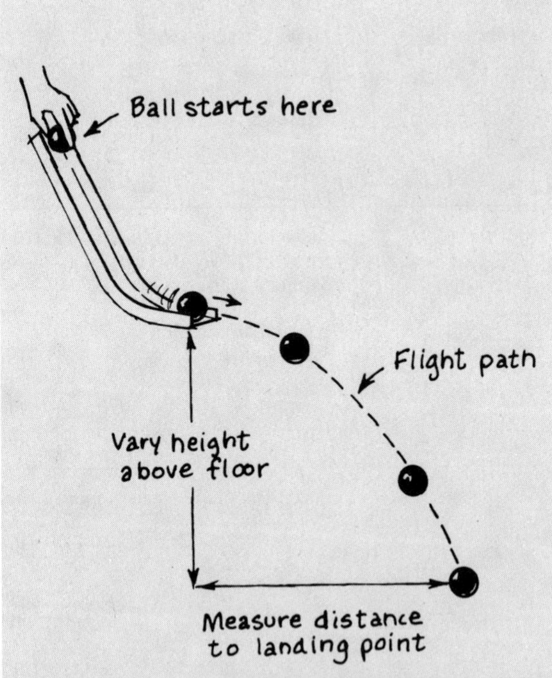

Figure 2-2 *Galileo's apparatus for studying projectile motion.*

Source: Robert H. March, *Physics for Poets,* 3d ed., McGraw-Hill, New York, 1992, p. 23. Reproduced with permission of McGraw-Hill.

© 1994 by Sidney Harris
S. Harris
"HERE WE ARE, CONWAY – THE FINANCIAL DISTRICT. KEEP YOUR EYES OPEN FOR ANY SHADY DEALS AND VIOLATIONS OF THE SECURITIES BUSINESS."

White-collar crime has become a widespread and disturbing reality in the nation's top corporate and financial circles.

Source: Richard T. Schaefer and Robert P. Lamm, *Sociology: A Brief Introduction*, McGraw-Hill, New York, 1994, p. 124. Reproduced with permission of McGraw-Hill.

Developmental tests are designed to chart the progress of infants—like 7-month-old Adam—and toddlers.

Source: Diane E. Papalia and Sally Wendkos Olds, *Human Development*, 5th ed., McGraw-Hill, New York, 1992, p. 119. Reproduced with permission of McGraw-Hill. *Photo:* Courtesy of Safra Nimrod.

Cartoons are a popular feature because they can make a point quickly and humorously. To be sure the reader will understand how a cartoon relates to the chapter material, the author may provide a legend (a comment or explanation) in addition to the caption (as in the example above left). Often, however, a cartoon is simply allowed "to speak for itself," and the reader must infer its relationship to the text.

Some photographs in textbooks (like the example above right) are included to enrich the text, to provide an example of a concept or situation, or to give the "flavor" of a time or place. Other photographs are informational and should be studied as carefully as the text itself: photos of paintings, statues, and buildings in an art appreciation text (like Selection 3-2 in *Opening Doors*) would be a good example. Of course, photos often fall somewhere between these two categories. Be sure to read photo legends (the words accompanying the photograph).

KEY TERMS

ambient system	dynamic visual acuity	group movement
apparent motion	element movement	induced motion
critical flicker frequency (CFF)	flicker	motion aftereffect
direction-selective cell	focal system	motion capture
	global motion	optic ataxia

Vocabulary Aids

Key term

Vocabulary aids: Textbook devices that highlight important terms and definitions.

Among the most common and most helpful textbook features are ***vocabulary aids,*** devices that highlight important terms and definitions. Authors highlight vocabulary in a variety of ways. Important terms may be set in **boldface,** *italic,* or color. They may also be printed in the margins (like *Key Terms* in *Opening Doors,* one of which appears here). There may be a list of terms, perhaps with definitions, at the end of a chapter (like the example at the top of this page) or after reading a selection (like the example below). These lists can also appear at the beginning of a chapter or reading. They may be called *Key Terms, Basic Terms, Terms to Know, Vocabulary, Terms to Remember,* and so on.

A list of important terms and definitions from the entire textbook may appear near the end of the book in a mini-dictionary, the *glossary.* (Shown opposite is the first page of the glossary of a psychology text.)

It is important to pay attention to vocabulary aids, because instructors expect you to know important terms, and often include them on tests.

VOCABULARY

delineate	to explain point by point
dialect	a manner of speaking common only to people from, or living in, a specific area
eloquent	able to speak (or write) in an especially moving and effective way
envoy	a messenger from, or representative of, a higher authority
flunkie	a person who does small, boring, or meaningless tasks at the orders of someone else; a "go-fer" (also spelled "flunky," "flunkey")
heresy	a belief or action that contradicts the official or strongly held beliefs of a society or organization, especially a church
japonica	a shrub that flowers profusely in spring
relentless	untiring, unwavering, ceaseless, persistent
sepulchral	like a tomb; having a tomblike atmosphere
whence	from which; where something came from
writ	a legal document, usually ordering some specific action

GLOSSARY

absolutist view of deviance The view that deviance is intrinsic to certain actions. In this view, right and wrong exist independently of arbitrary, human-created social judgments.

accounts Explanations that we offer for our behaviors. Accounts take four forms: excuses, justifications, concessions, and refusals.

additive task A task in which the performance of the group is measured in terms of the sum of the members' responses.

affect control theory (ACT) David Heise's theory offering a model of attitudes which suggests that the meanings we assign to identities and behaviors shape our social interactions. The theory uses the concepts of fundamental sentiments, transient sentiments, and deflection to describe the relationship between attitudes and behaviors.

affirmative action A government policy aimed at ending discriminatory practices by employers, as well as requiring them to take additional steps necessary to overcome the effects of past discrimination and give minorities "equal opportunity."

age grading The classification of individuals into age categories which divide the life course into meaningful stages and establish timetables for life events.

ageism Society's denial of privileges to a category of people because of their age.

agents of socialization The individuals, groups, and institutions that play a part in the transmission of culture to the new generation.

aggregate A unit of two or more persons whose interaction is minimal.

aggression Intentional harm done by one party to another.

alternative sources All the sources of rewards available to a person.

anticipatory socialization A phase of socialization in which individuals fantasize about, experiment with, and try on the behaviors associated with role expectations for future roles.

attitude consistency The organization of attitudes in a harmonious manner so that attitudes are not in conflict with each other (inconsistency or imbalance). Attitude consistency theories suggest that we strive to maintain consistency and to avoid inconsistency, which is experienced as an uncomfortable psychological state.

attitude toward the behavior In the reasoned action model, the behavioral-intention factor consisting of a person's beliefs and evaluations of the possible outcomes of the behavior. It is estimated by summing the person's evaluations of the consequences of the behavior, weighted by the likelihood of each consequence.

audience task A task involving performance in the presence of others who are observing the behavior but not performing the same task.

authoritarian parenting style A style of parenting in which parents rely on a combination of normative, reward, and coercive resources to produce their children's strict obedience.

authoritative parenting style A style of parenting in which parents rely on a combination of expert, informational, reward, and coercive resources to persuade their children to behave in a certain manner, taking into account the child's explanation for noncompliance.

backchannel feedback Any subtle vocal or nonverbal response that a listener makes while a speaker is talking that signals to the speaker whether he or she is keeping the listener's interest and being understood.

balance Balance theory's term for attitude consistency.

balance theory The original formulation of attitude consistency theory, developed by Fritz Heider, which focused on three elements: (1) the person who is the focus of attention, *P*; (2) some other person, *O*; and (3) an impersonal entity, *X*. The theory posits that *P* strives to maintain consistency among the attitudes connecting these elements, that is, *P*'s attitude toward *O*, *P*'s attitude toward *X*, and *P*'s perception of *O*'s attitude toward *X*.

behavioral intentions Our plans to perform a behavior. In the reasoned action model, behavioral intention is a function of the person's attitude toward the behavior and his or her subjective norm regarding it.

behavioral perspective An approach to social psychology proposing that our social behavior can best be understood by focusing on directly observable behavior and the environment that causes our behavior to change.

biological maturation The more or less automatic unfolding of biological potential in a set, predictable sequence.

birth cohort A category of people who were born in the same year or period and who age together.

body language The nonverbal communication of meaning through physical movements and gestures.

bonding The effort or desire to maintain a relationship.

catharsis A lessening of aggressive energy (anger) by discharging it through aggressive behavior.

civil inattention Form of body language in which we give others enough visual notice to signal to them that we recognize their presence, but then we quickly withdraw visual contact to show that we pose no threat to them and that we do not wish to interact with them.

coaction task A task involving performance in the presence of others with whom one has little interaction but who are performing the same task.

coalition An alliance of two or more parties who coordinate their efforts in order to achieve their ends against the

Sources: (Opposite page) Robert Sekuler and Randolph Blake, *Perception,* 3d ed., McGraw-Hill, New York, 1994, p. 25 *(top);* Susan Day and Elizabeth McMahan, *The Writer's Resource: Readings for Composition,* 4th ed., McGraw-Hill, New York, 1994, p. 340 *(bottom). (Above)* James A. Wiggins, Beverly B. Wiggins, and James Vander Zanden, *Social Psychology,* 5th ed., McGraw-Hill, New York, 1994, p. 551. Reproduced with permission of McGraw-Hill.

Study Questions and Activities

Many textbooks include ***study questions and activities,*** such as *exercises, drills,* and *practice sections.* These can be among the most important features you use, because they direct you to essential information you will be expected to know. Generally, if you are able to answer study questions and exercises, you will be able to do well on an actual test.

Study questions and activities may appear at the beginning or end of a chapter, a reading, or other subdivisions of the text. (In *Opening Doors,* for instance, questions appear preceding and following each reading selection.) In addition to the terms noted above, questions or activities may be called *Questions for Study and Review, Review, Ask Yourself, Self-Test, Check Your Mastery, Mastery Test, Learning Check, Check Your Understanding, Topics for Discussion, Problems,* etc. The examples shown here are typical.

Don't neglect study questions and activities; take the time to work on them. They provide valuable practice and give you a way to monitor your learning. Also, instructors often use these same items, or similar items, on tests.

PROBES

1 Briefly explain the objectives of the introduction.
2 Briefly describe five parts of an introduction.
3 Briefly describe five ways of getting the attention of the audience.
4 Describe three ways of preparing the audience for the body of the speech.
5 Briefly explain the objectives of the conclusion.
6 Describe four types of conclusions.
7 Briefly describe the idea of common ground.

APPLICATIONS

1 For each of the following subjects, create a method for getting the attention of the audience: (**a**) Preventing AIDS. (**b**) Date rape. (**c**) Applying first aid to a wound. (**d**) Joining the Peace Corps.
2 What kinds of conclusions could you use for each of the following topics? (**a**) Preventing child abuse. (**b**) Learning to use a computer. (**c**) Supporting affirmative action. (**d**) How to improve memory.
3 Read some issues of *Vital Speeches* and see how the speakers opened and closed their speeches.

Source: James A. Byrns, *Speak for Yourself: An Introduction to Public Speaking,* McGraw-Hill, New York, 1994, p. 178. Reproduced with permission of McGraw-Hill.

QUESTIONS FOR CRITICAL READING, THINKING, DISCUSSION, AND WRITING

Analyzing Content and Technique

1. Why, according to Taylor, is television so concerned with depicting family life?
2. What were the main characteristics of the television families of the 1950s?
3. What did the television industry realize in the 1970s? How did this change the type of family shows being produced? What happened in the 1980s?
4. What are some of the differences between *All in the Family* and *The Cosby Show?* How does Taylor evaluate each show?
5. In her conclusion, Taylor states, "Today, the generous space that was opened up then for public discussion is again being narrowed . . . [to] sentimentality and a profound horror of argument." What evidence does she provide? Do you find her evidence adequate or inadequate? Explain.

Making Connections

1. Describe two or three current television shows about family life, analyzing the characters, the situations, and the implied values. What do these shows reveal to you about social trends? Which show do you prefer, and why?
2. Write an essay comparing and contrasting your own family with one specific television family. How realistic is the television family? Have you learned anything from it, either positive or negative, that you can apply to your own family situation?

Source: Chitra B. Divakaruni, *Multitude: Cross-Cultural Readings for Writers,* McGraw-Hill, New York, 1993, p. 86. Reproduced with permission of McGraw-Hill.

REVIEW QUESTIONS

1. Distinguish between passionate and companionate love. Describe how you feel physically and emotionally when in passionate love. Have you ever loved another passionately, only to have the passion fade? Explain.

2. Think of a romantic relationship you once had and draw a love triangle to represent the extent of your passion, intimacy, and decision/commitment. What shape does the triangle take? Which component—passion, intimacy, decision/commitment—was the most prominent; least prominent? Now draw your partner's love triangle. Which component was most prominent; least prominent? Are there differences between the two triangles? Do you think these differences had anything to do with the breakup of the relationship?

3. How does the "feminization of love" affect romantic relationships? What are some strategies couples might use to counteract this tendency in their own relationships?

4. Why is it important to self-disclose in relationships? What are the risks of self-disclosure? Have you ever been in a relationship in which your partner seemed to disclose too much, too soon? Describe the situation and how you felt. Is the relationship ongoing or did it end?

5. What is relationship equity? Equity theory? When an individual is underbenefitted in a relationship, how does he or she typically react?

6. What is the difference between normal and pathological jealousy? What causes a person to feel jealous? How does a person usually react when confronted by a jealous partner? Are there ways to keep normal jealous reactions under control?

Source: Gloria Bird and Keith Melville, *Families and Intimate Relationships,* McGraw-Hill, New York, 1994, p. 84. Reproduced with permission of McGraw-Hill.

Chapter Summaries

Key term

Chapter summary: Textbook feature in which the author collects and condenses the most essential ideas.

A ***chapter summary*** is one of the most helpful textbook features because in it the author collects and condenses the most essential ideas. Many students find it useful to read a chapter summary both before and after studying a chapter. Of course, when you read a summary before you read the chapter, you may not understand it completely, but you will have a general idea of the most important material in the chapter.

Summaries can be short (like the first example below, from a public speaking text) or a full page or more in length (like the example opposite from a text on family life). A summary may also be called *Conclusion, Recapitulation, Looking Back, Summing Up, Key Points, Key Concepts,* etc. Summaries may be written as paragraphs or lists, and they may contain special aids. The second example below, from a sociology text, highlights key terms, for instance.

SUMMARY

Telling, showing, and doing are three important types of supporting information and should be used in every speech. Verbal channels include definitions, examples, stories and anecdotes, comparison and contrast, description, statistics, and testimony. Doing includes planning activities and leading groups through structured experiences.

SUMMARY

Culture is the totality of learned, socially transmitted behavior. This chapter examines the basic elements which make up a culture, social practices which are common to all cultures, and variations which distinguish one culture from another.

1 The process of expanding human culture has already been under way for thousands of years and will continue in the future.
2 Anthropologist George Murdock has compiled a list of general practices found in every culture, including courtship, family, games, language, medicine, religion, and sexual restrictions.
3 Societies resist ideas which seem too foreign as well as those which are perceived as threatening to their own values and beliefs.
4 ***Language*** includes speech, written characters, numerals, symbols, and gestures and other forms of nonverbal communication.
5 Sociologists distinguish between ***norms*** in two ways. They are classified as either ***formal*** or ***informal*** norms and as ***mores*** or ***folkways.***
6 The most cherished ***values*** of a culture will receive the heaviest sanctions; matters that are regarded as less critical, on the other hand, will carry light and informal sanctions.
7 Generally, members of a ***subculture*** are viewed as outsiders or deviants.
8 From a conflict perspective, the social significance of the concept of the ***dominant ideology*** is that the most powerful groups and institutions in a society control the means of producing beliefs about reality through religion, education, and the media.
9 Advocates of ***multiculturalism*** argue that the traditional curricula of schools and colleges in the United States should be revised to include more works by and about African Americans, other racial and ethnic minorities, and women.

Sources: (Above) James A. Byrns, *Speak for Yourself: An Introduction to Public Speaking,* 3rd ed., McGraw-Hill, New York, 1994, p. 139 *(top);* Richard T. Schaefer and Robert P. Lamm, *Sociology: A Brief Introduction,* McGraw-Hill, New York, 1994, p. 52 *(bottom). (Opposite)* Gloria Bird and Keith Melville, *Families and Intimate Relationships,* McGraw-Hill, New York, 1994, p. 340. Reproduced with permission of McGraw-Hill.

SUMMARY POINTS

- There are three types of power: social power, latent power, and manifest power. Social power refers to cultural beliefs and norms that, through socialization, influence women and men to devalue women's status and assign them fewer resources and less power. Latent power is present when the less powerful partner anticipates the reaction of the more powerful partner and adjusts her or his course of action without the partner having to say a word. Manifest power relies on the use of particular tactics or strategies to bring issues forward or keep them from being raised.

- Power strategies fall into four general categories: direct-cooperative, direct-uncooperative, indirect-cooperative, indirect-uncooperative.

- Men more often rely on direct power strategies based on concrete resources that emphasize their individual competencies. Women more often use indirect strategies based on personal resources that exaggerate their powerlessness.

- Employed women typically have higher self-esteem, use more direct strategies, report that marital issues are settled more fairly, and indicate that their needs are more often taken into account during marital negotiation.

- Cooperative power strategies are the most beneficial to relationships and usually result in the greatest satisfaction of partners. When cooperative strategies (bargaining, reasoning) do not get results, competitive strategies (coercion, manipulation) may be used. Should these strategies also fail, some partners resort to threats. Finally, if verbal means of influence are not successful, physical means of asserting power may be employed.

- The First and Second National Violence Surveys carried out by Murray Straus and his colleagues are valuable sources of information about violence in the American family.

- These national surveys are one of the few sources of information about violence in both black and white families. Some scholars, however, caution that race is only one of the factors, and not among the most critical, to consider when trying to understand family violence.

- Violence is not limited to any particular social class.

- Use of alcohol or drugs is not a cause of abusive behavior in families. Rather, drinking and using drugs are socially accepted *excuses* for bad behavior.

- Violence is influenced by sociocultural factors and the family is where people get their "basic training" in the use of violence. The marriage license is considered by some to be a "hitting license."

- The Conflict Tactics Scales were developed by Murray Straus to assess marital violence. Although the scales have been criticized, they continue to be the instruments used most frequently in measuring violence in the family.

- Lenore Walker proposes that most incidents of wife battering proceed through three distinct stages: tension building, acute battering, and loving contrition. She calls this three-stage sequence of events the cycle of violence.

- Women stay in violent relationships for many reasons. Among them are social isolation from kin and friends; lack of reliable community support systems; fear that their abusive partner will find them and punish them if they leave; dependence on the partner for money, food, shelter, and love; and learned helplessness.

- Men who batter tend to downplay and trivialize the seriousness of their violent behavior. Potential batterers share some common identifiable characteristics, including advocating traditional gender roles, externalizing problems, being unreasonably jealous, handling life problems in a physically aggressive manner, believing that battered women cause their own abuse, and being impulsive and manipulative.

- When a woman reacts violently, it is usually to break out of her partner's grasp, to "fight back" during an abusive episode, or to protect herself from being more seriously injured by her batterer.

- Suzanne Steinmetz argues that no matter how small the percentage of female batterers compared to male batterers, all battering should be taken seriously because of its effects on the family. Men say that they stay in battering relationships to maintain their standard of living, out of a need to be good fathers and keep the family together, and, in some cases, to protect their children from the mother's abuse.

Appendixes

Key term

Appendix: Section at the end of a book that includes supplemental material or specialized information.

An ***appendix*** is a section at the end of a book which includes supplemental material or specialized information. (Information may be presented as an appendix so that it can be referred to conveniently, or because it is too long to be included in any single chapter, or because it relates to more than one chapter.) The appendix is a useful textbook feature because it presents additional information that you may need to refer to repeatedly.

In an American history or American government text, the Declaration of Independence and the Constitution may appear as appendixes. Physics and chemistry texts may have formulas in appendixes. In texts with self-tests, an answer key may appear as an appendix. A very helpful appendix in some history texts is a chronology or "time line" like the one shown opposite. Shown below is the first page of an important appendix in a theater text that students would refer to often.

Opening Doors has three appendixes: a list of word parts, a master vocabulary list, and a glossary of key terms.

APPENDIX 5
REALISM AND NONREALISM

The distinction between realism and nonrealism in theater becomes clearer when the two approaches are placed side by side. They are present in all aspects of theater, as the following table illustrates.

REALISTIC TECHNIQUES	NONREALISTIC TECHNIQUES
STORY	
Events which the audience knows have happened or might happen in everyday life: Blanche DuBois in Tennessee Williams's *A Streetcar Named Desire* goes to New Orleans to visit her sister and brother-in-law.	Events which do not occur in real life but take place only in the imagination: Emily in Thornton Wilder's *Our Town*, after she has died, returns to life for one day.
STRUCTURE	
Action confined to real places; time passes normally as it does in everyday life: in *The Little Foxes* by Lillian Hellman, the activity occurs over several days in Regina's house as she takes control of her family's estate.	Arbitrary use of time and place: in Strindberg's *The Dream Play*, walls dissolve and characters are transformed, as in a dream.
CHARACTERS	
Recognizable human beings, such as the family—mother, father, and two sons—in O'Neill's *Long Day's Journey into Night*.	Unreal figures like the Ghost of Hamlet's father in *Hamlet*, the Three Witches in *Macbeth*, and the people who turn into animals in Ionesco's *Rhinoceros*.

CHRONOLOGY [APPENDIX 2]

MIDDLE AGES (450–1450)

Musicians	Artists and Writers	Historical and Cultural Events
		Sack of Rome by Vandals (455)
		Reign of Pope Gregory I (590–604)
		First Crusade (1096–1099)
Perotin (late twelfth century)		Beginning of Notre Dame Cathedral in Paris (1163)
		King John signs Magna Carta (1215)
	Dante (1265–1321)	
	Giotto (1266–1337)	
Guillaume de Machaut (c. 1300–1377)		
	Boccaccio (1313–1375)	
	Chaucer (c. 1343–1400)	Hundred Years' War (1337–1453)
		Black death (1348–1350)

RENAISSANCE (1450–1600)

Musicians	Artists and Writers	Historical and Cultural Events
Guillaume Dufay (c. 1400–1474)		Fall of Constantinople (1453)
Josquin Desprez (c. 1440–1521)	Leonardo da Vinci (1452–1519)	Gutenberg Bible (1456)
		Columbus discovers America (1492)
	Michelangelo (1475–1564)	
	Raphael (1483–1520)	Martin Luther's ninety-five theses (1517)
	Titian (c. 1477–1576)	
	François Rabelais (c. 1494–c. 1553)	
Andrea Gabrieli (c. 1520–1586)		

Sources: (Above) Roger Kamien, *Music: An Appreciation,* 2d Brief ed., McGraw-Hill, New York, 1994, p. 381. *(Opposite)* Edwin Wilson, *The Theater Experience,* 6th ed., McGraw-Hill, New York, 1994, p. 455. Reproduced with permission of McGraw-Hill.

Bibliographies and Suggested Readings

Key term

Bibliography: List of sources from which the author of the text has drawn information.

A ***bibliography*** (which usually appears near the end of a textbook) is a list of sources: books, articles, and other works from which the author of the text has drawn information. A bibliography may also be called *References, Works Cited,* or *Sources.* A bibliography sometimes lists works the author recommends for further (supplemental) reading. In this case it may be called *Select Bibliography* (like the example opposite, from a theater text), *Selected Works,* etc. Of course, some bibliographies serve both functions and are called *Bibliography and Selected Readings* or *References and Bibliography.*

A list of ***suggested readings*** often appears at the end of chapters (or parts), where it may be called *Additional Readings, Suggestions for Further Reading, Supplementary Readings,* etc. Suggested readings may be annotated, like the examples below. That is, the textbook author may provide brief descriptions and explain why each work is listed.

Bibliographies and suggested readings can be especially helpful for research assignments, such as papers and reports; or when you want or need to read other material to improve your understanding of the text.

SUGGESTIONS FOR FURTHER READING

DeVito, Joseph A.: *The Elements of Public Speaking,* HarperCollins, New York, 1991. Helpful for speakers who find it difficult to select a topic.

Ehninger, Douglas, Bruce Gronbeck, Ray McKerrow, and Alan Monroe: *Principles and Types of Speech Communication,* HarperCollins, New York, 1992. Includes useful material on subjects for speeches and occasions for public speaking.

Fletcher, Leon: *How to Design and Deliver a Speech,* 4th ed., HarperCollins, New York, 1990. Offers step-by-step procedures for making a topic manageable.

Ilardo, Joseph: *Speaking Persuasively,* Macmillan, New York, 1981. Provides a detailed theory of topic selection.

Osborn, Michael, and Suzanne Osborn: *Public Speaking,* 2d ed., Houghton Mifflin, Boston, Mass., 1991. Provides helpful strategies for determining the purpose of a speech.

ADDITIONAL READINGS

Huber, Joan, and Beth E. Schneider (eds.). *The Social Context of AIDS.* Newbury Park, Calif.: Sage, 1992. This anthology addresses a variety of issues as they relate to AIDS, including race, gender stratification, education, and persistent poverty.

Kephart, William, and William M. Zellner. *Extraordinary Groups: An Examination of Unconventional Lifestyles* (4th ed.). New York: St. Martin's, 1991. Among the groups described in this very readable book are the Amish, the Oneida community, the Shakers, the Mormons, Hasidic Jews, Jehovah's Witnesses, and the Romani (commonly known as *Gypsies*).

Majors, Richard, and Janet Mancini Bellson. *Cool Pose: The Dilemmas of Black Manhood in America.* New York: Lexington, 1992. An African American psychologist and a White sociologist analyze the ways in which African American adolescent males present themselves in everyday life.

Scheff, Thomas J. *Microsociology: Discourse, Emotion, and Structure.* Chicago: University of Chicago Press, 1992. An examination of sociological treatment of self and society.

Tannen, Deborah. *You Just Don't Understand: Women and Men in Conversation.* New York: Ballantine, 1990. A popularly written book that provides an overview of how men and women in the United States differ in their styles of communication.

SELECT BIBLIOGRAPHY

Allen, John: *Theatre in Europe,* J. Offord, Eastbourne, England, 1981.

Aristotle: *Aristotle's Poetics,* S. H. Butcher (trans.), Introduction by Francis Fergusson, Hill and Wang, New York, 1961.

Aronson, Arnold: *American Set Design,* New York, 1985.

Artaud, Antonin: *The Theater and Its Double,* Mary C. Richards (trans.), Grove, New York, 1958.

Atkinson, Brooks: *Broadway,* rev. ed., Macmillan, New York, 1974.

Austen, Gayle: *Feminist Theories for Creative Criticism,* University of Michigan Press, Ann Arbor, 1990.

Bartow, Arthur: *The Directors' Voice: 21 Interviews,* Theatre Communications Group, New York, 1988

Bay, Howard: *Stage Design,* Drama Book Specialists, New York, 1974.

Beckerman, Bernard: *Dynamics of Drama: Theory and Method of Analysis,* Drama Book Specialists, New York, 1979.

Benedetti, Jean: *Stanislavski: An Introduction,* Theatre Arts, New York, 1982.

Benedetti, Robert: *The Actor at Work,* Prentice-Hall, Englewood Cliffs, N.J., 1971.

Bentley, Eric: *The Life of the Drama,* Atheneum, New York, 1964.

——— (ed.): *The Theory of the Modern Stage,* Penguin, Baltimore, 1968.

Brecht, Bertolt: *Brecht on Theatre,* John Willett (trans.), Hill and Wang, New York, 1965.

Betsko, Kathleen, and Koenig, Rachel: *Interviews with Contemporary Women Playwrights,* Beech Tree, New York, 1987.

Bradby, David, and Williams, David: *Director's Theater,* St. Martin's, New York, 1988.

Brockett, Oscar G.: *History of the Theatre,* 5th ed., Allyn & Bacon, Boston, 1991.

——— and Robert R. Findlay: *Century of Innovation: A History of European and American Theatre and Drama Since the Late 19th Century,* 2d ed., Allyn and Bacon, Boston, 1990.

Brook, Peter: *The Empty Space,* Atheneum, New York, 1968.

———: *The Shifting Point,* HarperCollins, New York, 1987.

Burns, Elizabeth: *Theatricality,* Harper & Row, New York, 1973.

Case, Sue-Ellen: *Feminism and Theatre.* Routledge, Chapman, and Hall, New York, 1987.

Chinoy, Helen K., and Jenkins, Linda W.: *Women in American Theatre,* rev. ed., Theatre Communications Group, New York, 1987.

Clark, Barrett H. (ed.): *European Theories of the Drama,* rev. ed., Crown, New York, 1965.

Clurman, Harold: *On Directing,* Macmillan, New York, 1972.

Cohen, Robert: *Acting Power,* Mayfield, Palo Alto, Calif., 1978.

Cole, Toby: *Playwrights on Playwriting,* Hill and Wang, New York, 1961.

———, and Helen Krich Chinoy: *Actors on Acting,* Crown, New York, 1970.

Corrigan, Robert (ed.): *Comedy: Meaning and Form,* Chandler, San Francisco, 1965.

Sources: (Opposite) Teri Kwal Gamble and Michael Gamble, *Communication Works,* 4th ed., McGraw-Hill, New York, 1993, p. 339 *(top);* Richard T. Schaefer and Robert P. Lamm, *Sociology: A Brief Introduction,* McGraw-Hill, New York, 1994, p. 107 *(bottom). (Above)* Edwin Wilson, *The Theater Experience,* 6th ed., McGraw-Hill, New York, 1994, p. 461.

Indexes

Key term

Index: Alphabetical listing of topics and names in a textbook, with page numbers, usually appearing at the end of the book.

At the end of a textbook you will usually find one or more indexes. An ***index*** is an alphabetical listing of topics and names in the text, giving the specific pages on which you can find information about them. The index is a useful textbook feature because it helps you locate information quickly.

On the opposite page is an example of a general index, from a history text. Some textbooks have a separate *name index* and *subject index,* like the examples below from a psychology text. Anthologies and other textbooks with reading selections often have an *index of authors and titles.*

Indexes sometimes include special features. For instance, in the example from the history textbook, the notations *f* and *m* tell readers where they will find figures and maps. The index for *Opening Doors* begins on page 595.

Name Index

Subject Index

Source: John J. Shaughnessy and Eugene B. Zechmeister, *Research Methods in Psychology,* 3d ed., McGraw-Hill, New York, 1994, pp. 489, 494. Reproduced with permission of McGraw-Hill.

INDEX

Note: Page numbers followed by the letter *f* or *m* indicate figures or maps, respectively.

Source: Richard E. Sullivan, Dennis Sherman, and John B. Harrison, *A Short History of Western Civilization*, 8th ed., McGraw-Hill, New York, 1994, p. I-1. Reproduced with permission of McGraw-Hill.

Additional Features and Supplements

There are numerous other types of textbook features. Many texts (such as *Opening Doors*) include *epigraphs,* quotations at the opening of chapters (or other sections) that suggest overall themes or concerns. Some texts put vivid or provocative quotations in the margins.

Depending on the subject matter, a text may include special *exhibits* or *examples* such as student papers, plot summaries, profit-and-loss statements, documents, forms, and printouts. Useful material (such as the periodic table of the elements in a chemistry text) may even appear on the inside of the cover. Sometimes a textbook has a unique feature, like the chapter review cards in *Opening Doors.*

Finally, some textbooks have *supplements,* separate aids that accompany the text. These might include *study guides, supplemental readings, student workbooks,* and *computer diskettes.* Supplements are a good investment, since they have been developed to help you guide your own learning, test yourself, and check your progress.

All these textbook features can help you use your study time effectively and efficiently. Students often remark that in college textbooks "everything seems important." They find it hard to get a sense of how the facts and concepts add up to a coherent whole. Taking advantage of textbook features as you read can enable you to identify the essential information in a chapter and to understand its organization. Remember that authors and publishers want to help you study and learn from their textbooks. For this reason, they put a great deal of time, effort, and thought into designing textbook features.

Study Tips for Using Textbook Features

Prefaces

Read the preface to see what the book contains, how it is organized, and what its special features are.

Tables of contents

Use the table of contents, particularly if no chapter outlines are given. Your chapter study notes should cover each item listed in the table of contents. Pay attention to the size and type style, which indicate major and minor headings.

Part openings

Reading a part opening will help you understand the scope of what is contained in the section, how the section is organized, and how its chapters are interrelated.

Chapter outlines

Pay attention to major topics in a chapter outline. Your notes should also include all subtopics. The author has done some of your selecting for you, so take advantage of it.

Chapter objectives and introductions

Use objectives and introductions to test yourself on the chapter material. Try to write out the answers from memory.

Lists and sequences

Use mnemonic devices (memory devices) to help you remember information.

Boxes

Pay attention to boxed information. It helps you understand the text. Also, you may be tested on boxed material.

Tables

Pay attention to tables. They consolidate important information and help you understand relationships among ideas. Instructors may base test questions on them.

Graphic aids

Watch for graphic aids. Figures, cartoons, and photographs present important information or explain the text.

Vocabulary aids

Write down the definition for each term included in a vocabulary aid. It is your responsibility to learn the special vocabulary of each subject you study. Expect to be asked about these terms on tests.

Study questions and activities

Take the time to answer study questions and work on exercises, especially if your instructor has not provided study questions. Think carefully about discussion topics. Items like these may appear on tests.

Chapter summaries

Read the chapter summary both *before and after* you read the chapter itself.

Appendixes

Use appendixes for reference and as a source of additional information.

Bibliographies and suggested readings

Use source lists when you are doing papers, reports, and other research assignments. You can also use supplementary readings to improve your understanding of the textbook.

Indexes

Indexes will help you find specific material quickly.

Additional features

Look for epigraphs (quotations), exhibits, and examples in the text. Don't neglect special reference material that may appear on the inside of the cover.

Supplements

Study guides, study guides with supplemental readings, workbooks, and software accompanying your textbooks will usually prove to be a good investment. Use supplements like these to direct and focus your study, to test yourself, and to evaluate your learning.

MARKING TEXTBOOKS: UNDERLINING, HIGHLIGHTING, AND ANNOTATING

Key terms

Underlining **and** ***highlighting:*** Techniques for marking topics, main ideas, and definitions.

Annotation: Explanatory notes written in the margins of a textbook to organize and remember information.

It has been estimated that as much as 80 percent of the material on college tests comes from textbooks. For this reason alone, you need to be able to underline, highlight, and annotate your textbooks effectively.

Underlining and ***highlighting*** are techniques for marking topics, main ideas, and important definitions in reading materials. ***Annotation*** refers to explanatory notes you write *in the margins of your textbook* to help you organize and remember important information that appears within paragraphs. Taking a moment to annotate information (write or jot it down) also helps you concentrate. When you are reading a difficult textbook, you need to concentrate on one paragraph at a time. Effective students mark their textbooks by both underlining or highlighting *and* annotating.

Here are some considerations for *underlining and highlighting.* First, you need to avoid the most typical mistake students make in marking textbooks: *overmarking* (underlining or highlighting too much). Students often make this mistake because they try to underline or highlight *while* they are reading the material instead of *after* they have read it. The process of underlining and highlighting a textbook is a very selective one. Further, you cannot know what is important in a paragraph or section until you have *finished* reading it. Remember, for example, that the main idea sometimes does not appear until the end of a paragraph. Remember, too, that you may not be able to understand some paragraphs until you have read an entire section. The rule, then, is this: *Read first, and underline only after you have identified the important ideas.* A word of caution: Some students substitute underlining and highlighting for *thinking.* They mistakenly believe that if they have marked a lot in a chapter, they must have read it carefully and found the important information. To avoid this error, follow these steps: Read and *think; then* underline or highlight *selectively.*

Second, you need to know the kinds of things you *should* underline or highlight. As mentioned above, underline or highlight the *topic* of a paragraph. Underline or highlight the *main idea* of a paragraph if it is stated directly. Keep in mind that often you will not need to underline every word of a main idea sentence to capture the idea it is expressing. Underline or highlight important *definitions.* You may find it helpful to mark important terms as well.

Third, you need to know the kinds of things you should *not* underline or highlight. Do *not* underline or highlight supporting details, since this results in overmarking. (As you will see below, annotation can be used effectively to indicate supporting details.)

Once you have underlined and highlighted topics, main ideas, and important terms, you will want to *annotate:* that is, write explanatory notes and symbols in the margins. If a textbook has narrow margins, you may prefer to use notebook paper or even stick-on notes for your annotations, to give yourself more room.

The box on the opposite page shows how a passage from a human development textbook (about different forms of marriage) could be underlined and annotated.

An Example of Underlining and Annotation

A life-style that apparently exists in all societies is marriage—a socially sanctioned union between a woman and a man with the expectation that they will play the roles of wife and husband. After studying extensive cross-cultural data, the anthropologist George P. Murdock (1949) concluded that reproduction, sexual relations, economic cooperation, and the socialization of offspring are functions of families throughout the world. We now recognize that Murdock overstated the matter, since there are a number of societies—for instance, Israeli kibbutz communities—in which the family does not encompass all four of these activities (Spiro, 1954; Gough, 1960). What Murdock describes are commonly encountered tendencies in family functioning in most cultures.

(def.) marriage: socially sanctioned union of a woman and a man with the expectation they will play the roles of wife and husband

4 tendencies in functions of families:*
—reproduction
—sexual relations
—economic cooperation
—socialization of offspring

Societies differ in how they structure marriage
(1.) relationships. Four patterns are found: monogamy,
(2.) one husband and one wife; polygyny, one husband
(3.) and two or more wives; polyandry, two or more
(4.) husbands and one wife; and group marriage, two or more husbands and two or more wives. Although monogamy exists in all societies, Murdock discovered that other forms may be not only allowed but preferred. Of 238 societies in his sample, only about one-fifth were strictly monogamous.

(def.)
Four patterns of marriage:*
—monogamy: 1 husband/1 wife
—polygyny: 1 husband/2+ wives
—polyandry: 2+ husbands/1 wife
—group marriage: 2+ husbands/2+ wives

Polygyny has been widely practiced throughout the world. The Old Testament reports that both King David and King Solomon had several wives. In his cross-cultural sample of 238 societies, Murdock found that 193 of them permitted husbands to take several wives. In one-third of these polygynous societies, however, less than one-fifth of the married men had more than one wife. Usually it is only the rich men in a society who can afford to support more than one family.

Old Testament kings with several wives:
—Solomon
—David
—Murdock study: 193/238 societies permitted polygyny

—Usually only rich were polygynous

In contrast with polygyny, polyandry is rare among the world's societies. And in practice, polyandry has not usually allowed freedom of mate selection for women; it has often meant simply that younger brothers have sexual access to the wife of an older brother. Thus where a father is unable to
(?) afford wives for each of his sons, he may secure a wife for only his oldest son.

—women not usually allowed to choose mates

—often simply means younger brothers have sexual access to wife of older brother

Source: James Vander Zanden, *Human Development,* Knopf, New York, 1985.

You may be wondering what types of annotations are helpful and why it is necessary to annotate as well as to underline or highlight. For one thing, writing out an *important term* and its *definition* in the margin helps you remember it. When your instructor uses these terms in class, you will recognize them and be able to record them more easily in your lecture notes. And, of course, you will need to know these terms for tests.

Also, you may choose to list essential *supporting details* in shortened form in the margin. Annotating is an effective, convenient, concise way to organize supporting details; and jotting details down in the margin will help you connect them with the main ideas they support.

Formulated main ideas are another type of helpful annotation. Your formulated main idea sentence can be written in the margin next to the paragraph.

Symbols and *abbreviations* are still another helpful form of annotation. Your symbols and abbreviations will enable you to locate important material quickly and (if necessary) return to passages that need further study. Here are a few examples of abbreviations and symbols you can use in the margins:

def *Definition.* Use *def* when an important term is defined.

? *Question mark.* Use this when you do not understand something and need to study it further or get help with it.

1, 2, 3 . . . *Numbers.* Use numbers when an author gives items in a list or series.

***** *Asterisk.* Use an asterisk to mark important information.

TAKING NOTES FROM TEXTBOOKS: OUTLINING, MAPPING, AND SUMMARIZING

In addition to underlining, highlighting, and marginal annotations, *taking notes from textbooks* is another important study skill. Three very useful forms of textbook note-taking are outlining, mapping, and summarizing.

Guidelines for Outlining

Key term

Outlining: Formal way of organizing main ideas and supporting details to show relationships among them.

Outlining is a formal way of organizing main ideas and the supporting details that go with them. Even if you underline main ideas in your textbook and annotate supporting details in the margin, there may be times when it is helpful to outline a section or chapter. Outlines are especially useful for organizing complex material. Outlining is best done on separate paper rather than written in the textbook.

When should you outline? Obviously, you will not need to outline every section or every chapter. As mentioned above, outlining can be appropriate for complex material. It is also helpful when you need to condense a lengthy section or chapter in order to give yourself an overview. Because outlining condenses information and lets you see and understand how an entire section or chapter is organized, an outline makes the material easier to study and remember.

How do you create an outline of textbook material? To outline a paragraph, you need to write its main idea. Then, on separate, indented lines below the main idea, write the supporting details that go with it, like this:

I. Main idea sentence

  A. Supporting detail
  B. Supporting detail
  C. Supporting detail
  D. Supporting detail

For longer passages consisting of several paragraphs, continue your outline in the same way:

I. First main idea sentence

  A. Supporting detail for main idea I
  B. Supporting detail for main idea I
  C. Supporting detail for main idea I
  D. Supporting detail for main idea I

II. Second main idea sentence

  A. Supporting detail for main idea II
  B. Supporting detail for main idea II

III. Third main idea sentence

  A. Supporting detail for main idea III
  B. Supporting detail for main idea III
  C. Supporting detail for main idea III

The purpose of your study outline is to show you how ideas are related. Making your outline look perfect is not as important as making sure that the relationships are clear to *you.* Main ideas should stand out, and it should be obvious which details go with each main idea. Roman numerals (I, II, III) are often used for main ideas, and uppercase letters (A, B, C, D) are used for supporting details. This notation helps you see how ideas are related.

An outline can consist of phrases or sentences. However, when you have complex material, a sentence outline works well because it gives complete thoughts.

The box on page 478 shows a sentence outline of a passage from Selection 7-3. Notice also the identifying title: *Reactions to Impending Death.*

Use the same title for your outline as the one that appears in the original material. Do not entitle your outline "Outline." (It will be obvious that it is an outline!)

Sample Outline:

▪ ▪ ▪ ▪ ▪ ▪ ▪

Reactions to Impending Death

I. Elisabeth Kübler-Ross, a thanatologist, found in her research on the terminally ill that they tend to have certain basic emotional reactions as they prepare for death.
   A. There are five types of reactions: denial and isolation, anger, bargaining, depression, and acceptance.
   B. Different patients display different emotions.
   C. Reactions may occur in various orders, although the general pattern is shock, denial, anger, and acceptance.
   D. Several factors influence a person's type and sequence of emotional reactions.
   E. Overall, a person's approach to dying reflects his or her approach to living.
   F. These same emotions are characteristic of anyone who has experienced a major loss.

II. There are several uses of Kübler-Ross's research.
   A. It can be used to help the dying cope with their emotions by enabling them to discuss these emotions.
   B. It can be used to help survivors cope with the dying person's emotions as well as their own.

III. A hospice is a special hospital for the terminally ill.
   A. A hospice can enhance a dying person's final days.
   B. Life goes on more normally in this pleasant, informal environment.
   C. There are many supportive people, including personnel and family members.

IV. Survivors normally go through a period of grieving or bereavement following an ill person's death.
   A. Grief follows the pattern of shock or numbness; pangs of grief; apathy, dejection, and depression; and resolution.
   B. Survivors' reactions vary, but survivors are usually able to discharge their anguish by grieving, and thus prepare to go on living.
   C. Each person must grieve at his or her own pace and in his or her own way.

Guidelines for Mapping

Key term

Mapping: Informal way of organizing main ideas and supporting details by using boxes circles, lines, arrows, etc.

Another form of textbook note-taking is mapping. ***Mapping*** is an informal way of organizing main ideas and supporting details by using boxes, circles, lines, arrows, and the like. The idea is to show information in a way that clarifies relationships among ideas. Like outlining, mapping is done on separate paper rather than in the margins of the textbook.

One simple type of map consists of the topic or main idea in a circle or box in the middle of the sheet of paper, with supporting details, radiating out from it. Another type has the main idea in a large box at the top of the paper, with supporting ideas in smaller boxes below it and connected to it by arrows or "leader lines." If the information is sequential (for instance, significant events in World War I), a map can take the form of a flowchart. Samples of these kinds of maps are shown on page 480.

A study map for the passage on reactions of dying patients is shown on page 481. It condenses all the important information on a single page. A complete study map like this requires considerable thought and effort.

Since outlines and study maps both show relationships among important ideas in a passage, how can you decide which to use for a particular passage? Your decision will depend on how familiar you are with each technique, and on how the passage itself is written. Keep in mind that mapping is an informal study technique, whereas outlining can be formal or informal. When you are asked to prepare a formal outline in a college course, do not assume that you can substitute a study map.

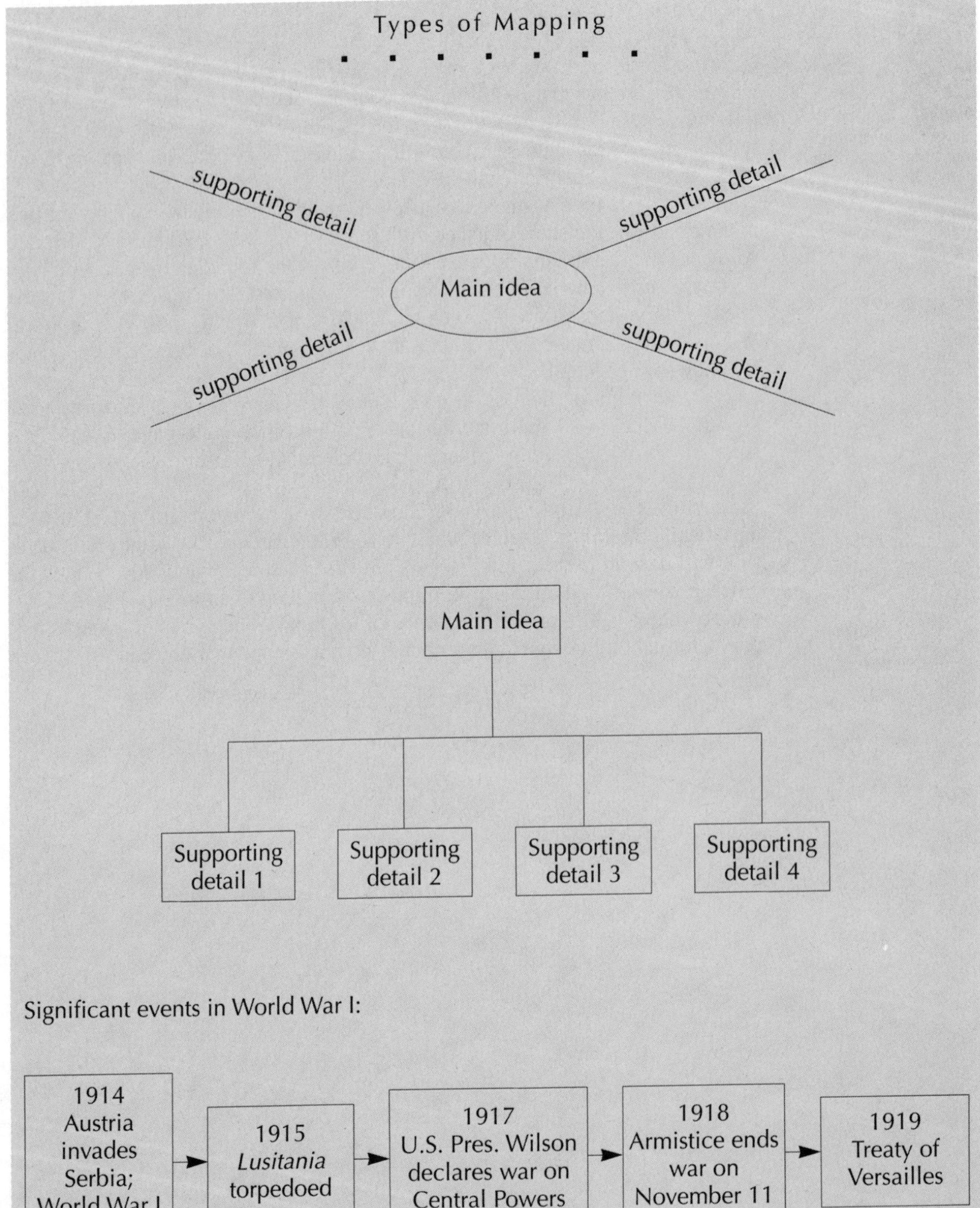
Types of Mapping
supporting detail
supporting detail
Main idea
supporting detail
supporting detail
Main idea
Supporting detail 1
Supporting detail 2
Supporting detail 3
Supporting detail 4
Significant events in World War I:
1914 Austria invades Serbia; World War I begins
1915 *Lusitania* torpedoed
1917 U.S. Pres. Wilson declares war on Central Powers
1918 Armistice ends war on November 11
1919 Treaty of Versailles

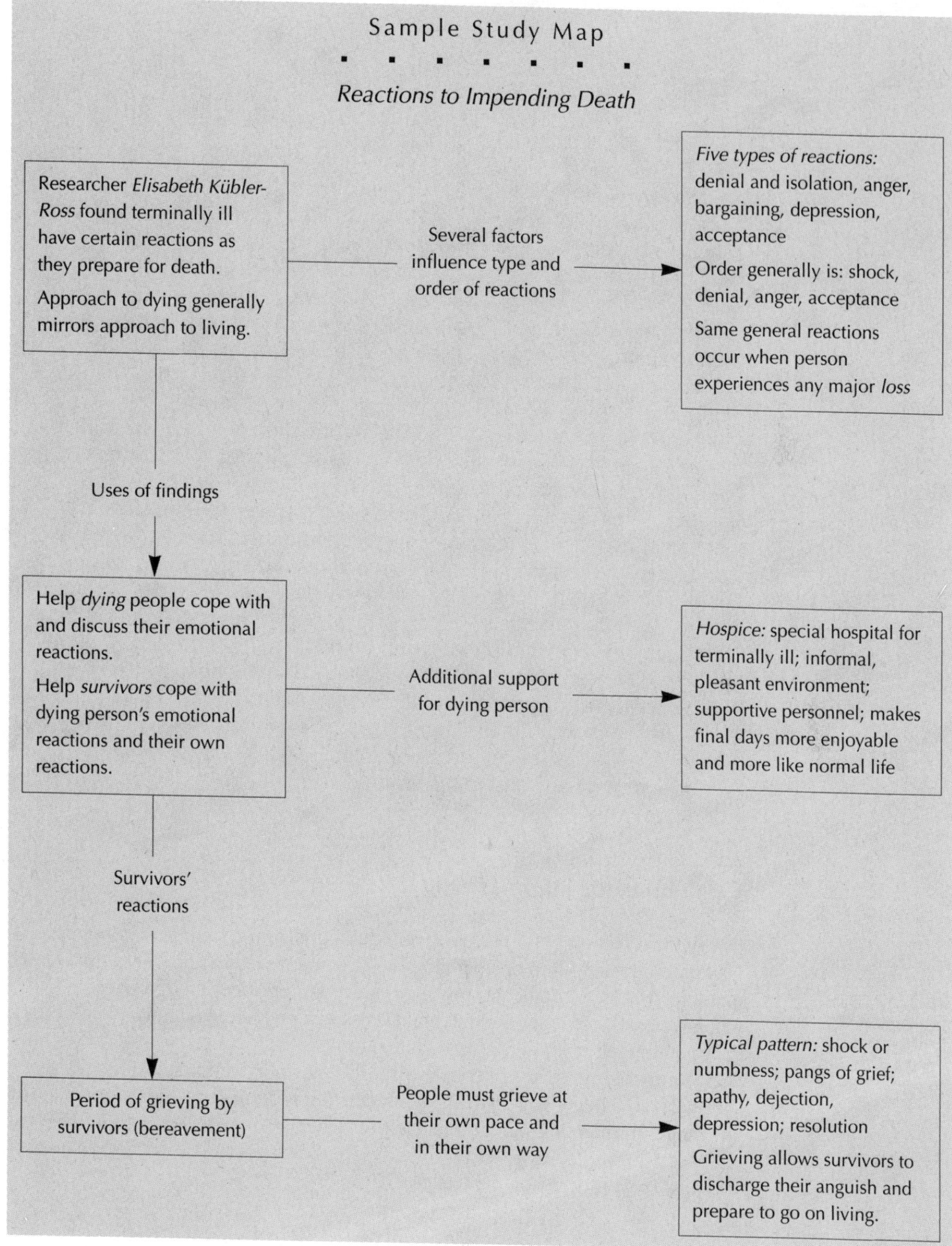
Sample Study Map
Reactions to Impending Death
Researcher Elisabeth Kübler-Ross found terminally ill have certain reactions as they prepare for death.
Approach to dying generally mirrors approach to living.
Several factors influence type and order of reactions
Five types of reactions: denial and isolation, anger, bargaining, depression, acceptance
Order generally is: shock, denial, anger, acceptance
Same general reactions occur when person experiences any major loss
Uses of findings
Help dying people cope with and discuss their emotional reactions.
Help survivors cope with dying person's emotional reactions and their own reactions.
Additional support for dying person
Hospice: special hospital for terminally ill; informal, pleasant environment; supportive personnel; makes final days more enjoyable and more like normal life
Survivors' reactions
Period of grieving by survivors (bereavement)
People must grieve at their own pace and in their own way
Typical pattern: shock or numbness; pangs of grief; apathy, dejection, depression; resolution
Grieving allows survivors to discharge their anguish and prepare to go on living.

Sample Summary

▪ ▪ ▪ ▪ ▪ ▪ ▪

Reactions to Impending Death

Elisabeth Kübler-Ross is a thanatologist whose research with terminally ill patients revealed that they tend to display several emotional reactions as they prepare for death. The five basic responses she found were (1) *denial and isolation,* (2) *anger,* (3) *bargaining,* (4) *depression,* and (5) *acceptance.* Different patients display different emotions. These may occur in various orders, although the general pattern is shock, denial, anger, and acceptance. Several factors influence a person's types and sequence of emotions. Overall, the individual's approach to dying reflects his or her approach to living. Emotions displayed by a dying person are the typical, appropriate ones that accompany any major loss. This information can be used to help dying persons and survivors cope with their emotional reactions. Most important, knowledge of these emotions can enable others to be supportive of dying people and help them discuss death and their feelings. The hospice, a hospital for the terminally ill, can enhance a dying person's last days. The ill person is offered emotional support and guidance from family as well as from other people. Life goes on more nearly as normal in this informal, pleasant environment. A period of bereavement (grieving) by survivors normally follows the death of the ill person. Grief also follows a pattern: *shock or numbness; pangs of grief; apathy, dejection, and depression;* and *resolution.* Survivors' reactions vary but survivors are usually able to discharge their anguish by grieving, and thus prepare to go on living. Each person must grieve at his or her own pace and in his or her own way.

Guidelines for Summarizing

Key term

Summary: Single-paragraph condensation of all the main ideas presented in a longer passage.

A third technique of textbook note-taking is summarizing. A ***summary*** is a way of condensing into one paragraph all the main ideas an author has presented in a longer selection (such as an essay or article) or a section of a chapter. When you have correctly identified the main ideas in a passage, you have identified the information necessary to prepare your summary.

Summarizing is an effective way to check your comprehension. Writing a summary also helps you transfer the material into your long-term memory. You will find summarizing particularly helpful when you know you will be answering essay questions on a test. Summarizing allows you to "rehearse" an answer you may have to write on the test.

Here are some things to keep in mind when you are preparing a summary:

- *Include all the main ideas.* You must include *all* the main ideas the author presents in the section. Include a supporting detail (such as the definition of an important term) if a main idea cannot be understood without it.
- *Do not add anything.* You must not add anything beyond the author's ideas (such as your own opinions).
- *Keep the original sequence.* Present the ideas in the same order that the author has used. In other words, you must keep the author's organization.
- *Reword as necessary, providing connections.* You must reword (paraphrase) the main ideas if necessary and supply clear connections among these ideas.
- *Give your summary a title.* Use the same title that appears in the original material. Do not entitle it "Summary."

The box at the top of the opposite page shows a sample summary for the passage on dying patients.

INTERPRETING GRAPHIC MATERIAL

Nearly every textbook contains graphic aids: tables, graphs (such as bar graphs, pie charts, and line graphs), time lines, diagrams, charts, maps, cartoons, photographs, flowcharts, and so forth. ***Graphic aids*** provide visual explanations of concepts and relationships in ways that are often more concise and easier to understand than words alone. For example, graphic aids can be used to illustrate numerical relationships (such as profits and losses), sequences (such as stages of cognitive development), processes (such as how a bill becomes a law), and spatial relationships (such as a floor plan). Writers include graphic aids precisely because they enable students to grasp and recall information more easily.

Although graphic aids contain important information, they can appear difficult unless you know how to interpret them. The following strategies will enable you to interpret graphic material more effectively and efficiently.

- Read the *title* and any *explanation* that accompanies the graph. The title tells you what aspect of the writer's topic is being clarified or illustrated by the graph or table.
- Check the *source* of the information presented in the graphic aid to see if it seems current and reliable.
- Read all the *headings* in a table and all the *labels* that appear in a graph (such as those on the bottom and side of a graph) to determine what is being presented or measured. For example, the side of a bar graph may be labeled "Annual Income in Thousands of Dollars" and the bottom may be labeled "Level of Education."

- Examine the *units of measurement* in a graph (for example, decades, percents, thousands of dollars, per hour, kilograms, per capita, milliseconds).
- Finally, use the information provided by the title and explanation (if any), the source, the headings and labels, and the units of measurement to help you determine the *important points or conclusions* that the writer is conveying. Try to understand how the information in the graph clarifies or exemplifies the written explanation. See if there are patterns or trends in the data that allow you to draw a general conclusion.

Here are explanations and examples of five commonly used graphic aids. Along with each graphic aid is a summary of its important elements as well as the conclusions that can be drawn from the graph.

Bar Graphs

A ***bar graph*** is a chart in which the length of parallel rectangular bars is used to indicate relative amounts of the items being compared. The bars in a bar graph may be vertical or horizontal. The bar graph here comes from a textbook on human development.

Population of the United States Aged 65 and Over (*Source:* U.S. Bureau of the Census, 1992)

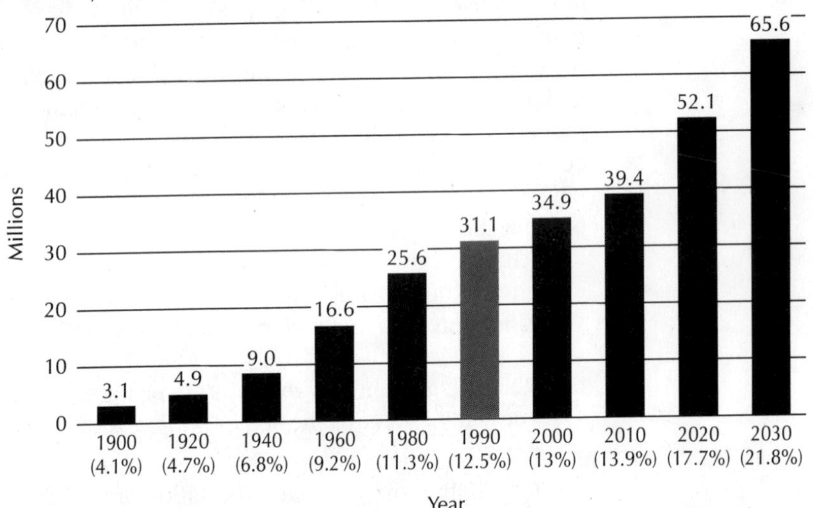

Source: Diane E. Papalia and Sally Wendkos Olds, *Human Development,* 6th ed., McGraw-Hill, New York, 1995, p. 528.

Title or explanation. Population of the United States aged 65 and over, 1900–2030 (projected).

Source. U.S. Bureau of the Census, 1992.

Headings and labels. Millions (of people), years (1900–2030; bar for 1990 differs from the other bars to indicate that figures beyond it are projections).

Units of measurement. Millions (increments of 10 million), years (20-year increments from 1900 to 1980; 10-year increments from 1980 to 2030), percents (of population aged 65 and over).

Important points or conclusions. Since the beginning of this century, the number of people aged 65 and over has continued to increase. This trend is expected to continue through the aging of the 'baby boom' generation. The number of people 65 and over will more than double by 2030.

Line Graphs

A ***line graph*** is a diagram whose points are connected to show a relationship between two or more variables. There may be one line or several lines, depending on what the author wishes to convey.

Percentage of the Labor Force in Various Sectors of the U.S. Economy
(*Source:* U.S. Bureau of Labor Statistics)

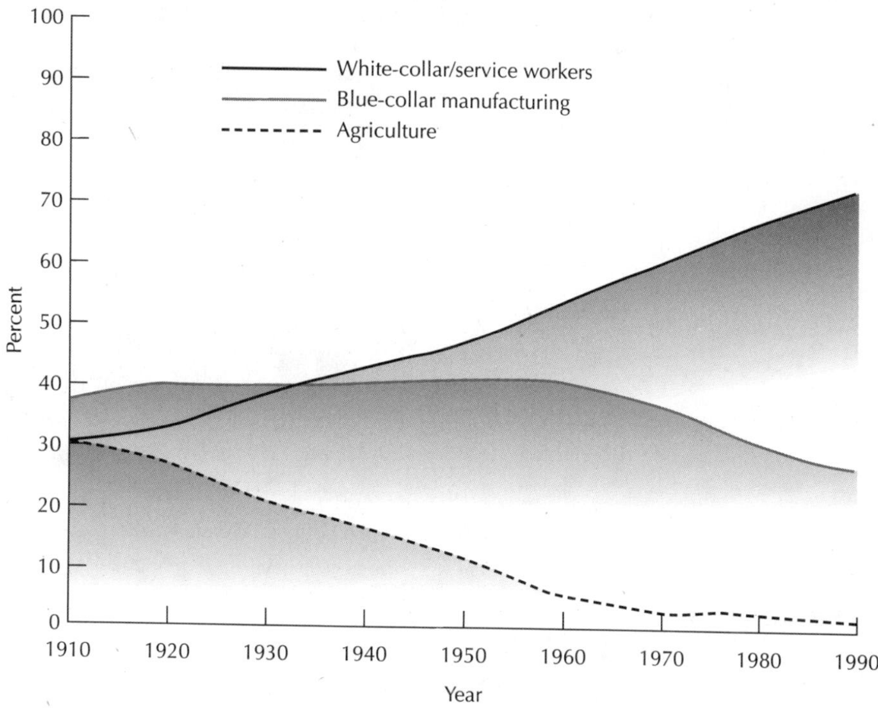

Source: Craig Calhoun, Donald Light, and Susanne Keller, *Sociology*, 6th ed., McGraw-Hill, New York, 1994, p. 420.

Title or explanation. Percentage of the Labor Force in Various Sectors of the U.S. Economy, 1910–1990.

Source. Data from U.S. Bureau of Labor Statistics.

Headings and labels. Year, percent; Agriculture, Blue-collar manufacturing, White-collar/Service workers.

Units of measurement. Decades, percent in increments of ten.

Important points and conclusions. During this century there has been a sharp drop in agricultural work and manufacturing jobs, and a striking increase in white-collar/service jobs. These trends seem likely to continue. Therefore, Americans today need higher educational / training levels to successfully enter and remain in the workforce.

Pie Charts

A ***pie chart,*** as its name suggests, is a circle graph in which the sizes of the "slices" represent parts of the whole. Pie charts are a convenient way to show the relationship among component parts as well as the relationship of each part to the whole. The example here comes from a sociology textbook.

People of Hispanic Origin in the United States (*Source:* U.S. Dept. of Commerce and Bureau of the Census)

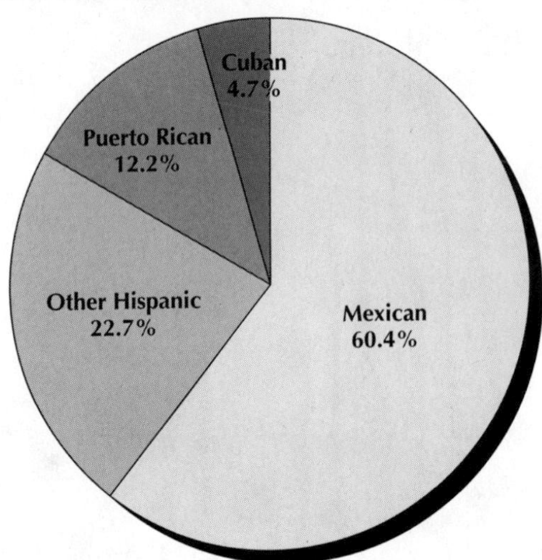

Source: Craig Calhoun, Donald Light, and Susanne Keller, *Sociology,* 6th ed., McGraw-Hill, New York, 1994, p. 64.

Title or explanation. People of Hispanic Origin in the United States.

Source. U.S. Department of Commerce, Bureau of the Census, Release CB91-216 (June 12, 1991).

Headings and labels. Mexican, Cuban, Puerto Rican, Other Hispanic.

Units of measurement. Percentage.

Important points and conclusions. The majority of people of Hispanic origin in the United States are of Mexican descent.

Flowcharts

A ***flowchart*** shows steps in procedures or processes by using boxes, circles, and other shapes that are connected with lines or arrows. The example here is from the *Dictionary of Cultural Literacy* and presents the legislative process (how a bill becomes a law).

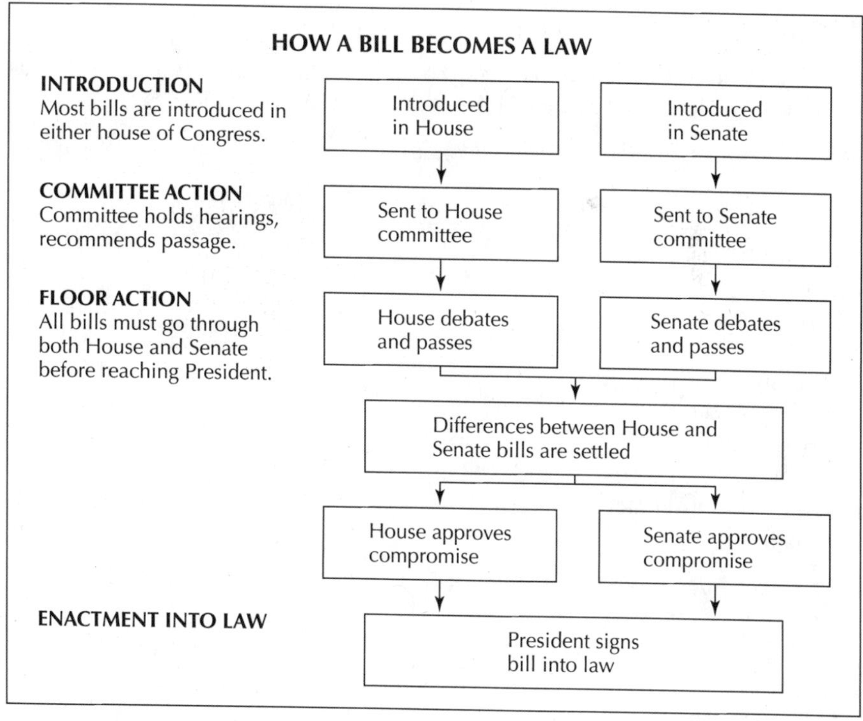

Source: E. D. Hirch, Jr., Joseph Kett, and James Trefil, *The Dictionary of Cultural Literacy,* Boston, Houghton-Mifflin, 1988, p. 319.

Title or explanation. How a Bill Becomes a Law.

Source. None given.

Headings and labels. Introduction, Committee Action, Floor Action, Enactment into Law.

Units of measurement. None.

Important points and conclusions. Although bills can be introduced in either the House or the Senate, all bills must go through committee hearings and through floor action in both the House and Senate, before the bill is submitted to the president for enactment into law.

Tables

A ***table*** is a systematic listing of data in rows and columns. The example below, from a textbook on human development, presents data about how school-age children spend their time. (Textbook features, including tables, are discussed earlier in this chapter.)

Table 9-1

How School-Age Children Spend Their Time: Children's Top 10 Activities (Average Hours and Minutes Per Day)

	Weekdays		Weekends	
Activity	Ages 6–8	Ages 9–11	Ages 6–8	Ages 9–11
Sleeping	9.55	9.09	10:41	9:56
School	4:52	5:15	—	—
Television	1:39	2:26	2:16	3:05
Playing	1:51	1:05	3:00	1:32
Eating	1:21	1:13	1:20	1:18
Personal care	0:49	0:40	0:45	0:44
Household work	0:15	0:18	0:27	0:51
Sports	0:24	0:21	0:30	0:42
Religious observance	0:09	0:09	0:56	0:53
Visiting	0:15	0:10	0:08	0:13

Source: Adapted from Institute for Social Research, 1985.

Source: Diane E. Papalia and Sally Wendkos Olds, *Human Development,* 6th ed., McGraw-Hill, New York, 1995, p. 312.

Title or explanation. How School-Age Children Spend Their Time: Children's Top 10 Activities (Average Hours and Minutes Per Day).

Source. Adapted from Institute for Social Research, 1985.

Headings or labels. Activity, Weekdays / Weekends, Ages 6–8 / Ages 9–11.

Units of measurement. Average Hours and Minutes per Day.

Important points and conclusions. Children spend about two-thirds of their time on necessary or required activities (sleeping, eating, school, personal care, housework, and religious observance). The two main things that children choose to do in their free time are playing and watching television. Both age groups watch more television on weekends and amount of television watching increases with age.

The reading selection in this chapter (Selection 9-1, beginning on page 495) is itself a complete chapter from a communications textbook. It will give you an opportunity to try out the study skills in Chapter 9, and it will also help you gain a realistic idea of how much time is needed to master a textbook chapter. Then, whenever a course involves mastering textbook information, you will know *how* to master it and will feel confident that you *can* master it.

DEVELOPING CHAPTER REVIEW CARDS

Review cards, or *summary cards,* are an excellent study tool. They are a way to select, organize, and review the most important information in a textbook chapter. The process of creating review cards helps you organize information in a meaningful way and, at the same time, transfer it into long-term memory. The cards can also be used to prepare for tests (see Chapter 10). The review card activities in this book give you structured practice in creating these valuable study tools. Once you have learned how to make review cards, you can create them for textbook material in your other courses.

Now, complete the seven review cards for Chapter 9 by supplying the important information about each topic. When you have completed them, you will have summarized important information about the skills in this chapter.

Three Keys to Studying College Textbooks

1. ____

____

____

____

2. ____

____

____

____

3. ____

____

____

____

Chapter 9: Selecting and Organizing Textbook Information

Underlining and Highlighting Textbook Material

Chapter 9: Selecting and Organizing Textbook Information

Annotating Textbooks

Chapter 9: Selecting and Organizing Textbook Information

Outlining

Chapter 9: Selecting and Organizing Textbook Information

Mapping

Chapter 9: Selecting and Organizing Textbook Information

Summarizing Textbook Information

Chapter 9: Selecting and Organizing Textbook Information

Interpreting Graphic Material

Chapter 9: Selecting and Organizing Textbook Information

READING

INTERCULTURAL COMMUNICATION

BY STEWART L. TUBBS AND SYLVIA MOSS

Prepare Yourself to Read

Directions: Do these exercises *before you read Selection 9-1.*

1. First, read and think about the title. What do you already know about the media in intercultural communication?

   ____

   ____

2. Next, complete your chapter preview by reading the following:

   Chapter objectives
   Section headings
   First sentence of each paragraph
   Words in **boldface** or *italic*
   Illustrations and their legends
   Chapter summary
   Review questions

   On the basis of your preview, what aspects of intercultural communication does this chapter seem to be about?

   ____

   ____

Apply Comprehension Skills

Directions: Do these exercises *as you read Selection 9-1.*

- Budget your time for reading this selection. It has four sections. If you wish, divide the selection into shorter reading sessions.
- As you read, apply the skills of selectivity and organization you have learned in this chapter. To remember essential information, underline, highlight, annotate, and take notes.

Intercultural Communication

CHAPTER OBJECTIVES

After reading this chapter, you should be able to:

1. Discuss how cultural groups differ from other groups with shared characteristics, and define "intercultural communication."
2. State three broad communication principles that have important implications for intercultural communication.
3. Identify and explain at least three ways in which language can interfere with communication between cultures.
4. Explain how nonverbal messages, including those that express emotion, vary from culture to culture and can be misinterpreted.
5. Describe how cultural roles and norms, including norms about conflict, affect intercultural communication.
6. Discuss the effects of differences in beliefs and values on people from different cultures.
7. Explain the concept of ethnocentrism and discuss two reasons for stereotyping of groups.
8. Describe some of the personal, political and social effects of intercultural communication.
9. Identify seven principles that would promote community building.

Source: Stewart L. Tubbs and Sylvia Moss, *Human Communication,* 7th ed., McGraw-Hill, New York, 1994, pp. 419–447 (chap. 13). Reproduced with permission of McGraw-Hill. (For additional sources, see page 492.)

The 1965 revision of U.S. immigration policies is changing the character of some of our major cities. For example, during the last two decades over a million immigrants have come to New York City, most of them from the West Indies, Latin America, and Asia (Foner, 1987, p. 1). Today the other new leading immigrant city is Los Angeles, and other cities receiving large numbers of immigrants include Chicago, Houston, Miami, and San Francisco (p. 4). In *The Middleman and Other Stories* (1988), Bharati Mukherjee portrays some of these new immigrants "trying on their new American selves, shouldering into their new country." She is writing, she explains, of "the eagerness and enthusiasm and confidence with which the new immigrants chase the American dream. But sometimes they get the American codes wrong, by being too aggressive, for example" (quoted in Healy, 1988, p. 22).

When members of different cultures communicate, getting the codes wrong is a common experience. Throughout this book we have discussed cultural differences in connection with many aspects of communication. As we have seen, intercultural communication can occur in any of the contexts we have discussed in the past few chapters, from intimate two-person communication to formal organizational and mass communication. Whenever intercultural communication occurs, the differences in the participants' frames of reference make the task of communication more complicated and more difficult, especially since participants may not be aware of all aspects of each others' cultures. In fact, one reason intercultural communication has fascinated scholars in the past few years is that it reveals aspects of our own communication behavior that we might not otherwise notice as distinct, such as our attitude toward time.

From another perspective, adjustment to a foreign culture often includes experiences of *culture shock:* "feelings of helplessness, withdrawal, paranoia, irritability, and a desire for a home" (Koester, 1984, p. 251). To compound the problem, readjustment to one's home culture after an experience in another culture produces a shock of its own: *reverse culture shock.* This may result from changes in attitudes, ways of interacting, and the like. In fact, those of us who are most adaptable to the foreign culture will probably experience the greatest *unanticipated* reentry shock (Koester, 1984).

Over 20 million people from outside the United States visit each year, and during 1991 to 1992, the number of foreign students attending colleges and universities in the United States was 419,585. The five leading countries from which these students came were China, Japan, Taiwan, India, and the Republic of South Korea (Zikopoulos, 1992). As the amount of intercultural communication we engage in increases, it becomes more important for each of us to understand some of its problems and implications.

A Definition of Culture

In Chapter 1 we defined **intercultural communication** as *communication between members of different cultures (whether defined in terms of racial, ethnic,* *or socioeconomic differences).* As this definition suggests, the divisions between cultural groups are not established or absolute; we may choose one or more of a variety of characteristics to identify a group of people as having a common culture. We may, for instance, speak of natives of California, Nebraska, and New Hampshire as being from different regional cultures (West Coast, Midwest, and New England); we may identify each of them as a member of an urban or rural culture, or as a member of a Jewish or Irish culture; we may speak of them all as members of a broader Western culture. Although scholars disagree as to which of these designations may properly be said to be a cultural group, to a certain extent all of them are.

Culture is *a way of life developed and shared by a group of people and passed down from generation to generation.* It is made up of many complex elements, including religious and political systems, customs, and language as well as tools, clothing, buildings, and works of art. The way you dress, your relationships with your parents and friends, what you expect of a marriage and of a job, the food you eat, the language you speak are all profoundly affected by your culture. This does not mean that you think, believe, and act exactly as everyone else in your cultural group. Not all members of a culture share all its elements. Moreover, a culture will change and evolve over time. Still, a common set of characteristics is shared by the group at large and can be traced, even through great changes, over many generations.

Culture As Learned

A popular cartoon that appeared during a period when many Americans were adopting Vietnamese War orphans depicted a woman announcing to her husband that the daughter they had adopted as a Vietnamese infant had spoken her first words that day. "English or Vietnamese?" he asked. Language, like culture, is so much a part of us that we tend to think of it as genetically transmitted, like the more physiological characteristics of race and nationality. As we attempt to communicate with people from other cultures and reconcile our differences, it is important that we remember culture is *learned.*

Because culture is learned, not innate, an infant born in Vietnam of Vietnamese parents but brought to the United States and raised as an American will be culturally an American. Because culture is learned, it also changes as people come into contact with one another or as their experiences change their needs. *The Covenant,* a novel by James Michener, describes how various cultural groups in South Africa changed as they came in contact with one another. Influenced by the demands of the new world and by their contact with the tribes who were there before them, the early Dutch settlers and their descendants became a separate cultural group, distinct in their way of living and speaking, from the Dutch in the homeland they had left behind them.

Some of the reasons people have so many problems communicating across cultural boundaries is suggested in this definition of culture:

> A culture is a complex of values polarized by an image containing a vision of its own excellence. Such a "tyrannizing image" takes diverse forms in various cultures such as "rugged individualism" in America, an individual's "harmony with nature" in Japan, and "collective obedience" in China. A culture's tyrannizing image provides its members with a guide to appropriate behavior and posits a super-sensible world of meaning and values from which even its most humble members can borrow to give a sense of dignity and coherence to their lives. (Cushman and Cahn, 1985, p. 119)

In a sense, then, it is the culture that provides a coherent framework for organizing our activity and allowing us to predict the behavior of others. People from other cultures who enter our own way may be threatening because they challenge our system of beliefs. In the same way, we ourselves may become threatening to others as we enter a foreign culture and challenge the cultural foundations of their beliefs.

Distinctions among Cultures

Differences between two cultural groups range from the slight to the very dramatic. The culture of the Yanomami people, a Stone Age tribe in Brazil, has little in common with the highly industrialized cultures of Japan or the United States. Many Americans, with their heritage of sympathy for union organization and antipathy toward big business, are amazed at such Japanese work customs as employees' beginning the day by singing a company song and the expectation that employees will stay with one company for life.

In recent years many Europeans and Americans have been shocked by the continuing Islamic death threat against novelist Salman Rushdie because of his novel *Satanic Verses.* The book outraged followers of Islam, who considered it blasphemous. Rushdie, a British subject, has lived in hiding since 1989.

Radical differences among cultures usually occur when there has been little exchange between them or, in some cases, with other cultures in general. What distinguishes one cultural group from another, however, is not always so evident. A New Yorker and a Californian will have cultural differences and similarities. Both may celebrate Thanksgiving and the Fourth of July with much the same sense of tradition associated with those holidays. On a day-to-day basis, however, they are likely to eat somewhat different foods, although probably with the same kind of utensils. They are likely to speak the same language but with different accents and a few different words or phrases. Both will speak more or less the same language as people who have always lived in England and Ontario, and they may even share many of the same values, but cultural differences are likely to become more evident as the Americans, Canadians, and British communicate with one another. Similarly, differences among cultures do not occur abruptly at regional or national borders but gradually, over a range (Samovar and Porter, 1991*a*).

MEANS OF INTERCULTURAL COMMUNICATION

Because of the technological innovations of the last two decades, writes Gergen, "contemporary life is a swirling sea of social relationships" (1991, p. 61). In that sea we must place the growing number of intercultural relationships. A dramatic increase in intercultural communication has come about primarily through high-tech developments in both aviation and electronic communication networks.

Consider first the extraordinary rise in our use of air transportation. Once an experience for the privileged few, international air travel is now routine and accessible to millions. We vacation in foreign capitals, we attend professional conferences and trade fairs, we fly to business meetings. Students in high school as well as college participate in study-abroad programs. Members of the scientific community attend international conferences on medical and

New technology is creating many opportunities for intercultural communication—for example, this "spacebridge" class with simultaneous translation between Tufts University and the University of Moscow.

environmental issues. Tourist groups from Europe and Asia are a common sight in large American cities.

We have come to take for granted the use of telephone, radio, newspaper, books, wireless services, and network television. Now satellite technology has brought the immediacy of political events into our homes—whether it be in the unprecedented coverage of the Gulf War by CNN or in the televised images of Bosnia's suffering people. As we saw in Chapter 12, the expansion of a vast electronic communications network has linked peoples of the world many times over. And the technologies of computers, electronic mail, teleconferencing, and fax, we are told, are only the beginning.

OBSTACLES TO INTERCULTURAL COMMUNICATION

Although modern means of travel and communication have brought us into contact with virtually the whole world, the technical capacity to transmit and receive messages is not, in itself, enough to allow people who have vastly different cultures to communicate with one another. Dramatic improvements in the technological means of communication have in many instances outstripped our abilities to communicate effectively with people who have different languages, different beliefs and values, and different expectations of relationships. Repeatedly, interaction between people of different cultures has created far more misunderstanding than understanding.

Of the many principles used by theorists to describe the communication process, several clearly apply to intercultural exchanges. The first is *a shared code system,* which of course will have *two aspects—verbal and nonverbal.* Sarbaugh (1979) argues that without such a shared system, communication will be impossible. There will be degrees of difference, but the *less* a code system is shared, the *less* communication is possible.

In his work anthropologist Edward Hall makes the distinction between high- and low-context cultures (1976). We can think of them along a continuum as, for example, in Figure 13.1. High- and low-context cultures have several important differences in the way information is coded. Members of **high-context cultures** are more skilled in reading nonverbal behaviors "and in reading the environment"; and they assume that other people will also be able to do so. Thus they speak less than members of low-context cultures; and in general their communication tends to be indirect and less explicit. **Low-context cultures** on the other hand, stress direct and explicit communication: "verbal messages are extremely important . . . and the information to be shared is coded in the verbal message" (Samovar and Porter, 1991*b*, pp. 234–235; Gudykunst and Kim, 1992, pp. 44–45).

Among members of high-context cultures are the Chinese, Korean, and Japanese. Notice our own position in Figure 13.1—within the low-context end of the spectrum, yet not at the very bottom. In comparing Americans with

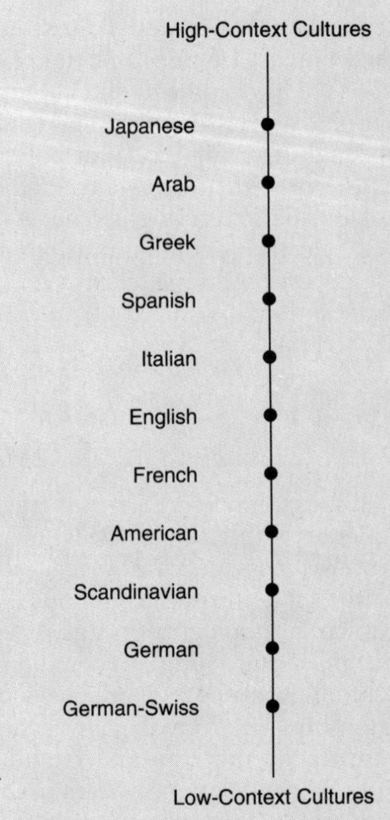

FIGURE 13.1 Sampling of Cultures Arranged along the High-Context/Low-Context Dimension (*Source:* Larry A. Samovar and Richard E. Porter, *Communication Between Cultures,* Belmont, CA: Wadsworth, 1991, p. 235.)

Malays and Japanese, Althen offers a clear example of the high-context/low-context dimension:

> Americans focus on the words people use to convey their ideas, information and feelings. They are generally quite unskilled in "reading" other people's non-verbal messages. "Oh, you Americans!" said an exasperated Japanese woman who was being pressed to express some details about an unpleasant situation, "You have to say everything!" (Althen, 1992, p. 416)

Second, different *beliefs and behaviors* between communicators establish the basis for different assumptions from which to respond. In fact, our own beliefs and behaviors influence our perceptions of what other people do. Thus two people of different cultures can easily attribute different meanings to the same behavior. If this happens, the two behave differently with neither being able to predict the other's response. Yet as we saw in Chapter 7, predictions are an integral part of being able to communicate effectively. Writing of his trip to East Africa, American essayist Edward Hoagland described how Gabriel, who was from the Sudan, served him a drink:

> Gabriel explained that it was his duty as a host to make me want to share with him whatever he had. I suggested that it was foolish for us to argue about the nature of hospitality in our two countries. . . . This sufficed for a while, but because I was not drinking my share of the sherry he became agitated again that I was not participating in the ritual of being his guest. I didn't know whether the way he knitted his forehead was from a host's unease, from empathy with my discomfort with . . . [my] headache, or from real twinges of a kind of pain of his own. (1979, p. 213)

A third principle discussed by Sarbaugh that has important implications for intercultural communication is the *level of knowing and accepting the beliefs and behaviors of others.* Notice that there are two components: knowledge and acceptance. It isn't so much the catalogue of differences—that is, the knowledge of such differences—that creates a problem. It's also the level of your acceptance. For example, writing about a tribe of African hunters called the Ik, anthropologist Colin Turnbull tried to come to terms with his own feelings of repulsion. The Ik, he knew, were uprooted hunters and the violent way they now lived—stealing each other's food, killing, and so on—could be explained by the fact that their entire society had been uprooted. Turnbull *knew* a great deal about the beliefs and behaviors of the Ik, but he could not *accept* the people of that culture. As an anthropologist, however, he still brings to his perceptions a certain objectivity—simply in declaring his responses.

The degree to which we judge a culture by our own cultural values and refuse to consider other cultural norms will determine how likely it is that effective communication takes place. At one extreme, we have participants in a transaction who both know and accept the beliefs and behaviors of others; at the other, we have those who neither know nor accept. And in this instance the probability of a breakdown in communication is extremely high (Sarbaugh, 1979).

Adopting a shared code system, acknowledging differences in beliefs and behaviors, and learning to be tolerant of the beliefs and behaviors of others all contribute to effective communication.

American anthropologist Mary Catherine Bateson tells of visiting her husband's family in Beirut on her honeymoon and being frustrated because, although she spoke to them in Armenian, her in-laws kept responding in English:

> Then, on the fourth or fifth day of our visit, his mother set out to make *chee kufta,* a dish in which finely ground lamb is kneaded at length with bulgur wheat, parsley, and onions until the raw meat simply disappears into the wheat. It's one of those dishes, shaped by their mother's hands, that sons go home to eat. Greatly daring, I went into the kitchen and

> took over the kneading. After that day, my in-laws began to answer me in Armenian, the handling of the meat and grain and the sharing of what I had prepared having transformed me into a different person. . . . (1990, p. 126)

Verbal Messages

The European Community's translation service in Brussels recently held an exhibition of signs that had been translated into English with some hilarious results including "Please leave your values at the front desk" (from a Paris hotel) and "Our wines leave you nothing to hope for" (this from a Swiss restaurant) (Goldsmith, 1992, B1). On a personal level, learning a foreign language improperly, even if just a few words are involved, can create immediate difficulties. For example, a Japanese businessman who was transferred to the United States explained his frustration in trying to find affordable housing; he kept asking about renting a "mansion," the word he had been taught instead of "apartment."

Language differences can go much deeper than simple translation ambiguities, however. Have you ever asked someone to translate a word from another language to you, only to have him say "Well, it doesn't translate into English exactly, but it means something like . . ."? As we saw in our discussion of the Whorf hypothesis in Chapter 3, languages differ more than strict word-for-word translations often indicate because the people who speak the languages have different needs.

Even when we can manage to translate from one language to another with literal accuracy, the deeper meanings are often lost because they are rooted in the culture of the language. Consider the following description of how the failure to understand the deeper meanings of words may interfere with communication between people who do not share a culture:

> There may be no better example to illustrate cultural mistranslation than the word *Red*. To Westerners "the Reds" conjures up images of blood, fire, fierceness, e.g., *red with anger, . . . seeing red,* but the Russian translation *krasnyi* has a different aura. For example, to a Russian
>
> krasnyi = beautiful
> pryekrasnyi = exquisite
> krasnaya ryiba = fine fish (e.g., salmon)
> krasnoye zoloto = pure gold ("red" gold)
> krasna devitza = beautiful girl
>
> Rather than *Red,* a far, far better symbolic translation of this word into English is *Golden,* as in a *Golden opportunity, . . . The Golden Age,* etc.

> No doubt a Russian might translate this word back into Russian to mean "the color of money!" . . .
>
> I was once highly embarrassed when using our common term *Red Indian* (American Indian, in British usage) to an American audience, some of whom took it to refer to an Indian communist. Colors are no more translatable than words. (Cherry, 1971, pp. 16–17)

Literal translations from one language to another often create misunderstandings because they do not account for culture-based linguistic styles. The elaborate style used in Arabic with its rhetoric of exaggeration, compliment, and multiple extended metaphors is puzzling to those unfamiliar with it. Even a yes-or-no answer can be misconstrued:

> An Arab feels compelled to overassert in almost all types of communication because others expect him to. If an Arab says exactly what he means without the expected assertion, other Arabs may still think that he means the opposite. For example, a simple "No" by a guest to a host's request to eat or drink more will not suffice. To convey the meaning that he is actually full, the guest must keep repeating "No" several times coupling it with an oath such as "By God" or "I swear to God." (cited in Gudykunst and Ting-Toomey, 1992, p. 227)

You can also get an inkling from this of how an Arab might interpret a single succinct "No" from someone speaking in English.

A grasp of the subtleties in language style is particularly important in matters of diplomacy. For example, Sir Hamilton Gibb of Oxford University suggests that "the medium in which the aesthetic feeling of the Arabs is mainly . . . expressed is that of word and language—the most seductive, it may be, and certainly the most unstable and even dangerous of all the arts" (cited in Kaplan, 1992, p. 41). In general, many career diplomats feel that our embassies need more foreign service officers proficient in foreign languages—particularly Arabic (p. 61).

When two cultures vary widely in their perceptions of how language functions in communication—and certainly this is true of high- and low-context cultures—there may even be differences in how the very act of *asking* a question is evaluated. For example, the person asking a question may think it necessary and innocuous; the person being asked may be offended and even avoid telling the truth. In Japanese business transactions, for example,

> one avoids the direct question unless the questioner is absolutely certain that the answer will not embarrass the Japanese businessman in any way whatsoever. In Japan for one to admit being unable to perform a given operation or measure up to a given standard means a bitter loss of face. Given a foreigner so stupid, ignorant, or insensitive to ask an embarrassing question, the Japanese is likely to choose what appears to him the lesser of two evils. (Hall and Whyte, in Mortensen, 1979)

Nonverbal Messages

Kurt Vonnegut, in his novel *Jailbird,* describes a woman attempting to interview a refugee of undetermined national origin. She tries a number of languages, looking for one they might have in common, and as she changes from one language to another, she changes her gestures as well.

Nonverbal communication systems vary from culture to culture just as verbal systems do, but we often overlook the symbolic nature of nonverbal systems. Many American travelers abroad have been embarrassed when they discovered that the two-fingered gesture they use to mean "Give me two" is assigned a different, obscene meaning in many countries. They have also been mistaken when they assumed that a nod always means yes. In some countries, a nod means "no"; in others a nod, or yes, simply indicates that a person understood the question. In this country, the gesture for "okay" is made by forming a circle with the thumb and forefinger while the other fingers are held up. But in France this gesture means "you're worthless," and in Greece it's a vulgar sexual invitation (Ekman et al., 1984).

Confusion in nonverbal indicators may be much more complex. In Chapter 4 we considered some of the different ways that cultures regard such nonverbal factors as the use of time and space. As we discussed then, we rely on nonverbal cues to give us information about the meaning we are to assign to a verbal message. Because we often interpret these nonverbal cues unconsciously, the message received is often very different from the one the speaker intended.

As we noted in Chapter 4, vocal cues such as volume are used differently in different cultures. In the Arab countries, men are expected to speak loudly to indicate strength and sincerity, at a volume that Americans consider "aggressive, objectionable, and obnoxious." A Saudi Arab may also lower his voice to indicate respect to a superior. In an exchange between an American and an Arab, the confusion of signals is likely to be disastrous. If the Arab speaks softly to indicate respect, the American is likely to raise his voice, because in *his* culture, one asks another person to speak more loudly by raising one's own voice. The Arab, thinking the American is suggesting that he is not being respectful enough, will lower his voice even more. The American responds by raising his voice again, and the cycle continues until the American is shouting and the Arab is no longer audible. "They are not likely to part with much respect for one another" (Hall and Whyte, in Mortensen, 1979, pp. 408–409).

The expression of emotion is also regulated by culture. For example, a gesture that Americans often misunderstand is the Japanese smile, cultivated for use as a social duty in order to appear happy and refrain from burdening friends with one's unhappiness. There are several cross-cultural studies of attitudes toward the display of emotion. For example, one study of people in England, Italy, Japan, and Hong Kong (Argyle et al., 1986) found that the Italians and the English allow more expressions of distress and anger than the Japanese. In fact, another study found that Japanese children are slower than North American children to identify anger—probably because "Japanese are socialized from an early age to avoid the expression of emotions like anger" (Gudykunst and Ting-Toomey, 1988*a*, p. 386). Moreover, it seems that in some cultures the display of emotions is limited to emotions that are "positive" and do not disturb group harmony (p. 396).

One aspect of a shared code system that contributes to the smooth flow of conversation and ultimately to understanding is **synchrony,** *the sharing of rhythms* (Gudykunst and Kim, 1992; Douglis, 1987). When people speak, they develop a rhythm, a dancelike beat that emphasizes and organizes meaning during conversation—a phenomenon to be observed between family members, friends, and lovers—even business associates. It is during a beat or stress that a speaker will often reveal important information or introduce a new topic into the conversation. It seems that timing in conversation can be affected even by a few microseconds and speakers who stay in sync not only have better understanding but a better relationship.

This rhythmic pattern is also seen in the nonverbal behavior that accompanies conversation: Speaking patterns are accented by nonverbal gestures and movements that follow the beat. But when two people are from different cultures or linguistic backgrounds, even their expectations for speech rhythms and nonverbal behaviors may be vastly different. Consciousness about synchrony also seems to vary from culture to culture. Hall has found people from Northern Europe and North America less aware of such rhythms than people from Asia, Latin America, and Africa:

> The fact that synchronized rhythmic movements are based on the "hidden dimensions" of nonverbal behavior might explain why people in African and Latin American cultures (as high-context nonverbal cultures) are more in tune and display more sensitivity toward the synchronization process than people in low-context verbal cultures, such as those in Northern Europe and the United States. (Gudykunst and Ting-Toomey, 1992, p. 281)

Relationships: Norms and Roles

Cultures also vary in the contexts in which verbal and nonverbal systems are used. When we think of making friends with a foreign student or of working with people abroad in business situations, it is important to remember that personal and working relationships are not the same and do not develop the same way in every culture. People in different cultures expect different behaviors from one another in a relationship. One culture's friendly gesture might be considered aggressive or impertinent in another culture, for example, while a gesture of respect or deference might be interpreted as inappropriate reticence or as defiance, depending on the cultural context.

Norms

Norms, as we discussed in Chapter 7, are *established rules of what is accepted and appropriate behavior.* Although we often use these rules as if they are absolute or instinctive standards, they are actually culturally developed and transmitted. If you grew up in the United States, for instance, you were probably taught to "speak up" clearly and to look at a person who is speaking to you, and that mumbling and looking away when someone addresses you is disrespectful. These norms would seem natural and logical to you, but not all cultural groups interpret these behaviors as good manners. We have already seen that people in some cultures drop their voices as an indication of respect and deference. White American police officers patrolling Hispanic neighborhoods have often misinterpreted a similar gesture: Hispanic children are taught to lower their eyes, as a gesture of respect, when a person in authority addresses them. The police, who had been brought up with opposite norms, interpreted the gesture as sullen and resentful, and reacted accordingly.

"A smile is the same in any language," is a saying that was popular a few years ago and that still shows up occasionally. In fact, though, a smile and related attempts to be friendly are interpreted in cultural contexts. An American student's smile of greeting to a non-Western student might be interpreted as superficial, sexually suggestive, or even rude; the American student, in turn, is likely to interpret the other's failure to return the smile as unfriendly or even hostile (Samovar and Porter, 1991*a*, pp. 346–347).

Understanding **conflict norms** becomes particularly important when a disagreement seems to be brewing between two people from different cultures. Sillars and Weisberg (1987) identify at least two important variables that distinguish how members of a given culture view interpersonal and family conflicts: (1) expressivity, and (2) privacy and individuality.

Even in this country there is considerable cultural variation in the amount of emphasis placed on **expressive communication** about conflict. Studies have shown that "North American and Black American males may regard deep personal feelings as too personal to express openly"; that Jews frequently value discussion and analysis so highly that by "mainstream" standards they may seem argumentative; that Irish families in family therapy dealt with conflicts through allusion, sarcasm, and innuendo rather than engage in verbal confrontations. In each instance we see a set of assumptions about what constitutes conflict and how it should be negotiated or resolved—or perhaps ignored.

One reason we cannot apply the expressive norms of mainstream America to other groups is that so many cultures place far less value on individual self-disclosures. Talking about feelings and being open about one's dissatisfactions—even with a member of your family, for example—is not always considered appropriate behavior, and many of the suggestions for resolving conflict mentioned in Chapter 6 would be difficult to apply to intercultural contexts. In fact, in many cultures keeping problems to oneself is strongly favored, and a stoic attitude often develops. For example, in working-class families, problems are frequently regarded as "lying outside the family and within the realm of natural economic, social, and biological conditions that are futile for the family to address. Thus [family members] may adopt a passive problem-solving style that emphasizes family cohesion over active problem solving" (p. 159).

The direct expression of conflict is also considered inappropriate in cultures that deemphasize explicit verbal coding of information and pay more attention to subtle cues and indirect messages. In such cultures, discretion and indirectness are the norms for dealing with conflict, and they of course are upheld and understood by members. This is true, as we have seen, of the Chinese and Japanese (Chapter 6). So while we might perceive the indirect treatment of conflict as cowardly, members of another type of culture might view our more confrontational approach as lacking in taste (Gudykunst and Ting-Toomey, 1988*b*, p. 160).

Cultural norms about **privacy and individuality** are equally variable. In the two-person and familial relationships of mainstream America, a great deal of autonomy is expected—especially among the middle class. Thus during a conflict, advice from friends and others outside the immediate family may be looked upon as an infringement of privacy. They are certainly not expected to intervene. In extended families, however, there is a more public aspect of relationships: "Because extended networks promote communal and traditional norms, there are more definite guidelines for resolving conflicts" (p. 161). There are even times when conflicts are settled not through personal communication but through the intervention of a third party. In Japan this is sometimes the case.

According to Sillars and Weisberg's survey of research, emphasis on cooperation, affiliation, and dependence is stressed by such groups as Africans, Native Americans, Asians, West Indians, Japanese, Mexicans, Mormons, and Catholics. Their norms dictate that some conflicts will be minimized or even solved indirectly for the good of the group. For example, in the tribal meetings of Native Americans or native Alaskans, it is expected that the individual will put group goals before personal ones and reach consensus (pp. 160–162). Sometimes the mainstream American ideal of agreeing to disagree becomes "an impractical and even undesirable goal" (p. 162).

Roles

Roles, as we discussed in Chapter 7, are *sets of norms that apply to specific groups of people in a society.* Roles, too, vary markedly among cultures. Differences in the respective roles of men and women may represent some of the most apparent cultural differences in human relationships: how unmarried couples should behave and whether they should be chaperoned, how men and women should behave toward each other in business situations, what a husband's and wife's responsibilities are to one another and to their respective families.

Researchers from several disciplines acknowledge that dual-culture marriage is different from a marriage in which both partners share a common culture. For example, there are cultural differences in decision-making power and self-disclosure patterns, and there is general agreement that there is less use of self-disclosure among northern Europeans than among people from Mediterranean cultures. "Perhaps," writes Rohrlich, "what is lacking is a set of Johari windows . . . which graphically depict the amount of open, blind, hidden and unknown areas of disclosure representative of cultures" (1988, p. 41). The author stresses that to marry someone from another culture is, in effect, marrying that culture. When one spouse fails to communicate interest or assumes that the other is not attached to his or her culture, there may be serious problems. In this view, an awareness of cultural differences must precede the development of appreciation and sensitivity: "The cultural difference is what makes the fabric of the marriage more varied, interesting, and richer" (p. 42).

Many other roles are dictated culturally. For example, the director of a conversant program (a program in which foreign students learning English were matched with native-speaking American students for informal practice in the language) at a major U.S. university routinely cautioned American women students not to meet their male Algerian conversants alone in their homes because their (the Americans') intentions would be misconstrued.

Many international students who come to this country for graduate study support themselves with jobs as teaching assistants. In interviews with graduate students (TAs) from England, Thailand, Japan, and China, Ross and Krider (1992) found how different their expectations are about the roles of teacher and student and about procedures in the classroom. For example, the assistants were not prepared for the degree of verbal interaction between student and teacher that takes place in the American classroom. Although all thought this to be positive, some felt challenged. One teaching student said:

> I felt that sometimes with their comments, I was being made fun of and not taken seriously. . . . I always felt like they were trying to test my knowledge base with all their questions. (p. 284)

Accustomed to far greater formality in the university, assistants were also surprised to see students eating and drinking during class though some seem to have grown accustomed to the practice.

Beliefs and Values

Even if you've never traveled outside of the United States, you have heard stories about how American politicians and presidents have inadvertently insulted Polish or Latin American audiences when trying to speak to their audiences in the unfamiliar languages. Movies and television shows provide a glimpse of many ways of life, including the roles and norms of Hawaiian-American, Asian, Native American, and numerous other cultures. Although the portrayals are not always accurate, they help to give us a sense of some cultural differences.

It is much more difficult to comprehend and accept the values of another culture when they differ from our own. More than any other aspect of the culture taught us from birth, our values seem to be universal absolutes. Values determine what we think is right, good, important, beautiful; we find it difficult to accept that what is right or good is as relative to culture as the word for "book" or "stove," or as the way our food is prepared or our clothes are made. It may be difficult for a Westerner to adjust to the combinations or seasonings of an unfamiliar Middle Eastern or Asian cuisine. It is even more difficult to accept that some cultures eat plants or animals that we do not classify as food, and still more difficult to understand why, in the face of mass starvation in India, cattle wander the streets unrestrained, protected by religious taboos. People of other cultures, meanwhile, may be appalled at Americans' willingness to eat meat, or at the casualness with which we often have meals "on the run," without ceremony.

Nonetheless, living in another country over a long period of time sometimes leads to changes in value systems—particularly when people do not remain insulated within their own cultural group. In a recent study DiMartino (1991) examined the effect of culture on moral values—specifically, through the interpretation of moral and conventional dilemmas. Her subjects, Sicilian-American men and women, had all come to the United States as young adults. She found that the women relied more on reasoning and used more moral than conventional adjectives in their interpretations whereas Sicilian-American men seemed to "retain the thinking patterns acquired as children in Sicily" (p. 318). DiMartino explains that while the men seemed to have stayed within a "cultural cocoon," spending all their leisure and work time with other Sicilian Americans, their wives—because of their involvement with children and community—negotiated two different social systems and thus had to develop other values and moral standards (p. 318). In fact, these women often complained "that their husbands were too conservative and too tied to the 'old' ways" (p. 318).

Other recent cross-cultural research suggests that sometimes our system of beliefs and values can improve our ability to adapt to living in another country. A study of Tibetan refugees who resettled in India shows that they have been extremely successful in adjusting to their new environment and have made many economic and social gains. Mahmoudi (1992) found that Tibetan views and institutions concerning religion, government, economics, and education were critical to their adjustment. Most important, it seems, was the sense of community engendered by Tibetan religious beliefs:

> Mahayana Buddhism provides the Tibetans not only with a design for living but also with a rather positive, industrious, pragmatic, and balanced view of life. . . .
>
> [For the Tibetans] actions promote life affirmation based on the good deeds performed by the individual and the community. The Tibetan Buddhism worldview promotes a "can do" attitude with a healthy dose of cheerfulness. (p. 23)

Mahmoudi believes that Tibetans can provide a model for other international refugee populations.

BARRIERS TO INTERCULTURAL UNDERSTANDING

We cannot learn another language by simply memorizing its vocabulary and grammatical structures. A language is a complex system, intricately related to culture, and it cannot be mastered by simple substitutions. Nor can we master a culture by memorizing a list of symbols, norms, and values, even if it were possible to memorize all of them. The meaning of "red" and "gold," the proper amount of time to devote to a business transaction, the appropriate way to behave toward a person in authority—these are not isolated factors; they are all part of the intricate pattern of a culture (Hall, 1959, pp. 99–105). Learning aspects of a given culture, therefore, will not allow you to understand that culture in the same way you understand your own.

The book *Blue Collar Worker,* by John Coleman (1974), illustrates some of the difficulties of understanding another culture. Coleman, a university president, spent some months working at a number of menial jobs, including collecting garbage, digging ditches, and working in a restaurant kitchen. Although the jobs and his contact with the people he worked with (none of whom knew he was a university president) taught him a great deal about the way of life of an unskilled worker, his understanding was ultimately very limited. He lived on his wages from his blue-collar jobs, but his salaries from the university and from the companies on whose boards he served supported his family, paid his children's tuitions, and met his insurance payments; as a result, he had no firsthand experience of living on an unskilled worker's pay. He learned how a garbage collector is supposed to act and how his supervisors, coworkers, and the people whose garbage he collected behaved toward him, but the roles he played ultimately had little effect on his self-concept because when his leave from the university ran out, he would go back to his job as university president. In many ways, Coleman was never "really" a blue-collar worker.

If you have spent summers in an unskilled job in a restaurant or factory, you may have noticed that the summer-employed college students and the more regular, full-time employees tend to form separate groups at lunchtime and after work. Although both groups of people hold similar jobs at the same place, they generally feel they have little in common. If you are returning to school after some years of working in or outside your home, you may feel quite isolated from the younger students around you, at least at first. You probably feel that you have very different ways of life outside of class, different roles in your families, different ways of spending your leisure time, and different expectations of your education. Not all these differences are necessarily cultural, but in both cases, the groups of people are divided by more than a collection of differences; their entire ways of life are different.

The more diverse two cultures are, the wider the division between their people, and the less they can come to really understand one another. Coleman's blue-collar coworkers shared, in most cases, Coleman's language, many of his social and political values, and the same national heritage, yet Coleman could never understand what it was to be a blue-collar worker. The division between cultural groups who have less contact with one another is likely to be greater and even more difficult to reconcile. As much as a native United States citizen of non-Asian heritage may study Korean culture, for example, he or she can never really understand what it is to be brought up in that culture.

Ethnocentrism

We are not aware of the many aspects of our culture that distinguish it from others; in fact, many of the aspects of communication and culture discussed in this book came to be recognized not through the direct study of communication but through the study of other cultures. Culture, as Hall (1976) describes it, "can be understood only by painstaking or detailed analysis." As a result, a person tends to regard his or her own culture "as though it were innate. He is forced into the position of thinking and feeling that anyone whose behavior is not predictable or is peculiar in any way is slightly out of his mind, improperly brought up, irresponsible, psychopathic, politically motivated to a point beyond all reason, or just plain inferior" (p. 38).

The tendency to judge the values, customs, behaviors, or other aspects of another culture *"using our own group and our own customs as the standards for all judgments"* is **ethnocentrism.** Because culture is unconscious, it may be inevitable that we regard "our own groups, our own country, our own culture as the best, as the most moral" (Samovar and Porter, 1991*a*). Psychologist Roger Brown (1986) puts it another way: "It is not just the seeming universality of ethnocentrism that makes us think it ineradicable but rather that it has been traced to its source in individual psychology, and the source is the individual effort to achieve and maintain positive self-esteem. That is an urge so deeply human that we can hardly imagine its absence" (p. 534).

An Australian-born historian recalls her visit to England after graduating from the University of Sydney and writes of weekend visits with her English hosts:

> They could not have been kinder, but I resented their air of superiority toward Australians. . . . I came to wait for the ultimate compliment which could be counted on by Sunday breakfast. I knew the confidential smile and the inclination of the head would be followed by "You know, my dear, one would hardly know you were not English." I couldn't control the irritation produced by such accolades, and would usually begin by telling preposterous stories about life in the outback to emphasize how different I was. (Conway, 1990, p. 206)

In a recent study of intercultural anxiety, Stephan and Stephan (1992) looked at a group of American college students who had been in Morocco on a four-day visit. One finding was that students who tested high in ethnocentrism tended to have a higher level of anxiety. The researchers used these six statements to measure ethnocentrism, asking students to rate each response on a ten-point scale from strongly disagree to strongly agree:

1. Americans have been very generous in teaching other people how to do things in more efficient ways.
2. English should be accepted as the international language of communication.
3. Primitive people have unsophisticated social and political systems.
4. The fact that America was able to put a man on the moon is evidence of America's technological superiority.
5. Minority groups within a country should conform to the customs and values of the majority.
6. In many countries people do not place a high value on human life—to them, life is cheap. (Adapted from p. 93)

It seems that, to some degree, every group teaches its members to be ethnocentric.

Hall (1976) believes that ethnocentrism complicates intercultural communication even when both parties in the interaction attempt to keep open minds:

> Theoretically, there should be no problem when people of different cultures meet. Things begin, most frequently, not only with friendship and good will on both sides, but there is an intellectual understanding that each party has a different set of beliefs, customs, mores, values, or what-have-you. The trouble begins when people start working together, even on a superficial basis. Frequently, even after years of close association, neither can make the other's system work! . . . Without knowing it, they experience the other person as an uncontrollable and unpredictable part of themselves. (p. 210)

Stereotyping

As discussed in Chapter 2, we tend to impose stereotypes on groups of people, which limits our communication with those groups. It is almost impossible for us *not* to stereotype a group of people with whom we have no personal contact; furthermore, without personal contact, it is almost impossible for us to dispel the stereotypes we acquire about the group. We saw in

Chapter 2 that stereotypes are inadequate because they are generalizations based on limited experience. Certainly, the sources of our information about people of different cultures are often inaccurate. For example, Driessen (1992) writes about the stereotyping of people from Mediterranean cultures:

> The stereotype of the excessively gesticulating Spaniard linked to his spontaneous, emotional, quick-tempered and high-spirited disposition . . . persists in the images of Spain created by the tourist industry but also surfaces in recent ethnographies. (p. 242)

Gumpert and Cathcart (1984) identify our main source of information about foreigners as television. According to their finding, the stereotyped images from the media even influence our face-to-face interaction with people of other cultures. Along with French and Japanese teams, the two researchers conducted a cross-cultural study of television stereotyping of American, French, and Japanese people.

Recently, content analyses (Dominick, 1993) show that Arab men tend to be presented on television by one of three negative stereotypes:

> (1) terrorists (although only a miniscule amount of real Arabs fit this category, it is prevalent in the media); (2) oil sheik (not too many fit in here either); and Bedouin desert nomad (only 5 percent of Arabs in real life are Bedouin). (p. 515)

Theorists emphasize that in addition to creating expectations about how people will behave, stereotypes often set in motion self-fulfilling prophecies because we act on information we believe to be true (Hamilton et al., 1992). This is especially the case in intercultural communication, where our information about others tends to be so limited.

EFFECTS OF INTERCULTURAL COMMUNICATION

Effects on the Individual

Although intercultural communication increasingly affects the world we live in, most scholars agree that the obstacles to intercultural communication and understanding will probably always mean that little of that communication will occur at a personal level. Travel is easier and more feasible economically than it was for our parents and grandparents, for example, but few people travel extensively enough to have much personal acquaintance with people of other cultures.

Even within our own country we tend to stay within our own groups and subgroups. Today the needs and desires of people of many groups to affirm and preserve their cultures are reflected in demands for more bilingual education, multicultural programs and curriculums, and textbooks that better represent all cultural contributions to our literature and history. Among the swelling immigrant population in this country's largest cities we find ethnic groups clustering in their own neighborhoods. New York, for example, has its Russian, Korean, and Indian sections, as in "Little Bombay," a densely packed area with row on row of stores stocking Indian spices, saris, videos, newspapers—every imaginable evidence of this thriving culture.

For anyone who reads books and newspapers, who watches television and is concerned with international events, the world has grown larger. The mass media have brought us images of Chinese students demonstrating in Tiananmen Square, the events leading up to the dismantling of the Soviet Union, and a starving Somalian population. We can no longer escape knowledge of world hunger or turn away from the impact of international events.

Although it is often assumed that international understanding increases as a result of cultural and educational exchanges over an extended period of time, scholars believe that this hoped-for goal must be demonstrated empirically. Thus there have been several studies of student exchange programs. For example, Rohrlich and Martin (1991) studied the adjustment of U.S. college students to studying abroad as well as their readjustment to returning home; they found women to be more satisfied than men upon returning, perhaps because their life-style at home was more independent than when living with a host family (pp. 178–179). Another investigation (Carlson and Widaman, 1988) compared 450 students from the University of California who spent their junior year studying at a European university (Sweden, Spain, France, the Federal Republic of Germany, Italy, and the United Kingdom were the countries involved) with students who remained on campus during the junior year. At the end of the school year, the study-abroad group had higher levels of cross-cultural interest, international political concern, and cultural cosmopolitanism. And when compared with students who remained at home, students who studied abroad also reported significantly more positive and more critical attitudes toward their own country (p. 14)—a finding consistent with earlier research. So relatively long-term study abroad may contribute to more favorable attitudes and increased international understanding, but there is still much to be learned about how such attitudes develop.

Social and Political Effects

We are no longer limited to being members of our own small community; we are citizens of the world as well, affected by political, economic, and social changes.

Communications, banking, and manufacturing have become increasingly international. Companies that deal in many commodities usually have offices, factories, and distributors in several countries or all over the world. As a result, the economies of the world's nations have become more and more intertwined, and the goods available in the nations that trade freely are drawn from the world at large. American companies have built plants and oil wells and in doing so created jobs in other countries. Similarly, companies from many parts of the world have created jobs for people in the United States. There have been multinational manufacturing efforts, and consortiums involving goods and services of every kind. Airbus Industrie, for example, is a consortium made up of the English, the French, the Germans, the Spanish, and the Dutch. Now, that joint venture may be extended to include the United States—and perhaps other international partners: In 1993 Boeing and Airbus agreed to explore the possibility of building an 800 passenger "superjumbo" airliner.

Not all the implications of an international economy are positive, however. When Iraq invaded Kuwait in 1990, for instance, there was much concern that the world's oil would be restricted and increasingly subject to Iraq's political actions. Economic problems in many areas of the world have resulted in repeated incidents of racial and ethnic conflict. Following several years of

No amount of information we read about intercultural communication can substitute for face-to-face encounters with people of other cultures and backgrounds.

recession and widespread unemployment, U.S. attitudes toward Japan have become extremely negative with Japan bashing characterized by one writer as "the national sport" (Krauthammer, 1992), and in the last few years a number of books have been published that many critics feel demonize the Japanese.

Yet our interdependence is clear. The United Nations, one of the most famous international organizations, is far more than a forum for political debate. Like many other international agencies, it deals actively with "the mechanics of living," such as the needs for food, health care, and education in many countries. International organizations also work on behalf of international refugees who, according to U.N. statistics, number between 15 and 20 million. Some international organizations provide such services as literacy training, education in such areas as modern agricultural methods, and help in organizing the local craft production into profitable cottage industries that market their goods beyond the immediate community. These services help to increase productivity and raise standards of living.

Cultural Effects

From the earliest times, cultures have been affected by contact with one another. Traders and the Mongol invasions once brought gunpowder, macaroni, and other Asian goods from Asia to Europe; later, immigrants brought these and other goods and customs to the United States. The Norman invasion of England in the eleventh century permanently affected the English language, not only from contact with the French language but because French became the language of the aristocracy and English the language of the peasants. European explorers brought horses to Native Americans, Native Americans taught early settlers how to grow corn and tobacco, and those settlers and their descendants drove the Native Americans westward. These are only a few examples of how trade, war, conquest, and migration have affected cultures throughout history.

As intercultural communication becomes more common and widespread, the effects of cultural contact are more pronounced and rapid. These are evident in the increased availability of goods that once would have been available, if at all, only to the very rich: tea from India, coffee from Brazil, woolen cloth from Britain, wine from France and Italy. It is also apparent in the spread of Western technology, health care methods, and Hilton Hotels in the "underdeveloped" nations, and the spread of Japanese industry and business methods in the United States.

Most people would not question the value of some aspects of cultural exchange, such as the introduction of sanitation methods that curb epidemics, or agricultural methods that save thousands from starvation. But many, including a number of scholars of culture, question the value of other aspects of cultural exchange. They ask whether certain so-called Stone Age and aboriginal communities that have been isolated for hundreds of years truly benefit from sudden contact with the outside world—whether, for example, exposure to war as well as sources of illness and pollution might outweigh what we consider the "advances" of civilization. The possibilities raise many ethical questions.

Intercultural exchange leads to **cultural homogenization,** *the tendency for cultures in contact with one another to become increasingly similar to one another.* Cultural homogenization implies that some aspects of one culture will dominate and eliminate the corresponding aspects of the other. The "standard American" voices we hear on television, for instance, are responsible for a standard American dialect and the disparagement of nonstandard dialects spoken by people who live in specific regions of the country. As a result of mass communication and travel, columnist Ellen Goodman notes, "We dress alike, we eat alike, and I guess we are destined to sound alike" (1981).

But even if we are familiar with foods from all over the world and blue jeans are as popular in Russia as in the United States, emphasis today is increasingly on our diversity. It is *differences* that have become the issue in conflicts not only between racial and ethnic groups in our own country but in those of other countries. Robert Jay Lifton, a psychiatrist who has written on the holocaust, believes that our discomfort at seeing televised images of human suffering can be a catalyst for change by evoking empathy and compassion:

> The evidence is there, on the screens, and in millions of human minds. Televised images can change the world.
>
> As survivors by proxy, can our witness be transformed into life-enhancing action—in Bosnia in this case, but also in other areas of death and suffering such as the famine in Somalia? (1992, p. 24)

Given enough understanding of regional as well as national cultures, it is possible to preserve individual differences of many kinds and allow members of various subcultures or groups to coexist and flourish. Indeed, Gudykunst and Kim maintain that "cultural and ethnic diversity are necessary for community to exist" (1992, p. 255); and they propose seven principles for building community, principles for which each of us must be responsible:

1. *Be committed.* We must be committed to the principle of building community in our lives, as well as to the individuals with whom we are trying to develop community.

2. *Be mindful.* Think about what we do and say. Focus on the process, not the outcome.

3. *Be unconditionally accepting.* Accept others as they are; do not try to change or control them. . . . Value diversity and do not judge others based only on their diversity.

4. *Be concerned for both ourselves and others.* Avoid polarized communication and engage in dialogue whenever possible. Consult others on issues that affect them and be open to their ideas.
5. *Be understanding.* Recognize how culture and ethnicity affect the way we think and behave. Search for commonalities. . . . Balance emotion, anxiety, and fear with reason.
6. *Be ethical.* Engage in behavior that is not a means to an end but behavior that is morally right in and of itself.
7. *Be peaceful.* Do not be violent or deceitful, breach valid promises, or be secretive. Strive for harmony. (Adapted from pp. 267–268)

SUMMARY

In this chapter, we discussed intercultural communication, which has become increasingly prevalent in the last few decades. We defined "culture" as the way of life developed and shared by a people and passed down from generation to generation. Because cultures vary along a range, the differences between two cultures may be slight or very dramatic. Even when two cultural groups are very similar, however, the differences between them are likely to become more evident in intercultural communication.

Intercultural communication has increased rapidly because of technological advances that have made long-distance communication more feasible and more available to the general public. Despite the advances in the means of sending and receiving messages, however, there are still many obstacles to intercultural communication. Differences in cultural factors such as language, nonverbal communication systems, relational roles and norms (particularly conflict norms), and beliefs and values that are deeply rooted in the whole cultural system often lead to intercultural misunderstanding.

Because we are not aware of the aspects of our own cultures in ourselves, the barriers to intercultural communication are complex and formidable. Ethnocentrism and stereotyping both limit our ability to deal with people beyond our own communities.

REVIEW QUESTIONS

1. Explain the difference between culture shock and reverse culture shock.
2. How do cultural groups differ from other groups that have shared characteristics?

3. Why is it important for effective intercultural communication to understand that culture is learned, rather than innate?
4. Why do cultures vary along a range, rather than being clearly distinct from one another?
5. What are the two major reasons that intercultural communication has increased in the last decades?
6. State three communication principles with significant implications for intercultural communication.
7. Identify at least three aspects of culture.
8. Explain the major difference between high-context and low-context cultures.
9. Explain at least three ways in which language is an obstacle to intercultural communication.
10. Describe at least three aspects of nonverbal communication that vary from culture to culture.
11. How can cultural roles and norms affect communication between cultures?
12. What are two variables that influence how members of a culture view conflict. Give an example of each.
13. Explain how differences in beliefs and values can prove to be obstacles in intercultural communication.
14. What is ethnocentrism? Why does it interfere with intercultural communication? Give an example.
15. Give two reasons for the stereotyping of cultural groups.
16. Identify several personal, political, and social effects of intercultural communication.
17. What is meant by "cultural homogenization"?
18. Explain the need for community building and state seven principles that have been proposed.

EXERCISES

1. Make a list of some of the cultural groups in your own region or state, including the group (or groups) that founded your community. To what extent have these groups been in contact with one another? To what extent

have they remained distinct from one another? List some ways in which these cultural groups have affected your own culture, such as your traditions, religious beliefs, and language.

2. Find three current articles about a cultural group, such as a group in Japan or Saudi Arabia, that has recently come into extended business or diplomatic contact with the United States. List at least five ways in which that culture, or that of the United States, has been affected by this contact.

3. List at least eight cultures, both inside and outside the United States, with which you communicate in some way (through personal contact, your work or business communication, or mass media). With which of these groups is your communication personal? With which is it institutional? In at least one case in which your contact with the other culture is primarily institutional, describe some ways in which your understanding of the people in that group is limited by your communication with them.

4. Think of a group of people that you feel have specific, shared, cultural characteristics, for example, Californians, southerners, New Yorkers, blacks, whites, Amish, Japanese, Russians, Chinese. Describe the people as a group, and list the characteristics that you think distinguish that group from others. To what extent is your description a stereotype? What is the source of your information about the group? Can you think of some reasons why your stereotype might be inaccurate? Can you think of some ways in which it might affect your communication with individual members of that group?

5. Listen to a national newscaster report the news on television. Do you think that such newscasters' use of language has affected the way you speak? Do you think their use of language affects what you consider to be good English? Why?

Suggested Readings

Baldwin, James. "Stranger in the Village." In *The Price of the Ticket*. By James Baldwin. New York: St. Martin's, 1985.

This is a moving essay on the experience of a black American who comes to live in an isolated European village.

Barnlund, Dean C. *Communicative Styles of Japanese and Americans: Images and Realities*. Belmont, CA: Wadsworth, 1989.

A comparative study that is thorough and clear-sighted. The author examines many stereotypical notions about the Japanese and the Americans.

Carroll, Raymonde. *Cultural Misunderstandings.* Translated by Carol Volk. Chicago: University of Chicago Press, 1988.

The author, who is French, has written a fascinating analysis of many of the cultural differences between the French and the Americans that generate so much misunderstanding on both sides.

Cushman, Donald P., and **Dudley D. Cahn, Jr.** *Communication in Interpersonal Relationships.* Albany, NY: SUNY Press, 1985.

An excellent book for the advanced student. There are good summaries of intercultural material in Chapter 8, "Cultural Communication and Interpersonal Relationships," and Chapter 9, "Cross-cultural Communication and Interpersonal Relationships."

Foner, Nancy, ed. *New Immigrants in New York.* New York: Columbia University Press, 1987.

This collection of essays by scholars from several disciplines examines the influence of New York City on its new immigrants as well as their influence on city life.

Gudykunst, William B., and **Young Yun Kim.** *Communicating with Strangers: An Approach to Intercultural Communication.* 2d ed. New York: McGraw-Hill, 1992.

The authors approach this excellent introduction to intercultural communication by providing students with a solid grounding in theoretical issues. Building community through diversity is the subject of the final chapter.

Gudykunst, William B., and **Young Yun Kim,** eds. *Readings on Communicating with Strangers: An Approach to Intercultural Communication.* New York: McGraw-Hill, 1992.

These readings have been selected to illustrate concepts across cultures or ethnic groups. The editors have an interdisciplinary focus which makes the book an invaluable resource.

Hall, Edward T. *Beyond Culture.* Garden City, NY: Doubleday, 1976.

The author of this book, an anthropologist, is an important researcher in cultural aspects and differences and in their affects on intercultural communication in business and diplomacy.

Hall, Edward T. *The Silent Language.* New York: Doubleday, Anchor, 1973.

This is one of the earliest books on nonverbal communication and its relationship to culture. The author describes a number of aspects of culture, such as the use of time and space, and discusses their implications for intercultural communication.

Kaplan, Robert. "Tales from the Bazaar." *The Atlantic,* 270 (August 1992): 37–61.

A fascinating report on Arabists, U.S. diplomats in the Middle East, and the long-term effects of their immersion in Arab culture.

Samovar, Larry A., and **Richard E. Porter**, eds. *Intercultural Communication: A Reader*. 6th ed. Belmont, CA: Wadsworth, 1991.

An outstanding collection of readings. Coverage is comprehensive and timely.

Additional sources: Photo, p. 468, J.D. Sloan, Picture Cube; *photo,* p. 485, Gloria Carlson, Picture Cube; *Figure 13-1* used by permission.

Comprehension Quiz: Textbook Chapter

Directions: Refer to Selection 9–1 as necessary to complete the following activities.

Options for collaboration: For some of these exercises, your instructor may prefer that you work collaboratively, that is, with other students. These exercises are identified in the margin. *If your instructor directs you to work collaboratively on any of these items,* form groups of three or four classmates to complete the exercise together. Discuss your answers with each other and have one member of the group record the answers. A member of the group may be asked to share the group's answers with the class.

Option

Exercise 1 may be completed collaboratively.

1. Complete an outline or study map for *one* of these subsections in Selection 9–1:

   "A Definition of Culture" (pages 497–501)

   "Obstacles to Intercultural Communication" (501–502)

   "Barriers to Intercultural Understanding" (512–515)

   "Effects of Intercultural Communication" (515–520)

   Note: Your instructor will give you specific instructions about this assignment.

Option

Exercise 2 may be completed collaboratively.

2. Your instructor will distribute one or more quizzes on Selection 9–1. Use the materials you have prepared to study for it. You will be allowed to use your outlines or maps.

REHEARSING TEXTBOOK INFORMATION AND PREPARING FOR TESTS

IN THIS CHAPTER YOU WILL LEARN THE ANSWERS TO THESE QUESTIONS:

Why is rehearsal important to memory?

What are important guidelines for test preparation?

What is the five-day test review plan?

How can I use review cards to prepare for a test?

How can I consolidate important information on test review sheets?

CHAPTER 10 CONTENTS

▪ ▪ ▪ ▪ ▪ ▪ ▪

No great thing is created suddenly.
Epictetus

REHEARSAL AND MEMORY

As you may have discovered, it is difficult to memorize information that you do not understand. This is why you must focus on understanding material before attempting to memorize it. Thorough comprehension enables you to memorize more efficiently.

Even when you understand material, however, you should not underestimate the time or effort needed to memorize it. To do well on tests, you must study information effectively enough to store it in ***long-term memory,*** or permanent memory. One serious mistake students make is leaving too little study time before the test to transfer material into long-term memory. Instead, they try to rely on ***short-term memory.*** However, as the term implies, material remains in short-term memory only temporarily. If you rely only on short-term memory (this kind of studying is called *cramming*), the information you need may not be there later when you try to recall it on a test.

Key terms

Long-term memory: Permanent memory.

Short-term memory: Temporary memory.

To understand the difference between long-term and short-term memory, consider a telephone number that you have just heard on the radio. The number is only in your short-term memory and will be forgotten in a matter of minutes or even seconds *unless you do something to transfer it into long-term memory.* In other words, you will forget the number unless you "rehearse" it in some way.

Rehearsal refers to taking specific steps to transfer information into long-term memory. Typical steps include writing information down and repeatedly reciting it aloud. In the example above, for instance, rehearsing the telephone number would probably involve writing it, saying it aloud several times, or both. Consider how much information you already have stored in long-term memory: the alphabet; the multiplication tables; names of thousands of people, places, and things; meanings and spellings of thousands of words. You have successfully stored these in your long-term memory because you rehearsed them again and again.

Key term

Rehearsal: Steps taken to transfer information into long-term memory; techniques include saying the information aloud and writing it down.

As noted in Chapter 9, rehearsal is the third key to effective studying. When you are preparing for a test, you should study over several days, enough days to enable you to transfer information from short-term memory into long-term memory. Psychologists who study how people learn emphasize that both sufficient time and ample repetition are needed to accomplish this transfer.

Before you can rehearse the information in a textbook chapter efficiently, you need to *organize* it. Obviously, the better you organize material, the more efficiently you will be able to memorize it. If you organize the material in your assignments consistently as you study, right from the beginning of the semester, you will be prepared to rehearse and memorize material for each test. You can organize material by using any of these techniques:

- Underlining and annotating textbook material
- Outlining or mapping information
- Preparing summaries
- Making review cards
- Making test review sheets

Underlining, annotating, outlining, mapping, and summarizing are discussed in Chapter 9; review cards and sheets are discussed below. The very act of preparing these study tools helps you store information in long-term memory.

After you have organized material, you should *rehearse* by doing one or more of the following:

- Reciting from review cards
- Reciting from test review sheets
- Reciting from your notes
- Writing out information from memory

Too often, students try to review for a test simply by rereading their notes and their textbook over and over again. But rereading is a time-consuming process and does not automatically result in remembering. It has been estimated that 80 percent of the time spent studying for a test should be used for memorizing, that is, for transferring information into long-term memory. Here is an example of how you could apply this "80 percent rule." If you need 5 hours to study for a test, you should spend the first hour organizing the material and getting help with, or clarification of, things you do not understand. The remaining 4 hours would be spent rehearsing the material in order to memorize it.

You may be wondering, "How can I tell when I have successfully transferred information into long-term memory?" The way to find out is to test yourself. Try to write the information from memory on a blank sheet of paper. If material is in your long-term memory, you will be able to recall it and write it down. If you cannot write it, or if you are able to write only a part of it, then not all of the information is in your long-term memory yet; you need to rehearse it further.

These steps may sound like a lot of work, but they are necessary if you want to lock information into long-term memory. It is precisely this type of study effort that leads to mastery.

STUDYING FOR TESTS

General Guidelines

This chapter presents a five-day test review plan, but the day to begin studying for a test is actually the first day of the semester! That means taking good notes, reading every assignment, reviewing regularly, and attending all classes. The review plan described here is designed to complement your careful day-to-day preparation. No review plan can replace or make up for inadequate daily studying and preparation. Following are a few more points you should be aware of before you examine the review plan itself.

First, one reason for starting to review several days ahead of time is that the amount of material covered is too much to learn at the last minute. In fact, in college you are typically given new material right up to the day of a test.

Second, it is appropriate to ask your instructor what type of test will be given and what will be included on it. Usually, instructors are willing to give a fairly complete description of tests. Don't miss the opportunity to ask questions about a test. For example, you might ask:

- Will the test be based on textbook material, on class material (lectures, demonstrations, etc.), or on both?
- How many textbook chapters will the test cover?
- What will be the format of the test (multiple-choice questions, essay questions, etc.)?
- How many questions will be asked?
- Should certain topics be emphasized in studying?

Third, be realistic about "test anxiety," or "freezing up," when you take a test. Students often complain that they "go blank" on tests, but what really happens is that they discover during the test that they did not rehearse and learn the material well enough. They did not actually forget; after all, a person cannot forget something he or she never knew. Good daily preparation and an effective test review plan are the best ways to prevent test anxiety. Knowing what to expect on a test can also leave you feeling calmer, and this is another reason for asking questions about tests, as noted above.

Key term

Distributed practice: Study sessions that are spaced out over time; a more efficient study method than massed practice.

Fourth, research studies have found that ***distributed practice*** is more effective than *massed practice.* This simply means that studying and reviewing sessions which are spaced out over time are more effective than a single session done all at once. Above, *cramming* was described as trying to rely on short-term memory when you should be putting the information into long-term memory. It can also be thought of as massed rather than distributed practice. Frantic last-minute cramming usually results in faulty understanding, poor recall, increased anxiety, and lower grades.

Fifth, to study and review efficiently, you must be rested. Cramming typically involves going without sleep, but staying up late or all night can do more harm than good. Late-night or all-night cramming overtires you, increases your stress level, and contributes to test anxiety. Cramming forces you to rely on short-term memory, which can fail under the pressure of fatigue and stress. Try to get at least 8 hours of sleep the night before a test. On the day of the test, eat a good breakfast: for example, fruit or juice, whole-grain cereal or bread, yogurt or low-fat milk. Don't rely on caffeine; avoid sugary, salty, or fatty foods. Getting enough rest and eating a nourishing breakfast will give you sustained energy and help you concentrate and think clearly.

A final word: Your attitude toward tests can make a big difference. Students often see tests as negative and threatening—even as punishment. Instead, try to think of a test as a learning experience. Try also to consider it an opportunity to demonstrate to yourself and your instructor how much you have learned. Remember that a test can tell you what you understand and how well you understand it. When you get a test back from an instructor, don't look at just the grade. Study the test carefully to see what you missed and why. A test also gives you an opportunity to evaluate the effectiveness of your test preparation techniques.

Five-Day Test Review Plan

Here is a detailed description of an effective five-day plan for preparing for a test. Although you may need more than five days, that is the least amount of time you should allow.

Five days before the test

Get an overview of all the material that will be on the test. This includes text material, class notes, handouts, etc. Identify important main ideas and details and prepare review cards and one or more test review sheets for the material to be covered. (Such cards and sheets summarize all the important points you expect to encounter on the test. You will learn to construct review cards and test review sheets later in this chapter.) You might also have a study guide that accompanies your textbook, or perhaps your instructor has given you a special review guide. In any case, try to anticipate questions that may be asked on the test. This is also the time to identify questions and problem areas you need further help on. By starting five days ahead, you will have allowed yourself enough time to get any help you need. You will have time to ask the instructor or a classmate, or to get help from a tutor. Plan to spend at least 2 hours studying. Take a 5- to 10-minute break after each hour.

Four days before the test

Briefly overview all the material that will be covered on the test; then review and rehearse the first third of the material in detail. First review all the material on your review cards and your test review sheet or sheets. Then, as you carefully study the first third of the material, use rehearsal techniques to memorize it and test yourself on it: that is, write and recite. Remember that you want to transfer the material into long-term (permanent) memory. Write the information; recite the information; test yourself by taking a blank sheet of paper and writing from memory what you have learned. Plan to spend at least 2 hours studying. If there are problem areas, get extra help or clarification from a tutor, a classmate, or your instructor.

Three days before the test

After a brief overview of all the material, review and rehearse the second third of the material in detail. Use the rehearsal techniques of writing and reciting to memorize and test yourself on the material. Plan to spend at least 2 hours studying. If any problem areas still remain, this is the time to clear them up. If you still don't understand, make another attempt at getting some additional help.

Two days before the test

After a brief overview of all the material, review and rehearse the last third of the material in detail. Use the rehearsal techniques of writing and reciting to memorize and test yourself on the material. Plan to spend at least 2 hours studying. Rehearse material in the problem areas that you cleared up earlier.

One day before the test

Make a final review of all of the material. Rehearse! Write! Recite! Test yourself! This is your final study session for the test, a full "dress rehearsal." Use this session to study your review cards and your test review sheet or sheets, covering all the important information in the material. At this point you should be feeling confident about the test. At the end of the day, right before you go to sleep, look through the material one last time; then get a good night's rest. Resist any temptation to relax or celebrate the completion of your review by watching television or going to a movie. These activities create interference that can make it harder to recall information when you take the test.

Using Review Cards to Prepare for a Test

As suggested above, one highly effective way to prepare for a test is to make review cards. You already have some experience with such cards, since you have been completing your chapter-by-chapter review cards throughout *Opening Doors.*

Key term

Test review card: Index card with an important question on the front and the answer on the back.

Another kind of ***review card,*** especially useful in preparing for tests, is an index card with an important question on the front and the answer on the back. The question and answer may have to do with a single main idea and its supporting details, a term and its definition, a name and an identification, a mathematical or chemical formula, and so on. Review cards are an efficient, effective, and convenient way to study for tests. Review cards can be prepared from a textbook or from lecture notes.

The boxes on page 532 show an example of a review card for an important concept presented in a sociology textbook. Notice how this card focuses on one main idea and its two supporting details. Notice also the format of this card: one side presents a probable test question, and the other side answers the question.

Sample Review Card: Front

Card 5
What are the two levels of sociological analysis?

Sample Review Card: Back

The two basic levels of sociological analysis are microsociology and macrosociology.

Microsociology: Small-scale analysis of data derived from the study of everyday patterns of behavior.

Macrosociology: Large-scale analysis of data in which overall social arrangements are scrutinized.

Just as outlining, mapping, and summarizing help you organize material, review cards allow you to arrange material clearly and concisely. Most students prefer to use 3- by 5-inch or 4- by 6-inch index cards. Cards of this size are convenient to carry and can be reviewed whenever you have spare moments. Index cards are available in several colors, and some students find it helpful to use a different color for each chapter or course. Other students use different colors for different categories of study material; for instance, vocabulary terms might be on cards of one color and key people on cards of another color. You may want to number your review cards so that they can be easily rearranged and then put back in order. For instance, you may want to set aside cards with especially difficult questions so that you can give them special attention before the test.

Review cards are helpful in numerous ways. First, since preparing these cards involves writing out certain information, the very act of making them will help you rehearse material and commit it to long-term memory. Do not assume, though, that simply making the review cards is a substitute for rehearsing the information on them.

Second, review cards let you concentrate on one small, manageable part of the material at a time. Lecture and textbook material can seem overwhelming if you try to review it all at once before a test or at the end of a semester, but it can be quite manageable in small parts.

Third, review cards can be especially useful for memorizing key terms, key people, formulas, and the like. For example, a college instructor might require students to learn math or chemistry formulas or to memorize a set of important terms. Learning 10 definitions, names, or formulas a week is much easier than trying to learn 150 of them just before a final exam.

Fourth, review cards can be a good way to review material with a study partner. When you are studying for a test, working with a partner can be highly effective. In fact, even when you use review cards by yourself, it is helpful to say the answers out loud, as you would if you had a partner.

Fifth, effective students try to anticipate test questions, and review cards are a good way to guide this effort. Writing an anticipated test question on the front of a card, with the answer on the back, allows you to test yourself on material before the instructor tests you.

Sixth, review cards can help you monitor your learning by measuring what you know and what you still need to learn or rehearse further.

To sum up, if you prepare your review cards carefully and use them to rehearse and learn information, they can be an important key to success.

Using Test Review Sheets

Suppose that you are going to be given a test in a sociology course. The test will cover a full chapter of your sociology textbook and the corresponding class sessions. Your instructor has announced that you will be allowed to prepare one sheet of notes (front *and* back) to use while you are taking the test. How could you consolidate an entire chapter's worth of information on one sheet of paper?

To begin with, consolidating all this information on a single test review sheet would *not* mean trying to recopy all the lecture notes, handouts, and textbook material in tiny handwriting. In other words, the question really is, "What kind of information would you include on this review sheet?" Preparing the sheet would mean being very selective; it would mean summarizing essential information from different sources, such as the chapter, your own class and textbook notes, and your instructor's handouts.

Key term

Test review sheet: Single sheet of paper consolidating and summarizing, on its front and back, the most important information to be covered on a test.

This example is imaginary, but in fact you should create a real ***test review sheet*** whenever you prepare for a test. You should try to restrict yourself to a single sheet (front and back) consolidating all the crucial information you would bring to the test if you could. (If a test will cover several chapters, though, you might want to prepare several review sheets: one sheet for each chapter.) Preparing such a review sheet is in itself a way of selecting, organizing, and rehearsing the material you must learn.

Obviously, you need to start by identifying major topics that you know will be on the test. Remember that you must be selective, because you cannot include everything. If you have been preparing review *cards* as you went along, then you have already taken the first step in preparing a test review *sheet,* because you have already identified most of the important information you need for the sheet. However, you will probably have to condense this information even more to create your test review sheet.

Another way to proceed with the first step in making a test review sheet is to list the major topics and the most important points about each. If your instructor does not identify the major topics for you, you should check your lecture notes. You should also refer to the main table of contents or to the chapter-opening contents in the textbook for an overview of the material that will be covered. The main headings and subheadings of the chapter are the major topics. If there is no detailed main table of contents or chapter-opening contents, you will need to check the text itself for titles and headings.

Your next step is to organize the material that you will include on the sheet. There is no one "correct" way to organize a test review sheet. However, the chapter material itself may often suggest logical ways in which the sheet can be organized. For example, a test review sheet can be as simple as a list of major topics with key words beside or beneath each topic. It could also consist of a grid of rows and columns, a set of mapped notes, a list of formulas, important terms (with or without definitions), a diagram or sketch, or some combination of these. The key is to organize the test review sheet in some way that is meaningful to *you.* Moreover, since this is your personal review sheet, you should feel free to use abbreviations, symbols, and highlighting in different colors to make this review sheet as clear and helpful to you as possible.

The boxes on pages 535–537 show entries in a table of contents for one chapter of a sociology text (note the major headings and subheadings) and the front and back of a test review sheet that could be prepared for this chapter.

Example: Chapter Table of Contents Used to Prepare a Test Review Sheet

▪ ▪ ▪ ▪ ▪ ▪ ▪

Source: Donald Light, Susanne Keller, and Craig Calhoun, *Sociology,* 5th ed., Knopf, New York, 1989, pp. xi, 3–25.

Sample Test Review Sheet
Front of Page

▪ ▪ ▪ ▪ ▪ ▪ ▪

Chapter 1—Approaches to Sociology

1. SOCIOLOGICAL PERSPECTIVE

Social Facts & Social Causes

Sociology—systematic study of human societies & behavior in social settings
Sociological perspective—lets us see how our background, social position, time, & place affect how we view world & act—also, who we interact with & how others see us
Sociological facts—properties of group life that can't be explained by indiv traits, actions, or feelings. Soc facts emerge from social forces (e.g., concept of beauty, romantic love)

Sociological Imagination

Soc imag—ability to see personal experience in world context (pers ex is limited, so we shouldn't make hasty generalizations)

Science, Sociology, & Common Sense

Scientific method used by sociologists—collect data (facts, statistics); develop theories
Theory—systematic formal explanation of how two or more phenomena are related. Local th = narrow aspect; middle-range th = broader; general th = most comprehensive (explain how several ths fit together). (Contrast w common sense—from pers ex, facts not checked, no organization into ths to be tested.)

Levels of Sociological Analysis

Microsociology—small-scale analysis of data from everyday behavior patterns.
Macrosociology—large-scale anal of data on overall social arrangements.

2. BASIC SOCIOLOGICAL QUESTIONS

What Holds Society Together?

Functional perspective—different parts of society contribute to whole
Power pers—those who control resources prob will shape society to their own advantage

What Is Relationship between Individual & Society?

Structural perspective—indiv choices explained by forces arising from soc organization
Action pers—society shaped by people's actions

Sample Test Review Sheet
Back of Page

▪ ▪ ▪ ▪ ▪ ▪ ▪

3. ORIGINS OF SOCIAL THEORY

Rational-Choice Th

Founder—Adam Smith. People choose & decide for own advantage;
soc = self-regulating system; all parts act in own int; market forces mesh pts into whole.
Expanded by Jeremy Bentham—govt intervention needed to help soc function & let people benefit from resources.

Th of Karl Marx

Economic system shapes soc life, breeds conflict; proletariat (workers) should overcome capitalists (oppressors—owners of resources)

Th of Émile Durkheim

Human behav explained by soc forces binding society (social solidarity); society held together by interrelated working of pts

Th of Max Weber

Power comes from dif factors—education, soc connections, etc.; society produced by actions of indivs. Stressed politics & culture (not only econ like Marx).

Interactionist Th

George Herbert Mead—people interact depending of how they interpret soc situations; we learn our place in world thru soc interactions. Th developed from phenomenology.

4. FOUNDING THEORIES & CONTEMPORARY SOCIOLOGY

Sociologists still influenced by ths above—have expanded orig ths to apply to modern issues. Some try to combine functional and power pres; structural & action-oriented pres.

DEVELOPING CHAPTER REVIEW CARDS

Review cards, or *summary cards,* are an excellent study tool. They are a way to select, organize, and review the most important information in a textbook chapter. The process of creating review cards helps you organize information in a meaningful way and, at the same time, transfer it into long-term memory. The cards can also be used to prepare for tests. The review card activities in this book give you structured practice in creating these valuable study tools. Once you have learned how to make review cards, you can create them for textbook material in your other courses.

Now, complete the five review cards for Chapter 10 by supplying the important information about each topic. When you have completed them, you will have summarized important material about the study skills in this chapter.

Rehearsal and Its Importance to Memory

Chapter 10: Rehearsing Textbook Information and Preparing for Tests

Studying for Tests: General Guidelines

Chapter 10: Rehearsing Textbook Information and Preparing for Tests

Five-Day Test Review Plan

Chapter 10: Rehearsing Textbook Information and Preparing for Tests

Test Review Cards

Chapter 10: Rehearsing Textbook Information and Preparing for Tests

Test Review Sheets

Chapter 10: Rehearsing Textbook Information and Preparing for Tests

READING

Selection 10-1

Psychology

COMMUNICATION, FROM *SOCIAL PSYCHOLOGY*

BY JAMES A. WIGGINS, BEVERLY B. WIGGINS, AND JAMES VANDER ZANDEN

Prepare Yourself to Read

Directions: Do these exercises *before you read Selection 10-1.*

1. First, read and think about the title. What do you already know about communication?

 ____

 ____

2. Next, complete your chapter preview by reading the following:

 First paragraph (chapter introduction)
 Headings in each section
 Words in **bold print** or *italics*
 Illustrations and their legends
 Chapter summary

 On the basis of your preview, what aspects of communication does this chapter seem to be about?

 ____

 ____

Apply Comprehension Skills

Directions: Do these exercises *as you read Selection 10-1.*

- Budget your time for reading this selection. It has four subsections. If you wish, divide your reading time into four sessions.
- To remember essential information, underline or highlight and annotate or take notes on a separate sheet of paper.
- Apply the skills you have learned in this chapter. Create test review cards for one or more of the four sections, making at least one card for every heading within each section. (Your instructor will give you specific directions.)

CHAPTER 5

COMMUNICATION

In Chapter 4, "Social Relationships and Groups," we discussed how people are linked by social relationships—patterns of social interaction and sets of expectations (norms and roles) reflecting and shaping these interaction patterns. We noted that social relationships go through cycles of negotiation and renegotiation. But we said very little about *how* this is accomplished. In this chapter we will focus on the important contribution of **communication**, the process by which people interact and interpret their interactions.

Symbols

When people interact, much of the language, behavior, and appearance of each party constitutes **symbols**—objects or actions that, by social convention, stand for or represent something else. Symbols are *arbitrary* stand-ins for other things; their meanings are not *givens*. Rather, they come to have meaning by virtue of socially shared conventions, that is, understandings between users. For example, you and a friend might agree that if you wink at him at a party, the wink means you're having a good time and want to stay longer. You could just as easily agree that the wink means you're bored and want to escape as soon as possible. Through socialization we learn the meanings assigned by our culture to many symbols. Spoken and written words, for example, are symbols, as are clothing styles and actions such as handshakes and frowns. The traditions and consensus within a society give symbols their meanings. As a result, many symbols have different meanings in different cultures.

Sometimes the parties to an interaction interpret aspects of it differently, and as a consequence, their interaction does not run smoothly. What interests social psychologists is how we negotiate meanings and the implications of this process for our continued interaction. Consider the following newspaper account:

> Stockton, Calif.—The worst possible fate befell two young masked robbers last night. They tried to hold up a party of thirty-six prominent, middle-aged women, but couldn't get anybody to believe they were for real.
>
> One of the women actually grabbed the gun held by one of the youths.
>
> "Why," she said, "that's not wood or plastic. It must be metal."
>
> "Lady," pleaded the man, "I've been trying to tell you, it is real. This is a holdup."

Source: James A. Wiggins, Beverly B. Wiggins, and James Vander Zaden, *Social Psychology,* 5th ed., 1994, pp. 135–170 (chap. 5). Reproduced with permission of McGraw-Hill. (For additional sources, see page 578.)

"Ah, you're putting me on," she replied cheerfully.

The robbers' moment of frustration came about 9:00 p.m. at the home of Mrs. Florence Tout . . . as she was entertaining at what is called a "hi-jinks" party. Jokes and pranks filled the evening. Thus not one of the ladies turned a hair when the two men, clad in black, walked in.

"All right now, ladies, put your rings on the table," ordered the gunman [the women were prominent in Stockton social circles].

"What for?" one of the guests demanded.

"This is a stickup. I'm serious!" he cried.

All the ladies laughed.

One of them playfully shoved one of the men. He shoved her back.

As the ringing laughter continued, the men looked at each other, shrugged, and left empty-handed. (*San Francisco Examiner*, April 4, 1968)*

In this example, interaction was problematic because the participants did not share meanings. The failure of the robbery attempt can be attributed to the *different meanings* that the robbers and the women at the party assigned to the robbers' message. The robbers thought that their symbols—masks, guns, and the words "This is a stickup"—would lead the partygoers to define the situation as a robbery and to give up their valuables.

But that's *not* how the women interpreted the symbols. They saw the masks and guns and heard the words, but these happened in the context of a "hi-jinks" party, where several pranks had already occurred. The women interpreted the robbers' symbols as part of still another joke. Moreover, in the women's minds, the joke did not call for them to actually hand over their valuables. In other words, the robbers and the women arrived at different meanings for the same symbols because they interpreted them in terms of different definitions of the situation. A **definition of the situation** is the meaning we give to an entire situation.

* Reprinted with permission from the San Francisco Examiner. © 1968 San Francisco Examiner.

DEFINITIONS OF THE SITUATION

What we are trying to arrive at when we send and receive various types of symbols is a definition of the situation. We might, for example, have definitions for such situations as a prayer meeting, a camping trip, an accident, an argument, a seduction, a friendly conversation, a tennis match, a robbery, a party, a social psychology class, and so forth. We use whatever information we can to help us define the situation we are in or are about to enter. Some of this information comes in the form of symbols provided by others—communication. Once we arrive at a definition of the situation, we interpret other information in terms of that definition. In other words, the definition of the situation constitutes a type of context for our interpretation of events. If we define the situation as a wedding, for example, and observe that a woman in the front row is weeping, we may interpret her tears as tears of joy. If we define the situation as a funeral, we may be more likely to define her tears as tears of grief.

Arriving at a definition of a situation gives us insight as to the roles people are going to play—allowing us to anticipate the actions of others and adjust our own actions accordingly. Much human interaction occurs among people who do not know one another and who, consequently, have no direct experience on which to base predictions about one another's behavior. *Scripts* are mental representations of sequences of interaction over a period of time. They allow us to quickly and easily fit our behavior with that of others in a situation. We feel quite comfortable going to an appointment with a new dentist, going to a new restaurant, or attending a class for the first time because we know the scripts. This allows us to take for granted certain expectations for our own behavior and the behavior of others in the situation.

When behavior follows a script, interaction proceeds smoothly. This is highlighted by cases in which we *don't* know the script for the situation. If we received an invitation to a state dinner at the White House and planned to attend, we would probably try to find out as much as we could about the script for state dinners. We'd want to know "who does what when?" (See the Student Observation: "Scripts.")

We are, of course, also interested in information not provided by the script for a particular definition of a situation. When visiting the dentist, for example, a patient might also be attentive to symbols indicating whether the dentist intended to carry out a complicated procedure, liked him, seemed competent and professional, or was in a bad mood. He would use this additional information to modify his interaction in that particular encounter with the dentist.

SIGNIFICANT SYMBOLS—SHARED MEANINGS

Because appearances and behaviors — indeed, all the things that can serve as symbols in communication — are interpreted, people may perceive and interpret the same information in different ways. Interpretation provides meaning for the symbol. When a symbol is interpreted similarly by several persons, the symbol is said to be a significant symbol. In other words, **significant symbols** are symbols whose meaning is *shared* by the parties in question. For example, for most Americans, the American flag stands for the country and our pride in it. But for some, it stands for aspects of the American government to which they object. When members of these two groups interact, the American flag will not be a significant symbol. In other words, they will not agree on its meaning.

Significant symbols are important because they allow us to anticipate one another's behavior and, therefore, to coordinate our behaviors. If the symbols we choose are *not* significant symbols — if their meanings are not shared — the chances of coordinating our actions with those of others is greatly diminished.

Subgroups within language groups often have specialized vocabularies or other symbols that emphasize the concepts that are most important to them. In this course, you are learning many of terms which social psychologists use regularly but which are relatively unknown to others. Similarly, physicists, farmers, truck drivers, cooks, physicians, and construction workers all have special vocabularies that allow them to efficiently communicate with one another about the things that are important to them.

STUDENT OBSERVATION

Scripts

People fail to realize how important scripts are until they come into a situation for which they don't have one. A few weeks ago I was reminded of this fact when I attended a retreat of the co-chairs of the committees of the Campus-Y. I was one of the very newest members of the Y, and I didn't know any of the other co-chairs. I had never been to one of the retreats before. When I arrived at the campground, I was painfully aware that I had no *script* — no mental representation of sequences of behavior over time — for this occasion. As all the other committee chairs boldly slung their bags and other gear in a corner of the big log cabin meeting room and laughed and hugged one another in a presumably Campus-Y co-chair fashion, *I was so uncomfortable*! I did not know what an appropriate greeting would be for me, a new, unfamiliar member, nor had I the faintest idea what to do with my camping stuff. I stood very awkwardly — scriptless — until a facilitator, someone who obviously had a script, introduced herself and kindly showed me where to put my backpack and sleeping bag. After watching the others for a while, I began to piece together a script so that I could fit my behavior to theirs. However, I was never more grateful for directions than I was those first minutes at the rustic retreat.

THE TWO SIDES OF WARSPEAK

During the 1991 Persian Gulf War, a *Time* magazine article pointed out that the top brass and the GIs seemed to be speaking two different languages, neither of them English. William Lutz, a Rutgers University English professor, noted that military strategists seemed to have adopted M.B.A.-style buzzwords that reflected an "emphasis on managerial skills," a depersonalization of the enemy, and a distancing from violence, while the men and women in the ranks adopted a more colorful and less distanced way of communicating. Here's a sampler:

Top Brass

Incontinent ordinance: Bombs and artillery shells that fall wide of their targets and hit civilians.
Area denial weapons: Cluster bombs with the ability to wreak great damage over a particular zone.
Ballistically induced aperture in the subcutaneous environment: A bullet hole in a human being.
Coercive potential: The capability of bombs to harm and demoralize soldiers.
Suppressing assets: The destruction of sites containing antiaircraft weaponry.
Unwelcome visit: British term for any foray into enemy territory.
Scenario-dependent, post-crisis environment: Conditions after the war.

Grunts

Echelons beyond reality: The source of orders from superior officers.
High speed, low drag: Phrase indicating that an operation went exactly according to plan.
Micks: Abbreviation of minutes, as in "Give me five micks."
9-4: A more chummy version of the traditional "10-4" radio sign-off.
Suicide circles: Nickname for Saudi traffic roundabouts. A number of allied soldiers died in road accidents in Saudi Arabia.
180 out: The coordinate-minded soldier's term for the wrong answer—180 degrees from the truth.
Strack: To get on the right track, or frame of mind, for battle.

Source: Reprinted from D. Ellis, "The Two Sides of Warspeak," *Time*, February 25, 1991 p. 13. Copyright 1991 Time, Inc. Reprinted by permission.

These special vocabularies are sometimes disparagingly referred to as *jargons*, because the meanings these words have are not shared by the larger population. Thus, although they increase the efficiency of communication among those who share them, they are not effective symbols for communication with those who don't. During the 1991 war against Iraq in the Persian Gulf, the public was exposed to military jargon during the many briefings on the progress of the war. Interested observers noted that the jargons of the commanders and those of the lower-level soldiers differed, perhaps reflecting the two groups' different concerns and perspectives on the situation (see the box "The Two Sides of Warspeak").

KINDS OF SYMBOLS—CHANNELS OF COMMUNICATION

Talking and listening are the activities that we most often associate with communicating. But speech is only one of the kinds of symbols we use to communicate with others. Besides using words, we communicate with qualities of our voices and through nonverbal channels—our facial expressions, body movements, the distances and orientations with which we position ourselves relative to others, and our physical appearance and such personal attributes as hair styles and clothing. Social psychologists and linguists note that these kinds of symbols constitute the *channels of communication* available to us. They distinguish between the verbal and nonverbal channels.

Verbal Symbols

Verbal symbols are of two main types: language and paralanguage. **Language** is our principal vehicle for communication, finding expression in speech and writing. Language allows us to denote abstract ideas and events that are distant in time or place. A single word may have a complex meaning. For example, you may associate the word "home" not only with the house you live in but also with your family and dinnertime, with conflict or happiness and security. So the word "home" may represent more than "bricks and mortar" if it pertains to these other things as well.

We learn words and their meanings from agents of socialization (see our discussion in Chapter 2, "Early Socialization," for details). Because these meanings are largely shared, we are able to communicate with others in our language group. However, we sometimes create new symbols, such as new words, or assign words new meanings that are shared only by members of a particular relationship or group. Such symbols are part of the internal culture of our relationships and groups. They are significant symbols for members of the group, but not for others. For example, you may have a special name for a loved one that stands for your special feelings for that person. (We discussed internal culture in Chapter 4, "Social Relationships and Groups.")

Paralanguage consists of the nonsemantic aspects of speech – the stress, pitch, and volume of speech – by which we communicate meaning. Paralanguage has to do with *how* we say something, not with *what* we say. Tone of voice, inflection, pacing of speech, silent pauses, and extralinguistic sounds (such as sighs, screams, laughs) constitute paralanguage. Paralanguage is what we are referring to when we say, "It wasn't *what* she said; it was the *way* she said it." Consider, for instance, the difference in the meaning of the response "Oh yeah" under the following circumstances:

1. As a retort to the threat "Stop it or I'll smash you!" (hostile intonation)
2. As a response to the sexual invitation "Let's make love." (seductive intonation)
3. As a response to the suggestion "Won't it work if you hold that button down?" (embarrassed acknowledgement)
4. As a response to the question "Are you coming with us?" (affirmation)

Baby talk is a type of paralanguage (Caporael, 1981, Caporael and Culbertson, 1986; DePaulo and Coleman, 1986). While baby talk contains unique words (for example, "choo-choo" for train

STUDENT OBSERVATION

Paralanguage

My roommate provides a good example of the use of paralanguage in his telephone conversations. When he talks to his relatives, he speaks at a higher volume than in normal conversation. He also uses a higher pitch and a very happy tone of voice. When he talks to his girlfriend, he raises his pitch still higher and slows his rate of speech. When speaking to friends, he lowers his pitch and varies his tone of voice more frequently. The variation in paralanguage is really evident when one of his male friends calls when he is expecting his girlfriend. He answers with a high-pitched "Hey!" – but quickly "corrects" his pitch and tone when he realizes who the caller actually is.

and "tum-tum" for stomach), it is also distinctive in its paralinguistic features, especially its high pitch and exaggerated intonations. Indeed, baby talk has been documented in numerous languages. The higher pitch of baby talk may serve to hold babies' attention. Studies show that babies prefer to listen to baby talk (Fernald, 1985). (Before reading further, see the Student Observation: "Paralanguage.")

Nonverbal Symbols

Suppose you can see, through a window across the street, a young man and woman interacting in an apartment. Because of the noise of the traffic below, you can't hear their words, or even their voices, but you can see their faces and movements quite clearly. Without any verbal or paralinguistic cues, do you think you could tell whether the couple was having an argument or beginning a romantic evening together? Your guess just might be correct. This is because, besides speech and paralanguage, we use several kinds of nonverbal symbols to convey or amend meaning. These include body language, interpersonal spacing, and physical characteristics and personal effects. (Before reading further, see the Student Observation: "Symbols.")

Body language (also called **kinesics**) is the nonverbal communication of meaning through physical movements and gestures. We tap our fingers to show impatience. We shrug our shoulders to indicate indifference. We nod our heads to mean "yes" or "um-hum, I'm paying attention." We scratch our heads in puzzlement. We maneuver our bodies to negotiate a crowded setting without touching others. We avoid eye contact to indicate an unwillingness to interact. Through the motions of our bodies, limbs, faces, and eyes we communicate information about our feelings, attitudes, and intentions. This is not to say that we easily decipher the motions, wiggles, and fidgets accompanying ordinary speech. A nonverbal behavior may represent many different meanings, depending on the context in which it occurs – its timing and intensity, and its combination with other verbal and nonverbal behaviors (Zuckerman et al., 1981; Harper, 1985; O'Sullivan et al., 1985).

Eye contact frequently functions as a type of body language. Depending on how people define the situation, eye contact may signal an aggressive or dominating intent, as in a staredown; intimacy or close bonding, as among lovers; or a fervent call for assistance, as with a prisoner of war ap-

STUDENT OBSERVATION

Symbols

When I was about four years old, I attended a wonderful playschool. However, one afternoon my mother was late picking me up. Of course, I was hysterical – I thought my mother was never coming back to get me! From that point on, the playschool was a terrifying place to me. I began to have temper tantrums in the mornings before going, and I cried all day until my mother came to pick me up. Finally, my mother figured out a plan to ease my fear of being left and forgotten. She devised a symbol to represent the fact that she wasn't going to forget about me in the afternoons – she might be late, but she wasn't going to forget and leave me.

The symbol was nothing but a simple lipstick kiss on the back of my hand. It may sound silly, but it worked. Every day when she left me at the playschool, my mother would kiss my hand and leave her lipstick print. This "silly" mark meant the world to me. It was a symbol of security, of my mother's love, and of her promise that she would never forget me.

STUDENT OBSERVATION

Civil Inattention

One interesting example of civil inattention takes place in automatic teller lines. In lines for other kinds of service, people tend to stand with about 1 or 2 feet between them. In automatic teller lines, however, the distance between the person completing the transaction and the next one in line greatly increases. The "next up" must stand at least 4 to 5 feet away and make an obvious effort to gaze at something other than the person completing the transaction, in effect saying, "Don't worry about me. I'm just waiting for my turn – I'm not trying to see your number or how much money you're taking out. I'm no threat."

The other day I was in one of these lines. The next-up man was obviously in a hurry and violated the interpersonal spacing norms either out of carelessness or an effort to hurry the woman completing her transaction. She looked over her shoulder with a sharp, nervous expression on her face, obviously perceiving the opposite of the benign, adequately spaced message: "I'm too close to be normal – I'm looking to see your number or how much money you are taking out. I'm a threat." As soon as he saw her look back, the man sheepishly backed up to the appropriate distance – now saying, "No, I'm really *not* a threat. Sorry!" – and concentrated on the bush to the left, looking embarrassed about having communicated such a threatening message unintentionally.

pearing before a television camera. Gazes come in many variations. We can glare, gawk, ogle, or leer. We alter the symbolism of a gaze by tilting our heads, widening or narrowing our eyes, or lowering or raising our eyebrows. For instance, we typically perceive the lowering of brows as more assertive and domineering than the raising of brows (Mazur et al., 1980).

Eye contact assumes considerable importance in public settings. We employ it to assess strangers and define their intentions. Consider our behavior on a city bus, a subway, or an elevator. We view these forms of public transportation as means of moving from one place to another. Therefore, within such contexts we usually aim to protect our own rights and to maintain a proper social distance from strangers.

One way to achieve these outcomes is through **civil inattention**: we give others enough visual notice to signal to them that we recognize their presence, but then we quickly withdraw visual contact to show that we pose no threat to them and that we do not wish to interact. We do this by cutting off eye contact, a maneuver of civil inattention that Erving Goffman dubs "a dimming of the lights" (1963*b*: 84). Thus, despite the closeness of our bodies and our mutual vulnerability, little focused interaction occurs, few of us are accosted, and few friendships arise. We project cues to ensure that these things *do not take place*. (See the Student Observation: "Civil Inattention.")

Social contexts vary in permissible *looking time* – the amount of time that we can hold another person's gaze without being rude, aggressive, or intimate. The permissible looking time is zero on an elevator; it is a little longer in a crowded subway or bus; and it is still longer out on the street. Apparently, greater leeway is permitted to pedestrians in "looking one another over."

Interpersonal spacing (also termed **proxemics**) is nonverbal communication involving the distances and angles at which people position themselves relative to others. We invite interaction by angling our bodies toward others and discourage it by angling away. We position ourselves closer to those we like and farther from those we don't like.

We also use *markers* – signs that communicate the fact of ownership or legitimate occupancy to keep others at a distance from the territory we want to claim. As markers we use symbols such as nameplates, fences, hedges, and personal belongings. We place a book, handbag, or coat on a table or an empty chair to reserve a place in the library, sunglasses and lotion on a towel to lay claim to a spot on the beach, and a drink on a bar to assert "ownership" of a bar stool (Becker, 1973; Shaffer and Sadowski, 1975). We also use touch to communicate territorial control. For instance, at a game arcade, others are less likely to attempt to use a machine if a person stands near it and touches it than if a person stands off and does not touch it (Werner, Brown, and Damron, 1981).

Physical characteristics and personal effects. We also communicate through the way we look. This includes not only our physical characteristics (such as hair color, skin color, body build, height, the way we groom our bodies) but also the personal effects we choose and display (clothing, jewelry, makeup, choice of beverage, car, the way we decorate our living quarters, and so on). A ring on the fourth finger of the left hand suggests, in our culture, that a person is married. A uniform communicates that the wearer occupies a specific role, such as police officer, airline attendant, or physician. Thus, the uniform sets our expectations for the behavior of the wearer.

Note that some of these aspects of appearance are easily changed. We *choose* our clothing, makeup, grooming styles, and sometimes even hair color. Other aspects of our appearance are not easily changed—such as skin color, height, and body build. Even those aspects of our appearance over which we have little control are used by others to make judgments about us. Black males, for example, sometimes find that their race and gender are viewed as symbols of threat or danger (see the box "Just Walk on By: A Black Man Ponders His Power to Alter Public Space").

Norms define what is considered to be "appropriate dress" in various situations. That's why we tend to have different clothes for different occasions—some for work, some for leisure, some for dress-up nights out. For example, we would think it very odd if a friend attended our backyard cookout in sequined evening dress or a job applicant showed up for an interview in swim trunks and flip-flops. We would probably think such persons socially inept.

Within the range considered situationally appropriate, individuals choose their clothing and other personal effects partly to make a statement about who they are. A woman who wants to be taken seriously as a supervisor at work probably should not wear childish clothing. A manager who

If others attribute meaning to such social characteristics as race and gender, aspects of our appearance serve as symbols for these social categories and communicate information about us.

JUST WALK ON BY: A BLACK MAN PONDERS HIS POWER TO ALTER PUBLIC SPACE

My first victim was a woman—white, well dressed, probably in her early twenties. I came upon her late one evening on a deserted street in Hyde Park, a relatively affluent neighborhood in an otherwise mean, impoverished section of Chicago. As I swung onto the avenue behind her, there seemed to be a discrete, uninflammatory distance between us. Not so. She cast back a worried glance. To her, the youngish black man—a broad six feet two inches with a beard and billowing hair, both hands shoved into the pockets of a bulky military jacket—seemed menacingly close. After a few more quick glimpses, she picked up her pace and was soon running in earnest. Within seconds she disappeared into a cross street.

That was more than a decade ago. I was 22 years old, a graduate student newly arrived at the University of Chicago. It was in the echo of that terrified woman's footfalls that I first began to know the unwieldy inheritance I'd come into—the ability to alter public space in ugly ways. It was clear that she thought herself the quarry of a mugger, a rapist, or worse. Suffering a bout of insomnia, however, I was stalking sleep, not defenseless wayfarers. As a softy who is scarcely able to take a knife to a raw chicken—let alone hold it to a person's throat—I was surprised, embarrassed, and dismayed all at once. Her flight made me feel like an accomplice in tyranny. It also made it clear that I was indistinguishable from the muggers who occasionally seeped into the area from the surrounding ghetto. That first encounter, and those that followed, signified that a vast, unnerving gulf lay between nighttime pedestrians—particularly women—and me. And I soon gathered that being perceived as dangerous is a hazard in itself. I only needed to turn a corner into a dicey situation, or crowd some frightened, armed person in a foyer somewhere, or make an errant move after being pulled over by a policeman. Where fear and weapons meet—and they often do in urban America—there is always the possibility of death. . . .

The fearsomeness mistakenly attributed to me in public places often has a perilous flavor. The most frightening of these confusions occurred in the late 1970s and early 1980s when I worked as a journalist in Chicago. One day, rushing into the office of a magazine I was writing for with a deadline story in hand, I was mistaken for a burglar. The office manager called security and, with an ad hoc posse, pursued me through the labyrinthine halls, nearly to my editor's door. I had no way of proving who I was. I could only move briskly toward the company of someone who knew me. . . .

I began to take precautions to make myself less threatening. I move about with care, particularly late in the evening. I give a wide berth to nervous people on the subway platforms during the wee hours, particularly when I have exchanged business clothes for jeans. If I happen to be entering a building behind some people who appear skittish, I may walk by, letting them clear the lobby before I return, so as not to seem to be following them. I have been calm and extremely congenial on those rare occasions when I've been pulled over by the police.

And, on late-evening constitutions along streets less traveled by, I employ what has proved to be an excellent tension-reducing measure: I whistle melodies from Beethoven and Vivaldi and the more popular classical composers. Even steely New Yorkers hunching toward nighttime destinations seem to relax and occasionally they even join in the tune. Virtually everybody seems to sense that a mugger wouldn't be warbling bright, sunny selections from Vivaldi's *Four Seasons*. It is my equivalent of the cowbell that hikers wear when they know they are in bear country.

Source: Brent Staples, "Just Walk on By: A Black Man Ponders His Power to Alter Public Space," *Ms.*, September 1986, pp. 54, 88. Used by permission of the author.

wants to be seen as "one of the guys" probably should not dress too differently from them.

INTENDED AND UNINTENDED SYMBOLS

Communication involves a behavior or an attribute capable of being perceived by someone else — something that can serve as a symbol. Sometimes we *intend* for our behavior or attribute to be interpeted by others; sometimes we do not. Sociologist Erving Goffman (1959) distinguishes between *expressions given* — intended symbols — and *expressions given off* — symbols we transmit unintentionally. Communication occurs whenever some other person perceives and interprets a symbol we transmit, whether we *intended* to transmit that symbol or not.

We usually consider communication to be an intentional process, and it often is. For example, a graduate who majored in accounting may explain to a job interviewer, "In addition to my coursework, I did the accounting for student government during my junior and senior years at college. I think this experience makes me more prepared than many other graduates to enter a job with substantial responsibility." Here, the speaker is sending verbal signals that she hopes will serve as symbols of her suitability as a job candidate. She is also likely to have sent nonverbal messages intended to convey the same meaning — such as dressing in a suit, presenting a neatly prepared résumé, and being punctual for the interview.

But a sender may also deliver messages *without* intending to. The woman in our example almost certainly does *not* intend to send signals indicating that she is extremely nervous during the job interview. Nevertheless, her unsteady voice and trembling hands might communicate her nervousness to the interviewer. Similarly, the woman's wedding band might communicate her maturity and responsibility to the interviewer, even though she hasn't thought about communicating this or may not even be aware that her wedding band has been noticed by the interviewer. In most situations, we both give and give off expressions — through our appearance and behavior — that are interpreted by others. We communicate both intentionally and unintentionally.

MULTICHANNEL COMMUNICATION

Ordinarily, communication takes place through several communications channels simultaneously. Even on the telephone, both linguistic and paralinguistic cues are available to us, although body movements, facial expressions, spacing, and personal effects are not. In face-to-face conversation, we may use all the channels of communication. Sometimes, the information provided by a single channel can be interpreted in more than one way. For example, intense looking may indicate either love or hostility. A tense body posture may signal respect or hostility. The meaning of such behaviors is usually clarified when we look at the context provided by additional behavior channels. Thus we often impute love to an intense gaze when it is combined with close distance and relaxed posture (Schwarz, Foa, and Foa, 1983). In contrast, intense gaze coupled with loud speech and negative facial expression would probably be interpreted as anger. Thus, we decode most accurately when multiple communication channels convey what appears to be consistent information.

But if we had access to only a single channel of communication, which channel would give us the best (most accurate) assessment of a person's emotion? Research suggests that judgments based on verbal content are the most accurate. One such study presented subjects with passages from the 1976 televised debate between vice-presidential candidates Walter Mondale and Robert Dole. The researchers selected twelve passages for each speaker, half of which seemed to convey positive emotions and half negative. Subjects were presented with only one of several channels of communication available in the standard videotape of the passages: (1) verbal only — a written transcript; (2) video only — with audio removed; or (3) paralinguistic only—the audio track with content filtered out but with paralinguistic features such as pitch, loudness, rate, and so forth, preserved. The subjects' judgments about the positivity or negativity of the emotions being expressed were compared to those of another group of subjects who viewed the standard videotape, which contained both audio and video. The judgments of subjects who read the written transcript—the verbal content—most closely matched the judgments of subjects with complete information (Krauss et al., 1981). The results of this study indicate that when the information provided by various channels is reasonably consistent, the verbal channel contributes most to the *accuracy* of our judgments of positivity and negativity of emotion.

But sometimes the information conveyed through various channels appears *inconsistent*. What do we do when that happens? Albert Mehrabian (1972) designed a study to answer this question. He had actors display contradictory verbal, paralinguistic, and facial cues. In deciding which emotions were the true ones, subjects judging the actors' emotions assigned the most importance to facial cues, less to paralinguistic cues, and the least importance to verbal cues. Although they may disagree on the exact proportion of meaning attributable to verbal and to nonverbal cues, many researchers have found evidence that when observers are faced with inconsistent information, they weigh nonverbal symbols most heavily and tend to give very little weight to verbal symbols (Argyle, Alkema, and Gilmour, 1971; Archer and Akert, 1977; DePaulo, et al., 1978). Perhaps we believe that nonverbal channels are more likely to reveal a person's "true" feelings when we don't trust the verbal channel.

In real life, of course, much depends on the situation, the kind of behavior being judged, and the availability of multiple channels of information. Studies suggest that, when they are available, we make use of multiple channels of information, interpreting each within the context of the others (Zuckerman, Depaulo, and Rosenthal, 1981; Harper, 1985; O'Sullivan et al., 1985).

What We Communicate

The previous section focused on the different types of symbols we use to communicate with others. Now let's turn to *what* we communicate—the various types of meaning we can convey through the use of symbols.

TASK INFORMATION

Some communicative behavior is, of course, task-oriented, or aimed at getting something done. For example, a boss communicates on the job in order to coordinate her actions with those of co-workers to produce a product, such as an automobile or a report. Thus, the boss tells her secretary when a report is needed and specifies the typeface and margins she requires. Or you might communicate with your friends about plans for a party in order to coordinate your actions with theirs so that everyone knows when and where the party will be and so that you don't end up with lots of munchies but no beer. A student calls his parents to tell them that he is working hard, but that this is a particularly difficult semester, in order to prepare them for the disappointing grades he anticipates.

Task information is perhaps the most obvious kind of information we communicate. But we inevitably communicate several kinds of meanings at once. Our communicative behavior reflects the intimacy of our relationships with other persons, reflects and reinforces our relative status in the group, and provides information about ourselves (Patterson, 1988).

EXPRESSIONS OF INTIMACY

Relationships vary in terms of intimacy, or closeness, and we provide symbols to communicate degrees of intimacy and liking to our partners and other, third-party observers. For example, a man might choose particular verbal and nonverbal behaviors to encourage observers of his interaction to perceive him as a loving spouse, a devoted friend, or a disinterested date.

Relationship partners sometimes cooperate to present a particular image of their relationship. A feuding marital couple might agree to present a harmonious image when they are in public. Their nonverbal behaviors, such as hand-holding and mutual gazing, serve to promote the desired image of their relationship. When partners in a close relationship enter a setting where their closeness is unknown to others, they often display "withness cues" (Scheflen and Ashcraft, 1976) or "tie-signs" (Goffman, 1971) to signal that they are a "couple." A jealous partner may initiate higher levels of nonverbal involvement toward his or her partner in order to "stake a claim" to the partner. On the other hand, exaggerated noninvolvement, such as sitting far apart, may be used to signal to others that the relationship is *not* a close one.

We use both verbal and nonverbal symbols to express and promote intimacy.

Intimacy with Words

Some languages, such as French and Spanish, have formal and familiar forms of second-person pronouns. In intimate relationships, the familiar form is used. Similarly, in most languages, forms of address indicate intimacy. We frequently use only first names in interactions with intimates, while titles and last names are more commonly used with strangers or those with whom we have only formal relationships. Imagine your mother's reaction if you were to insist on addressing her as "Mrs." followed by her last name – a more intimate form of address for your own mother is expected. But when you first meet a friend's mother, the formal "Mrs." would be considered appropriate.

Intimacy also affects conversational style. Analyses of telephone conversations have showed that, in comparison to strangers and casual acquaintances, friends use more implicit openings, such as "Hi" or "Hi. It's me." They also introduce more topics into their conversations and are more responsive to their friends (Hornstein, 1985). Other studies suggest that as closeness increases, partners develop communication patterns (part of their internal culture) – including speech rhythms, pitch, and movements – that are increasingly personalized, synchronized, and efficient (Baxter and Wilmot, 1985).

Intimates often develop their own jargon – private symbols, including words and phrases commonly used by others, that have special meanings for them. When these words or phrases are used publicly, intimates may exchange a knowing glance, a wink, or a smile. A person is likely to feel disappointment if her or his partner uses these special words or way of talking with someone else.

Intimacy Without Words

Nonverbal behaviors can also indicate the closeness of relationships. In several studies, observers inferred stronger liking and higher levels of sexual involvement between partners whose level of reciprocated gaze was higher (Kleinke, Meeker, and LaFong, 1974; Thayer and Schiff, 1977). Other studies suggest that postural congruence or matching – in which participants assume postures that are carbon copies or mirror images of one another – reflect greater rapport or the desire to promote a closer relationship (LaFrance and Ickes, 1981).

In close relationships touch signals positive affect, such as support, appreciation, inclusion, sexual involvement, or affection (Jones and Yarbrough, 1985). Support touches are intended to nurture or reassure the other. Appreciation touches, which signal gratitude, are often accompanied by a verbal expression of thanks. Inclusion touches, such as holding hands or putting an arm around a partner, emphasize closeness. Touches signaling sexual interest usually involve holding or caressing the partner on the chest, pelvis, or buttocks. Affection touches are used to express general positive regard toward the partner.

EXPRESSIONS OF STATUS

An individual's status is his or her relative standing vis-à-vis others, and a person's status may differ from one social situation to the next. A college sophomore may have relatively low status compared with seniors but high status relative to freshmen. The same person may have high status among the friends with whom he plays poker on Thursday nights but lower status among those with whom he plays softball on Tuesday afternoons. In social situations, persons with higher status generally exercise greater power and control. Status is reflected and reinforced through communicative behaviors.

Status with Words

Relative status in relationships is clearly communicated by forms of address. People with lower status use formal forms of address for those with higher status. People with higher status often use familiar forms to address those whose status is lower. Two people with equal status tend to employ the same form of address with each other. Both will use either formal ("Dr.," "Mrs.," "Ms.," "Professor") or familiar ("John," "Pat") forms, depending on how well they know each other. When we are unsure about our status relative to someone else, we are faced with a dilemma. A familiar example is the problem of what to call our in-laws – "Mr. and Mrs."? "Mom and Dad"? or (after the arrival of grandchildren) "Grandma and Grandpa"? When we feel uncertain about how to address someone, we sometimes avoid calling him or her anything at all (Little and Gelles, 1975). Other strategies for masking our uncertainty without using a formal title that confers too much status or a familiar address that confers too little include using ambiguous forms of address (such as "Sir," "Miss," "Ma'am," or "Ms.") or inventing an in-between form (such as "Doc" for a physician or professor).

Our choices of vocabularies and pronunciations reflect our relative status and, consequently, influence our relationships. We often adjust our speech to express status differences appropriate to changing situations (Stiles et al., 1984). For example, there are words and phrasings we would use with our children but not with our spouses, and vice versa. A person might tell a child, "Pick up all those magazines you left in the living room, right now!" but the same person would probably address a spouse more politely: "The living room sure is getting messy." In our culture, polite, indirect phrasing is considered more appropriate between equal-status adults.

Similarly, social class and racial, ethnic, and regional differences in vocabulary, pronunciation, and speech style can have a large impact on communication. Recall our discussion in Chapter 3, "Socialization over the Life Course," regarding class differences in communication styles that not only reflect but also perpetuate status differences from one generation to the next.

Paralinguistic behaviors also communicate status. Higher-status speakers talk more frequently, longer, and more loudly and interrupt their partners more in conversations than do lower-status speakers (Brown, 1980; Street and Brady, 1982; Cappella, 1985; Street and Cappella, 1985; Weimann, 1985; Street and Buller, 1988). People with lower status show that they are paying attention by such responses as "Mmmm" at appropriate times. When people of the same status interact, they use these paralinguistic cues more equally (Leffler, Gillespie, and Conaty, 1982). Studies suggest that influence is enhanced by using the paralinguistic behaviors deemed appropriate to one's status in the group (Ridgeway, 1987).

Status Without Words

Status is also communicated through body language (Mazur et al., 1980; Edinger and Patterson, 1983; Givens, 1983). When a person in authority talks to a subordinate, the lower-ranking person listens intently and keeps his or her eyes riveted to the superior. Looking about would indicate disrespect. But when the subordinate is speaking, it is deemed appropriate for the boss to look around or gaze at his or her watch. And people in submissive roles tend to crouch slightly and display self-protective stances (e.g., folding their arms or hugging themselves, crossing their legs, or reaching up and touching their throats). People in dominant roles typically use more expansive gestures, (such as spreading their arms and legs, thereby creating an air of assurance) (Leffler, Gillespie, and Conaty, 1982).

A person can convey his or her higher status by patting a low-status person on the back or shoulder, a behavior not permitted to a person of subordinate rank. And the high-status person takes the lead. If he or she remains standing, then the subordinate is also expected to stand. Only when the high-status person sits can the lower-status person feel free to sit down.

INFORMATION ABOUT OURSELVES: FACEWORK

Some of our communication behavior is designed to deliberately present or enhance an identity or image we have of ourselves or of our relationships. Such actions illustrate that meanings are not fixed entities that set in motion an automatic unfolding of behavior. The activities of others enter as factors in the formation of our own conduct.

The need for the negotiation occurs when interactants do not share definitions of the situation. For example, suppose that Linda, the chairperson of a committee, is making a request of Paul, an older colleague on the committee. If Paul defines the situation as one in which he, an older, experienced committee member, should be advising an inexperienced younger committee member, he and Linda are likely to see each other as being too directive. When this happens, each is likely to ask, "What's going on here?" By getting additional information from each other and making adjustments, Linda and Paul may reach a shared definition of the situation – or they may not. The flow of the interaction will be affected by their ability or inability to arrive at a single script to govern the interaction.

Upon discovering that something is wrong – in this case, each one's thinking that the other is being too directive – Linda and Paul might respond by providing additional information about their own meanings. Linda might say, "Well, as chair of the committee, I think we should . . . ," or Paul might say, "If you had more experience, I think you would see that. . . ." These phrases would at least let each of them know where the other was "coming from."

From here, they might come to agreement by either one's giving up his or her own position in favor of the other's or by reaching a compromise (e.g., the young, inexperienced chair of the committee is making a polite request of the older, experienced, distinguished member of the committee). On the other hand, each might cling to his or her early meanings or adjust them so that they are even more discrepant. For example, Linda might change her definition of the situation to portray herself as the young, promising chair of the committee arguing with an old stick-in-the-mud committee member. Paul's definition might depict himself as the experienced, distinguished committee member being insulted by the uppity young chairperson. Whether Linda's interaction with the older committee member proceeds smoothly or problematically or is terminated altogether depends in part on whether she and Paul can arrive at a mutually acceptable definition of the situation.

In Chapter 1, we first mentioned sociologist Erving Goffman and his ideas about "impression management" – the routine ways in which we try to manage the impressions of ourselves as well as those of others. In everyday life, we often explain our own and other people's behavior through appeals to "face" (Tracy, 1990; Holtgraves, 1992): I was trying to give him a way to *save face*. *Face* is a social phenomenon referring to our concern with personal reputation – the public images we claim for ourselves or attribute to others. The communication strategies we use to enact, support, or challenge these public images are called **facework** (Goffman, 1955). Facework is one of the ways we negotiate with others about the meanings of our actions. The goal of such conduct is to enhance or protect our own face claims and/or to support or challenge others' face claims. According to Goffman (1971), these strategies are either "corrective" or "preventive."

Corrective Facework

Corrective facework consists of practices we employ to restore face *after* it has been attacked or threatened. Sociologist C. Wright Mills noted, in a classic article, that along with learning norms of action for various situations we learn acceptable explanations, which he called "vocabularies of motive" (1940: 909). For example, we often use *accounts* — explanations we offer to make our inappropriate behavior appear more reasonable (Cody and McLaughlin, 1985; Snyder, 1985). Accounts take four forms: excuses, justifications, concessions, and refusals. *Excuses* are statements admitting the inappropriateness of our behavior or its consequence but denying our responsibility for it. For instance, "I know you had to wait a long time because I was late, but I had a flat tire." *Justifications* are statements we provide that admit responsibility for our behavior or its consequence but deny its inappropriateness, reinterpreting it in a more socially acceptable manner: "You would have hit him too if he had said that about your wife."

In a *concession*, we neither deny responsibility nor attempt to justify our conduct. Rather, we simply admit to the failure in question and frequently offer an apology or expression of remorse or offer to make restitution: "I acted foolishly; I'm sorry." On the other hand, *refusals* involve denying that the act in question was actually committed: "I was *not* late! I said I'd be here at 3:30!" Refusals may also include a denial of the other party's right to punish; "Don't you dare scold *me* for being late! How late were *you* last night?" Accounts are discussed further in the box "Facework by Students: Accounts for Absences."

To minimize threats to others' face, we are often studiously inattentive to small lapses in their behavior (Edelman, 1985; Cupach, Metts, and Hazelton, 1986; Knapp, Stafford, and Daly, 1986). For example, we might pretend not to notice the quiet burp emitted by the person seated next to us at the table. We sometimes provide facework to protect the reputations of others. "It's OK, I know you are busy" may give a spouse a (corrective) excuse for her or his failure to pick up the dry cleaning.

Preventive Facework

Whereas corrective facework consists of the practices we engage in *after* our face is damaged or threatened, *preventive facework* consists of the things we do *when we anticipate* damage to face. We use such practices to avoid punishment for a future behavior or to assess the consequences of our actions. For example, asking someone to do something for us reduces our face if we are seen to have acted inappropriately. We can reduce the face threat of making such requests in several ways: (1) by seeking permission to make the request in the first place — "May I ask you a favor?"; (2) by offering an excuse for making the request — "I'm going to *have* to miss our next class because I have a job interview at that time"; or (3) by pleading — "Please, this is very important to me."

We also protect our face by using *disclaimers* intended to convey that, despite our present behavior, we normally abide by the rules: "I normally wouldn't ask to be excused from class, but. . . ." When making what another person might consider a negative statement or criticism, we might use a disclaimer such as, "I know I shouldn't say this, but . . ." or "I'm not prejudiced, but. . . ." When offering advice that may not be well received, we might say, "I know I'm not an expert, but . . ." or "I know it's none of my business, but. . . ." These tactics take away the other person's ability to damage our face by pointing out our weakness: "You're no expert!" or "It's none of your business!"

We may protect the face claims of ourselves and others by preceding a request with a question that suggests to them an excuse for their refusal. For example, "Are you going to be home tonight?" allows the person to answer "No" (without embarrassment to either party) before being placed in the position of refusing a request to pay the person a visit.

Individuals differ in the face concerns they bring to each interaction (O'Keefe and Shepherd, 1987; O'Keefe, 1988). An insecure person may approach the interaction hoping only to avoid embarrassment, while a confident, outgoing person may want to be the focus of attention. And the face wants that individuals pursue may be different in different contexts. For example, sometimes we want to be seen as fun and likable, and other times we want to be seen as firm or even intimidating. This means that communicators need to

FACEWORK BY STUDENTS: ACCOUNTS FOR ABSENCES

Kathleen Kalab (1987) studied the "vocabularies of motive" provided by students when they missed her introductory sociology and social psychology classes. She told her students on the first day of class that they would be expected to give her a written reason for any missed class. Over two semesters, she received 270 notes.

When she analyzed the notes, Kalab found that only about 8 percent contained *justifications.* All of the justifications used by Kalab's students were "appeals to higher loyalties." They suggested that although the student was responsible for missing class – normally a bad thing – doing so was necessary because obligations to relatives and friends had to be placed ahead of the obligation to be in class on a particular date: "The reason I wasn't in your class last Friday and Monday is because my grandmother had a stroke and I had to fly home early." "On [date] I had to attend the funeral of a friend's mother." "Here we go again! I really am sorry to have missed your class [date]. Believe it or not, a friend of mine (not myself) got stranded? at a motel. She called me up Friday morning and like a fool I missed class to pick her up in Russellville. What else could I do?" (Kalab, 1987: 74–75).

Most of the accounts Kalab received were *excuses.* In these notes students admitted to the negative aspect of missing class but attempted to lessen their individual responsibility through the use of five major themes: reference to biological factors, control by another person, oversleeping, other coursework, and accidents. It is not surprising that students made illness their number-one excuse, because illness is commonly recognized as an excuse for not fulfilling various social obligations. It is also an excuse that can be used more than once without being viewed skeptically – and it was used more than once by many of Kalab's students.

Excuses involving control by another person included organizational demands ("The reason for missing your class on Friday, [date] was because I had a cross-country meet to run and we left at 10:30 a.m."); appointments set by others with higher status ("I missed your class on Friday in order to make a doctor's appointment."); and ride providers ("I was absent Friday [date] because my only ride home was leaving at 1:00. I hadn't been home in an awfully long time. Thanks.").

A third, and less common, theme among excuses was oversleeping. Intentional wit and humor were more likely to be used in notes about oversleeping than in those for other excuses. One student wrote, "I'm sorry I missed Friday. My id took over and wouldn't let my superego in until it was too late. Basically I overslept. (I had no intention of missing.) Thank you." Most students who used oversleeping as a reason seemed to recognize it as a rather weak excuse for missing class; very few students used it as an excuse more than once.

Some students' excuses involved missing class in order to do other classwork: "I am sorry that I was not in class on Wednesday [date]. I was studying for a very very important test. Thank you." When using the "other classwork" excuse, students were more serious than when writing about oversleeping. Only one student used this excuse more than once.

The final, and least used, type of excuse Kalab identified in her study involved accidents. Accounts that attribute responsibility to accidents emphasize hazards in the environment. The appeal to accidents often works because we all know that we cannot totally control our environment. Almost half the students' accident notes referred to faulty alarm clocks. The most unique excuse Kalab received was in the accident category:

> I was absent Friday, [date] because the dye I used Thursday night to turn my hair black somehow changed to green when I washed it Friday morning. I'm talking green-bean green! I spent 3 hours and 36 dollars to return my hair to a normal hair color. (Kalab, 1987: 80)

As with oversleeping and other coursework, accident excuses were not used more than once. Kalab notes that accident excuses are not likely to work if they are overused. We honor such excuses precisely because they do not occur often.

A few of the notes Kalab received provided neither excuses nor justifications for missing class. For whatever reason, on these occasions, the students didn't try to explain their negative act in a way designed to protect or restore their face. One note said:

> Yes, I was absent from your class on Friday, [date]. (Bet it was a whole lot quieter!) I have no good excuse. I didn't go home. I blew off *all* my classes Friday. And I'll be honest – I enjoyed every minute of it. Thank you. (Kalab, 1987: 82)

And another simply stated, "I can't remember why I was absent Wed."

decide which aspect of another's identity is governing the other's face claims in a particular situation. In fact, orienting remarks to a contextually inappropriate face of the other may be (or may be seen as) a strategy to attack the other or to enhance one's own face.

Even in a single situation, our face needs may conflict. We want to be connected to, and intimate with, others, but we also want to be independent and autonomous. We might want to be both fair and firm. We want to be honest *and* considerate. Behaviors that support one of the face needs can undermine the other. We sometimes deal with such conflict through a kind of facework called *equivocating* (Bavelas, 1983, 1985; Bavelas and Chovil, 1986; Bavelas et al., 1988). For example, if someone gives us a gift that we don't really like, we might equivocate by responding, "Oh, how thoughtful of you!"

Social situations also sometimes involve tensions between the face needs of interactants. In some situations, to protect our own face, we must challenge someone else's (Craig, Tracy, and Spisak, 1986). For example, to protect her identity as a competent student, a woman who has just received a failing grade on an exam might portray her professor as incompetent by suggesting that he gave inadequate instructions about what the exam would cover, wrote unclear questions on the exam, or misgraded.

Nothing guarantees that our facework, whether corrective or preventive, will soothe the interaction and allow us to avoid or reduce the disruptive consequences of our actions. Instead, the facework itself may become a *second* source of controversy: "You are always late! I'm sick of your excuses!"

We have seen that communication takes place through the exchange of various types of symbols, both verbal and nonverbal, which convey various types of meaning—about tasks, intimacy, status, and self. We have noted that communication involves the negotiation of meanings and have discussed some of the processes through which negotiation takes place. Now let's turn to a discussion of *how* we communicate—the rules of conversation.

How We Communicate: Rules of Conversation

All human encounters involve, in one way or another, the transfer of information. If we were capable of sending and receiving information simultaneously, regardless of the complexity and amount of information presented, we would not need rules governing the flow of information. However, because humans have finite information-processing capacities, human interactions must be governed by some rules of procedure that control the flow of information and signal when speaking and listening roles are to be switched. Besides solving technical problems of sequencing, so that communication can take place more smoothly, these rules of procedure also influence our impressions of who is in control of a situation, who is a competent social actor, who is friendly, and who is shy. Thus, interpersonal power, status, competence, and attraction depend, at least partly, on our ability to control speaking and listening roles (Cappella, 1985).

Both verbal behavior and nonverbal behaviors such as gaze, touch, facial expressions, postural shifts, gestures, and paralinguistic cues often signal immediate or impending changes in the state of conversation (Button and Lee, 1987; Leeds-Hurwitz, 1989; Goodwin and Heritage, 1990; Boden and Zimmerman, 1991; Maynard and Clayman, 1991). The regulation of conversation, such as who should speak when and about what, usually occurs without our awareness. As an analogy, consider how we navigate a crowded sidewalk. Through mutual glances and gestures we communicate with one another about our speed and direction of movement so as to minimize collisions. In effect, these glances and gestures function as routing or crash-avoidance devices. Just as we want to avoid collisions on sidewalks and streets, it is desirable to avoid simultaneous talking in conversations. Typically, we take turns in speaking and listening. We spend relatively little time in mutual silence or simultaneous talking, and usually the transitions from one speaker to another are without perceptible speaker overlap or pause (Trimboli and Walker, 1982, 1984).

How do we manage to avoid verbally bumping into one another in our conversations? The answer lies in the rules and signals with which we regulate conversation.

INITIATING CONVERSATIONS

When and how to start a conversation is governed by several rules. *Initiation rules* encourage us to initiate conversations in some situations and discourage us from doing so in others. For example, whenever we encounter friends or acquaintances we are almost always expected to say "Hi" and are frequently expected to initiate small talk or conversation. We are expected *not* to begin conversations with strangers in the same settings.

Conversations may be initiated with an *attention-getting sequence* such as a greeting, question, knock on the door, or ring of the telephone. Such efforts may be successful or not. In response to an attention-getting attempt, the person being addressed may signal that he or she is paying attention and is ready to interact. In face-to-face interaction, eye contact is a critical signal of availability. For example, a voice from down the hall calls "Sally!" Sally looks toward the voice and sees John, and she returns the greeting, "Hi, John!" John smiles and waves and then turns his gaze back to the bulletin board in front of him. No further interaction takes place. If John smiles and waves and *holds* Sally's gaze, Sally is under an obligation to interact further (Goffman, 1981). When people ignore our attention-getting attempts—violating the rules of conversation—we consider them rude, snobbish, or psychologically absent (absorbed in other thoughts, asleep, intoxicated, and so on).

If the attention-getting sequence is successful, it will probably be followed by a "*how are you*" *sequence* before another topic is introduced. For example:

J: Sally!
S: Hi, John! What's up?
J: Not much. What about with you?
S: Been studying for my physics exam. Are you going to the party on Friday?

Most telephone conversations begin with an attention-getting/answer sequence, followed by an *identification-recognition sequence*, and then by a "how are you" sequence, before another topic is introduced (Schegloff, 1979):

[Ring]
W: Hello.
S: Dr. Wiggins?
W: Yes.
S: Hi. This is Mary Jenkins . . . from your Soc. 51 class. How are you?
W: Fine, thanks, Mary. What can I do for you?
S: Well, um . . . I'm not going to be able to be in class on Friday for the exam.

In face-to-face situations that do not offer us much information about *who* the other person is (such as at a large party where most of the other guests are strangers to us), we may also proceed with an identification-recognition sequence, in part as a search for an opening topic of conversation:

A: Hi, I'm Todd Baker.
B: Hello, I'm Joanne Summers.
A: Are you a friend of Joe's [the party's host]?
B: I guess you could say so. I'm his fiancée. What about you?
A: Oh, I just met Joe. I came to the party with a mutual friend—Paul Andrews.

This sequence offers enough information to continue the conversation if the two participants desire to do so. For example, Todd could ask Joanne about her wedding plans. Joanne could ask how Todd knows Paul Andrews or how Paul Andrews knows Joe. On the other hand, Todd may be hoping for a romantic encounter with someone at the party, and discovering that Joanne is Joe's fiancée may squelch his interest in pursuing the conversation. Similarly, if Joanne doesn't know Paul Andrews, Todd and Joanne's conversation topics are limited, and they may begin to look elsewhere for conversation partners.

In special situations, we dispense with most, if not all, of these initiation sequences. We seldom engage in them with our intimates. In emergencies, we dispense with them even when initiating a conversation with a stranger. For example, Whalen and Zimmerman (1987) have observed that emergency phone calls dispense with greetings in order to get more quickly to the reason for the call:

[Ring]
P: Newton Police.
C: I'd like to report a stolen car.
P: Your name?
C: Jack Jones.
P: Address?

The first response to the attention getter (ring) also verifies for the caller that he has reached the intended party (the police). The caller immediately states his reason for calling. Then the police officer asks questions to obtain the critical information needed to respond to the request for help. A similar modification of face-to-face interaction patterns occurs in emergency situations:

A: Hey! I can use some help here. This woman has fainted.
B: Have you called an ambulance?

Some role relationships allow us to skip initiation sequences. For example, it is acceptable for a waiter to skip the initiation rituals and ask a customer, "Are you ready to order?" Although the customer is otherwise a stranger, his or her strangeness is not absolute. The waiter and customer each are aware of the role of the other, and being in these reciprocal roles makes an initiation ritual unnecessary.

Initiation rules also *discourage* us from initiating conversations in some situations. For example, most of us are hesitant to interrupt when someone is busy, to initiate conversations with strangers, or to talk during class, a movie, or a church service.

However, violations of these rules may be excused if prefaced by *intrusion sequences* which offer an acknowledgment or apology for the intrusion: "Excuse me" or "Sorry to bother you." This may be followed by a signal from the person being addressed which indicates that the speaker can proceed with her or his intended conversation ("That's OK, what is it you want?") or by a signal indicating that the intrusion is not welcome ("I'm busy. What do you want?")

In some encounters with strangers, the rules against initiating conversations are relaxed. Simply sharing a situation with others provides us with some information about them, offering us an excuse for initiating conversation. For example, we may be attending a party, waiting in line for a bus or basketball tickets, or sharing a view of the Grand Canyon. In such situations we probably could comment on the particular situation we are currently sharing without breaching an intrusion rule: "Why don't they stop those guys from breaking into the line?" "Nice camera!" While these comments probably would not be considered offensive, they may or may not lead to an extended conversation, and we would be expected to respect the other's privacy if he or she did not encourage us to pursue the conversation.

KEEPING CONVERSATIONS GOING

We have described how we initiate conversations, but how do we keep them going? Communication is a shared social accomplishment. Through verbal and nonverbal feedback, listeners help us assess how effectively we are communicating. Any subtle vocal or nonverbal response that a listener makes while a speaker is talking is called **back-channel feedback**. This feedback helps us know whether we are keeping our listeners' interest and being understood. Listeners may signal their *attention* to us by simply looking at us, perhaps occasionally nodding their heads. To indicate that they *understand* us, they may use brief vocal insertions such as "Oh," "Yeah," "OK," or "I see"; complete our unfinished sentences; or restate in a few words our preceding thoughts (Kraut, Lewis, and Swezey, 1982; Jefferson, 1984; Heritage, 1984*b*). Smiles and laughs as well as frowns and tears may indicate understanding *if they are appropriate to the speaker's topic*. For example, a listener's laugh following a speakers's joke indicates understanding. However, if it follows a serious comment, it indicates that the listener does not understand or is trying to disrupt the speaker's talking (Jefferson, 1985; Drew, 1987). Listeners also unconsciously display subtle rhythmic body movements — such as swaying, rocking, and blinking — that are precisely synchronized with the speech sounds of the speaker when communication is going well (Kendon, Harris, and Key, 1970).

The timing of feedback is also important, often occurring when the speaker pauses or turns his or her head toward the listener. When listener feedback is mistimed or absent, the speaker may undertake some "repair work" in order to regain the listener's attention and involvement — by inserting "You know," "You see," or "Understand?" prior to or after pauses (Fishman, 1980) or by asking simple yes-no questions such as "OK so far?" or "Are you with me?" (Goodwin, 1987*a*). If we feel the listener is not paying attention or doesn't understand, we may restart the conversation with such phrases as "What I mean to say . . ." or "My point is. . . ." If these efforts fail to repair the conversation, our speech is likely to deteriorate, becoming more wordy, less efficient, and more general. We may hesitate or even stop talking.

REGULATING TURN TAKING

As speakers, we are interested not only in maintaining our listeners' attention and understanding but also in keeping the floor. We do not want to be interrupted until we have made our points, and we exhibit cues that maintain our turns. One way to do this is to verbally indicate that we intend to make a series of remarks, for example, "First of all" or "To begin with," followed by "Another thing." We may signal our desire to keep speaking by maintaining the same voice pitch and keeping our heads straight, our eyes unchanged, and our hands gesturing. As we near what would normally be the point where someone else would talk, we may talk faster, filling the pauses with sounds such as "uh" and "umm" or deliberately avoid finishing a sentence by ending each utterance with "and . . ." or "but the umm. . . ." At the same time, our listeners signal their willingness to allow us to continue speaking by using some of the same cues they use to indicate attention and understanding — for example, an "mm-hmm" or a nod of the head (Schegloff, 1987*a*, *b*).

However, turns at talking do not always proceed smoothly. Sometimes we are interrupted. As with intrusions in initiating conversations, some interruptions of ongoing talk evoke an apology — an intrusion ritual; others do not. When seeking a point of clarification, a listener may interrupt a speaker by raising a hand and/or saying, "Excuse me. What do you mean?" When attempting to challenge a speaker's information, a listener forgoes the pleasantries of an intrusion ritual; the intruding listener may try to complete the speaker's sentence and then continue on with his or her own sentence, may say something like "Just wait a minute. Do you really believe that? That's absurd," or may laugh when the speaker is obviously being serious. Of course, a speaker can attempt to rebuff an interruption with a raised hand, indicating "Let me finish," or may increase the volume of her or his voice to drown out the interruption.

Some interruptions are more permanent than others. An interruption that takes the floor from the original speaker for a brief time and then returns it to the speaker is called a *side sequence*. A side sequence may be initiated by a listener. For example, a listener might attempt to correct a speaker with a brief phrase: "Classes begin on *Wednesday*, not *Monday*." The length of the side sequence depends on how the speaker responds to the correction. The speaker might accept the correction immediately and proceed without missing a beat, or the speaker could reject the correction, diverting the original conversation to a discussion of the side sequence (Jefferson, 1987; Cheepen, 1988).

A side sequence can be initiated by the speaker as well as the listener. For example, as speakers, we might initiate a side sequence if we are forgetful or uncertain about a piece of information we need to continue talking (Goodwin, 1987*a*). We may turn to a potentially knowledgeable person and invite that person (with nothing more than a gaze) to share in our search for the information. This has the effect of elevating the status of listener to that of informed speaker. Or when a telephone call interrupts a conversation, the speaker may use an expression such as "Excuse me, please" to initiate the side sequence and another such as "Sorry. Now where were we?" to mark its end and the return to the original conversation.

Having taken a turn at conversation, we can signal that it is the listener's turn to talk. Turn-taking signals involve a number of behavioral cues that are displayed either singly or simultaneously during a conversation. A speaker can indicate a willingness to yield a turn by any of the following signals (Duncan, 1972; Schegloff, 1987*a*; Sachs, 1990):

1. *Gaze:* The speaker gazes directly at the listener toward the end of an utterance.
2. *Body motion:* The speaker ends the hand gesturing he or she used while talking or relaxes tensed hands. If the speaker asks a question such as "What time is it?" or "Where are you going?" his or her head comes up on "it" or on the *ing* in "going." The speaker's eyes also tend to open wider with the last note of a question, as a signal for the other person to start his or her answer.
3. *Paralingual drawl:* The speaker utters the final syllable or a stressed syllable of a terminal clause in a slow, drawn-out manner.
4. *Intonation:* The speaker raises or lowers his or her voice as evidence of a terminal (ending) clause. An example would be raising the voice on "this" in the question "Do you like this?"
5. *Verbal clues:* The speaker utters a stereotyped expression— "but uh" or "you know"— followed by a phrase: "But uh, I guess that's just the way he is." Questions are also an important turn-yielding signal.

Listeners can signal that they are seeking a turn through cues such as inhaling audibly, gesturing with their hands, beginning a vocalization while shifting their heads away from us, or expressing especially loud vocal responses indicating interest— "Yes!" Such subtle and taken-for-granted (unconscious) mechanisms make communication easier. They make possible back-and-forth exchange without the need of saying, "Are you finished? Now I will talk."

Because of the absence of nonverbal cues, we might expect more turn-taking problems in telephone conversations. However, research does not support this expectation (Rutter, 1987). In fact, the only clear difference supported by research is that there are *fewer* interruptions on the telephone. Thus, although successful turn taking can be accomplished using nonverbal cues, such cues are not necessary, as interruptions can be avoided through the exclusive use of verbal cues.

TERMINATING CONVERSATIONS

We do not conclude conversations any more arbitrarily than we begin, continue, or interrupt them. Two people do not simply stop talking and abruptly walk away from each other. Just as there are initiation rituals, there are also *termination rituals.* Some rituals are short; others, particularly those that require the negotiation of a conversation closure, take more time (Button, 1987). The length of the termination ritual is influenced by such factors as the status of the participants, the setting, and the willingness of a participant to violate the termination rules.

Termination rituals between persons of equal status usually involve some prepping before the final goodbyes. Such rituals are initiated by one of the participants and may involve many components. For example, a person might close a conversation with an acquaintance by saying, "I'd better be going. Nice talking with you. See you." In this case, the final goodbye was preceded by an initiation of the closing ("I'd better be going") and an appreciation statement ("Nice talking with you").

With friends or intimates, a termination ritual might be more elaborate. For example, a student might say, "Sorry! Gotta run. Okay? Thanks for the help. See you after class. Bye." In this example, not only did the closing include an initiation ("Gotta run"), an appreciation ("Thanks for the help"), and a final goodbye ("Bye"), but it was extended by a request for the friend to approve terminating the conversation ("Okay?") as well as an arrangement for initiating the next conversation ("See you after class"). Some termination rituals might be punctuated with a hug or kiss.

In some situations we terminate conversations with friends or intimates more abruptly. For example, if two friends are accustomed to routinely terminating their conversations at a particular point — during a walk to class or work together, for instance — their termination ritual may be as brief as a nod of the head, "Bye," or "See ya." Other components of the ritual are assumed and therefore not spoken; for example, there is no need to include the explanation for closing and an arrangement for reopening the conversation in the future. On another occasion, the closing may be no more than "Oh, no! I forgot about the pie in the oven!" as the person turns and dashes away. Although the words suggest an explanation for the departure, the loss of eye contact suggests that the person is not asking for anyone's approval to leave (Goodwin, 1987*b*).

A termination attempt may be resisted whether or not it includes an actual request of the other party to approve it. It may be countered with "Oh, just one more thing. . . ." Such resistance is usually hard to overcome, whether it occurs in a face-to-face conversation or on the telephone. There isn't much the participant making the attempt can do other than repeat the termination ritual, emphasizing his or her explanation. The person might suggest another conversation in the near future: "I'll call you back tomorrow." In a face-to-face conversation, he or she can slowly decrease eye contact and move farther away from the other person. But abruptly turning away — or hanging up — without waiting for the other person's goodbye is "against the rules" and therefore requires repair work in the next conversation.

Termination rituals are somewhat different when the parties are of unequal status. For example, a superior may conclude a conversation with a subordinate abruptly, with little fanfare. On the other hand, you know your status is higher when the other person — instead of closing the conversation abruptly — asks if you want to extend the conversation. This occurs, for example, when a salesperson asks, "Can I help you with anything else?"

However, other factors may override the effects of status differences. Television news interviews, for example, usually operate with prespecified closing times (Clayman, 1989). It would be considered rude for either the interviewer or the interviewee to leave early. However, once the agreed-upon ending time arrives, it is often the higher-status person who exercises the right to terminate the interaction. You have probably noticed that it is not uncommon for the president to leave his press conferences with the press's questions still ringing in his ears.

TALK IN INSTITUTIONAL SETTINGS

The conversational rules we have been discussing apply to mundane (everyday) conversations; thus they apply to a diversity of roles and conversation topics. In social institutions, which involve a narrower range of topics and relatively specialized identities, these conversational rules are often modified to better address the interactional contingencies of the particular setting (Heritage, 1984*a*; Whalen and Zimmerman, 1987; Zimmerman and Boden, 1991). For example, turn taking is governed by different rules within the settings of particular institutions, such as classrooms, courtrooms, emergency rooms, and corporate boardrooms. Institution-specific rules may specify the order of speakers as well as how long each can talk, who can interrupt whom in what manner, and, sometimes, what the topic of conversation is (West and Frankel, 1991). The rules may also specify who can make or enforce these kinds of rules, for example, the judge in a courtroom (Philips, 1990). The incumbents of particular roles such as police officers, teachers, doctors, lawyers, and interviewers typically begin the conversation, ask the questions, sometimes interrupt or select the next speaker, and decide when the conversa-

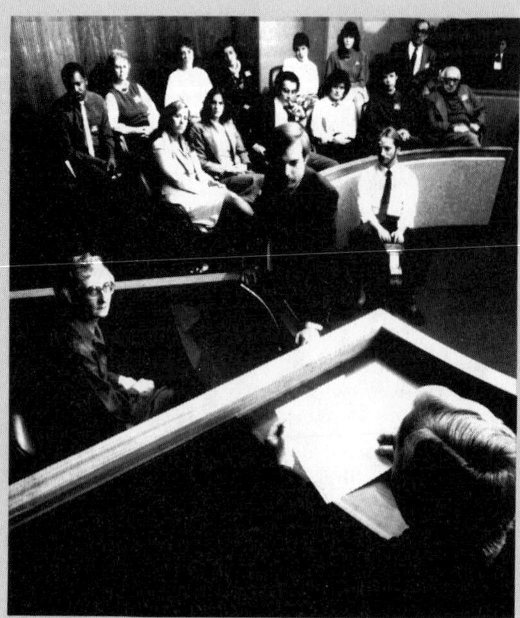

In social institutions, conversational rules are often modified to better address the interactional contingencies of the particular setting.

tion will end. These are the people in charge. On the other hand, others such as students, patients, witnesses, and interviewees follow the formers' initiatives. In some instances, the question-answer activities are reversed. For example, in a classroom or at a press conference the teacher or the politician/expert becomes the interviewee, while the students or the press become the interviewers. However, the teacher or politician still initiates the conversation by selecting the questioner and probably sets most of the agenda of the interview.

To the extent that participants in an institutional setting, such as a courtroom, organize their conversations in a way that is distinctive from everyday conversation, they are both *displaying* and *creating* the unique institutional character of that setting (Heritage and Greatbatch, 1991). Each institution has its own unique pattern of modifications. These vary from culture to culture, and they are subject to processes of social change.

THE COOPERATIVE PRINCIPLE

To make their purposes understood, speakers sometimes explicitly state their intent: "I am asking for your help." "I am telling you to stop right now." "I insist that you leave now." "I invite you to come tomorrow." "I apologize for being late." "I promise to get the paper." "I'm warning you that it is not enough." Most languages also provide standard ways of combining words and intonation to convey a speaker's purpose. In English, for example, there are standard ways of using word order, verb forms, and intonation to convey asking ("Is Wendy here?"), telling ("Wendy is here"), and commanding ("Come here, Wendy!").

More often, however, we indicate our intentions much more indirectly. For example, when Carol telephones Tricia and Jonathan answers, she might ask, "Is Tricia there?" Carol expects Jonathan to understand from this that she wants to speak to Tricia; she isn't simply asking for a yes or no answer. If Tricia is home, Carol expects Jonathan to reply, "Yes, I'll get her." If she isn't home, Carol expects something like, "No, may I take a message?" or "No, she'll be back about nine." These answers acknowledge that Carol wants to speak to Tricia, even though she didn't say so directly. Similarly, when you say to your roommate, "I'm hungry," you expect him to know that you are not simply stating a fact but want the two of you to start doing something about it. Depending on the setting, you might mean "Is there anything in the refrigerator that I could eat?" or "Let's stop what we're doing and go get some dinner."

Obviously, people often mean much more than they actually say. How do listeners figure out the more indirect meanings? Philosopher H. Paul Grice (1975, 1978) has argued that we do this, partly, by relying on a **cooperative principle** – an assumption that speakers are trying to be (1) informative (but not overly informative), (2) truthful, (3) relevant, and (4) clear (unambiguous and brief).

Consider this example: Adam is standing by a car on the side of a dusty rural road as Bob comes along on foot. Adam says, "I'm out of gas." Bob replies, "There's a fruit stand around the corner and another one a little farther down the road on the left." How should Adam interpret Bob's reply? Taking Bob's remarks at face value, Adam might think that Bob is entirely unconcerned with his problem and wants him to buy some fruit at the local stand. But if Adam relies on the cooperative principle, his thinking may be along these lines: Bob thinks the fruit stands are my closest sources of help (he is trying to help by giving good information; he knows and is being truthful about where they are). Maybe the fruit stands also sell gas or have a phone I can use to call for help (they must be relevant to my being out of gas). Why did Bob mention two fruit stands? He must think it's possible that the closest stand won't solve the problem (it might be closed), so he gave me more information, just in case. (Adam assumes Bob wouldn't give unnecessary information because the principle of cooperation says speakers should be brief.)

Suppose you point toward a group of ten dancers and say to the friend next to you, "*That* is Sandra's brother." Your friend assumes that, if you are acting cooperatively, you have given her all the information she needs to pick out the unique dancer to whom you are referring. If nine of the dancers are female, your friend will know that Sandra's brother is the sole male dancer. But what if all the dancers are male? She will look for something that sets one dancer apart from the others. ("Really? The *naked* one?")

Cooperation is essential to language use and, more generally, to all communication. Speakers say what they say intending it to be understood a certain way by their listeners. We talk to convince, request, apologize, warn, and promise. To succeed, we have to rely on the cooperative principle (Clark, 1985; Schiffrin, 1990).

Group Differences in Communication

Not everyone uses the same style of communication. We do not all share the same interpretation of particular cues; in other words, not all cues are significant symbols. Nor do we necessarily interact using the same rules of conversation (e.g., some of us use repair work, which others ignore). Some of these differences occur between individuals; others are differences between groups of people. There are several explanations for the communication differences that distinguish groups (Coupland, Giles, and Weimann, 1991): (1) People use different communication styles (including different languages and jargon) because they come from different cultures or have specialized socialization and training. (2) Different developmental levels of the "same" language may account for different communication styles, such as those seen in conversations between adults and children. (3) People may use different channels of communication because of physical restriction; for example, the sight-, hearing-, or speech-impaired who cannot receive or send information through particular channels and, at the same time, may use cues that the nonimpaired have difficulty interpreting. (4) Biological explanations suggest that genetic differences between categories of persons result in different communication styles. (5) As we have discussed previously, communication differences can be a vehicle for the display of one person's power or status over another. When we encounter someone whose symbols or communication style is different from our own, we often make the judgment that our own style of communication is "the correct one" and other styles are "deviant" – not just different, but bad or *inferior* (Henley and Kramarae, 1991).

Obviously, communication differences, whatever their source, can lead to communication problems between people who have occasion to interact with one another. Our reactions to others whose communication styles are different vary. Sometimes we lower our expectations of the abilities of those using other styles; for example, we may use baby talk when interacting with children, the elderly, the impaired, and even those whose native language is different from our own. Sometimes we attempt to change the communication styles of those whose styles differ from our own; for instance, we may oppose bilingual education. A third way we react to these differences is by avoiding opportunities to interact with dissimilar others; for example, we may adhere to the segregation of ingroup and outgroup members (a topic discussed in Chapter 4, "Social Relationships and Groups"). Of course, segregation can be the *cause* as well as the *effect* of communication differences.

We expect differences when we talk to people who grew up in a different country but not when we talk to people who grew up in "the same culture" and who speak "the same language" as ourselves. So it is perhaps surprising that social psychologists devote a great deal of attention to gender differences in communication.

GENDER DIFFERENCES IN COMMUNICATION

Folklore has long attributed "female intuition" to women. According to this view, women are more adept than men in nonverbal communication. An accumulating body of research supports this popular belief (Hall, 1984). On the whole, psychologists find that women are more visually attentive to other people than are men. And women are better judges than men of the meanings behind voice tones, facial expressions, and body movements — the sorts of cues people cannot or will not put into words.

One explanation for women's superior nonverbal decoding skills and different conversational style is that they are socially oppressed and hence must give greater attention to an accurate reading of the needs and demands of more powerful others. Another speculation is that women in male-dominated societies usually find themselves watching and listening and might therefore develop greater nonverbal ability through sheer practice. Still another is that the ability is genetic, or "prewired," because nonverbal sensitivity on a mother's part might permit her to detect distress in her children or threatening signals from adults, thus enhancing the survival chances of her offspring.

In contrast to these "oppression" and "biological" explanations, another thesis is that gender differences in communication styles emerge from male and female *subcultures* whose norms are learned from, and reinforced by, gender mates from early childhood on (Maltz and Borker, 1982; Maccoby, 1990; Tannen, 1990). According to this explanation, gender differences in communication behavior stem from adherence to the norms of one's own gender group, not so much from status differences that may become salient when men and women interact with one another.

Women's style is seen as reflecting females' greater concern with *intimacy*, or connection with others. This style focuses on minimizing differences and avoiding the appearance of superiority, which would highlight differences among the members of complex networks of friends. Communication, for women, is frequently directed toward establishing connections with others, building relationships, and preserving intimacy.

Men's communication style reflects their greater concern with *status* and independence, with being up rather than down in the hierarchical social order. Thus, men's conversations are negotiations in which they try to achieve and maintain the upper hand if they can and protect themselves from others' attempts to put them down or push them around. This is not to say, of course, that women are entirely unconcerned with status or that men are unconcerned with intimacy. The difference is one of focus and degree — women's primary concern is intimacy, while men's primary concern is status — and this leads to dramatic gender differences in communication styles.

Notice that the difference in the concerns of the two genders reflects two of the main "things we communicate" discussed earlier in the chapter — intimacy and status. Men's greater use of filled pauses (which permit them to keep the floor), faster speech, and interruptions follows from their concern with status: they are competing for conversational floor time and respect. Women's greater use of questions, briefer speech, and more direct gazes reflects their concern with egalitarianism and connection. In this view, men and women come together as citizens of different cultures — thinking that they speak the same language when, in fact, they do not (Hall, 1978).

Perhaps because females are more concerned with interpersonal harmony and/or are more skilled at affecting it, both sexes find interactions with women to be more pleasant and satisfying than interactions with men. Social psychologist Harry Reis (1986) suggests that males and females make different contributions to social interaction. He and his colleagues asked subjects — forty-three male and fifty-three female college seniors — to complete a series of ratings for each interaction of ten minutes or longer that they were involved in during a two-week period.

The researchers found that interactions involving at least one female were rated by the subjects of both sexes as more intimate, more pleasant, and more satisfying. In such interactions, subjects indicated that they and the others involved in the interaction disclosed more. Even when a male interacted with his best male friend, the interaction was rated as less intimate, disclosing, pleasant, and satisfying than interactions between females or between opposite-sex partners. Additionally, among both male and female subjects, the more time they spent interacting with females, the less lonely they reported themselves to be. Reiss's study, however, did not attempt to identify the particular behaviors that made interaction with females more positive.

Gender Differences in Meaning

Because of gender differences in communication skills and approaches to interpersonal interaction, males and females sometimes view the same interaction quite differently. For example, backchannel responses such as "yeah" and "um-hum" have different meanings for men and women. For women, these mean "I'm listening, please continue." For men, they mean "I agree." So, in a male-female conversation, the man may think he is listening but not agreeing, but the woman will think he is not listening. Women frequently ask questions to maintain conversations — to show interest and encourage the speaker to continue. Men are more likely to see questions as requests for information. Women often respond to shared experiences and problems by offering reassurance. Men see the presentation of problems as requests for solutions and respond by giving advice, lecturing, or acting as experts (Aries, 1987). Women who think they are displaying a positive quality — connection — are misjudged by men who see them as lacking independence, which men regard as synonymous with incompetence and insecurity. Men who think they are displaying a positive quality — independence — are misjudged by women who see them as insensitive and uncaring. It is not surprising that communication between men and women is sometimes difficult.

Deborah Tannen, a linguist who has studied gender differences in conversational styles, illustrates how men's and women's different cultural backgrounds can lead to miscommunication:

> When Josh's old high-school chum called him at work and announced he'd be in town on business the following month, Josh invited him to stay for the weekend. That evening he informed Linda that they were going to have a houseguest, and that he and his chum would go out together the first night to shoot the breeze like old times. Linda was upset. . . . Josh had made these plans on his own and informed her of them, rather than discussing them with her before extending the invitation. . . . But when she protests, Josh says, "I can't say to my friend, 'I have to ask my wife for permission'!"
>
> To Josh, checking with his wife means seeking permission, which implies that he is not independent, not free to act on his own. It would make him feel like a child or an underling. To Linda, checking with her husband has nothing to do with permission. She assumes that spouses discuss their plans with each other because their lives are intertwined, so the actions of one have consequences for the other. . . . Linda was hurt because she sensed a failure of closeness in their relationship: He didn't care about her as much as she cared about him. And he was hurt because he felt she was trying to control him and limit his freedom. (1990: 26–27)*

Miscommunication between the genders is not limited to the interactions of husbands and wives. Antonia Abbey (1982) got her idea for a study about miscommunication between men and women from an encounter she had with strangers. Abbey was with some female friends at a crowded campus bar, sharing a table with two male strangers. While Abbey thought that she and her friends were merely being "friendly," the men appeared to interpret the women's behavior as an indication of sexual interest. She reports that she and her friends finally had to excuse themselves from the table in order to avoid an awkward scene. This made Abbey wonder: Do men often see women's words and actions as more seductive than the women intend?

Abbey designed a study to answer this question. She assigned two males and two females to each of twenty-six four-person groups. When each group arrived for the study, Abbey randomly selected one male and one female to engage in a brief conversation (the actors) while the other male and female observed the conversation from another room (the observers). After the conversation, all four subjects filled out questionnaires indicating their perceptions of the actors' personality traits and chose from among a list of characteristics those that they thought described how each actor was "trying to behave." Although these terms were included with many others, Abbey was particularly interested in how "flirtatious," "seductive," and "promiscuous" the four subjects perceived the two actors to be.

Abbey found that the behavior of the female actor was rated more promiscuous and seductive by both the male actor and the male observer than by either the female actor or the female observer. Overall, the male observers saw the female actors as more interested in and attracted to their partners than did the female observers. The males and females in this study either participated in or observed the same interaction, but both as actors and as observers the males and females perceived it quite differently—mutual understanding was not reached. As Abbey's experience in the bar indicates, this gender difference in "meaning" can lead to problems.

Differences in Conversational "Work" and Control

As we noted earlier in this chapter, the maintenance of a conversation is somewhat problematic and requires the continual, turn-by-turn efforts of the participants. However, this does not mean that there is an equal distribution of work in a conversation. For instance, Pamela Fishman finds that a woman typically carries the greater burden in keeping a conversation moving with a man. Fishman (1978) analyzed fifty-two hours of tapes made in the apartments of three middle-class couples between the ages of twenty-five and thirty-five. The women raised nearly twice as many topics of conversation as the men because many of the women's topics failed to elicit any response. Besides exercising their right to inject new topics, men controlled topics by veto: they would refuse to become full-fledged conversational participants. Both men and women regarded topics introduced by women as tentative, and many of these topics were quickly dropped. In contrast, topics introduced by men were seldom rejected and frequently resulted in a lengthy exchange.

The tapes revealed that the women resorted to attention-getting devices when faced with the men's grunts or long silences. The women asked three times as many questions as did the men. Asking a question is conversational "work"; it is a device used to keep conversation going by eliciting a response from the other party. And more often than the men, the women prefaced their remarks with comments like "D'ya know what?" and "This is interesting"; as talk lagged, the women used the interjection "you know" with considerable frequency. Such phrases function as "go-ahead" signals, indicating that the other party may speak up and that what is said will be heeded.

Deborah Tannen suggests that men see communication as a way to gain status by showing that they know more. Women, on the other hand, see communication as a way to build connections, so they tend to play down their own expertise rather than display it. Because of these differences, men are often more comfortable, and more talkative, in public situations that allow them to "show off." Women are often more comfortable, and more talkative, in private situations that allow them to build rapport. Men are inclined to jockey for position and challenge the authority of others. Women are more likely to avoid confrontation because they feel it is more important to be liked than to be respected. Men see disagreement as more interesting—and more status enhancing—than agreement. Women see disagreement as a threat to intimacy and strive to be more accommodating. Because they are not struggling to compete with others in conversation, women are often seen by men as being powerless or inept.

A number of studies have found that men account for the vast majority of the interruptions in a conversation. One early study found that in cross-sex conversations in public places, over 90 percent of the interruptions were made by men (Zimmerman and West, 1975). A recent study (Smith-Lovin and Brody, 1989) found that, while male and females interrupt at almost identical rates, males are more than twice as likely to interrupt a female as they are to interrupt another male. Females, in contrast, interrupt male and female speakers equally. The men were also found to be more successful at interrupting women.

Some researchers conclude from these findings that women, who do the routine maintenance work in conversations, neither control nor necessarily benefit from the conversational process (West and Zimmerman, 1983; Kollock, Blumstein, and Schwartz, 1985; Pfeiffer, 1985). One explanation for these findings is that widely held beliefs in our society attribute more status, or power, to men than to women and that this difference is reflected in conversational dynamics (Ridgeway and Diekema, 1992). According to this view, differences in communication styles are essential to the maintenance of male dominance (Henley and Kramarae, 1991). A second explanation proposes that these differences are not so much a reflection of or a mechanism for maintaining male dominance but are, instead, another result of the different socialization and resulting cultures of the two genders.

These two explanations are not necessarily mutually exclusive (Smith-Lovin and Robinson, 1992). Both early *socialization* and peer-group interaction may lead boys and girls to develop gender identities that differ substantially in *power*. Although parents don't directly or intentionally socialize children to play or interact differently on the basis of their gender (Maccoby, 1990), they do communicate, subtly, that girls are nicer, less powerful, and less lively than boys. These early experiences shape our views of ourselves and others as males and females. These gender identities are reinforced in same-sex play groups. In adulthood, men's and women's definitions of "male" and "female" differ substantially. When these gender identities are activated, men and women behave differently in carrying out social roles. Thus, according to this view, it is gender-differentiated *identities*, which we hold for ourselves and others, that shape our interactions, including whether we interrupt, encourage someone else to speak, nod attentively, actively disagree, and so on.

Gender Stereotypes and Communication

One conclusion that we might draw from these studies on gender differences in the use of verbal and nonverbal cues is that women should try to adopt the culturally recognized male patterns in order to reap the same rewards. But would they?

When social psychologists began looking for objective cues to identify who would emerge as leader in an initially unstructured group, they found that the emergent leader was often the one centrally located in the group and that group members seated at the ends of the table became leaders more often than those occupying side positions. Psychologist Robert Pellegrini (1971) had subjects rate each person in photographs of five college women seated around a rectangular table, one at the head and two on each side. The woman seated at the head of the table was identified as the most influential, talkative, and leaderlike and as the one who had contributed most to the group. Pellegrini reasoned that we expect the high-status member of a group to be seated at the head of the table in our society, so we automatically attribute status and dominance to the person who occupies that position. The head of the table thus serves as a nonverbal cue to leadership status.

Natalie Porter and Florence Geis (1981) devised a study to determine whether the cues identifying a man as a leader would equally confer leadership on a woman. They decided to use position at the head of the table as the cue they would study, since it would be unlikely that, in photographs of seating position, males and females would seem to be doing this "differently." The research described above showed that the position at the head of the table serves as a leadership cue in same-sex groups. Porter and Geis hypothesized that in *mixed-sex* settings, sex-role stereotypes that define women as nonleaders when a man is available would cause leadership cues to be interpreted differently for males and females.

Using the same procedure that Pellegrini had used, Porter and Geis showed subjects a slide of five individuals seated at a rectangular table, two on each side and one at the head. To make sure that results were not due to a particular stimulus person, the researchers used several slides, with the seating positions of particular individuals varied in each one. Subjects viewed one slide and then rated each group member shown.

As they had predicted, the researchers found that the person at the head of the table was seen as the leader in the all-female, all-male, and mixed-sex groups with a male at the head of the table but not in mixed-sex groups with a female at the head of the table. In fact, a woman at the head of the table in a mixed-sex group was less than half as likely to be seen as the leader as was the person at the head in the other three conditions. This was true among both male and female subjects, including those with feminist as well as those with nonfeminist beliefs. The researchers concluded that "seeing is not believing" when the objective evidence seen is not consistent with the beliefs encoded in cultural stereotypes. This suggests that women cannot get the same treatment as men simply by displaying the same nonverbal cues.

Men and women are judged differently when they use the same verbal cues as well. Women who attempt to adjust their styles by speaking louder, longer, and more assertively are judged to be acting in an "unfeminine" manner (Tannen, 1990). They may command more attention and respect, but they are likely to be disliked and disparaged as "aggressive" and "unfeminine." A man acting the same way is merely being a masculine male, and he is judged positively as a result. Indeed, women do not have to be particularly aggressive to be criticized.

A study by Harriet Wall and Anita Barry (1985) found that we define success in masculine terms and see these traits as incompatible with femininity. The researchers gave students information about prospective professors — their academic backgrounds, publications, and letters of recommendation — and asked the students to predict how well the candidates would do if hired and what their chances were of winning a distinguished teaching award. Some of the students were given a woman's name and others a man's name for the candidate. Those who believed the materials described a woman candidate were more likely to predict that she would not win the teaching award because, as one student put it, there was "too much business, not enough personality." None of the students who read exactly the same file under a man's name made these negative inferences about personality. In addition, students who believed they were evaluating a woman expected her to be more nurturing and to devote more time to her students outside of class than those who thought they were evaluating a man.

When women use stronger, more direct power cues — cues considered inappropriate to their gender — they often receive negative evaluations (Burgoon and Miller, 1985; Russell, Rush, and Herd, 1988; Heilman et al., 1989; Powell, 1990). This produces a double-bind dilemma for women who aspire to positions of leadership or responsibility. If they use typical female cues, they are ignored—considered "nice mice" who don't possess the necessary leadership qualities. If they use stronger signals, they are viewed as overly emotional, arrogant, and abusive—"dragons" who are trespassing on territory regarded as inappropriate for women. No "right" demeanor can be achieved (Fogarty, Rapaport, and Rapaport, 1971). Consider, for example, the plight of Geraldine Ferraro as the first female candidate for vice president of the United States. The press made much of the fact that in her debate with then Vice President Bush, she had difficulty creating a public image that would be authoritative but not "too masculine" (Epstein, 1988).

Even when journalists set out to praise Ferraro, they often used terms that highlighted the incongruity between her gender and the office she was seeking. Linguist Michael Geis (1987) points out in his book *The Language of Politics* that she was called "spunky" and "feisty"—words, Geis observes, that are used only for small, powerless creatures: for a Pekingese but not a Great Dane, perhaps for Mickey Rooney but not for John Wayne. Our language has built-in gender distinctions that shape our attitudes. It appears that gender is itself a cue that, in some situations, conflicts with or even overrides other communication cues to determine the responses of others (Eagly and Karau, 1991; Eagly, Makhijani, and Klonsky, 1992).

RACE AND CLASS DIFFERENCES IN COMMUNICATION

Race and social class are also sources of communication differences and, as a result, sources of communication problems when members of different races or social classes come together. Although the research literature on racial and social class communication styles is less extensive than that on gender differences in communication, several interesting observations have been made.

In his classic study, anthropologist William Labov (1972) found that African-American males (in this case, young, urban, and mainly lower class) exchanged insults, often in the presence of other peers who served as an audience. This activity was usually competitive in nature, in that each man tried to top the previous insult with one that was more clever, outrageous, or elaborate. The audience members acted as judges in deciding who won the competition of insults. Labov referred to this style of verbal exchange as "ritual insults."

Labov's observations were followed by research aimed at discovering the communication styles of females, whites, and members of the middle class (whatever their gender or race). Researchers observing African-American females found that they adopted the ritual-insult style when interacting with African-American males, and their communication with one another was typified by play songs and cheers that incorporated several aspects of insulting, such as assertive and mocking tones (Goodwin, 1980; Heath, 1983). Studies of white females found that the use of assertive and mocking play songs was not common (Heath, 1983) and that middle-class white females were often intimidated by the more aggressive style of their African-American peers (Schofield, 1982). However, still another study of the interaction among groups of white females found that ritual insulting *was* common among girls who came from working- or lower-class backgrounds but not among those from the middle class (Eder, 1990). The researcher concluded that social class (not gender or race) was the major determinant of ritual insulting and that communication problems arise when persons from different social classes interact largely because middle-class people interpret working- and lower-class speech styles as both rude and assertive.

In a similar vein, Thomas Kochman (1981) observed differences in the communication styles used by African-Americans and whites in conflict situations. According to Kochman, blacks more frequently use a loud, animated, and confrontational style, while whites more frequently use a quiet, dispassionate, and nonchallenging style. The observations of a second researcher (Donohue, 1985) support those of Kochman: he found that in conflicts between members of the two races, African-Americans tend to be loud while whites are more likely to be extremely solicitous and friendly. Kochman proposes a cultural explanation for the communication differences. He contends that in African-American culture, loudness is viewed as an expression of sincerity and conviction of action – and therefore is positively valued. African-Americans tend to interpret whites' solicitous and friendly style of conflict communication as a mask of hypocrisy and weakness. On the other hand, whites interpret the loudness of African-Americans as overly aggressive and hostile.

Again, however, it is important to note that these studies compare working- and lower-class African-Americans to middle-class whites. Thus, the observed differences in communication styles may reflect *social class* differences rather than *racial* differences. In one study of middle-class college students, males of both races tended to use the quiet, nonchallenging style (there were only a small number of African-American males in the study), and the style differences between the females of the two races were small, although African-American females used the intense, confrontational style somewhat more frequently (Ting-Toomey, 1986).

Several studies suggest that racial differences in the cues that listeners and speakers provide for one another can also cause difficulties in interracial interaction (LaFrance and Mayo, 1976; Erickson, 1979). For example, African-American speakers tend to give fewer and more subtle cues indicating that they expect listener feedback. White speakers tend to look *away* from the listener while talking, whereas African-American speakers look *at* the listener more. White listeners, on the other hand, look at the speaker almost continuously, while African-American listeners look down or away and give fewer and more subtle listening cues (such as nods) than do whites. For example, for white speakers, listening is signaled by gaze, combined with *both* verbal and nonverbal back-channel cues. For African-American speakers, *either* a vocal ("um-hmm") *or* a nonvocal (head nod) cue signals listening; these cues are rarely given together. White speakers infer from this that the African-American listener is not paying attention or doesn't understand. Consequently, they often repeat points and overexplain, making the African-American listener feel that the speaker thinks she or he is stupid. On the other hand, African-American speakers often feel that a white listener's "staring" indicates hostility.

CULTURAL UNIVERSALS AND DIFFERENCES

As we noted at the beginning of this chapter, the meanings that symbols come to have are arbitrary in the sense that they result from cultural conventions. A symbol can have any meaning that a group of people agree on. This means, of course, that a single symbol may have different meanings for different groups. Our discussion of gender, race, and class differences provides many examples of this. However, there are some commonalities in the use of symbols among various cultures and subcultures. In this section we'll explore both these commonalities and the cultural differences in the use of various kinds of symbols for communication.

Language

Human communities develop languages in order to express thoughts and feelings. All human groups have some features in common, and these are reflected in **linguistic universals** – features common to every language. Every language has nouns and verbs, for example, because all people must refer to objects and actions. Every language has terms for such spatial dimensions as direction (right, left; up, down; front, back), distance, height, and length, because all people use basically the same perceptual capacities to orient themselves to the physical world (Clark and Clark, 1977). Similarly, every language has terms to distinguish between past, present, and future – universally experienced dimensions of time.

Some linguistic universals result from common experiences of social life. These are of particular interest to social psychologists. For example, all cultures have some sort of family structure, although the structures themselves vary. All languages contain terms that allow speakers to distinguish three characteristics of family members—sex, generation, and blood relationship. All languages have precise, simple terms for relatives who spend the most time together, but they usually string together several terms to specify one's exact relationship to relatives who are less central to the family structure. For example, in English, the term "grandmother" designates a female, two generations prior to the referent, and a blood relationship. But the term "cousin" designates only two of the three characteristics—generation and blood relationship but not gender; it takes two words, "female cousin," to completely describe the cousin relationship. All languages have pronouns that facilitate references to self and other—for example, in English, "I/we," "you," and "he/she/they." Other universal language concepts include certain body parts (head, foot, belly, mouth), colors (red, green, black, white), common human actions (eat, sleep, hear, walk), and features of the environment (cloud, earth, rain, moon, fire) (Swadesh, 1971).

All languages have terms for concepts that are central to daily activities. As we have seen, the *common* capacities and experiences of humans lead to the incorporation of certain features in all languages—linguistic universals. But human groups also *differ* in terms of the physical environments they inhabit and the activities they undertake. These differences are also reflected in their languages. The Arabs have some 6,000 different terms for camels. The Hanunoo, a people of the Philippine Islands, have a term for each of ninety-two varieties of rice. Having precise words for frequently needed concepts makes communication easier and more accurate.

When learning to speak a new language, people generally do not pick up all the cultural conventions about how it should be used in different contexts. As a result, they may accidentally send the wrong message. For example, German allows more direct phrasing of requests and complaints than English does (House and Kasper, 1981). Thus, when Germans speak English, they sometimes sound domineering to Americans accustomed to the English convention that considers it impolite to be too direct with status equals. Similarly, research suggests that Israelis are concerned with appearing to be honest and forthright in their communications, while Americans and the British are more concerned with appearing to be polite and considerate (Katriel, 1986). Israeli speakers, in striving to maximize the attributes of honesty and forthrightness, which are valued in their culture, may come across to American and British listeners as rude and inconsiderate.

Body Language

Some gestures have the same or similar meanings in several cultures. An example is the side-to-side head motion meaning "no." However, some behaviors have a specific meaning in one culture but not in another. The French gesture of putting one's fist around the tip of the nose and twisting to signify that a person is drunk is not employed in other cultures. And a gesture may have one meaning in one culture and a different meaning in another culture. Thus, Roman emperors gave the thumbs-up gesture to spare the lives of gladiators in the Colosseum. Today the same gesture is favored by American and Western European airline pilots, truck drivers, and others to mean "all right." But in Sardinia and northern Greece, it is an insulting gesture, paralleling the insulting middle-finger gesture of American society (Ekman, Friesen, and Bear, 1984).

One aspect of body language, however, does seem to have common meanings in different cultures—the *facial expression* of emotion. Paul Ekman (1980) and his associates showed subjects from widely different cultures photographs of individuals' faces that in Western societies are judged to display six basic emotions: happiness, sadness, anger, surprise, disgust, and fear (see photo). The researchers found that college-educated subjects in the United States, Brazil,

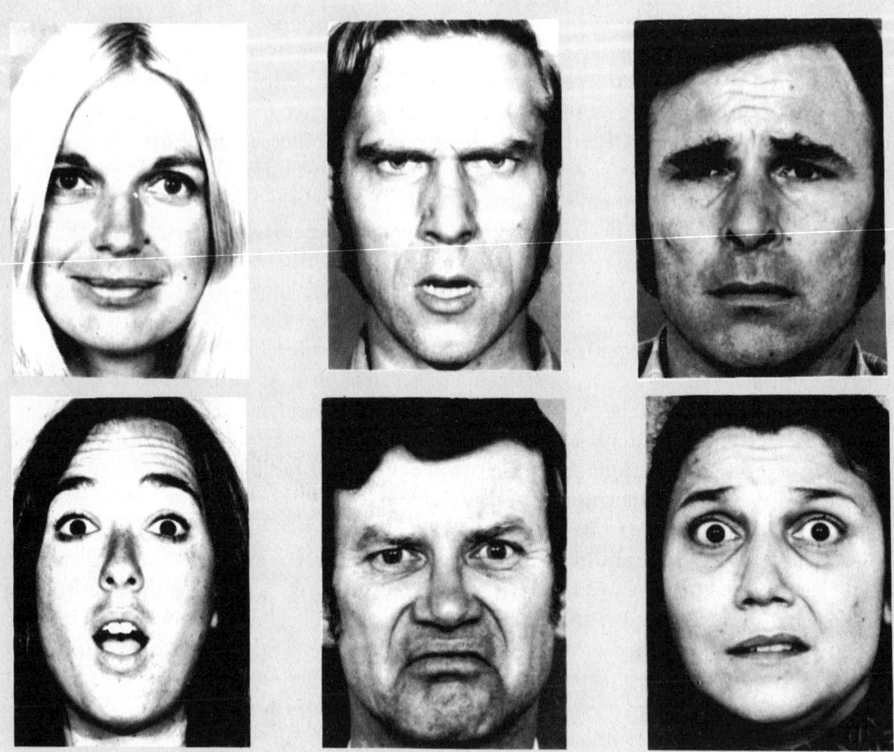

People in many cultures recognize the emotions of happiness, anger, sadness, surprise, disgust, and fear in these photos.

Argentina, Chile, and Japan ascribed the same emotions to the same faces. Moreover, with the exception of their failure to discriminate fear from surprise, even the isolated and preliterate Fore of New Guinea made similar distinctions. (Among the Fore, surprising events are almost always fearful, such as the sudden appearance of a hostile member of another village or the unexpected meeting of a "ghost.")

In a more recent study, Ekman and his colleagues showed photographs depicting the six emotions to college-student observers in ten countries (Ekman et al., 1987). The observers were asked to rate *how intensely* the person in the photo was experiencing the emotion, as well as *which* emotion the person was feeling. Although there were high levels of agreement across cultures about which emotion was being expressed, judgments of intensity showed much lower levels of agreement. The greater variation in intensity than in type of emotion may be a result of cultural differences in "display rules."

Ekman believes this evidence demonstrates that our central nervous systems are genetically prewired for the facial expression of emotion. However, he does not rule out the influence of environment. Learning determines which circumstances will elicit a given emotional expression, and cultures formulate their own display rules to regulate the expression of emotion. For example, in our culture, norms prescribe that even though a guest might feel intense disgust at the thought of eating the specific food served by his hostess, politeness requires that he attempt to mask the expression of this emotion. The guest shouldn't leap back from the table exclaiming, "Oh, yuck, how revolting!" or even sit quietly and wrinkle his nose like the person in the "disgust" photo on page 544. Instead, he should pretend to be delighted by the feast or at least make a polite excuse for not eating the disgusting item ("Oh, that looks delicious, but my doctor has told me I absolutely mustn't eat pickled frog eyes any more") and, at the same time, should make every effort to have his facial expression match his insincere words. Some other cultures might allow freer expression of disgust in this situation.

Interpersonal Spacing

Anthropologist Edward T. Hall (1966) has shown that there are cultural differences in interpersonal spacing. Hall observes that Americans commonly consider Arabs to be pushy and rude. Paradoxically, Arabs also consider Americans to be pushy. This is because interpersonal spacing has different meanings in the two cultures. For example, the visual interaction of Arabs is intense: they stare; Americans do not. Further, Arabs bathe the other person in their breath. To smell another is not only desirable but mandatory; to deny another one's breath is to act ashamed. Whereas Arabs stay inside the olfactory bubble of others, Americans stay outside of it. Hence an American communicates shame to the Arab when, in fact, the American is trying to be polite. These behaviors, Hall explains, derive from the fact that the typical Arab lacks a sense of a private spatial bubble that envelops the body. Rather than viewing a person as extending in space beyond the body, Arabs see the person as existing somewhere down *inside* the body. Thus, they violate the American ego by invading Americans' private space.

In summary, human communication is characterized by both cultural universals and differences. These interest social psychologists because they illustrate the complexity of human experience. On the one hand, we have much in common with others. We inhabit the same earth and are subject to its physical laws. Even some features of social experience are common to all cultures. We all have parents and other kin, for example; we all feel certain basic emotions, and we must all communicate with others in order to negotiate and align our actions.

On the other hand, members of different cultural groups have different concerns and these are reflected in their communications. Different cultural groups have devised different symbols even for the universal aspects of human experience. Consider, for example, all the different words for mother in the world's languages. Subcultures within a cultural group may assign different meanings to certain symbols and may have jargons all their own. Even a brother and sister growing up in the same family, who have in common not only the larger culture but also the group culture of the family itself, may experience the world very differently from each other – and develop different communication styles and concerns – due to a factor such as gender. Why is this so? It is because our culture assigns meanings to such characteristics as gender, race, social class, and physical beauty, and these meanings affect the way we experience the world – how others react to us and how we come to see ourselves. We'll discuss the process by which this occurs in our next two chapters: Chapter 6, "Social Attitudes and Attributions," and Chapter 7, "The Social Nature of Self."

Summary

1. Communication is the process by which people interact and interpret their interactions. Symbols are objects or actions that stand in, or substitute, for something else. Significant symbols are symbols for which several people share meanings. They are important because they allow us to coordinate our behaviors with those of others.
2. We communicate through several kinds of symbols: language, paralanguage, body language, interpersonal spacing, physical characteristics, and personal effects.

3. We communicate multiple meanings with a single message. Besides conveying task information, our communicative behavior reflects the intimacy of our relationships with other persons, as well as our relative status within the group, provides information about ourselves and our feelings, and is used to manage impressions of ourselves and our relationships. We use facework to support or challenge the public images we claim for ourselves or attribute to others.
4. Our behavior also provides cues to regulate the interaction itself: we signal the initiation of interaction, indicate our willingness to stop or start speaking, and provide feedback to the speaker to indicate our interest and understanding. We often indicate our intentions indirectly, relying on the cooperative principle to decipher a speaker's meaning.
5. Different gender, racial, and social class groups have different norms for regulating conversation. Therefore, when members of these different groups interact, miscommunication may result. Some explanations for gender differences in communication styles relate to women's disadvantaged position in society or their biological role as mothers. The socialization or cultural explanation suggests that males and females interact, as children, in same-gender subgroups whose different norms they learn. Working- and lower-class persons use a loud interaction style in conflict situations which middle-class persons interpret as overly aggressive and hostile. Middle-class persons use a friendly and solicitous conflict style which lower- and working-class persons interpret as hypocritical and weak. African-Americans and whites tend to use different speaking and listening cues — sometimes leading to difficulties in interracial interaction.
6. Common human concerns are reflected in linguistic universals — features that exist in all languages. Language differences also reflect the different concerns of various human groups. Even subgroups of a language group have specialized vocabularies which reflect their particular concerns.

Additional sources:
Photo, p. 551, Robert Kalman, Image Works.
Photo, p. 566, Jim Pickerell/Stock, Boston.
Photos, p. 576, Modified and reproduced by special permission of the publisher, Consulting Psychologist Press, Inc., Palo Alto, CA 94303. From *Pictures of Facial Affect* by Paul Ekman and Wallace V. Friesen. Copyright 1976 by Paul Ekman. All rights reserved. Further reproduction is prohibited without the publisher's consent.
Excerpt, pp. 544–545, with permission of San Francisco Examiner.
Box, p. 547, with permission of Time.
Box, p. 552, with permission of Brent Staples.
Excerpt, p. 569, with permission of William Morrow and Co., Inc.

Comprehension Quiz: Textbook Chapter

Directions: Refer to Selection 10-1 as necessary to complete this quiz.

Options for collaboration: For some of these exercises, your instructor may prefer that you work collaboratively, that is, with other students. These exercises are identified in the margin. *If your instructor directs you to work collaboratively on any of these items,* form groups of three or four classmates to complete the exercise together. Discuss your answers with each other and have one member of the group record the answers. A member of the group may be asked to share the group's answers with the class.

Option

Exercises 1 and 2 can be completed collaboratively.

1. Create a test review sheet for one or more of the four main sections of Selection 10-1:

   "Symbols" (pages 544–554)
   "What We Communicate" (pages 554–560)
   "How We Communicate: Rules of Conversation" (pages 560–567)
   "Group Differences in Communication" (pages 567–577)

   Note: Your instructor will give you specific instructions about this assignment.

2. Your instructor will distribute one or more quizzes on the sections in Selection 10-1. You will be allowed to use your review cards and your test review sheet.

APPENDIX 1

A LIST OF WORD PARTS

IN THIS APPENDIX . . .

Understanding the meaning of various word parts can help you define many unfamiliar words, especially in context. Most of the word parts listed in this appendix are Greek and Latin; a few are Old English or Slavic. Try to associate each word part (left column) and its meaning (middle column) with the example (right column). Associating the part, definition, and example in this way will help you remember word parts that are new to you.

	Word part	*Definition*	*Example*
1.	a	without, not	amoral
2.	ab	from	abstain
3.	acou	hear	acoustic
4.	acro	high	acrobat
5.	alter	another	alternate
6.	ambi	both; around	ambivalent
7.	ambul	walk; go	ambulatory
8.	andr	man (human)	android
9.	annu, anni	year	annual, anniversary
10.	ante	before, forward	antebellum, antecedent
11.	anthrop	humankind	anthropology
12.	anti	against	antifreeze
13.	aqua	water	aquarium
14.	arch	rule, chief	archbishop
15.	astro	star	astronomy
16.	aud	hear	auditory
17.	auto	self	automatic
18.	avi	bird	aviary
19.	belli	war	belligerent
20.	bene	well, good	beneficial
21.	bi	two	bicycle
22.	bio	life	biology
23.	bov	cattle	bovine
24.	by	secondarily	by-product
25.	camera	chamber	bicameral
26.	cani	dog	canine
27.	capit	head	decapitate
28.	card	heart	cardiac
29.	carn	flesh	carnivorous
30.	caust, caut	burn	caustic, cauterize
31.	cav	hollow	cavity
32.	cent	hundred	century
33.	chromo	color	monochromatic
34.	chrono	time	chronology
35.	cide	kill	homicide
36.	contra	against	contraceptive
37.	cosm	universe	microcosm
38.	counter	against	counteract
39.	crat, cracy	rule	democratic
40.	cred, creed	belief	credibility, creed
41.	crypt	secret, hidden	cryptography
42.	cycl	circle	tricycle
43.	deca	ten	decade
44.	dei	god	deity
45.	demo	people	democracy
46.	dent	tooth	dentist
47.	derm	skin	dermatology
48.	di	two, double	dichotomy
49.	dict	speak	diction

	Word part	Definition	Example
50.	dorm	sleep	dormitory
51.	dyna	power	dynamo
52.	dys	bad, difficult	dysfunctional
53.	enni	year	centennial
54.	epi	upon, outer	epidermis
55.	equ	horse	equine
56.	esque	like, resembling	statuesque
57.	ethn	race, nation	ethnic
58.	eu	good, well	eulogy
59.	ex	out	exit
60.	extra	beyond, over	extravagant
61.	fer	carry, bear	conifer
62.	ferr	iron	ferrous
63.	fid	faith, trust	fidelity
64.	fini	limit	finite
65.	flagr	burn	conflagration
66.	flect, flex	bend	reflect, flexible
67.	fore	before	forewarn
68.	fort	strong	fortress
69.	frater	brother	fraternity
70.	gamy	marriage	monogamy
71.	gastr	stomach	gastric
72.	gene, gen	origin, race, type	genesis, genocide, genre
73.	geo	earth	geography
74.	geronto	old	gerontology
75.	grad, gress	go, step	regress
76.	graph, gram	write, record	telegraph
77.	gyne	woman	gynecology
78.	helio	sun	heliocentric
79.	hemi	half	hemisphere
80.	hemo	blood	hemophilia
81.	hetero	other, different	heterosexual
82.	homo	same	homosexual
83.	hydr	water	hydrant
84.	hyper	over, above	hyperactive
85.	hypo	under, less than	hypodermic
86.	ign	fire	ignite
87.	in, il, im, ir	not	inactive
88.	inter	between	intercept
89.	intra	within	intravenous
90.	itis	inflammation	tonsilitis
91.	ject	throw	eject
92.	junct	join	junction
93.	kilo	thousand	kilometer
94.	later	side	lateral
95.	leg	law	legal
96.	liber	free	liberate
97.	libr	book	library
98.	lingua	tongue, language	bilingual

	Word part	Definition	Example
99.	lith	stone	lithograph
100.	locu, loqu, log	speak	elocution, colloquial, dialogue
101.	logy	study of	psychology
102.	luc	light, clear	lucid
103.	macro	large	macrocosm
104.	magn	great	magnify
105.	mal	bad, ill	malfunction
106.	mamma	breast	mammal
107.	mania	craving for	kleptomania
108.	manu	hand	manual
109.	matri, mater	mother	maternal
110.	mega	large	megaphone
111.	meter, metr	measure	thermometer, metric
112.	micro	small	microscope
113.	milli	thousand, thousandth	millenium, millimeter
114.	mini	less	minimal
115.	miso	hatred of	misogamy
116.	miss, mit	send	dismiss, transmit
117.	mob, mov, mot	to move	mobile, movable, motion
118.	mono	one	monotone
119.	morph	form	amorphous
120.	mort	death	mortal
121.	multi	many	multitude
122.	nat	born, birth	prenatal
123.	naut	sail	nautical
124.	neo	new	neophyte
125.	nox	harmful	noxious
126.	noct	night	nocturnal
127.	ob, oc, of, op	against	object, occlude, offend, oppress
128.	oct	eight	octopus
129.	ocul	eye	oculist
130.	oid	resembling	humanoid
131.	omni	all	omnipotent
132.	onym	name, word	pseudonym
133.	ortho	correct, straight	orthodontist
134.	osis	condition	psychosis
135.	osteo, ost	bone	osteopath
136.	out	better than	outrun
137.	pac, pax	peace	pacifist
138.	pan	all	panorama
139.	para	beside	parallel, parapsychology
140.	path	feeling, illness	sympathy, pathology
141.	patri, pater	father	paternity
142.	ped, pod	foot	pedal, tripod
143.	pel	drive	repel
144.	pend	hang	pendulum, pending
145.	penta	five	pentagon
146.	per	through	perspire
147.	peri	around	perimeter

	Word part	Definition	Example
148.	petr	rock	petrified
149.	philo	love	philosophy
150.	phobia	fear of	acrophobia
151.	phono	sound	phonics, phonograph
152.	photo	light	photograph
153.	pneum	air	pneumatic
154.	poly	many	polygon
155.	port	carry	portable
156.	pos	place	position
157.	post	after	postwar
158.	pre	before	prewar
159.	primo	first	primitive, primordial
160.	pro	forward, in favor of	progress, pro-American
161.	pseud	false	pseudoscience
162.	psych	mind	psychic
163.	pugn	fight	pugnacious
164.	punct	point	puncture
165.	purg	cleanse	purge
166.	pyre	fire	pyromania
167.	quad, quart	four	quadruplets, quartet
168.	quint	five	quintet
169.	re	back, again	return, repeat
170.	reg	rule, kingly	regal
171.	rupt	break	rupture, disrupt
172.	scend	climb	descend
173.	scope	see; view	telescope
174.	scribe, scrip	write	scribble, prescription
175.	sequ	follow	sequence, sequel
176.	semi	half	semicircle
177.	seni	old	senile
178.	simil	like	similar
179.	sol	sun	solar
180.	soli	alone	solitude
181.	somni	sleep	insomnia
182.	soph	wise	sophomore, sophisticated
183.	spect	see	spectator
184.	spir	breathe	respiratory
185.	strict	tighten	constrict
186.	sub	under	submarine
187.	super, sur	over	supervisor, surpass
188.	surg	rise	surge, resurgent
189.	tang, tact	touch	tangible, tactile
190.	tech, tect	skill	technician
191.	tele	far	telepathy
192.	tend, tens	stretch	tendon, tension
193.	terri	earth	territory
194.	tert	third	tertiary
195.	theo	god	theology
196.	therm	heat	thermometer

	Word part	*Definition*	*Example*
197.	tomy	cut	vasectomy
198.	tors, tort	twist	distort
199.	toxi	poison	toxic
200.	tract	pull	tractor, extract
201.	tri	three	trio
202.	ultra	beyond, over	ultramodern
203.	unct, ung	oil	unctuous, unguent
204.	uni	one	unity
205.	vacu	empty	vacuum
206.	veni, vent	come	convene, convention
207.	verd	green	verdant
208.	vers, vert	turn	reverse
209.	vid, vis	see	video, vision
210.	vinc	conquer	invincible
211.	vit, viv	life	vitality, vivacious
212.	voc, voke	voice, call	vocal, evoke
213.	voli, volunt	wish	volition, volunteer
214.	volv	roll, to turn	revolve
215.	zoo	animal	zoology

APPENDIX 2

MASTER VOCABULARY LIST

IN THIS APPENDIX . . .

Appendix 2 lists all the terms covered in "Extend Your Vocabulary by Using Context Clues" in Parts One and Two. This master list will be useful for review and self-testing. The listing is alphabetical; the numbers in parentheses indicate the selections in which the words appear.

reprimand (1–1)
resolved (7–3)
rigidity (3–1)
rooted (2–2)
rote (4–3)
sector (7–1)
secular (4–2)
simulations (1–1)
sluggish (4–1)
societal (8–2)
solitude (2–2)
stagnated (6–3)
strategically (4–1)
subordinates (5–1)
succeeding (1–2)
supposition (3–2)
supremely (6–2)
surging (6–3)
sustain (7–2)
swig (2–2)
tenure (5–3)
terminal (2–2)
theology (4–2)
transcendence (3–2)
transition (3–3)
treacherous (8–2)
triggered (5–2)
underestimate (1–3)
uneventful (8–3)
universal (3–3)
unleashes (7–3)
unmet (3–3)
vanished (2–2)
vast (2–3)
veneration (3–2)
vital (2–3)
vocational (6–2)
weighing (8–2)
widespread (8–2)
willed (1–2)

APPENDIX 3

GLOSSARY OF KEY TERMS

IN THIS APPENDIX . . .

Appendix 3 lists key terms from Opening Doors, *with definitions. This listing will help you review text material and monitor your understanding of the concepts and skills you have studied. The listing is alphabetical; the numbers in parentheses indicate chapters where the key terms are found.*

Annotation: Explanatory notes written in the margins of a textbook to organize and remember information. (Chapter 9)

Appendix: Section at the end of a book which includes supplemental material or specialized information. (9)

Argument: Point of view or postition the author wants to persuade the reader to believe. (8)

Average reading: Rate used for textbooks and more complex material in periodicals (200–300 words per minute). (2)

Bar graph: Chart in which the length of parallel rectangular bars is used to indicate relative amounts of the items being compared. (9)

Bibliography: Textbook feature near the end of the book, giving a list of sources: books, articles, and other works from which the author of the text has drawn information; it may also be called *references, works cited,* or *sources.* Bibliographies sometimes include works the author recommends for further (supplemental) reading. (9)

Box: Textbook feature consisting of supplementary material separated from the regular text; also called a *sidebar.* (9)

Cause-effect pattern: Writing pattern presenting reasons for (causes of) events or conditions and results (effects) of events or conditions. (7)

Chapter introduction: Textbook feature opening a chapter, describing the overall purpose and major topics or "setting the scene" with a case study, anecdote, etc. (9)

Chapter objectives: Textbook features at the beginning of a chapter, telling you what you should know or be able to do after studying the chapter; also called *preview questions, what you'll learn, goals,* etc. (9)

Chapter outline: Textbook feature at the beginning of a chapter, listing the chapter topics or headings in their order of appearance; also called *chapter contents, preview, overview,* etc. (9)

Chapter review cards: Study tool and special textbook feature in *Opening Doors;* a way to select, organize, and review the most important information in a chapter; also called *summary cards.* (1)

Chapter summary: Textbook feature at or near the end of a chapter, in which the author collects and condenses the most essential ideas. (9)

Comparison-contrast pattern: Writing pattern used to present similarities (comparisons), differences (contrasts), or both. (7)

Connotation: Additional, nonliteral meaning associated with a word. (8)

Context clues: Other words in a sentence or paragraph which help the reader deduce the meaning of an unfamiliar word. (1, 2)

Critical reading: Going beyond basic comprehension to gain additional insights. (8)

Credibility: Believability of an author's argument. (8)

Definition pattern: Writing pattern presenting the meaning of an important term discussed throughout a passage. (7)

Denotation: Literal, explicit meaning of a word; its dictionary definition. (8)

Dictionary pronunciation key: Guide to sounds of letters and combinations of letters in words. A full pronunciation key usually appears near the beginning of a dictionary; an abbreviated key, showing only vowel sounds and the more unusual consonant sounds, usually appears at or near the bottom of each page. (2)

Distributed practice: Study sessions that are spaced out over time; a more efficient study method than massed practice. (10)

Epigraphs: Quotations that suggest overall themes or concerns of a chapter; this kind of textbook feature is usually found at chapter openings or in the margins. (9)

Etymology: Origin and history of a word. (2)

Examples: See *exhibits.* (9)

Exhibits: Special textbook features such as student papers, plot summaries, profit-and-loss statements, documents, forms, and printouts. (9)

Fact: Something that can be proved to exist or have happened or is generally assumed to exist or have happened. (8)

Figurative language: Imagery; words that create unusual comparisons, vivid pictures, and special effects; also called *figures of speech.* (2)

Flow chart: Diagram that shows steps in procedures or processes by using boxes, circles, and other shapes connected with lines or arrows. (9)

Glossary: Mini-dictionary at end of a textbook, listing important terms and definitions from the entire text. (9)

Graphic aids: Illustrations that consolidate information and present it more clearly than words alone; graphic aids include figures, cartoons, and photographs. (9)

Hyperbole: Figure of speech using obvious exaggeration for emphasis. (2)

Illustrations: See *graphic aids.* (9)

Implied main idea: Main point that is not stated directly as one sentence and therefore must be inferred and formulated by the reader. (5)

Index: Alphabetical listing of topics and names in a textbook, with page numbers, usually appearing at the end of the book. (9)

Inference: In reading, a logical conclusion based on what an author has stated. (8)

Intended audience: People an author has in mind as readers; the people he or she is writing for. (8)

Intended meaning: What an author wants you to understand even when his or her words seem to be saying something different. (8)

Intermediate goal: Goal you want to accomplish in the next 3 to 5 years. (1)

Learning style: Way in which an individual learns best. (1)

Line graph: Diagram whose points are connected to show a relationship between two or more variables. (9)

List pattern: Series of items in no particular order, since order is unimportant. When set off from the text in some special way, a list is also a useful textbook feature. (7, 9)

Long-term goal: Goal you want to accomplish during your lifetime. (1)

Long-term memory: Permanent memory, as contrasted with short-term (temporary) memory. (10)

Mapping: Informal way of organizing main ideas and supporting details by using boxes, circles, lines, arrows, etc. (9)

Metaphor: Figure of speech implying a comparison between two essentially dissimilar things, usually by saying that one of them *is* the other. (2)

Mixed pattern: Combination of two or more writing patterns. (7)

Monitoring comprehension: Evaluating your understanding as you read and correcting the problem whenever you realize that you are not comprehending. (2)

Monthly assignment calendar: Calendar showing test dates and due dates in all courses for each month of a semester. (1)

Opinion: Belief or judgment that cannot be proved or disproved. (8)

Organization: Arranging main ideas and supporting details in a meaningful way. Second of three essential study strategies. (9)

Outlining: Formal way of organizing main ideas and supporting details to show relationships between them. (9)

Paraphrasing: Rewriting someone else's material in your own words. (6)

Part opening: Textbook feature that introduces a section (part) consisting of several chapters. (9)

Personification: Figure of speech giving human traits to nonhuman or nonliving things. (2)

Pie chart: Circle graph in which the sizes of the "slices" represent parts of the whole. (9)

Point of view: An author's position (attitude, belief, or opinion) on a topic. (8)

Predicting: Anticipating what is coming next as you read. (2)

Preface: Introductory section in which authors tell readers about a book. (9)

Prefix: Word part attached to the beginning of a root that adds its meaning to the root. (2)

Preparing to read: Previewing a chapter, assessing your prior knowledge, and planning your time.

Previewing: Examining reading material to determine its subject matter and organization. Previewing is step 1 of the three-step reading process in *Opening Doors.* (3)

Prior knowledge: What you already know about a topic; background knowledge. (3)

Purpose: An author's reason for writing. (8)

Rapid reading: Rate used for easy or familiar material (300–500 words per minute). (2)

Rehearsal: Saying or writing material to transfer it into long-term memory. Third of three essential study strategies. (3, 9, 10)

Review: See *rehearsal.* (3, 9)

Review card: Index card with an important question on the front and the answer on the back. (9) Also, throughout *Opening Doors,* a technique for reviewing a chapter; *chapter review cards* summarize the most important information in the chapter and therefore are also called *summary cards.*

Root: Base word that has a meaning of its own. (2)

Scanning: Information-gathering technique used to locate specific information quickly and precisely. (2)

Selectivity: Identifying main ideas and important supporting details. First of three essential study strategies. (9)

Sequence pattern: List of items in a specific, important order. When set off from the text in some special way, a *sequence* is also a useful textbook feature. (7, 9)

Short-term goal: Goal you want to accomplish in the next 3 to 6 months. (1)

Short-term memory: Temporary memory. (10)

Sidebar: See *box.* (9)

Simile: Figure of speech stating a comparison between two essentially dissimilar things by saying that one of them is *like* the other. (2)

Skimming: Information-gathering technique that involves moving quickly and selectively through material to find only important material. (2)

Stated main idea: Sentence in a paragraph that expresses the most important point about the topic. (4)

Study questions: General term for textbook features such as *activities, exercises, drills,* and *practice sections.* These features may also be called *questions for study and review, review, ask yourself, self-test, check your mastery, mastery test, learning check, check your understanding, topics for discussion, problems,* etc. (9)

Study reading: Rate used for material that is complex, technical, new, demanding, or very important (50–200 words per minute). (2)

Study schedule: Weekly schedule with specific times set aside for studying. (1)

Suffix: Word part attached to the end of a root word. (2)

Suggested readings: Textbook feature, often at the end of chapters (or parts), listing the author's recommendations for supplemental reading or research, sometimes with annotations (comments); may be called *additional readings, suggestions for further reading, supplementary readings,* etc. (9)

Summary cards: See *chapter review cards.* (1)

Summary: Single-paragraph condensation of all the main ideas presented in a longer passage. (9)

Supplements: Separate aids accompanying a textbook; supplements include *study guides, supplemental readings, student workbooks,* and *computer diskettes.* (9)

Supporting details: In a paragraph, additional information necessary for understanding the main idea. (6)

Table of contents: Textbook feature at the beginning of the book, listing chapter titles and sometimes including headings within chapters as well. (9)

Table: Material arranged in rows and columns. (9)

Test review card: Index card with an important question on the front and the answer on the back. (10)

Test review sheet: Single sheet of paper consolidating and summarizing, on its front and back, the most important information to be covered on a test. (10)

Textbook feature: Device used by an author to emphasize important material and show how it is organized.

"To do" list: Prioritized items to be accomplished in a single day. (1)

Tone: Manner of writing (choice of words and style) that reflects an author's attitude toward a topic. (8)

Topic: Word or phrase that tells what an author is writing about. (4)

Underlining and highlighting: Techniques for marking topics, main ideas, and definitions. (9)

Vocabulary aids: Textbook devices that highlight important terms and definitions. Vocabulary aids may be called *key terms, basic terms, terms to know, vocabulary, terms to remember,* etc. (9)

Word-structure clue: Root, prefix, or suffix that helps you determine a word's meaning. (2)

Writing patterns: Ways authors organize and present their ideas. (7)

INDEX